Cambridge Studies in the History of Psychology
GENERAL EDITORS: WILLIAM R. WOODWARD AND
MITCHELL G. ASH

Metaphors in the history of psychology

Metaphors in the
history of psychology

Edited by
David E. Leary

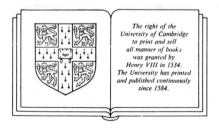

The right of the
University of Cambridge
to print and sell
all manner of books
was granted by
Henry VIII in 1534.
The University has printed
and published continuously
since 1584.

Cambridge University Press

Cambridge

New York   Port Chester   Melbourne   Sydney

Published by the Press Syndicate of the University of Cambridge
The Pitt Building, Trumpington Street, Cambridge CB2 1RP
40 West 20th Street, New York, NY 10011, USA
10 Stamford Road, Oakleigh, Melbourne 3166, Australia

First published 1990

Printed in the United States of America

Library of Congress Cataloging-in-Publication Data
Metaphors in the history of psychology/edited by David E. Leary.
p. cm. – (Cambridge studies in the history of psychology)
ISBN 0-521-37166-X
1. Psychology – Philosophy – History.   2. Metaphor – History.
I. Leary, David E.   II. Series.
BF38.M482   1990
150′.1 – dc20   89-27215
                                                      CIP

British Library Cataloguing in Publication Data
Metaphors in the history of psychology. – (Cambridge studies
in the history of psychology).
1. Psychology. Role of metaphor.
I. Leary, David E.
150

ISBN 0-521-37166-X hard covers

Contents

About the authors

James R. Averill is Professor of Psychology at the University of Massachusetts, Amherst. A Fellow of the American Psychological Association and past member of the Board of Directors of the International Society for Research on Emotion, Averill is the author of *Anger and Aggression: An Essay on Emotion* (New York: Springer, 1982) and editor of *Patterns of Psychological Thought: Readings in Classical and Contemporary Texts* (Washington, DC: Hemisphere, 1976). He has also published numerous research articles and chapters on stress and emotion.

Jerome Bruner is Research Professor of Psychology at New York University and a Visiting Scholar of the Russell Sage Foundation. A former president of the American Psychological Association, he has also held professorships at Harvard University, Oxford University, and the New School for Social Research. Widely recognized as one of the pioneers in the field of cognitive psychology, Bruner has been honored by the Distinguished Scientific Contribution Award of the APA, by the Gold Medal of the CIBA Foundation, and by the 1987 Balzan Prize "for a lifetime's contribution to human psychology." Among his recent books are *In Search of Mind* (New York: Harper & Row, 1983), *Child's Talk* (New York: Norton, 1983), and *Actual Minds, Possible Worlds* (Cambridge, MA: Harvard University Press, 1986).

Edward L. Cochran supervises a group of cognitive scientists and human factors specialists in the Artificial Intelligence Department at Honeywell's Corporate Systems Development division in Minneapolis. The department develops advanced user interfaces, expert systems, user interface development environments, and knowledge-based software. A former faculty member of the Department of Psychology at Adelphi University, Cochran has published articles on various aspects of cognitive science and artificial intelligence.

Kurt Danziger is Professor of Psychology at York University in Toronto. The author of many articles on experimental and social psychology, Danziger is also well known for his research and publications in the history and philosophy of psychology, on such topics as the history of introspection, the role of positivism in the development of psychology, and the social context of early scientific psychology, including especially its investigative practices. His most recent book is *Constructing the Subject: Historical Origins of Psychological Research* (Cambridge University Press, 1990).

Carol Fleisher Feldman began studying philosophy but ended up taking her Ph.D. in psychology at the University of Michigan. Her research has focused primarily on the relation of language and thought, a subject on which she has written extensively. Feldman has taught at the University of Chicago, Harvard University, and Yale University, and she is presently Senior Research Associate at New York University and an occasional Adjunct Professor at the Graduate Center of the City University of New York.

Kenneth J. Gergen is Professor of Psychology at Swarthmore College. He is a Fellow of the American Psychological Association and has served as president of its Psychology and the Arts division and its Theoretical and Philosophical Psychology division. Widely known for his research on the self, on historical psychology, and on social constructionism, Gergen has been a leader in the exploration of new approaches to understanding the nature and development of psychological phenomena as well as the nature and development of the subject matter and methods of the discipline of psychology. Among many other publications, Gergen has written *Toward Transformation in Social Knowledge* (New York: Springer, 1982), and he has coedited *Historical Social Psychology* (Hillsdale, NJ: Erlbaum, 1984) with Mary M. Gergen.

Robert R. Hoffman is Associate Professor of Psychology at Adelphi University. Currently serving as associate editor of the journal *Metaphor and Symbolic Activity,* Hoffman is a leading researcher in the psychology of figurative language. Recently his research has focused on the problem of knowledge acquisition in general and on the development of expert knowledge in particular, largely from the viewpoint of artificial intelligence. The author of many papers on the history and philosophy of psychology, Hoffman has also coedited *Cognition and Figurative Language* (Hillsdale, NJ: Erlbaum, 1980) with Richard P. Honeck and *Memory and Learning: The Ebbinghaus Centennial Conference* (Hillsdale, NJ: Erlbaum, 1987) with David S. Gorfein.

David E. Leary is Professor of Psychology and Dean of the Faculty of Arts and Sciences at the University of Richmond. Previously he was Professor of Psychology, History, and the Humanities, chairperson of Psychology, and codirector of the History and Theory of Psychology Program at the University of New Hampshire. He is a Fellow of the American Psychological Association, past president of its History of Psychology division, and a former Fellow at the Center for Advanced Study in the Behavioral Sciences in Stanford, California. Leary is the coeditor (with Sigmund Koch) of *A Century of Psychology as Science* (New York: McGraw-Hill, 1985), and he has published various articles and chapters on the history, philosophy, and theory of psychology.

Paul McReynolds is Emeritus Professor of Psychology at the University of Nevada-Reno, where in 1987 he was the recipient of the university's Outstanding Researcher Award. He is a Fellow of the American Psychological Association and of the Society for Personality Assessment, and he has served on the editorial board of *Motivation and Emotion*. An editor of a number of books, including *Four Early Works on Motivation* (Gainesville, FL: Scholars' Facsimiles and Reprints, 1969), McReynolds is also the author of many articles and chapters on motivation, personality, and the historical background of psychology.

James M. Nead is a computer scientist at UNISYS Corporation in Minneapolis, where he works on the automatic synthesis of digital computer hardware and on the automatic verification of digital hardware designs. Trained in psychology as well as computer science, Nead has been studying the broad area of meaning in artificial and natural languages in an attempt to produce a semantic model that captures the insights of metaphor studies and contextualism.

Karl H. Pribram is James P. and Anna King University Professor and Eminent Scholar for the State of Virginia at Radford University. He spent many years at Stanford University, where he is now Professor Emeritus, and he has received many fellowships and honors, including a Lifetime Career Research Award in Neuroscience from the National Institutes of Health. He was the first president of the International Neuropsychological Society and has served as president of the Division of Physiological and Comparative Psychology and of the Division of

Theoretical and Philosophical Psychology of the American Psychological Association. Pribram is the coauthor (with George Miller and Eugene Galanter) of *Plans and the Structure of Behavior* (New York: Holt, 1960), and he is the author of *Languages of the Brain,* rev. ed. (New York: Brandon House, 1988), of *Brain and Perception: Holonomy and Structure in Figural Processing – The MacEachran Lectures* (Hillsdale, NJ: Erlbaum, 1988), and of many other articles, chapters, and books.

Theodore R. Sarbin is Professor Emeritus of Psychology and Criminology at the University of California, Santa Cruz. He is a Fellow of the American Psychological Association and past president of its Psychological Hypnosis division. He has been a Fulbright Fellow at Oxford University and a Fellow of the Social Science Research Council, the John Simon Guggenheim Memorial Foundation, and the Center for the Humanities at Wesleyan University. Sarbin is the editor of *Narrative Psychology: The Storied Nature of Human Conduct* (New York: Praeger, 1986), coeditor (with Karl E. Scheibe) of *Studies in Social Identity* (New York: Praeger, 1983), coauthor (with James C. Mancuso) of *Schizophrenia: Medical Diagnosis or Moral Verdict?* (New York: Pergamon, 1980), and author or coauthor of other books, essays, and research articles.

Laurence D. Smith is Associate Professor of Psychology at the University of Maine. He holds a master's degree in the history and philosophy of science from Indiana University and a Ph.D. in the history and theory of psychology from the University of New Hampshire, where he was a National Science Foundation Graduate Fellow. Smith is the author of *Behaviorism and Logical Positivism: A Reassessment of the Alliance* (Stanford, CA: Stanford University Press, 1986), as well as articles on the history and philosophy of psychology, and he is currently serving as assistant editor of the *Journal of Mind and Behavior.*

Preface

This volume reflects at least three trends that have become increasingly apparent over the past several decades: the development of interest in the history of psychology; the development of interest in the nature of cognitive processes, particularly those underlying creative activity; and the development of interest in the nature of language, especially the incidence and functions of metaphor. Although these trends overlap in various regards, the chapters in this volume tighten their association by explicating the role of metaphors in the thinking and behavior of psychologists. As a whole, this volume should raise the consciousness of psychologists, historians of science, students, and interested laypersons regarding the uses – and abuses – of metaphor in the history of psychology.

As the book's progenitor and editor, I am particularly grateful for the cooperation, diligence, and scholarship of my collaborators; for the interest and support of the director, staff, and my fellow fellows (in 1982–3) at the Center for Advanced Study in the Behavioral Sciences, Stanford, California; for the encouragement and feedback of many persons who attended a series of symposia entitled "Metaphors in the History of Psychology" that were held at the annual meetings of the American Psychological Association between 1983 and 1986; for the intellectual and financial assistance of the Department of Psychology, Dean Stuart Palmer of the College of Liberal Arts, and the Research Administration Office of the University of New Hampshire; for the reference checking and proofreading done by Trey Buchanan and Linda Pertsch; for the patience and secretarial help of Shirley Norton, Donna Hardy, and especially Anna Moses; for the expert and timely editorial work of Helen Wheeler and

xi

Mary Nevader of Cambridge University Press; and for the forbearance of all those, from collaborators to strangers, who kept asking, "When is that book on metaphor going to come out?" Finally, I would like to acknowledge a very personal debt to my wife, Marge, and to my children, Emily, Elizabeth, and Matthew. I would not have had the satisfaction of being associated with this work if they had not continually supported my scholarly efforts.

Perhaps a few words about the chapters in this volume are in order. My introductory chapter, "Psyche's Muse," is meant simply to draw you, the reader, into the subject and concerns of this volume by presenting a brief, preliminary discussion on metaphor and by pointing to illustrative instances of its historical role in fields other than psychology as well as in psychology itself. The objective of this introductory chapter is simply to set the scene for the subsequent chapters in such a way that no reader will put down this volume with the idea that psychology is somehow alone in its reliance on metaphor. However unique its particular uses of metaphor, psychology has had no monopoly on metaphorical thinking. As a result, even though this volume focuses primarily on the role of metaphors in psychology, its analyses are relevant to an understanding of intellectual life in general, both inside and outside the domain of science.

Whereas my introductory chapter seeks to elicit your interest and to set wider boundaries for your thoughts, my concluding chapter briefly summarizes the major metaphors and sources of metaphors covered in each chapter, sharpens an important point that is not emphasized in the foregoing chapters, and indicates the scholarly work that remains to be done. Since the chapters of this volume provide in each case something akin to initial reconnaissance, I have resisted the impulse – and the weight of custom – to "tie it all together." Such considerable unity as this volume enjoys inheres in its common subject and in the common objective toward which the chapters point. There is no need to hasten closure at this time.

As for the chapters between my introduction and conclusion, you will discover that they are the heart and soul of this book. They describe in considerable detail the uses of metaphor in different areas of psychology. Other areas might have been represented, either instead of or in addition to those actually chosen. But those surveyed herein constitute a very reasonable selection from among the many subspecialties encompassed by the contemporary discipline of psychology. In any case, by offering such a rich and varied diet, the contributors to this volume have provided plenty of food for you to digest, with profit, for a good long time.

This book is intended primarily for those whose interests intersect one or more of the trends listed at the beginning of this preface. But even if you are not among these many individuals, I join my fellow collaborators in hoping that you will be informed, stimulated, and challenged by this volume.

As for ourselves, the authors of this volume, we have enjoyed producing this book, and if anything, we are now more conscious than before that our topic is important – and that our contributions are all too preliminary. As Philip Wheelwright once noted in a similar context, we can only murmur with the Hindu sages of the Upanishads, "*Neti neti*," which is to say, "Not quite that! Not quite that!"

We thank those who have been patient as we traveled toward this milestone in our efforts to comprehend the role of metaphor in the history of psychology, and we are grateful in advance to those who will read this volume with tolerance as well as vigilance. However fallible our analyses and arguments may be, we are convinced that they deal with topics and concerns that deserve – and will repay – the effort of sustained attention.

1

Psyche's muse: the role of metaphor in the history of psychology

DAVID E. LEARY

Ever since Aristotle asserted that "the greatest thing by far is to be a master of metaphor," numerous scholars have studied and written about the nature and functions of metaphor.[1] The vast majority of these scholars have focused on metaphor as a distinctive use of language that has various rhetorical functions.[2] Recently, however, some scholars have begun to dig deeper into the topic, investigating the possibility that metaphor is not only a form of *speech,* but more fundamentally a form of *thought,* having basic epistemological functions.[3] With regard to science, for instance, such scholars as Arbib and Hesse (1986), Barbour (1974), Black (1962, 1979), Bohm and Peat (1987), Boyd (1979), Farber (1950), Gerschenkron (1974), Gould (1977a,b, 1983), Hesse (1955, 1966, 1980), Hoffman (1980, 1984b), R. S. Jones (1982), Kuhn (1979), Leatherdale (1974), MacCormac (1976, 1985), Martin and Harré (1982), Nisbet (1976), North (1980), Oppenheimer (1956), and Temkin (1977) have begun to study the ways in which metaphorical thinking, broadly conceived, has helped to constitute, and not merely reflect, scientific theory and practice.[4] Following upon such work, this volume has been organized with the intention of raising and answering questions about the role of metaphor in the history of psychology, while also providing analyses of some of the major metaphors that have guided – and sometimes preempted – investigation in selected areas of psychology.

My own orientation, as organizer and editor of this volume, should bear some preliminary scrutiny, though my views about metaphor and its role in the history of psychology do not necessarily reflect those of other contributors to this volume. (No contributor had to sign an oath of

1

egiance in order to participate in this intellectual venture.) The purpose
this introductory chapter, therefore, is to describe the orientation
‿nderlying my involvement in this collaborative project, to provide a
brief opening discussion on metaphor (as it is generally understood in this
volume), and to give a historical survey of selected uses of metaphor in
various disciplines of thought, including but not limited to psychology.
This survey will occupy most of the chapter and will provide a running
start into the chapters that follow. I hope it will also obviate a conclusion
that might be reached on the basis of the title and coverage of this
volume, namely, that metaphor plays a role in psychology but not necessarily in other disciplines. It would be indefensible if this volume invited
or left room for the impression that psychology stands alone in its reliance
on metaphorical thinking.

Preliminary distinctions and discussions

My own thesis

To start things off, I shall state my own thesis as baldly as I can: All
knowledge is ultimately rooted in metaphorical (or analogical) modes of
perception and thought. Thus, metaphor necessarily plays a fundamental
role in psychology, as in any other domain. In other words, the inspiration of psychological thought, which I have symbolized as "Psyche's
Muse" in the title of this chapter, derives from the comparative, relational mode of understanding that I presume to be fundamental to
human cognition.

The simplest and most appropriate way to elucidate this thesis is by
means of an analogy. If I am confronted with a word that I do not understand, I will either ask someone what it means or look it up in a dictionary. In either case, I will keep asking and searching until the word is
defined in terms of other words that are better known to me. This simple
example can serve as a paradigm for the many ways in which we confront
and come to understand "reality." When any aspect of our experience
strikes us as worth understanding, either for the first time or in a new
way, we begin to search for "similar instances," as William James (1890)
called them (chaps. 13, 19, and 22). Only when we have found an apt
"peg" or "pigeonhole" for this aspect of our experience do we feel the
subjective satisfaction that brings our search to an end.[5] It is my contention that the similar instances that serve as our pegs and pigeonholes –
as our categories of understanding – are either explicitly or implicitly
metaphorical in nature and function.

To express this contention in slightly different terms, I would say that
just as we turn to a dictionary for the definition of unknown words in
terms of more familiar words, so we look to phenomena of other sorts,

whether natural or artificial, for analogs of things, qualities, and events – including aspects of our own experience and activity – that we wish to comprehend. And conversely, we often look to our own experience and activity for analogs of other natural and artificial phenomena. For instance, Aristotle (ca. 330 B.C./1931) explained mental functioning through the use of biological metaphors, while recent cyberneticists (e.g., Wiener, 1961) have revised our notion of biological organisms through the use of mechanical and cognitive metaphors. Thus, to Aristotle the mind is a *living thing,* whereas to cyberneticists living things are information-processing *machines.* Consequences of both a moral and an aesthetic nature result from such conceptual differences.

This general contention regarding the fundamentally metaphorical nature of human thought seems obvious to me, but it is nevertheless worth stating and considering, since forgetting the metaphorical nature of our concepts invites "hardening of the categories" and the various sorts of myths and cults – such as the myth of objectivity and its associated cult of empiricism – that have characterized so much of twentieth-century thought, in the social and behavioral sciences as elsewhere (see Toulmin & Leary, 1985).

Of course, I am far from the first to propose that human language and thought are ultimately metaphorical. Indeed, I have some very good company. If Aristotle is not foursquare among this company (see Levin, 1982; Lloyd, 1987), he at least started the ball rolling by pointing out that "it is from metaphor that we can best get hold of something fresh" (Aristotle, ca. 330 B.C./1924a, l. 1410). Still, it is only in modern times, beginning with the etymological, rhetorical, and historical analyses of Giambattista Vico (1744/1948), that many scholars have come to share the view that metaphor characterizes human thought and language in a truly fundamental way. This view, which usually presupposes that analogy is included in the broader category of metaphor, has been held by many theorists of various persuasions – by empiricists and pragmatists as well as by idealists and intellectual anarchists: by David Hume, Jeremy Bentham, Alexander Bain, and Charles Peirce (for instance) as well as by Immanuel Kant, Friedrich Nietzsche, Hans Vaihinger, and Ernst Cassirer.[6] In point of fact, this view has become so widespread and has been expressed by theorists of so many orientations that the twentieth-century psychologist Kenneth Craik seems to have uttered a mere commonplace when he suggested that "the brain is a machine for making analogical models."[7] This view has been reinforced in recent years by a host of studies conducted by investigators from many disciplines (e.g., Holland, Holyoak, Nisbett, & Thagard, 1986). In sum, the postulate that metaphorical or analogical thinking plays a fundamental role in the acquisition and extension of knowledge has been broadcast far and wide.

Nonetheless, this view is not unanimously held. The contention that all language and thought is ultimately metaphorical or analogical is controversial, even though it is common. To give the critics their due, two major distinctions must be acknowledged and addressed: (1) the distinction between metaphor and other figures of speech and thought and (2) the distinction between metaphorical as opposed to literal language and thought. These distinctions can and, in some contexts, certainly should be made, but in relation to my thesis, I believe that by and large they can be ignored. In the following sections I shall try to justify this belief by arguing (1) that metaphor is not simply one among many figures of speech and thought, but rather, that it can be reasonably considered to be the primary figure of speech and thought and (2) that there is no absolute chasm between metaphorical and literal language and thought.

The definition of metaphor and its relation to other figures of speech and thought

Consistent with my thesis, metaphor has been defined through the use of comparisons – indeed, *many* comparisons: Metaphor has been likened to a filter, a fusion, a lens, a pretense, a screen, a tension, a displacement, a stereoscopic image, a form of linguistic play, a false identity, a semantic fiction, a contextual shift, a translation of meaning, a twinned vision, and an incongruous perspective, to mention only a few of its common metaphors. This range of images and their correlative definitions is so great that one student of metaphor, Janet Martin Soskice (1985), has commented that "anyone who has grappled with the problem of metaphor will appreciate the pragmatism of those who proceed to discuss it without giving any definition at all. One scholar claims to have found 125 different definitions, surely only a small fraction of those which have been put forward" (p. 15). Still, even allowing for alternatives, it will be useful for me to provide a general definition, if only to move our discussion along.

Soskice's own "working definition" is that "metaphor is that figure of speech whereby we speak about one thing in terms which are seen to be suggestive of another" (p. 15, italics deleted). This definition is similar to that of Richard Brown (1977), who asserts simply that "metaphor is seeing something from the viewpoint of something else" (p. 77). Like most definitions of metaphor, these reflect Aristotle's (ca. 330 B.C./ 1924b) definition, according to which metaphor is constituted by giving to something "a name that belongs to something else" (l. 1457). Following Soskice and so many others, I shall stay within Aristotle's ambit by offering the following, slightly modified definition: Metaphor consists in giving to one thing a name or description that belongs by convention to something else, on the grounds of some similarity between the two. In considering this definition, one should realize that the thing metaphorized need not be a material object. Qualities, events, and any other aspect of experience are included among the innumerable "things" that can be rendered through metaphor. This definition also suggests that Aristotle's "denomination" theory is inadequate, if understood in a restricted sense. Metaphor often involves more than the mere transfer of a *name* from one object to another. As Paul Ricoeur (1977, 1979) has noted, metaphor can also involve the transfer of predicates or descriptions. Indeed, anything associated with the metaphorical term, in its original context, can be implied of its new referent. Thus, when Aristotle treated the mind as a living thing, he invited the inference that it can develop and change over time, and when cyberneticists make information central to biological functioning, they set the stage for questions about the relationship between the "noise" and "messages" involved in the regulation of living bodies.

This definition of metaphor also highlights the fact that convention – one's understanding of the "normal" usage of language – plays a role in the creation of metaphor. I will say more about this in the next section. Finally, this definition suggests that similarity – or analogy – is the bond between the two things compared in a metaphor. As Aristotle (ca. 330 B.C./1924b) said, "A good metaphor implies an intuitive perception of the similarity in dissimilars" (1. 1459). Thus, the notion of similarity or analogy is included in the concept of metaphor. To say that the mind is a living thing or that a living thing is a machine – as also to say that emotions are forces, or that the senses are signal detection devices, or that behavioral problems are illnesses – is to suggest a set of resemblances between the members of each of these pairs of terms.

The inclusion of analogy in the concept of metaphor underscores the fact that I am proposing a broad definition of "metaphor" that encompasses a variety of other figures of speech. Indeed, according to the above definition, metaphor can hardly be distinguished from trope (figure of speech) in general.[8] Furthermore, a consequence of this definition is that such things as fables, parables, allegories, myths, and models, including scientific models, can be seen, by implication, as "extended and sustained metaphors" (Turbayne, 1970, pp. 11–20; see also Barbour, 1974, pp. 42–5; Black, 1962, p. 237; Shibles, 1974, p. 27).

Others before me have argued for giving this sort of generous sway to the concept of metaphor. Traditional rhetoricians, for instance, have allowed metaphor to stand for figure of speech in general as well as for one particular figure of speech among others (see, e.g., Fogelin, 1988, p. 28; Hawkes, 1972, p. 2; Lanham, 1968, pp. 123–4; Perelman & Olbrechts-Tyteca, 1959/1969, pp. 398–9).[9] This does not mean, of course, that nothing could be gained by using the term, in a study like the present one, with a narrow rather than broad signification. Future studies might well investigate the role that metaphor, as *distinct* from analogy, simile, metonymy, synecdoche, and so on, has played in the history of psychology. However, I believe that there is good reason to proceed here with a broader view, not only because of scholarly precedent, but because the evidence (as I see it) supports David Cooper's (1986) conclusion that "usually one gains rather than loses by employing 'metaphor' in a gener-ous way" (p. 196). I believe that this is surely the case in an admittedly preliminary study like the present one. At the start, it is critical to make certain that there is a general phenomenon of some interest and import, however blunt our means of identification and exploration. As a result, I am quite content that the contributors to this volume, for the most part, have assumed a broad rather than narrow definition of metaphor and that some have felt free to use analogy as virtually equivalent to metaphor. In my judgment, that is as it should be.[10]

Metaphorical versus literal language and thought

The key to the relationship between the metaphorical and the literal is provided by the concept of conventionality. Metaphor is constituted, I claimed in my definition, by the attribution to one thing of a name or description that belongs *by convention* to something else. Although the problem of reference is a thorny one, it is nevertheless commonly assumed that descriptions as well as names are *assigned* to things by social practice rather than *discovered* through some sort of raw experience, as if they were somehow embedded for all time in their objects. What counts as literal language, in the now standard account, is language usage to which a particular linguistic community has grown accustomed. Thus, when English speakers refer to the "leg" of a chair, they need not worry that other skilled English speakers will think their expression rather oddly metaphorical. However, as in so many instances, it is nonetheless true that the term of reference – in this case *leg* – was originally an imaginative metaphor. It is only with repeated usage over time that such terms are transformed by custom into "literal" terms with virtually unanimously understood referents. The implication, as Ralph Waldo Emerson (1836/1983a, 1837/1983b, 1844/1983c) noted more than once, is that metaphor is the fertile soil from which all language is born, and literal language is the graveyard into which all "dead metaphors" are put to rest.[11]

What this means is that there is no sharp division between metaphorical and literal language. At the opposite ends of a single continuum, relative-ly clear instances of metaphorical and literal language are fairly easy to recognize, but – except in truly dead languages – there is continual commerce between these two poles, as metaphorical concepts become more common (i.e., literal) through use and as literal concepts are used in unexpected (i.e., metaphorical) ways. In this manner, the metaphorical concept of "cognitive input" has lost most of its novelty and awkwardness over the past decade, and the once literal (physiological) concept of "neural connections" has taken on an entirely new (cognitive) meaning, at least for many members of the psychological community.

This contention about the permeable boundaries between the metaphorical and the literal is hardly new. In 1927, for instance, Mortimer Adler noted that "the distinction between literal and metaphorical statements cannot be defended when the symbolism of all language is revealed" (p. 94). His claim is consonant with a great deal of recent scholarship. Carol Kates (1980) epitomized this scholarship when she said that "narrowly semantic theories of metaphor are unable to distinguish metaphorical structures from ordinary literal (empirical) statements" and that the distinction between the metaphorical and literal "can only be captured by a pragmatic model of the metaphorical function" (p. 232). "Captured" may be too strong a metaphor: The most Kates feels able to claim is that "one is *intuitively* aware of a difference between a metaphorical utterance and a literal empirical statement, or between a living and a dead metaphor" (p. 233, italics added). To say that the distinction between the metaphorical and literal depends on "intuition" is to say that it depends on a very subtle, acquired sense or taste – that one "knows" what is metaphorical and what is literal because one has become a sensitive connoisseur of the language. This supports my argument, though it might not represent the entire story behind the ability to "intuit" the distinction between metaphorical and literal statements. Sensitivity to a speaker's *intention* may be as important as sensitivity to linguistic *usage* in this regard (see Gibbs, 1984). In any case, a good deal of recent research suggests that the distinction between the metaphorical and literal is relative rather than absolute and that the distinction has "little psychological reality" (Gibbs, 1984, p. 275).

Be that as it may, the distinction does have the sort of *practical* reality that is born of repetition and ritualization. As Cynthia Ozick (1986) has put it, metaphor "transforms the strange into the familiar" (p. 67) – and sometimes into the *all too familiar*. The problems that may result from such familiarization, or literalization, will be discussed later in this chapter and at various places throughout this volume. For now, I hope we can simply agree that the distinction between the metaphorical and literal need not stand in the way of my central thesis that human language and thought are fundamentally metaphorical.[12] In any case, it is time to move on to the selective historical survey that I promised to provide.

A selective and illustrative historical survey: metaphor in the history of Western thought and science

Thoughts about metaphor in early Greek philosophy

To get a running start, I shall go back to the ancient Greeks and begin with Plato, who is important in the history of metaphor, particularly for installing a deep ambivalence about it at the very core of the Western intellectual tradition. It was Plato (ca. 375 B.C./1961a, ca. 360 B.C./

1961b), you will recall, who said that the true essences of things are pure
ideas that we can and should strive to attain (or, rather, to remember),
but that in practice will remain (for most of us) forever beyond our
complete grasp (or recall). All that we can know empirically, said Plato,
are the reflections of these ultimate essences – reflections that are embedded in the material objects accessible to our senses. Since these
reflections are only copies or likenesses of true reality, what we take to be
our knowledge of things is actually only opinion. At best, our theories –
and he referred in the *Timaeus* (ca. 355 B.C./196lc) specifically to our
scientific theories – are "likely stories." In other words, they are myths,
or extended metaphors.[13]

Thus, Plato degraded the only kind of knowledge we are likely to have
in this finite world of ours. Setting the framework for the views of
knowledge and science that were to come, he established the heuristic
goal of certain truth and placed beside it the ineluctable actuality of
tentative stories. In so doing he besmirched the reputation of the very
sort of knowledge he so astutely analyzed, and so beautifully exemplified
in his own work (e.g., see Bambrough, 1956).

Aristotle, Plato's student, served in his own way to delay the consideration of metaphorical thinking as fundamental to all knowledge. For all his
importance as the first serious student and most enduring figure in the
history of research on metaphor, Aristotle focused primarily on the role
of metaphor in poetry and rhetoric, and thus helped establish the several-
millennium emphasis on metaphor as a mere rhetorical device (see Kennedy, 1980). Typically overlooked has been the fact that metaphor can
also serve as a means of discovery. Although Aristotle himself pointed
toward this fact, it was not until the work of Giambattista Vico (1744/
1948) that it received any significant attention – and not until the work of
Samuel T. Coleridge (1817/1975), I. A. Richards (1936), and others that
it was more fully explored.[14] Thus, only in relatively recent times has the
study of metaphor begun to move back into the central place it occupied,
at least implicitly, in Plato's pragmatic philosophy of science.

Metaphor and the rise of modern science

Of course, when we think about the philosophy of science, we naturally
think of modern science, not of Plato, Aristotle, Vico, Coleridge, or I. A.
Richards. As is commonly known, the emergence of modern science in
the seventeenth century coincided with a good deal of antimetaphorical
rhetoric (see R. F. Jones, 1963). Thomas Sprat captured the tone of this
rhetoric in his *History of the Royal Society of London* (1667/1702), when
he wrote that the members of this new scientific society had "endeavor'd,
to separate the knowledge of *Nature* from the colours of *Rhetorick,* the
devices of *Fancy,* [and] the delightful deceit of *Fables*" (p. 62). In their

place, he said, they had substituted "a close, naked, natural way of speaking" (p. 113).[15]

Thomas Hobbes (1651/1968) expressed the same attitude when he compared "metaphors, and senslesse and ambiguous words" to "*ignes fatui.*" Reasoning with metaphors, he said, "is [like] wandering amongst innumerable absurdities"; and the end of metaphorical thinking is "contention, and sedition, or contempt" (pp. 116–17).

It is instructive that all this antimetaphorical talk was rhetorical in the extreme, its goal being to reapportion the strictures on thought and discourse. Indeed, it is a delicious irony that the "new language" of both Sprat and Hobbes was thoroughly infused with metaphors – about the "colours" of rhetoric, the "devices" of fancy, the "deceit" of fables; about metaphors being "foolish fires" (*ignes fatui*); and about metaphorical thinking being a path to strife, treason, and all sorts of woe.[16]

Even more to the point, Hobbes's own physiological and social theories were based on metaphors, the central ones being mechanical in nature, thus reflecting his fascination with artificial automata and in particular his love affair with clocks (see McReynolds, 1980). On the very first page of his masterpiece, for instance, Hobbes (1651/1968) laid out the metaphoric assumptions underlying his way of thought – and that of so many other adherents of the "mechanical philosophy" that accompanied the Scientific Revolution:

> Seeing life is but a motion of Limbs, the begining whereof is in some principall part within; why may we not say, that all *Automata* (Engines that move themselves by springs and wheeles as doth a watch) have an artificiall life? For what is the *Heart,* but a *Spring;* and the *Nerves,* but so many *Strings*; and the *Joynts,* but so many *Wheeles,* giving motion to the whole Body, such as was intended by the Artificer? . . . [So too] by Art is created that great LEVIATHAN called a COMMON-WEALTH, or STATE, (in latine CIVITAS) which is but an Artificiall Man . . . in which, the *Soveraignty* is an Artificiall *Soul,* as giving life and motion to the whole body; The *Magistrates,* and other *Officers* of Judicature and Execution, artificiall *Joynts; Reward* and *Punishment* . . . are the *Nerves* [and so on]. (p. 81)

Of course, when we think of the "clockwork universe," we think almost immediately of Sir Isaac Newton, even though Newton's perspective was thoroughly mathematical rather than mechanical. Indeed, the central concept in his system of thought – universal gravitation – is far from mechanistic (Newton, 1687/1974; see Cohen, 1980). In fact, the history of this concept, which is one of the most fundamental in modern science, illustrates neatly how natural philosophers and scientists often utilize metaphors from the social world.[17] When Newton first pondered the fact that no detectable mechanical force accounted for the tendency of masses of matter to move toward one another, he conceptualized this mysterious movement as analogous to the "attraction" of human persons toward one another. In his early notebooks he even used the term "sociability" in addition to "attraction" (Manuel, 1968, p. 68). Later, he preferred to speak of "gravity," despite its mechanistic connotation, on the assumption that this metaphor could be used neutrally, which is to say, in a purely descriptive manner. But though "gravity" was certainly less anthropomorphic than "sociability" or "attraction," its subsequent history shows that it was rarely taken neutrally.[18] Indeed, as I have already suggested, no term, no sign, no metaphor is so translucent that it can convey a pure idea without some sort of clothing. Numbers may come closest to being translucent, but even they, as we now know, bring along a wardrobe of assumptions that shroud their objects, however sparely, in one fashion or another.[19]

In sum, we need not select a Neoplatonic mystic like Johannes Kepler in order to illustrate the impact of metaphorical thinking in the history of the physical sciences (see Koestler, 1959). Quite the contrary. It would be easy to provide examples ad nauseam of the constitutive and regulative metaphors of modern physical science, accompanied by extended analyses of and quotations from the works of such respectable scientists as James Clerk Maxwell, William Thomson (Lord Kelvin), and Albert Einstein. For the sake of preserving the necessarily selective character of my historical survey, however, I shall simply refer to the works of Hesse (1966), Hoffman (1980), Leatherdale (1974), MacCormac (1976), and North (1980), which provide many lucid and compelling examples of the contributions of metaphorical thinking to the development of the natural sciences.

Metaphor in biological science

If there was a Newton of biology, that person was Charles Darwin, whose published works (despite his sometimes positivist rhetoric) are replete with metaphors, often – indeed generally – social in origin: metaphors of struggle, competition, organization, and division of labor; metaphors regarding the economy and polity of nature; and so on.[20] But more significant than the mere abundance of metaphors in Darwin's writing is the essential role that metaphors played in the conceptual development of his thinking, as clearly shown in his notebooks (see, e.g., Barrett, 1974; De Beer, 1960–1, 1967; Herbert, 1980; Vorzimmer, 1977). Far from being merely illustrative, Darwin's metaphors constitute the very foundation of his theory (see Evans, 1984; Gruber, 1974, 1980; Manier, 1978).

Most fundamental, of course, is Darwin's metaphor of natural selection. Does *Nature* – with a capital *N,* as he typically had it – really *select*?

Not really, but Darwin's articulation of evolutionary theory was dependent on his sustained analogical – and rhetorical – comparison between the so-called artificial selection (or breeding) of animals as controlled by humans, on the one hand, and the putatively natural selection of variants carried out by Nature, on the other. Thus, the human metaphor (as nicely analyzed by Robert Young, 1971) was central and critical to Darwin's thought, in this as in other ways. And it is worth noting that Darwin was no more able to forestall unintended, sometimes even teleological readings of his metaphor than Newton was able to keep the mechanists at bay (see Glick, 1974; D. Hull, 1973; Vorzimmer, 1970). If I may use a current Darwinian metaphor, I would say that the history of Darwinian thought suggests that ideas (like offspring of a different sort) develop according to their own genetic endowments, environments, and life histories, tending to move in directions unanticipated (and sometimes even vigorously opposed) by their parents.[21]

Also important in Darwin's creative thinking was the role of imagery, which often initially took the form of visual metaphor and was soon articulated into verbal metaphor. I am thinking primarily of the image of an irregularly branching tree, although other examples could be cited as well. As Gruber (1978) has shown, the metaphor of a tree helped Darwin at a crucial point to make sense of a good deal of untidy and problematic data regarding the evolutionary history and relationships of various species. The tree metaphor did not, and does not, work perfectly. Darwin (1859/1964) himself claimed only that it "*largely* speaks the truth" (p. 129, italics added).[22] And yet, whatever its imperfections, the tree metaphor continues to this very day – like imperfect metaphors in other disciplines – to provide a cognitive framework for both scientists and laypersons alike.

Before turning from the biological to the social sciences, I want to say a few words about one aspect of the physiological theory of Herbert Spencer, whose life and work overlapped significantly with Darwin's. I wish to do so in order to focus attention briefly on the relationship between metaphors and empirical research. To account for the multiplicity of neural functions, which clearly outnumber the finite number of the nervous system's organic parts, Spencer (1870) suggested that the brain (with its neurological extensions) resembles a piano. Though the piano has fewer than one hundred keys, its potential combinations of notes are so numerous that it can produce a virtual infinitude of sounds. So it is (Spencer said) with the brain, whose extensions and parts can be "played" in innumerable ways (pp. 562–3). To be sure, this is an innocent-seeming metaphorical comparison, but it inspired some of the important neurological work of John Hughlings Jackson, and through Jackson its impact was felt by Sigmund Freud and many others (see

Forrester, 1980, chap. 1; Fullinwider, 1983; C. U. M. Smith, 1982a,b; Young, 1970, chaps. 5 and 6).

The point I would like to emphasize here is that there are many different ways to look at the brain, or at anything else. Spencer suggested one of them, on the basis of an analogy with a piano. He used many other analogies as well – his railroad metaphor is perhaps the best known. Other theorists and researchers in his time used battery and dam metaphors, which soon gave way to telephone metaphors and eventually to other telecomunications and information measurement metaphors, a variety of thermostat and feedback metaphors, computer hardware and software metaphors, and now hologram, pattern analysis, and parallel distributed processing metaphors (see Pribram, Chapter 2, this volume). It is important to realize that all these metaphors have had historically significant *directive* functions: They have directed the gaze – not to mention the theoretical and practical activities – of researchers toward different aspects of the nervous system. Indeed, it seems safe to say that, as a general rule, phenomena (such as the brain and its extensions) look somewhat different to – and tend to be conceptualized and treated some-what differently by – possessors of different metaphorical frameworks.[23]

A graphic demonstration of this point could be provided by a historical survey of neurological illustrations, which would show how researchers of different theoretical persuasions produce different "objective" repre-sentations of the brain. It may not be so surprising that hand-drawn illustrations (even by well-trained draftsmen) are susceptible to stylization along the lines dictated by theoretical gravity and technical facility, but few people stop to consider that even photographic illustrations are based on "prepared" brains, cut in sections and carefully displayed along lines dictated by current theory. Although we cannot pursue this topic further, it is relevant to observe that different and even opposing theoretical views, grounded on very different sets of analogies, can be illustrated and corroborated at one and the same time, for what counts as "relevant evidence" varies in relation to one's theoretical vision. A good example is provided by the simultaneous confirmation of both John Hughlings Jackson's decentralized (British) model of brain functioning and Eduard Hitzig and Gustav Fritsch's centralized (Prussian) model, both of which were elaborated on the basis of explicitly sociopolitical analogies (Pauly, 1983; C. U. M. Smith, 1982b). (Outside the biological sciences, the contemporaneous confirmation of both Wilhelm Weber's particle-oriented theory and James Clerk Maxwell's field theory of electromagnet-ism provides another good example; see Hiebert, 1980, p. 188.) Obviously the "givenness" of facts is not such that it rules out the possibility of selective perception and alternative interpretation, guided (I would main-tain) by differing metaphoric assumptions about reality.

Metaphor in social science

About the metaphors of social science – mechanistic, organic, linguistic, ludic, dramaturgical, and so on – much could be said.[24] However, I prefer to focus on a single historical case and an issue that it raises – an issue that will bear further attention when we turn to psychology and its metaphors. As I have already noted, Newton derived his original notion of gravity from the analog of human attraction. I want now to point out the ironical legacy of this concept, which was soon utilized as an analog in theories of social dynamics. As an example, I shall refer to the social theory of Bishop George Berkeley, because it illustrates the point so clearly. It should be understood, however, that Berkeley was only one of many post-Newtonian thinkers and social scientists for whom the metaphor of Newtonian gravity, or some related concept, served as a template for construing human action in the aggregate.

The essence of Berkeley's social theory is expressed in his posthumously titled essay "The Bond of Society" (1713/1955). As set forth in typically succinct Berkeleyan fashion, this theory is based on the simple, straightforward contention that there is a "certain correspondence" or "similitude of operation" between the natural and human worlds. Just as natural philosophers (following Newton) agreed that natural bodies exert a "mutual attraction upon each other," so too, Berkeley asserted, can we observe a "like principle of attraction" in the moral world. In fact, the "social appetite in human souls" – that "greatest spring and source of moral actions" – is the very bond of society, just as gravity is the bond of nature (pp. 225–8).[25]

So in Berkeley's theory of social interaction, the "social appetite" that binds humans together is likened to the "physical gravity" that draws bits of matter toward one other. Need I explicate the irony? Newton had used the analog of human attraction precisely because he could think of no mechanical or physical force capable of accounting for the natural phenomena he was studying. But even before his death in 1727, his supposedly issue-begging metaphor, backed by the authority he himself had conferred on it, was turned full circle and used as an analog by which human attraction could be understood. And going a step further, the use of this metaphor would soon contribute to the questioning of the very conception of human nature, as nonmechanical and nonmaterialistic, that Newton had found pertinent to his formulation of the concept of gravity in the first place. Although Berkeley himself, as an idealist, sidestepped the physicalist, reductionist connotations of his "Newtonian" way of thinking about social behavior, the same could not be said for many of his contemporaries and successors. Before long, social dynamics (and mental dynamics, for that matter) were being discussed as if humans (or ideas) were so many billiard balls bumping into one another.[26] As we shall remark again later on, this sort of ironical boomerang effect, by which a human metaphor is reflected back on the human condition in a nonhumanist, reductionist form, is not as rare as one might wish in the history of the social and psychological sciences.

Metaphor and the origin of psychological concepts

We come now, at last, to psychology, but only after having devoted the first portions of our brief historical survey to pointing out examples of the way the other physical, biological, and social sciences have developed on the basis of certain root, or founding, metaphors. It is important to remember these examples, lest unwarranted conclusions be drawn about psychology's reliance on metaphorical thought and expression.

We should begin our consideration of metaphors in the psychological domain by focusing on the concepts of the soul, or mind, and its various intellectual and emotional processes – in other words, by focusing on the conceptual foundations of traditional mentalistic psychology. Where do these concepts and terms come from? My answer is quite simple: They come, historically, from the elaboration of metaphorical modes of comprehending human experience.

Like other claims in this chapter, this one is not new. John Locke (1690/1959), who was himself a proponent of many influential metaphors of the mind,[27] made the same claim – and presaged the conclusion of numerous linguistic historians, philosophers, and psychologists (e.g., Müller, 1867, and Whitney, 1896, pp. 88–90; Nietzsche, 1873/1979, and Reid, 1785/1969, p. 51; Asch, 1955, 1958, and Skinner, 1989, respectively) – when he noted how "sensible ideas are transferred to more abstruse significations, and made to stand for ideas that come not under the cognizance of our senses" (vol. 2, p. 5). Locke's point was simply that terms referring originally to sensible objects and actions have often come to stand for processes that are not accessible to sensory experience. To illustrate his point, Locke cited such psychological concepts as imagination, apprehension, comprehension, conception, disgust, disturbance, and tranquility, each of which had originally signified physical states and processes.[28] Furthermore, Locke went on to say (with considerable foresight) that he was confident that "if we could trace them to their sources, we should find, in all languages, the names for things that fall not under our senses to have had their first rise from sensible ideas" (vol. 2, p. 5).

In other words, Locke recognized that our basic mentalistic concepts are metaphorical – transferred from the physical to the psychological realm in an attempt to express what our inner experience is *like*. But these metaphorical concepts are not simply *descriptive*; they have also been *transformative*: Their use has led to changes in human self-reference and hence to human self-consciousness. This is a major claim, but one that has the substantial backing of such respected classical scholars as R. B. Onians (1951) and Bruno Snell (1953). The nub of the argument is that it was only over time that such physicalist terms as *pneuma* and *psyche* came to have explicitly psychological meanings and that it was during the same time that humans began to think of themselves as having a distinctive soul or identity – something "solid" and "tangible" at their very core.[29] Thus, as Brewster Smith (1985) has argued, explicit self-consciousness seems to be the *result,* not simply the progenitor, of metaphorical thinking. This is apparently true not only on the phylogenetic level – a level on which generic self-consciousness originated when humans began to think about themselves with reference to other things, activities, and persons – but also on the ontogenetic level; As George Herbert Mead (1924–5), Harry Stack Sullivan (1953), Lev Vygotsky (1934/1986), and others have proposed, the origin of individual selves seems to occur in the context of relationships with "others" and with the "outer world."

I would like to make two other points of more general applicability: (1) Metaphors can have an impact on practical as well as theoretical developments, and (2) metaphorical concepts can undergo progressive, historical development, changing their analogical clothing (as it were) from time to time. Both points can be illustrated with psychological concepts rooted in ancient times. For instance, given the association of "spirit" (or breath) and "life," which was common in a variety of ancient cultures (see Bremmer, 1983; Rohde, 1894/1925), it was natural for our forebears to think that if the quality of their lives took a turn for the worse it was somehow related to a change in the quality of their spirit. One practical result of such thinking was the institution of trephining – the drilling of a hole in the skull – as a technique for releasing "evil spirits" from patients suffering psychic disturbance.[30] It is relevant to emphasize that this practice was reasonable within the conceptual (i.e., metaphorical) context in which it was formulated.[31] But the major point I wish to make, with the assistance of this example, is that metaphors can have a significant impact in the realm of practical activity. As we shall see later in this chapter and book, this is as true in the twentieth century as it was in ancient times.

To illustrate the historical transformation of metaphorical concepts, I will refer again to the notion of "spirit" or "breath," with its originally physical referent. Over time, this referent "became" less and less physical, at least in the Western tradition, until it was thoroughly "immaterialized" into the Christian concept of the soul (see Baker, 1947; Knowles, 1962, chap. 17; Tillich, 1972). "Spirit" now meant something different from before, yet, interestingly, many of the psychological practices associated with the earlier concept of the spirit were transformed and maintained in a strikingly parallel manner. For example, the surgical release of evil spirits was replaced by the "casting out of devils," which involved spiritual purifications and incantations rather than surgical intervention.[32]

Not surprisingly, the historical transformation of metaphorical concepts and practices is not an all-at-once or all-or-none process. Despite the immaterialization of the concept of the soul, for instance, minutely physical "animal spirits" were still part of the basic explanatory framework of psychology in the seventeenth century, when René Descartes assigned them a central role in the tipping of his infamous pineal gland (see the illustrations as well as the text of Descartes, 1662/1972, pp. 91–2). Soon afterward, however, the remaining animal spirits were transmogrified into electrical currents, which in turn were transformed into biochemical solutions, and so on. Thus, the theoretical legacy moves forward – with clinical practice following suit – from ancient times right down to the present.

Descartes and the mechanistic metaphor in psychology

Descartes, to whom I have just referred, is particularly important in the history of psychology for having solidified – for better or worse – the radical distinction between mind and body (see Descartes, 1644/1911c, esp. pp. 221–2; Keeling, 1968, chap. 6). As is well known, Descartes explained all bodily functioning, including emotion and behavior, in mechanistic terms. It is not as well known that Descartes's postulation of a mechanistic psychology was inspired, like Hobbes's, by artificial automata, though more by the water-driven figures in the grottoes of the Royal Gardens at Saint-Germain-en-Laye than by clocks (see Jaynes, 1970; Price, 1965; and the illustration opposite the title page of Descartes, 1662/1972). Having seen these remarkable automated statues, Descartes (1662/1972) reasoned that if mere men could make mechanical devices that acted in such lifelike fashion, then surely it was – and had been – a simple thing for God to make living bodies that acted according to the principles of basic mechanics (pp. 1–5).[33]

Descartes's metaphorical reasoning provides another example of someone taking a humanly constructed analog – this time an animated statue made in the image and likeness of human beings – and then using this analog as a means of reflecting on human nature, that is, on the very same aspect of nature that had been the model for the analog in the first place. Of course, Descartes himself (1637/1911b) felt that no merely mechanical creature would have – nor could have – created an external image of itself, and he continued to believe in the autonomy of the human mind (see esp. pp. 115–18). But once the possibility of a mechanistic explanation of mind was proposed, as it was by many in the eighteenth century (see Rosenfield, 1968), the paradoxical import of

Descartes's use of the mechanical metaphor had a deep and lasting effect on the estimation of human nature reached by many scientific and non-scientific thinkers, right up to our own day. Thus, not for the last time in the history of psychology, a caricature of the human mind served as a model for its theoretical portrait. As a result, the mind was not portrayed as being *like* a machine built to mimic human behavior; it was pictured *as* a machine (e.g., La Mettrie, 1748/1912).

It was a merely logical consequence when David Hartley, among others, began to speculate about the possible physiological basis of Lockean associationism, which became the most popular psychological theory of mental dynamics in the eighteenth century and beyond (see Gay, 1969; Ong, 1951; Randall, 1962; Warren, 1921). After first conceptualizing associationism on an explicitly social model, Hartley (1749/1966) followed a suggestion of Newton's and conjectured that "vibrations" are set off in the brain by the "impact" of sensations and that these physical movements leave "traces" representing the "pathways" that constitute the associative links between ideas (see Walls, 1982). Such metaphorical thinking – about vibrations, impacts, traces, and pathways – stimulated numerous developments in psychoneurological theory and motivated a great deal of empirical research (see, e.g., French, 1969, chaps. 10 and 11; Rather, 1965). Although such research revealed the limitations of these metaphors, there is no denying their important role in the history of physiological psychology.[34] Nor, for that matter, should one overlook their role in the history of behavioral psychology, for these metaphors, and the associationist theory by which they were linked to psychology, eventually fed into the development of behaviorism, which was first based on the concept of the physiological reflex (see Watson, 1916) and then developed further on the basis of its critique (e.g., by Skinner, 1931).

Of course, not all post-Cartesian mechanists tried to physiologize psychology or to translate associationism into a behavioristic psychology (see Rachlin, 1970, chap. 1). Some remained steadfast mentalists, even though they were committed to the notion that mental phenomena are products of mechanical processes. One such person was Johann Friedrich Herbart (1816/1891), who referred to these psychomechanical processes as the "statics and dynamics of the mind." I need not remind most readers that "mental mechanics" is now a mainstay of twentieth-century cognitive psychology. Indeed, if there were any utility in attaching such metaphoric labels, I would suggest that Herbart was the "great-grandfather" of contemporary information-processing approaches to the mind.[35] Besides this somewhat distant progeny, his "mental mechanics," with its postulated "threshold" between consciousness and unconsciousness, is also related (along uncular if not paternal lines) to Sigmund Freud's approach to the "statics and dynamics of the mind."

Freud and the metaphors of psychoanalysis

Not too long ago, when positivist strictures were more strongly held, Freud was often charged with serious violations of scientific method (see, e.g., Popper, 1963; Skinner, 1954). Today, however, a somewhat different assessment is coming to the fore, and there is even occasional talk about how advanced his philosophy of science was![36] In any case, whatever criticisms may still be leveled against his work, Freud was unusually astute in his awareness that psychoanalytic theory, like any theory, constitutes what he called a "mythology," in the sense that it inevitably involves speculation. He also realized that there is no way for psychologists to operate without the metaphorical expressions that are, as he said, "peculiar to psychology" (1920/1955e, p. 60). "In psychology," Freud (1926/1959c) wrote, "we can only describe things by the help of analogies. There is nothing peculiar in this; it is the case elsewhere as well. But we have constantly to keep changing these analogies, for none of them lasts us long enough" (p. 195).[37]

This is a remarkable and by no means isolated statement.[38] More explicitly perhaps than any other psychologist, Freud gave analogical thinking center stage in his theoretical ruminations. Beyond that, he let analogies guide his practical work in therapy, where he countered "resistance" with freedom and overcame "repression" with disclosure (see Freud, 1915/1957c, 1926/1959b, esp. pp. 157–64; Laplanche & Pontalis, 1973, pp. 390–7).

It is noteworthy in this context that Freud was a devotee of Plato.[39] In effect, he accepted Plato's pragmatic, rather than his idealistic, philosophy of science. If human knowledge at best is a "likely story," Freud strove to make psychoanalysis the most likely story possible. In his continuous struggle to improve this story, he tried out any metaphor that promised to move his thinking forward.

Indeed, a taxonomist would have to work long and hard to classify Freud's many metaphors, which were drawn from social and political life, from the fields of physical dynamics and hydraulics, physiology and natural history, anthropology and mythology, archeology and ancient history, military life and technology, the classics and popular literature, and from other realms as well. As Freud utilized these metaphors – of energy and force, flow and resistance, repression and conversion, defense and aggression, and all the rest – he was clearly following his own advice to change analogies and comparisons as often as necessary.[40]

Freud's use of multiple metaphors was occasioned by his awareness of the insufficiency of any single metaphor. He did not seek multiplicity for its own sake. Instead, as already noted, he constantly strove to find the most appropriate and useful metaphors for his particular concerns and subject matter. For example, in his major treatise, *The Interpretation of*

Dreams (1900/1953a), Freud worked through a series of metaphors in order to arrive at a much more restricted core of basic comparisons (see esp. chap. 7). He did so largely through his explication of the analogy between perception, thought, and writing, which resolved some of the conceptual and empirical problems with which he had been struggling (for an insightful analysis, see Derrida, 1978). Matthew Erdelyi (1985) has argued that our contemporary computer model solves these problems even more economically. This may be so, but we can expect computational theory in its turn to be found wanting, for like all other theories, including Freud's, it is ultimately metaphorical and fallible (see note 35). What is distinctive about Freud is his explicit understanding and acceptance of this metaphoricity and fallibility, and his persistent efforts – however successful – to improve the comparisons that oriented his theory and practice.[41]

Perhaps even more important, Freud frequently attempted to specify the limitations of his analogs, often within the very context in which he used them. As much as any other psychiatrist or psychologist, he wanted to be persuasive, but he rarely presented his metaphors and analogies as anything other than imperfect. For instance, in his *Interpretation of Dreams* (1900/1953a), Freud openly admitted that his metaphors needed improvement, but he said that he saw "no necessity to apologize" for that fact since they were only provisional aids, intended to assist his initial descriptions and thoughts about previously unremarked psychic processes (p. 536).[42] Even granting that this sort of self-disclosure serves a rhetorical purpose of its own, it also invited others to examine, to improve, and sometimes to reject his work in favor of other metaphorical schemes of psychological understanding and practice. That is not a bad way to conduct the business of science.[43]

James and the metaphorical nature of scientific thought

Even so, until just a decade or two ago, many persons would have been bothered by the suggestion that human thought, including scientific thought, is necessarily perspectival, approximal, and incomplete. But not William James, the most frequently and most justifiably cited "father" of modern American psychology. The expectation that someone might present a theory that would end all theoretical argument was foreign to James's temperament and, as he pointed out, unfaithful to the historical record of science itself. Following in the footsteps of his beloved Ralph Waldo Emerson, James believed that "science is nothing but the finding of an analogy" and that the analogies of science – indeed, the analogies underlying all forms of knowledge – are "fluxional" rather than "frozen" (Emerson, 1837/1983b, p. 55; 1844/1983c, p. 463). In other words, although he was a staunch empiricist – or rather, as he saw it, *because* he

was a staunch empiricist – James insisted that there is always a new way
to experience any reality and a new way to categorize any experience. A
creative genius in any field, in science as in the arts, is simply someone
who has an unusual native talent for perceiving analogies that have not
yet occurred to others but that, upon presentation, are seen by them to
reveal something salient about experience (James, 1890, vol. 1, pp. 423–
4, 529–30; vol. 2, pp. 109–10, 360–5).[44]

Salience, as James knew, is not something that is absolute. It cannot be
judged once and for all. Even James's well-known pragmatic criterion of
truth is susceptible to variable interpretation: What "works" for one
person may not "work" for someone else, given different fundamental
concerns. In the end, James felt, humans – scientists included – must
humbly accept the fact that the salience of their creative ideas will
ultimately be judged by the "consensus" of their social or professional
group (James, 1880; 1890, vol. 1, p. 192; 1907/1975).[45]

The achievement of scientific consensus, from this point of view, depends to a significant degree on the rhetorical power of particular analogies or, rather, of the particular stories based on these analogies. This
power draws on the experiential sensitivities of the particular scientific
community, but it is not reducible in any simple or direct fashion to the
"brute facts of the matter." No analogy – which is to say, no *likeness* of
reality – is identical with reality. As another of James's admired men put
it, "No likeness goes on all fours" (Coleridge, ca. 1823/1981, p. 132).
Therefore, no story developed from analogical premises can be definitive
or final. This is the same view expressed by Plato long ago: We should
expect no more than a likely story from those who construct theories
about the natural world (see note 13 and the text associated with it).
Consequently, James (1890) concluded, "the best mark of health that a
science can show is this unfinished-seeming front," even though it is
useful for each science to have as its heuristic goal the attainment of
"conceptions so adequate and exact that we shall never need to change
them" (vol. 1, p. vii; vol. 2, p. 109). In other words, in James's view as
well as my own, we should continue to search for perfectly adequate
metaphors or maps of reality, thus continually improving our stock of
metaphors, but we should not expect to discover an analog that will
provide the "final word" about our experience of reality.[46]

James's belief in the analogical or metaphorical foundation of knowledge is richly illustrated in his own psychological writings. His treatment
of thought or consciousness as a "stream" rather than a "chain" or
"train" is well known (see James, 1890, chap. 9), and his discussion of
other psychological topics is similarly informed by underlying analogies
and metaphors.[47] The ultimate metaphors that founded and framed his
psychological thinking, and that came to undergird his pragmatism, pluralism, and radical empiricism, were the Darwinian metaphors of varia-

tion, selection, and function.[48] All psychological states and actions, according to James, are products of spontaneous variation and/or selection in terms of their consequential utility. This "functionalist" orientation has been shared by many other American psychologists and has structured much of the theoretical argumentation in modern psychology, leading historically from mentalistic functionalism to functionalistic behaviorism and back again. Its rhetorical power is clearly dependent on the authority that Darwinian modes of analysis, because of their success in making sense of a vast array of biological phenomena, have come to enjoy (see, e.g., E. Mayr, 1982). Often taken, despite James's intention, as a definitively true story rather than as a usefully likely story, the functionalist account of mind and action has led to some of the central psychological theories – and myths – of our time.[49]

Conclusion: Psyche's muse in the twentieth century and beyond

Now that we have reviewed Freud and James on the role of metaphorical thinking in science and psychology (as well as in cognition in general), we have reached a point at which we can halt our very selective historical survey with the realization that, around the turn of the century, some psychologists, at least, were keenly aware of the metaphorical nature of psychological knowledge. Although other twentieth-century psychologists have shared this awareness,[50] psychologists for the most part have tended to flow with the positivist tide. As a result, until recently, data gathering – generally presumed to be an activity that can and should be pursued without any theoretical preconceptions – was frequently considered to be the source of psychological theory and practice (see Toulmin & Leary, 1985). In this regard, the naive empiricist view of James McKeen Cattell, another founder of modern American psychology, is much more emblematic of twentieth-century psychology than the more sophisticated empiricism of James. For Cattell, scientific activity was *work*, pure and simple. Rather than the spontaneous flashes of metaphoric insight that James touted, Cattell (1896) saw "men of science" engaging in the "every-day up-hill work of the laboratory." This work, in his opinion, was "scarcely more stimulating than the routine of the factory or the farm" (p. 139).[51] With such a stoic, antimetaphorical view of science (structured by the metaphor of piecework labor), it is not surprising that the "work" of Cattell and far too many of his contemporaries and successors has provided little more than well-organized catalogs of "facts," largely devoid of long-range theoretical significance.[52]

Given the positivist mentality of so many twentieth-century psychologists, it was natural enough that awareness of the metaphoricity of psychological concepts and terms receded over the middle portion of this century, leaving the impression that both scientific and applied psychology, unlike earlier philosophical psychology, rested on an unambiguously rooted conceptual foundation. Perhaps the best example of the solidification of this conceptual foundation is the literalization of "stimulus" and "response," surely the most used and abused terms in twentieth-century psychology. When John B. Watson (1919) first recommended these terms, he admitted that in introducing them from physiology into psychology "we have to extend somewhat" their usage (p. 10), which is to say (quite properly) that *psychological* "stimuli" and "responses" – as well as the *psychological* "reflexes" (or correlations between stimuli and responses) about which they allow us to speak – are somehow *like* their physiological counterparts, but also *unlike* them. But Watson never defined the exact ways in which psychological stimuli and responses are unlike their originating analogs, thus setting the scene for a simple-minded literalization of these terms,[53] and leaving room for subsequent variations or "extensions." Indeed, as Koch (1959) has persuasively shown, we have not lacked such extensions. In fact, these two reputedly "objective" and "neutral" terms, so basic to behavioral science in this century, have been used over the past half-century in *myriad* ways, and rarely in precisely the same way by any two theorists. The variety is not necessarily bad – let the mutants contend and the fittest variant(s) survive! But when the variation goes unrecognized, a presumption of monolithic unanimity is (and has been) created – a presumption that does not reflect disciplinary reality, however much we might wish that it did.

Fortunately, in more recent years, the variation or pluralism of twentieth-century psychology, which is evident at so many levels of the discipline, has come to be recognized (e.g., see Koch, 1976), and not unrelatedly, awareness of the metaphorical nature of psychological theory, and of the metaphorical framing of psychological practice, has increased significantly. Where this will lead, whether to the dismemberment of psychology (long since predicted by Dunlap, 1938, and others) or to a revivification of psychology, we cannot yet say. (Are neuroscience, cognitive science, and the new health sciences at the "growing edges" or on the "fraying ends" of psychology?) In either case, in the elaboration of these and other developments, we can be confident that Psyche's Muse – muted and hemmed in, but far from inactive during much of this century – will have her say. Or rather, *we* will have our say, at least a *chance* to have our say; for, as I have tried to show, Psyche's Muse, the fount of psychological theory and practice, is none other than *we ourselves*, using what the empiricist David Hume called "Analogy, that great principle of Reasoning" and what the rationalist Immanuel Kant, though in an unfortunately transcendentalist mood, called the "Analogies of Experience."[54]

I have said a number of times that my thesis is hardly new: Many scholars and scientists have recognized that our thoughts, feelings, and behavior are informed by metaphors. Still, given the stakes in the domain of psychology, it seems more than reasonable that we should pause and reflect on the nature and consequences of these metaphors. That is what this book is all about. Insofar as the quality of life of many individuals and groups, as well as the future of the discipline itself, will be affected by the choices of metaphor that psychologists make, this book has a very serious purpose. By focusing on the role of metaphor in the history of psychology, the following chapters suggest that it is through the judicious choice and use of metaphor that psychologists will deal more or less effectively with the estimable challenges and opportunities that lie ahead.

Acknowledgments

An early version of this chapter was shared with many of my fellow members of the Center for Advanced Study in the Behavioral Sciences in Stanford, California, in February 1983. I am especially grateful to Matthew H. Erdelyi, James W. Fernandez, and Howard M. Spiro for their supportive and thoughtful feedback at that time. Intermediate versions were presented before the Western Psychological Association in April 1983 and before the American Psychological Association in August 1984. The latter occasion was my presidential address before the APA's Division of the History of Psychology. I thank all of those who listened patiently and responded critically. I am also grateful to the other contributors to this volume, who have provided support, feedback, and stimulation, and to the *Journal of the History of the Behavioral Sciences* for permission to use portions of an article of mine (1987).

Notes

1 Most of these scholars have taken their lead from Aristotle, especially from his treatises on rhetoric and poetics (Aristotle, ca. 330 B.C./1924a; ca. 330 B.C./ 1924b). The quotation in the text is from the former work (l. 1410).

2 Aristotle (ca. 330 B.C./1924a), for instance, said that metaphor confers "clearness, charm, and distinction [to discourse] as nothing else can" (l. 1405). For a review of the history of scholarship of metaphor, see Johnson (1981a). For a survey of the literature up to 1970, see Shibles (1971); for that from 1970 into the mid-1980s, see van Noppen, De Knop, and Jongen (1985). Johnson (1981b), Miall (1982), Ortony (1979), and Sacks (1979) provide convenient access into, and examples of, the recent literature on metaphor. Billow (1977), Hoffman (1984a), and Ortony, Reynolds, and Arter (1978) provide overviews of the psychological literature. Vosniadou and Ortony (1988) represent some of the latest developments, and Winner (1988) discusses some of the onto-genetic factors that underpin the use of metaphor in adult life, by scientists as well as others.

3 I. A. Richards's chapters on metaphor in *The Philosophy of Rhetoric* (1936) are at the root of much of this recent work, which stems more proximately

from Max Black's *Models and Metaphors* (1962). Richards (1936) argued that "metaphor is the omnipresent principle of language" (p. 92) and, subsequently, that it is also the fundamental principle of thinking: "Thinking is radically metaphoric. Linkage by analogy is its constituent law or principle, its causal nexus, since meaning only arises through the causal *contexts* by which a sign stands for (takes the place of) an instance of a sort. To think of anything is to take it *as* of a sort (as a such and such) and that 'as' brings in (openly or in disguise) the analogy, the parallel, the metaphoric grapple or ground or grasp or draw by which alone the mind takes hold. It takes no hold if there is nothing for it to haul from, for its thinking is the haul, the attraction of likes" (I. A. Richards, 1938, pp. 48–9).

4 Despite the criticisms directed at his (1962) position, Black (1979) has continued to argue that "a metaphorical statement can sometimes generate new knowledge and insight by *changing* relationships between the things designated" and, furthermore, that "some metaphors enable us to see aspects of reality that the metaphor's production helps to constitute" (pp. 37, 39) Someone adopting a less radical position would agree with Black's contention that metaphors can direct our attention to formerly *unnoticed* aspects of reality, and are thus important in the development of new insights into – or visions of – reality, but would eschew the idea that metaphors actually help to constitute reality. Even someone holding this more moderate view, however, would credit metaphor with an essentially epistemological function.

Of the many books and articles stimulated by Black's work, Mary B. Hesse's *Models and Analogies in Science* (1966) deserves mention, not least for its highlighting of relevant issues by means of an insightful rendition of a hypothetical debate between Pierre Duhem and N. R. Campbell regarding the role of models in the construction of theories in physics. Duhem's (1906/1962) and N. R. Campbell's (1920) works provide additional context for the deliberations in this volume. See L. D. Smith's comments (Chapter 7, this volume) on Duhem's metaphorical statements against the use of metaphorical statements in science. Also see Hesse (1955), which shows that Hesse was "on the right track" long before Black's (1962) work appeared.

Finally, Black's work, together with several essays by Saul Kripke and Hilary Putnam, has inspired Thomas Kuhn's recent assignment of preeminence to metaphor in the process of "revolutionary" change in science. As Kuhn said in 1979, reacting to a similarly relevant essay by Richard Boyd (1979), "The view toward which I grope would also be Kantian but without 'things in themselves' and with categories of the mind which could change in time as the accommodation of language and experience proceeded. A view of that sort need not, I think, make the world less real" (pp. 418–19). By 1987, Kuhn would say that, of the three characteristics shared by his illustrative revolutions, the one that "has been the most difficult... for me to see, but now seems the most obvious and probably the most consequential," is the common occurrence of a "central change of model, metaphor, or analogy – a change in one's sense of what is similar to what, and of what is different" (p. 20). The crux of Kuhn's analysis is that the groupings or categorizations of phenomena change radically and holistically in the course of a scientific revolution, so that what once were "natural categories" of perception and understanding no longer are such. Aristotle, for instance, found it quite natural to assume that "the falling stone was *like* the growing oak, or *like* the person recovering from illness," and thus that all three were instances of "motion" (p. 20). Newton's alignment of like and unlike, however, was completely different. After his review of other instances of scientific change,

Kuhn (1987) noted that "all these cases display interrelated features familiar to students of metaphor. In each case two objects or situations are juxtaposed and said to be the same or similar.... The juxtaposed items are exhibited to a previously uninitiated audience by someone who can already recognize their similarity, and who urges that audience to learn to do the same.... Thus, the education of an Aristotelian associates the flight of an arrow with a falling stone and both with the growth of an oak and the return to health.... the student learns what categories of things populate the world, what their salient features are, and something about the behavior that is and is not permitted to them. In much of language learning these two sorts of knowledge – knowledge of words and knowledge of nature – are acquired together, not really two sorts of knowledge at all, but two faces of the single coinage that a language provides" (pp. 20–1).

Kuhn's relevant conclusion is simply that "the metaphorlike juxtapositions that change at times of scientific revolution are thus central to the process by which scientific and other language is acquired" (p. 21). As these statements and his examples show, Kuhn's position is now virtually identical to Black's radical position, described at the beginning of this note. Though I stand in close proximity to them, I want to repeat that sharing this position is not a prerequisite for according metaphor an important role in the history of thought and science.

5 The necessity of allowing our search for meaning to rest on the achievement of subjective satisfaction, intuition, or belief was suggested long ago by Montaigne (1587–8/1958): "I ask what is 'nature,' 'pleasure,' 'circle,' 'substitution.' The question is one of words, and is answered in the same way. 'A stone is a body.' But if you pressed on: 'And what is a body?' – 'Substance.' – 'And what is substance?' and so on, you would finally drive the respondent to the end of his lexicon" (pp. 818–19). To say that our knowledge rests, ultimately, on a basis secured by satisfaction, intuition, or belief is not to admit that our knowledge is insecure in any devastating sense. I think it was Karl Popper, or perhaps one of his students, who suggested several images that, at least in my rendition, express my own view of the matter: Our knowledge is like a house built on pilings driven into quicksand. No individual piling is absolutely secured, and any given piling may – and probably will – fail and have to be replaced, yet the pilings are sunk into "reality" and manage *as a group and with our ongoing vigilance and repair* to keep us in touch with "reality" without allowing us to sink so far into it that we lose our overarching perspective. An alternative image is quite similar: It is as if we are in a boat whose various planks must be replaced from time to time; though in need of constant repair, our boat manages to keep us afloat. The point in each case is that our knowledge is not supported by any single satisfaction, intuition, or belief, nor by any rock-solid foundation, but by a coordinated system of satisfactions, intuitions, and beliefs, each of which has stood the test of experience, at least up to the present moment. As William James (1897/1979) put it, the "final truth" will not be known "until the last man has had his experience and had his say" (p. 141). In the meantime, the "circle of knowledge" is repeatedly broken and reconnected as we continue to "bootstrap" our understanding of the world and ourselves. Metaphors, I am suggesting, provide one of the major means of this ever-ongoing process.

6 The commonality of this view is rarely appreciated, partly because of the difference in vocabulary favored by theorists of different persuasions. As Newell and Simon (1972) have noted, with reference to an earlier article

(Simon & Newell, 1956), there is no set "terminology nor metatheory of science to explicate the roles of metaphors, analogs, models, theories and descriptions, or the passage from one category to another" (p. 5) – hence the cacophony of voices, each trying to express a similar insight. For instance, a justification of the references made in the text would proceed through the explication of the following core statements: *Hume* (1748/1972): "All arguments from experience are founded on the similarity which we discover among natural objects" (p. 36). *Bentham* (1841/1962): "In the use made of language, fiction . . . becomes a necessary resource" (p. 331). *Bain* (1855): "Some discoveries turn upon this [use of the law of similarity] exclusively; and no succession of discoveries can proceed without it" (p. 508). *Peirce* (1932): "Upon finding himself confronted with a phenomenon unlike what he would have expected . . ., he [the reasoner] looks over its features and notices some remarkable character or relation among them, which he at once recognizes as being characteristic of some conception with which his mind is already stored. . . . Presumption [or the 'abducting' of similarities] is the only kind of reasoning which supplies new ideas" (pp. 776–7). *Kant* (1781/1965): "We are justified in combining appearances [in order to arrive at concepts] only according to what is no more than an analogy" (p. 212). *Nietzsche* (1873/1979): "The drive toward the formation of metaphors is the fundamental human drive" (p. 88). *Vaihinger* (1911/1924): "All cognition is the apperception of one thing through another. In understanding, we are always dealing with an analogy, and we cannot imagine how otherwise existence can be understood . . . all conception and cognition are based upon analogical apperception" (p. 29). *Cassirer* (1925/1946): "Myth and language [the roots of human cognition] may differ, yet the same form of mental conception is operative in both. It is the form which one may denote as *metaphorical thinking*" (p. 84).

Regarding the thoughts of Peirce, Nietzsche, and Cassirer on metaphor and related topics, which have proved particularly stimulating to many individuals, see Burks (1946), Fann (1970), and Fisch (1986); Blondel (1977), Breazeale (1975), Cantor (1982), Schrift (1985), and Stern (1978); and Langer (1942), respectively. Ogden (1932) offers an interesting overview of Bentham's theory of fictions, including a section titled "Fictions and Metaphors" (pp. 70–4), and McReynolds (1970) discusses the application of this theory to psychological concepts.

Of course, to say that language and thought are ultimately metaphorical leaves unresolved the precise nature of this metaphoricity (see Leatherdale, 1974, pp. 172–3). In this regard I would simply argue, conservatively, that the acquisition of new knowledge is always based on the forward "reach" of metaphorical or analogical perception and thought. This leaves room for the additional claim, which I would also endorse, that such "metaphorical" knowledge can become "literal" knowledge once it is confirmed by continued use and general acceptance: Indeed, it sometimes becomes *all too literal* in the sense discussed later in the text and in note 49.

Again, I would like to point out that my thesis is hardly novel. More than a century ago, the great comparative linguist Max Müller (1867) noted that "no advance was possible in the intellectual life of man without metaphor" (p. 370), and Fritz Mauthner, the writer and philosopher, argued that "without exception every word in its individual usage is metaphorical" and that "we have learnt to understand the metaphor as the term for the phenomenon which others call the growth or the development of language" (quoted in Gerschenkron, 1974, p. 432). Among psychologists, as we shall see, William

James (1890) was among the first to assert that "a native talent for perceiving analogies is . . . the leading fact in genius [creative thinking] of every order" (vol. 1, p. 530, italics deleted).

7 I have been unable to relocate the source of this quotation, but it is attributed to Craik somewhere in McCulloch (1965) (see Pribram, 1971, p. 97). In any case, it fits Craik's (1943) general point of view, not to mention his own analogical extrapolations about the brain and its functions (see Craik, 1966, chaps. 4–6).

8 A "figure of speech" is any of the various forms of linguistic expression that deviate from the usual arrangement or use of words. The term "trope" is generally treated as a synonym for "figure of speech," and it can be so understood here. Ricoeur (1977) has noted the circular intertwining of "metaphor" and "figure." As he says, "Metaphor is a figure and the word *figure* is metaphorical" (p. 53). The figures of speech that are generally considered closest to, yet distinguishable from metaphor, narrowly defined, are analogy, metonymy, simile, and synecdoche. These and other "metaphorical substitutions and puns" are defined in Lanham (1968).

9 As observed years ago by Stanford (1936), the more tolerant use of the term "metaphor" has been favored by most of those who have investigated metaphor from the viewpoint of philology and etymology, whereas the opponents of the equation of metaphor and trope have tended to come (like Stanford himself) from the ranks of literary critics, whose job it is to make finer distinctions about the use of language (p. 100). This is not to say that all literary critics oppose a broad conception of metaphor and its relation to discourse. M. H. Abrams (1953), surely a leading literary critic, has written that metaphor, "whether alive or moribund, is an inseparable element of all discourse, including discourse whose purpose is neither persuasive nor aesthetic, but descriptive and informative. Metaphysical systems in particular are intrinsically metaphorical systems. . . . Even the traditional language of the natural sciences cannot claim to be totally literal, although its key terms often are not recognized to be metaphors until, in the course of time, the general adoption of a new analogy yields perspective into the nature of the old. . . . [Some analogs are] *constitutive* [not simply illustrative]: they yield the ground plan and essential structural element of a . . . theory . . . they select and mold those 'facts' which a theory comprehends. For facts are *facta,* things made as much as things found, and made in part by the analogies through which we look at the world as through a lens" (p. 31).

This statement, especially the latter part, is remarkably prescient of subsequent "postpositivist" philosophy of science (see H. I. Brown, 1977, for a succinct summary; Suppe, 1977, for more details). Even earlier, Kenneth Burke (1935/1965), another leading literary critic, expressed a similar conviction: "As the documents of science pile up, are we not coming to see that whole works of scientific research, even entire *schools,* are hardly more than the patient repetition, in all its ramifications, of a fertile metaphor? Thus we have, at different eras in history, considered man as the son of God, as an animal, as a political or economic brick, as a machine, each such metaphor, and a hundred others, serving as the cue for an unending line of data and generalizations" (p. 95).

Similarly, literary writers, as opposed to literary critics, have shown little hesitation in accepting the wider notion of metaphor. For instance, Robert Frost (1931/1956) found that "in late years" he wanted "to go further and further in making metaphor the whole of thinking" (p. 37), and Walker Percy (1958) has argued that metaphor "is the true maker of language" and that the mind's "favorite project" is a "casting about for analogies and connections" (pp. 96–7).

10 I should reiterate, however, that the broad use of metaphor and its frequent equation with analogy throughout this volume do not mean that any of the volume's other contributors necessarily accept my contention that all language and thought are fundamentally metaphorical.

It is not only metaphor and analogy that can be considered interchangeable for purposes like those pursued in this volume. Howard Gruber, on the basis of his long-term study of creative thinking in science (e.g., Gruber, 1974), has concluded, in harmony with the thrust of my own thought, that "metaphors, analogies, and models are part of a group of comparison processes by which we use some parts of our knowledge to illuminate others. There are many names for such comparison processes, but there is no adequate taxonomy of them. Indeed, since they have almost always been treated singly, we have no adequate overview of the way in which groups of such comparison processes function in intellectual work. Lacking any such systematic treatment, it is idle to fuss over definitions. We need a large and generous term to cover the whole family of comparison processes.... I will use *metaphor, image, figure of thought*, and the abbreviated *figure* interchangeably for such comparison processes" (Gruber, 1980, p. 122).

Gruber's use of "comparison processes" is similar to my own inclination to use "comparative thinking" as a generic term that encompasses and thus avoids the distinction between metaphor, analogy, simile, and so on. In this regard, it is interesting that Kant (1797/1974) used "comparison," as opposed to "distinction." in much the same way (pp. 89–92). However, I only suggest this term here, rather than insist on it, since there is already a long tradition of using "metaphor" to represent the same overarching concept. For a similar blending of "analogies," "models," "hypotheses," and "theories" under the generic concept of "representation," see Wartofsky (1979, esp. pp. 1–11, 24–39). See also Fogelin (1988, chaps. 3–6) and O. Mayr (1986, p. 204, note 1).

11 As MacCormac (1985) has said, "Metaphors that were false seem to become true, and metaphors that were ungrammatical seem to become grammatical, both through usage" (p. 27). A related point regarding supposedly literal *thought* has been made by Bloor (1971): "After something has been said by means of a metaphor it is easy to think that it could have been said without it, because one's understanding of the literal concepts undergoes a change under the impact of the metaphor" (p. 441). In other words, since the idea expressed by a metaphor can soon come to seem "natural" and "literal" and can then be expressed (however partially) by different metaphors, it is easy to overlook the creative role of the original metaphor. A recent, effective argument for the thesis that "all language is metaphorical" has been offered by Arbib and Hesse (1986), who admit that this thesis "will appear shocking to those writers who have labored to provide careful distinctions between the literal and metaphoric in traditional grammar and semantics" (p. 150). Their argument hinges on their carefully considered rejection of the literal view of language, a rejection based (among other foundations) on a review of the research on language acquisition. See also Barfield (1960), Benjamin, Cantor, and Christie (1987), and Rumelhart (1979).

12 I cannot resist a few parting shots before moving on to the promised historical survey. These shots take the form of corroborative statements by four scholars of rather different orientations – Isaiah Berlin, Nelson Goodman, Robert Nisbet, and Stephen Pepper:

> The notion that . . . it is possible to think without such analogies in some direct fashion – "face-to-face" with the facts – will not bear criticism. To think is to generalise, to generalise is to compare. To think of one phenomenon or cluster of phenomena is to think in terms of its resemblances and differences with others. This is by now a hoary platitude. It follows that without parallels and analogies between one sphere and another of thought and action, whether conscious or not, the unity of our experience – our experience itself – would not be possible. All language and thought are, in this sense, necessarily "metaphorical." (Berlin, 1981, p. 158)

> Metaphor permeates all discourse, ordinary and special. . . . This incessant use of metaphor springs not merely from love of literary color but also from urgent need of economy. If we could not readily transfer schemata to make new sortings and orderings, we should have to burden ourselves with unmanageably many different schemata, either by adoption of a vast vocabulary of elementary terms or by prodigious elaboration of composite ones. (Goodman, 1976, p. 80)

> Human thought in the large is almost inconceivable apart from the use in some degree of metaphor. Whenever we identify one thing with another – one commonly better known in nature than the other – we are engaging in metaphor. "The mind is a machine." "Societies are organisms." "A mighty fortress is our God." All of these are instances of metaphoric construction. Metaphor is no simple grammatical device, a mere figure of speech; not, that is, in its fullness. Metaphor is a way of knowing – one of the oldest, most deeply embedded, even indispensable ways known in the history of human consciousness. . . . It is easy for the positivist to dismiss metaphor as "unscientific." . . . . But from metaphor proceed some of the dominating themes of Western science and philosophy, as well as art. (Nisbet, 1976, pp. 32–3)

> A man desiring to understand the world looks about for a clue to its comprehension. He pitches upon some area of common-sense fact and tries if he cannot understand other areas in terms of this one. This original idea becomes then his basic analogy or root metaphor. He describes as best he can the characteristics of this area, or, if you will, discriminates its structure. A list of its structural characteristics becomes his basic concepts of explanation and description. We call them a set of categories. In terms of these categories he proceeds to study all other areas of fact whether uncriticized or previously criticized. He undertakes to interpret all facts in terms of these categories. (Pepper, 1942, p. 91)

I realize that the mere quotation of these sources, without further explication, constitutes a form of *argumentum ad hominem* (or *ab auctoritatibus*), but I trust that the gentle use of such argumentation is not too offensive when it draws on sources of such proven worth.

13 I like Plato's definition of scientific theories as "likely stories," though I would insist that likely stories are not myths in the derogatory sense. For a use of "likely stories" as an orienting conceptual device, see Leary (1987). With regard to Plato's ambivalence about metaphor and rhetoric, see Havelock (1963) and Lloyd (1987). The psychological and social context of this ambivalence is described by Dodds (1951) and B. Simon (1978).

14 Aristotle's (ca. 330 B.C./1924a) point in saying that "it is from metaphor that we can best get hold of something fresh" (l. 1410) was that "strange words" are "unintelligible" whereas "current words" are "commonplace." It is midway between these two extremes of the bizarre and the rote use of words that metaphor serves both to please and to instruct. Wallace Stevens (1930–55/ 1982) expressed a similar thought when he wrote that "reality is a cliché from which we escape by metaphor" (p. 179).

The secondary literature on Vico's "metaphoric turn" is so vast and readily available that I shall mention only the recent, excellent book by Mooney (1985). Coleridge's insights and convictions regarding the role of metaphor in the development of human thought and sensibility were further developed in his *Logic* (ca. 1823/1981) and his *Aids to Reflection* (1825/1884), about which Jackson (1983) has written. Coleridge's ideas influenced I. A. Richards as well as many others, including Owen Barfield (1977).

15 "Nakedness" was and remains a common metaphor for "plain," "unclothed," and hence supposedly "objective" discourse. A later scientist, Charles Darwin (1876/1887), used a related metaphor when he claimed to have written his autobiography "as if I were a dead man" (p. 27). "Lifelessness" or "passivity" fits the assumptions of positivist rhetoric, which was further exemplified by Darwin's statement that the *Origin of Species* (1859/1964) began to take shape when he was "*struck* with certain facts in the distribution of the inhabitants of South America" (p. 1, italics added). The intended image is clear: He was simply standing there, on Her Majesty's ship the *Beagle,* when nature of its own accord *came to him.* By implication, he did no *looking* or *searching about* for information. "Certain facts" simply spoke for themselves.

Regarding Darwin's rhetoric, see J. A. Campbell (1987), Cannon (1966), and H. White (1978). The fact that this rhetoric ill fitted the historical record of Darwin's own creative activity (as discussed by Leary, 1988b) is another similarity between Darwinian discourse and that of his seventeenth-century forebears. As for the rhetoric of these forebears, Dear (1985) has suggested that, on the basis of their actual practice, the Royal Society's motto should have been *Totius in verba* rather than *Nullius in verba.*

16 This ironically metaphorical opposition to the use of metaphor and related modes of thought and language was typical of Reformation figures as well as the "new philosophers" who ushered in the age of modern science. In the sixteenth century, for instance, Martin Luther (ca. 1542/1968) condemned allegory as a "beautiful harlot who fondles men in such a way that it is impossible for her not to be loved" (p. 347). A similar opposition was mounted by persons who might have been expected to use metaphor somewhat more freely – by the Paracelsian-influenced J. B. van Helmont, for instance (see Vickers, 1984, pp. 143–9). Given the widespread concern about potential abuses of figures of speech and thought, it is not surprising that the seventeenth century witnessed the "rationalization of myth" as well as the "end of allegory" as a widely accepted form of extended metaphor (see Allen, 1970, chap. 10).

Other important persons who were ambivalent about the use of metaphor and analogy included Francis Bacon, Galileo, and René Descartes (see Jardine, 1974; Park, Daston, & Galison, 1984). Bacon, for instance, granted that "there is no proceeding in invention of knowledge but by similitude," but he worried that "all perceptions as well of the sense as of the mind are according to the measure of the individual and not according to the measure of the universe [ex *analogia hominis, et non ex analogia universi*]" (quoted by Park in Park et al., 1984, pp. 294, 295). It was his skepticism about anthropomorphically biased concepts that stimulated his fear of the "idols of the Tribe," not any doubt that the human mind operates through analogy. This was a typical sixteenth- and seventeenth-century fear (see Popkin, 1964). Thus, skepticism should be added to the incipient versions of scientific realism, the positivist theory of knowledge, and the literalist view of language that Arbib and Hesse (1986) have listed as significant correlates of the Scientific Revolution (pp. 148–9).

It is unfortunate that skeptical concerns have not kept pace with the historical elaboration of these other three commitments. If they had been kept in mind – and turned against later versions of realism, positivism, and literalism – modern-day proponents of linguistic purity (such as B. F. Skinner, 1987) might have established a more propitious balance of commitments and concerns, not to mention a greater awareness of the rhetorical devices in their own linguistic behavior. As it is, they tend to see the mote in other people's eyes, but not the metaphor on their own tongues (see Leary, 1988a).

17 Newton's thought does not provide the only example of the transfer of a concept from a social to a natural scientific context. Indeed, as a number of scholars have pointed out (Adkins, 1972, esp. chap. 5; Collingwood, 1945, pp. 3–4; Cornford, 1912; Frank, 1945, pp. 116–17; Huizinga, 1944/1955, p. 117; Jaeger, 1934/1945, pp. 158–61; Snell, 1953, chap. 10; Zilsel, 1942), the very notions of "nature," "cause," and "law," which are so central to our conception of natural science, were drawn originally from the social realm. In more recent times, one of the most critical transferences has involved the use of statistics and the attendant notion of probability, originally developed in the study and conceptualization of human thought and social behavior (see Daston, 1988; Hacking, 1975; Porter, 1986; Stigler, 1986). Although the importation of the social-statistical metaphor initially met considerable resistance within the natural scientific community, its eventual acceptance has significantly changed the character of the physical sciences. (For general background and surveys of the impact on individual sciences, see Krüger, Daston, & Heidelberg, 1987; Krüger, Gigerenzer, & Morgan, 1987; for an overview, see Gigerenzer et al., 1989; for a specific analysis of "social law and natural science," see Porter, 1986, chap. 5; for a specific example of the use of a social metaphor in the study of physical phenomena, see Gentner & Gentner, 1983.)

Other social metaphors are frequently encountered in the physical sciences. See, e.g., Prigogine and Stengers's (1984) discussion of how order emerges from chaos in the physical world. This Nobel laureate and his colleague propose that the ordered universe is built on the existence of "hypnons" (fundamental "sleepwalking" or "dancing" units).

Human artifacts are also common metaphorical fodder for the physical as well as biological and social sciences. Clocks and various other devices and machines are too obvious to enumerate, but for their historical context, see Beniger (1986), Dijksterhuis (1969), O. Mayr (1986), and Price (1965). Koyré (1950/1968) has shown that, from the very start, the relatively unstructured quality of social life created problems for the assumption that such mechanistic metaphors (and the metaphysical principles based on them) are universal in application (see esp. pp. 22–4).

Finally, social metaphors also play a fundamental role in our understanding of natural scientific activity, which should not be surprising since scientific activity is, of course, social in nature. Think, for example, of all the recent talk of "revolutions" in science (Cohen, 1985; Hacking, 1981; Kuhn, 1970). Whether fortunately or not, the often muted implications of social conflict and aggression that are associated with this political metaphor rest on a much more substantial basis than many might suppose or wish to admit (see D. Hull, 1988). And as Cohen (1985) notes, this political metaphor incorporates an even more fundamental religious metaphor insofar as scientific revolutions have been seen (even by scientists themselves) to depend on the personal "conversions" of individual scientists (pp. 467–72). Berman (1983) discusses the historical relation between revolutions and religious reformation (pp. 18–23).

18 As Guerlac (1965) and Schofield (1970) have shown, British philosophers and scientists tended to develop the mechanistic and materialistic implications of Newton's work.

As is often the case in the history of science, Newton's ideas were "over-determined" by a variety of overlapping metaphors and modes of thought. Alchemical, biological, and theological metaphors blended with the social metaphor of "attraction" in the development of his understanding of the laws of nature (see Dobbs, 1975; Guerlac, 1983; Westfall, 1987). In all these areas of thought, anthropomorphism was clearly evident. "Sociability," for instance, was a construct used in alchemy – and in Newton's own correspondence regarding alchemy (see Dobbs, 1975, pp. 207–9). Although Cohen (1987) reports that "until his death Newton was deeply troubled by the concept [of universal gravity]," and in particular by his inability to give it a (presumably mechanistic or materialistic) explanation (p. 587), Newton's deep and sustained interest in alchemy seems to have been associated with his *rejection* of materialism and his corresponding *preference* for a "picture of reality in which spirit dominates" (Westfall, 1987, p. 565). This accords with the stance taken in Newton's stead by Samuel Clarke in the famous Leibniz–Clarke debates, which showed the extent to which theological voluntarism – the belief in the sustaining potency of God's will – lurked behind, and supported, Newton's mature vision of the universe (see Alexander, 1956). It is appropriate to add, as Guerlac (1983) has shown, that "God's active will was understood by Newton through an analogy with human will and animal motion" (p. 228).

This interweaving of alchemical, biological, theological, social, and psychological metaphors with natural scientific concepts suggests the reiterative nature of what soon became the dominant world view in the Western intellectual tradition. Virtually by definition, this world view *qua* world view (or "root metaphor") became the source of derivative metaphors (see Pepper, 1942). To select but one family of derivative metaphors, the Newtonian concepts of "inertia" and "momentum" have been used in a great deal of subsequent psychological and social theorizing. See e.g., Atkinson and Cartwright (1964), Frijda (1988), Nevin (1988), and Parsons, Bales, and Shils (1953). Of course, with Einstein's amendments of the Newtonian world view, alternative metaphors, such as those used in Lewin's (1936, 1951) field-theoretic approach to psychology, became available for behavioral and social scientists.

19 The decision to use *this* number system instead of another, *this* statistical procedure instead of another, *this* means of measurement instead of another can make a considerable difference in the results of one's analysis. Mathematics, whether pure or applied, is no singular, once-and-for-all language that maps all aspects of the world in a perfect one-to-one relationship. Rather, as recognized since the introduction of noncommutative algebras and non-Euclidean geometries in the nineteenth century, mathematics is (in Poincaré's words) a "free invention of the human mind" whose "truth" is not and cannot be absolute (Wilder, 1981, pp. 78–9). "Gradually," as Morris Kline (1980) has put it, "mathematicians granted that the axioms and theorems of mathematics were not necessary truths about the physical world." Rather, mathematics "offers nothing but theories or models" that can be replaced as demanded by the requirements of given situations (p. 97). The same view is accepted by mathematical physicists. Einstein, for instance, said that "insofar as the propositions of mathematics give an account of reality they are not certain; and insofar as they are certain they do not describe reality" (quoted by Kline, 1980, p. 97). In summary, "the attempt to establish a universally acceptable, logically sound body of mathematics has failed. Mathematics is a human activity and is subject to all the foibles and frailties of humans. Any formal, logical account is a pseudo-mathematics, a fiction, even a legend, despite the element of reason" (Kline, 1980, p. 331). As with any metaphorical system, mathematics becomes a myth (in the derogatory sense) if its metaphoricity is forgotten (see Turbayne, 1970, and note 49). The attempt to counter the myth of mathematics, by the way, started before the nineteenth century with Vico, who recognized that mathematics is an "experimental science" created by humans rather than the gods (see Corsano, 1969).

The nature of mathematics' metaphoricity is suggested by a statement attributed to Bertrand Russell, to the effect that mathematics began "when it was discovered that a brace of pheasants and a couple of days have something in common: the number two" (Koestler, 1964, p. 200). The point is simply that numbers are signs of similarity between things, whether between two objects, between two sets of objects, or between an object and a particular code of reference (one of the many alternate numerical systems). Two ideas, two cars, and two historians of science have at least this in common: Their existence can be "figured" in the same way. (The overlap among our concepts and terms for "number," "figure," and "metaphor" is no mere coincidence.) This numerical figure is the most abstract characteristic that they share (other than existence per se). Such abstraction allows the ultimate degree of precision – and the lowest amount of substantive specificity. "Two" tells you nothing about the nature of the objects compared other than their quantity: *Anything* that can appear in duplicate form, whether "real" or "ideal," can be represented by this figure. Although history testifies to the theoretical and practical benefits that can be gained by utilizing this kind of abstraction, that does not make number any less metaphorical.

Even those who might balk at considering number itself to be metaphorical would probably agree that the process of *applying* numbers is metaphorical (see McCloskey, 1985, pp. 79–83). Beyond that, the application of numbers is inherently *rhetorical* – i.e., meant to be persuasive – even though it cannot lead to totally definitive accounts of reality (see Davis & Hersh, 1986, 1987). Relatedly, the development of new forms of mathematics – e.g., the mathematics of probability – can be shown to have changed the ways in which we think about ourselves, the world around us, and everyday life (see Daston, 1988; Gigerenzer et al., 1989). For discussions of the role of analogical thinking in mathematics, see Mach (1905/1976) and Polya (1954); for a discussion of mathematics as a cognitive activity, see Lakoff (1987, chap. 20); for a discussion of the locus of mathematical reality by a nonmathematician, see L. A. White (1949); for an offbeat, but interesting discussion of number as metaphor, see R. S. Jones (1982); for a relevant discussion of the aesthetics, as opposed to the logic, of mathematics, see Papert (1978); and for discussions of the quantification of psychology, see Danziger (1987), Gigerenzer (1987), Hornstein (1988), and Leary (1980a). Regarding the "unreasonable effectiveness of mathematics in the natural sciences," see Wigner (1960); for a somewhat converse argument, see Sharma (1982); and for a cultural explanation of the symbiosis of mathematics and physics, see Wilder (1981, pp. 45–6). The main thrust of Wilder's analysis of mathematics as a cultural system is seconded by the work of MacKenzie (1981). Perhaps, since "proof" is considered such a hallmark of absolute truth, I should end this note by quoting Wilder's (1981) comment that "it seems to be a commonly held belief, chiefly outside the mathematical community, that in the realm of mathematics can be found absolute truth.... [But as we have seen] 'proof' in mathematics is a culturally determined, relative matter. What constitutes proof for one generation, fails to meet the standards of the next or some later generation" (pp. 39–40). For more on this topic, see Davis and Hersh (1986) and the final paragraph of note 44.

20 Regarding Darwin's sometimes positivist rhetoric, see note 15. But also note that, despite this rhetoric, Darwin believed that "without the making of theories I am convinced there would be no observation" (letter to C. Lyell, 1 June 1860, in F. Darwin, 1887b, vol. 2, p. 315). Indeed, his son recalled that Darwin often said that "no one could be a good observer unless he was an active theoriser.... it was as though he were charged with theorising power ready to flow into any channel on the slightest disturbance, so that no fact, however small, could avoid releasing a stream of theory, and thus the fact became magnified into importance" (F. Darwin, 1887a, p. 149). That it was not simply theory but theoretically pregnant metaphors that were so readily set loose in Darwin by the process of observation can be seen from Darwin's own comments and notebook annotations: "There is an extraordinary pleasure in pure observation; not but what I suspect the pleasure in this case is rather derived from comparisons forming in one's mind with allied structures" (letter to J. D. Hooker, ca. 1847, in F. Darwin, 1887b, vol. 1, p. 349). But despite his son's recollection of the facility of Darwin's theorizing power, Darwin himself reported that making original conjectures was by no means easy: "Perhaps one cause of the intense labour of *original inventive* thought is that none of the ideas are habitual, nor recalled by obvious associations" (notebook entry, 16 August 1838, in Barrett, 1974, p. 282); that is, Darwin had to make his novel comparisons in the face of habitual associations, which work by their nature toward nonoriginal ends. Still, the effort did not squelch his pleasure: "I remember my pleasure in Kensington Gardens has often been greatly excited by looking at trees at [i.e., as] great compound animals united by wonderful & mysterious manner" (notebook entry, 15 July 1838, in Barrett, 1974, p. 273). All in all, Darwin would probably have agreed with T. H. Huxley, who wrote that "the great danger which besets all men of large speculative faculty, is the temptation to deal with the accepted statements of facts in natural science, as if they were not only correct, but exhaustive.... In reality, every such statement, however true it may be, is true only relatively to the means of observation and the point of view of those who have enunciated it" (quoted by F. Darwin, 1887b, vol. 1, p. 347).

Darwin's sensitivity to rhetorical style is revealed in his reply to a young naturalist who had sent him a manuscript for review: "Shall you think me impertinent ... if I hazard a remark on the style, which is of more importance than some think? In my opinion (whether or no worth much) your paper would have been much better if written more simply and less elaborated" (letter to J. Scott, 11 December 1862, in F. Darwin & A. C. Seward, 1903, vol. 1, p. 219–20). Later he wrote: "I never study style; all that I do is to try to get the subject as clear as I can in my own head, and express it in the commonest language which occurs to me. But I generally have to think a good deal before the simplest arrangement and words occur to me.... writing is slow work; it is a great evil, but there is no help for it.... I would suggest to you the advantage, at present, of being very sparing in introducing theory in your papers.... *let theory guide your observations,* but till your reputation is well established be sparing in publishing theory. It makes persons doubt your observations" (letter to J. Scott, 6 June 1863, in F. Darwin & A. C. Seward, 1903, vol. 2, pp. 322–3).

21 Regarding the evolutionary epistemology on which this comment draws, an epistemology developed on an explicitly Darwinian model, see D. Campbell (1960, 1974), Popper (1979), R. J. Richards (1977), and Toulmin (1972). Also see Simontin (1988) for a psychology of science based on this epistemology and Cohen (1985) for a discussion of the earlier "Darwinian" philosophies of science of Ludwig Boltzmann and Ernst Mach (pp. 534–40). For other impacts of Darwinism on diverse fields of thought, often mediated by the metaphorical extension of Darwinian concepts, see Appleman (1970), Beer (1983), G. M. Edelman (1987), Leatherdale (1983), Oldroyd (1980), R. J. Richards (1987), Seward (1909), and Wiener (1949). Twentieth-century American psychology in particular is based on Darwinian premises. Two of the most self-conscious of these extensions are those of William James, discussed below in the text, and B. F. Skinner, discussed in note 49.

22 Darwin had previously tried to "fit" or "map" his data on a more or less linear time–line. With the image of the tree, he was able to *imagine* a much more complex set of relationships among his data. Although he realized early on that coral, with which he was quite familiar, provided a better image than did a tree (since the branches at the base of coral die off, obscuring the earlier connections between subsequent branches, as occurs analogously in evolutionary history), and although he realized later that seaweed provides an even better image than coral (in that seaweed is "endlessly branching" in every possible direction), Darwin seems to have liked and used the "tree of life" image because of its biblical connotations (see Beer, 1983, p. 37; Gruber, 1978). This suggests a more general rule: that the choice of any given metaphor can depend on more than simply its structural characteristics. Aesthetic and other characteristics can – and probably often do – play a role, as they did in this case. For further discussion of the role of visualization in science (often in the form of visual metaphors), see Arnheim (1969), Koestler (1964, bk. 1, chap. 21), Langley, Simon, Bradshaw, and Zytkow (1987, chap. 10), A. I. Miller (1984), Randhawa and Coffman (1978), Roe (1951), Root-Bernstein (1985), and Shepard (1978). Regarding the role of visual representation in the history of psychology and psychiatry, see Gilman's (1976, 1982, 1988) pathbreaking works.

23 This is not to say that phenomena can look any way we want them to look. Except for those who are psychotic or similarly impaired, there are limits to the extent to which "reality" can be assimilated to subjective suppositions, fears, and desires. At the same time, however, the "resistance" of phenomena to being "taken" in a variety of ways, whether perceptually or cognitively, is far from absolute. See Barnes and Shapin (1979, pt. 1), Cooter (1984), and Shapin (1979).

24 The literature on social scientific metaphors (other than those used in psychology) includes Barrows (1981), R. H. Brown (1976, 1977, 1987), Deutsch (1951), Felstiner (1983), Gerschenkron (1974), Goldstein (1984), Harré and Secord (1972), H. Jones (1906), Kahn (1965), Martin Landau (1961), Misia Landau (1984), Lasky (1976), Leiber (1978), McCloskey (1985), E. F. Miller (1979), Nisbet (1976), Olson (1971), Saccaro-Battisti (1983), and Stepan (1986). Buck (1956), Chapman and Jones (1980), and Gergen (Chapter 8, this volume) are also very relevant. The literature on premodern and a-modern social metaphors includes Agnew (1986), Alford (1982), Bambrough (1956), Curtius (1953, esp. pp. 138–44), Douglas (1982), Jaynes (1976), Kantorowicz (1957), and Tillyard (1944). Medical metaphors that verge on and overlap with social metaphors are discussed in Figlio (1976), Harrington (1987), Rather (1982), Sontag (1978, 1988), and Temkin (1977). The role of metaphors in social policy making is the special province of Schön (1963, 1979), but Gusfield (1976) has also made a significant contribution. The metaphors of day-to-day political discourse – so redolent of "battles," "races," "trading," and other forms of contest and compromise – await someone's sustained attention. To date, Burke (1945) has pointed toward, and Lakoff and Johnson (1980) have provided examples of, the sort of metaphors that would result from such an analysis.

25 For further discussion of Berkeley's social theory and its historical context, see Leary (1977) and Macklem (1958). On Berkeley's use of other metaphors, see Brykman (1982) and Turbayne (1970), and on the metaphors underlying various modern philosophies of the social sciences, see Shapiro (1985–6).

26 David Hume is the best known representative of the many individuals who wished to be the Newton of the social (or moral) sciences. Not only does the subtitle of Hume's major treatise (1739–40/1978) identify the work as an "attempt to introduce the experimental method of reasoning into moral subjects," but Hume explicitly indicates that his hypothesized "principle of association" is meant to be the principle of gravity of the mental world. The sequence of Hume's metaphorical thoughts is quite revealing. He begins by talking about the principle of association as a "gentle force" that unites ideas in the mind (p. 10); suggests that association represents "a kind of ATTRACTION, which in the mental world will be found to have as extraordinary effects as [does gravity] in the natural, and to shew itself in as many and as various forms" (pp. 12–13); then says that he "cannot compare the soul more properly to any thing than to a republic or commonwealth, in which the several members are united by the reciprocal ties of government and subordination" (p. 261); and ends by claiming that the principles of association "are the only links that bind the parts of the universe together, or connect us with any person or object exterior to ourselves," which is to say that these principles of association "are really *to us* the cement of the universe" ("Abstract," p. 662). In a very real sense, Hume brings the attraction metaphor full circle – back from the natural philosophy of Newton to the social and mental realms in which Newton's universe inheres. Along the way, he characterizes ideas and perceptions, and distinguishes beliefs and fantasies, by their various degrees of "force," "vitality," "solidity," and "firmness." We shall have occasion to reflect on such physicalist metaphors for mental phenomena in the next section of this chapter.

I should also note that an entirely *social* metaphor guides Hume's understanding of reason and its relations to other human faculties: "Reason is, and ought only to be the slave of the passions, and can never pretend to any other office than to serve and obey them" (p. 415). Although many others, from Plato to Freud, have expressed the relation of reason to other dynamic factors through the use of similar social metaphors, Hume was distinctive in regarding the "enslavement" of reason to be appropriate and acceptable.

Finally, another reaction to the clockwork universe, wittily expressed by Thomas Reid (1785/1969), points toward the inverse social metaphor at the foundation of the mechanistic world view:

> Shall we believe with Leibnitz, that the mind was originally formed like a watch wound up; and that all its thoughts, purposes, passions and actions, are effected by the gradual evolution of the original spring of the machine, and succeed each other in order, as necessarily as the motions and pulsations of a watch?
>
> If a child of three or four years, were put to account for the phenomena of a watch, he would conceive that there is a little man within the watch, or some other little animal that beats continually, and produces the motion. Whether the hypothesis of this young philosopher in turning the watch spring into a man, or that of the German philosopher in turning a man into a watch spring, be the most rational, seems hard to determine. (p. 444)

Reid granted that "it is natural to men to judge of things less known by some similitude they observe, or think they observe, between them and things more familiar or better known," and he acknowledged that "where the things compared have really a great similitude in their nature, when there is reason to think that they are subject to the same laws, there may be a considerable degree of probability in conclusions drawn from analogy" (p. 48); but he also noted that "men are naturally disposed to conceive a greater similitude in things than there really is" (p. 49), and he insisted that "all arguments, drawn from analogy, are still the weaker, the greater the disparity there is between the things compared" (p. 50). Amen.

27 Locke is perhaps best known for his metaphor of the mind as a tabula rasa, or blank tablet (or more precisely, "white paper, void of all characters"; see Locke, 1690/1959, vol. 1, p. 121), but he used many other metaphors as well, including a metaphorical comparison of the mind, or understanding, to a *"dark room"* or "closet wholly shut from light, with only some little opennings [i.e., sensory channels] left, to let in visible resemblances, or ideas of things without" (p. 212). Reid (1785/1969) recognized that this metaphor was no mere rhetoric device, but embodied a central assumption underlying Locke's theory of perception (p. 124). By popularizing this and other assumptions, Locke helped to establish the representationalist tradition of perceptual theory, with its metaphorical treatment of ideas as "resemblances," "pictures," "copies," and "likenesses" of reality (see Hamlyn, 1961, chaps. 6 and 8). The larger question of psychology's borrowing of such metaphors from the realm of the arts, especially in the pivotal eighteenth century, when the boundaries between aesthetics and psychology were so fluid, deserves study. The full story promises to be quite fascinating, reaching back to the original Greek concept of *idola* and forward to the latest "picture theory" of semantics.

Besides our notions of "copies," "likenesses," and such, we have derived our sense of "perspective" – so fundamental to modern consciousness – from the history of drawing and painting (see Guillén, 1968). Drawing and painting, of course, are not the only sources of these art-related metaphors. Architecture has also long been a favorite source of psychological (as well as epistemological) metaphors, according to which we "construct" our mental life from the "ground up" – or "top down" – following "plans," "blueprints," and so on (see, e.g., Anderson, 1983). Less well known, but historically important metaphors have been drawn from music, covering the range from "harmony" to "rhythm." When brain researchers recently "scored" brain-wave harmonies (see, e.g., the "cerebral symphony" in Pribram, 1971, p. 75), it is likely that few people realized the rich tradition they had joined (see, e.g., Heelan, 1979; Kassler, 1984; Levarie, 1980).

Beyond the tabula rasa, "dark room," and representational metaphors of the mind, Locke helped to establish the "atomistic" or "corpuscular" approach to the mind, according to which the mind is analyzed into its presumably elemental ideas (Locke, 1690/1959, vol. 1, pp. 121–9; see Buchdahl, 1969, chap. 4). He was also responsible for the influential view that the mind is characterized and motivated by its fundamental "uneasiness" (Locke, 1690/1959, vol. 1, pp. 332–9; see Hazard, 1935/1963, chap. 5). These basic metaphorical assumptions informed many of the psychologies that came after Locke's.

28 Locke could have added moral concepts, such as dependability, reliability, and forthrightness, to this list of psychological concepts. As Whitney (1896) wrote, "A conspicuous branch of the department of figurative transfer, and one of indispensable importance in the history of language, is the application of terms having a physical, sensible meaning, to the designation of intellectual and moral conceptions and their relations. . . . In fact, our whole mental and moral vocabulary has been gained precisely in this way. . . . there is a movement in the whole vocabulary of language from the designation of what is coarser, grosser, more material, to the designation of what is finer, more abstract and conceptional, more formal. . . . there is no grander phenomenon than this in all language-history" (pp. 88–90). Whitney provided examples to support his contention.

On the use of "botanomorphic" metaphors in the description of traits and types, see Sommer (1988).

29 For some interesting conjectures on the development of the ancient Greek mind, coupled with a very sensitive awareness of the role of metaphor in self-understanding, see Jaynes (1976).

30 See Fletcher (1882) and Majno (1975), both of whom include illustrations in their discussions of trephining or trepanation (as Majno calls it).

31 Should trephining seem unreasonable, or even inconceivably primitive, see Valenstein (1986) on twentieth-century psychosurgery. (The illustrations on p. 210, regarding the use of electroconvulsive shock as an anaesthetic and the use of transorbital lobotomy as a cure for schizophrenia, are particularly emblematic.) It is also humbling to compare other twentieth-century practices with earlier ones that seem prima facie rather "backward." It is not clear, for instance, that the rationale behind the nineteenth-century practices of douching and rotating (see Howells & Osborn, 1984, vol. 1, pp. 260–1; vol. 2, pp. 799–801, for brief descriptions and illustrations) is significantly different in kind or quality from the rationale behind many of the therapeutic practices that are common in the late twentieth century. Although Gross (1978) is admittedly critical in orientation, his description of our "psychological society," with its "new therapies" and "new messiahs," can hardly be ignored as completely off the mark. At the same time, however, it is unlikely that all of the parallels between current and past practices should be seen as an indictment of twentieth-century practice. Almost certainly, some of them should be regarded as a complement to earlier therapeutic interventions that had a more solid basis than we generally recognize.

32 On the various forms of possession and exorcism, in other cultures as well as in the history of the Western world, see Ellenberger (1970, pp. 13–22).

33 Descartes's reliance on metaphorical thinking may seem to clash with his self-proclaimed image as a thoroughly skeptical, cautious, and hence conservative thinker. But like Francis Bacon, who has also been misunderstood in this regard (see note 16), Descartes (1628/1911a) was quite aware that "all knowledge whatsoever, other than that which consists in the simple and naked intuition of single independent objects, is a matter of the comparison of two things or more, with each other. In fact practically the whole of the task set the human reason consists in preparing for this operation" (p. 55). For a discussion of Descartes's use of other metaphors, see N. Edelman (1950). On the use of human artifacts, especially machines, as analogs of physical, biological, social, bahavioral, and mental phenomena, see Boring (1946), Chapanis (1961), and note 17. One of the strong advocates of the metaphorical use of such artifacts in psychology, Clark Hull (1943), sought to combine both "objectivity" and "modelling" by considering "the behaving organism as a completely self-maintaining robot." This, he thought, would serve as an effective "prophylaxis against anthropomorphic subjectivism" (p. 27). The next question, I suppose, regards who and what will provide a safeguard against the excesses of "mechanomorphic objectivism." (For a similar comment on the uncritical physicomorphism of psychological language, see Asch, 1958, p. 87.)

34 The discovery of the limitations of these and other correlates of the mechanistic metaphor in eighteenth-century physiology and psychology contributed to the emergence of a very different root metaphor – that of "sensibility" or "sensitivity" (see Moravia, 1978, 1979; Rousseau, 1976). Of course, no matter how delimited, the mechanistic metaphor was far from dead: It was transmogrified in the nineteenth century to fit the new demands and possibilities suggested by the laws of thermodynamics. In unwitting anticipation of the metaphor's further transformation into Freudian *psycho*dynamics, Helmholtz (1861/1971) even argued that "the human body is . . . a *better* machine than the steam engine" (p. 119, italics added). Note that it was now the steam engine, not the clock or the hydraulic statue, that was the preferred analog. As this updated comparison implies, the mechanistic metaphor has proved to be immensely protean, changing shape whenever there is an advance in physical science or engineering technology (see Wiener, 1961, chap. 1).

35 For an overview of the recent cognitive revolution and some of the variant forms of contemporary cognitive psychology and cognitive science, see Baars (1986) and Gardner (1987). For a general discussion and more details regarding cognitive metaphors, see Bruner and Feldman (Chapter 6, this volume) and Hoffman, Cochran, and Nead (Chapter 5, this volume), respectively. Cognitive metaphors are also usefully and interestingly tabulated and discussed by Estes (1978), Gentner and Grudin (1985), Lakoff and Johnson (1981), and Roediger (1980). The current dominance of cognitivism in psychology is reflected in the fact that cognitive metaphors are frequently assumed to be literal descriptors of mental entities and processes (see, e.g., Newell & Simon, 1972; Pylyshyn, 1984). Although the literalization (in the sense

described earlier in this chapter) of the new cognitive metaphors of input, storage, retrieval, output, and all the other argot of computation and instrumentation is perhaps to be expected, given the frequent usage of these metaphors, I cannot help but join H. Jones (1906) and Berggren (1962) in worrying about the potential *misuse* and *abuse* of metaphors. Nor can I resist joining Turbayne (1970) in fearing the danger of creating a *myth* out of metaphors when such literalization occurs. A myth in this instance would be the result of assuming that a set of "likenesses" between (say) computation and mentation provide adequate grounds for an inference of complete, or at least essential, *identity*. For a further discussion of "myth," used in a negative rather than positive sense, see note 49.

Once again, as in the discussion of Berkeley's gravitational theory of human attraction, I feel compelled to point out the paradox that a machine made to mimic *some* of the human mind's activities has come to serve as the standard *against which* the human mind's activities – *and potential* – are measured. Despite all the marvelous advances in information-processing theory and technology – no, *because* of them – it would seem wise to avoid the temptation to think that we have finally reached the end of the road in understanding our mental life. To anyone with historical awareness and sensitivity, it should seem premature, as William James would put it, to assume that the final word has been spoken on this matter (see note 5).

I do not wish to be misunderstood. Even granting that its fruitfulness could be recognized only in a technologically advanced – and obsessed – culture, the information-processing metaphor (in its computationist and other guises) has been extraordinarily fruitful. It has even found its way into the study of personality (Powell, Royce, & Voorhees, 1982), the psychology of induction and creativity (Holland et al., 1986; Langley et al., 1987), and the philosophy of science (Thagard, 1988). My concern is focused not on what this metaphor and its derivatives offer, but on what alternative metaphors may be *cut off* if they are taken to be definitive. This is a basic motivating concern behind my own research on the use – and abuse – of metaphor in science. The *use* of metaphor is necessary and wonderful to behold; but the *abuse* of metaphor – its use as a tool of presumptuous prescription rather than tentative description – concerns me a great deal. At worst, the metaphors bandied about today with such confidence by psychologists and cognitive scientists may infiltrate public consciousness (and personal self-consciousness) and remain lodged there, long after these same psychologists and cognitive scientists have adopted a new set of metaphors. Do we really want our children and fellow citizens to think of themselves as more or less adequately networked information systems and computational devices? There are surely worse metaphors to live by, but *any* prescriptive metaphor is, I believe, one too many.

It should be obvious that I am very sympathetic when Lakoff and Johnson (1981) state that they

> are not suggesting that there is anything wrong with using such [cognitive] metaphors.... [But] the metaphors of a science, like any other metaphors, typically hide indefinitely many aspects of reality.
>
> The way ordinary people deal implicitly with the limitations of any one metaphor is by having many metaphors for comprehending different aspects of the same concept.... These clusters of metaphors serve the purpose of understanding better than any *single* metaphor could.... the insistence on maintaining a consistent extention of one metaphor may blind us to aspects of reality that are ignored or hidden by that

metaphor.... The moral: Cognitive Science needs to be aware of its metaphors, to be concerned with what they hide, and to be open to alternative metaphors – even if they are inconsistent with the current favorites. (p. 206)

Theirs is not the only such cautionary comment (see, e.g., Crosson, 1985; Weizenbaum, 1976; on the "high cost of information," see Haraway, 1981–2; and for a critique of the "mind-as-machine paradigm," see Lakoff, 1987, chap. 19). It should be added that history suggests that *no* metaphor, however mythologized, is likely to stifle all dissent and creative thinking. Thus, we can always expect that new metaphors will be found. Just how fair a hearing new metaphors will receive, however, will vary according to the degree of "true believing" that stands in their way.

Finally, having asserted this caveat, I must give credit where credit is due: Much of the recent revival of interest in analogy and metaphor has been spurred by those committed to the information-processing, computational-calculus, artificial-intelligence approaches to mental dynamics (see, e.g., Arbib, 1972; Boden, 1977, chap. 11; 1988, chap. 6; Russell, 1986; Sternberg & Rifkin, 1979).

36 Certainly, in comparison with the naive empiricism of some of his well-known scientific contemporaries, Freud fares well in this regard. Else Frenkel-Brunswik (1954), trained in the philosophy of science as well as in psychology at the University of Vienna in the late 1920s, was one of the first to note that "Freud, in contrast to some of his followers, was keenly aware of logical and epistemological problems," including those pertaining to the conventionality of scientific definitions (p. 294). Relatedly, in a critique of Skinner's (1954) criticism of Freud's scientific method, Scriven (1956) argued that "the language of psychoanalysis . . . is very open-textured; it is a first approach. Being so, it runs the risk of becoming empirically meaningless, a ritual form of mental alchemy. But the *approach* is fully justifiable; and it is as wrong to suggest that Freud should have pinned his terms down to infant neurology or, by the 'simple expedient of an operational definition,' to physical and biological science, as it would be to insist that the founders of radio astronomy should have early said whether a radio star was a solid body or a region of space" (p. 128). More recently, MacIntyre (1967), among others, has pointed out the blindness of commentators who seem not to have noticed that, after all, "Freud brought to light and described a huge variety of hitherto unrecognized types of behavior," thus giving psychology "a new subject matter to explain" (p. 252). He also noted that the ritualistic criticism regarding the untestability of Freud's theory is simply false – much of Freud's theory *has* been rejected and/or modified as a result of such testing. Other philosophers who have shown an increased interest in Freud's work include Wollheim (1971) and the contributors to Wollheim (1974). Among the latter, Glymour (1974) explicitly defends Freud's bootstrapping verification procedure, if not all of his logical arguments.

Meanwhile, Ricoeur (1970) and Spence (1982, 1987) represent a school of philosophers and psychologists who are taking a new hermeneutic approach to psychoanalysis, trying to elucidate the ways in which psychoanalysis represents an *interpretive* enterprise par excellence. Although some are critical of this new approach (see esp. Grünbaum, 1984, who presents an updated version of the old empiricist critique) and although others present a very different view of Freud's work (see esp. Sulloway, 1979, who places Freud squarely *and only* in the biological tradition), the hermeneutic understanding of Freud's work as essentially interpretive in orientation is more in line with Freud's intentions and background than these critics recognize or allow. As early as 1895 Freud realized that he was groping toward an approach that resulted in case histories that were more novelistic than scientistic in format (Freud, 1895/1955a, pp. 160–1), and by 1896 he had already clarified that psychological processes involve "rearrangement" and "retranscription" of memory traces – that is, a "revision" of sensations, images, ideas, and words (see his letter to Wilhelm Fliess, 6 December 1896, in Masson, 1985, p. 207). When Freud subsequently remarked that psychoanalysis was concerned with *reconstructing* these same displaced "traces" into coherent stories in which the missing elements had been reinserted into their proper places (as he did in the famous case of Dora, 1905/1953b, e.g., pp. 16, 116, in which he used the concepts of "censors," "new editions," and "facsimiles" as well as "revised editions"), he was simply closing the circle of a long-standing position. That Freud himself studied the science of language and drew on relevant aspects of the philological tradition is clear (see Forrester, 1980), and that he was conversant with the philosophical literature – and was confident in his own epistemological position – is shown by his comment that he did not have to refer to Vaihinger's (1911/1924) work in order to legitimate his own use of "fictions." All sciences, Freud argued (1926/1959c, p. 194), depend on such "fictions." Most recent philosophers of science would agree, even if they would use different terms.

To review briefly three salient points in Freud's philosophy of science: (1) He did not feel that precise definitions should be the sine qua non of scientific work. In fact, he felt just the opposite – that premature definition serves only to retard open and unfettered research (see, e.g., Freud, 1914/1957a, p. 77; 1915/1957b, p. 117; 1917/1963, p. 304; 1925/1959a, pp. 57–8). (2) He did not feel that certainty is a necessary characteristic of science. In fact, he doubted that it could be reached. Instead, he proposed that science should aim for highly probable knowledge – for better and better analogies that provide ever closer "resemblances" and "approximations" of reality (see, e.g., Freud, 1895/1955b, p. 291; 1917/1963, pp. 51, 296). (3) He took a completely pragmatic approach to science. He freely admitted that his metaphorical concepts were "nothing but constructions," but he insisted that psychoanalytic practice showed them to be "necessary and useful constructions," at least for the time being (1917/1963, p. 326). He presumed that one must make many assumptions in order to get on with scientific work and that the way to justify any given assumption (or metaphorical conception) was simply "to see what comes of it. The outcome of our work will decide whether we are to hold to this assumption and whether we may then go on to treat it in turn as a proved finding. But what is it actually that we want to arrive at? What is our work aiming at? We want something that is sought for in all scientific work – to understand the phenomena, to establish a correlation between them and, in the latter end, if it is possible, to enlarge our power over them" (p. 100). Freud's criterion of psychological health was similarly pragmatic: It is "a practical question and is decided by the outcome – by whether the subject is left with a sufficient amount of capacity for enjoyment and of efficiency" (p. 457). Of course, he related this outcome to a metaphorical premise regarding the "relative sizes of the quota of energy that remains free" (p. 457).

37 Bettelheim's (1983) translation of this passage is less awkward and more apt: "In psychology we can describe only with the help of comparisons. This is nothing special, it is the same elsewhere. But we are forced to change these

comparisons over and over again, for none of them can serve us for any length of time" (p. 37).

That there was nothing unusual, so far as Freud was concerned, about psychology's reliance on metaphorical comparisons is made clear by these two passages:

I know you will say that these ideas [about "resistance" and "repression"] are both crude and fantastic. . . . more than that, I know that they are incorrect, and, if I am not very much mistaken, I already have something better to take their place. Whether it will seem to you equally fantastic I cannot tell. They are preliminary working hypotheses, like Ampère's manikin swimming in the electric current [in one of the founding studies in the science of electromagnetism], and they are not to be despised in so far as they are of service in making our observations intelligible. (Freud, 1917/1963, p. 296)

We need not feel greatly disturbed . . . by the fact that so many bewildering and obscure processes occur [in our scientific speculations]. . . . This is merely due to our being obliged to operate with the scientific terms, that is to say with the figurative language, peculiar to psychology (or, more precisely, to depth psychology). We could not otherwise describe the processes in question at all, and indeed we could not have become aware of them. The deficiencies in our description would probably vanish if we were already in a position to replace the psychological terms by physiological or chemical ones. It is true that they too are only part of a figurative language; but it is one with which we have long been familiar and which is perhaps a simpler one as well. (Freud, 1920/1955e, p. 60)

The critical "mechanism" of scientific creativity for Freud was, as he wrote to Sándor Ferenczi on 8 April 1915, the "succession of daringly playful fantasy and relentlessly realistic criticism" (quoted by Grubrich-Simitis, 1987, p. 83).

38 As he said elsewhere, "What is psychical is something so unique and peculiar to itself that no one comparison can reflect its nature" (Freud, 1919/1955d, p. 161). Freud was keenly sensitive to the need for multiple comparisons – and to the insufficiency of the ones he had so far located – from very early in his career. As he said, "I am making use here of a number of similes, all of which have only a very limited resemblance to my subject and which, moreover, are incompatible with one another. I am aware that this is so, and I am in no danger of over-estimating their value. But my purpose in using them is to throw light from different directions on a highly complicated topic which has never yet been represented. I shall therefore venture to continue in the following pages to introduce similes in the same manner, though I know this is not free from objection (1895/1955b, p. 291). He made such statements throughout his career, as he struggled for more and more adequate analogs of the psychological processes he studied and dealt with. This was a never-ending struggle for him, not confined to his early works. In just three of the final pages of *The Ego and the Id* (1923/1961a), for instance, Freud compared the ego to a constitutional monarch, a servant of three masters, a psychoanalyst, a politician, and protozoans (pp. 55–7)!

39 Freud's love of antiquity and of Greek history and literature is well conveyed by Gay's (1976) text and the accompanying pictures of the ancient statues and other antiquities in Freud's Viennese home and offices. Indeed, it is for good

reason that Freud's thought has been studied in relation to Greek mythology, philosophy, and rhetoric (see, e.g., Mahoney, 1974; Tourney, 1965). Freud's relation to the classical humanist tradition – a tradition that is overlooked in Sulloway's (1979) attempt to reduce Freudian thought to its biological roots – is discussed by Bettelheim (1983) and by the contributors to Gedo and Pollock (1976). It is also elucidated in Rieff's (1979) masterful analysis. Among the various passages in which Freud indicated his debt to Plato, and specifically to Platonic myths, the following is particularly telling: "What psycho-analysis called sexuality was by no means identical with the impulsion towards a union of the two sexes or towards producing a pleasurable sensation in the genitals; it had far more resemblance to the all-inclusive and all-preserving Eros of Plato's *Symposium*" (Freud, 1925/1961b, p. 218).

40 To get a quick sense of the role of metaphors and analogies in Freud's work, see A. Richards's (1974) compilation of "some of the more striking of Freud's analogies and extended similes" (p. 179). On Freud's metaphors, see, e.g., Badalamenti (1979), Bloom (1982), Browning (1987), Derrida (1978), Edelson (1983), Erdelyi (1985), Mahoney (1982, chap. 5), Nash (1962, 1963), Pederson-Krag (1956), Shengold (1979), Spence (1987), and Wilden (1980). On the psychoanalytic approach to metaphor, see Rogers (1978).

One of Freud's fundamental metaphors – "translation" or "transcription," used in reference to the revision of one's life story that takes place in the course of psychoanalysis – was mentioned in note 36. Another fundamental metaphor, or rather family of metaphors, comes from archeology (see note 41). Another has to do with the analogies between the ontogenetic development of the individual and the phylogenetic history of the human race (see, e.g., the subtitle and analysis of Freud, 1913/1955c, and the title and analysis of Freud, 1915/1987). And, of course, Freud's metaphorical transformation of thermodynamics into psychodynamics is signaled throughout his work in such passages as "The prime factor is unquestionably the process of getting rid of one's own emotions by 'blowing off steam'" (Freud, 1905/1953c, p. 305).

41 Despite (or perhaps because of) Freud's frequent changes in what might be called his "surface metaphors," we can see a smaller set of "deep metaphors" that persist, with amendments, throughout the development of his thought. This suggests a difference between metaphors that are relatively more expository or elaborative and those that are more basic, though I would not want to reduce expository metaphors to nonconsequential status. One example is Freud's reliance on the archaeological metaphor – or family of metaphors – according to which the mind is like an archaeological dig, with various layers or historical sediments being buried at different levels (though because of occasional upheavals they are sometimes displaced in relation to the original line of sediment) and being "unearthed" and "reconstructed" in the course of psychoanalysis. This basic metaphorical scheme, which clearly oriented Freud's aptly designated "depth psychology," was obvious as early as 1897 (see Freud's comments and drawing in Masson, 1985, pp. 246–8), and it was still critical at the end of his career (see, e.g., Freud, 1930/1961c, pp. 69–71). Regarding Freud's abiding interest in archaeology, including Heinrich Schliemann's highly suggestive discovery of the many-layered city of Troy, see Bernfeld (1951) and Gay (1976).

The fact that Freud readily changed *his own* metaphors does not mean, of course, that he always welcomed changes made or suggested by others. Although he certainly had the right to argue for his own preferred concepts and theories, his tendency to be dogmatic toward others in this regard is not easily justified. However, though Freud sometimes fell below the mark that many of us would endorse at our point in time, the personal, interpersonal, and historical contexts of Freud's dogmatism – not to mention the character of this dogmatism itself – have not yet been adequately assessed. Meanwhile, Gay's (1988) recent work compensates for earlier treatments of this matter.

42 This is not to deny that many of his followers – and many commentators on psychoanalysis – have been less careful, nor that Freud himself was occasionally less careful, nor that Freud's rhetoric at times invited misunderstanding. For example, Freud's frequent and graphic use of synecdoche (e.g., labeling developmental stages, which he had already shown to be much more complicated, as simply "oral," "anal," "phallic," and "genital") both aided the popularization and encouraged the trivialization of his ideas (see Rieff, 1979, pp. 44–5). But a distinctive aspect of Freud's rhetoric is his almost obsessive criticism and qualification of his own metaphors (see, e.g., Freud, 1900/1953a, p. 536; 1913/1955c, pp. 160–1; 1917/1963, pp. 295–6; 1919/1955d, p. 159; 1926/1959c, pp. 194–5, 254; 1930/1961c, pp. 70–1, 144; and Freud's appreciative footnote quotation from Sir James G. Frazer in 1913/1955c, p. 108). Freud continually pointed out the *dis*analogous dimensions of his metaphors – where and to what extent they fell short of the mark. Unfortunately, as Mahoney (1982) has noted, "All too often, commentators paraphrasing Freud leave out the figure of speech, the *what if,* the *possible* or *probable,* by which his own statements are qualified, thus obscuring the suppositional character of the original" (p. 117).

43 Perhaps I should clarify that I am neither for nor against psychoanalysis per se, but I am appreciative of Freud's broadening and deepening of psychological understanding and of his insight and courage regarding metaphorical and analogical thinking. I hardly presume that Freud's metaphors are definitive, but I have no doubt that he pursued and shed light on topics of great significance and relevance.

44 James (1878/1983a) reached the conviction that analogical thinking is fundamental to human knowledge, including science, very early in his career: "Every phenomenon or so-called 'fact' has an infinity of aspects.... What does the scientific man do who searches for the reason or law embedded in a phenomenon? He deliberately accumulates all the instances he can find which have any analogy to that phenomenon, and, by simultaneously filling his mind with them all, he frequently succeeds in detaching from the collection the peculiarity which he was unable to formulate in one alone.... our only instrument for dissecting out the special characters of phenomena, which... are [then] used as reasons, is this association by similarity.... the mind in which this mode of association most prevails will... be one most prone to reasoned thinking" (pp. 12, 21–2, italics deleted).

A mind *less* prone to analogical thinking is more prone, according to James, to "association by contiguity," which is to say, to a mental life constituted by sequences of thought that are automatically, or irrationally, determined by the past order of experience. James (1880) described this latter, "non-thinking" type of mind as "dry, prosaic, and matter of fact" – in a word, "very literal." Human intelligences of such a "simple order" are, he said, "slaves of habit" who "take the world for granted" (p. 456). "But turn to the highest order of mind, and what a change!" (p. 456). Here, "instead of thoughts of concrete things patiently following one another in a beaten track of habitual suggestion," there are "the most abrupt cross-cuts and transitions from one idea to another, the most rarefied abstractions and discriminations, the most unheard-of combinations of elements, the subtlest associations of analogy; in a word, we seem suddenly introduced into a seething caldron of ideas, where . . . partnerships can be joined or loosened in an instant, treadmill routine is unknown, and the unexpected seems the only law" (p. 456).

Interestingly, James (1883–4/1988) noticed that, although "the world may be a place in which the same thing never did & never will come twice," the human mind nonetheless constantly tries to find similarities among these ever-novel phenomena. Indeed, instead of the "psychological principle of sameness," James suggested that it would be more precise to speak of the "law of constancy in our meanings," which he took to be "one of the most remarkable features, indeed one might well say the very backbone, of our subjective life" (p. 285). It is only through the operation of this "law," James argued, that generalization, abstraction, reasoning, and other forms of higher cognition can take place.

This emphasis on the centrality of association by similarity – or analogical thinking – continued throughout James's works, including his philosophical works. Regarding metaphysical knowledge, for example, he agreed with Harald Höffding (1905a,b) – and foreshadowed Stephen Pepper (1928, 1942) – when he argued that "all our attempted definitions of the Whole of things, are made by conceiving it as analogous in constitution to some one of its parts which we treat as a type-phenomenon" (James, 1905, p. xi).

In corroboration of points made elsewhere in this chapter, it is relevant to note that James agreed that (1) mathematics, as well as classification and logic, is fundamentally metaphorical, that is, based on comparison or analogical thinking (see James, 1890, vol. 2, pp. 641–69); (2) our terms and concepts for mental phenomena are derived from physical analogs (see James, 1883–4/1988, p. 256; for a possibly influential precedent, besides Locke, see Emerson, 1836/1983a, p. 20); (3) alternative theoretical frameworks can be simultaneously verified (see James, 1890, vol. 2, p. 312; 1907/1975, p. 104); (4) human understanding, or knowledge, can be usefully considered to be a "translation" of "sensible experiences into other forms" (see James, 1890, vol. 2, pp. 640, 669); and (5) the disanalogous dimensions of metaphorical comparisons must be clarified along with the analogous dimensions (see, e.g., James, 1890, vol. 1, pp. 6–7, and note 49).

45 Early on, James (ca. 1879/1978) recognized that "universal acceptance" is the "only mark of truth which we possess" (p. 360). Pointing toward a sociology of knowledge, he came to realize how complex and interdependent the matter of acceptance is: "You accept my verification of one thing. I yours of another. We trade on each other's truth. . . . All human thinking gets discursified; we exchange ideas; we lend and borrow verifications, get them from one another by means of social intercourse. All truth thus gets verbally built out, stored up, and made available for everyone" (1907/1975, pp. 100, 102).

Simplistic interpretations of what James meant when he spoke about an idea "working" or "paying off" have led to some grotesque distortions of the thought of one of the greatest intellects in American history – in philosophy as well as psychology. (Alfred North Whitehead, 1938, pp. 3–4, even argued that James was one of the four great intellects of the Western tradition, along with Plato, Aristotle, and Leibniz.) The social dimension of James's thought, as exemplified above by the notion of verification by social intercourse, has often been underestimated. Even though James emphasized the individual over the group, this does not excuse some of the simple-minded claims that have been made about James's disregard of the social nature of psychological phenomena, including knowledge. He was a leader, for instance, in arguing for the social dimension of the self (1890, vol. 1, pp. 293–6).

46 Although "the ideal of every science is that of a closed and completed system of truth" (James, 1890/1983c, p. 247), experience is ever open-ended, ever promising and yielding new phenomena and new aspects of phenomena (see James, 1890, vol. 1, p. 233; 1897/1979, p. 141). Thus, the quest for "'absolutely' true" concepts is an "ideal vanishing-point towards which we imagine that all our temporary truths will some day converge" (James, 1907/1975, pp. 106–7). We must remember that absolute truth is a goal, not an achievement, so that when we "lay hold of" reality from a particular "angle," we will not unduly persist in treating reality "as if . . . it were nothing but that aspect" (James, 1890, vol. 2, p. 648; 1907/1975, p. 103). How far can and will nature be "remodelled" by human understanding? That is "a question which only the whole future history of Science and Philosophy can answer" (James, 1890, vol. 2, p. 671).

47 See, e.g., James (1878/1983a. pp. 35–6; 1884/1983b, pp. 152–3; 1890, vol. 1, pp. 26–7, 234–5, 288–9, vol. 2, pp. 450, 481; 1902/1985, pp. 380–1; 1907/ 1982; 1909/1986, pp. 374–5) and the metaphors highlighted in E. Taylor (1982, e.g., on p. 18). On the evolution of various "ensembles and families of metaphors" in James's work, see Osowski (1986). On the influence of James's "fluid symbols" (e.g., his famous analysis of and emphasis on the "stream of consciousness"), see Ruddick (1981).

48 On the Darwinian background of James's thought, see Hofstadter (1955), Perry (1935, vol. 1, chap. 27), R. J. Richards (1987, chap. 9), Russett (1976), Wiener (1949), and Woodward (1983). The classic exposition of James's thought is provided by Perry (1935), but for a more recent, lengthy explication and analysis, see Myers (1986); and for a much briefer summary of James's philosophical principles, see Suckiel (1982). Bjork's (1988) treatment is relevant insofar as it focuses on the centrality of James's cognitive theory to his overall intellectual position. In all of these works, it is rarely, if ever, noted that James was one of the first to see and to accept the larger significance of Darwinian natural selectionism. Darwin (1859/1964) convinced many, rather quickly, of evolutionism, but natural selection – Darwin's own theory of evolution – was not so quickly accepted (see D. Hull, 1973). Long before selectionism was accepted by the majority of biological scientists as one of the primary mechanisms of biological evolution, James (1880) had accepted it and was drawing out its implications for the theory of social evolution. One would hope that R. J. Richards's (1987, chap. 9) recent work will inaugurate a revival of interest in this aspect of James's work.

49 I mean "myth" here not simply in the more positive sense intended earlier in this chapter, but also in a more derogatory sense, according to which myth is the taking of an analogy or metaphor as an identity – and, by extension, the taking of its elaboration as a completely true story. Another way of saying this is that myths (in the negative sense) arise when people forget to say "like" or "as if" when proposing a metaphorical comparison and when they neglect to define the ways in whch analogous things or processes are also *dis*analogous or *dis*similar, as they are by definition as well as experience. For related discussions, see Burke (1935/1965, p. 97) and Turbayne (1970, esp. pt. 1). Royce's (1964) discussion of "encapsulation" – the taking of "*one* approach to reality as if it were *the* approach" (p. 164) – is also relevant. You might also recall Thomas Carlyle's (1829/1971) comment on all the early-nineteenth-century talk about the "Machine of Society": "Considered merely as a metaphor, all this is well enough; but here, as in so many other cases, the 'foam hardens itself into a shell,' and the shadow we have wantonly evoked 'stands terrible before us and will not depart at our bidding. Government includes much also that is not mechanical, and cannot be treated mechanically; of which latter truth, as appears to us, the political speculations and exertions of our time are taking less and less cognisance" (p. 70). The modern preference for representing reality in terms of "differences and identities" rather than "comparisons and similarities" (a preference analyzed by Foucault, 1970, chap. 3) accounts, somewhat tautologically, for the contemporary tendency toward literalization, which is the modern version of mythical thinking. This preference for what Kant (1797/1974) called "distinctions" (the noting of differences and identities rather than comparisons and similarities) does not eliminate the actual process of comparison that underlies cognition, but it does tend to obscure it. With regard to the dangers of not discriminating between similarities and identities, it is interesting that Descartes (1628/1911a) began his first philosophical work with a warning against taking similarities as identities (p. 1).

James frequently pointed out the dangers of literalization – of taking metaphors as definitive, literal statements of truth. For example, regarding two of the major psychological theories of the nineteenth century, he wrote: "I do not mean to say that the 'Associationist' manner of representing the life of the mind as an agglutination in various shapes of separate entities called ideas, and the Herbartian way of representing it as resulting from the mutual repugnancies of separate entities called *Vorstellungen,* are not convenient formulas for roughly symbolizing the facts. So are the fluid-theories of electricity, the emission-theory of light, the archetype-theory of the skeleton, and the theory that curves are composed of small straight lines. But, if taken as literal truth, I say that any one of these theories is just as false as any other, and leads to as pernicious results.... Associationism and Herbartianism [like other scientific theories] are only schematisms which, the moment they are taken literally, become mythologies, and had much better be dropped than retained" (1884/1983b, pp. 147, 153).

James's caveat did not foreclose the tendency toward literalization. To give but one example, B. F. Skinner's (1938, 1981) radical behaviorism is founded – as is James's psychology, though with very different results – on the central Darwinian metaphors of variation, selection, and utility. Skinner supposes that there are spontaneous, blind variations in behavior, some of which are selected (i.e., reinforced) because of their utility. But despite the fact that he transfers Darwin's concepts from the context of phylogenetic history to that of ontogenetic development, and despite the fact that he applies these concepts to the arena of behavioral learning rather than that of biological speciation, Skinner makes no qualification in his literalist appeal to Darwinian authority. He is, he claims, simply drawing out the ineluctable consequences of Darwin's evolutionary theory. I would say that he is making an interesting and potentially informative extrapolation from Darwin's theory, but that he is mistakenly equating the evolution of species over millennia with the evolution of an individual's behavior over a single lifetime; and I would suppose that the conceptual framework adequate for the one will not be identically adequate for the other. It is precisely the specification of some of the major *differences* – that is, the specification of the extent to which variation, selection, and utility are *not* preemptive concepts for the understanding of organic behavior – that would help fill in and round out Skinner's psychology.

What adds a bit of pathos to all this is the fact that Skinner uses Darwinian theory in support of a completely determinist view of human nature, a view that allows for no freedom or self-control, as traditionally understood. Once again we see an ironical conceptual boomerang. Darwin, you will remember, reached his theory by looking specifically at how human breeders control nature by *intentionally* selecting the characteristics they want to enhance in future generations. Now Darwin's metaphor of natural selection, which is based on the notion of human control over nature in the breeding of domestic animals, is used to support the argument that nature controls humans, and thus to discredit the very conception of conscious intentionality that grounded Darwin's theory.

James (1890), by the way, was more faithful than Skinner – or Darwin – to Darwin's originating insight. He explicitly used selection *by means of conscious attention* (or intention) to explain what he regarded to be the relatively small, *but very significant* amount of human freedom (chap. 26).

Regarding Skinner's attitude toward metaphor and Skinner's own metaphoric language, see Leary (1988a) and L. D. Smith (Chapter 7, note 4, this volume). Staddon and Simmelhag (1971), in their attempt to account for behavioral *variation* as well as behavioral *selection,* provide one of many examples of the amplification of the Darwinian metaphor that lies at the heart of Skinnerian psychology.

50 For instance, G. Stanley Hall, one of the founders of scientific psychology in America, felt as strongly as Freud and James about the analogical or metaphorical basis of all knowledge. In a manner reminiscent of both James and Emerson, Hall (1904) claimed that metaphors are among the mind's "first spontaneous creations" and that they provide the basis for the development of language, which is therefore essentially "fossil poetry." With reference to psychological knowledge in particular, Hall noted that through the "widening circle of objects and events" linked by metaphorical thinking, "scores of objects are no longer mere things of sense, but are words in the dictionary of psychic states and moral qualities" (vol. 2, p. 145). In saying this in his typically obscure manner, Hall had in mind the same fact noted by Locke, James, and others (see note 28 and the last paragraph of note 44): that psychological concepts such as "imagination," "apprehension," and "emotion," and moral concepts such as "dependability," "reliability," and "forthrightness," were drawn originally from physical analogs.

Whatever their similarity, Hall's approach was also markedly different from those of Freud and James. Rather than assume that there is always more than one salient metaphorical view of reality, Hall supposed that one particular metaphorical approach could be the definitively correct one. A monist rather than a Jamesian pluralist in this regard, he proposed his own recapitulation theory of psychological development as the ultimate scientific theory of human personality and character (1897, 1904, 1922). Transforming a metaphor into a principle, he extrapolated theories of childhood, adolescence, and aging from the premise that the phylogenetic history of the species provides a literal, completely accurate analog of the developmental stages in the life of the individual. Similar recapitulationist theories have been proposed by others in the history of psychology and have been much more influential than usually recognized. See Gould (1977a) for general background on recapitulationist theory; see Sulloway (1979) on Freud's recapitulationism; and see Jung (1917/ 1966) and Piaget (1967/1971, chap. 4, esp. pp. 158–64; 1969) for other theories with recapitulationist elements that continue to attract attention. As for Hall's developmental theory, both its largely speculative nature and its spare empirical backing help account for its downfall.

51 Elsewhere, Cattell (1898) noted that the experimental psychologist's "regard for the body of nature becomes that of the anatomist rather than that of the lover" (p. 152). Though perfectly understandable, Cattell's choice of metaphors is emblematic of the professionalization of psychology (more hoped for than actual when Cattell wrote these words). No longer an "amatuer" (or lover) of human nature, Cattell wanted to move beyond even T. H. Huxley (1898), "Darwin's bulldog," who for all his fierce commitment to science still felt that "living nature is not a mechanism but a poem; not merely a rough engine-house for the due keeping of pleasure and pain machines, but a palace whose foundations, indeed, are laid on the strictest and safest mechanical principles, but whose superstructure is a manifestation of the highest and subtlest art" (p. 311).

The loss of aesthetic feeling for one's subject matter – the dulling of the eye, as William Wordsworth (1814/1977) put it with special reference to materialistic science (p. 155) – is a loss of significant import, as both Darwin and James would have agreed (Leary, 1988c). Such aesthetic loss is frequently tied to the "overt" rejection of metaphoric language – and the "covert" or unrecognized use of empiricist metaphors, such as those associated with "taking nature apart" and "reconstructing it" with the "bare essentials," generally "from the bottom up." It is worth considering the nature of the supposed "nonessentials" that are omitted by and from classic scientific study and the actual and potential damage done to psychology – not to mention our scientific and technological culture – by their omission, especially since many of these "nonessentials" (e.g., emotional, aesthetic, and moral reactions and interests) are related to the so-called secondary qualities of experience that were banished from the realm of scientific theory and research at the time of Galileo, Descartes, and Newton (see Burtt, 1925/1954, esp. pp. 180–4, 231–9, 303–25; Koyré, 1950/1968, 1957). Although strides are being made toward returning these "qualities" to their rightful place in the realm, and study, of reality, we seem not to have tapped the full dimensions of the "human metaphor" (Sewell, 1964). With William James and others, I doubt we ever will, but we ought not close the door to the attempt: We ought instead to strive, through the metaphors we create and use, to enrich and empower rather than to restrict and desiccate human potential, experience, and action. Such enrichment and empowering would pay double dividends insofar as richness of experience and emotion are among the most important factors that enable and motivate metaphoric, or creative, expression (see MacCormac, 1986).

52 In fact, Cattell's near decade of "mental testing" left little more than a warehouse of meaningless data (see Sokal, 1987). In contrast, the works of Freud and James continue to be sources of theoretical ideas fifty and eighty years after the respective deaths of these two thinkers. It is also relevant that even an antimetaphorist leaves metaphorical traces, and in Cattell's case these traces have dug deeply into psychological practice. The empiricist rhetoric of scientific inquiry – like the methodological practices it corroborates – is age-old, but the rhetoric of modern psychological diagnosis and treatment is much more recent. Though this is a huge topic, what is most pertinent – and will

serve as an illustration – is the rhetoric (and myths) that grew up around Cattell's concept of "mental testing." From its original metaphorical basis in the "anthropometric" work of Francis Galton, the "psychometry" of the "mental testing" movement begun in America by Cattell was soon enveloped in a rhetoric of social doctoring and human engineering. Drawing attention and power from its numerous linguistic and conceptual references to the two most conspicuous fields in which modern science has proved its worth (medicine and engineering), an entire rhetoric of abnormal and clinical psychology was elaborated. As doctors tested for disease and engineers for stress, so psychologists came to think of themselves, and presented themselves, as being capable of testing for intelligence or insanity or any number of psychological properties. They were not simply *like* doctors and engineers; they *were* doctors and engineers, testing "patients" for "mental disease" and designing "solutions" for their "mental stress." More significantly, a whole set of practical routines has been tied to this conceptual framework – routines that still direct the professional activities of many psychologists, even though the conceptual framework itself (at least the portion drawing on medical analogs) has received some well-publicized criticism (particularly after Szasz, 1961). On the rhetoric of mental testing and of professionalization in general, see J. Brown (1985, 1986); on applied psychology earlier in this century, see O'Donnell (1985), Napoli (1981), and Samelson (1979); and on the development of psychology's (or more particularly, psychiatry's) professional jurisdiction over "personal problems," see Abbott (1988, chap. 10).

53 Such subtle movement from metaphorical to supposedly literal conceptualization of psychological phenomena is typical of the historical development of twentieth-century psychological rhetoric. The apparently pure, neutral psychological language mandated earlier in the century by the dominant positivist philosophy of science was always, deeper down, informed by comparative thinking (see note 10); and many of the theoretical arguments and developments over the past century have been the result of what might be called *analogical redescription* of psychological phenomena. For example, much of the turn-of-the-century awareness of, and framework for understanding, the phenomena of nonnormal psychology (e.g., regarding different levels of consciousness and dual personality) was "translated" into the new scientific language of psychology, with little acknowledgment, from psychic research (Leary, 1980b). Another example is provided by a truncated argument made by John B. Watson (1916) in his presidential address to the American Psychological Association. "It seems to me," he said, "that hysterical motor manifestations may be looked upon as conditioned reflexes" (p. 99). This is not an unreasonable analogy, and pursuing it might have enlightened our understanding of hysteria, but Watson slid without further justification from this suggestive analogy to a matter-of-fact declaration that "the conditioned reflex can be used as an explanatory principle in the psychopathology of hysteria" (p. 99).

This sort of linguistic sleight of hand, by which an analogical redescription is taken to be a new theoretical explanation, was noted in 1934 by a perceptive observer who complained that "psychology, for all its theories, has performed no miracles. It has renamed our emotions 'complexes' and our habits 'conditioned reflexes,' but it has neither changed our habits nor rid us of our emotions. We are the same blundering folk that we were twelve years ago, and far less sure of ourselves" (Adams, 1934, p. 92). Even those who would be more generous in their assessment of modern psychology and its effects will probably sympathize with this critique. Still, it is a measure of the success of modern psychology's rhetoric that so many people now turn to psychology both in health and in distress. Indeed, many Americans now approach psychology as their predecessors approached religion. Not coincidentally, a great deal of religious rhetoric – for example, about the means of personal enlightenment and salvation – has found its way into psychological treatises.

The persuasiveness of twentieth-century psychology, like that of any other discipline, is clearly related to its choice of metaphors. By drawing on culturally salient and popular metaphors, psychologists have created a salient and popular discipline. I shall give three examples based on the fact that our culture places a high value on *efficiency,* that our society is *capitalistic,* and that we are obsessed with *technology* (facts that are admittedly interrelated): (1) In our efficiency-conscious culture, psychologists have used metaphors of efficiency at the very core of their thinking and rhetoric. Nurtured by the Puritan ethic as well as by the capitalist marketplace, the cult of efficiency has influenced both applied psychology (e.g., industrial and educational psychology) and more theoretical psychology (e.g., abnormal and personality psychology). As correlates of the metaphor of efficiency, with its criteria of economy of effort and directedness of purpose, "mental deficiency" became the effective synonym for subnormal mental functioning, while the leading of an "integrated" and "productive" life became the major criterion of psychological normality. (2) In this capitalist society, psychologists have given metaphors of productivity and exchange a prominent place in their analyses of social behavior. Although theories of social exchange (in social psychology) and theories of optimization (in behavioral psychology) have been given their mature form only in recent decades, the implicit assumptions of cost–benefit analysis have guided theoretical work in psychology for much longer. (3) In this technological society, psychologists have turned to cybernetic, computational, and other such analogs of neurological, cognitive, emotional, and behavioral functioning. (The computer is but one of many technical devices that have provided critical analogs for the theoretical ruminations of twentieth-century psychologists.) Clearly, no one would or could have thought of our senses, for example, as "signal detection devices" without the prior invention of radar, nor would the methodological and quantitative techniques necessary to study the senses as signal detectors have been available without the previous development of radar and similar technology.

On psychological efficiency and deficiency, see Goddard (1920), Hollingworth (1912, 1914), Judd (1918, chaps. 4 and 5), Witmer (1915, 1919), and Woodworth (1901). Dewey's (1896/1972a) description of "good character" as having as its first attribute "1. Efficiency, force. To be good for something, not simply to mean well" (p. 326), and his subsequent (1897/1972b) remark that "force, efficiency in execution, or overt action, is the necessary constituent of character" (p. 78), provide a context for his later (1900) concern about such things as "waste in education" (chap. 3). The "progressivist" cultural context of this "cult of efficiency" (as Callahan, 1962, has called it) is reflected in works such as that of E. H. Richards (1910), in Frederick W. Taylor's "Scientific Management Movement" (see May, 1959, pp. 132–6; Schwartz, 1986, chap. 8; F. W. Taylor, 1911), and in various educational concerns and reforms (see Callahan, 1962; Tyack & Hansot, 1982). The long-term legacy of this cult was still visible in the 1950s (see Wallin, 1956). Indeed, it is visible today, transmogrified into ergonomics, cost–benefit analyses, optimization theories, and so on, which continue to influence theories of individual and social behavior, both inside and outside psychology proper (see, e.g., Haraway, 1981–2; Wilson, 1968, 1971, 1975, 1978).

As I have indicated, optimization theories are related to earlier concerns about efficiency and come primarily from economic theory. The exchange metaphor is also rooted in economic (capitalist) theory and was introduced formally into psychology in works such as that of Thibaut and Kelley (1959). Regarding later developments, see Gergen, Greenberg, and Willis (1980). With regard to technological metaphors, see Pribram (Chapter 2, this volume) and N. Wiener (1961). The complete and fascinating story of the dialectic between ideas and devices in psychology – how ideas lead to the invention of devices and how devices lead to the modification and extension of ideas – has not yet been adequately told, though the interaction of thoughts and things (including in some cases political theory, daily patterns of behavior, and everyday technical devices) is beginning to be the focus of historical scholarship in other realms (e.g., Beniger, 1986; Gimbel, 1976; Landes, 1983; O. Mayr, 1986). The overlap between the American cult of efficiency and the American obsession with machines was well expressed in Santayana's classic analysis, "The Intellectual Temper of Our Times" (1913/1940), in which Santayana noted that in America (as opposed to Europe) "the mind is recommended rather as an unpatented device for oiling the engine of the body and making it do double work" (p. 17).

There is no *necessary* problem involved in drawing on culturally popular metaphors, but the dangers associated with it, especially the danger of literalization, are quite real: When metaphors seem "obvious," they can easily be "taken for granted" and can be very persuasive to a great many people. Furthermore, when a culturally prominent metaphor is literalized, this tends to legitimate as well as draw on cultural values and arrangements. To this extent, culturally based metaphors have ideological dimensions and political ramifications no less than do metaphors that purposely cut against the grain of standard cultural assumptions. In this situation it seems all the more important that theoretical metaphors be clearly seen and identified for what they are, namely, historically contingent modes of perception, cognition, and (so far as they are implemented) action. That well-socialized Americans tend to engage in social interactions in "capitalistic" ways, expecting a profitable – and perhaps a more than equitable – exchange of goods and services, should not be surprising. But to "prove" the validity of exchange theory by observation of *American* social-behavior patterns, and then to propose exchange theory *on this basis* as a *universal* explanation of human behavior, is to prescribe uncritically one particular cultural pattern as the "normal" mode of human behavior. This not only canonizes one particular cultural arrangement, it shields it from criticism and by implication damns alternative social arrangements as "unnatural," deviant, or less than optimal. The case is similar regarding other sorts of metaphors. For example, our culture favors novelty ("signals" or "messages") over constancy ("background noise"), and we learn to focus, to think about, and to study our senses accordingly. But "signal detection" hardly exhausts the range and possibility of sensory experience.

Still, have signal detection theory and social exchange theory helped us understand, control, and even extend certain dimensions of our experience? Absolutely. And provided that they are not seen as definitive, they even provide the grounds for a *critique* of our sensory and social experience. But insofar as they become prescriptive, they narrow rather than expand our options, and there, I believe, is the rub: metaphor, yes; prescription, no.

A historiographical postscript: The intimate connection between culture and psychology that is so obvious *in* metaphor – and instrumentally accomplished, in part, *through* metaphor (see MacCormac, 1985, p. 2) – makes metaphor an extremely useful tool for the historian who wishes to study the impact of culture upon psychological theory and practice and the converse impact of psychology upon culture. The latter influence results from the energizing and popularizing that can begin within the domain of psychology, as, for instance, when Freud helped make awareness – or the supposition – of sexual motives, dream symbols, and various sorts of symptoms and defenses part of our cultural heritage. Although more strictly academic and scientific psychology has had less obvious influence on culture at large, it has contributed to our culture's sensitivity to the ways in which our lives are "shaped" by the environmental "reinforcements" that we receive. Indeed, the entire Head Start Program and much of the Peace Corps movement have been energized by hopes and techniques derived at least in part from academic psychology. The historical charting of this mutual influence of psychology and culture, which is surely dialectic, constitutes one of the major challenges for historians of psychology. As this history is charted, the old distinctions between intellectual, social, and cultural history will become less and less useful, and metaphor will be seen as one of the sinews that bind this history together.

The degree of intimacy between cognition and culture is reflected in the title of a recent book that focuses on cultural models *in* rather than *of* language and thought (Holland & Quinn, 1987), and it is clearly implicated in Geertz's (1983) call for an "ethnography of modern thought."

54 Or what we can call, more simply, the human imagination. The modern ambivalence toward the "imagination" as a presumptive human faculty has been well documented (see, e.g., Costa-Lima, 1988; Engell, 1981; Gay, 1969, pp. 208–15; Johnson, 1987; Kearney, 1988; Schulte-Sasse, 1986–7, 1988). Even though science contributed in some ways to a rediscovery of the imagination (see Rousseau, 1969), it is nonetheless true that the imagination has generally been considered to lack the methodological rigor and reliability demanded by science and, consequentially, that the imagination is a "faculty seldom encountered in modern treatments of analogy in science" (Park et al., 1984, p. 287). However, the imagination's fortunes seem to be changing. (In this regard, see all the works previously cited in this note as well as Boulding, 1956, chap. 11; Hesse, 1955; Holton, 1978; Koestler, 1964; Ricoeur, 1979.) I hope this trend continues. An unembarrassed admission of the reality and role of the human imagination seems to me to be perfectly in tune with the discussions of "fact, fiction, and forecast" (Goodman, 1954), "personal knowledge" (Polanyi, 1958), "plans" (Miller, Galanter, & Pribram, 1960), "foresight and understanding" (Toulmin, 1961), "the logic of scientific discovery" (Hanson, 1961), "conjectures and refutations" (Popper, 1963), "posits and reality" (Quine, 1966), "paradigms" (Kuhn, 1970), "the thematic imagination in science" (Holton, 1973), "ways of worldmaking" (Goodman, 1978), "the construction of reality" (Arbib & Hesse, 1986), "science as creative perception-communication" (Bohm & Peat, 1987, chap. 2), "constructive realism" (Giere, 1988), and "imagistic and analogical reasoning" (Nersessian, in press) that, from my perspective, express the central thrusts and trajectories of recent and current musings about the nature of knowledge and science. It is not only the "poet's pen" that gives "shapes" to "things unknown." The scientist too has an imagination that "bodies forth the forms of things unknown" and gives to them a "local habitation and a name" (Shakespeare, 1598/1936, p. 406). The scientist too is a "maker." Indeed, the modern scientist has demonstrated the awesome truth of Wallace Stevens's (1930–55/1982) contention that "the imagination is man's power over nature" (p. 179).

That I turn to poetry to express the heart of the matter is no accident. As Sewell (1985) has argued, the sooner the "uneven dance" between psychology and poetry is rechoreographed, the better; and as Asch (1958) noted years ago, the study of metaphor could contribute not only to "our knowledge of cognitive functions" but also to a "lessening of a gap that has, too long, continued between psychology and the humanities" (p. 94). Indeed, psychology, like science more generally, is one of the humanities – one of the major products of the human imagination. We should remember, ponder, and act according to this fact. John Dewey (1891/1969), in arguing that "we must bridge this gap of poetry from science" and thus "heal this unnatural wound," said much the same thing: "This division of life into prose and poetry [or science and the humanities], is an unnatural divorce of the spirit" (p. 123).

In this context, it is symbolically apt that Marx Wartofsky concludes his too neglected (1979) collection of papers on representation and the scientific understanding with an essay titled "Art as Humanizing Process" (pp. 357–69). If we can understand more fully how art humanizes us, we can begin to fathom some of the less commonly recognized ways in which science can contribute to the expansion of human awareness, understanding, discrimination, choice, and action.

References

Abbott, A. (1988). *The system of professions: An essay on the division of expert labor.* Chicago: University of Chicago Press.

Abrams, M. H. (1953). *The mirror and the lamp: Romantic theory and the critical tradition.* New York: Oxford University Press.

Adams, G. (1934). The rise and fall of psychology. *Atlantic Monthly, 153,* 82–92.

Adkins, A. W. H. (1972). *Moral values and political behaviour in ancient Greece.* New York: Norton.

Adler, M. (1927). *Dialectic.* New York: Harcourt, Brace.

Agnew, J.-C. (1986). *Worlds apart: The market and the theater in Anglo-American thought, 1550–1750.* Cambridge University Press.

Alexander, H. G. (Ed.). (1956). *The Leibniz–Clarke correspondence.* Manchester: Manchester University Press.

Alford, J. A. (1982). The grammatical metaphor: A survey of its use in the Middle Ages. *Speculum, 57,* 728–60.

Allen, D. C. (1970). *Mysteriously meant: The rediscovery of pagan symbolism and allegorical interpretation in the Renaissance.* Baltimore, MD: Johns Hopkins University Press.

Anderson, J. R. (1983). *The architecture of cognition.* Cambridge, MA: Harvard University Press.

Appleman, P. (Ed.). (1970). *Darwin: A Norton critical edition.* New York: Norton.

Arbib, M. A. (1972). *The metaphorical brain: An introduction to cybernetics as artificial intelligence and brain theory.* New York: Wiley.

Arbib, M. A., & Hesse, M. B. (1986). *The construction of reality.* Cambridge University Press.

Aristotle (1924a). Rhetorica (W. R. Roberts, Trans.). In W. D. Ross (Ed.), *The works of Aristotle* (vol. 11, ll. 1354–1420). Oxford: Clarendon Press. (Original work written ca. 330 B.C.)

(1924b). De poetica (I. Bywater, Trans.). In W. D. Ross (Ed.), *The works of Aristotle* (vol. 11 ll. 1447–62). Oxford: Clarendon Press. (Original work written ca. 330 B.C.)

(1931). De anima (J. A. Smith, Trans.). In W. D. Ross (Ed.), *The works of Aristotle* (vol. 3, ll. 402–35). Oxford: Clarendon Press. (Original work written ca. 330 B.C.)

Arnheim, R. (1969). *Visual thinking*. Berkeley and Los Angeles: University of California Press.

Asch, S. E. (1955). On the use of metaphor in the description of persons. In H. Werner (Ed.), *On expressive language* (pp. 29–38). Worcester, MA: Clark University Press.

(1958). The metaphor: A psychological inquiry. In R. Taguiri & L. Petrullo (Eds.), *Person perception and interpersonal behavior* (pp. 86–94). Stanford, CA: Stanford University Press.

Atkinson, J. W., & Cartwright, D. (1964). Some neglected problems in contemporary conceptions of decision and performance. *Psychological Reports, 14,* 575–90.

Baars, B. J. (1986). *The cognitive revolution in psychology*. New York: Guilford Press.

Badalamenti, A. F. (1979). Entropy in Freudian psychology. *Methodology and Science, 12,* 1–16.

Bain, A. (1855). *The senses and the intellect*. London: Parker.

Baker, H. (1947). *The dignity of man: Studies in the persistence of an idea*. Cambridge, MA: Harvard University Press.

Bambrough, R. (1956). Plato's political analogies. In P. Laslett (Ed.), *Philosophy, politics and society* (pp. 98–115). New York: Macmillan.

Barbour, I. G. (1974). *Myths, models, and paradigms*. New York: Harper & Row.

Barfield, O. (1960). The meaning of the word 'literal'. In L. C. Knights & B. Cottle (Eds.), *Metaphor and symbol* (pp. 48–63). London: Butterworth.

(1977). *The rediscovery of meaning, and other essays*. Middletown, CT: Wesleyan University Press.

Barnes, B., & Shapin, S. (Eds.). (1979). *Natural order: Historical studies of scientific culture*. Beverly Hills, CA: Sage.

Barrett, P. H. (Ed.). (1974). Darwin's early and unpublished notebooks. In H. E. Gruber & P. H. Barrett, *Darwin on man* (pp. 259–474). New York: Dutton.

Barrows, S. (1981). *Distorting mirrors: Visions of the crowd in late nineteenth-century France*. New Haven, CT: Yale University Press.

Beer, G. (1983). *Darwin's plots: Evolutionary narrative in Darwin, George Eliot and nineteenth-century fiction*. London: Routledge & Kegan Paul.

Beniger, J. R. (1986). *The control revolution: Technological and economic origins of the information society*. Cambridge, MA: Harvard University Press.

Benjamin, A. E., Cantor, G. N., & Christie, J. R. R. (Eds.). (1987). *The figural and the literal: Problems of language in the history of science and philosophy*. Manchester: Manchester University Press.

Bentham, J. (1962). Essay on language. In E. Bowring (Ed.), *The works of JeremyBentham* (vol. 8, p. 295–338). New York: Russell & Russell. (Original work published posthumously 1841.)

Berggren, D. (1962). The use and abuse of metaphor. *Review of Metaphysics, 16,* 237–58, 450–72.

Berkeley, G. (1955). The bond of society. In A. A. Luce & T. E. Jessop (Eds.), *The works of George Berkeley, Bishop of Cloyne* (vol. 7, pp. 225–8). London: Nelson. (Original work published 1713.)

Berlin, I. (1981). *Concepts and categories* (H. Hardy, Ed.). Harmondsworth: Penguin.

Berman, H. J. (1983). *Law and revolution: The formation of the Western legal tradition*. Cambridge, MA: Harvard University Press.

Bernfeld, S. C. (1951). Freud and archeology. *American Imago, 8*, 107–28.

Bettelheim, B. (1983). *Freud and man's soul.* New York: Knopf.

Billow, R. M. (1977). Metaphor: A review of the psychological literature. *Psychological Bulletin, 84*, 81–92.

Bjork, D. W. (1988). *William James: The center of his vision.* New York: Columbia University Press.

Black, M. (1962). *Models and metaphors.* Ithaca, NY: Cornell University Press.
 (1979). More about metaphor. In A. Ortony (Ed.), *Metaphor and thought* (pp. 19–43). Cambridge University Press.

Blondel, E. (1977). Nietzsche: Life as metaphor (M. Macrae, Trans.). In D. B. Allison (Ed.), *The new Nietzsche: Contemporary styles of interpretation* (pp. 150–75). New York: Dell.

Bloom, H. (1982). Freud's concepts of defense and the poetic will. In *Agon: Towards a theory of revisionism* (pp. 119–44). New York: Oxford University Press.

Bloor, D. (1971). The dialectics of metaphor. *Inquiry, 14*, 430–44.

Boden, M. A. (1977). *Artificial intelligence and natural man.* New York: Basic Books.
 (1988). *Computer models of mind: Computational approaches in theoretical psychology.* Cambridge University Press.

Bohm, D., & Peat, F. D. (1987). *Science, order, and creativity: A dramatic new look at the creative roots of science and life.* New York: Bantam Books.

Boring, E. G. (1946). Mind and mechanism. *American Journal of Psychology, 59*, 173–92.

Boulding, K. E. (1956). *The image: Knowledge in life and society.* Ann Arbor: University of Michigan Press.

Boyd, R. (1979). Metaphor and theory change: What is a "metaphor" a metaphor for? In A. Ortony (Ed.), *Metaphor and thought* (pp. 356–408). Cambridge University Press.

Breazeale, D. (1975). The word, the world, and Nietzsche. *Philosophical Forum, 6*, 301–20.

Bremmer, J. (1983). *The early Greek concept of the soul.* Princeton, NJ: Princeton University Press.

Brown, H. I. (1977). *Perception, theory and commitment: The new philosophy of science.* Chicago: University of Chicago Press.

Brown, J. (1985). *The semantics of profession: Metaphor and power in the history of psychological testing, 1890–1929.* Ph. D. dissertation, University of Wisconsin.
 (1986). Professional language: Words that succeed. *Radical History Review, 34*, 33–51.

Brown, R. H. (1976). Social theory as metaphor: On the logic of discovery for the sciences of conduct. *Theory and Society, 3*, 169–97.
 (1977). *A poetic for sociology: Toward a logic of discovery for the human sciences.* Cambridge University Press.
 (1987). *Society as text: Essays on rhetoric, reason, and reality.* Chicago: University of Chicago Press.

Browning, D. S. (1987). Metaphors, models, and morality in Freud. In *Religious thought and the modern psychologies* (pp. 32–60). Philadelphia, PA: Fortress Press.

Brykman, G. (1982). Microscopes and philosophical method in Berkeley. In C. M. Turbayne (Ed.), *Berkeley: Critical and interpretive essays* (pp. 69–82). Minneapolis: University of Wisconsin Press.

Buchdahl, G. (1969). *Metaphysics and the philosophy of science: The classical origins, Descartes to Kant.* Oxford: Blackwell Publisher.

Buck, R. C. (1956). On the logic of general behavior systems theory. In H. Feigl & M. Scriven (Eds.), *Minnesota studies in the philosophy of science* (pp. 223–38). Minneapolis: University of Minnesota Press.

Burke, K. (1945). *A grammar of motives.* New York: Prentice-Hall.

(1965). *Permanence and change: An anatomy of purpose* (2d rev. ed.). New York: New Republic. (Original work published 1935.)

Burks, A. W. (1946). Peirce's theory of abduction. *Philosophy of Science, 13,* 301–6.

Burtt, E. A. (1954). *The metaphysical foundations of modern physical science* (2d rev. ed.). New York: Doubleday. (Original work published 1925.)

Callahan, R. E. (1962). *Education and the cult of efficiency.* Chicago: University of Chicago Press.

Campbell, D. (1960). Blind variation and selective retention in creative thought as in other knowledge processes. *Psychological Review, 67,* 380–400.

(1974). Evolutionary epistemology. In P. Schilpp (Ed.), *The philosophy of Karl Popper* (pp. 413–63). La Salle, IL: Open Court.

Campbell, J. A. (1987). Charles Darwin: Rhetorician of science. In J. S. Nelson, A. Megill, & D. N. McCloskey (Eds.), *The rhetoric of the human sciences: Language and argument in scholarship and public affairs* (pp. 69–86). Madison: University of Wisconsin Press.

Campbell, N. R. (1920). *Physics: The elements.* Cambridge University Press.

Cannon, W. F. (1966). Darwin's vision in *On the origin of species.* In G. Levine & W. Madden (Eds.), *The art of Victorian prose* (pp. 154–76). New York: Oxford University Press.

Cantor, P. (1982). Friedrich Nietzsche: The use and abuse of metaphor. In D. S. Miall (Ed.). *Metaphor: Problems and perspectives* (pp. 71–88). Sussex: Harvester Press.

Carlyle, T. (1971). Signs of the times. In A. Shelston (Ed.), *Thomas Carlyle: Selected writings* (pp. 59–85). Harmondsworth: Penguin. (Original work published 1829.)

Cassirer, E. (1946). *Language and myth* (S. K. Langer, Trans.). New York: Harper Bros. (Original work published 1925.)

Cattell, J. M. (1896). Address of the president before the American Psychological Associaton, 1895. *Psychological Review, 3,* 135–48.

(1898). The biological problems of today: Psychology. *Science, 7,* 152–4.

Chapanis, A. (1961). Men, machines, and models. *American Psychologist, 16,* 113–31.

Chapman, A. J., & Jones, D. M. (Eds.). (1980). *Models of man.* Leicester: British Psychological Society.

Cohen, I. B. (1980). *The Newtonian revolution.* Cambridge University Press.

(1985) *Revolution in science.* Cambridge, MA: Harvard University Press.

(1987). Newton's third law and universal gravity. *Journal of the History of Ideas, 48,* 571–93.

Coleridge, S. T. (1884). Aids to reflection. In W. G. T. Shedd (Ed.). *The complete works of Samuel Taylor Coleridge* (vol. 1, pp. 117–416). New York: Harper Bros. (Original work published 1825.)

(1975). *Biographia literaria.* London: Dent. (Original work published 1817.)

(1981). Logic. In J. R. de J. Jackson (Ed.), *The collected works of Samuel Taylor Coleridge* (vol. 13). Princeton, NJ: Princeton University Press. (Original work written ca. 1823.)

Collingwood, R. G. (1945). *The idea of nature.* Oxford: Clarendon Press.

Cooper, D. E. (1986). *Metaphor.* Oxford: Blackwell Publisher.

Cooter, R. (1984). The social sense of brain. In *The cultural meaning of popular* science: *Phrenology and the organization of consent in nineteenth-century Britain.* Cambridge University Press.

Cornford, F. M. (1912). *From religion to philosophy: A study in the origins of Western speculation.* London: Arnold.

Corsano, A. (1969). Vico and mathematics. In G. Tagliacozzo & H. V. White (Eds.), *Giambattista Vico: An international symposium* (pp. 425–37). Baltimore, MD: Johns Hopkins University Press.

Costa-Lima, L. (1988). *The control of the imaginary: Reason and imagination in modern times* (R, Sousa, Trans.). Minneapolis: University of Minnesota Press.

Craik, K. J. W. (1943). *The nature of explanation.* Cambridge University Press. (1966). *The nature of psychology: A selection of papers, essays and other writings* (S. L. Sherwood, Ed.). Cambridge University Press.

Crosson, F. J. (1985). Psyche and the computer: Integrating the shadow. In S. Koch & D. E. Leary (Eds.), *A century of psychology as science* (pp. 437–51). New York: McGraw-Hill.

Curtius, E. R. (1953). Metaphorics. In *European literature and the Latin middle ages* (W. R. Trask, Trans.; pp. 128–44). Princeton, NJ: Princeton University Press.

Danziger, K. (1987). Statistical method and the historical development of research practice in American psychology. In L. Krüger, G. Gigerenzer, & M. S. Morgan (Eds.), *The probabilistic revolution* (vol. 2, pp. 35–47). Cambridge, MA: MIT Press.

Darwin, C. (1887). Autobiography. In F. Darwin (Ed.), *The life and letters of Charles Darwin* (2d ed., pp. 26–107). London: Murray. (Original work written 1876.)

(1964). *On the origin of species* (facsimile of 1st ed.). Cambridge, MA: Harvard University Press. (Original work published 1859.)

Darwin, F. (1887a). Reminiscences of my father's everyday life. In F. Darwin (Ed.), *The life and letters of Charles Darwin* (2d ed.; vol. 1, pp. 108–160). London: Murray.

Darwin, F. (Ed.). (1887b). *The life and letters of Charles Darwin* (2d ed.). London: Murray.

Darwin F., & Seward, A. C. (Eds.). (1903). *More letters of Charles Darwin.* New York: Appleton.

Daston, L. (1988). *Classical probability in the Enlightenment.* Princeton, NJ: Princeton University Press.

Davis, P. J., & Hersh, R. (1986). *Descartes's dream: The world according to mathematics.* Boston: Houghton Mifflin.

(1987). Rhetoric and mathematics. In J. S. Nelson, A. Megill, & D. N. McCloskey (Eds.), *The rhetoric of the human sciences: Language and argument in scholarship and public affairs* (pp. 53–68). Madison: University of Wisconsin Press.

Dear, P. (1985). *Totius in verba:* Rhetoric and authority in the early Royal Society. *Isis, 76,* 145–61.

De Beer, G. (Ed.). (1960–1). Darwin's notebooks on transmutation of species. *Bulletin of the British Museum (Natural History),* Historical Series 2, 23–183.

(1967). Darwin's notebooks on transmutation of species: Pages excised by Darwin. *Bulletin of the British Museum (Natural History),* Historical Series 3, 133–75.

Derrida, J. (1978). Freud and the scene of writing. In *Writing and difference* (A. Bass, Trans.; pp. 198–231). Chicago: University of Chicago Press.

Descartes, R. (1911a). Rules for the direction of mind. In E. S. Haldane & G. R. T. Ross (Eds. and Trans.), *The philosophical works of Descartes* (vol. 1, pp. 1–77). Cambridge University Press. (Original work written 1628.)

(1911b). Discourse on the method of rightly conducting the reason and seeking truth in the sciences. In E. S. Haldane & G. R. T. Ross (Eds. and Trans.), *The philosophical works of Descartes* (vol. 1, pp. 79–130). Cambridge University Press. (Original work published 1637.)

(1911c). The principles of philosophy. In E. S. Haldane & G. R. T. Ross (Eds. and Trans.), *The philosophical works of Descartes* (vol. 1, pp. 201–302). Cambridge University Press. (Original work published 1644.)

(1972). *Treatise of man* (T. S. Hall, Trans.). Cambridge, MA: Harvard University Press. (Original work published posthumously 1662.)

Deutsch, K. W. (1951). Mechanism, organism, and society: Some models in natural and social science. *Philosophy of Science, 18,* 230–52.

Dewey, J. (1900). *The school and society.* Chicago: University of Chicago Press.

(1969). Poetry and philosophy. In J. Boylston (Ed.), *The early works of John Dewey, 1882–1898* (vol. 3, pp. 110–24). Carbondale: Southern Illinois University Press. (Original work published 1891.)

(1972a). Educational psychology: Syllabus of a course of twelve lecture-studies. In J. Boylston (Ed.), *The early works of John Dewey, 1882–1898* (vol. 5, pp. 303–27). Carbondale: Southern Illinois University Press. (Original work pubished 1896.)

(1972b). Ethical principles underlying education. In J. Boylston (Ed.), *The early works of John Dewey, 1882–1898* (vol. 5, pp. 54–83). Carbondale: Southern Illinois University Press. (Original work published 1897.)

Dijksterhuis, E. J. (1969). *The mechanization of the world picture* (C. Dikshoorn, Trans.) New York: Oxford University Press.

Dobbs, B. J. T. (1975). *The foundations of Newton's alchemy, or "The hunting of the greene lyon."* Cambridge University Press.

Dodds, E. R. (1951). *The Greeks and the irrational.* Berkeley and Los Angeles: University of California Press.

Douglas, M. (1982). The two bodies. In *Natural symbols: Explorations in cosmology* (2d ed., pp. 65–81). New York: Pantheon Books.

Duhem, p. (1962). *The aim and structure of physical theory* (P. P. Wiener, Trans.). New York: Atheneum. (Original work published 1906.)

Dunlap, K. (1938). *The impending dismemberment of psychology.* Unpublished manuscript, Knight Dunlap Papers, Box M570.2, Archives of the History of American Psychology, Akron, OH.

Edelman, G. M. (1987). *Neural Darwinism: The theory of neuronal group selection.* New York: Basic Books.

Edelman, N. (1950). The mixed metaphor in Descartes. *Romantic Review, 41,* 165–78.

Edelson, J. T. (1983). Freud's use of metaphor. *Psychoanalytic Study of the Child, 38,* 17–59.

Ellenberger, H. F. (1970). *The discovery of the unconscious: The history and evolution of dynamic psychiatry.* New York: Basic Books.

Emerson, R. W. (1983a). Nature: Chapter 4, Language. In *Essays and lectures* (J. Porte, Ed.; pp. 20–5). New York: Literary Classics of the United States. (Original work published 1836.)

(1983b). The American scholar. In *Essays and lectures* (J. Porte, Ed.; pp. 51–71). New York: Literary Classics of the United States. (Original work published 1837.)

(1983c). The poet. In *Essays and lectures* (J. Porte, Ed.; pp. 445–86). New York: Literary Classics of the United States. (Original work published 1844.)

Engell, J. E. (1981). *The creative imagination: Enlightenment to romanticism.* Cambridge, MA: Harvard University Press.

Erdelyi, M. H. (1985). Models of mind and the language of the models. In *Psychoanalysis: Freud's cognitive psychology* (pp. 197–44). New York: Freeman.

Estes, W. K. (1978). The information processing approach to cognition: A confluence of metaphors and methods. In W. K. Estes (Ed.), *Handbook of learning and cognitive processes* (vol. 5, pp. 1–18). Hillsdale, NJ: Erlbaum.

Evans, L. T. (1984). Darwin's use of the analogy between artificial and natural selection. *Journal of the History of Biology, 17,* 113–40.

Fann, K. T. (1970). *Peirce's theory of abduction.* The Hague: Nijhoff.

Farber, E. (1950). Chemical discoveries by means of analogies. *Isis, 41,* 20–6.

Felstiner, M. L. (1983). Family metaphors: The language of an independence revolution. *Comparative Studies in Society and History, 25,* 154–80.

Figlio, K. M. (1976). The metaphor of organization: An historiographical perspective on the bio-medical sciences of the early nineteenth century. *History of Science, 14,* 17–53.

Fisch, M. H. (1986). *Peirce, semeiotic, and pragmatism* (K. L. Ketner & C. J. W. Kloesel, Eds.). Bloomington: Indiana University Press.

Fletcher, R. (1882). *On prehistoric trephining and cranial amulets.* Washington, DC: Government Printing Office.

Fogelin, R. J. (1988). *Figuratively speaking.* New Haven, CT: Yale University Press.

Forrester, J. (1980). *Language and the origins of psychoanalysis.* New York: Columbia University Press.

Foucault, M. (1970). *The order of things: An archaeology of the human sciences.* New York: Random House.

Frank, J. (1945). *Fate and freedom.* New York: Simon & Schuster.

French, R. K. (1969). *Robert Whytt, the soul, and medicine.* London: Wellcome Institute of the History of Medicine.

Frenkel-Brunswik, E. (1954). Meaning of psychoanalytic concepts and confirmation of psychoanalytic theories. *Scientific Monthly, 79,* 293–300.

Freud, S. (1953a). The interpretation of dreams. In J. Strachey (Ed., and Trans.), *The standard edition of the complete psychological works of Sigmund Freud* (vols. 4 and 5, pp. 1–627). London: Hogarth Press. (Original work published 1900.)

(1935b). Fragment of an analysis of a case of hysteria. In J. Strachey (Ed. and Trans.), *The standard edition of the complete psychological works of Sigmund Freud* (vol. 7, pp. 1–122). London: Hogarth Press. (Original work published 1905.)

(1953c). Psychopathic characters on the stage. In J. Strachey (Ed. and Trans.), *The standard edition of the complete psychological works of Sigmund Freud* (vol. 7, pp. 303–10). London: Hogarth Press. (Original work published 1905.)

(1955a). Studies on hysteria: Case 5 – Fraülein Elizabeth von R. In J. Strachey (Ed. and Trans.), *The standard edition of the complete psychological works of Sigmund Freud* (vol. 2, pp. 135–81). London: Hogarth Press. (Original work published 1895.)

(1955b). Studies on hysteria: IV. The psychotherapy of hysteria. In J. Strachey (Ed. and Trans.), *The standard edition of the complete psychological works of Sigmund Freud* (vol. 2, pp. 253–305). London: Hogarth Press. (Original work published 1895.)

(1955c). Totem and taboo: Some points of agreement between the mental lives of savages and neurotics. In J. Strachey (Ed. and Trans.), *The standard edition of the complete psychological works of Sigmund Frued* (vol. 13, pp. vii–162). London: Hogarth Press. (Original work published 1913.)

(1955d). Lines of advance in psycho-analytic therapy. In J. Strachey (Ed. and Trans.), *The standard edition of the complete psychological works of Sigmund Freud* (vol. 17, pp. 157–68). London: Hogarth Press. (Original work published 1919.)

(1955e). Beyond the pleasure principle. In J. Strachey (Ed. and Trans.), *The standard edition of the complete psychological works of Sigmund Freud* (vol. 18, pp. 1–64). London: Hogarth Press. (Original work published 1920.)

(1957a). On narcissism: An introduction. In J. Strachey (Ed. and Trans.), *The standard edition of the complete psychological works of Sigmund Freud* (vol. 14, pp. 67–102). London: Hogarth Press. (Original work published 1914.)

(1957b). Instincts and their vicissitudes. In J. Strachey (Ed. and Trans.), *The standard edition of the complete psychological works of Sigmund Freud* (vol. 14, pp. 109–40). London: Hogarth Press. (Original work published 1915.)

(1957c). Repression. In J. Strachey (Ed. and Trans.), *The standard edition of the complete psychological works of Sigmund Freud* (vol. 14, pp. 141–58). London: Hogarth Press. (Original work published 1915.)

(1959a). An autobiographical study. In J. Strachey (Ed. and Trans.), *The standard edition of the complete psychological works of Sigmund Freud* (vol. 20, pp. 1–74). London: Hogarth Press. (Original work published 1925.)

(1959b). Inhibitions, symptoms and anxiety. In J. Strachey (Ed. and Trans.), *The standard edition of the complete psychological works of Sigmund Freud* (vol. 20, pp. 75–175). London: Hogarth Press. (Original work published 1926.)

(1959c) The question of lay analysis: Conversations with an impartial person. In J. Strachey (Ed. and Trans.), *The standard edition of the complete psychological works of Sigmund Freud* (vol. 20, pp. 177–258). London: Hogarth Press. (Original work published 1926.)

(1961a). The ego and the id. In J. Strachey (Ed. and Trans.), *The standard edition of the complete psychological works of Sigmund Freud* (vol. 19, pp. 1–66). London: Hogarth Press. (Original work published 1923.)

(1961b). The resistances of psycho-analysis. In J. Strachey (Ed. and Trans.), *The standard edition of the complete psychological works of Sigmund Freud* (vol. 19, pp. 213–24). London: Hogarth Press. (Original work published 1925.)

(1961c). Civilization and its discontents. In J. Strachey (Ed. and Trans.), *The standard edition of the complete psychological works of Sigmund Freud* (vol. 21, pp. 57–145). London: Hogarth Press. (Original work published 1930.)

(1963). Introductory lectures on psycho-analysis. In J. Strachey (Ed. and Trans.), *The standard edition of the complete psychological works of Sigmund Freud* (vols. 15 and 16). London: Hogarth Press. (Original work published 1917.)

(1987). *A phylogenetic fantasy: Overview of the transference neuroses* (I. Grubrich-Simitis, Ed.; A. Hoffer & P. T. Hoffer, Trans.). Cambridge, MA: Harvard University Press. (Original work written 1915.)

Frijda, N. H. (1988). The laws of emotion. *American Psychologist, 43,* 349–58.

Frost, R. (1956). Education by poetry. In H. Cox & E. C. Lathem (Eds.),

Selected prose of Robert Frost (pp. 33–46). New York: Holt, Rinehart & Winston. (Original work published 1931.)

Fullinwider, S. P. (1983). Sigmund Freud, John Hughlings Jackson, and speech. *Journal of the History of Ideas, 44,* 151–8.

Gardner, H. (1987). *The mind's new science: A history of the cognitive revolution* (enl. ed.). New York: Basic Books.

Gay, P. (1969). The science of man. In *The enlightenment: An interpretation* (vol. 2, pp. 167–215). New York: Knopf.

(1976). Freud: For the marble tablet. In *Bergasse 19: Sigmund Freud's home and offices, Vienna 1938 – The photographs of Edmund Engelman* (pp. 13–54). New York: Basic Books.

(1988). *Freud: A life for our time.* New York: Norton.

Gedo, J. E., & Pollock, G. H. (Eds.). (1976). *Freud: The fusion of science and humanism – The intellectual history of psychoanalysis.* New York: International Universities Press.

Geertz, C. (1983). The way we think now: Toward an ethnography of modern thought. In *Local knowledge: Further essays in interpretive anthropology* (pp. 147–63). New York: Basic Books.

Gentner, D., & Gentner, D. (1983). Flowing waters or teeming crowds: Mental models of electronic circuits. In D. Gentner & A. Stevens (Eds.), *Mental models* (pp. 99–129). Hillsdale, NJ: Erlbaum.

Gentner, D., & Grudin, J. (1985). The evolution of mental metaphors in psychology: A 90-year perspective. *American Psychologist, 40,* 181–92.

Gergen, K. J., Greenberg, M. J., & Willis, R. H. (Eds.). (1980). *Social exchange: Advances in theory and research.* New York: Plenum.

Gerschenkron, A. (1974). Figures of speech in social sciences. *Proceedings of the American Philosophical Society, 118,* 431–48.

Gibbs, R. W., Jr. (1984). Literal meaning and psychological theory. *Cognitive Science, 8,* 275–304.

Giere, R. (1988). *Explaining science: A cognitive approach.* Chicago: University of Chicago Press.

Gigerenzer, G. (1987). Probabilistic thinking and the fight against subjectivity. In L. Krüger, G. Gigerenzer, & M. S. Morgan (Eds.), *The probabilistic revolution* (vol. 2, pp. 11–33). Cambridge, MA: MIT Press.

Gigerenzer, G., Swijtink, Z., Porter, T., Daston, L., Beatty, J., & Krüger, L. (1989). *The empire of chance: How probability changed science and everyday life.* Cambridge University Press.

Gilman, S. L. (Ed.). (1976). *The face of madness: Hugh W. Diamond and the origin of psychiatric photography.* New York: Brunner/Mazel.

(1982). *Seeing the insane: A cultural history of madness and art in the Western world, showing how the portrayal of stereotypes has both reflected and shaped the perception and treatment of the mentally disturbed.* New York: Brunner/ Mazel.

(1988). *Disease and representation: Images of illness from madness to AIDS.* Ithaca, NY: Cornell University Press.

Gimbel, J. (1976). Reason, mathematics, and experimental science. In *The medieval machine: The industrial revolution of the Middle Ages* (pp. 171–98). New York: Holt, Rinehart & Winston.

Glick, T. (Ed.). (1974). *The comparative reception of Darwinism.* Austin: University of Texas Press.

Glymour, C. (1974). Freud, Kepler, and the clinical evidence. In R. Wollheim (Ed.), *Freud: A collection of critical essays* (pp. 285–304). Garden City, NY: Anchor Books.

Goddard, H. H. (1920). *Human efficiency and levels of intelligence*. Princeton, NJ: Princeton University Press.

Goldstein, J. (1984). "Moral contagion": A professional ideology of medicine and psychiatry in eighteenth- and nineteenth-century France. In G. L. Geison (Ed.), *Professions and the French state, 1700–1900* (pp. 181–222). Philadelphia: University of Pennsylvania Press.

Goodman, N. (1954). *Fact, fiction, and forecast*. London: Athlone Press.
    (1976). *Languages of art: An approach to a theory of symbols*. Indianapolis, IN: Hackett.
    (1978). *Ways of worldmaking*. Indianapolis, IN: Hackett.

Gould, S. J. (1977a). *Ontogeny and phylogeny*. Cambridge, MA: Harvard University Press.
    (1977b). Eternal metaphors of paleontology. In A. Hallam (Ed.), *Patterns of evolution: As illustrated by the fossil record* (pp. 1–26). Amsterdam: Elsevier.
    (1983). For want of metaphor. *Natural History, 92,* 14–19.

Gross, M. L. (1978). *The psychological society: A critical analysis of psychiatry, psychotherapy, psychoanalysis and the psychological revolution*. New York: Simon & Schuster.

Gruber, H. E. (1974). A psychological study of scientific creativity. In H. E. Gruber & P. H. Barrett, *Darwin on man* (pp. 1–257). New York: Dutton.
    (1978). Darwin's "tree of nature" and other images of wide scope. In J. Wechsler (Ed.), *On aesthetics in science* (pp. 121–40). Cambridge, MA: MIT Press.
    (1980). The evolving systems approach to creative scientific work: Charles Darwin's early thought. In T. Nickles (Ed.), *Scientific discovery: Case studies* (pp. 113–30). Boston: Reidel.

Grubrich-Simitis, I. (1987). Metapsychology and metabiology: On Sigmund Freud's draft overview of the transference neuroses. In S. Freud, *A phylogenetic fantasy: Overview of the transference neuroses* (I. Grubrich-Simitis, Ed.; A. Hoffer & P. T. Hoffer, Trans.; pp. 73–107). Cambridge, MA: Harvard University Press.

Grünbaum, A. (1984). *The foundations of psychoanalysis: A philosophical critique*. Berkeley and Los Angeles: University of California Press.

Guerlac, H. (1965). Where the statue stood: Divergent loyalties to Newton in the eighteenth century. In E. R. Wasserman (Ed.), *Aspects of the eighteenth century* (pp. 317–34). Baltimore, MD: Johns Hopkins University Press.
    (1983). Theological voluntarism and biological analogies in Newton's physical thought. *Journal of the History of Ideas, 44,* 219–29.

Guillén C. (1968). On the concept and metaphor of perspective. In S. G. Nichols, Jr., & R. B. Vowles (Eds.), *Comparatists at work: Studies in comparative literature* (pp. 28–90). Waltham, MA: Blaisdell.

Gusfield, J. (1976). The literary rhetoric of social science: Comedy and pathos in drinking driver research. *American Sociological Review, 41,* 16–34.

Hacking, I. (1975). *The emergence of probability* (2d ed.). Cambridge University Press.
    (Ed.) (1981). *Scientific revolutions*. New York: Oxford University Press.

Hall, G. S. (1897). A study of fears. *American Journal of Psychology, 8,* 147–249.
    (1904). *Adolescence: Its psychology and its relations to physiology, anthropology, sociology, sex, crime, religion and education*. New York: Appleton.
    (1922). *Senescence: The last half of life*. New York: Appleton.

Hamlyn, D. W. (1961). *Sensation and perception: A history of the philosophy of perception*. London: Routledge & Kegan Paul.

Hanson, N. R. (1961). Is there a logic of scientific discovery? In H. Feigl & G. Maxwell (Eds.), *Current issues in the philosophy of science* (pp. 20–35). New York: Holt, Rinehart & Winston.

Haraway, D. J. (1981–2). The high cost of information in post–World War II evolutionary biology: Ergonomics, semiotics, and the sociobiology of communication systems. *Philosophical Forum, 13,* 244–78.

Harré, R., & Secord, P. F. (1972). *The explanation of social behaviour.* Oxford: Blackwell Publisher.

Harrington, A. (1987). *Medicine, mind and the double brain.* Princeton, NJ: Princeton University Press.

Hartley, D. (1966). *Observations on man, his frame, his duty, and his expectations.* Delmar, NY: Scholars' Facsimiles and Reprints. (Original work published 1749.)

Havelock, E. A. (1963). *Preface to Plato.* Cambridge, MA: Harvard University Press.

Hawkes, T. (1972). *Metaphor.* London: Methuen.

Hazard, P. (1963). *The European mind, 1680–1715* (J. L. May, Trans.). Cleveland, OH: World. (Original work published 1935.)

Heelan, P. A. (1979). Music as basic metaphor and deep structure in Plato and in ancient cultures. *Journal of Social and Biological Structures, 2,* 279–91.

Helmholtz, H. von (1971). The application of the law of the conservation of force to organic nature. In R. Kahl (Ed.), *Selected writings of Hermann von Helmholtz* (pp. 109–21). Middletown, CT: Wesleyan University Press. (Original work published 1861.)

Herbart, J. F. (1891). *A textbook of psychology: An attempt to found the science of psychology on experience, metaphysics, and mathematics* (2d ed.; W. T. Harris, Ed.; M. K. Smith, Trans.). New York: Appleton. (Original work published 1816.)

Herbert, S. (Ed.). (1980). *The red notebook of Charles Darwin.* Ithaca, NY: Cornell University Press.

Hesse, M. B. (1955). *Science and the human imagination.* New York: Philosophical Library.

(1966). The explanatory function of metaphor. In *Models and analogies in science* (pp. 157–77). Notre Dame, IN: University of Notre Dame Press.

(1980). *Revolutions and reconstructions in the philosophy of science.* Bloomington: Indiana University Press.

Hiebert, E. N. (1980). Boltzmann's conception of theory construction: The promotion of pluralism, provisionalism, and pragmatic realism. In J. Hintikka, D. Gruender, & E. Agazzi (Eds.), *Pisa Conference proceedings* (vol. 2, pp. 175–98). Boston: Reidel.

Hobbes, T. (1968). *Leviathan* (C. B. Macpherson, Ed.). Harmondsworth: Penguin. (Original work published 1651.)

Höffding, H. (1905a). *The problems of philosophy* (G. M. Fisher, Trans.). New York: Macmillan.

(1905b). On analogy and its philosophical importance. *Mind, 14,* 199–209.

Hoffman, R. R. (1980). Metaphor in science. In R. P. Honeck & R. R. Hoffman (Eds.), *Cognition and figurative language* (pp. 393–423). Hillsdale, NJ: Erlbaum.

(1984a). Recent psycholinguistic research on figurative language. *Annals of the New York Academy of Sciences, 433,* 137–66.

(1984b). Some implications of metaphor for philosophy and psychology of science. In W. Paprotte & R. Dirven (Eds.), *The ubiquity of metaphor* (pp. 327–80). Amsterdam: Benjamins.

Hofstadter, R. (1955). *Social Darwinism in American thought* (rev. ed.). Boston: Beacon Press.

Holland, D., & Quinn, N. (Eds.) (1987). *Cultural models in language and thought.* Cambridge University Press.

Holland, J. H., Holyoak, K. J., Nisbett, R. E., & Thagard, P. R. (1986). *Induction: Processes of inference, learning, and discovery.* Cambridge, MA: MIT Press.

Hollingworth, H. L. (1912). The influence of caffein on mental and motor efficiency. *Archives of Psychology,* No. 12.

(1914). Variations in efficiency during the working day. *Psychological Review, 21,* 473–91.

Holton, G. (1973). The thematic imagination in science. In *Thematic origins of scientific thought, Kepler to Einstein* (pp. 47–68). Cambridge, MA: Harvard University Press.

(1978). *The scientific imagination: Case studies.* Cambridge, MA: Harvard University Press.

Hornstein, G. (1988). Quantifying psychological phenomena: Debates, dilemmas, and implications. In J. Morawski (Ed.), *The rise of experimentation in American psychology* (pp. 1–34). New Haven, CT: Yale University Press.

Howells, J. G., & Osborn, M. L. (1984). *A reference companion to the history of abnormal psychology.* Westport, CT: Greenwood Press.

Huizinga, J. (1955). *Homo ludens: A study in the play element in culture* (R. F. C. Hull, Trans.). Boston: Beacon Press. (Original work published 1944.)

Hull, C. L. (1943). *Principles of behavior: An introduction to behavior theory.* New York: Appleton-Century-Crofts.

Hull, D. (1973). *Darwin and his critics.* Cambridge, MA: Harvard University Press.

(1988). *Science as a process.* Chicago: University of Chicago Press.

Hume, D. (1972). An enquiry concerning human understanding. In *Enquiries concerning the human understanding and concerning the principles of morals* (L. A. Selby-Bigge, Ed.; pp. 1–165). Oxford: Clarendon Press. (Original work published 1748.)

(1978). *A treatise of human nature* (P. H. Nidditch, Ed.). Oxford: Clarendon Press. (Original work published 1739–40.)

Huxley, T. H. (1898). *Scientific memoirs* (M. Foster & E. R. Lankester, Eds.; vol. 1). London: Macmillan Press.

Jackson, H. J. (1983). Coleridge, etymology and etymologic. *Journal of the History of Ideas, 44,* 75–88.

Jaeger, W. (1945). *Paideia: The ideals of Greek culture* (G. Highet, Trans.; 2d ed., vol. 1). New York: Oxford University Press. (Original work published 1934.)

James, W. (1880). Great men, great thoughts, and the environment. *Atlantic Monthly, 46,* 441–59.

(1890). *The principles of psychology.* New York: Holt.

(1905). Preface. In H. Höffding, *The problems of philosophy* (G. M. Fisher, Trans.; pp. v–xiv). New York: Macmillan.

(1975). Pragmatism's conception of truth. In *Pragmatism: A new name for some old ways of thinking* (pp. 95–113). Cambridge, MA: Harvard Unversity Press. (Original work published 1907.)

(1978). Notes for "The sentiment of rationality." In *Essays in philosophy* (F. H. Burkhardt, Ed.; pp. 339–71). Cambridge, MA: Harvard University Press. (Original work written ca. 1879.)

(1979). The moral philosopher and the moral life. In *The will to believe and other essays in popular philosophy* (pp. 141–62). Cambridge, MA: Harvard University Press. (Original work published 1897.)

(1982). The energies of men. In *Essays in religion and morality* (F. H. Burkhardt, Ed.; pp. 129–46). Cambridge, MA: Harvard University Press. (Original work published 1907.)

(1983a). Brute and human intellect. In *Essays in psychology* (F. H. Burkhardt, Ed.; pp. 1–37). Cambridge, MA: Harvard University Press. (Original work published 1878.)

(1983b). On some omissions of introspective psychology. In *Essays in psychology* (F. H. Burkhardt, Ed.; pp. 142–67). Cambridge, MA: Harvard University Press. (Original work published 1884.)

(1983c). The hidden self. In *Essays in psychology* (F. H. Burkhardt, Ed.; pp. 247–68). Cambridge, MA: Harvard University Press. (Original work published 1890.)

(1985). *The varieties of religious experience.* Cambridge, MA: Harvard University Press. (Original work published 1902.)

(1986). The confidences of a "psychical researcher." In *Essays in psychical research* (F. H. Burkhardt, Ed.; pp. 361–75). Cambridge, MA: Harvard University Press. (Original work published 1909.)

(1988). The object of cognition and the judgment of reality. In *Manuscript essays and notes* (F. H. Burkhardt, Ed.; pp. 261–92). Cambridge, MA: Harvard University Press. (Original work written 1883–4.)

Jardine, L. (1974). *Francis Bacon: Discovery and the art of discourse.* Cambridge University Press.

Jaynes, J. (1970). The problem of animate motion in the seventeenth century. *Journal of the History of Ideas, 31,* 219–34.

(1976). *The origin of consciousness in the breakdown of the bicameral mind.* Boston: Houghton Mifflin.

Johnson, M. (1981a). Introduction: Metaphor in the philosophical tradition. In M. Johnson (Ed.), *Philosophical perspectives on metaphor* (pp. 3–47). Minneapolis: University of Minnesota Press.

(Ed.). (1981b). *Philosophical perspectives on metaphor.* Minneapolis: University of Minnesota Press.

(1987). Toward a theory of imagination. In *The body in the mind: The bodily basis of meaning, imagination, and reason.* Chicago: University of Chicago Press.

Jones. H. (1906). The misuse of metaphors in the human sciences. *Hibbert Journal, 4,* 294–313.

Jones, R. F. (1963). The rhetoric of science in England of the mid-seventeenth century. In R. F. Jones (Ed.), *The rhetoric of science in the mid-seventeenth century* (pp. 5–24). Chicago: University of Chicago Press.

Jones, R. S. (1982). *Physics as metaphor.* Minneapolis: University of Minnesota Press.

Judd, C. H. (1918). *Introduction to the scientific study of education.* Boston: Ginn.

Jung, C. G. (1966). On the psychology of the unconscious. In *Two essays on analytical psychology* (R. F. C. Hull, Trans.; 2d rev. ed., pp. 1–119). Princeton, NJ: Princeton University Press. (Original work published 1917.)

Kahn, H. (1965). *On escalation: Metaphors and scenarios.* New York: Praeger.

Kant, I. (1965). *Critique of pure reason* (N. K. Smith, Trans.). New York: St. Martin's Press. (Original work published 1781.)

(1974). *Anthropology from a pragmatic point of view* (M. J. Gregor, Trans.). The Hague: Nijhoff. (Original work published 1797.)

Kantorowicz, E. H. (1957). *The king's two bodies: A study in mediaeval political theology.* Princeton, NJ: Princeton University Press.

Kassler, J. C. (1984). Man – A musical instrument: Models of the brain and mental functioning before the computer. *History of science, 22,* 59–92.

Kates, C. A. (1980). The constitution of novel utterance meanings: The metaphorical function. In *Pragmatics and semantics: An empiricist theory* (pp. 209–234). Ithaca, NY: Cornell University Press.

Kearney, R. (1988). *The wake of the imagination.* Minneapolis: University of Minnesota Press.

Keeling, S. V. (1968). *Descartes* (2d ed.). New York: Oxford University Press.

Kennedy, G. A. (1980). *Classical rhetoric and its Christian and secular tradition from ancient to modern times.* Chapel Hill: University of North Carolina Press.

Kline, M. (1980). *Mathematics: The loss of certainty.* New York: Oxford University Press.

Knowles, D. (1962). *The evolution of medieval thought.* London: Longman Group. *

Koch, S. (1959). Epilogue. In S. Koch (Ed.), *Psychology: A study of a science* (Vol. 3, pp. 729–88). New York: McGraw-Hill.

(1976). Language communities, search cells, and the psychological studies. In W. J. Arnold (Ed.), *Conceptual foundations of psychology* (Nebraska Symposium on Motivation, 1975; pp. 477–559). Lincoln: University of Nebraska.

Koestler, A. (1959). *The sleepwalkers: A history of man's changing vision of the universe.* New York: Macmillan.

(1964). *The act of creation.* New York: Macmillan.

Koyré, A. (1957). *From the closed world to the infinite universe.* Baltimore, MD: Johns Hopkins University Press.

(1968). The significance of the Newtonian synthesis. In *Newtonian studies* (pp. 3–24). Chicago: University of Chicago Press. (Original work published 1950.)

Krüger, L., Daston, L. J., & Heidelberger, M. (Eds.). (1987). *The probabilistic revolution* (vol. 1). Cambridge, MA: MIT Press.

Krüger, L., Gigerenzer, G., & Morgan, M. S. (Eds.). (1987). *The probabilistic revolution* (vol. 2). Cambridge, MA: MIT Press.

Kuhn, T. S. (1970). *The structure of scientific revolutions* (2d enl. ed.). Chicago: University of Chicago Press.

(1979). Metaphor in science. In A. Ortony (Ed.), *Metaphor and thought* (pp. 409–19). Cambridge University Press.

(1987). What are scientific revolutions? In L. Krüger, L. J. Daston, & M. Heidelberger (Eds.), *The probabilistic revolution* (vol. 1, pp. 7–22). Cambridge, MA: MIT Press.

Lakoff, G. (1987). *Women, fire, and dangerous things: What categories reveal about the mind.* Chicago: University of Chicago Press.

Lakoff, G., & Johnson, M. (1980). *Metaphors we live by.* Chicago: University of Chicago Press.

(1981). The metaphorical structure of the human conceptual system. In D. A. Norman (Ed.), *Perspectives on cognitive science* (pp. 193–206). Norwood, NJ: Ablex.

La Mettrie, J. O. (1912). *Man a machine* (G. C. Bussey & M. W. Calkins, Trans.). Chicago: Open Court. (Original work published 1748.)

Landau, Martin (1961). On the use of metaphor in political analysis. *Social Research, 28,* 331–53.

Landau, Misia. (1984). Human evolution as narrative. *American Scientist, 72,* 262–8.

Landes, D. (1983). *Revolution in time: Clocks and the making of the modern world.* Cambridge, MA: Harvard University Press.

Langer, S. K. (1942). *Philosophy in a new key: A study in the symbolism of reason, rite, and art.* Cambridge, MA: Harvard University Press.

Langley, P., Simon, H. A., Bradshaw, G. L., & Zytkow, J. M. (1987). *Scientific discovery: Computational explorations of the creative processes.* Cambridge, MA: MIT Press.

Lanham, R. A. (1968). *A handlist of rhetorical terms.* Berkeley and Los Angeles: University of California Press.

Laplanche, J., & Pontalis, J.-B. (1973). *The language of psycho-analysis* (D. Nicholson-Smith, Trans.). New York: Norton.

Lasky, M. J. (1976). *Utopia and revoluton: On the origins of a metaphor.* Chicago: University of Chicago Press.

Leary, D. E. (1977). Berkeley's social theory: Context and development *Journal of the History of Ideas, 38,* 635–49.

   (1980a). The historical foundation of Herbart's mathematization of psychology. *Journal of the History of the Behavioral Sciences, 16,* 150–63.

   (1980b, September 3). *William James, psychical research, and the origins of American psychology.* Invited address presented at the annual meeting of the American Psychological Association, Montreal.

   (1987). Telling likely stories: The rhetoric of the new psychology, 1880–1920. *Journal of the History of the Behavioral Sciences, 23,* 315–31.

   (1988a). A metaphorical analysis of Skinner's verbal behavior. *Theoretical and Philosophical Psychology, 8,* 12–15.

   (1988b, April 7). *On the origin of evolutionary theory: The influence of the humanities on the development of Darwin's thought.* Annual Phi Beta Kappa Lecture, University of New Hampshire, Durham.

   (1988c, August 14). *Poetry and science: William Wordsworth's influence on Charles Darwin and William James.* Invited address presented at the annual meeting of the American Psychological Association, Atlanta, GA.

Leatherdale, W. H. (1974). *The role of analogy, model and metaphor in science.* Amsterdam: North-Holland.

   (1983). The influence of Darwinism on English literature and literary ideas. In D. Oldroyd & I. Langham (Eds.), *The wider domain of evolutionary thought* (pp. 1–26). Dordrecht: Reidel.

Leiber, J. (1978). Universal structuralism and the waning of the game metaphor. In *Structuralism: Skepticism and mind in the psychological sciences* (pp. 121–38). Boston: Twayne.

Levarie, S. (1980). Music as a structural model. *Journal of Social and Biological Structures, 3,* 237–45.

Levin, S. R. (1982). Aristotle's theory of metaphor. *Philosophy and Rhetoric, 15,* 24–46.

Lewin, K. (1936). *Principles of topological psychology* (F. Heider & G. M. Heider, Trans.). New York: McGraw-Hill.

   (1951). *Field theory in social science: Selected theoretical papers* (D. Cartwright, Ed.). New York: Harper Bros.

Lloyd, G. E. R. (1987). Metaphor and the language of science. In *The revolutions of wisdom: Studies in the claims and practice of ancient Greek science* (pp. 172–214). Berkeley and Los Angeles: University of California Press.

Locke, J. (1959). *An essay concerning human understanding* (A. C. Fraser, Ed.). New York: Dover. (Original work published 1690.)

Luther, M. (1968). Lectures on Genesis, chapters 26–30. In J. Pelikan (Ed.), *Luther's works* (vol. 5; G. V. Schick, Trans.). Saint Louis, MO: Concordia. (Original work written ca. 1542.)

MacCormac, E. R. (1976). *Metaphor and myth in science and religion.* Durham, NC: Duke University Press.

(1985). *A cognitive theory of metaphor.* Cambridge, MA: MIT Press.

(1986). Creative metaphors. *Metaphor and Symbolic Activity, 1,* 171–84.

Mach, E. (1976). Similarity and analogy as a leading feature of enquiry. In *Knowledge and error: Sketches on the psychology of enquiry* (T. J. McCormack, Trans.; pp. 162–70). Dordrecht: Reidel. (Original work published 1905.)

MacIntyre, A. (1967). Sigmund Freud. In P. Edwards (Ed.), *The encyclopedia of philosophy* (vol. 3, pp. 249–52). New York: Macmillan.

MacKenzie, D. A. (1981). *Statistics in Britain, 1865–1930: The social construction of scientific knowledge.* Edinburgh: Edinburgh University Press.

Macklem, M. (1958). Moral gravitation: A metaphor of moral order. In *The anatomy of the world: Relations between natural and moral law from Donne to Pope* (pp. 100–2). Minneapolis: University of Minnesota Press.

Mahoney, P. (1974). Freud in the light of classical rhetoric. *Journal of the History of the Behavioral Sciences, 10,* 413–25.

(1982). *Freud as a writer.* New York: International Universities Press.

Majno, G. (1975). *The healing hand: Man and wound in the ancient world.* Cambridge, MA: Harvard University Press.

Manier, E. (1978). *The young Darwin and his cultural circle.* Dordrecht: Reidel.

Manuel, F. (1968). *A portrait of Isaac Newton.* Cambridge, MA: Harvard University Press.

Martin, J., & Harré, R. (1982). Metaphor in science. In D. S. Miall (Ed.), *Metaphor: Problems and perspectives* (pp. 89–105). Sussex: Harvester Press.

Masson, J. M. (Ed. and Trans.). (1985). *The complete letters of Sigmund Freud to Wilhelm Fliess, 1887–1904.* Cambridge, MA: Harvard University Press.

May, H. F. (1959). *The end of American innocence: A study of the first years of our own time, 1912–1917.* New York: Knopf.

Mayr, E. (1982). *The growth of biological thought: Diversity, evolution, and inheritance.* Cambridge, MA: Harvard University Press.

Mayr, O. (1986). *Authority, liberty, and automatic machinery in early modern Europe.* Baltimore, MD: Johns Hopkins University Press.

McCloskey, D. N. (1985). *The rhetoric of economics.* Madison: University of Wisconsin Press.

McCulloch, W. S. (1965). *Embodiments of mind.* Cambridge, MA: MIT Press.

McReynolds, P. (1970). Jeremy Bentham and the nature of psychological concepts. *Journal of General Psychology, 82,* 113–27.

(1980). The clock metaphor in the history of psychology. In T. Nickles (Ed.), *Scientific discovery: Case studies* (pp. 97–113). Dordrecht: Reidel.

Mead, G. H. (1924–5). The genesis of the self and social control. *International Journal of Ethics, 35,* 251–77.

Miall, D. S. (Ed.). (1982). *Metaphor: Problems and perspectives.* Sussex: Harvester Press.

Miller, A. I. (1984). *Imagery in scientific thought: Creating 20th-century physics.* Boston: Birkhaüser.

Miller, E. F. (1979). Metaphor and political knowledge. *American Political Science Review, 73,* 155–70.

Miller, G. A., Galanter, E., & Pribram, K. H. (1960). *Plans and the structure of behavior.* New York: Holt.

Montaigne, M. de (1958). Of experience. In D. M. Frame (Ed. and Trans.), *The complete essays of Montaigne* (pp. 815–57). Stanford, CA: Stanford University Press. (Original work written 1587–8.)

Mooney, M. (1985). *Vico in the tradition of rhetoric.* Princeton, NJ: Princeton University Press.

Moravia, S. (1978). From *homme machine to homme sensible:* Changing eighteenth-century models of man's image. *Journal of the History of Ideas, 39,* 45–60.

(1979). 'Moral'-'physique': Genesis and evolution of a 'rapport.' In A. J. Bingham & V. W. Topazio (Eds.), *Enlightenment studies in honour of Lester G. Crocker* (pp. 163–74). Oxford: Voltaire Foundation.

Müller, M. (1867). Metaphor. In *Lectures on the science of language* (vol. 2, pp. 351–99). New York: Scribner's.

Myers, G. E. (1986). *William James: His life and thought.* New Haven, CT: Yale University Press.

Napoli, D. S. (1981). *Architects of adjustment.* Port Washington, NY: Kennikat.

Nash, H. (1962). Freud and metaphor. *Archives of General Psychiatry, 7,* 25–7.

(1963). The role of metaphor in psychological theory. *Behavioral Science, 8,* 336–45.

Nersessian, N. J. (in press). Methods of conceptual change in science: Imagistic and analogistic reasoning. *Philosophica.*

Nevin, J. A. (1988). Behavioral momentum and the partial reinforcement effect. *Psychological Bulletin, 103,* 44–56.

Newell, A., & Simon, H. A. (1972). *Human problem solving.* Englewood Cliffs, NJ: Prentice-Hall.

Newton, I. (1974). *Mathematical principles of natural philosophy* (A. Motte, Trans.). Berkeley and Los Angeles: University of California Press. (Original work published 1687.)

Nietzsche, F. W. (1979). On truth and lies in a nonmoral sense. In D. Breazeale (Ed. and Trans.), *Philosophy and truth: Selections from Nietzsche's notebooks of the early 1870's* (pp. 79–97). Atlantic Highlands, NJ: Humanities Press. (Original work written 1873.)

Nisbet, R. (1976). *Sociology as an art form.* New York: Oxford University Press.

North, J. D. (1980). Science and analogy. In M. D. Grmek, R. S. Cohen, & G. Cimino (Eds.), *On scientific discovery* (pp. 115–40). Dordrecht: Reidel.

O'Donnell, J. M. (1985). *The origins of behaviorism: American psychology, 1870–1920.* New York: New York University Press.

Ogden, C. K. (1932). *Bentham's theory of fictions.* London: Routledge & Kegan Paul.

Oldroyd, D. R. (1980). *Darwinian impacts: An introduction to the Darwinian revolution.* Milton Keynes: Open University Press.

Olson, R. (Ed.). (1971). *Science as metaphor: The historical role of scientific theories in forming Western culture.* Belmont, CA: Wadsworth.

Ong, W. J. (1951). Psyche and the geometers: Associationist critical theory. *Modern Philology, 49,* 16–27.

Onians, R. B. (1951). *The origins of European thought.* Cambridge University Press.

Oppenheimer, J. R. (1956). Analogy in science. *American Psychologist, 11,* 127–35.

Ortony, A. (Ed.). (1979). *Metaphor and thought.* Cambridge University Press.

Ortony, A., Reynolds, R. E., & Arter, J. A. (1978). Metaphor: Theoretical and empirical research. *Psychological Bulletin, 85,* 919–43.

Osowski, J. V. (1986). *Metaphor and creativity: A case study of William James.* Ph. D. dissertation, Rutgers University, Newark, NJ.

Ozick, C. (1986). The moral necessity of metaphor: Rooting history in a figure of speech. *Harper's, 272,* 62–8.

Papert, S. A. (1978). The mathematical unconscious. In J. Wechsler (Ed.), *On aesthetics in science* (pp. 104–19). Cambridge, MA: MIT Press.

Park, K., Daston, L. J., & Galison, P. L. (1984). Bacon, Galileo, and Descartes on imagination and analogy. *Isis, 75,* 287–326.

Parsons, T., Bales, R. F., & Shils, E. A. (Eds.). (1953). *Working papers in the theory of action.* New York: Free Press.

Pauly, P. J. (1983). The political structure of the brain: Cerebral localization in Bismarckian Germany. *International Journal of Neuroscience, 21,* 145–50.

Pederson-Krag, G. (1956). The use of metaphor in analytic thinking. *Psychoanalytic Quarterly, 25,* 66–71.

Peirce, C. S. (1932). Elements of logic. In C. Hartshorne & P. Weiss (Eds.), *Collected papers of Charles Sanders Peirce* (vol. 2). Cambridge, MA: Harvard University Press.

Pepper, S. C. (1928). Philosophy and metaphor. *Journal of Philosophy, 25,* 130–2.

(1942). *World hypotheses: A study in evidence.* Berkeley and Los Angeles: University of California Press.

Percy, W. (1958). Metaphor as mistake. *Sewanee Review, 66,* 79–99.

Perelman, C., & Olbrechts-Tyteca, L. (1969). *The new rhetoric: A treatise on argumentation* (J. Wilkinson & P. Weaver, Trans.). Notre Dame, IN: University of Notre Dame Press. (Original work published 1959.)

Perry, R. B. (1935). *The thought and character of William James.* Boston: Little, Brown.

Piaget, J. (1969). Genetic epistemology. *Columbia Forum, 12,* 4–11.

(1971). *Biological knowledge: An essay on the relations between organic regulations and cognitive processes* (B. Walsh, Trans.). Chicago: University of Chicago Press. (Original work published 1967.)

Plato (1961a). The republic (P. Shorey, Trans.). In E. Hamilton & H. Cairns (Eds.), *The collected dialogues of Plato* (pp. 575–844). Princeton, NJ: Princeton University Press. (Original work written ca. 375 B.C.)

(1961b). Theaetetus (F. M. Cornford, Trans.). In E. Hamilton & H. Cairns (Eds.), *The collected dialogues of Plato* (pp. 845–919). Princeton, NJ: Princeton University Press. (Original work written ca. 360 B.C.)

(1961c). Timaeus (B. Jowett, Trans.). In E. Hamilton & H. Cairns (Eds.), *The collected dialogues of Plato* (pp. 1151–211). Princeton, NJ: Princeton University Press. (Original work written ca. 355 B.C.)

Polanyi, M. (1958). *Personal knowledge: Towards a post-critical philosophy.* Chicago: University of Chicago Press.

Polya, G. (1954). *Mathematics and plausible reasoning.* Princeton, NJ: Princeton University Press.

Popkin, R. H. (1964). *The history of scepticism from Erasmus to Descartes.* New York: Humanities Press.

Popper, K. R. (1963). Science: Conjectures and refutations. In *Conjectures and refutations* (pp. 33–65). New York: Harper & Row.

(1979). *Objective knowledge: An evolutionary approach* (rev. ed.). Oxford: Clarendon Press.

Porter, T. M. (1986). *The rise of statistical thinking, 1820–1900.* Princeton, NJ: Princeton University Press.

Powell, A., Royce, J. R., & Voorhees, B. (1982). Personality as a complex information-processing system. *Behavioral Science, 27,* 338–76.

Pribram, K. H. (1971). *Languages of the brain: Experimental paradoxes and principles in neuropsychology.* Englewood Cliffs, NJ: Prentice-Hall.

Price, D. J. (1965). Automata and the origins of mechanism and mechanistic philosophy. *Technology and Culture, 5,* 9–23.

Prigogine, I., & Stengers, I. (1984). *Order out of chaos: Man's new dialogue with nature.* New York: Bantam Books.

Pylyshyn, Z. W. (1984). *Computation and cognition: Toward a foundation for cognitive science.* Cambridge, MA: MIT Press.

Quine, W. V. O. (1966). Posits and reality. In *The ways of paradox and other essays* (pp. 233–41). New York: Random House.

Rachlin, H. (1970). *Introduction to modern behaviorism.* San Francisco: Freeman.

Randall, J. H., Jr. (1962). The science of human nature: The associationist psychology. In *The career of philosophy* (vol. 1, pp. 921–39). New York: Columbia University Press.

Randhawa, B. S., & Coffman, W. E. (Eds.). (1978). *Visual learning, thinking, and communication.* New York: Academic Press.

Rather, L. J. (1965). *Mind and body in eighteenth century medicine.* Berkeley and Los Angeles: University of California Press.

  (1982). On the source and development of metaphorical language in the history of Western medicine. In L. G. Stevenson (Ed.), *A celebration of medical history* (pp. 135–56). Baltimore, MD: Johns Hopkins University Press.

Reid, T. (1969). *Essays on the intellectual powers of man.* Cambridge, MA: MIT Press. (Original work published 1785.)

Richards, A. (1974). List of analogies. In J. Strachey (Ed. and Trans.), *The standard edition of the complete psychological works of Sigmund Freud* (vol. 24, pp. 177–83). London: Hogarth Press.

Richards, E. H. (1910). *Euthenics: The science of controllable environment – A plan for better living conditions as a first step toward higher human efficiency.* Boston: Whitcomb & Barrows.

Richards, I. A. (1936). *The philosophy of rhetoric.* New York: Oxford University Press.

  (1938). *Interpretation in teaching.* New York: Harcourt, Brace.

Richards, R. J. (1977). The natural selection model of conceptual evolution. *Philosophy of Science, 44,* 494–501.

  (1987). *Darwin and the emergence of evolutionary theories of mind and behavior.* Chicago: University of Chicago Press.

Ricoeur, P. (1970). *Freud and philosophy: An essay on interpretation* (D. Savage, Trans.). New Haven, CT: Yale University Press.

  (1977). *The rule of metaphor* (R. Czerny, Trans.). Toronto: University of Toronto Press.

  (1979). The metaphorical process as cognition, imagination, and feeling. In S. Sacks (Ed.), *On metaphor* (pp. 141–57). Chicago: University of Chicago Press.

Rieff, P. (1979). *Freud: The mind of the moralist* (3d ed.). Chicago: University of Chicago Press.

Roe, A. (1951). A study of imagery in research scientists. *Journal of Personality, 19,* 459–70.

Roediger, H. L., III (1980). Memory metaphors in cognitive psychology. *Memory & Cognition, 8,* 231–46.

Rogers, R. (1978). *Metaphor: A psychoanalytic view.* Berkeley and Los Angeles: University of California Press.

Rohde, E. (1925). *Psyche: The cult of souls and belief in immortality among the Greeks* (W. B. Hillis, Trans.). New York: Harcourt, Brace. (Original work published 1894.)

Root-Bernstein, R. S. (1985). Visual thinking: The art of imagining reality. *Transactions of the American Philosophical Society, 75,* 50–67.

Rosenfield, L. C. (1968). *From beast-machine to man-machine: Animal soul in French letters from Descartes to La Mettrie* (enl. ed.). New York: Octagon Books.

Rousseau, G. S. (1969). Science and the discovery of the imagination in Enlightened England. *Eighteenth-Century Studies, 3,* 108–35.

(1976). Nerves, spirits, and fibres: Towards defining the origins of sensibility. *The Blue Guitar, 11,* 125–53.

Royce, J. R. (1964). *The encapsulated man: An interdisciplinary essay on the search for meaning.* New York: Van Nostrand Reinhold.

Ruddick, L. (1981). Fluid symbols in American modernism: William James, Gertrude Stein, George Santayana, and Wallace Stevens. In M. W. Bloomfield (Ed.), *Allegory, myth, and symbol* (Harvard English Studies, vol. 9, pp. 335–53). Cambridge, MA: Harvard University Press.

Rumelhart, D. E. (1979). Some problems with the notion of literal meanings. In A. Ortony (Ed.), *Metaphor and thought* (pp. 78–90). New York: Cambridge University Press.

Russell, S. W. (1986). Information and experience in metaphor: A perspective from computer analysis. *Metaphor and Symbolic Activity, 1,* 227–70.

Russett, C. E. (1976). *Darwin in America: The intellectual response, 1865–1912.* San Francisco: Freeman.

Saccaro-Battisti, G. (1983). Changing metaphors of political structures. *Journal of the History of Ideas, 44,* 31–54.

Sacks, S. (Ed.). (1979). *On metaphor.* Chicago: University of Chicago Press.

Samelson, F. (1979). Putting psychology on the map: Ideology and intelligence testing. In A. R. Buss (Ed.), *Psychology in social context* (pp. 103–68). New York: Irvington.

Santayana, G. (1940). The intellectual temper of our times. In *Winds of doctrine: Studies in contemporary opinion* (pp. 1–24). New York: Scribner's. (Original work published 1913.)

Schofield, R. E. (1970). *Materialism and mechanism: British natural philosophy in an age of reason.* Princeton, NJ: Princeton University Press.

Schön, D. A. (1963). *The displacement of concepts.* London: Tavistock.

(1979). Generative metaphor: A perspective on problem setting in social policy. In A. Ortony (Ed.), *Metaphor and thought* (pp. 254–83). Cambridge University Press.

Schrift, A. D. (1985). Language, metaphor, rhetoric: Nietzsche's deconstruction of epistemology. *Journal of the History of Philosophy, 23,* 371–95.

Schulte-Sasse, J. (1986–7). Imagination and modernity: Or the taming of the human mind. *Cultural Critique, 5,* 23–48.

(1988). Afterword: Can the imagination be mimetic under conditions of modernity? In L. Costa-Lima, *The control of the imaginary: Reason and the imagination in modern times* (R. Sousa, Trans.; pp. 203–25). Minneapolis: University of Minnesota Press.

Schwartz, B. (1986). *The battle for human nature: Science, morality and modern life.* New York: Norton.

Scriven, M. (1956). A study of radical behaviorism. In H. Feigl & M. Scriven

(Eds.), *Minnesota studies in the philosophy of science* (vol. 1, pp. 88–130). Minneapolis: University of Minnesota Press.

Seward, A. C. (Ed.) (1909). *Darwin and modern science.* Cambridge University Press.

Sewell, E. (1964). *The human metaphor.* Notre Dame, IN: University of Notre Dame Press.

  (1985). Psychology and poetry: The uneven dance. In S. Koch & D. E. Leary (Eds.), *A century of psychology as science* (pp. 921–7). New York: McGraw-Hill.

Shakespeare, W. (1936). A midsummer-night's dream. In W. A. Wright (Ed.), *The complete works of William Shakespeare* (pp. 387–411). New York: Doubleday. (Original work written 1598.)

Shapin, S. (1979). The politics of observation: Cerebral anatomy and social interests in the Edinburgh phrenology disputes. *Sociological Review Monographs, 27,* 139–78.

Shapiro, M. J. (1985–6). Metaphor in the philosophy of the social sciences. *Cultural Critique, 2,* 191–214.

Sharma, C. S. (1982). The role of mathematics in physics. *British Journal of the Philosophy of Science, 33,* 275–86.

Shengold, L. (1979). The metaphor of the journey in *The interpretation of dreams.* In M. Kanzer & J. Glenn (Eds.), *Freud and his self-analysis* (pp. 51–65). New York: Aronson.

Shepard, R. (1978). The mental image. *American Psychologist, 33,* 125–37.

Shibles, W. A. (1971). *Metaphor: An annotated bibliography and history.* Whitewater, WI: Language Press.

  (1974). The metaphorical method. *Journal of Aesthetic Education, 8,* 25–36.

Simon, B. (1978). *Mind and madness in ancient Greece: The classical roots of modern psychiatry.* Ithaca, NY: Cornell University Press.

Simon, H. A., & Newell, A. (1956). Models: Their uses and limitations. In L. D. White (Ed.), *The state of the social sciences* (pp. 66–83). Chicago: University of Chicago Press.

Simontin, D. K. (1988). *Scientific genius: A psychology of science.* Cambridge University Press.

Skinner, B. F. (1931). The concept of the reflex in the description of behavior. *Journal of General Psychology, 5,* 427–58.

  (1938). *The behavior of organisms: An experimental analysis.* New York: Appleton-Century.

  (1954). Critique of psychoanalytic concepts and theories. *Scientific Monthly, 79,* 300–5.

  (1981). Selection by consequences. *Science, 213,* 501–4.

  (1987). Whatever happened to psychology as a science of behavior? *American Psychologist, 42,* 780–6.

  (1989). The origins of cognitive thought. *American Psychologist, 44,* 13–18.

Smith, C. U. M. (1982a). Evolution and the problem of mind: Part I. Herbert Spencer. *Journal of the History of Biology, 15,* 55–88.

  (1982b). Evolution and the problem of mind: Part II. John Hughlings Jackson. *Journal of the History of Biology, 15,* 241–62.

Smith, M. B. (1985). The metaphorical basis of selfhood. In A. J. Marsella, G. DeVos, & F. L. K. Hsu (Eds.), *Culture and self: Asian and Western perspectives* (pp. 56–88). London: Tavistock.

Snell, B. (1953). *The discovery of mind: The Greek origins of European thought* (T. G. Rosenmeyer, Trans.). Oxford: Blackwell Publisher.

Sokal, M. M. (1987). James McKeen Cattell and mental anthropometry: Nineteenth-century science and reform and the origins of psychological testing. In M. M. Sokal (Ed.), *Psychological testing and American society, 1890–1930* (pp. 21–45). New Brunswick, NJ: Rutgers University Press.

Sommer, R. (1988). The personality of vegetables: Botanical metaphors for human characteristics. *Journal of Personality, 56,* 665–83.

Sontag, S. (1978). *Illness as metaphor.* New York: Farrar, Straus & Giroux.

(1988). *AIDS and its metaphors.* New York: Farrar, Straus & Giroux.

Soskice, J. M. (1985). *Metaphor and religious language.* Oxford: Clarendon Press.

Spence, D. P. (1982). *Narrative truth and historical truth: Meaning and interpretation in psychoanalysis.* New York: Norton.

(1987). *The Freudian metaphor: Toward paradigm change in psychoanalysis.* New York: Norton.

Spencer, H. (1870). *The principles of psychology* (2d ed.; vol. 1). London: Williams & Norgate.

Sprat, T. (1702). *The history of the Royal Society of London* (2d ed.). London: Scot. (Original work published 1667.)

Staddon, J. E. R., & Simmelhag, V. L. (1971). The "superstition" experiment: A reexamination of its complications for the principles of adaptive behavior. *Psychological Review, 78,* 3–43.

Stanford, W. B. (1936). *Greek metaphor: Studies in theory and practice.* Oxford: Blackwell Publisher.

Stepan, N. L. (1986). Race and gender: The role of analogy in science. *Isis, 77,* 261–77.

Stern, J. P. (1978). Nietzsche and the idea of metaphor. In M. Pasley (Ed.), *Nietzsche: Imagery and thought* (pp. 64–83). Berkeley and Los Angeles: University of California Press.

Sternberg, R. J., & Rifkin, B. (1979). The development of analogical reasoning processes. *Journal of Experimental Child Psychology, 27,* 195–232.

Stevens, W. (1982). Adagia. In *Opus posthumous* (S. F. Morse, Ed., pp. 157–80). New York: Vintage. (Original work written 1930–55.)

Stigler, S. M. (1986). *The history of statistics: The measurement of uncertainty before 1900.* Cambridge, MA: Harvard University Press.

Suckiel, E. K. (1982). *The pragmatic philosophy of William James.* Notre Dame, IN: University of Notre Dame Press.

Sullivan, H. S. (1953). *The interpersonal theory of psychiatry* (H. S. Perry & M. L. Gawel, Eds.). New York: Norton.

Sulloway, F. J. (1979). *Freud, biologist of the mind: Beyond the psychoanalytic legend.* New York: Basic Books.

Suppe, F. (Ed.). (1977). *The structure of scientific theories* (2d enl. ed.). Urbana: University of Illinois Press.

Szasz, T. S. (1961). *The myth of mental illness.* New York: Harper & Row.

Taylor, E. (1982). *William James on exceptional mental states: The 1896 Lowell lectures.* New York: Scribner's.

Taylor, F. W. (1911). *The principles of scientific management.* New York: Harper Bros.

Temkin, O. (1977). Metaphors of human biology. In *The double face of Janus and other essays in the history of medicine* (pp. 271–83). Baltimore, MD: Johns Hopkins University Press.

Thagard, P. R. (1988). *Computational philosophy of science.* Cambridge, MA: MIT Press.

Thibaut, J. W., & Kelley, H. H. (1959). *The social psychology of groups.* New York: Wiley.

Tillich, P. (1972). *A history of Christian thought from its Judaic and Hellenistic origins to existentialism* (C. E. Braaten, Ed.). New York: Simon & Schuster.

Tillyard, E. M. W. (1944). *The Elizabethan world picture.* New York: Macmillan.

Toulmin, S. (1961). *Foresight and understanding: An enquiry into the aims of science.* Bloomington: Indiana University Press.

——— (1972). *Human understanding: The collective use and evolution of concepts.* Princeton, NJ: Princeton University Press.

Toulmin, S., & Leary, D. E. (1985). The cult of empiricism in psychology, and beyond. In S. Koch & D. E. Leary (Eds.), *A century of psychology as science* (pp. 594–617). New York: McGraw-Hill.

Tourney, G. (1965). Freud and the Greeks: A study of the influence of classical Greek mythology and philosophy upon the development of Freudian thought. *Journal of the History of the Behavioral Sciences, 1,* 67–85.

Turbayne, C. M. (1970). *The myth of metaphor* (rev. ed.). Columbia, SC: University of South Carolina.

Tyack, D., & Hansot, E. (1982). Schooling by design in a corporate society, 1890–1954. *Managers of virtue: Public school leadership in America, 1820–1980* (pp. 105–211). New York: Basic Books.

Vaihinger, H. (1924). *The philosophy of 'as if'* (C. K. Ogden, Trans.). New York: Harcourt, Brace. (Original work published 1911.)

Valenstein, E. S. (1986). *Great and desperate cures: The rise and decline of psychosurgery and other radical treatments for mental illness.* New York: Basic Books.

van Noppen, J.-P., De Knop, S., & Jongen, R. (1985). *Metaphor: A bibliography of post-1970 publications.* Amsterdam: Benjamins.

Vickers, B. (1984). Analogy versus identity: The rejection of occult symbolism, 1580–1680. In B. Vickers (Ed.), *Occult and scientific mentalities in the Renaissance* (pp. 95–163). Cambridge University Press.

Vico, G. (1948). *The new science of Giambattista Vico* (rev. ed.; T. G. Bergin & M. H. Fisch, Eds. and Trans.). Ithaca, NY: Cornell University Press. (Original work published 1744.)

Vorzimmer, P. (1970). *Charles Darwin: The years of controversy.* Philadelphia, PA: Temple University Press.

——— (Ed.). (1977). The Darwin reading notebooks (1838–60). *Journal of the History of Biology, 10,* 106–53.

Vosniadou, S., & Ortony, A. (Eds.). (1988). *Similarity and analogical reasoning.* Cambridge University Press.

Vygotsky, L. (1986). *Thought and language* (A. Kozulin, Trans.). Cambridge, MA: MIT Press. (Original work published 1934.)

Wallin, J. E. W. (1956). *Mental deficiency.* Brandon, VT: Journal of Clinical Psychology.

Walls, J. (1982). The psychology of David Hartley and the root metaphor of mechanism: A study in the history of psychology. *Journal of Mind and Behavior, 3,* 259–74.

Warren, H. C. (1921). *A history of association psychology.* New York: Scribner's.

Wartofsky, M. W. (1979). *Models: Representation and the scientific understanding.* Dordrecht: Reidel.

Watson, J. B. (1916). The place of the conditioned-reflex in psychology. *Psychological Review, 23,* 89–116.

——— (1919). *Psychology from the standpoint of a behaviorist.* Philadelphia, PA: Lippincott.

Weizenbaum, J. (1976). *Computer power and human reason: From judgment to calculation.* San Francisco: Freeman.

Westfall, R. S. (1987). Newton's scientific personality. *Journal of the History of Ideas, 48,* 551–70.

White, H. (1978). The fictions of factual representation. In *Topics of discourse: Essays in cultural criticism* (pp. 121–34). Baltimore, MD: Johns Hopkins University Press.

White, L.A. (1949). The locus of mathematical reality. In *The science of culture: A study of man and civilization* (pp. 282–302). New York: Farrar, Straus.

Whitehead, A. N. (1938). *Modes of thought.* New York: Macmillan.

Whitney, W. D. (1896). *The life and growth of language: An outline of linguistic science.* New York: Appleton.

Wiener, N. (1961). *Cybernetics: Or control and communication in the animal and the machine* (2d rev. ed.). Cambridge, MA: MIT Press.

Wiener, P. P. (1949). *Evolution and the founders of pragmatism.* Cambridge, MA: Harvard University Press.

Wigner, E. P. (1960). The unreasonable effectiveness of mathematics in the natural sciences. *Communications on Pure and Applied Mathematics, 13,* 1–14.

Wilden, A. (1980). Metaphor and metonymy: Freud's semiotic model of condensation and displacement. In *Structure and system: Essays in communication and exchange* (2d ed., pp. 31–62). London: Tavistock.

Wilder, R. L. (1981). *Mathematics as a cultural system.* Elmsford, NY: Pergamon.

Wilson, E. O. (1968). The ergonomics of caste in living insects. *American Naturalist, 102,* 41–66.

(1971). Compromise and optimization in social evolution. In *The insect societies* (pp. 336–48). Cambridge, MA: Harvard University Press.

(1975). *Sociobiology: The new synthesis.* Cambridge, MA: Harvard University Press.

(1978). *On human nature.* Cambridge, MA: Harvard University Press.

Winner, E. (1988). *The point of words: Children's understanding of metaphor and irony.* Cambridge, MA: Harvard University Press.

Witmer, L. (1915). On the relation of intelligence to efficiency. *Psychological Clinic, 9,* 61–86.

(1919). Efficiency and other factors of success. *Psychological Clinic, 12,* 241–7.

Wollheim, R. (1971). *Freud.* London: Fontana.

(Ed.) (1974). *Freud: A collection of critical essays.* Garden City, NY: Anchor Books.

Woodward, W. R. (1983). Introduction. In W. James, *Essays in psychology* (F. H. Burkhardt, Ed.; pp. xi–xxxix). Cambridge, MA: Harvard University Press.

Woodworth, R. S. (1901). The influence of improvement in one mental function upon the efficiency of other functions. *Psychological Review, 8,* 247–61, 384–95, 553–64.

Wordsworth, W. (1977). The excursion. In *Poems* (J. O. Hayden, Ed.; Vol. 2 pp. 35–289). Harmondsworth: Penguin. (Original work published 1814.)

Young, R. M. (1970). *Mind, brain and adaptation in the nineteenth century: Cerebral localization and its biological context from Gall to Ferrier.* Oxford: Clarendon Press.

(1971). Darwin's metaphor: Does nature select? *Monist, 55,* 442–503.

Zilsel, E. (1942). The genesis of the concept of physical law. *Philosophical Review, 52,* 245–79.

2

From metaphors to models: the use of analogy in neuropsychology

KARL H. PRIBRAM

Many scientists feel uncomfortable with the explicit use of analogy in their work. Brain scientists are no exception: They want to understand the results of their experiments solely in terms of those results. This may be possible when data concern one level of inquiry, but it becomes infeasible whenever an attempt is made to relate several levels of inquiry, as in neuropsychology. In such instances, some metaphor, analogy, or model often serves as a useful tool for organizing the relationships among data so that they reflect the organization of data at adjacent levels of inquiry.

Brain scientists have, in fact, repeatedly and fruitfully used metaphors, analogies, and models in their attempts to understand their data. The theme of this essay is that *only* by the proper use of analogical reasoning can current limits of understanding be transcended. Furthermore, the major metaphors used in the brain sciences during this century have been provided by inventions that, in turn, were produced by brains. Thus, the proper use of analogical reasoning sets in motion a self-reflective process by which, metaphorically speaking, brains come to understand themselves.

Analogical reasoning in science typically begins with metaphors that are only loosely coupled to the data to be organized and ends ideally by furnishing precise models of the fit of those data to the type of organization suggested by the original metaphor. This essay provides examples of how this process has worked and is working in the field of neuropsychology. Specifically, it reviews the influence of metaphors taken from telecommunications, control systems engineering, computer science, and holography.

First, however, a qualification is in order. The kind of understanding often achieved by metaphor – what we might call existential understanding – is not the kind that is the goal of science. When I listen to a symphony or feel the intimacies of a relationship or enjoy a good meal, I experience a sense of tacit understanding of the symphony, the interpersonal experience, the food before me. This sort of existential understanding can be enhanced by metaphor and complemented by the study of musical form and of the ear and auditory nervous system; the analysis of the constraints and freedoms in interpersonal relationships and of the emotional and motivational makeup of the persons involved; or the caloric content and constituent composition of foods and their metabolism. Such knowledge does not detract from, and may even enhance, each of the existential processes described. It is clear, however, that existential understanding is essentially private, whereas scientific understanding is essentially and eminently shareable.

Once we distinguish between existential and scientific understanding, we can see that skeptics are indeed correct in doubting our ability to achieve an existential understanding of our own brains. Brain tissue is peculiar because, in contrast to other tissues, it is largely insensitive to probing even by neurosurgeons. We cannot, therefore, sense our brains as such. Only the brain's processes are accessible to experience. As an example, when the somatosensory area of the cortex is electrically stimulated, a sensation of tingling in the toes is produced; when the classical motor region is excited, the toes actually move. In epileptic patients, whole trains of remembered experiences can be elicited when the cortex of the temporal lobes of the brain is probed electrically. The patient never exclaims that he feels his brain. He simply feels, and that feeling is referred to those parts of "him" that make neuronal connections with the brain tissue under the probe (see Libet, 1966).

Yet although the brain appears inaccessible to existential understanding, there seem to be no barriers to a scientific understanding. As in other scientific endeavors, such understanding comes from a propitious blend of the three modes of reasoning that guide research and provide some understanding of its results: the induction of principles from data; the deduction of logical relationships among principles; and reasoning by analogy, which attempts to place the relationships in a wider context. This essay is concerned chiefly with reasoning by analogy, not only because it is most closely related to the theme of this volume, but also because – as pointed out above and by C. S. Peirce (1932) – innovation stems almost exclusively from the proper use of analogy. Induction systematizes the familiar; deduction casts it into formal relationships.

Reasoning by analogy, by contrast, brings to bear on the familiar a new perspective derived from another realm of inquiry.

The use of analogy has been fruitful in neuropsychology from its beginning. Often the analogical thinking is implicit. Sometimes it is explicit, as when the brain is compared to a telephone switchboard or to the central processing unit of a computer. In either case, the analogy provides a step in the understanding of how the human brain functions.

The impact of telecommunications

The contribution of telecommunications to neuropsychology came in the form of techniques for measuring the flow of signals. The contribution of Bell Laboratory's Claude Shannon and his collaborator Warren Weaver is a landmark in the development of modern thinking. Shannon and Weaver (1949) developed a measure of signal patterns in impulses of energy transmitted over a given time in a limited communication channel, using a binary Boolean algebra as a base for that measure. Thus, a bit (*bi*nary di*git*) of information was first conceived as a unit indicating the match between the signal patterns produced by a sender and those received at the other end of the communication channel. The measure of information related the number of possible understandings (alternatives) contained in the message to those understood by the receiver. When the number of alternatives or possibilities (uncertainties) had been reduced by half, one bit of information was said to have been transmitted. Shannon and Weaver noted that such a measure was related to the idea of entropy. Entropy measures the disorder of a system. The idea is taken from thermodynamics, where it is used to describe the efficiency (or inefficiency) with which energy is used by a machine. Measures of order in the use of energy and in the flow of information promised to yield interesting results when applied to other fields of inquiry.

But this line of thinking ran into difficulties. Shannon noted that the measure of information depends on the uncertainty (the number of alternatives) in a system. For him, the measures of information and entropy were positively correlated – more information implies greater entropy. However, others, like Brillouin (1962), pointed out that an increase in the measure of information involves uncertainty *reduction* and is therefore more appropriately related to the opposite of entropy. This view has become prevalent: Information is now conceived as the measure of order, and entropy as the measure of disorder, of a system.

In the brain sciences the information measurement concepts became especially powerful in the hands of Warren McCulloch and his collaborators (see McCulloch, 1945). They described the brain as an organ where communication functioned both internally in the network of neurons and as a means of providing the order of external (psychological) communications among individuals.

The impact of these formulations has been paradoxical. On the one hand, the idea has taken root that a level of organization beyond that of electrical nerve impulses exists and can be dealt with in quantitative terms as "information." On the other, specific contributions of information measures to the understanding of brain function or to psychology have been meager. Ross Ashby (1963), one of the foremost exponents of information measurement theory, has remarked that the strength of the theory lies not in providing answers but in allowing the reformulation of questions in more precise terms.

The concept of channel capacity is an example of the failure of information measurement theory to provide specific answers while sharpening the framing of questions. This concept was devised to handle the organization of energy patterns in fixed channels of limited capacity. But this is an oversimplification in brain science, because fixed channels of limited capacity do not exist in the brain (Pribram, 1976), nor do they operate in personal communication, in which the context of transactions is continually influenced by information received (Miller, 1953). Neurological and psychological systems operate within flexible constraints that shift, expand, and contract, as they do, for instance, when attention becomes focused. It is a common mistake at present to attribute *all* processing limitations to restricted channel capacity (see, e.g., Kahneman, 1973). Although central-brain-processing limitations are real (Broadbent, 1974; Pribram, 1974), the idea of "competency" based on contextual structuring (Chomsky, 1963; Pribram, 1977b; Pribram & McGuinness, 1975) or "chunking" (Garner, 1970; Miller, 1956; Simon, 1974) is more productive.

The move from a concept of a restricted channel capacity to the concept of a flexible competency capable of being "reprogrammed" to meet changing conditions heralds a shift from viewing the brain as a telephone-like system to regarding it as computer-like. Before discussing this shift we must clarify another related problem plaguing the application of information measurement theory.

The impact of control systems engineering

Cybernetics, "the science of information and control," raises the new problem. Intuitively, we may feel that the greater the amount of information available to a system, the more precisely that system can be controlled. However, since information can be defined as a measure of the amount of uncertainty in a system (as suggested earlier), it would appear that the more information there is in a system, the harder that system is to control.[1]

The difficulty is resolvable. Shannon in his original paper (Shannon & Weaver, 1949) distinguished between two types of information: The first reduces uncertainty; the second is concerned with repetitions. In a telephone communication disturbed by excessive noise, the receiver often shouts, "What did you say? I can't hear you. Please repeat." When the sender hears this, he or she repeats the message. The effect of repetitions is to reduce noise and error, which is not the same as reducing the uncertainty contained in the original communication. Error reduction is accomplished by repetition, or redundancy, rather than by changing the structure of the communication. Since error-reducing signals were not an intrinsic part of uncertainty-reducing communications, they were of secondary concern to Shannon and Weaver. However, error-reducing signals are, as we shall see, the critical operators in control systems.

The original idea behind cybernetic control systems is twofold: (1) The current state of a system can be compared with a desired state, and (2) the current state can be brought closer to the desired state through adjustments (repetitions) based on the magnitude of an "error signal" that denotes the discrepancy between the current state and the desired state. The process of adjustment that reduces the error signal is called "negative feedback."

Norbert Wiener in *Cybernetics* (1948) notes the relationship between cybernetics and the concept of homeostasis. Homeostasis describes the maintenance of a constant internal environment in the body by compensatory mechanisms brought into play when shifts occur in chemical or physical conditions. This is an old concept, developed originally by the physiologist Claude Bernard (1858) and given precision by Walter B. Cannon (1932). Wiener extended the concept of physiological homeostasis into control systems engineering. The thermostat, which maintains a temperature within assigned limits, is an example of such a control system.

The idea of physiological homeostasis played a role in the development of the more comprehensive ideas of cybernetics. The concept of negative feedback that developed out of control systems is, in turn, applicable to neurophysiology. In a sense, an engineering idea that was in part based on physiological observations returns to physiology on a higher level. Negative feedback is currently invoked to explain regulation by the brain of sensory input from the external environment (Pribram, 1967) and the fine tuning of muscle activity (Miller, Galanter, & Pribram, 1960; Pribram, 1977b).

The first evidence of negative feedback in the operations of the nervous system came from work on muscle spindles, receptors in the muscles that signal the degree of muscle stretch (Kuffler, 1953; Matthews, 1964). These muscle spindles are directly controlled from the spinal cord and brain, forming a loop that ensures smooth and coordinated movements.

Feedback from the brain also regulates receptors of other sensory systems. Signals originating in the brain can alter the input of signals from tactile (Hagbarth & Kerr, 1954), auditory (Galambos, 1956), olfactory (Kerr & Hagbarth, 1955), and visual (Spinelli & Pribram, 1966; Spinelli & Weingarten, 1966) receptors. The association areas of the brain, which lie adjacent to the somatosensory cortex, are potential sources of these signals that influence sensory input (Lassonde, Ptito, & Pribram, 1981; Reitz & Pribram, 1969; Spinelli & Pribram, 1967).

This evidence of central control over receptors revolutionized the concept of the reflex in neurophysiology and thus affected the picture of the stimulus–response relationship that had dominated psychology for decades (see Miller et al., 1960). No longer could the organism and its brain be thought of as a passive switchboard on which environmental contingencies might play at will. A new, active image of a self-setting, homeostatically controlled organism that searched for and selectively accepted environmental events replaced the old passive stimulus–response image. Now, instead of responses elicited by discrete stimuli, as in the old physiology and psychology, the response was seen as initiating further nervous system activity that altered future responses. In biology, this change in thinking flourished in the studies of animal behavior known as ethology. In psychology, the change was reflected in an abandonment of stimulus–response learning theories in favor of the ideas of operant conditioning and cognitive conceptualization (Pribram, 1977b).

The thermostat embodies these principles. The set point of the thermostat determines the level at which changes in temperature will be sensed by the system and regulates (starts and turns off) the operation of the furnace. The operation of the furnace depends on temperature changes within chosen limits rather than on a simple on–off switch. Homeostatically controlled systems, like the thermostatically controlled furnace, provide a tremendous saving in memory load. Von Foerster (1965) called this mechanism a "memory without record." There is no need to keep track of the vagaries and variabilities of the temperatures external to the system: The homeostatic system operates on the hottest summer days and in the coldest winter months. Only the deviations of temperature from the set point need be sensed.

Cybernetics attempted to combine the insights derived from telecommunications with those derived from servocontrol. As noted earlier, this created problems. Some of these were anticipated by Shannon (Shannon & Weaver, 1949) when he used the term "information" in two technical senses, neither of which corresponds to the popular sense. As we have seen, in one technical sense information is a measure of the reduction of the number of alternative choices, that is, of uncertainty. In the second, information is a measure of the failure to reduce a discrepancy between two ongoing processes. But the distinction goes even deeper. The first measure specifies chiefly the complexity of a process. It can be precisely and quantitatively stated in bits. The second measure is an error signal that specifies little or nothing about complexity, but deals only with discrepancy and changes in discrepancy. Usually it is measured in continuous analog terms, since it is *change* that is of central concern. As noted earlier, when digital measures are applied to this second kind of information, it is seen to be more akin to the concept of redundancy than to the concept of information! It is this redundant error signal that is the critical component of homeostatic mechanisms and is involved in the negative feedback process of cybernetic control systems.

Error signals, which specify changes in redundancy rather than in uncertainty, provide the link between cybernetic concepts and information measurement theory. Cybernetic systems use redundant error signals to maintain stability. They have little to do with "uncertainty" or complexity. Brain systems that operate solely on homeostatic principles are technically not information-processing systems in the sense of reducing or enhancing uncertainty. Information measurement theory is therefore not applicable to internal homeostasis and external sensory processing unless the homeostatic principle is supplemented in some way.

These ideas characterized the brain and behavioral sciences almost three decades ago and are detailed in *Plans and the Structure of Behavior* (Miller et al., 1960). Roger Brown (1962) rightly criticized this book for the homeostatic cast it shares with psychoanalytic theory (see Freud, 1895/1966). The notion of "drives and habits" in Hullian stimulus–response psychology (Hull, 1943) and Skinner's concept of the "conditionable operant" (Skinner, 1938) share this slant. Even ethological formulations of "eliciting stimuli" and "action-specific energies" are essentially modeled on the homeostatic principle (Hinde, 1954a, 1960; Lorenz, 1969; Tinbergen, 1951). But the capacity of homeostatic systems to alter their set points is implicit in all of these theories (Pribram & Gill, 1976). This capacity was emphasized by Waddington (1957) in his concept of homeorhesis: a flow toward an ever-changing set point rather than a return to a static stable one. Homeorhetic systems are open, helical, future-oriented, feed-forward systems (as opposed to homeo*static* systems, which are closed loops), because the changes in set point can be programmed. In biological systems, prime examples of helical organizations are the DNAs that program development. Engineers have developed nonbiological programmable systems, the currently ubiquitous computers.

The impact of computer science

Computers are information-processing devices that have been heralded as harbingers of the second industrial revolution, the revolution in the communication of information. This revolution can be compared to the communications revolution that occurred at the dawn of history with the invention of writing or, earlier, when linguistic communication among humans began. The revolution depended largely on stepwise serial processing. Despite prodigious speed, serial processing is considerably less nimble than the brain's facility, which, as we shall see in the next section of this essay, is based to a large extent on parallel procedures carried out simultaneously. Nevertheless, as a model for brain activity, computer programming has produced three decades of intense research (Anderson & Bower, 1973; Miller et al., 1960; Neisser, 1967; Newell, Shaw, & Simon, 1958). More recently, the field of artificial intelligence has attempted to enhance computer capabilities by patterning computers after natural intelligence (Schank & Abelson, 1977) or possible brain organizations (Winograd, 1977). What has generated such sweeping changes in the way we view communication and computation?

Von Neumann (1951/1963) contributed a major innovation by devising a computational configuration that could be programmed by a system of lists in which each item in a list was prefixed by an address and suffixed by an instruction to proceed to another address. List programming was then developed by Newell and Simon (1956) to allow any item in any list to be addressed by (follow) any other item and in turn to address (precede) any other item. Items and lists of items were thereby endowed with the capacity to address themselves (often after running through several other lists). In the jargon of programming, this was called "recursiveness." As Turing (1937) pointed out, self-reflective programs endowed with recursiveness can locate any item stored in them and can associate any group of items. Such a network of lists is a far cry from the stimulus–response type of communication based on the model of the early simple telephone connection.

Structures embodying lists of the sort necessary for program construction have been shown to exist in the brain cortex. The cellular organization of the cerebral cortex of the brain shows both a vertical and a horizontal patterning. There are vertical columns of cells, perpendicular to the surface of the cortex, in which each cell responds to a different aspect of sensory input from a small group of receptor cells on the surface of the body – from a small area of the retina, for example. The columns can be thought of as lists containing items, namely, the cells (Edelman & Mountcastle, 1978; Hubel & Wiesel, 1968). The horizontal organization of the cortex reflects the arrangement of receptors on the surface of the body. The somatosensory area of the cerebral cortex, which lies directly behind the central fissure, receives sensory signals from the body surface projected in a pattern that mimics a tiny human figure, or "homunculus." The items (cells), therefore, also form horizontal lists. Interconnections between the cells in columns or arranged within a single horizontal layer enable the brain to interpret moving sensory signals. Thus, some cells in the vertical lists show sensitivity to movement of the stimulus from one surface touch receptor to another. Movement in one direction can trigger the brain cells, while movement in another has no effect, a finding that can be interpreted as suggesting a set of prefixes and suffixes as in von Neumann's analysis (Pribram, 1977b; Werner, 1970). In the visual part of the cortex, *each* cell (item) in the cortical column (list) appears to be endowed with such prefixes and suffixes. Most of these cells respond selectively to movement, direction, and even velocity changes (Pribram, Lassonde, & Ptito, 1981), which suggests a richer, more finely grained network of connection than is present in the somatosensory system.

Characterization of cortical cells of the brain as similar to items in a program list is often described as *feature analysis,* since each item represents one feature of a sensory input. In fact, the prevailing school of neurophysiological thinking currently favors the view that these cells are feature detectors (Barlow, 1972), that is, that each brain cell is uniquely responsive to one – and only one – feature. A competing view is that each cell has multiple selectivities and that its output is not unique to any one type of stimulus, as would be required of a feature detector. In the visual cortex, for example, a cell may select on the basis of the orientation of lines, their width and spacings, luminance, color, the direction of movement, the velocity of movement, and even the frequency of auditory tones.

It appears, therefore, that each cortical cell is a member of an associative network of cells (perhaps a set of list structures, as the evidence noted above would suggest) rather than a single-feature detector. Feature analysis must therefore be a function of the entire network of cells that is addressed by the total pattern of sensory input. The brain thus differs from current computers in that the initial stages of processing occur simultaneously, that is, in parallel rather than serially. Feature analysis, therefore, results from pattern matching rather than from single-feature detection. To return to an earlier analogy, the thermostat is a primitive pattern-matching device that "selects" deviations from a set point. It thus reduces the memory load that would otherwise be required to "detect" the occasion of every new temperature that required a response. An association of homeostatic devices, that is, columns of brain cells, thus can serve as a pattern-matching device that selects features from the sensory input.

Even the concept of list structures of homeostatic devices does not solve all the problems raised by viewing the brain as an associative network of cells. Ashby (1960) noted that such associative networks tend to be hyperstable and thus intolerably slow to modify; they seem to be unable to learn. To paraphrase Lashley (1950), even though one may be driven at times to consider such a model in the classroom, it should not be forgotten that one of the brain's distinguishing features is its capacity to learn. Two choices are open to the model builder. The evidence for homeostatic organization of the brain can be ignored, as Edelman and Mountcastle (1978) have done in their proposal for a "degenerative" (a many-to-one mapping) model in which feedback becomes a secondary rather than a primary constituent. Or, as Ashby (1960) and Miller et al. (1960) have done, one can start with an associative net made up primarily of homeostatic elements and add constraints (Pribram, 1977b). These constraints are based on invariant properties of the stimulus. The structures within the brain that recognize invariant stimuli or test–operate– test–exit units (TOTES, as Miller, Galanter, & Pribram call them) cut the associative net into pieces (to paraphrase Ashby) and can be shown to be organized hierarchically (Gelfand, Gurfinkel, Tsetlin, & Shik, 1971; Miller et al., 1960; Pribram, 1977b; Turvey, 1973). A definition of the "invariant properties," or features, of stimuli now becomes critical. Turvey (1973) and Gibson (1979) describe such properties as localized in the environment of the organism, while nativists (e.g., Chomsky, 1972) describe them as selected by the organism in the face of an environmental cornucopia.

The computer model of brain structure and function suggests an intermediate stance. In a computer the selection of a workable program depends on a "good fit," a match between input and central processor. The brain's "central processor" may be considered to have become adapted during evolution to an ecological niche, and it should be possible to determine the "invariant properties" (features) of that niche that have effected the adaptation. But with as general purpose a computer as the human brain, the responsible environmental features may be as difficult to delimit as the specifications of the adapting mechanisms of the brain that are concerned with identifying these invariances.

The impact of holography (parallel distributed processing)

Mechanisms of extracting invariances ("features") from sensory input have been of considerable interest to neuroscientists and psychologists. As we have seen, a brain cell organization based on an associative net with hierarchic constraints can serve as a useful model. Certain problems exist with this model. There is, for example, the need to postulate an analytic mechanism that is relatively sparing in its use of neurons so that invariance can be detected without invoking a "one neuron–one feature" equivalency. A successful model must also explain the speed and immediacy with which perception occurs and its high resolving power (see Gibson, 1979).

Historically, three sorts of answers have been given to the question raised. At one extreme is the "feature detector," or "one neuron–one feature" answer, which (as just noted) is untenable in the light of current neurological evidence. This model can also be faulted on the basis of behavioral evidence (Rock, 1970). At the other extreme is the model proposed by Wolfgang Köhler (Köhler & Held, 1949) to account for the distortions of physically measured stimulation found in illusions. Köhler emphasized the configurational aspects of perception and suggested that direct current (DC) fields result when sensory input arrives in cortical tissue. The low resolving power of the DC fields casts doubt on the efficacy of such machinery and its capacity to account for texture perception. A series of experiments was therefore set up to test the issues involved. The results of these experiments were as follows: (1) DC shifts *did* accompany the desynchronization of the cortical electrical record (EEG) induced by sensory (visual and auditory) stimulation; (2) disruption of DC electrical activity by epileptogenic agents placed on, or injected into, the cortex failed to impair pattern perception; and (3) such disruption did impair learning. Subsequently, it was shown that imposing a cathodal (negative) DC polarization across the cortex would slow learning, whereas imposing anodal (positive) DC polarization would speed learning (Stamm & Rosen, 1973). In short, DC shifts in the cortex bias learning, not perception, and are thus unlikely candidates for the critical machinery of pattern perception.

Between the extremes of the "one neuron–one feature" (usually referred to as the "pontifical" or "grandfather" cell dogma) and the DC field theory, a pair of more moderate views has been proposed. Each of these stems from one of the extreme positions. Neurophysiologist Horace Barlow (1972) has suggested that the idea of "one neuron–one feature" be dropped in favor of a set of cells that together can recognize a feature. This proposal is little different from that made by psychologist Donald Hebb (1949), who suggested that a cell assembly becomes constituted in response to sensory input. In these proposals "one neuron–one feature" is replaced by "one cell assembly–one feature." Barlow's and Hebb's proposals differ in that Barlow's cell assembly has a relatively fixed range of sensitivities – propensities to respond – whereas Hebb's "phase-sequenced" cell assemblies vary with respect to their constituent neurons and change with experience.

A quite different point of view was offered by Karl Lashley (1942) in his proposal that waves of activity are generated in the cortex by sensory input and that these waves interact to produce interference patterns. Lashley, however, did not develop his suggestion at either the neuronal or the perceptual level. He was attracted by the possibility suggested by Goldscheider (1906) at the turn of the century that the brain's organization of the perceptual field might display some of the same characteristics as the organization of embryonic developments. (Lashley was a zoologist by training.)

In several essays I have developed in detail the "interference pattern" model for brain function (Pribram, 1966, 1977b; Pribram, Nuwer, & Baron, 1974). At the neuronal level, the model interprets electrical changes in the cell membranes of neurons on the far side of synapses (or interneuronal junctions) as constituting wave fronts. These electrical changes, known as "hyperpolarizations" and "depolarizations," are not themselves nerve impulses. Depolarizations increase the likelihood that a neuron will increase its generation of nerve impulses; hyperpolarizations decrease this likelihood. My proposal is somewhat similar to that made in quantum physics, where the wave equation is treated as a vector based on the probability of occurrences of quantal events. The neural "quantal events" are those hyperpolarizations and depolarizations that, taken as a pattern occurring in an area of the cortex, can be described in terms of nodes created by reinforcement and extinction among interfering micro-wave forms. These patterns of polarization form a microprocess of fluctuating polarizations. Molecular storage, perhaps in the form of a conformational change in the proteins of the cell membranes at neuron-to-neuron synapses, is assumed to result from repetitions of particular patterns in the neuroprocess (Pribram, 1977b; Pribram et al., 1974).

At the perceptual level, the model implies that sensory input becomes encoded in synaptic membranes by these microprocesses in such a fashion that image reconstruction can be readily accomplished. This can be done by storing the Fourier or similar transform (see later in this section) of a sensory signal, which involves storing the coefficients that represent the interference nodes of the microprocess (Pribram, 1988; Pribram et al., 1974), rather than representing it by simple point-to-point intensive dimensions. In order to read out an image from such a store, all that is necessary is to invoke the inverse transform to restore an image.

Over the past century evidence has been accumulating that such harmonic analysis of the neural process entailed in sensory processing is valid. Ohm (of Ohm's law) suggested in 1843 that the auditory system operates as a frequency analyzer, perhaps according to Fourier principles. Fourier theory states that *any* pattern, no matter how complex, can be separated into a set of component regular waves of different frequencies, amplitudes, and relations to one another. Helmholtz (1857/1971) developed Ohm's suggestion by a series of experiments that provided evidence that such separation takes place in the cochlea, the part of the inner ear where the sound receptors are located. Helmholtz proposed that the cochlea operates much like a piano keyboard, a proposal that was subsequently modified by Georg von Bekesy (1960), who demonstrated that the cochlea resembled more closely a stringed instrument brought to vibrate at specific frequencies. Nodes of excitation developing in the vibrating surface (the "strings") accounted for the piano-keyboard-like qualities described by Helmholtz.

Bekesy further developed his model by actually constructing a surface bearing five vibrators, which he placed on the forearm of a subject. The periods of vibration of the five vibrators could be adjusted so that the five showed a variety of phase relationships to one another. The phase relationship could be adjusted so that a single point of tactile excitation was perceived (Bekesy, 1967). It was then shown that the cortical response evoked by such vibrations was also located in a single area: The pattern evoked resembled the perceptual response in its singleness rather than the multiplicity of the physical stimuli (Dewson, 1964). Somewhere between skin and cortex, inhibitory (hyperpolarizing) interactions among neurons had produced a transformation.

Bekesy went on to show that by applying two such vibrator-bearing surfaces, one to each forearm, and once again making the appropriate adjustments of phase, the subject could be made to experience the point source alternately on one arm, then on the other, until, after some continued exposure, the source of stimulation was projected outward into space between the two arms. Bekesy noted that we ordinarily "project" our somatosensory experience to the end of writing and surgical instruments. The novelty in his experiments was the lack of solid physical continuity between the perceived source and the actual physical source. Stereophonic high-fidelity music systems are based on a similar principle: By appropriate phase adjustment, the sound is projected to a location between and forward of the acoustical speakers, away from the physical source of origin.

Over the past two decades, it has been shown that the visual system operates along similar principles in its processing of spatial patterns. In an elegant series of experiments, Fergus Campbell (1974) and John Robson (1975) found anomalous responses to sets of gratings (sets of lines or bars) of various widths and spacings. The anomalies were reconciled when it was realized that the widths and spacings of the bars could be treated as having a frequency of alternation over space – that is, the width of bars and the distance between them formed a pattern that, when scanned, showed a frequency in the change from bar to spacing. The anomalous results were obtained when these "spatial frequencies" formed harmonics.

Then it was shown that certain cells in the visual cortex encode such "spatial frequencies" (De Valois, Albrecht, & Thorell, 1977; Movshon, Thompson, & Tolhurst, 1978; Pollen & Taylor, 1974; Schiller, Finlay, & Volman, 1976). Most telling are the results of experiments pitting the standard neurophysiological hypothesis that these cortical cells are line (bar or edge) detectors against the hypothesis that they are selective of one or another bandwidth of spatial frequency. De Valois and his colleagues showed that cortical cells were insensitive to bar width and that, when the bars were crossed with others in a pattern such as a plaid, the response of the cortical cells changed to reflect the total pattern. Specifically, each cortical cell was shown to be selectively sensitive to lines (gratings) oriented in a particular direction, a finding that had been instrumental in generating the feature detector proposal (Hubel & Wiesel, 1959). If the cells were operating as feature detectors, additions to the initial display pattern of lines should not alter the orientation in which the display has to be shown in order to match the selectivity of the cell. Additional lines in the pattern would be processed by additional units whose orientation matched that of the additional lines. If, however, the total pattern of the plaid was being processed by the brain cell, the orientation of the whole pattern would have to be altered to match the orientation of the major components of the Fourier (i.e., spatial frequency) transform of the pattern. De Valois performed a Fourier transform by computer on each plaid displayed. Such transforms showed radii at various angles from the original perpendicular pattern of the plaid. De Valois found that all plaid display patterns had to be rotated to bring these radii into line with the special selectivity for orientation of the brain cells. Furthermore, the rotation was exactly that (to the degree and the minute of visual arc) predicted by the proposal that the Fourier transform of the total plaid (and not its separate lines) is encoded.

There thus remains little doubt that descriptions in terms of harmonic analysis are valid models of the processing of sensory stimuli in audition, touch, and vision. Such descriptions can also be compared to image formation in the processing devices called holograms. Holograms were so named by their inventor, Dennis Gabor (1948), because each part of the hologram is representative of the whole. In a hologram each quantum of light acts much like a pebble thrown into a pond. The ripples from one pebble spread over the entire surface of the pond. (The mathematical expression for this is, in fact, called a spread function, and the Fourier transform is a prime example of such a function.) If there are several separate pebbles, the ripples produced by one pebble will originate in a different location than those produced by another pebble. The ripples will intersect and form interference patterns, with nodes where the ripples add, and sinks where they cancel. If "ripples" are produced by light falling on film (instead of pebbles falling into water), the nodes can be captured as reductions of silver grains on the film. Note that the information from the impact of each pebble or light ray is spread over the "recording" surface; thus, *each portion* of that surface can be seen as encoding the whole. And as noted earlier, performing the inverse Fourier transform reconstructs the image of the origin of that information. Thus, the whole becomes enfolded in each portion of the hologram since each portion "contains" the spread of information over the entire image.

The principle of the hologram is different from the earlier Gestalt view that wholes develop properties in addition to the sum of their parts. The properties of holograms are expressed by the principle that "the whole is contained or enfolded in its parts," and the very notion of "parts" is altered, because parts of a hologram do not have what we think of as boundaries.

The following properties of holograms are important for brain function: (1) the distribution and parallel content-addressable processing of information – a characteristic that can account for the failure of brain lesions to eradicate any specific memory trace (or engram); (2) the tremendous storage capacity of the holographic domain and the ease with which information can be retrieved (the entire contents of the Library of Congress can currently be stored on holofische, or microfilm recorded in holographic form, taking up no more space than is contained in an attaché case); (3) the capacity for associative recall that is inherent in the parallel distributed processing of holograms because of the coupling of separate inputs; and (4) the provision by this coupling of a powerful technique for correlating (cross-correlations and autocorrelations are accomplished almost instantaneously).

It is important to realize that holography is a mathematical invention and that its realization in optical systems through the use of laser beams is only one product of this branch of mathematics. Fourier transforms also play a role in modern computer technology as in the parallel distributed processing algorithms of neural network simulations of cognitive processing (Rumelhart, McClelland, & the PDP Research Group, 1986), in X-ray tomography, and (as demonstrated by the evidence described earlier) in understanding the results obtained in experiments on brain function.

Let us return for a moment to the classes of neural models that have been proposed for perception. Recall that the holographic model (i.e., of interference pattern processing of Fourier coefficients) was derived from dissatisfaction with both the "feature detector" and "cell assembly" theories. John (1967) and Uttal (1978) have also developed sophisticated statistical correlation models, which differ from the holographic model, however, in that they do not rely primarily on harmonic analysis of brain function. The most efficient manner of achieving statistical correlations is to transform the data (the sensory input, in the case of the nervous system) into the Fourier domain. There is thus a convergence of the statistical and harmonic models when they are followed to their logical and neurological conclusion: Nerve impulses arriving at synaptic junctions are converted to postsynaptic depolarizations and hyperpolarizations, which can best be described as Fourier transforms of those impulses. Repetitions of impulse patterns result in information storage of as yet undetermined nature, possibly alterations in the cell membranes of neurons. Subsequent sensory stimuli are cross-correlated with the stored residual from former inputs, and the inverse transform of the results of the correlation form our perceptions. The perceptions are then projected away from the brain itself by appropriate phase relationships, as in Bekesy's experiments, in stereophonic sound equipment, and in holograms.

There are important differences between the brain process and the optical information procedure, however. First, in an ordinary hologram the wave form is spread more or less over the entire surface of the film. In the brain each individual cortical cell reflects a particular pattern of depolarizations and hyperpolarizations in the dendritic network. If this is compared to encoding in a hologram, it is seen that the cortical "hologram" must be a patchwork (Robson, 1975) in which the Fourier transform of any specific input pattern becomes encoded in an overlapping set of patches, each patch corresponding to the receptive field of a particular cortical neuron. But such composite holograms, called strip or multiplex holograms, are commonly employed to provide three-dimensional *moving* images (see Leith, 1976). The process of adding together strips representing Fourier-transformed sections of space was invented by Bracewell (1965) to compose a high-resolution image of the heavens by radio astronomy. Pollen and Taylor (1974) interpreted some of their neurophysiological results in terms of a strip hologram in which each elongated receptive field served as a strip in the total pattern. Thus, the neural hologram, because of its patchwork nature, shows properties that are purely holographic (discussed later) as well as properties that are due to the spatial arrangement of the patches or strips. These spatial arrangements form the basis of the list structures described earlier and account for such nonholographic properties of perception as location and movement in the space and time domain.

Further, as noted earlier, each cortical cell is selective of several features of a stimulus. In the visual system these can include spatial frequency, color, directional movement, and velocity. Recordings from small groups of neurons in the visual cortex suggest that other aspects of situations are also encoded: In a problem-solving task, wave forms indicating the presence or absence of expected reinforcement are recorded (Pribram, Spinelli, & Kamback, 1967). The aspects of brain function that are encompassed by the neural holographic model are not exhaustive of all that the brain accomplishes, and the relationship of the model to the information and control models presented earlier must not be forgotten. The holographic model does, however, account for hitherto unexplained aspects of brain functioning, and it brings brain science into relationship with the revolution in modern physics occasioned by quantum and relativity theory (Pribram, 1988).

This relationship to physics is brought out when a particularly vexing question is faced. In all of the holographic systems other than neural that have been described here, an observer is assumed. Who and where is the observer of the image constructed by the neural hologram? Where is the little man or woman in the head? Who is the "I," the "self," that experiences the results of the holographic process?

To try to answer this question one must first ask what it is that is being observed. The assumption has been that an isomorphism (identical form) exists between a sensory perception and some physical "reality" (Köhler & Held, 1949). But as the Bekesy experiment with multiple vibrators makes clear, physical reality and perceptual reality may differ substantially. The sensory apparatus appears to be lenslike as it focuses an input, but the focusing produces an image that is decomposed by subsequent neural activity into the Fourier transform domain – that is, into a distributed holographic form. In view of the invertibility of *image domain* ⇄ *holographic domain*, one may ask in what form the input to the senses arrives. Is this input holographic, and does it become organized into images (thereby revealing the objects of which the images are formed) only by the lenslike capabilities of our senses?

This view is probably too extreme. The only way we can answer these questions is through the evidence of the senses and the instruments devised to augment them. This evidence suggests an ordinary level of reality to which the senses have become adapted through evolution. "Ordinary reality" is the reality of Newton's mechanics and Euclid's geometry. It is grasped through consensual validation – by bringing to bear the several senses and inferring a reality that partakes of them all. We see a moon in the sky and send a man to palpate it. We bump into unseen obstacles and invent radar and sonar to discover them. As infants, we hear our mothers, and see and touch them. At another level, smell and taste are based on our perceptions of dissolved molecules – a chemical level of an unseen, unheard, and untouched reality.

More recently, physicists have probed ever smaller components and have taken a new look at the evidence about a spatially distant reality presumably palpable but beyond our reach. The evidence about this macrouniverse comes to us by way of the very same electromagnetic components that make up the microuniverse. It should come as no great surprise, therefore, that the laws that relate to us the nature of the macrouniverse, such as the special and general laws of relativity, and those that relate the nature of the microuniverse, that is, quantum and nuclear mechanics, provide a somewhat similar conception of reality. This reality, highly mathematical in nature, departs considerably from ordinary sensory experience.

David Bohm (1971, 1973) has noted that, although the mathematics of relativity and of quantum theory are thoroughly worked out, the conceptual representation of what that mathematics might mean has lagged seriously. He has suggested that this lag is caused by our propensity to use lens systems to construct our conceptual reality. He proposed that the hologram might provide a better conceptual model for understanding both the macrouniverse and microuniverse! His proposal strikes a responsive chord in the neuroscientist, who has also found a level of organization in the nervous system that is more appropriately modeled by the hologram than by the senses (i.e., lenses). After all, the brain is a part of physical reality.

What are the characteristics of this holograph-like order of reality? First, it does not correspond to sense perception and is thus counterintuitive. Second, this order, which Bohm calls "implicate" to distinguish it from the ordinary "explicate" sensory order, is nonobjective. The objective, explicate order is made up of the images by which we know objects. These images are constructed by lenses: the lenses and lenslike characteristics of our senses as well as the lenses, often called "objectives," of our microscopes and telescopes. By contrast, the holograph-like implicate nonobjective reality is not composed of things but of quantally constituted microwaves and their interactive constituents such as constructive (nodal) and destructive interferences. Leibniz (1714/1973) described such a reality in his *Monadology*, in which the whole universe was represented in each monad, a windowless portion of the whole. Substitute lensless for windowless, and the monad becomes holographic.

Finally, in the reality described in this domain, the ordinary dimensionalities of space and time become enfolded (implicated). Thus, a different set of dimensions must be invoked in order to specify its characteristics. Time and space can be read out, but the readout may show peculiarities such as the complementary nature of measures of location in space and of moment (momentum), so that in specifying one, the other becomes elusive. "Particles," or rather events, in this microuniverse appear to influence one another in situations where a causal connection between them cannot be traced (see d'Espagnat, 1971). An implicate order composed of the probabilities of fluctuations in interference nodes, related by their wave equations, was proposed to account for the peculiarities resulting from observations of the microuniverse. The implicate order is therefore not static, and "holographic" is a somewhat inappropriate term. A hologram is only a frozen record of an ever-changing scene. The term "holonomic," used in physics to describe linear dynamical processes, would be preferable (Pribram, 1977a).

The fact that the holonomic implicate order is without boundaries, that every part enfolds or "contains" the whole, and that therefore the distinction between observer and observed is blurred so that observations no longer result in objects (i.e., observables) has led some physicists to note the intrinsic interweaving of perception and consciousness on the one hand and macrophysical and microphysical reality on the other. Thus, Bohm includes an appendix titled "Perception" in his book *The Special Theory of Relativity* (1965), and Wigner (1967) exclaims that modern physics deals with "relations among observations," not among "observables." An observable is characterized by invariance across observations;

in his famous principle Heisenberg (1930/1984) pointed out that, in microphysics, the observed varies with the instrumentation of the observer. Bohr (1928/1985) enunciated his principle of complementarity on the same grounds. And, of course, Einstein (1917/1961) made the same point with regard to the macrouniverse in his general theory of relativity.

This enfoldment of observation into the observable has led some physicists and some philosophers (e.g., Whitehead, 1938) into a panpsychism in which consciousness is a universal attribute rather than an emergent property of brain organization. Such views have interesting consequences for the analysis of the mind–brain issue (Pribram, 1979, 1986), bringing the concept of consciousness closer to that enunciated in the Eastern mystical tradition and the spiritual religious views of the West. Thus, Capra (1975) can proclaim a Tao of Physics in which the details of modern macrophysics and microphysics are matched to those of the mystical tradition. Science of this sort appears far removed from the objective operationism of the positivist and critical philosophers of the Vienna circle (e.g., Carnap, 1939; Feigl, 1954) and of likeminded psychologists (e.g., Hull, 1943; Skinner, 1938).

Summing up: how human beings go about understanding themselves

It is incredible to think that the major impacts on neuropsychology and the brain sciences that we have reviewed have occurred in less than half a century. Of course, the modes of thought that made these advances possible could be traced much further back in time, but enough history has been covered to allow a return to the issue raised at the beginning of this essay. If you will recall, I said that I would review the impact of certain modes of thought, which had been stimulated by several new inventions, in an attempt to trace the manner in which human brains go about understanding themselves. I also foreshadowed my thesis, stating that reasoning by analogy is one of the most powerful tools for innovative thought and scientific progress. The subsequent historical review of major developments in neuropsychology should have provided ample illustration of this claim, even for the most intractable skeptic. Now I want to review this thesis.

I find it useful to distinguish between *metaphor* (the larger concern of this volume), *analogy* (a way of reasoning about metaphor), and *model* (a precise coupling of an organization of data to another mode of organization such as a mathematical formulation). It seems to me that the historical episodes I have just recounted show (1) how a group of investigators can begin with a general metaphor – a broad and somewhat undefined sense of the similarities between two things (in our cases between some newly invented technological device or concept and some aspect of brain function), (2) how they can "trim" this metaphor into more and more precise shape, primarily through reasoning by analogy back and forth between the two things being compared, and (3) how, once they have gone far enough, the original metaphor is transformed into a precise scientific model, a theoretical framework that can be shared with and tested by the larger scientific community. I submit that my historical account of developments in the brain sciences over the past half-century shows that this simple scheme is a straightforward and accurate way of tracing the manner in which human brains have gone about understanding themselves.

So, in sum, metaphorical insight, reasoned analogy, and empirical modeling are woven together in the fabric of scientific innovation, in the "hard" areas of psychology as in the "soft" areas. I have emphasized the process of proper analogical reasoning – the process leading from metaphor to model – because, although metaphorical insight is fundamental, it will not get us far in achieving scientific understanding unless we subject it to the sort of sustained reasoning by analogy that has been illustrated throughout this essay.

Looking to the future, there is no reason to expect that the sort of reasoning by analogy that has wrought current scientific understanding in neuropsychology will cease. New developments, technical and theoretical, in engineering, chemistry, interpersonal psychology, and other yet unspecified domains, will continue to cross-fertilize the brain sciences – leading from vague but pregnant metaphors to more precise and testable models – provided that scientists continue to reason, carefully, by analogy.

Acknowledgment

This chapter is based largely on my (1980) article in *Daedalus*, journal of the American Academy of Arts and Sciences. I am grateful to *Daedalus* for permission to reproduce extensive portions of this article.

Note

1 I once posed the problem of specifying the relationship between information measurement and the control of systems to Norbert Wiener, Warren McCulloch, Don Mackay, and other cyberneticians. After many hours of discussion, everyone agreed that it was indeed a most perplexing issue that had at that time no direct answer.

References

Anderson, J. R., & Bower, G. H. (1973). *Human associative memory*. New York: Wiley.
Ashby, W. R. (1960). *Design for a brain: The origin of adaptive behavior*. New York: Wiley.
(1963). *An introduction to cybernetics*. New York: Wiley.

Barlow, H. B. (1972). Single units and sensation: A neuron doctrine for perceptual psychology? *Perception, 1,* 371–94.

Bekesy, G. von. (1960). *Experiments in hearing.* New York: McGraw–Hill.

(1967). *Sensory inhibition.* Princeton, NJ: Princeton University Press.

Bernard, C. (1858). *Leçons sur la physiologie et la pathologie du système nerveux* [Lectures on the physiology and pathology of the nervous system]. Paris: Baillière.

Bohm, D. (1965). *The special theory of relativity.* New York: Benjamin.

(1971). Quantum theory as an indication of a new order in physics: A. Development of new orders as shown through the history of physics. *Foundations of Physics, 1,* 359–81.

(1973). Quantum theory as an indication of a new order in physics: B. Implicate and explicate order in physical law. *Foundations of Physics, 3,* 139–68.

Bohr, N. (1985). The quantum postulate and the recent development of atomic theory. In J. Kalcker (Ed.), *Neils Bohr: Collected works* (vol. 6, pp. 113–36). Amsterdam: North-Holland (Original work published 1928.)

Bracewell, R. (1965). *The Fourier transform and its applications.* New York: McGraw-Hill.

Brillouin, L. (1962). *Science and information theory.* New York: Academic Press.

Broadbent, D. E. (1974). Division of function and integration of behavior. In F. O. Schmitt & F. G. Worden (Eds.), *The neurosciences: Third study program* (pp. 31–41). Cambridge, MA: MIT Press.

Brown, R. (1962). Models of attitude change. In R. Brown, E. Galanter, E. Hess, & G. Mandler (Eds.), *New directions in psychology* (vol. 1, pp. 1–85). New York: Holt, Rinehart & Winston.

Campbell, F. W. (1974). The transmission of spatial information through the visual system. In F. O. Schmitt & F. G. Worden (Eds.), *The neurosciences: Third study program* (pp. 95–103). Cambridge, MA: MIT Press.

Cannon, W. B. (1932). *The wisdom of the body.* New York: Norton.

Capra, F. (1975). *Tao of physics.* Boulder, CO: Shambhala.

Carnap, R. (1939). *Science and analysis of language.* The Hague: van Stockum & Zoon. (Preprinted for distribution at the Fifth International Congress for the Unity of Science, Cambridge, MA, 3–9 September 1939, from the *Journal of Unified Science* [*Erkenntnis*], *9,* which was never published.)

Chomsky, N. (1963). Formal properties of grammars. In R. D. Luce, R. R. Bush, & E. H. Galanter (Eds.), *Handbook of mathematical psychology* (pp. 323–418). New York: Wiley.

(1972). *Language and mind.* New York: Harcourt Brace Jovanovich.

d'Espagnat, B. (1971). The quantum theory and reality. *Scientific American,* 158–81.

De Valois, R. L., Albrecht, D. G., & Thorell, L. G. (1977). Spatial tuning of LGN and cortical cells in monkey visual system. In H. Spekreijse (Ed.), *Spatial contrast* (pp. 60–3). Amsterdam: North-Holland.

Dewson, J. H., III (1964). Cortical responses to patterns of two-point cutaneous stimulation. *Journal of Comparative and Physiological Psychology, 58,* 387–9.

Edelman, G. M., & Mountcastle, V. B. (1978). *The mindful brain.* Cambridge, MA: MIT Press.

Einstein, A. (1961). *Relativity, the special and the general theory* (R. W. Lawson, Trans.). New York: Crown. (Original work published 1917.)

Feigl, H. (1954). Scientific method without metaphysical presuppositions. *Philosophical Studies, 5,* 17–32.

Freud, S. (1966). Project for a scientific psychology. In J. Strachey (Ed. and Trans.), *The standard edition of the complete psychological works of Sigmund*

Freud (vol. 1, pp. 281–397). London: Hogarth Press. (Original work written 1895.)

Gabor, D. (1948). A new microscopic principle. *Nature, 161,* 777–8.

Galambos, R. (1956). Suppression of auditory nerve activity by stimulation of efferent fibers to cochlea. *Journal of Neurophysiology, 19,* 424–37.

Garner, W. R. (1970). The stimulus in information processing. *American Psychologist, 25,* 350–8.

Gelfand, I. M., Gurfinkel, V. S., Tsetlin, M. L., & Shik, M. L. (1971). Some problems in the analysis of movements. In I. M. Gelfand, V. S. Gurfinkel, S. V. Fomin, & M. L. Tsetlin (Eds.), *Models of the structural-functional organization of certain biological systems* (C. R. Beard, Trans., pp. 329–45). Cambridge, MA: MIT Press.

Gibson, J. J. (1979). *The ecological approach to visual perception.* Boston: Houghton Mifflin.

Goldscheider, A. (1906). Ueber die materiellen Veranderungen bei der Associationsbildung [Concerning the material changes accompanying the establishment of associations]. *Neurologie Zentralblatt, 25,* 146.

Hagbarth, K. E., & Kerr, D. I. B. (1954). Central influences on spinal afferent conduction. *Journal of Neurophysiology, 17,* 295–307.

Hebb, D. O. (1949). *The organization of behavior: A neuropsychological theory.* New York: Wiley.

Heisenberg, W. (1984). The physical principles of the quantum theory (C. Eckart & F. C. Hoyt, Trans.). In W. Blum, H.-P. Durr, & H. Rechenberg (Eds.), *Werner Heisenberg: Gesammelte Werke/Collected works* (pp. 117–66). Berlin: Springer-Verlag. (Original work published 1930.)

Helmholtz, H. L. F. von. (1971). The physiological causes of harmony in music. In R. Kahl (Ed.), *Selected writings of Hermann von Helmholtz* (A. J. Ellis, Trans., pp. 75–108). Middletown, CT: Wesleyan University Press. (Original work published 1857.)

Hinde, R. A. (1954a). Factors governing the changes in the strength of a partially inborn response, as shown by the mobbing behavior of the chaffinch (*Fringilla coelebs*): I. The nature of the response, and an examination of its course. *Proceedings of the Royal Society, B, 142,* 306–31.

(1954b). Factors governing the changes in strength of a partially inborn response, as shown by the mobbing behavior of the chaffinch *(Fringilla coelebs)*: II. The waning of the response. *Proceedings of the Royal Society, B, 142,* 331–58.

(1960). Factors governing the changes in strength of a partially inborn response, as shown by the mobbing behavior of the chaffinch *(Fringilla coelebs)*: III. The interaction of short-term and long-term incremental and decremental effects. *Proceedings of the Royal Society, B, 153,* 398–420.

Hubel, D. H., & Wiesel, T. N. (1959). Receptive field of single neurones in the cat's striate cortex. *Journal of Physiology, 148,* 574–91.

(1968). Receptive fields and functional architecture of monkey striate cortex. *Journal of Physiology, 195,* 215–43.

Hull, C. L. (1943). *Principles of behavior.* New York: Appleton-Century.

John, E. R. (1967). *Mechanisms of memory.* New York: Academic Press.

Kahneman, D. (1973). *Attention and effort.* Englewood Cliffs, NJ: Prentice-Hall.

Kerr, D. I. B., & Hagbarth, K. E. (1955). An investigation of olfactory centrifugal fiber system. *Journal of Neurophysiology, 18,* 362–74.

Köhler, W., & Held, R. (1949). The cortical correlate of pattern vision. *Science, 110,* 414–19.

Kuffler, S. W. (1953). Discharge patterns and functional organization of mammalian retina. *Journal of Neurophysiology, 16,* 37–69.

Lashley, K. S. (1942). The problem of cerebral organization in vision. *Biological Symposia, 7,* 301–22.

(1950). In search of the engram. *Symposium of the Society of Experimental Biology, 4,* 454–82.

Lassonde, M. C., Ptito, M., & Pribram, K. H. (1981). Intracerebral influences on the microstructure of visual cortex. *Experimental Brain Research, 43,* 131–44

Leibniz, G. W. F. von. (1973). Monadology. In G. H. R. Parkinson (Ed.). *Leibniz: Philosophical writings* (M. Morris & G. H. R. Parkinson, Trans., pp. 179–94). London: Dent. (Original work published 1714.)

Leith, E. N. (1976). White-light holograms. *Scientific American, 235*(2), 80–95.

Libet, B. (1966). Brain stimulation and conscious experience. In J. C. Eccles (Ed.), *Brain and conscious experience* (pp. 165–81). New York: Springer.

Lorenz, K. (1969). Innate bases of learning. In K. H. Pribram (Ed.), *On the biology of learning* (pp. 13–94). New York: Harcourt, Brace & World.

Matthews, P. B. C. (1964). Muscle spindles and their motor control. *Physiological Review, 44,* 219–88.

McCulloch, W. S. (1945). A heterarchy of values determined by the topology of nervous nets. *Bulletin of Mathematics and Biophysics, 7,* 89–93.

Miller, G. A. (1953). What is information measurement? *American Psychologist, 8,* 3–11.

(1956). The magical number seven, plus or minus two, or, some limits on our capacity for processing information. *Psychological Review, 63,* 81–97.

Miller, G. A., Galanter, E., & Pribram, K. H. (1960). *Plans and the structure of behavior.* New York: Holt.

Movshon, J. A., Thompson, I. D., & Tolhurst, D. J. (1978). Receptive field organization of complex cells in the cat's striate cortex. *Journal of Physiology, 283,* 79–99.

Neisser, U. (1967). *Cognitive psychology.* New York: Appleton-Century-Crofts.

Newell, A., Shaw, J. C., & Simon, H. A. (1958). Elements of a theory of human problem solving. *Psychological Review, 65,* 151–66.

Newell, A., & Simon, H. A. (1956). The Logic Theory Machine: A complex information processing system. *IRE Transactions on Information Theory,* vol. IT-2, no. 3, 61–79.

Ohm, G. S. (1843). Ueber die Definition des Tones, nebst daran geknüpfter Theorie der Sirene und ähnlicher tonbildener Vorrichtungen [On the definition of tones, with a related theory of sirens and similar amplifying devices]. *Annalen der Physik und der physikalischen Chemie, 135,* 513–65.

Peirce, C. S. (1932). Elements of logic. In C. Hartshorne & P. Weiss (Eds.), *Collected papers of Charles Sanders Peirce* (vol. 2). Cambridge, MA: Harvard University Press.

Pollen, D. A., & Taylor, J. H. (1974). The striate cortex and the spatial analysis of visual space. In F. O. Schmitt & F. G. Worden (Eds.), *The neurosciences: Third study program* (pp. 239–47). Cambridge, MA: MIT Press.

Pribram, K. H. (1966). Some dimensions of remembering: Steps toward a neuropsychological model of memory. In J. Gaito (Ed.), *Macromolecules and behavior* (pp. 165–87). New York: Academic Press.

(1967). The new neurology and the biology of emotion. *American Psychologist, 22,* 830–8.

(1974). How is it that sensing so much we can do so little?. In F. O. Schmitt & F. G. Worden (Eds.), *The neurosciences: Third study program* (pp. 249–61). Cambridge, MA: MIT Press.

(1976). Self-consciousness and intentionality. In G. E. Schwartz & D. Shapiro (Eds.), *Consciousness and self-regulation* (pp. 51–100). New York: Plenum.

(1977a). Holonomy and structure in the organization of perception. In J. M. Nicholas (Ed.), *Images, perception, and knowledge* (pp. 155–85). Dordrecht: Reidel.

(1977b). *Languages of the brain* (rev. ed.). Monterey, CA: Brooks/Cole.

(1979). Transcending the mind/brain problem. *Zygon, 14,* 19–30.

(1980). The role of analogy in transcending limits in the brain sciences. *Daedalus, 109,* 19–38.

(1986). The cognitive revolution and mind/brain issues. *American Psychologist, 41,* 507–20.

(1988). *Brain and perception: Holonomy and structure in figural processing – The MacEachran Lectures.* Hillsdale, NJ: Erlbaum.

Pribram, K. H., & Gill, M. M. (1976). *Freud's project re-assessed.* New York: Basic Books.

Pribram, K. H., Lassonde, M., & Ptito, M. (1981). Classification of receptive field properties. *Experimental Brain Research, 43,* 119–30.

Pribram, K. H., & McGuinness, D. (1975). Arousal, activation, and effort in the control of attention. *Psychological Review, 82,* 116–49.

Pribram, K. H., Nuwer, M., & Baron, R. (1974). The holographic hypothesis of memory structure in brain function and perception. In R. C. Atkinson, D. H. Krantz, R. C. Luce, & P. Suppes (Eds.), *Contemporary developments in mathematical psychology* (pp. 416–67). San Francisco: Freeman.

Pribram, K. H., Spinelli, D. N., & Kamback, M. C. (1967). Electrocortical correlates of stimulus response and reinforcement. *Science, 157,* 94–6.

Reitz, S. L., & Pribram, K. H. (1969). Some subcortical connections of the inferotemporal gyrus of monkey. *Experimental Neurology, 25,* 632–45.

Robson, J. G. (1975). Receptive fields: Neural representation of the spatial and intensive attributes of the visual image. In E. C. Carterette & M. P. Friedman (Eds.), *Handbook of perception* (vol. 5, pp. 82–116). New York: Academic Press.

Rock, I. (1970). Perception from the standpoint of psychology. *Proceedings of the Association for Research in Nervous and Mental Disease, 48,* 1–11.

Rumelhart, D. E., McClelland, J. L., & the PDP Research Group (1986). *Parallel distributed processing: Explorations in the microstructure of cognition.* Cambridge, MA: MIT Press.

Schank, R. C., & Abelson, R. P. (1977). *Scripts, plans, goals and understanding.* Hillsdale, NJ: Erlbaum.

Schiller, P. H., Finlay, B. L., & Volman, S. F. (1976). Quantitative studies of single-cell properties in monkey striate cortex. *Journal of Neurophysiology, 39,* 1288–374.

Shannon, C. E., & Weaver, W. (1949). *The mathematical theory of communication.* Urbana: University of Illinois Press.

Simon, H. A. (1974). How big is a chunk? *Science, 183,* 482–8.

Skinner, B. F. (1938). *The behavior of organisms.* New York: Appleton-Century.

Spinelli, D. N., & Pribram, K. H. (1966). Changes in visual recovery functions produced by temporal lobe stimulation in monkeys. *Electroencephalography and Clinical Neurophysiology, 20,* 44–9.

(1967). Changes in visual recovery function and unit activity produced by frontal and temporal cortex stimulation. *Electroencephalography and Clinical Neurophysiology, 22,* 143–9.

Spinelli, D. N., & Weingarten, M. (1966). Afferent and efferent activity in single units of the cat's optic nerve. *Experimental Neurology, 3,* 347–61.

Stamm, J. S., & Rosen, S. C. (1973). The locus and crucial time of implication of prefrontal cortex in the delayed response task. In K. H. Pribram & A. R. Luria (Eds.), *The psychophysiology of the frontal lobes* (pp. 139–53). New York: Academic Press.

Tinbergen, N. (1951). *The study of instinct.* New York: Oxford University Press.

Turing, A. M. (1937). On computable numbers, with an application to the Entscheidungs Problem. *Proceedings of the London Mathematics Society, 2,* 230–65.

Turvey, M. T. (1973). Peripheral and central processes in vision: Inferences from an information processing analysis of masking with pattern stimuli. *Psychological Review, 80,* 1–52.

Uttal, W. R. (1978). *Psychobiology of emotion.* Hillsdale, NJ: Erlbaum.

Von Foerster, H. (1965). Memory without record. In D. P. Kimble (Ed.), *The anatomy of memory* (pp. 388–433). Palo Alto, CA: Science and Behavior Books.

von Neumann, J. (1963). The general and logical theory of automata. In A. H. Taub (Ed.), *John von Neumann: Collected works* (pp. 288–328). Oxford: Pergamon Press. (Original work published 1951.)

Waddington, C. H. (1957). *The strategy of the genes.* London: Allen & Unwin.

Werner, G. (1970). The topology of the body representation in the somatic afferent pathway. In F. O. Schmitt (Ed.), *The neurosciences: Second study program* (pp. 605–16). New York: Rockefeller University Press.

Whitehead, A. N. (1938). *Modes of thought.* New York: Macmillan.

Wiener, N. (1948). *Cybernetics, or control and communication in the animal and the machine.* New York: Wiley.

Wigner, E. (1967). *Symmetries and reflections: Scientific essays.* Bloomington: Indiana University Press.

Winograd, T. (1977). Framework for understanding discourse. *Stanford University Intelligence Monograph,* Stanford, CA.

3

Inner feelings, works of the flesh, the beast within, diseases of the mind, driving force, and putting on a show: six metaphors of emotion and their theoretical extensions

JAMES R. AVERILL

Probably no area of psychology is marked by more poetic and vivid metaphors than is the area of emotion. A person who is fearful is a "yellow-bellied," "lily-livered," "faint-hearted," "spineless" "chicken" – with "cold feet," no less. A person is "blue" when sad, "white" when fearful, and "red" when angry. Love may "blind" you, hope will "cloud your vision," and anger can prevent you from "seeing straight." If grief "weighs you down," hope will "buoy you up." You may be "full" of gratitude, "bursting" with joy, "exploding" with anger, "swelled" with pride; but disappointment can "let the air out of your sails," and despair may "crush" you. Pride "struts like a peacock"; you are happy "as a lark"; and when humbled, you "eat crow." Love can "consume" you; and jealousy can "eat your heart out." When sad, you are "down at the mouth"; when happy, you are "floating on air." This is only a small sample of the literally hundreds of metaphors of emotion found in colloquial English. Why are such metaphors so common? And what influence, if any, do they have on the way we conceptualize and investigate the emotions in a scientific context?

Before we can start to answer these questions, a few distinctions must be made. In the above examples, the emotions (fear, anger, love, etc.) are the *targets* of metaphor, whereas some other aspects of experience (anatomical structure, spatial direction, color, etc.) provide the *source*. The source presumably helps to clarify the meaning and significance of the target.

According to Lakoff and Johnson (1980), aspects of experience that are poorly delineated are especially likely to become the targets of metaphor.

104

Examples include physical objects that lack clear boundaries or orientation, abstract concepts such as time, many social practices, and mental activities – especially the emotions.

Lakoff and Johnson are undoubtedly correct, but their comments do not explain why the emotions are so frequently the target of metaphor. For one thing, many emotional syndromes are relatively well delineated (e.g., an angry person is seldom confused by a lack of structure; see Averill, 1982). For another thing, emotions often serve as the source as well as the target of metaphor. Consider the following examples: The sky "threatened"; the storm unleashed its "fury"; the "fierce" wind swirled; the young tree stood "defiantly" against the onslaught; eventually the storm "exhausted" itself; the sky "blushed" in "shame" as the sun sank below the horizon; the next day dawned bright and "cheerful"; the "mirthful" brook babbled "merrily" on its way; the branches of the trees intertwined in "fond" embrace; the hills stood "humble" against the sky; all the world seemed "calm" and "peaceful"; only the little flower bent its head "forlornly," its stem broken by the "cruel" storm.

The ascription of human emotions to inanimate objects is so common that it has even been given a formal name in logic – the "pathetic fallacy." Even more common is the ascription of human emotions to animals. Eagles are "proud," lions "courageous," deer "timid," cows "contented," doves "peaceful," and so forth.

The eighteenth-century theorist Giambattista Vico (1744/1948) saw in the pathetic fallacy (although he did not call it such) the origins of civil society. Vico used fear of thunder as a paradigm of his thesis. As early humans fled to caves to escape the thunder, they understood intuitively, through look and gesture, that they all feared the same thing. Their fear provided common ground, a "sensory topic" (to use Vico's term), which gave meaning to events. But what exactly was it that they feared? The thunder posed no immediate danger, nor was there anything specific to be done. These early people's fear pointed beyond the thunder to some unknown cause; and, according to Vico, when people are ignorant of natural causes, they tend to imbue nature with human attributes. For example, thunder may be attributed to the anger of some god. In this way, through the metaphorical extension of shared feelings to inanimate objects, mythologies supposedly were born, as, ultimately, were more highly developed forms of social organization.[1]

I am not concerned here with the accuracy of Vico's account as a bit of psychoarchaeology. For our purposes, it suffices to note that feelings and emotions often serve as the source as well as the target of metaphorical analyses. In fact, the same terms can serve both functions, depending on the context, as in the following examples: "The storm unleashed its fury" and "His fury was like a storm." In the first instance, "fury" helps clarify the nature of "storm"; in the second instance, the reverse is true. This "double duty" helps explain the frequency of emotional metaphors. But it is still not the entire story.

Metaphors serve two main functions beyond mere description or elaboration. Those functions are explanation and evaluation. *Explanatory* metaphors are concerned primarily with the transfer of knowledge from the target to the source domain. *Evaluative* metaphors, by contrast, are intended to convey an attitude or mood. Phenomena that call for both explanation and evaluation are especially likely to become a source and/or target of metaphor.

At the core of any emotion is an evaluative judgment. For someone to be angry, frightened, sad, in love, disgusted, proud, and so forth, requires that the situation be evaluated in a certain way – as good or bad, as beneficial or harmful, as just or unjust, as beautiful or ugly, and so forth. Because of this, emotions are a rich source of evaluative metaphors. However, the emotions are also the object of value judgments, and hence the target of evaluative metaphors. Consider, for example, the characterization of emotions as "diseases of the mind." As we shall see shortly, this is one of the major metaphors of emotion, historically speaking. It has an explanatory function (e.g., emotions can disturb orderly thought processes, just as diseases can disturb orderly physiological processes). However, the metaphor is also clearly evaluative. Emotions are "unhealthy."

Unfortunately, it is not always easy to distinguish explanatory from evaluative uses of a metaphor. And when the two are confused, value judgments may masquerade as objective explanations. I will argue below that this has been – and continues to be – a particularly vexing problem for theory and research in the psychology of emotion.

In the discussion thus far, the reader may have noted two rather distinct uses of the concept of emotion. These uses must be made explicit, for they plague nearly every discussion of this topic. In one sense, "emotion" is used as a generic term for such specific states as anger, fear, grief, love, and so forth. In the second sense, it is used to refer to the broad and diffuse matrix of experience, out of which more delineated thoughts and feelings arise. This second usage is illustrated by Pribram's (1980) contention that "only logic is limited, the world of emotion and practice is limitless" (p. 19). Pribram goes on to distinguish emotional ("tacit," "existential") understanding from scientific understanding: "When I listen to a symphony or feel the intimacies of a relationship or enjoy a good meal, I experience a sense of tacit understanding. . . . It is clear, however, that existential understanding is essentially private, while scientific understanding is essentially and eminently shareable" (p. 20).

Pribram's use of "emotion" in this context is quite common and understandable. Indeed, our language is replete with useful concepts that seem quite "limitless" in reference. This includes not only psychological concepts, such as "emotion" and "practice" (in Pribram's sense), but also such physical concepts as "thing" and "happening." Such concepts do not lend themselves well to logic or scientific understanding. However, this is not because they are too private or unshareable, as Pribram implies; rather, it is because their referents can vary widely depending on the context.

In any case, I am concerned in this chapter primarily with the first sense of emotion described above; that is, with "emotion" as a generic term for the class of psychological states that includes anger, fear, and so on. I will proceed as follows: First, I will examine the historical origins of some of the major metaphors of emotion. Next, I will explore the influence of these metaphors on five contemporary approaches to the study of emotion, namely, phenomenological, psychophysiological, ethological, psychodynamic, and drive theories. Finally, I will introduce yet another metaphor – emotions as social roles – and explore some of its implications.

Metaphors of emotion in historical perspective

Not all metaphors are introduced consciously, nor are their meanings transparent. To take a rather mundane example, the French word for head, *tête,* derives from the (late) Latin *testa,* meaning "earthen pot" or "urn." Similarly, the German word for head, *Kopf,* derives from the Latin *cupa* (a tub or cask), which in English has become "cup." The metaphorical relationship between head and vessel is obvious in these etymologies, although it need never have been introduced consciously or explicitly into the language. When metaphors evolve within the vernacular, their origins are frequently difficult to recognize; and when they embody seriously held beliefs (not superficial resemblances, as in the example of the head as a vessel), they may exert considerable influence on the direction of thought.

Many metaphors of emotion have become so deeply embedded in our ordinary language that their metaphorical connotations often go unrecognized. Yet, as I will argue later, those connotations have exerted, and continue to exert, considerable influence on the way we think about the emotions. Therefore, I will begin this analysis with a bit of history and etymology.

The term "emotion" is itself based on metaphor. It stems from the Latin, *e + movere,* which originally meant "to move out," "to migrate," or "to transport an object." Metaphorically, it was sometimes used to describe physical conditions, such as turbulent weather, or psychological states involving turmoil. It did not, however, become a common term for referring to human emotions until about the middle of the eighteenth century.[2] For most of Western history, the emotions have been referred to as passions.

"Passion" comes from the Greek *pathe,* by way of the Latin *pati* (which means "to suffer"; the perfect participle of *pati* is *passus,* from which the noun *passio* is formed). From *pathe,* we also get such emotional terms as "pathetic," "empathy," and "antipathy."

In its original Greek and Latin forms, "passion" had a very broad connotation. It could refer to any object, animate or inanimate, that was undergoing ("suffering") some change through the action of an external agent. A rock, for example, could suffer the blow of a hammer. Emotions in the contemporary sense were thus only one kind of passion, namely, passions of the soul (*psyche, animus,* self). In other words, emotions were understood to be "inner" changes, impressed on the soul by some external agent.

Two other categories of passion – sensory experience and disease states – are worthy of special note, because of their (metaphorical) influence on subsequent theories of emotion. Sensory experiences are also passions of the soul, broadly speaking. For example, when I look upon an object under normal lighting conditions, I cannot help but see the object. It is as though the image has been impressed upon my mind, independent of (or even against) my will. A person can demand of me, "Don't look"; but once I have looked, the demand "Don't see" is unintelligible.

Of the senses, touch has often been considered the most basic. To touch something is to feel it. Hence, by metaphorical extension, we get the conception of emotions as "inner feelings," as when we are "touched to the quick." I will have much more to say about this conception later, when I discuss the phenomenological tradition in contemporary psychology.

Another subcategory of *pathe* that has had a major impact on subsequent theories of emotion is that of disease. Diseases are passions of the body. This meaning of *pathe* is evident in such contemporary medical terms as "pathology," "pathogen," "idiopathy," and (via the Latin) "patient." In view of the fact that the same generic term was used to cover both emotion and disease,[3] it is not surprising that an association was often made between the two conditions. The Stoics, in particular, considered emotions to be diseases of the mind. I will also have much more to say about this association shortly.

To summarize these preliminary remarks, the emotions share with certain other conditions (sensations, feelings, diseases) a common meaning, namely, the connotation of passivity. This shared meaning has been the source of many metaphors throughout the ages, and it continues to shape our theories of emotion. It lies at the heart of what Solomon (1976) has aptly called the "myth of the passions," that is, the notion that emotions are irrational responses over which we have little control.

Historically, Plato (427–347 B.C.) provides the best introduction to this myth. Plato divided the soul (*psyche*) into two major parts. He localized the rational/immortal part in the head and the irrational/mortal part in the body below the neck.[4] The rationale behind this localization was explicitly metaphorical. Rational thought is the highest kind of thought; hence, its localization in the body should also be "highest" (i.e., nearest the heavens). More important, Plato conceived of thought as a kind of motion. Rational thought is self-initiated and self-sustaining; that is, it is an action and not a passion. Within Greek cosmology, circular motion was believed to have similar characteristics. Rational thought, therefore, should be located in the part of the body that is most spherical, namely, the head.[5]

Since the emotions interfere with deliberate, rational behavior, they should be located away from the head, where they can do as little harm as possible. Plato therefore located anger and related "spirited" emotions in the chest, separated from the head by an isthmus (the neck) but close enough to be called upon by reason when needed for the defense of the individual. The baser emotions were situated still farther away, below the midriff.

Plato also postulated a kind of reverse evolution. A man who failed to live a life of reason could be "punished" by reincarnation as a woman or as an animal – a bird, land mammal (quadruped or polypod), reptile, or fish, in descending order, depending on the passion that dominated his life and the severity of his transgressions. "These are the laws by which all animals pass into one another, now, as in the beginning, changing as they lose or gain wisdom and folly" (*Timaeus*, 92c; Hamilton & Cairns, 1961, p. 1211). Or, stated metaphorically, emotions are "bestial" as well as "gut" reactions.

It might be objected that Plato's analysis of emotion, although highly metaphorical, was not without empirical warrant. After all, physiological arousal often accompanies intense emotional arousal; and animals do show fear, rage, sexual desire, and so on, but not rationality (at least not in the same sense as humans). Moreover, Plato did not disparage the emotions and the body; his concern was, rather, that they be kept in balance or harmony, lest they usurp the power of reason. But most metaphors have some grounding in empirical relations; otherwise, they would not be effective. The important point is that Plato's analysis is primarily evaluative, although it is presented as explanatory (a "likely story").

As a counterpoint to Plato's physiologizing, let us consider briefly the views of the Stoics, whose analyses of the emotions were far more systematic than were those of Plato. According to the Stoics, the emotions are forms of false judgments. As such, they can be experienced only by a rational being, for only a being capable of making true judgments is also capable of making false judgments. It follows that emotions are not closely related to physiological activity in the manner postulated by Plato, nor are they animal-like in anything but an evaluative sense. However, the Stoics did adhere to the myth of the passions in one fundamental respect: The emotions are something we suffer, pathologies of the mind.[6]

Cicero (106–43 B.C.) was one of the persons most responsible for transmitting Greek thought to the Roman world (see, e.g., Lang, 1972). Although his primary leanings were with the followers of Plato, Cicero believed the Stoic analysis of emotion to be the more penetrating. He considered the more turbulent emotions to be disorders of the soul (*perturbationes animi*), but not diseases in the strict sense:

> These [terrors, lusts, fits of anger, and the like] belong, speaking generally, to the class of emotions which the Greeks term *pathe:* I might have called them "diseases" [*morbos*], and this would be a word-for-word rendering: but it would not fit in with Latin usage. For pity, envy, exultation, joy, all these the Greeks term diseases, movements that is of the soul, which are not obedient to reason; we on the other hand should, I think, rightly say that these same movements of an agitated soul are "disorders" [*perturbationes*], but not "diseases" in the ordinary way of speaking, unless you are of another opinion. (Cicero, 45 B.C./1966, bk. 3, chap. 4, p. 233)

Evidently, some were of another opinion, for as previously noted, *passiones animae* (passions of soul) came to be the more commonly used term for the emotions, in spite of – or perhaps because of – its connotation of morbidity.

One other historical line of thought deserves mention before we turn to an analysis of metaphors of emotion in contemporary psychological theory. An association of emotion with a motivating or driving force has been common throughout Western history, although the source of the metaphor has varied with the intellectual and technological conditions of the time. For example, in the *Phaedrus,* Plato compared the passions to two-winged steeds over which the charioteer – reason – must try to exercise control (Hamilton & Cairns, 1961, p. 493).

An association of emotion with motivation became especially prominent among Christian Neoplatonists, the most prominent of whom was St. Augustine. By way of background, it should be noted that the Greeks and their Roman followers generally considered reason to be the regnant faculty of the human mind. That view underwent fundamental change with the advent of Christianity. The idea that human reason is capable of comprehending an omniscient God was considered by early Christians to be akin to blasphemy; yet a person of good *will* could believe or have faith in that which he or she could not fully comprehend. In this sense, the will was regarded as equal, if not superior, to reason. This dethronement of reason also had implications for conceptions of emotion.

Turning now to Augustine (354–430 A.D.), we should note that he recognized a broad class of emotional phenomena – the affections *(affectiones)* – of which the passions are a subcategory. Many of the affections are necessary for human life, and some (e.g., love) even partake of the divine. Like the Stoics, Augustine (ca. 420/1966) considered the passions proper to be contrary to nature; but unlike the Stoics, he believed that they (and other affections) arise from the will, not reason:

> The character of a man's will [*voluntas*] makes a difference. For if it is wrong, these emotions will be wrong; but if it is right, they will be not only not blameworthy but even praiseworthy. The will is indeed involved in them all, or rather, they are all no more than acts of will. For what is desire or joy but an act of will in sympathy with those things that we wish, and what is fear or grief but an act of will in disagreement with the things that we do not wish?... And generally, even as a man's will is attracted or repelled in accordance with the diverse character of the objects that are pursued or avoided, so it shifts and turns into emotions of one sort or the other. (bk. 14, chap. 6, pp. 285–7)

Augustine went on to postulate love as the fundamental character of the will:

> A right will therefore is good love [*bonus amor*] and a wrong will is bad love. Hence the love that is bent on obtaining the object of its love is desire, while the love that possesses and enjoys its object is joy; the love that avoids what confronts it is fear, and the love that feels it when it strikes is grief. (bk. 14, chap. 7, p. 291)

The association of emotion with the will or volition remained a dominant theme throughout the Middle Ages.[7] However, with the advance of technology and the rise of modern science, the nature of the metaphor took another turn. During the sixteenth century, spring mechanisms came into widespread use as the motive power for clocks; by analogy, human motives came to be viewed as "springs of action" (McReynolds, 1980). To the extent that emotions had become identified with motivation, they too could be conceptualized as a kind of inner force.

There is not space to carry this historical survey further, nor is there need, for we can already see the roots of some of the major metaphors of emotion that have influenced contemporary thought. To recapitulate briefly, the emotions have traditionally been conceptualized as passions, things that happen to us as opposed to things we do in a rational, deliberate way (actions). Within the Western intellectual tradition, rationality and free will have been considered the hallmarks of humankind. They are what distinguish humans from animals. It is not surprising, therefore, that the emotions should be metaphorically linked to those aspects of human nature that are nonrational (noncognitive), involuntary yet "driven" (motivational), common to both animals and humans (instinctual), and, in their more extreme or disruptive manifestations, psychopathological. These are the core features of what may be called, borrowing Solomon's (1976) felicitous phrase, the myth of the passions. By calling these features a myth, I do not mean to downgrade their importance. Myths are what people live by, and sometimes die for. But as we shall see in subsequent sections, there is another reality behind the myth of the passions.

Needless to say, the myth of the passions is not peculiar to Western societies. No society could long endure if it emphasized the nonrational over the rational, the involuntary over the voluntary (deliberate), and the private over the public. However, the myth does take different forms in different societies. For example, Lutz (1982) reports that the Ifaluk, a people of Micronesia, view the emotions primarily in terms of inter-personal relations, and they place little emphasis on their physiological concomitants. Moreover, even within the Western cultural tradition, the myth of the passions has by no means remained unitary. We have already mentioned the Stoics, who maintained that the emotions are a peculiarly human affliction. And during periods of romanticism (e.g., through much of the nineteenth century) the "logic" of the emotions has often been valued more highly than the logic of reason. However, even among romantics, or perhaps especially among romantics, emotions are divorced from society – not because the latter is viewed as a civilizing influence, but rather because it distorts and inhibits the authentic expression of emotion.

Metaphors of emotion in contemporary psychological theory

On the basis of the preceding historical analysis, five major metaphors of emotion may be distinguished: Emotions are considered to be (1) inner feelings; (2) bodily responses, especially of the viscera; (3) the animal in human nature; (4) diseases of the mind; and (5) driving forces. For ease of reference, these five *abstract* metaphors are listed in Table 3.1, to-gether with some illustrative *basic-level* metaphors taken from colloquial English.

The distinction between *abstract* and *basic-level* metaphors deserves brief comment. Abstract metaphors represent superordinate categories and, for the most part, are not found in everyday speech. They provide the (often implicit) rationale for whatever explanatory function the basic-level metaphors presumably have. It will be recalled, however, that many metaphors have an evaluative as well as an explanatory function. The evaluative function is usually most evident in basic-level metaphors. For example, no one really believes that calling a fearful person "chicken shit" explains his behavior. It does, however, express a strong opinion.

Table 3.1. *Five major metaphors of emotion*

Emotions are inner feelings (experiences).
He "felt" his anger rising.
Her kindness "touched" him deeply.
He "listened" to his heart, not his head.
She is a real "pain."
He "ached" for her.

Emotions are physiological responses, especially of the viscera.
He had a "gut reaction."
Anger made his "blood boil."
She got "cold feet."
He had "butterflies in his stomach."
Her "heart broke" from grief.

Emotions are the animal in human nature.
Don't be a "brute."
She acted "like an animal."
He "subdued" his fear.
She was proud "as a peacock."
He responded "sheepishly."
Don't "ruffle her feathers."

Emotions are diseases of the mind.
He was "insane" with rage.
She fell "madly" in love.
He was "paralyzed" with fear.
She was "sickened" by despair.
He was "blind" with envy.
She was "crazy" with jealousy.
He was "foaming at the mouth."

Emotions are a driving force or vital energy.
He was "driven" by fear.
Love "makes the world go 'round."
He could not "rein in his anger."
She was "bursting" with joy.
He "blew his stack."
Hope "sustained" him.
Disappointment "took the wind out of his sails."
Jealousy only added "fuel" to his desire.

This evaluative function is usually less evident at higher levels of abstraction. Thus, to say that emotions are closely associated with bodily structures and physiological changes seems more explanatory than evaluative. I would suggest, however, that the evaluative function is not absent from the abstract level, only masked (and in some cases it is not even masked; see the emotion-as-disease category).

Other abstract metaphors of emotion could, of course, be mentioned. For example, emotions are often treated as though they were physical objects that can be lost, found, offered, relinquished, abandoned, and the like. Such hypostatizing of the emotions helps to divorce them from the self, and from rational, deliberate activity (what a person *does*). Spatial metaphors are also common (in addition to the inside–outside distinction). We have already noted that the emotions are generally considered "lower" than rational, deliberate responses (i.e., the "higher" thought processes). But within this lower domain, further distinctions can be made. In general, positive emotions (e.g., happiness) are "up," whereas negative emotions (e.g., grief) are "down." And, needless to say, each emotion has metaphors that are specific to it. Many of these are metonymic expressions, in which some aspect of behavior is made to stand for the whole (e.g., cold feet in the case of fear, a swelled chest in the case of pride, aggression in the case of anger, tears in the case of sadness).[8]

Given these qualifications, the five categories listed seem to encompass the most important abstract metaphors of emotion. This is true historically, as already discussed. It is also true in the sense that each abstract metaphor is associated with a major tradition in the psychology of emotion, namely, the phenomenological, psychophysiological, ethological, psychodynamic, and drive traditions, respectively. In what follows, I will say a few words about each of these traditions. In a subsequent section, I will consider a sixth tradition, namely, the dramaturgical, in which emotions are considered as social roles.

The phenomenological tradition

Spatial metaphors are among the most common in psychology (Gentner & Grudin, 1985). On an "inner–outer" dimension, emotions are "inner" (see Table 3.1). As described earlier, sensory experience as well as emotions are "passions of the soul," as traditionally conceived. We have also noted that the sense of touch (feeling) has often been considered the most basic of the senses. By metaphorical extension, we get the conception of emotions as inner feelings or experiences. Not only is this conception common in everyday speech; it is also central to many theories of emotion. For example, Clore and Ortony (1984) ask us to imagine an intelligent robot that, from a cognitive point of view, is indistinguishable from a human being. This robot is a perfect Turing machine. It can evaluate emotional stimuli just as you and I; it can plan emotionally relevant courses of action; and it can carry out those actions in an appropriate manner. "Yet, for all this display of appropriate behavior and expression, it does not follow that the robot ever actually *feels* anything" (p. 53). Moreover, Clore and Ortony (1984) suggest, "if there is no feeling, there is no emotion, regardless of anything else that might be going on" (p. 54).

This suggestion seems quite reasonable until we ask: What is a feeling? The term "feeling" is one of the most elastic in the English language. As already noted, its root meaning is "to touch," but through multiple extensions it has come to include a wide variety of psychological states. A person can feel a pinprick, feel a dull pain, feel cold, feel ill or healthy, feel rebellious, and so forth. Considering this wide applicability, the assertion that emotions are feelings is not particularly informative. The nature of the feeling must be specified.

Two broad approaches to the analysis of emotional feelings can be distinguished: the atomistic and the holistic. With regard to the atomistic approach, a further subdivision must be made, namely, (1) feelings are (nothing but) sensations, for example, of bodily changes; and (2) feelings are modes of experience sui generis, for example, of pleasure and displeasure. The first position was that adopted by William James (1890) in his famous psychophysiological theory of emotion; the second position was advocated by Wilhelm Wundt (1896/1897) in his equally famous tridimensional theory. After nearly three decades of careful introspective research, many psychologists came to believe that Wundt's dimensions were reducible to sensations in a Jamesian sense (Nafe, 1924). Be that as it may, neither position has proved to be particularly convincing on either logical or empirical grounds. (For general reviews and analyses, see Alston, 1969; Natsoulas, 1973; Solomon, 1976.)

Atomistic approaches, such as those of James and Wundt, presume that it is possible to analyze emotional feelings into more elementary units. Other phenomenological approaches would reject this presupposition, preferring instead to treat emotional feelings as experiential *Gestalten*. Indeed, in the strictest sense, a phenomenological analysis would reject all presuppositions and attempt to describe emotional consciousness *simpliciter*. That goal, however, has proved to be something of a chimera. Phenomenological analyses that adopt the holistic approach typically yield results remarkably similar to the linguistic analysis of emotional concepts. This is an important point that bears centrally on the relationship between metaphor and emotion. Therefore, let me expand on it briefly.

It is common among phenomenologists to distinguish between pre-reflective and reflective experience. The former is a kind of *ur*-awareness, presumably like that of a dog or bird. Reflective experience, by contrast, is a higher-order awareness, an awareness of being aware. This does not necessarily mean a self-conscious reflection on one's own experience. Rather, it means the subsumption of experience under a concept (see Kant, 1781/1966; Mill, 1869/1967). Stated somewhat differently, consciousness in the human sense, including feelings of emotion, is dependent on the same cognitive structures and capacities that underlie language. On this point there is widespread agreement, even among theorists of otherwise diverse persuasion:

Language is as old as consciousness, language is practical consciousness, as it exists for other men, and for that reason is really beginning to exist for me personally as well; for language, like consciousness, only arises from the need, the necessity, of intercourse with other men. (Marx & Engels, 1845–6/1939, p. 19)

The subtlety and strength of consciousness are always in proportion to the capacity for communication.... In short, the development of speech and the development of consciousness (not of reason, but of reason becoming self-conscious) go hand in hand. (Nietzsche, 1882/1960, p. 296)

The process of something becoming conscious is above all linked with the perceptions which our sense organs receive from the external world.... But in men there is an added complication through which internal processes in the ego may also acquire the quality of consciousness. This is the work of the function of speech, which brings material in the ego into a firm connection with mnemic residues of visual, but more particularly of auditory, perceptions. (Freud, 1940/1964, pp. 161–2)

Without the help of a verbal community all behavior would be unconscious. Consciousness is a social product. It is not only *not* the special field of autonomous man, it is not within the range of a solitary man. (Skinner, 1971, p. 192)

Freud claimed that dreams are the royal road to the unconscious. That claim may be disputed. What seems beyond dispute, however, is that language is the royal road to conscious experience, *including feelings of emotion*. It follows that the experience of emotion is not simply subjective ("inner"); it is intersubjective – a shared experience that is informed by many of the same conventions that govern the use of language.

If these observations are correct, a complete analysis of the emotions must proceed in two steps. The first step is to lay bare the metaphorical nature of emotional consciousness (e.g., as exemplified by the myth of the passions). The second step is to explore what lies behind the metaphors. Why do we experience emotions the way we do? This second step involves a careful analysis of the way particular emotions relate to the broader social-historical context of which they are a part.

I will return to a discussion of the social bases of emotional behavior in a subsequent section. For now, I will simply conclude this brief discussion of the phenomenological tradition with a few additional observations on why emotions are so frequently identified with inner feelings, when in fact feelings are neither necessary nor sufficient conditions for the attribution of emotion. (For example, the notion of "unconscious emotions" is perfectly intelligible, whereas that of "unconscious feelings" – i.e., unfelt feelings – involves a contradiction of terms.)

Needless to say, feelings (whether interpreted as bodily sensations or experiential *Gestalten*) are often prominent features of emotional episodes. It is therefore not surprising that, by metonymy of part for the whole, feelings have come to stand for emotions. But I believe emotions have become closely identified with feelings for another reason as well.

Both feelings and emotion are often contrasted with thinking (reason). For example, if I touch a rough surface, I do not have to think in order to feel the roughness. Thinking or reason enters when we must infer what is not evident to the senses. Similar considerations apply when "feeling" is used to refer to nonsensory events. Thus, if you ask me why I did something, and I can think of no special reason, I may reply, "I just felt like it." Such a reply has two effects: First, it implies that my behavior was not based on rational, deliberate processes (i.e., it was a passion rather than an action); and second, it tends to halt further inquiry. I would maintain that the appeal to feelings in the explanation of emotional behavior has often had similar effects on scientific inquiry.

The psychophysiological tradition

This tradition also looks to the inside, but to inner responses rather than inner feelings. Specifically, physiological change is considered a necessary condition for emotion – and sometimes even a sufficient condition (see Wenger, 1950). This tradition is often combined with the phenomenological, as when William James (1890) explained the *quale* of emotion as the awareness of bodily change added to the "cold" perception of the exciting event.

Needless to say, all psychological phenomena ultimately depend on physiological processes. However, in the case of the emotions, this dependency has been given special status. Why should this be so?

The functioning of the human body is of utmost importance, not only for the individual, but for society as a whole. Moreover, until relatively recently, presumed knowledge of the human body was often based on informal observations of slain animals. It is not surprising, therefore, that common-sense interpretative schemes (folk anatomies and physiologies) are heavily imbued with meaning that has less to do with the physiological functions of an organ or body part than with its use as food, its involvement in ritual sacrifice, its role in sexual activity, and the like. From a psychological point of view, our body is as much symbol as substance (Douglas, 1970; Onians, 1951; Thass-Thienemann, 1968).

Body symbolism can affect scientific activity in a variety of subtle ways. For example, Hudson (1972) has found that medical specialists from English private (as opposed to state-supported or public) schools are more likely to achieve eminence by working on the head as opposed to the lower body, on the surface as opposed to the inside of the body, and on the male as opposed to the female body. These and other relationships observed by Hudson defy analysis in terms of medical skill, but they do have obvious social implications. As Hudson notes:

> Parts of the body, evidently, possess symbolic significance – a significance that influences medical students when they are deciding to specialize. And, it would seem, students from an upper-middle-class background are more likely than those from a lower-middle or working-class background to find their way into specialities that are seen for symbolic reasons as desirable. (p. 71)

Body symbolism can influence not only the choice of scientific speciali-
ties, but also the nature of theoretical speculations. Our concern here is
with the way psychological processes (such as emotions) become associated with physiological processes (such as visceral responses) on the basis
of shared symbolic meaning rather than on any empirically demonstrated
functional relationship. Once such an association is made, it can be
extremely tenacious. Let me illustrate.

The term "hysteria" is derived from the Greek word for the womb or
uterus *(hystera)*. References to the womb as a cause of physical symptoms
can be found in Egyptian writings as early as 1900 B.C. From Egyptian
sources, this notion worked its way into Greek medicine (Veith, 1965).
Hippocrates was the first to call certain symptoms hysterical, in metonymic reference to their presumed cause. These early theorists did not seem
especially concerned about how the womb could wander so widely, producing symptoms throughout the body. The localization of function was
apparently based on the vague recognition that some types of symptoms
stem from sexual difficulties and that the uterus is an important organ of
female sexuality. It is more difficult to determine why such symptoms
became associated almost exclusively with female disorders. Perhaps it
had something to do with the status of women and their sex role; it might
also have been regarded as unseemly for a man to be so afflicted.
Moreover, downward movement of the uterus has some empirical foundation in uterine prolapse, whereas the male organ is obviously not free to
wander. Whatever the case, once the wandering womb came to symbolize
hysterical reactions, the notion that these symptoms are gender-linked
proved extremely tenacious, even after the uterus was made immobile
through advancing physiological knowledge. Freud (1925/1959) described
an "old surgeon" who exclaimed to him regarding the possibility of male
hysterics: "But, my dear sir, how can you talk such nonsense? *Hysteron*
[*sic*] means the uterus. So how can a man be hysterical?" (p. 15).

Elsewhere (Averill, 1974), I have referred to the metaphorical association of psychological with physiological processes as *psychophysiological
symbolism,* and I have traced the influence of such symbolism on theories
of emotion from the time of the ancient Greeks to present neurophysiological speculation. Suffice it here to note that the common assumption that
physiological change, especially that mediated by the autonomic nervous
system and its central neural representations (in the "visceral" brain), is
based more on the myth of the passions than on hard empirical evidence.

Needless to say, physiological responses are prominent features of
many emotional episodes. There are conditions, such as sudden fright,
nausea on smelling a putrid odor, lashing out against a painful stimulus,
depression following loss of a loved one, and so forth, that are accompanied by pronounced physiological changes. In such states, a person may
be struck by the autonomy of bodily responses. The body seems to

"know" something that the person does not, and it acts "on its own," sometimes against the person's will and desires. Such seemingly autonomous responses may appropriately be regarded as "happenings" – as passions rather than as actions. It should be emphasized, however, that noticeable physiological change is not a prominent feature of all emotional episodes (e.g., of fear), but only of those that are relatively intense; and, moreover, physiological change is not even characteristic of some emotional syndromes (e.g., hope), no matter how intense the episode.

Still, through the use of metonymy in common speech, we often allow presumed physiological responses to stand for the whole (e.g., "sweaty palms" for fear, a "broken heart" for grief, being "red in the face" for anger). The intuitive appeal of psychophysiological theories of emotion is based, in part, on such everyday metonymies. But in the process of abstraction and generalization, we tend to forget that we are dealing with only a part, and we assume that what is true of certain physiological responses (e.g., visceral change) is also true of whole emotional syndromes.

There is another aspect of physiological metaphors of emotion that deserves brief mention. Such metaphors are not *simply* metonymies; they are also veiled instructions about how a person should look and react when emotionally involved. It is not uncommon for people to "stoke the fires" of their passion in order to conform to such "instructions." The precise means by which people control their physiological responses are not well understood and are undoubtedly multiple. But that such control can and does occur is beyond dispute. Perhaps the most dramatic example of this is voodoo death. The person who is hexed adopts the role of a dying person – and dies (often with the unwitting and subtle assistance of those present). As a more mundane example, consider the Victorian lady who would faint "on demand," as for instance upon hearing a sexually suggestive remark. Such behavior has gone out of fashion, but it illustrates well the fine control that can be exerted over physiological response even by ordinary persons.

The ethological tradition

The ethological tradition derives in recent times from Darwin's *The Expression of the Emotions in Man and Animals* (1872/1965). In fact, the most dominant view in psychology today is probably that emotions are products of biological evolution – instinctive reactions that may be observed in "lower" animals as well as in humans. This, too, is part of our myth of the passions. (Recall Plato's postulation of a kind of reverse evolution, the *psyche* being reincarnated in an animal according to the dominant passion by which the person had lived.)

It is sometimes said that human beings are "unfinished" at birth, in the sense that many human characteristics are a product of socialization, not biological inheritance. It would probably be more accurate to say that humans are "partly finished" at birth, with biological maturation completing one part and socialization the other.

A problem with many traditional theories of emotion, especially those within the ethological tradition, is that they tend to identify the emotions with the biologically finished part, whereas reason (cognition, will, and the "higher" mental processes in general) is assigned to the unfinished portion. For example, the claim that intellectual processes are, in part, determined by heredity is often met with skepticism and even hostility. By contrast, the claim that the emotions are biologically primitive responses is often accepted uncritically. Both claims do an injustice – to reason as well as to the emotions.

Consider, first, the case of reason. As Midgley (1978) has argued, reason is not some deus ex machina granted to us by a benevolent deity so that we may be more in his image; nor (as some romantics would have it) is reason an alien force imposed on us by society in order to bridle our passions. Rather, reason is part of our nature, a reflection of and a means by which our needs are ordered into a coherent whole, among themselves and in relation to our environment. A porpoise does not manifest rationality in the human sense, not because it lacks the cranial capacity, but because it has a different nature, a different set of needs to meet.[9]

Just as it is a mistake to consider reason an entity apart from our biological nature, so too is it a mistake to consider emotion a thing apart from our social nature and our "higher" thought processes. Both reason and emotion partake of the "high" and the "low" of human nature. This fact is obscured by the many animal metaphors that we use when thinking and speaking of the emotions, metaphors whose function is more evaluative than explanatory.

In a frequently cited observation, Hebb and Thompson (1954) pointed out that human beings are the most emotional of animals, as well as the most intelligent. Why should such an obvious fact require mention and deserve frequent citation were it not that our way of thinking about the emotions as "animal-like" and "brutish" has conditioned us to overlook the obvious? It should go without saying (but seldom has) that the emotional and cognitive capacities of humans have coevolved, the distinction between the two spheres being more one of social interpretation than of underlying mechanisms (Averill, in press).

The psychodynamic tradition

This tradition draws much of its intuitive appeal from the metaphor of emotions as "diseases of the mind." In popular conception, "mental illness" is practically synonymous with "emotional disorder." By contrast, mental deficiency (abnormally low intelligence) is not usually considered an "illness," although it may require lifelong institutionalization (usually in a "school," not a "hospital"). A perusal of "self-help" books also suggests that such emotional states as anger, jealousy, envy, fear, anxiety, guilt, embarrassment, loneliness, and grief are on one "sick list" or another. Even such highly valued emotions as love have become the object of suggested "cures." And this is not just a peculiarity of pop psychology. As Thoits (1985) has observed, emotional variables enter into the diagnostic criteria for most forms of psychopathology, as listed in the *Diagnostic and Statistical Manual of Mental Disorders, DSM-III*, published by the American Psychiatric Association (1980).

To call this tradition *psychodynamic* is perhaps a bit misleading, for dynamic psychologies are by no means preoccupied with the notion of emotions as diseases of the mind. Yet most psychodynamic theories have their base in clinical phenomena; they are also among the most consistent and insightful approaches to the study of emotion.

Since psychoanalysis is a prime example of a psychodynamic theory, let us consider it briefly. During his long career, Freud developed a number of different, and not always compatible, views on emotion (Rapaport, 1953). I will consider only one strand in this complex web. In *Studies on Hysteria* (1895/1955), Breuer and Freud presented the hypothesis that hysterical symptoms result when emotions are aroused but not allowed a normal outlet, for example, because of psychological defenses. Freud frequently returned to this theme in later writings. For instance, this is how he summarized these earlier studies in his Clark lectures:

> One was driven to assume that the illness occurred because the affects generated in the pathogenic situations had their normal outlet blocked, and that the essence of the illness lay in the fact that these "strangulated" affects were then put to an abnormal use.... A certain portion of our mental excitation is normally directed along the paths of somatic innervation and produces what we know as an "expression of the emotions." Hysterical conversion exaggerates this portion of the discharge of an emotionally cathected mental process; it represents a far more intense expression of the emotions, which has entered upon a new path. (Freud, 1910/1957, p. 18)

At a still later date, Freud seemed to expand his views of hysteria to include normal, not just "strangulated," affect. Drawing on the view, common in his time, that experiences oft repeated could ultimately become inherited, Freud (1917/1963) described emotions as hysterical attacks that had become part of our biological inheritance. Conversely, he described hysterical reactions as a "freshly constructed individual affect" (p. 396).[10]

I emphasize these observations by Freud for two reasons. First, they illustrate well the close relationship between the psychodynamic tradition and the conception of emotions as diseases of the mind. Second, and more important, emotions *are* like hysterical conversion reactions in certain fundamental respects. In both cases, for example, the person seems to be "suffering" from some behavior that is, on a deeper level of analysis, an action that he or she is performing. In the case of hysterical conversion reactions, the behavior (neurotic symptom) is highly idiosyncratic and results from intrapsychic conflict. In the case of normal emotional reactions, by contrast, the behavior has become standardized and to a certain extent legitimated within society. I will return to this issue in a later section, when we discuss emotions as social roles. I believe the latter metaphor (emotions as social roles) better conveys Freud's basic insight than does his own variation of the emotion-as-disease metaphor.

The drive tradition

The conception of emotions as "driving forces" could also be illustrated by reference to Freud, who, in his more metatheoretical writings, postulated a kind of psychic energy derived from instinctual sources. This energy could vary quantitatively (i.e., in intensity), but it had few qualitative features of its own. Affect was experienced when energy was discharged, the quality of the affect (e.g., fear as opposed to anger) being determined by the ideas to which the energy had become cathected.

An interpretation of emotions as drives has also been common to behaviorists (of the Hullian, not the Skinnerian, variety). Fear is the "drive" that motivates avoidance behavior, anger is the "drive" that motivates aggression, and so forth. In some versions, the drive is conceptualized as an intervening variable (theoretical construct) without any substantive properties of its own. In other versions, the drive is given a physiological locus (e.g., arousal of the autonomic nervous system), and if it is considered a "primary drive," it is given a biological (hereditary) origin.

I do not wish to comment in any detail on the emotion-as-drive concept, in either its psychoanalytic or its behaviorist versions. Suffice it to note that, of all the traditions we have been considering (the phenomenological, psychophysiological, ethological, and psychodynamic), the drive tradition probably has been the least illuminating, and possibly the most obstructive, as far as our understanding of the emotions is concerned. I mention it here primarily because of its historical importance.

If this assessment seems a bit harsh, this is due in part to the fact that the emotion-as-drive concept derives considerable intuitive appeal from two metaphorical sources: first, our ordinary language (see Table 3.1); and, second, the language of physical theory, where "energy" and "force" have been central constructs. Neither source has transferred well into psychological theory. Particularly damaging has been the tendency to treat emotional "drives" in quantitative terms only, thus deflecting attention from detailed observations of the qualitative differences among emotions (whether those differences be phenomenological, physiological, or behavioral). Within the drive tradition, motivation was the primary concern; the emotions were "reduced" to motives and were largely ignored, not being considered worthy of study in their own right.

Some further observations on the relationship between theory and metaphor

The five theoretical traditions that we have discussed thus far are not independent. The phenomenological tradition, at least in its more atomistic version, has sometimes attempted to reduce the experience of emotion to the perception of physiological responses; those responses, in turn, have been related to the biologically more "primitive" parts of the nervous system (e.g., limbic and autonomic structures). Drive theories have also related emotions to physiological arousal and animal instincts; that is, when they have not treated emotions as pure intervening variables (theoretical constructs). And we saw in the case of Freud how these traditions can become intertwined in a psychodynamic approach to emotional disorders (diseases of the mind). What lies behind and helps provide some unity to these traditions is the myth of the passions and its many metaphorical extensions.

Simply by pointing out a parallel between the major (abstract) metaphors of emotion and some of the major traditions in emotional theorizing we do not demonstrate that the theoretical traditions are based on metaphor. However, scientific explanation, like any other kind of explanation, necessarily involves the use of metaphor. Indeed, some have argued that scientific theories are little more than extended metaphors. That is going too far, for there is certainly a useful distinction to be made between a scientific explanation and a *merely* metaphorical account of the same phenomenon. But at the very least, our metaphors help make certain kinds of theorizing seem more natural and intuitively obvious. Of course, emotions are noncognitive (feelings); of course, they are closely associated with visceral activity; of course, they are remnants of our evolutionary past; of course, they may lead to psychopathology (e.g., if too extreme or not allowed proper expression); and of course they motivate behavior. Everybody knows that. It is embedded in our common language.

Another metaphor: emotions as social roles

In this section, I wish to introduce still another metaphor of emotion, namely, emotions as social roles (Averill, 1980a, 1985, in press). This metaphor is no more "true" in an absolute sense than any of the five metaphors discussed earlier. However, it does reveal certain features of emotion that the others have tended to conceal. Perhaps most important, it takes the emotions out of the private realm and places them in the public ("outer") domain, and it treats the individual as the agent of his or her own emotional responses, rather than as a patient.

The concept of a social role is itself based on metaphor, the source of which is the theater. ("All the world's a stage....") However, the notion of emotions as social roles is not simply a metaphor on a metaphor. Some of the most insightful analyses of emotion can be found in books on acting, especially on the technique of method or "deep" acting pioneered by the Russian director Stanislavski (1936). Thus, when speaking of emotions as social roles, I am drawing on the theatrical tradition directly, as well as on the extension of that tradition within social psychology (Biddle, 1979; Sarbin & Allen, 1968).

If the role metaphor is to be useful in explicating the emotions, it must be made more precise. In this respect, Sarbin (1986) has made useful distinctions among four types of roles. The first is theatrical, namely, the part or character in a play. The second involves taking on another's identity in a social context, for instance, as a con artist. In the third sense, the concept of role is used to describe the expected conduct of a person, given his or her status in society. This is the usual social-psychological meaning of a role. Finally, there are stereotypic patterns of behavior, such as characterize the traditional lover or rogue, the jealous husband, and so forth. Behaviors of this type help preserve and enhance an actor's identity and moral values. Sarbin therefore calls such stereotypes identity roles. He suggests that emotions belong in this category, since emotions involve an assessment of the effect of an action on a person's sense of identity.

Sarbin's distinctions are useful in reminding us that not all social roles are alike. A more detailed discussion of emotions as social roles would have to take these and related distinctions into account. For the sake of simplicity, however, I will refer simply to social roles in a generic sense and to emotions as one variety of social role (metaphorically speaking). Some of the ways that emotions are similar to social roles are outlined in Table 3.2.

Needless to say, there are also limitations to the role metaphor. Emotions are presumably "authentic," "spontaneous," and "self-involving." By contrast, role behavior is regarded as "feigned," "deliberate," and "self-distanced" (divorced from the self). These contrasts are all legitimate at the level of everyday experience, but their theoretical significance requires critical analysis.

The anthropologist Hsu (1983) has written a short but revealing essay on the relation between social roles and emotions (or what he calls affects). Hsu cites excerpts from Malinowski's diaries, indicating that the latter had difficulty empathizing with the natives he was studying (Trobriand Islanders). "As for ethnography," Malinowski records in his diary,

Table 3.2. *Parallels between dramatistic and emotional roles*

Roles	Emotions
Role: A role is constituted by a set of instructions, i.e., the lines and stage settings.	An emotion is constituted by social rules and situations (and not simply by innate factors).
Play: A role does not exist in isolation, but is interwoven with other roles to form a whole.	An emotion does not exist as an isolated event; it is an interpersonal and intersubjective phenomenon.
Plot: A role is part of a larger story that gives it meaning.	An emotion is part of a larger cultural matrix that gives it meaning.
Actor: Persons can choose when and how to enact a role.	Persons are active participants in their emotions, not passive recipients ("patients").
Training: Acting is a skill that requires practice as well as innate ability.	Emotions are skilled performances and not unlearned, reflex-like responses.
Involvement: The actor identifies with the character of the role, experiencing events as the character might.	Involvement in the emotional role determines the nature and intensity of the emotional experience.
Interpreting the role: In order to become involved in a role, the actor must understand the plot of the play.	Emotional involvement requires an intuitive understanding of the cultural matrix that helps give the emotion its meaning.

"I see the life of the natives as utterly devoid of interest or importance, something as remote from me as the life of a dog." Hsu suggests that Malinowski lacked "truly *human* relations with the natives." Hsu then asks rhetorically, "What do we mean by truly *human* relations?" And he answers, "Truly *human* relations are characterized by affect (or feeling) in contrast to the not-so-human relations, characterized by role (or usefulness)" (p. 172).

At this point it might be asked, What is more peculiarly *human* than the social role? But leaving that question aside, let us continue with Hsu's account. Malinowski, we are led to presume, could understand (rationally?) the roles that the Trobriand Islanders adopted and that separated their culture from his, but he could not understand what he supposedly shared with them, namely, their emotional experiences:

> Cultures borrow much from each other in role matters such as foods, artifacts, etiquette, theories of nature, and tools for control of human beings and things. But there is little evidence that people change in any fundamental way, and, as a whole, their patterns of feeling about themselves, about each other, and about the rest of the world. (Hsu, 1983, p. 174)

Hsu concludes his essay with a paean to "our shift from a Melting Pot concept of America to that of Cultural Pluralism."

I take this last statement to mean that, by recognizing our common humanity (represented by feelings and emotions), we will be better able to accept cultural differences (represented by social roles). But if social roles are so superficial, characterized primarily by their "usefulness," why should we be concerned about their amalgamation in a "melting pot"? And why should Malinowski have had such difficulty understanding what he shared with the Trobriand Islanders, while being so astute in comprehending the differences?

The answer to both these questions lies, I believe, in the fact that the emotions are themselves cultural creations. Indeed, they are more central to a culture than they are to an individual. This is not to deny a common human nature. But it is to deny that the emotions are a more direct reflection of that nature than they are products of the culture in which a person is raised. The emotions are, in fact, one of the chief ways in which one culture differs from another.

Ironically, in his criticism of Malinowski, Hsu is drawing on a conception of emotion that is, to a large extent, culturally specific, one rooted in the Western myth of the passions. A study by Myers (1979) illustrates an alternative conception. When giving accounts of emotional reactions, for instance, to the death of a parent, the Pintupi (a group of Australian aborigines) do not emphasize "inner feelings." To quote Myers:

> The Aboriginal autobiographies I have seen, as well as those I tried to elicit, emphasize the cultural expectations much more than they do the specific experiences and interpretations of the individual; they seem illustrations rather than self-conscious introspections. It was frequently difficult to tell whether a person was genuinely "angry" (feeling anger) or whether the display was a "cultural performance," or finally *what sense it made to distinguish these.* Pintupi talk of emotion, then, is not necessarily the talk of "raw experience." (p. 348, italics added)

I would go further and suggest that emotions *are* "cultural performances," and not just among the Pintupi. The young man who says to his sweetheart, "I love you," is not simply describing some inner condition (a peculiar feeling or state of physiological arousal), nor are his words simply a substitute for more primitive expressions of sexual excitement, like the caterwauling of a civilized tomcat. Rather, by an avowal of love, the individual is expressing a willingness to enter into a certain kind of social relationship with the other, a relationship that varies from one culture to another and from one historical epoch to another (Averill, 1985).

Similar considerations apply to other emotions. Grief is not simply an inner wound caused by the loss of a loved one; it is also a duty imposed on the bereaved by the group, with accompanying rights, duties, and obligations (Averill, 1979; Averill & Wisocki, 1981). Anger, too, involves a transaction among individuals, a transaction that is constituted as well as regulated by social norms and rules (Averill, 1982). Even such a "primitive" emotion as fear is, in its most common manifestations, a social construction (Averill, 1987). Every social group has its appropriate fears (e.g., of God, pollution, communists, capitalists, certain natural phenomena), the experience of which certifies membership in and allegiance to the group.

There is not space here to pursue the way emotions are like, and the way they are unlike, social roles. The references cited in the preceding paragraphs provide detailed analyses of specific emotions from a social-constructionist point of view. There is, however, a final point worth making before I conclude this chapter.

Not only does the role metaphor help place emotional phenomena in a new light; it also suggests new sources of data relevant to the understanding of emotion. One of those new sources of data is metaphor itself. The general model of emotion held within a culture is encoded in the colloquialisms, maxims, and folk sayings common in everyday speech. Many of these expressions are metaphorical. Thus, an examination of common metaphors can help uncover the norms, rules, expectations, and values that define emotional roles. (Some analyses of this kind have already been mentioned in note 8.)

Concluding observations

Our most common metaphors depict the emotions as inherently private ("inner") events, a part of our human nature that is – in its purest form – unsullied by social influence and "higher" thought processes (reason, logic). To the extent that our metaphors help constitute the way we think and feel, they create the experience of emotion in their own image. And to the extent that we forget or fail to recognize the metaphorical nature of emotional experience, we are liable to develop theories that mystify more than they explain.

But people live at multiple levels of reality. To understand the emotions, we must take into account at least two levels. The abstract level is that depicted in metaphor, myth, and many of our scientific theories. It is important to understand this abstract level, for it guides our behavior and lends meaning to our experience. Yet we must also look at the more concrete level, at the role that emotions play within the social system, as well as any biological and psychological functions they might have.

The metaphor of emotions as social roles has been introduced to facilitate this task. It is meant not to replace the other major metaphors of emotion, but to complement them. In the final analysis, emotions are emotions, and our goal should be to understand them on their own terms. But that goal is perhaps too idealistic. In psychology, probably more than in most sciences, understanding proceeds by way of metaphor. That, at least, has been the history of theories of emotion, as the preceding analysis indicates. Still, as an ideal, we should always be searching for ways to make our metaphors more precise and, for scientific purposes, more explanatory and less evaluative.

Acknowledgment

Preparation of this chapter was supported, in part, by Grant MH40131 from the National Institute of Mental Health.

Notes

1 This brief summary of Vico is based on a recent analysis by Shotter (1986).

2 These remarks refer to the use of the term "emotion" in English. In modern French, *sentiment* and *emotion* are the terms most widely used to refer to emotional phenomena. (*Sentiment* has a connotation similar to the English "feeling.") In German, *Gefühl* and *Gemütsbewegung* are the vernacular terms corresponding roughly to "feeling" and "emotion," respectively; *Affekt* has also been commonly used in the psychological literature (e.g., by Freud), as has, more recently, *Emotion*. For related terms in other Indo-European languages, see Buck (1949).

3 The term "disease" originally had an emotional connotation. It stems from the Middle French, *des* (dis) + *aise* (ease), meaning "discomfort" or "uneasiness."

4 The irrational/mortal part of the soul was subdivided into a "spirited" aspect, localized in the region of the chest, and an appetitive aspect, localized below the midriff. The significance of this subdivision is explained below.

5 The most concise presentation of Plato's localization of function can be found in his dialogue *Timaeus* (Hamilton & Cairns, 1961, pp. 1151–1211).

6 For discussions of emotion by early Greek Stoics (e.g., Zeno and Chrysippus), see Gardiner, Metcalf, and Beebe-Center (1937) and Rist (1969). The assertion that only a rational being would be capable of making emotional judgments is well illustrated by Seneca's (ca. 50/1963) contention that reason and passion are not distinct, but are "only the transformation of the mind toward the better or worse" (p. 127). Thus, anger, although "it is the foe of reason, ... is nevertheless born only where reason dwells" (p. 115).

7 To the extent that emotions are passions (i.e., are things that happen to us and are beyond our control), they are *involuntary* and not voluntary. However, emotions are not involuntary in the sense that behavior induced, say, by external coercion is involuntary. The angry person *wants* to gain revenge; the fearful person *wants* to flee; and so forth. In other words, while experiencing an emotion a person is "coerced," if at all, by his or her own desires. In scholastic philosophy (O'Brien, 1948), this fact led to a distinction between

fully voluntary acts (to which the individual gives full assent, as when he or she is experiencing an emotion) and perfectly voluntary acts (which are performed after deliberation and forethought). The legacy of this distinction can be found today in the legal treatment of "crimes of passion." A homicide committed under sufficient emotion is adjudicated as voluntary manslaughter, as opposed to murder (premeditated) and involuntary manslaughter (due to negligence or culpable accident). In subsequent discussion, I will use "motivation" and "motive" as generic terms to refer to both fully (emotional) and perfectly (deliberate) voluntary acts, and in accordance with everyday speech, I will often refer to the emotions as involuntary. The context should make the meaning clear.

8 For detailed analyses of the metaphors of specific emotions, see Kovecses (1986, 1988) on anger, pride, and love, and see Averill, Catlin, and Chon (in preparation) on hope.

9 The sense of reason or rationality just described is not the only, or even the most common, one today. Usually, when we speak of rationality we imply some means-end relationship, following certain standards of efficacy. Rationality as harmony among one's basic needs and desires goes back to the original Greek meaning of *logos,* which meant to assemble or gather together the best of something or, alternatively, the principle by which such an assemblage is made (Karatheodoris, 1979). This meaning is evident in such current terms as antho*logy.* In one of its senses, the Latin root – *ratio* – also implied harmony and proportionate relations.

10 I am indebted to Bram Fridhandler (1985) for these comments by Freud.

References

Alston, W. P. (1969). Feelings. *Philosophical Review, 78,* 3–34.
American Psychiatric Association (1980). *Diagnostic and statistical manual of mental disorders, DSM-III* (3rd ed.). Washington, D.C.: Author.
Augustine (1966). *The city of God* (vol. 4; P. Levine, Trans.). Cambridge, MA: Harvard University Press. (Original work written ca. 420.)
Averill, J. R. (1974). An analysis of psychophysiological symbolism and its influence on theories of emotion. *Journal for the Theory of Social Behavior, 4,* 147–90.
  (1979). The functions of grief. In C. Izard (Ed.), *Emotions in personality and psychopathology* (pp. 339–68). New York: Plenum.
  (1980a). A constructivist view of emotion. In R. Plutchik & H. Kellerman (Eds.), *Theories of emotion* (pp. 305–40). New York: Academic Press.
  (1980b). On the paucity of positive emotions. In K. R. Blankstein, P. Pliner, & J. Polivy (Eds.), *Assessment and modification of emotional behavior* (pp. 7–45). New York: Plenum.
  (1982). *Anger and aggression: An essay on emotion.* New York: Springer.
  (1985). The social construction of emotion: With special reference to love. In K. Gergen & K. Davis (Eds.), *The social construction of the person* (pp. 90–109). New York: Springer.
  (1987). The role of emotion and psychological defense in self-protective behavior. In N. Weinstein (Ed.), *Taking care: Why people take precautions* (pp. 54–78). Cambridge University Press.
  (in press). Emotions as episodic dispositions, cognitive schemas, and transitory social roles: Steps toward an integrated theory of emotion. In D. Ozer, J. M.

Healy, & A. J. Stewart (Eds.), *Perspectives in personality.* Greenwich, CT: JAI Press.

Averill, J. R., Catlin, G., & Chon, K. K. (in preparation). The studies on hope.

Averill, J. R., & Wisocki, P. A. (1981). Some observations on behavioral approaches to the treatment of grief among the elderly. In H. J. Sobel (Ed.), *Behavior therapy in terminal care* (pp. 125–50). Cambridge, MA: Ballinger.

Biddle, B. J. (1979). *Role theory: Expectations, identities, and behaviors.* New York: Academic Press.

Breuer, J., & Freud, S. (1955). Studies on hysteria. In J. Strachey (Ed. and Trans.), *The standard edition of the complete psychological works of Sigmund Freud* (vol. 2, pp. 1–306). London: Hogarth Press. (Original work published 1895.)

Buck, C. D. (1949). *A dictionary of selected synonyms in the principal Indo-European languages.* Chicago: University of Chicago Press.

Cicero (1966). *Tusculan disputations* (J. E. King, Trans.). Cambridge, MA: Harvard University Press. (Original work written 45 B.C.)

Clore, G.L., & Ortony, A. (1984). Some issues for a cognitive theory of emotion. *Cahiers de Psychologie Cognitive, 4,* 53–7.

Darwin, C. (1965). *The expression of the emotions in man and animals.* Chicago: University of Chicago Press. (Original work published 1872.)

Douglas, M. (1970). *Natural symbols.* New York: Pantheon Books.

Freud, S. (1957). Five lectures on psycho-analysis. In J. Strachey (Ed. and Trans.), *The standard edition of the complete psychological works of Sigmund Freud* (vol. 11, pp. 1–55). London: Hogarth Press. (Original work published 1910.)

   (1959). An autobiographical study. In J. Strachey (Ed. and Trans.), *The standard edition of the complete psychological works of Sigmund Freud* (vol. 20, pp. 1–74). London: Hogarth Press. (Original work published 1925.)

   (1963). Introductory lectures on psycho-analysis: Part 3. In J. Strachey (Ed. and Trans.), *The standard edition of the complete psychological works of Sigmund Freud* (vol. 15, pp. 243–576). London: Hogarth Press. (Original work published 1917.)

   (1964). An outline of psycho-analysis. In J. Strachey (Ed. and Trans.), *The standard edition of the complete psychological works of Sigmund Freud* (vol. 23, pp. 141–207). London: Hogarth Press. (Original work published 1940.)

Fridhandler, B. M. (1985). *Outline of a psychoanalytic theory of emotion.* Unpublished doctoral dissertation, University of Massachusetts, Amherst.

Gardiner, H. M., Metcalf, R. C., & Beebe-Center, J. G. (1937). *Feeling and emotion: A history of theories.* New York: American Book.

Gentner, D., & Grudin, J. (1985). The evolution of mental metaphors in psychology: A 90-year retrospective. *American Psychologist, 40,* 181–92.

Hamilton, E., & Cairns, H. (Eds.). (1961). *The collected works of Plato.* Princeton, NJ: Princeton University Press.

Hebb, D. O., & Thompson, W. R. (1954). The social significance of animal studies. In G. Lindzey (Ed.), *Handbook of social psychology* (vol. 1, pp. 532–61). Cambridge, MA: Addison-Wesley.

Hsu, F. L. K. (1983). Role, affect, and anthropology. In *Rugged individualism reconsidered* (pp. 171–4). Knoxville: University of Tennessee Press.

Hudson, L. (1972). *The cult of the fact.* New York: Harper & Row.

James, W. (1890). *The principles of psychology.* New York: Holt.

Kant, I. (1966). *Critique of pure reason* (F. M. Muller, Trans.). Garden City, NY: Doubleday. (Original work published 1781.)

Karatheodoris, S. (1979). *Logos:* An analysis of the social achievement of rationality. In A. Blum & P. McHugh (Eds.), *Friends, enemies, and strangers: Theorizing in art, science, and everyday life* (pp. 175–214). Norwood, NJ: Ablex.

Kovecses, Z. (1986). *Metaphors of anger, pride, and love: A lexical approach to the structure of concepts.* Amsterdam: Benjamins.

   (1988). *The language of love: The semantics of passion in conversational English.* Lewisburg, PA: Bucknell University Press.

Lakoff, G., & Johnson, M. (1980). *Metaphors we live by.* Chicago: University of Chicago Press.

Lang, F. R. (1972). Psychological terminology in the Tusculans. *Journal of the History of the Behavioral Sciences, 8,* 419–36.

Lutz, C. (1982). The domain of emotion words on Ifaluk. *American Ethnologist, 9,* 113–28.

Marx, K., & Engels, F. (1939). *The German ideology* (R. Pascal, Ed.). New York: International. (Original work written 1845–6.)

McReynolds, P. (1980). The clock metaphor in the history of psychology. In T. Nickles (Ed.), *Scientific discovery: Case studies* (pp. 97–112). Dordrecht: Reidel.

Midgley, M. (1978). *Beast and man: The roots of human nature.* Ithaca, NY: Cornell University Press.

Mill, J. (1967). *Analysis of the phenomena of the human mind* (vol. 2, rev. 2d ed.; J. S. Mill, Ed.). New York: Kelley. (Rev. ed. originally published 1869.)

Myers, F. (1979). Emotions and the self: A theory of personhood and political order among Pintupi aborigines. *Ethos, 7,* 343–70.

Nafe, J. (1924). An experimental study of the affective qualities. *American Journal of Psychology, 35,* 507–44.

Natsoulas, T. (1973). Own emotion awareness. *Interamerican Journal of Psychology, 7,* 151–87.

Nietzsche, F. (1960). *Joyful wisdom* (T. Common, Trans.). New York: Ungar. (Original work published 1882.)

O'Brien, V. P. (1948). *The measure of responsibility in persons influenced by emotion.* Washington, D.C.: Catholic University of America Press.

Onians, R. B. (1951). *The origins of European thought about the body, the mind, the soul, the world, time, and fate.* Cambridge University Press.

Pribram, K. H. (1980). The role of analogy in transcending limits in the brain sciences. *Daedalus, 109,* 19–38.

Rapaport, D. (1953). On the psychoanalytic theory of affects. *International Journal of Psychoanalysis, 34,* 177–98.

Rist, J. M. (1969). *Stoic philosophy.* Cambridge University Press.

Sarbin, T. R. (1986). Emotion and act: Roles and rhetoric. In R. Harré (Ed.), *The social construction of emotions* (pp. 83–97). Oxford: Blackwell Publisher.

Sarbin, T. R., & Allen, V. L. (1968). Role theory. In G. Lindzey & E. Aronson (Eds.), *The handbook of social psychology* (vol. 1, pp. 488–566). Reading, MA: Addison-Wesley.

Seneca (1963). On anger. In J. W. Basore (Trans.), *Moral essays* (vol. 1, pp. 106–355). Cambridge, MA: Harvard University Press. (Original work written ca. A.D. 50.)

Shotter, J. (1986). A sense of place: Vico and the social production of social identities. *British Journal of Social Psychology, 25,* 199–211.

Skinner, B. F. (1971). *Beyond freedom and dignity.* New York: Knopf.

Solomon, R. C. (1976). *The passions.* Garden City, NY: Doubleday/Anchor.

Stanislavski, K. S. (1936). *An actor prepares* (E. R. Hapgood, Trans.). New York: Theatre Arts Books.

Thass-Thienemann, T. (1968). *Symbolic behavior.* New York: Washington Square Press.

Thoits, P. A. (1985). Social support processes and psychological well-being: Theoretical possibilities. In I. G. Sarason & B. R. Sarason (Eds.), *Social support: Theory, research and application* (pp. 51–72). The Hague: Nijhoff.

Veith, I. (1965). *Hysteria: The history of a disease.* Chicago: University of Chicago Press.

Vico, G. (1948). *The new science of Giambattista Vico* (T. G. Bergin & M. H. Fisch, Eds. and Trans.). Ithaca, NY: Cornell University Press. (Original work published 1744.)

Wenger, M. A. (1950). Emotions as visceral action: An extension of Lange's theory. In M. L. Reymert (Ed.), *Feelings and emotions: The Mooseheart–Chicago Symposium* (pp. 3–10). New York: McGraw-Hill.

Wundt, W. (1897). *Outlines of psychology* (C. H. Judd, Trans.). New York: Stechert. (Original work published 1896.)

4

Motives and metaphors: a study in scientific creativity

PAUL McREYNOLDS

My purpose in this chapter is to examine the role that metaphorical thought has played in the historical development of motivational psychology. The relation between motives and metaphors constitutes a particularly apt topic, since recently there has been growing interest in the significance of metaphors and analogies in scientific thought (e.g., Boyd, 1979; Gruber, 1980; Hesse, 1966; Kuhn, 1979; Leatherdale, 1974; MacCormac, 1985; McReynolds, 1980; Turbayne, 1962) and since the field of motivation is one of the most basic and venerable areas of psychology.

Rather than beginning with a predetermined conception of the utility of metaphors in motivational theorizing and then looking for historical instances that fit that conception, I will present a historical survey of different approaches to motivation, paying special attention to the use of metaphors and analogies, and I shall then draw such conclusions from the data as seem warranted. Though my survey is necessarily limited and selective, it covers a representative sample of motivational perspectives. Before beginning this survey, it will be useful to discuss briefly the concepts of motive and metaphor.

The concept of motive

Though a rigorous and completely defensible definition of motivation is not easily articulated, the general area demarcated by the term is clear enough, and theorists throughout history have found the notion of motive, or something like it, necessary for an explanation of behavior. If we think of behavior as being determined by factors of two kinds, those in the organism and those in the situation, then motivation falls in the former category. Thus, motivational influences are those behavioral determinants that an organism carries around within itself into different environments.

A key term here is the word "behavior." Generally speaking, this term is taken to refer to actions that are in some sense optional for the organism. Thus, an animal may or may not eat in a given situation, a person may or may not go to a given social function, and so on. To say that a behavior is optional is not to assert that it is necessarily, or even probably, consciously intended; rather, it is simply to imply that within the range of realistic possibilities, including relevant species-specific tendencies, the occurrence of the behavior is problematic and is significantly determined by variable factors within the organism. In contrast, such "automatic" functions as digestion, respiration, and cardiovascular processes are not ordinarily thought of as "behavior," though they may be, at least under certain circumstances and to a certain extent. Broadly conceived, behavior consists of actions, movements, motions, whatever the animal as a *whole* animal (as contrasted with a particular organ of the animal) *does,* whether overtly or covertly.

Essential, then, to the notion of motivation is the idea of organisms *doing* things, and doing them in large part under their own steam, to put it metaphorically. Thus, we can think of organisms as being constituted so as to have the capacity to perform certain behaviors; yet without some internal impetus, some inner push or pull, some tendency toward actualizing its potential actions, an organism would merely exist, inert and inactive. To be sure, it could still respond, in reflex fashion, to the world about it, but it would lack the characteristic capacity of animate beings to adjust their behavior to internal needs and deficits. What we think of as motivational tendencies do not exist in the abstract, independent of their context. Rather, they come into play only under certain conditions. For example, the motive to drink arises in response to a water deficit, the motive to flee in response to a perception of danger, and so on.

These inner impetuses to behavior – individually, in toto, and in the context of the overall state of an organism – constitute the essence of the concept of motivation. The base paradigm or metaphor for the notion of motive, then, is that of a force within an organism that leads to certain movements – hence the term "motive," something that produces motion, or movement.

The durability and tenacity of motivational concepts derive from the fact that motivational interpretations, in one form or another, have proved to be essential to the explication of behavior. Yet the precise nature and source of most motives are highly obscure and, of course, were even more so in earlier times. This obscurity should not be surprising given that motives are internal factors largely hidden from direct inspection. As a result, the variety of motivational formulations that have been proposed through the ages is enormous, and many of these conceptions have involved complex metaphors. This suggests that metaphors are most likely to occur in areas of science in which important questions are combined with limited knowledge.

Another reason for the prominence of metaphorical patterns of thought in motivational psychology lies in the kind of problems that are dealt with in the study of motivation. The area encompasses (but is not limited to) the topics of intentional (purposive) behavior, choice behavior, perceptions of personal control, and intrapsychic conflicts, and such topics inevitably raise difficult conceptual issues, including the problems of free will and determinism. In coping with these and related problems, motivation theorists have sometimes turned to anthropomorphism (e.g., referring to the ego as if it were animate) and reification (e.g., treating the unconscious as if it were a thing). Such patterns of thought are frequently expressed in figurative language.

The relation between motives and emotions deserves a brief introductory comment. The distinction – and overlap – between these two concepts have always posed something of a puzzle, and some authors have treated them as essentially interchangeable. In the seventeenth century the notion of a "passion" included both conative and affective aspects, and in the contemporary period motivation and emotion are sometimes brought together in the same text and in the same journal.[1] The problem is not so much that motivation and emotion are in principle indistinguishable, but rather that they frequently occur conjointly. Certain strong emotions (e.g., love or anger) have obvious impellent functions, and, conversely, certain motivational processes (e.g., success and failure) may have conspicuous emotional concomitants. The answer to this apparent problem is to recognize that the same phenomenon may from one perspective be motivational and from another be affective. Thus, to the extent that a given emotional state has motivational qualities it is also a motive, and vice versa.

The concept of metaphor

A metaphor is a particular type of cognitive construction. Ordinarily manifested verbally, it relates two items, not typically conceptualized as similar, in a relatively surprising and sometimes dramatic fashion.[2] Metaphorical thinking is prominent in ordinary human discourse, in literature, and in the arts, as well as in the sciences. For example, such figurative expressions as "My job is a rat race" and "He's a chip off the old block" are part of the standard repertoire of contemporary American speech. In literature the use of metaphor – as when Carl Sandburg (1916) refers to Chicago as "Hog Butcher for the World" (p. 3) and tells us that "The fog comes/on little cat feet" (p. 3) – is particularly striking and perhaps essential. Metaphor also plays a role in the arts. In painting, for instance, cubists saw the world as composed of cylinders, cones, and spheres, and in music a well-known composition is commonly referred to as the "Pastoral Symphony."

Though the utilization of metaphors was once considered relatively rare and somewhat inappropriate in the sciences, recent scholarship – as already noted – has strongly emphasized the prominent role that metaphors and analogies have played in scientific creativity. Instances are not hard to find. In the physical sciences one thinks, for instance, of August Kekulé's discovery of the structure of benzene on the basis of a dreamlike image of a snake gripping its own tail or of Lord Rutherford's hypothetical construction of the atom – as composed of electrons whirling around a nucleus – in terms of the structure of the solar system. An early and well-known metaphor in psychology, dating back to Plato and Aristotle, represents memory in terms of the impression of a seal on a wax tablet. A favorite contemporary psychological metaphor, in some quarters at least, is that of the brain or mind as a "black box."

The technical literature on metaphors, most of it concerned with logical and linguistic analyses and involving a number of conflicting interpretations and emphases, is enormous.[3] Fortunately, it is unnecessary for us to review this literature in detail here. Indeed, it is probably best to approach our historical survey without too many preconceived notions as to the nature of metaphors, lest those ideas inappropriately bias our search.[4] There are, however, several important introductory points to be made.

First, some comments on the usage of several words – in particular *simile, metaphor, analogy,* and *model* (as this term is used in science) – will be helpful. Each of these words refers to the comparison of two terms on the basis of similarity. In a simile the similarity is specifically stated, as in the expression "The brain is *like* a computer." If we change this slightly to suggest an identity, as in "The brain *is* a computer," we have a metaphor. And if we propose that the computer is in certain respects a representation of how the brain functions, we have made the computer a model of the brain. The term "analogy" is often employed when one wishes to draw attention to a relevant similarity between two things, while at the same time recognizing their differences. Note that all these uses are figurative. The brain is *not really* a computer; it does not have transistors, disk drives, and so on.

In practice the distinctions among similes, metaphors, models, and analogies are not always clear-cut. There is a growing tendency to employ the word "metaphor" as a generic term for all of the above dyadic expressions.[5] I will generally follow this convention in this chapter, though my main emphasis will be on the identification of what are technically analogies, similes, and metaphors. The term "model," it seems to me, should be (and typically is) restricted to the more complex, deliberative attempts to construct predictive replicas (physical, conceptual, or mathematical) of given natural domains.

How do metaphors exercise their influence on thought? In what manner can metaphors be productive, as contrasted with merely clever? Some insight into these questions is afforded by the view of Burke (1945/1969) that a metaphor "is a device for seeing something *in terms of* something else" (p. 503). Thus, to say that "the brain is a computer" is to lead one to think of the brain *from the perspective of* what computers are like: It causes one to conceptualize the brain in a new way. Similarly, the metaphorical expression "Sue has a warm personality" yields a quite different picture of Sue than the expression "Sue has a cold personality."

The essence of a metaphorical construction, in action, is that a person is interested, for one reason or another, in a given idea or topic, X, and elaborates this idea or topic by combining it with or relating it to another idea or topic, Y, thus extending or modifying the meaning of X. For this combination to qualify as a metaphor, it is further required that X and Y be from content areas that are not normally linked, so that at first their conjunction may seem paradoxical, or even absurd. The reason they *can* be linked, in spite of this disparity, is that they can be conceived as having *something* in common, and it is when one perceives what this commonality could be that he or she "gets" the metaphor. It is through this commonality that the meaning of X is modified by seeing it from the perspective of Y. Thus, in the utterance "John is a dormant volcano," it is clear that the person John (X) is not actually a dormant volcano (Y); but if it is perceived that the function of the expression is to imply that while normally John is placid he has the capacity to react violently, then this metaphorical characterization has successfully led to an elaborated and enhanced understanding of John. Writers on metaphor have employed a variety of terms to designate what I have referred to simply as X and Y. I find the labels proposed by Leatherdale (1974, p. 16), "topic analogue" and "imported analogue," to be particularly helpful, and I will employ these terms from time to time.

Metaphors sometimes undergo stages of development. In some instances this means that over time a metaphor comes to be taken literally.[6] For example, the expression "Man is a machine" was originally intended metaphorically, but is now believed by some persons to be a literal truth. Another similar, but subtly different type of change occurs when a "live" metaphor becomes a "dead" one, as exemplified by the short history of the term "skyscraper," which once had a certain shock value but which soon came to be used in reference to any tall building.[7] All languages are well stocked with such dead metaphors. Indeed, Jeremy Bentham insisted early in the nineteenth century that all strictly psychological terms in the common language were once figurative expressions based on corporeal analogies (McReynolds, 1970; Ogden, 1959).

It is useful to classify metaphors according to the extent of their coverage or application. In this regard two types have been distinguished. Pepper, in his *World Hypotheses* (1942), delineated the concept of "basic analogy or root metaphor" (p. 91), which can be contrasted with other, more specific metaphors. A root metaphor is a conception of broad theoretical generality that suggests, by analogy, other similarly broad conceptions. Although Pepper did not give a name to the more frequent, less encompassing metaphors, MacCormac (1985), following Pepper, has proposed that the broader class be termed "basic metaphors" and that the other, less encompassing class be called "conveyance metaphors" (p. 19). A basic metaphor, in MacCormac's dichotomy, serves "as a basic presuppositional insight or intuition that undergirds an entire theory." A conveyance metaphor, in contrast, is "employed to express a particular feeling or to suggest an individual possibility" (p. 19). As an example of a root or basic metaphor, MacCormac cites the computational metaphor, which has recently led to a variety of formulations regarding cognitive processing.[8]

What are the functions of metaphors in science? Park, Daston, and Galison (1984), in their stimulating discussion of the employment of analogies by Bacon, Galileo, and Descartes, distinguish between the use of analogies as vehicles for scientific explanation and their use as vehicles for scientific exposition. Thus, Galileo, though a master of expository analogies, tried to avoid their use in explanation, whereas Descartes emphasized their explanatory role. Of the two types, explanatory analogies are the more exciting to the historian because of their role in scientific discovery. What frequently appears to happen is something like this: A scientist trying to make sense of an inadequately charted domain finds that the conventional way of conceptualizing it leaves important issues unresolved, and then comes up with a way of seeing a particular problem as analogous to something from an entirely different domain, thus putting the whole matter into a new perspective. Sometimes this is helpful; sometimes it is not.

Metaphors in motivational psychology

Having examined the concepts of motives and metaphors, we are now ready to bring the two together in a primarily historical perspective. My approach will be to focus on certain key instances of metaphorical thought in the history of motivational psychology, since it would be impossible to trace this history comprehensively in a chapter-length study – and since, in any case, this would not necessarily be the best way to proceed, even if space permitted. In other words, I shall identify and describe what I conceive to be the major root or basic metaphors that have historically been involved in human motivation theory, and I shall organize my subsequent discussion in terms of these.

I discern five such underlying metaphors, though I do not insist that my list is absolutely comprehensive. Motivation is a very intricate affair, and efforts to fathom its mysteries have resulted in innumerable currents and cross-currents of thought. As a result, no reasonably finite set of categories can guarantee a definitive taxonomy of this highly complex and confused area. Certainly there is no single theme, except perhaps something that would be so broad as to be ineffectual, under which all motivational conceptions can be ordered. Even with my fivefold conceptualization there will be instances in which it is unclear whether a given conception fits into one category or another, as well as cases in which a particular motivational conception has some of the characteristics of two or more metaphoric themes.

The five basic metaphors of motivation that I propose are the following:

1. Controlling powers: persons as pawns[9]
2. Personal control: persons as agents
3. Inherent tendencies: persons as natural entities
4. Bodily processes: persons as organisms
5. Inner forces: persons as machines

These five basic metaphors can be thought of as the guiding themes in terms of which motivation theorists have tended to develop their conceptualizations.[10] In the following sections of this chapter, I will examine each of these themes, focusing on the use of metaphors in various motivation theories rather than on the theories themselves. Within each section, I will also include, as appropriate, instances of less encompassing (conveyance) metaphors.

Controlling powers: persons as pawns

It seems probable that human interest in the determinants of behavior reaches far back into prehistory, virtually to the dawn of the species. Our knowledge of the earliest conceptions of what we now term motivation is, of course, extremely sparse, but we can draw certain plausible inferences. It seems certain, on the basis of anthropological and linguistic analyses, that the present naturalistic era, which began in the first millennium B.C., was preceded by a long period during which the occurrence of important events, including significant human actions, tended to be attributed to the influences of "higher," supernatural powers.[11] Though it is not clear how widespread this pattern of thought was, it is evident, as I will document presently, that it was once very prominent. When applied to human behaviors, it amounts to a theory of motivation in which the basic paradigm is that the decisions an individual makes, when faced with important choices, are determined by the influences on his or her mental processes of certain controlling deities.

This conception of action, though present in a wide variety of early peoples, including the Norse, Slavs, Anglo-Saxons, Celts, ancient Persians, and Aryan invaders of early India, has been most definitively revealed in the works of Homer. As the classical scholar R. B. Onians (1951) put it:

> In Homer, one is struck by the fact that his heroes with all their magnificent vitality and activity feel themselves at every turn not free agents but passive instruments or victims of other powers.... A man felt that he could not help his own actions. An idea, an emotion, an impulse came to him; he acted and presently rejoiced or lamented. Some god had inspired or blinded him. (p. 303)

The same theme has been articulated by other authorities on the history of ideas, including E. R. Dodds (1951), who employed the term "psychic intervention" to refer to the conception of higher powers interfering with the course of behavior, and by Bruno Snell (1953), who concluded:

> In Homer a man is unaware of the fact that he may act spontaneously, of his own volition and spirit. Whatever "strikes" him, whatever "thought comes" to him, is given from without, and if no visible external stimulus has affected him he thinks that a god has stood by his side and given him counsel. (p. 123)

There are many examples of this folk motivation notion in Homer, but I will indicate only one here. Early in the *Iliad,* the hero Achilles, angry at Agamemnon for having taken from him the fair-cheeked Briseis, is torn "whether to draw from beside his thigh the sharp sword, driving/ away all those who stood between and kill the son of Atreus [Agamemnon],/or else to check the spleen within and keep down his anger" (bk. 1, 190–2; Lattimore, 1962, p. 64). In this situation of uncertainty, the goddess Athene appears to Achilles and directs him to stay his ire.

The extent to which the actions of the characters in the *Iliad* are conceived to be determined or at least influenced by divinities was first systematically explored by Nilsson (1925/1967) and was developed further by Dodds (1951), Onians (1951), and Snell (1953). Barbu (1960) as well as Simon and Weiner (1966) have related the conception more directly to psychology. Barbu, for instance, observed that "the people described by Homer did not feel that the 'motives' of their behavior lay in themselves; on the contrary, they believed that their behavior was determined from outside, by the gods" (p. 75). More recently, I have utilized this metaphor in tracing the history of the concept of anxiety (McReynolds, 1975). It was Julian Jaynes (1976), however, who carried the psychological implications of the *Iliad* to their extreme. In his stimulating but speculative theory of the historical origins of consciousness, he has proposed that people of the Homeric age lacked consciousness and that their voluntary behaviors were exclusively a function of felt directives from a god.

This interpretation, however, seems quite implausible. Certainly, Homer's characters manifest an abundance of very human motives and drives. Indeed, if this were not the case, readers today would hardly find the poems so compelling. The episode referred to above – in which Agamemnon has claimed Briseis simply because he desires her and is powerful enough to take her and in which Achilles reacts ambivalently, revealing conflicting motives – provides two cases in point. In my view, the evidence, interpreted conservatively, strongly supports the view that an early conception of what we now call motivation presupposed that many human inclinations to act arise from the intervention of divinities, but it does not support the further interpretation, proposed by Jaynes and implied to some degree by the other scholars quoted above, that *all* human actions were conceived in this manner.

In summary, there seems little doubt that in the early period *many* human motives for action were conceptualized in terms of what I have labeled the controlling-powers metaphor. Answers to questions concerning when, where, and how this mode of understanding motivation originated are lost in the mists of prehistory, but the paradigm appears to have been utilized in a considerable variety of early cultures.[12] As a basic metaphor for motivation, the theme is, of course, fundamentally flawed in that it does not lead to precise and accountable theories. With the advent of the materialistic era in ancient Ionia and Greece, the approach tended to disappear, and it never attained the status of a systematically delineated conception of human behavior.[13]

Personal control: persons as agents

The motivational conception of people being in charge, so to speak, of their own behavior has a long past. However, the person-as-agent paradigm was not systematized until the classical Greek period. Since then, in its various representations and reincarnations, it has continued to be a viable approach. Though different aspects of this theme have been emphasized by different authors, the essential core conception is that an individual's behavior is a function of his or her having and exercising the capacity to make voluntary choices and decisions and to act purposively on them.

The early development of the person-as-agent motivational paradigm occurred in what has been referred to by Jaspers (1953) as the "axial period" of human history, specifically in the era between 800 and 200 B.C. (see Parkes, 1959, p. 76). It was in this period that the earlier "preindividualistic" world view was succeeded, notably in the intellectual culture of the Greek world, by a conception of the individuality of human beings (Barbu, 1960, p. 71). This historical stage is thus to be strongly contrasted with the stage described earlier as underlying the higher-powers theme. With regard to human motivation, what we see in this transition is a shift from the assumption that important human decisions are made by the gods to the view that they are made by human beings themselves. Thus, the agency for important action was consciously and explicitly transferred from without to within.

According to the best classical authorities, the rise of individualism was stimulated and manifested by such lyric poets as Sappho and Pindar and by the great tragedies of Aeschylus, Sophocles, and Euripides. Snell, in his *Discovery of the Mind* (1953), and Barbu, in his chapter titled "The Emergence of Personality in the Greek World" (1960, chap. 4), have brilliantly described the dawning emphasis on internal human directives in classical Greek thought. This was the era of Socrates' concern with self-knowledge and of the admonition "Know thyself" over the entrance to the temple at Delphi. It was also the era of the first systematic psychological theories. Plato's was among the first.

Plato divided the soul into three parts or aspects: reason, high spirits (passions), and appetites. All of these have motivational significance, but it is the first – reason, or the rational mind – that corresponds ancestrally to the concept of personal agency. Plato was particularly interested in the relation of reason to the other aspects of mental life and motivation, and he portrayed this relationship with several striking metaphors. Perhaps the best known of these is the simile of the charioteer and two steeds (*Phaedrus*, 253–5; Hamilton & Cairns, 1961, pp. 499–500). In this simile, one of the horses is portrayed as highly spirited but manageable (passion), and the other as difficult and unruly (appetites). The charioteer, of course, represents reason. The point of the metaphor is that the charioteer (human agency), perhaps with some support from one of the horses (passion), controls the movement of the chariot. In other analogies, Plato compared the three motivational aspects to counselors (reason), helpers (passions), and money makers (appetites) in a city (*Republic*, 441; Hamilton & Cairns, 1961, p. 683) and to lovers of wisdom, lovers of honor, and lovers of gain (*Republic*, 581; Hamilton & Cairns, 1961, p. 808). One cannot know, of course, whether these metaphors were instrumental in the development of Plato's tripartite theory or whether their role was solely that of communicating his conception through vivid imagery. At minimum they performed the latter function.

Whereas the concept of human agency was only loosely delineated by Plato, it was spelled out explicitly and in considerable detail by Aristotle. In Aristotle's analyses the notion of agency entails the ideas of choice, end-oriented behaviors, and purpose. The following statements of Aristotle (ca. 335 B.C./1975) are illustrative: "It appears therefore... that a man is the origin of his actions... and all our actions aim at ends" (p. 139) and "The origin of the movement of the parts of the body instrumental to the act lies in the agent; and when the origin of an action is in oneself, it is in one's own power to do it or not" (p. 119).

Aristotle was more technical and less poetic in his writings than Plato. These facts, as well as the fact that Aristotle, coming after Plato, found knowledge more well ordered, may account for his less dramatic and apparently less frequent utilization of figurative language. Aristotle did, of course, employ metaphors.[14] With respect to the concept of agent, for example, Aristotle (ca. 335 B.C./1975) suggested that the process of deliberating about ends is analogous to the analysis of a figure in geometry (pp. 137–9). He also compared the process of an individual making a choice by and for himself to the procedure by which Homeric kings proclaimed decisions to the people (p. 141).

Since the time of St. Augustine, the notion of self-agency, in the sense of voluntarily choosing and intending, has often been discussed in terms of "the will."[15] Though this term is difficult to define in a rigorous manner and though it has been employed in a variety of ways by different authors, it typically carries the connotation of a distinct volitional power or faculty, as implied by "*the* will." In addition to Augustine, other prominent analysts of the will have been St. Thomas Aquinas, René Descartes, David Hume, Immanuel Kant, and William James. Perhaps in part because of its somewhat ambiguous and abstract nature, the history of the idea of the will is replete with metaphors, of which two may be noted here.

Pierre Charron, in his influential treatise *Of Wisdom* (1601/1707), contrasted the will with the nature of understanding and wrote with respect to the former, "Here the Soul goes as it were out of it self, it stretches and moves forward toward the Object; it seeks and runs after it with open Arms, and is eager to take up its Residence, and dwell with the Thing desir'd and belov'd" (p. 165). Edward Reynolds (1640/1971), writing a little later, conveyed his idea of will in the following way:

> the Will hath both an *Oeconomical* Government in respect of the Body, and the Moving Organs thereof, as over *Servants*: and it hath a *Politique* or Civill Government towards the *Understanding*, *Affections*, and *Sensitive Appetite*, as *Subjects*, with which by reason of their often Rebellions, it hapneth to have sundry conflicts and troubles: as Princes from their seditious and rebellious subjects. (pp. 541–2)

Though currently out of vogue as a topic of psychological inquiry, the term "will" remains a stable part of our language, as in such metaphorical expressions as willpower, weak willed,[16] and goodwill, and it continues to be a focal point in the ongoing discussion of free will.[17] Further, whereas concern with the faculty of will has faded in contemporary psychology, emphasis on the personal-control metaphor, in its broader sense, remains strong and indeed appears to be increasing.

Richard de Charms (1968), taking an individual-differences approach to personal causation, has employed the metaphors of Origins and Pawns to designate, respectively, individuals who feel that their behaviors are determined by their own choices and those who feel that their actions tend to be controlled by other persons or the environment. Julian Rotter (1966) utilized a spatial metaphor – locus of control – to differentiate similarly between feelings of internal (person-as-agent) and external (person-as-pawn) control. Another major contemporary metaphorical term that apppears to have at least some of the characteristics of self-agency is the concept of a Plan as introduced by Miller, Galanter, and Pribram (1960).[18]

The major current interest in the person-as-agent paradigm, however, has been in the form of philosophical examinations of the concept of agency (e.g., Harré, 1984; Harré & Secord, 1972; Taylor, 1977). Harré (1984) conceives of personal agency as a kind of release for potential action, and he has employed the following conveyance metaphor to elaborate his meaning: "In preparing to set off a race the starter creates a state of readiness in the runners with his 'Get Set.' The subsequent 'Go' can be thought of as a releaser" (p. 189).

Inherent tendencies: persons as natural entities

One of the oldest and still prevalent motivational conceptions is that people behave the way they do because it is *natural* for them to do so. Systems based on this root metaphor have difficulty explicating individual differences in behavior, but they do so to some extent by positing different natural behavior repertoires for men, women, and children. Conceptions of human nature – and hence of natural behavior – date back at least to ancient Sumer (Kramer, 1963), and there are numerous implicit allusions to the nature of man in Homer, in early biblical writings, and in the literature of early China and India.

It is important to emphasize that the term "natural" is not being employed here in the limited sense of "instinctive," "inherited," or "genetic." These concepts, reflective of more modern approaches to the continuity of human nature, were not involved in the formative stages of the inherent-tendencies metaphor, nor are they part of its essence. The reference of "natural," as applied to human beings, is simply to the way people intrinsically are, as represented in Aristotle's (ca. 330 B.C./1947) statement that "all men naturally desire knowledge" (p. 3). That is, people seek to learn new things because it is natural for them to do so. In discussing human nature, which has always been taken to refer primarily to the motivational makeup of human beings, some authors, like Aristotle, have described certain posited natural motives, whereas others have simply asserted that certain desires or tendencies were implanted by God or by an anthropomorphized Nature.

Systematic discussions of natural motives were inaugurated in the classical Greek period. The Greek word that we translate as "nature" is *phusis*. The etymology of this term suggests that its original meaning, later metaphorically extended, was "manner of growth" (Adkins, 1970, p. 79). Aristotle developed a large catalog of natural desires and behavioral tendencies (Griffin, 1931), including desires for food, warmth, sexual relations, care of the young, and many others. The early Stoic philosophers were primarily responsible for developing a speculative taxonomy of the human passions. Their general model, concerned with supposedly natural motivational affects, lasted – with numerous additions and variations – for two millennia. History, then, has witnessed the postulation of a wide assortment of motives held to be inherent in human nature. I will spotlight several of these to illustrate the role of metaphors in the historical development of the inherent-tendencies theme.

First, consider the passion of love, a broadly construed human inclination of tremendous interest to Renaissance philosopher-psychologists. The following selection, which I give at some length in order to convey its overall context, is from *A Table of Humane Passions* (1620/1621), by the French philosopher Nicolas Coeffeteau:

> As it is the custome of men to refer the noblest effects to the most excellent causes; many considering the dignity of *love*, have imagined that this *Passion* came from a particular impression, which God makes in our *Soules*, inspiring into them with the *nature*, the affections which transport them, and which makes them seeke the objects which are pleasing unto them. The which they strive to prove by the example of the naturall inclinations which he hath given to other Creatures. Wee see, say they, that God as the Author of *nature,* hath ingrafted into light things an inclination to rise upward, to seeke the place of their rest, by reason whereof the fire doth always send his flame towards *heaven*. And in like manner hee hath imprinted in heavy things a naturall inclination which makes them tend to the *center*: so as stones, marbles, and such like, do always bend downeward, & do not hang in the aire, but with violence and contrary to their inclination. In the same manner, say they, God hath ingrafted in man a certain inclination to those things

which have some beames of beauty or bounty, so as when these objects come to incounter his eyes or minde, he is ravished, and then presently there is framed in his heart an ardent desire to seek and pursue them. (pp. 83–5)

What is Coeffeteau's purpose in using this metaphor of "ingrafting"? It is not to introduce a new explanatory concept, or simply to clarify his exposition. I suggest that it is primarily *persuasive,* that is, to convince the reader of the plausibility of the view that the inclination to love is implanted by God. Coeffeteau tries to do so by showing that this proposition is analogous to something the reader (in that period) already took for granted, namely, the Aristotelean conception of upward and downward motion.

As a second example of metaphors used in the service of the inherent-tendencies theme, I refer to Coeffeteau's treatment of pleasure and pain. The passage, in the same book, reads as follows:

As this great *Fabricke* of the heavens [19] makes his motion upon the two Poles of the world, which are as it were the two points where it beginnes and ends: So it seemes that all the Passions of our soules depend upon *Pleasure* and *Paine,* which grow from the contentment or distaste which we receive from the diverse objects which present themselves to us in the course of this life. (pp. 244–5)

The contention that pleasure and pain are the natural arbiters of behavior is an old one. Perhaps its best-known formulation is Jeremy Bentham's (1789/1948) metaphorical expression that "Nature has placed mankind under the governance of two sovereign masters, pain and pleasure. It is for them alone to point out what we ought to do, as well as to determine what we shall do" (p. 1).[20]

For my next illustration I am indebted to David Leary (1977), who has called attention to an interesting employment of analogy in George Berkeley's social theory. (The very fact that Berkeley, famous for his idealism, had a social theory will perhaps surprise many.) The essence of Berkeley's (1713/1955) position was an emphasis on the inherent nature of human sociability. To portray his conception, Berkeley drew a parallel between social tendencies and gravitational concepts as then recently codified in Newtonian theory. The following, somewhat truncated selection expresses the analogy:

Philosophers are now agreed that there is a mutual attraction between the most distant parts at least of this solar system.... Now, if we carry our thoughts from the corporeal to the moral world, we may observe in the Spirits or Minds of men a like principle of attraction, whereby are drawn together in communities, clubs, families, friendships, and all the various species of society. As in bodies, where the quantity is the same, the attraction is strongest between those which are placed nearest to each other, so is it likewise in the minds of men, *caeteris paribus,* between those which are most nearly related. (pp. 225–6)[21]

An important contemporary of Berkeley was Francis Hutcheson. Hutcheson, in company with a number of other philosophers of his period, in particular Shaftesbury, espoused a natural human tendency toward benevolence, or what today is termed altruism. Like Berkeley and practically all other savants in the early eighteenth century, Hutcheson was influenced by Newton. It is therefore not surprising to find Hutcheson (1725) framing the following comparison:

> This *universal Benevolence* toward all Men, we may compare to that Principle of *Gravitation*, which perhaps extends to all Bodys in the *Universe*; but, like the *Love* of *Benevolence, increases* as the Distance is diminished, and is *strongest* when Bodys come to *touch* each other. . . . This *increase* of *Love* towards the *Benevolent* according to their *nearer Approaches to our selves* by their *Benefits*, is observable in the high degree of *Love,* which *Heroes* and *Law-givers* universally obtain in their own Countrys, above what they find abroad. (pp. 198–9)

It is instructive that both Berkeley and Hutcheson employed gravitational metaphors to state their cases. Although it would be difficult to prove, it seems that it was through the creative use of analogies from Newton's conception of gravitation (its postulated universality and its inverse square law) that Hutcheson, like Berkeley, came up with the ideas he proposed concerning sociability and benevolence. In any case, it is interesting to note how Berkeley and Hutcheson utilized the then very recent Newtonian theory of gravitation and how, at an earlier time, Coeffeteau used the then prevailing Aristotelean conception of forces. Clearly, the specific comparisons made by these theorists reflected the historical contexts in which they lived.

My final illustration of a productive analogy in the naturalistic mode is less clear-cut, but very interesting. In the year 1692, Christian Thomasius, a leading figure in the German Enlightenment, proposed a model of personality that postulated four inherent human inclinations: sensuousness, acquisitiveness, social ambition, and rational love. The strikingly innovative aspect of Thomasius's conceptualization is that it was proposed along with a method of systematically applying numerical rating scales in the assessment of these four motivational variables (McReynolds & Ludwig, 1984). In addition, Thomasius reported quantitative information derived from five persons, including what amounts to reliability data concerning one case. This work appears to constitute the first documented systematic collection and analysis of quantitative data on actual subjects in the entire history of psychology.

Thomasius's approach to reliability – having the same person rated independently by two judges – was suggested to him by the following analogy, as expressed in his own words (translated and quoted in Mc-Reynolds & Ludwig, 1984):

> Just as in mathematics, where there is no better way to check to see if one has calculated correctly than to repeat the process two or three times in order to find out if the sum is the same, I have thought that in the discovery of other truths, regardless of what discipline it may be, this method might be the best way of checking [the accuracy of this science]. (p. 551)

An intriguing question is, Where did Thomasius get the idea of rating psychological dimensions? In addition, why did he utilize a sixty-point scale rather than a scale of ten, twenty or some other number of points? Although we can only conjecture, there is no harm in exploring possible clues. Most likely Thomasius got his basic idea from an analogy based on temperature scales. Though accurate and standardized thermometers had not been developed by 1692, the idea of linear temperature scales was well established and presumably well known to Thomasius.[22] The subsequent choice of a sixty-point scale may have been based on an analogy with time measurement as carried out by mechanical clocks. The number 60 has, of course, been significant in Western culture since it served as the base for the number system of the ancient Sumerians, but it was in the latter part of the seventeenth century that clocks began to have minute hands that marked off hours in sixty equal units.

In the modern era the inherent-tendency approach to motivation was afforded strong support by the writings of Charles Darwin (1859, 1871) and William James (1890), both of whom emphasized instinctive factors in behavior. Though instinct theories are now out of style, they have been succeeded by analogous ethological conceptions (see Eibl-Eibesfeldt, 1970; Klopfer & Hailman, 1967). Though ethologists have concentrated on animal behavior, their work has definite implications for human motivation. Other inherent-tendency approaches (e.g., Cattell & Child, 1975; Eysenck, 1967) have been largely assimilated into genetic conceptualizations, though only in a very preliminary way. At the level of folk theories of motivation, interpretations of behavior in terms of conceptions of basic human nature are commonplace.

Bodily processes: persons as organisms

The essence of the bodily-processes metaphor for motivation – that humans are animate, organic beings – does not preclude the simultaneous application of the person-as-agent, person-as-natural-entity, and person-as-machine guiding metaphors. Conceptions of the nature of animate beings have changed over the centuries, but this fact need not trouble us here, since our goal is not an ultimate specification of what life is, but a clarification of the role that conceptions of the living organism have played historically in motivational theory.

In this context it is important to note that an animate world view, in which all reality is interpreted as being alive and as possessing feeling and wishes, has been prevalent throughout much of human history. This view was not limited to primitive peoples or to early civilizations. On the contrary, as we will see shortly, it persisted in some degree until the eighteenth century. Such a perspective obviously facilitated attempts to interpret behaviors in terms of organic processes, as these were understood at different times and in different places.

An early, though limited, organismic conception of motives was offered by Plato in his *Philebus* (31d–32d; Hamilton & Cairns, 1961, pp. 1109–10). In this dialogue Socrates proposes that a state of distress in a living creature follows a disturbance of harmony and that the distress caused by such a state (e.g., hunger or thirst) leads to restorative efforts. This formulation is clearly an adumbration of modern physiological-deficit models of motivation.

Aristotle, primarily a biological theorist, was strongly oriented toward an organismic motivational perspective. In his *Movement of Animals* (ca. 340 B.C./1968), he employs a number of metaphors to elaborate the nature of motivated behavior:

> The movement of animals resembles that of marionettes which move as the result of a small movement, when the strings are released and strike one another; or a toy-carriage which the child that is riding upon it himself sets in motion in a straight direction, and which afterwards moves in a circle because its wheels are unequal.... Animals have similar parts in their organs, namely the growth of their sinews and bones, the latter corresponding to the pegs in the marionettes and iron [presumably a reference to a part of the carriage], while the sinews correspond to the strings, the setting free and loosening of which causes the movement. (pp. 463–4)[23]

A contemporary reader coming upon these words for the first time is likely to see in them an early instance of the person-as-machine metaphor. This, however, would be incorrect. The machine paradigm was still some two millennia in the future (about two thousand years separate Aristotle from Hobbes and Descartes), and Aristotle's purpose in employing a mechanical metaphor was not to insist that animals are actually machines, but rather, as a biologist, to portray the nature of animal movement by relating it to something familiar to his audience. The fact that passages similar to the one just quoted were put forward in the

seventeenth and eighteenth centuries to argue for a machine model illustrates how similar metaphors can be employed for quite different
purposes and how the message intended by a metaphor is very much a
function of its context.

The major organismic conceptualization developed in the ancient world
was the theory of the humors. Originally systematized by Hippocrates as
an explanation of diseases, it was later elaborated and extended by Galen
and others to comprise a theory of temperament. The general notion
of the latter theory, as is well known, was that certain temperamental
orientations, such as cheerfulness and irritability, are determined by
bodily constituents of the kind that we nowadays would label biochemical.
Though primarily an affective theory, humorology also had obvious motivational implications. For instance, humoral theorists supposed that the
amount of phlegm affected the vigor of actions. So far as humorology
provided a motivational psychology, it is appropriate to note that Galen's
original development of the fourfold-temperament conception in the
second century A.D. appears to have been stimulated, at least in large
part, by an analogy with Hippocrates' disease model – and that the latter
was itself derived from the Greek conception of four primary organismic
qualities (hot, cold, dry, and wet). These four qualities were transferred
by Galen to the psychological realm when, for example, he attributed a
quickly changing mind to an excess of bodily heat, emotional stability
to coolness, and so on (Siegel, 1970, p. 210). These metaphors are still
embedded in our common language, as when we say that a person is hot-
tempered or is cool in the presence of danger.

As noted earlier, the concept of motivation encompasses the phenomenon of movement, and early writers who took the organismic perspective were especially interested in how animal motion could be explained.
It was recognized very early – by the Hellenistic period and possibly
before – that animal motion in some manner involves directives sent out
from the brain by means of the nerves to the musculature, which in turn
actually effect movement. A central problem in this analysis was the
means by which the messages travel along the nerves. The question was
not resolved, of course, until the modern era, with the understanding of
bioelectric processes, but the intervening centuries brought forth a variety
of speculations.

Galen conceived that some unspecified alteration in quality moves
along the nerve, and he likened this to the manner in which light and heat
are transmitted from the sun (Siegel, 1970, p. 194). The most general
approach until the modern period, however, was to picture the nerves as
tubes through which "animal spirits" pass from the ventricles of the brain
to the muscles. As the muscles supposedly fill with animal spirits they
expand, thus bringing about movement through an essentially hydraulic
process (Esper, 1964, p. 100; Jaynes, 1970). As an example of this notion

of neural transmission, I quote briefly from an anatomy lecture given in 1620: "Nerves have no perceptible cavity internally . . . but their internal substance is continuous and porous, whereby it gives a passage to the animal spirit, which is exceedingly rapid in motion and is carried through this substance with an irradiant rapidity, just as we see light moving through air" (quoted by French, 1975, p. 15).[24]

Before closing this section, I wish to comment briefly on the origins of hydraulic analogies, which have played so great a role in motivation theory. Empedocles (fifth century B.C.), so far as written evidence indicates, was the first philosopher to apply the hydraulic notion to organisms. In his *On Nature* (Esper, 1964, p. 96; Leonard, 1908, p. 47, fragment 100; Worthen, 1970), he compared the functions of passages (tubes) within the body to the phenomenon of a girl holding a container ("a water-clock of gleaming bronze") under water with her hand over an opening so that the air within prevents water from entering. Empedocles' somewhat ambiguous simile, and the fact that he is traditionally associated with the development of the pneumatic school of medicine, suggest that his thoughts may have been instrumental in the eventual development of systematic hydraulic theories. We may more safely presume that the actual hydraulic and pneumatic apparatuses, as described by Hero of Alexandria (ca. A.D. 62/1971), were of suggestive value to early motivation theorists.

Hydraulic analogies, it would seem, have proved almost essential to motivational psychologists, and their day in the sun has hardly ended. Without elaboration and without specifying whether they support the person-as-organism or the person-as-machine root metaphor, I shall simply list a number of quasi-hydraulic analogies recently or currently employed in motivational theory: Freud's (1940/1964) conception of cathexes, in which libidinal energies, in order to be invested in one object, must be withdrawn from another object; Jung's (1928/1960) principle of equivalence, according to which psychic energy can be attached to one interest only if released from another attachment; Hull's (1943) motivation theory, which assumes that the forces from several motives sum up to yield an overall drive (D); Lorenz's action-specific energy model, in which different energy sources, conceptualized as figuratively filling a reservoir, build up pressure to bring about release (see Klopfer & Hailman, 1967, pp. 42–3); and my own theory of anxiety, which attributes the intensity of that affect to the level of unassimilated experiences (McReynolds, 1976). The most common example of a hydraulic motivational metaphor lies in the popular notion that people need to "let off steam" from time to time as the pressure from accumulated irritations increases.[25]

Clearly, the organismic approach to human motivation is highly prominent in contemporary psychology. This biological emphasis underlies work on such topics as the role of hormonal factors, brain functions, and other physiological factors in behavior (for a review, see Mook, 1987). I should note too that there has been a concerted tendency to incorporate the organismic paradigm within the mechanistic paradigm.

Inner forces: persons as machines

The predominant contemporary motivational paradigm is based on the machine metaphor. People are conceived as machines, and the expression and interaction of motives are interpreted in terms of the operations and effects that characterize mechanisms. It is, to be sure, not easy to know precisely what constitutes a mechanism. There was a time when the word "machine" conjured up images of gear tracks, pulleys, levers, and the like, and perhaps it still does. Such a picture, however, is hardly adequate in a period in which the most sophisticated apparatuses include transistors, X-rays, and laser beams. Fortunately, it is not necessary for our present purposes that we have a rigorous definition of machines, since our concern is not primarily with machines per se, but rather with people's conceptions of machines.[26]

In this context let us briefly examine the history of the machine metaphor as applied to motivation and consider in particular how it came to be differentiated from the animate-being metaphor. For several millennia, probably since the beginnings of systematic human thought, there was a tendency (as we noted earlier) for people to attribute life, at least in some lower sense, to objects that we now consider inanimate. This perspective had remarkable staying power. For example, it was commonly assumed – and not just by the alchemists – that metals were in some sense alive. As late as the latter part of the seventeenth century, John Locke (ca. 1720/1877) wrote, "All stones, metals, and minerals are real vegetables; that is, grow organically from proper seeds, as well as plants" (p. 486). The animate paradigm began to be systematically supplanted by the mechanical paradigm in the seventeenth century, and by the nineteenth century the dominant world view, at least in the West, revolved around the machine analog. This transition, though somewhat abrupt in historical terms, did not occur overnight and is fascinating to study.

Today, with the dominance of the machine metaphor, we are likely to say that the human brain is like a computer, but in the transitional period, when the animate perspective was still powerful, one was just as likely to understand a physicalistic phenomenon by comparing it to something animate. For example, Arabian alchemists "compared the transmutation of diseased metals into gold to the medical cure of sickness. They thought of the furnace for the metal as if it were a hospital cot for the invalid" (J. C. Gregory, 1927, p. 301). Francis Bacon, though a strong harbinger of the developing mechanistic perspective, still thought, as Gregory puts it, in terms of an *"inanimate equivalent* of animate behavior" (p. 304). Thus, Bacon conceived that "inanimate bodies had a 'kind of appetite' to choose the pleasing or avoid the unacceptable.... Water would hang in droplets to avoid discontinuance ... gold leaves preferred the point of a finger to the neighbourhood of the atmosphere" (p. 304), and so on.

Perhaps the most intriguing instance of a physicalism-to-animism analogy is that believed to have been utilized by Newton (1687/1974) in the formative stages of his theory of gravitation. Though explicit documentary evidence is lacking, there is reason to believe that Newton's revolutionary insight grew out of analogies from the animate realm (see Dobbs, 1975; Guerlac, 1983; Manuel, 1968, pp. 73–4, 84–5; Westfall, 1980; see also Leary, Chapter 1, this volume). Before the *Principia*, the developing mechanistic philosophy of nature was framed in terms of particles in motion, acting directly on one another. Newton's epochal move was to posit that bodies attract each other at a distance, without necessary intermediary bridges. Though his notion was considered occult by many and had implications bothersome to Newton himself, its far-reaching influence cannot be doubted. How did Newton come upon such an idea? What was its germinal origin in his mind? Apparently, Newton reached this conception through analogical reasoning based on his intensive studies of alchemy, a field populated by such concepts such as "active principles," "attraction," "repulsion," and the "sociability"[27] of substances (Dobbs, 1975; Westfall, 1980). Ultimately, once his theory was further developed, Newton attributed the physical forces in the universe to God's will (Guerlac, 1983).

What factors led to the rise of the mechanistic world view and thus to a mechanistic conception of motivation in the seventeenth and eighteenth centuries? A partial answer seems to lie in the popularity during that period of lifelike, mechanically animated figures, or automata, which were sometimes found in public places. Such moving replicas of humans and animals, with their complex contrivances of wheels, cams, and levers, could well have suggested that humans and animals actually are machines, though somewhat more complex than the existent automata. Indeed, we know from Descartes's own testimony that analogies based on the automata found in the grottoes of Paris were instrumental in his conceptualization of animals as machines (Descartes, 1662/1972; Jaynes, 1970). This is particularly relevant testimony since Descartes's theories are usually accepted as seminal in the eventual development of the machine model.[28]

Nevertheless, and without depreciating the influence of automata, I am not inclined to assign them a singular role in the eventual triumph of the mechanistic world view. For one thing, seventeenth-century automata, though possibly more complex than those of previous eras, were hardly novel. It is now well documented that complex machines, including intricate automata (Bedini, 1964; Brumbaugh, 1966; Chapuis & Droz, 1958; Hero, ca. A.D. 62/1971; McReynolds, 1971; Price, 1964) and even an early computer-like device (Price, 1959), existed in ancient Greco-Roman culture. Thus, it is clear that factors other than the mere existence of automata are necessary to explain the emergence of the machine paradigm.

It is fairly obvious what these crucial factors were. Specifically, they were (1) the development of a new conception of motion and (2) the spread of mechanical clocks, many of which involved automata, including human figures constructed to strike the hours. Since both of these factors were intimately involved in the development of the mechanical metaphor for motivation, I will discuss each of them separately.

First, the concept of motion. Aristotle had proposed a theory of motion that dominated thought up to and in some respects beyond the time of Galileo. This conceptualization emphasized the inherent capacity of animals to engage in self-initiated movement, in contrast to inanimate objects, which move only when pushed or pulled or when seeking their natural position. This last point is important: It was assumed that heavy objects such as stones naturally move downward toward the center of the universe (conceived as the center of the earth) and that light objects, such as smoke, naturally move upward. An important exception to these generalities was the movement of the heavenly bodies, which were thought to be animate. For them the natural movement was supposed to be circular. Further, the natural state of all terrestrial bodies was considered to be rest, so that for an object to be kept in motion it was presumed that continuous force had to be applied. (For a psychological analogy based on Aristotle's conception, see the quotation from Coeffeteau that is given earlier.)

This complex, but highly influential model ran into certain problems even in Aristotle's day, and it came under increasing attack in the late medieval and Renaissance periods. The new paradigm of motion, represented most definitively in the work of Galileo and Newton, emphasized rectilinear motion and the tendency of bodies to stay at rest or to continue in motion, as the case might be, and erased any underlying difference between the movements of terrestrial and heavenly bodies. The long-term effects of this revolution in the conception of motion were extremely far reaching. Butterfield (1957) even concluded that "of all the intellectual hurdles which the human mind has confronted and overcome in the last fifteen hundred years, the one most stupendous in the scope of its consequences is the one relating to the problem of motion" (p. 15).

This paradigm shift in the conception of motion had important implications for psychology, and especially for motivation theory. This is not surprising given that the term "motive," in its psychological sense, originally referred to the nature and sources of animal and human movement. The influence of the new conception of motion was particularly apparent in the seventeenth-century writings of Thomas Hobbes, who was strongly influenced by Galileo. Hobbes, working from an analogy with the role of motion in physics, developed a materialistic theory in which mental activity was equated with infinitely small motions, or "endeavors," in the nerves and the brain. The concept of "endeavor," as we noted earlier, was subsequently used by Newton (see note 27). As employed by Hobbes, it had a distinctly motivational cast, being used, for instance, to explain appetitive and aversive tendencies. As Peters (1967) has observed, "The postulation of these minute movements in the bodies of animals and men made the suggestion plausible that human action as well as the movement of projectiles can be explained mechanically. After all men move forwards and away from objects and each other" (p. 87).[29]

The second important factor in the rise of the mechanistic world view, and more particularly of the mechanistic conception of motives, was the spread of mechanical clocks. Though horological devices of various sorts, some of them quite complex, can be traced well back into the medieval and ancient periods, it was in the fourteenth century and thereafter that large, mechanical, weight-driven clocks began to appear throughout Europe. For some time the more prominent of the clocks included complex automata, thus reflecting the persistence of the animistic world view. During the sixteenth century, or perhaps even before, a new form of motive force – the use of metal springs that could be tightened – was developed. This made it possible to construct much smaller as well as portable clocks.

As clocks improved in accuracy and portability, and became more widely disseminated, they came to be viewed as amazing, miraculous, even lifelike devices. This attitude was vividly expressed in a rhetorical question asked by the philosopher John Amos Comenius (1657/1910): "Is it not a truly marvelous thing that a machine, a soulless thing, can move in such a life-like, continuous, and regular manner?" (p. 96). It is not clear, this long after the event, who first had the creative inspiration that the human mind, or at least the animal mind, might be thought of as analogous to a clock, but eventually the clock metaphor became very prominent in psychological thought. Among the many seventeenth- and eighteenth-century authors who utilized the clock metaphor in explicating human behavior were Hobbes, Descartes, and La Mettrie.

It is important to emphasize the special relevance of the clock analogy to motivation theory. This relationship derives primarily from the significance of metaphors that focused on the analogy between the sources of power in clocks and the motive forces in animals and persons. Thus, we find Comenius stating, with respect to early clocks, that "the weights are the desires and affections which incline the will this way or that" (p. 48).

Later, as clocks became more sophisticated, it was the spring (specifically the mainspring) that constituted the imported analog for conceptualizing motivation in mechanical terms. Thus, Julien de La Mettrie, in his influential *Man a Machine* (1748/1912), referred to the human brain as the "mainspring of the whole machine" (p. 135), and William Paley (1825) noted that "when we see the watch *going,* we see proof . . . that there is a power somewhere . . . that there is a secret spring . . . in a word, that there is force, and energy, as well as mechanism" (p. 525).

As I have proposed elsewhere (McReynolds, 1980), the clock metaphor, including the provision of an internal power source that keeps the mechanism functioning, was instrumental in delineating the conception of inner forces, or motives, in humans and animals.[30] Though the general notion of motivation is an old one, and medieval and Renaissance philosophers posited a motivational faculty ("motiva") to carry out the directives of the soul, the idea of motives as inner forces or impetuses had to await not only the elucidation of the concept of force by Galileo, Newton, and others, but also the specific analog of the spring-driven clock. By the end of the eighteenth century the term "motive," in its modern psychological sense, had come into general use (e.g., Bentham, 1789/1948, 1815/1969; Hutcheson, 1725; Locke, 1690/1959). It is interesting that the term "motive power" also came to be employed in physics (e.g., Carnot, 1824/1960).

As the dominant world view shifted from that of an animate perspective to that of mechanism (Dijksterhuis, 1969), it began to seem natural to conceptualize different aspects of reality in mechanical terms. Thus, even after the use of the clock metaphor declined in the eighteenth and nineteenth centuries, other machine-like analogs were used to sustain and advance the mechanistic model of motivation.[31] The essence of this paradigm, as it developed, was the assumption of internal conditions or states that automatically drive or impel an animal or person into given behavioral channels. These inner motive forces were conceived as arising mechanically and necessarily within the individual. The grand success of Newton's (1687/1974) gravitational theory suggested to various philosophers that concepts and approaches analogous to those employed by Newton might be productive in the human sciences. Earlier quotations in this chapter, from the works of Berkeley and Hutcheson, reflect this view. More systematic attempts to borrow creatively from Newton were made by Locke, Hume, Hartley, Kant, and Herbert (see Lowry, 1971).

The nineteenth century saw the rapid development of thermodynamic theory in physics, which fostered the further delineation of the concepts of energy and entropy. These concepts were adapted analogically by certain theorists. Both Freud (see Holt, 1968) and Jung (1928/1960) utilized the notion of psychic energy, and McDougall (1933) posited the existence of mental energy. The principle of entropy and the conservation of energy contributed by suggestive example to a number of hydraulic motivational models, as discussed earlier in this chapter.

Coming to the present period we find that motivation theory in the twentieth century has been dominated by two broad conceptualizations: psychoanalytic theory and drive theory. Both of these approaches have involved the significant use of conveyance metaphors. Psychoanalytic motivation theory, developed by Freud (1917/1963, 1933/1964, 1940/1964) from the end of the last century into the 1930s, can be seen as an incongruous but productive marriage of the person-as-agent and person-as-machine metaphors. The concept of the ego is reflective of personal control, but the greater part of psychoanalytic motivation theory, with its emphasis on the interplay of inner forces, is clearly mechanistic. Freud himself was a prolific inventor and user of metaphors (Nash, 1962; Thomä & Kächele, 1987; see also Leary, Chapter 1, this volume). In this connection, one thinks not only of Freud's extensive hydraulic analogies, to which I alluded earlier, but also of his postulation of a "censor" guarding against the entry of "repressed" material into consciousness; his proposal of dramatic interrelations among the anthropomorphic ego, id, and superego; and so forth. As Leary has observed, Freud's use of metaphors was deliberate and nonapologetic. Further, as Nash has pointed out, "Freud not only illustrated by metaphor, he also conceived in metaphor" (p. 25).

Probably the most widely employed technical term in motivational psychology in this century has been "drive." This term was introduced by Woodworth in 1918, along with the companion term "mechanism." (The term "mechanism" failed to catch on in motivation theory.) It is interesting that Woodworth employed metaphors in order to delineate the meaning of these concepts. Using the example of a baseball pitcher, he described mechanism as the problem of aiming, gauging the distance, and coordinating movements, and drive as the answer to the questions why the man is pitching at all, why he pitches better on one day than another, and so on (pp. 36–7). "The distinction between drive and mechanism may become clearer," Woodworth (1918) wrote, "if we consider it in the case of a machine. The drive here is the power applied to make the mechanism go; the mechanism is made to go, and is relatively passive" (p. 37).[32] Following Woodworth, other psychologists developed drive theory. Most important among them was Clark Hull (1943, 1952), who revealed his early commitment to a mechanistic approach in the following diary entry for 1 March 1926: "It has struck me many times of late that the human organism is one of the most extraordinary machines – and yet a machine" (Hull, 1962, p. 820).

Though both psychoanalytic theory and drive theory are now less central to motivational psychology than before, they are still influential, and a number of newer mechanistic motivational conceptions have gained recognition. These include optimal-level theory and opponent-process theory. Optimal-level theory (summarized in Arkes & Garske, 1977, pp. 144–65) holds that individuals seek to maintain optimal levels (not too much and not too little) of certain psychological variables, such as the amount of novelty that one is experiencing or the extent that one is aroused. Though this theory has many roots, it was stimulated in part by an analogy with Cannon's (1932) conception of homeostasis (Mook, 1987; Stagner, 1977), which held that organisms are so constituted as to maintain a proper balance within physiological systems. Opponent-process theory, developed by Solomon and Corbit (1974), is concerned with the fact that certain experiences that are either pleasant or unpleasant tend, when terminated, to be followed by an opposite affect (see Mook, 1987). For example, certain drugs yield positive affects, but the withdrawal feelings are distinctly unpleasant. The essential theme of this theory was borrowed by analogy from sensory psychology (Hurvich & Jameson, 1957).

In conclusion, the person-as-machine metaphor has tended to dominate motivational theorizing in recent decades, and it has tended to incorporate both the person-as-natural-entity and the person-as-organism themes. Further, both contemporary behaviorism and current cognitive psychology are essentially mechanistic in style. The only serious rival to the machine analogy on the current scene is the person-as-agent metaphor, which (as noted earlier) has shown a striking resurgence in recent years.

Theoretical implications

Having completed our historical survey, we are now in a position to see what lessons and suggestions may be gleaned from the record of the past. Perhaps the most clear-cut and not unexpected conclusion is that analogical thinking has been widely employed throughout the two and a half millennia of formal thought about motivation. The specific examples that I have given constitute only a small fraction, though I think a representative fraction, of the metaphors that motivation theorists have devised. The general pattern has been that a particular way of conceptualizing motivation has been developed or modified by importing analogs from other content domains.

My primary purpose in taking a longitudinal approach in this survey has been to enable us to get an overall picture of the topic under review, to see – to put it figuratively – the forest rather than the trees. In this context, we may ask where the imported analogs for motivation metaphors have come from. Our review clearly indicates that they have come from all over – from wherever thinkers and scientists have found what seemed to be relevant instances. For example, motivation theorists have borrowed analogs from music (e.g., dissonance motivation), from politics (e.g., censoring motives), and even from other fields of psychology (e.g., the opponent-process motivational model). More generally, it appears that analogs have most frequently been drawn either from the fund of general wisdom and experience familiar to everyone or from nonpsychological areas that enjoy high prestige. Instances of the first sort include, for example, different versions of the clock analogy as well as most of the motivational metaphors employed by Plato, Descartes, and Freud. In contrast, metaphors of the second class include those adapted from the physical sciences, such as those relying on concepts from Newtonian theory. This reference to physical science analogs as examples of the second sort presumes, of course, that the prevailing world view accords higher prestige to the physical sciences than to psychology and the other life sciences. It is worth noting in this regard that in an earlier age, when the animistic perspective was dominant, physical scientists commonly imported analogies from the animate world in order to afford their concepts an aura of greater reality. The physical notion of force, for instance, was often explicated by analogy to human physical strength.

Thus, the typical *direction* of a scientific metaphor or analogy is from a *more* prestigious and credible domain to a *less* prestigious and credible domain. Consider, for instance, the expression "human benevolence is like gravity." One of the implications of this statement is that benevolence is universal, and one of the aims of its reliance on a scientific metaphor is to make this theoretical position seem more plausible, more convincing, by associating it with a proposition or phenomenon that the audience already takes for granted. Of course, what is taken for granted differs from one era and from one audience to another, so it should not be surprising that there has been a continual change over time in the choice of specific (conveyance) motivational analogies. Thus, whereas Newtonian mechanics once spawned a number of inertia analogies, more recently it has been physical field theories in the tradition of Einstein's relativity theory that have suggested newer motivational conceptions like those of Kurt Lewin (1939).[33] Currently, as noted earlier, a major development in motivational psychology is optimal-level theory. This approach utilizes analogs from both technology (e.g., the thermostat) and biology (Cannon's concept of homeostasis).

Taken together, these observations suggest that the metaphors employed in motivational psychology tend to be *topical*, to draw on relevant *new* sources as these become available. But though this is so, it is also true that certain metaphorical themes in the area of motivation are amazingly persistent. I am thinking, for example, of the innumerable restatements and reincarnations of the hydraulic analogy. Another enduring theme is the concept of various bodily or psychological deficits or needs. Further, the same theme may appear in similar metaphors at widely separated times. For example, in a dramatic description reminiscent of Plato's image of the two steeds, Freud (1933/1964) compared the ego's relation to the id to that of a rider on his horse. Similarly, the clock metaphor is still used, at least in common speech ("I wonder what makes him tick?"). However, fundamentally different underlying metaphors may be supported by essentially similar topical analogs. For example, the automata that Descartes and others used to support the machine paradigm were not radically different from the marionettes with which Aristotle illustrated the organismic paradigm.

Frequently, scientific metaphors appear to flow rather directly from prevailing world views – often, I suspect, without the theorist being aware of this fact. That the universe and all its parts, including persons, are basically mechanisms is the implicit assumption underlying most current motivational theorizing, but the majority of contemporary theorists probably do not realize that the mechanistic paradigm is itself a metaphor on the grand scale. This observation leads me to propose that metaphors can in principle be conceptualized hierarchically, from the most all-encompassing instances, such as the animistic paradigm and the machine paradigm, to the most particularistic and trivial ones, as when one might construct a metaphor that has meaning only for a very limited audience. It is, I suggest, the higher, broader analogies, which I have referred to as basic or root metaphors, that serve as guides, often implicitly, to theory construction. The lower-level, more particularistic metaphors are more likely to serve an expository role.[34]

An interesting question is, When do metaphors come into play? What occasions their construction? Metaphors are devised, of course, by persons acting under individual needs and whims. Consequently their advent cannot be predicted in any rigorous way. Yet certain generalities are suggested by our survey. One is that metaphors appear to arise in times and areas of ignorance and uncertainty and to persist as live metaphors for as long as the questions at issue remain clouded or undecided, and as long as the imported analog retains its credibility.[35] In other words, theorists are likely to reach for a metaphor when they are faced by a problem. Examples of this are provided by the great variety of metaphorical descriptions of neural transmission that were devised over the years until the problematic nature of bioelectrical transmission was finally resolved. A second kind of situation in which metaphors are likely to be generated is brought about by the introduction and development of a new high-order (or basic) metaphor. Thus, the person-as-machine conception stimulated, or was associated with, a great variety of mechanistic analogs – clocks, automata, mills, telephone switchboards, and other devices.

Further, on the basis of our foregoing survey, I believe that metaphors are less likely to appear in areas of immediate personal significance and/or experience than in domains that are more personally remote. That is, metaphors appear not to be as necessary for the elaboration of phenomena that are already personally meaningful. In support of this interpretation I refer to the fact that concepts of the soul and human agency, both of which refer to personal, inner experiencing and both of which have motivational significance, have generated relatively few metaphors. Similarly, directly experienced motivational tendencies, such as hunger, thirst, pain, and pleasure, have not frequently been described metaphorically.[36] In contrast, extensive use of figurative language has been employed for the person-as-machine paradigm, which seems a less "natural" and less immediately understandable way of construing human behavior.

What are the uses or functions of metaphors in science? The foregoing historical survey suggests that analogical thinking serves three distinct functions: descriptive, persuasive, and creative. The first and last of these correspond to what Park et al. (1984) refer to as the expository and explanatory roles of analogy.[37]

Descriptive uses of analogy are important didactically in *delineating* and *communicating* motivational conceptions. Descriptive metaphors tend to involve generally familiar analogs – analogs familiar, that is, to the theorist's intended audience. For example, consider Plato's metaphor of the chariot and Freud's comparison of the tie-up of psychic energy (in fixation) to the analog of a portion of an army staying behind the general advance in order to maintain control over a conquered territory. These metaphors were surely familiar to Plato's and Freud's diverse audiences and would have helped their audiences understand the phenomena they were trying to describe.

Persuasive analogies are intended to *convince* an audience. In the case of science the audience is typically the relevant scientific community, though it may (especially initially) be restricted to the theorist. Persuasive metaphors are argumentative and frequently syllogistic. They tend to take the following form: *A* is obviously true; *B* is like *A*; therefore *B* is probably true. Theories cannot be validated in analogistic arguments, but they can be made to seem plausible, aesthetically appealing, and worthy of further consideration. An example, presented earlier, would be Coeffeteau's analogical comparison between human love and the then highly credible Aristotelian conception of natural forces.

Of special interest is the third, explanatory function of metaphor, which suggests a truly *creative* use of analogy. The primary audience here is the scientist, and the aim is to *solve* a theoretical problem by coming to see the relevant phenomenon in a new way. Sometimes, of course, the theorist may have no specific aim – no explicit question to answer. On such occasions the new analog may appear adventitiously, as did the clock analog and more recently the computer analog, but in any case it opens up new and unexpected vistas for theoretical exploration. The virtue of the creative metaphor is that it permits the theorist to conceptualize data in a different way, to reexamine previously accepted verities. Some of the new directions opened up may lead to permanent advances; others may lead into blind alleys. Thus, if we think of creativity as being composed of two basic stages – first, the production of new ideas and, second, the critical examination and development of these ideas – then it is obvious that analogical thinking makes its major contribution in the first phase.

Have analogies led to any major creative advances or "breakthroughs" in motivation theory?[38] I think so, and as examples I cite the development of the concept of motivational force or strength and the distinction between force and direction in motivation, the first engendered by the clock metaphor and the second by Woodworth's drive versus mechanism analogy. For a recent example, I refer to the development of optimal-level motivation theory, a substantial theoretical advance. Though adumbrations of optimal-level conceptions can be found as far back as classical Greece,[39] the general notion did not become significant until the relevant biological and physical analog had been created.

Final comments

This chapter has examined the role of metaphors in motivation theory from a historical perspective. The material was organized in terms of five basic metaphors of motivation that have been influential during the course of history. On the basis of this survey, I have concluded that metaphors have served – and presumably will continue to serve – three different functions in motivation theory: descriptive, persuasive, and creative.

Though I have focused on metaphors in motivational psychology, I believe that most of the tentative generalizations I have put forward are relevant to other fields of psychology, and probably to the entire scientific enterprise.

Notes

1 For example, they are treated together in P. T. Young's *Motivation and Emotion* (1961) and in the journal *Motivation and Emotion*.

2 Many writers on metaphor (e.g., MacCormac, 1985; Sarbin, 1982) have commented on the fact that the paired referents in a metaphor, particularly when it is new, have a striking, unusual quality that contributes to an attention-getting tension or strain in the hearer. As a metaphor becomes "older" and more familiar, this novel quality weakens.

3 Among the general sources that I have found particularly informative and stimulating are Black (1962), Burke (1945/1969), Leatherdale (1974), MacCormac (1985), Mair (1977), Ortony (1979), Paprotte and Dirven (1985), Sarbin (1982), and Turbayne (1962). Important special-area sources, in addition to those already cited, include Hester (1967), Rogers (1978), and Sapir and Crocker (1977). Among those presenting psychological theories of metaphors are MacCormac (1985), Miller (1979), and Sarbin (1982).

4 Though exceptions exist (e.g., Gentner & Grudin, 1985; Park, Daston, & Galison, 1984), most analyses of metaphors and analogies have been based on instances selected to illustrate certain preconceived theoretical ideas rather than on surveys of metaphors as they actually occur. Gentner and Grudin's recent study presents an interesting analysis of changing trends in the use of metaphors in scientific psychology over the past ninety years.

5 Of the four concepts (simile, metaphor, model, and analogy), analogy is usually considered the most basic. As Leatherdale (1974) states, "Both the concept of metaphor and the concept of model include within their sense the concept of analogy. As far back as Aristotle one form of metaphor is described as 'giving the thing a name that belongs to something else . . . on the grounds of analogy'" (p. 1). The dependence of metaphor on analogy is also noted by MacCormac (1985, pp. 21–2), who suggests that the difference between the two terms of a metaphor is more marked than between the terms of simple analogies, which accounts for the more discernible shock provided by metaphor. The tendency of writers to consider simile, metaphor, model, and/or analogy as aspects of the same domain is reflected in several recent titles, including *Models and Metaphors* (Black, 1962), *Models and Analogies in Science* (Hesse, 1966), and *The Role of Analogy, Model and Metaphor in Science* (Leatherdale, 1974).

6 Sarbin (1968, 1977, 1982) refers to the process whereby metaphors are transformed into literal equations as the reification of metaphors. The frequent reification of psychoanalytic metaphors is discussed by Thomä and Kächele (1987). This problem was hardly unknown to Freud. As Thomä and Kächele observe (p. 33), Breuer, in his portion of the seminal work on psychoanalysis (Breuer & Freud, 1895/1955), cautioned against the danger of treating metaphorical concepts as if they were real (p. 169).

7 Transformation of a literal statement into a figurative one may also occur. For example, in pre-Copernican days the sentence "The sun is setting" was intended as a literal statement, whereas now it is generally understood to be metaphorical.

8 In further distinguishing basic and conveyance metaphors, MacCormac (1985) writes: "Conveyance metaphors usually propose a metaphoric insight limited in scope, whereas basic metaphors underlie an entire theory or discipline devoted to description of widespread phenomena." For example, "the scientist may adopt consciously or unconsciously the basic metaphor, 'The world is mathematical'" (p. 48). For a further discussion of Pepper's root-metaphor approach, see Sarbin (1977). Basic or root metaphors are, of course, not limited to science. They exist in all broad areas of human thought.

9 I am employing the term "pawn" in essentially the same metaphorical sense as de Charms (1968), except that my usage is set in a historical context.

10 My listing is different from the classification of root metaphors proposed by Pepper (formism, mechanism, contextualism, and organicism), though there are certain similarities, especially with respect to the mechanistic orientation. It should be noted that whereas Pepper's aim was to conceptualize and delineate all root metaphors that have logical and scientific merit and which can be defended in a fundamental sense, my aim here is to identify and describe particular root metaphors that motivation theorists have actually employed, regardless of their adequacy, during the course of history. My purpose is thus significantly different from that which guided Pepper.

11 "Supernatural" is, of course, *our* term. The distinction between natural and supernatural was not made in the prenaturalistic period.

12 There is no way of knowing with certainty how prominent was the tendency to attribute the origin of human motives to higher powers. Most scholars believe that the tendency existed to a significant degree, and this is my conclusion. Smith (1974) disagrees to some extent, concluding that "Homeric man was not a puppet of the gods as has been charged. But there are a number of ways in which the gods did exert influence" (p. 315). Dodds (1951) has convincingly argued that the instances of supernatural control recounted in the *Iliad* are not mere literary devices, but instead reflect the cultural views of that period. One may ask, What was the psychological basis of the attribution of personal decisions to the gods? The most plausible answer is that they were projections in the psychoanalytic sense. According to H. B. Parkes (1959), "Man's first answer to the social and political problems involved in the rise of civilization was to strip himself of all responsibility for his destiny and project all authority upon the gods" (p. 53). And B. Simon and H. Weiner (1966) state: "One can then view the gods as projections, not merely of unacceptable impulses or wishes, but more as projections of self-representations" (p. 308). The projection hypothesis is supported by the fact that the values attributed to the gods paralleled those of mortals.

13 Though all or most vestiges of the early controlling-powers conceptions have disappeared, instances of the underlying theme are by no means rare in modern society. Thus, it is not unusual for ordinary individuals to feel that a decision of theirs has been guided by a higher power. Further, paranoid delusions often take the form of a conviction that one's mind is being controlled by alien forces. In addition, modern empirical research has highlighted the extent to which individuals in contemporary society attribute control over themselves to such metaphorical entities as fate and destiny.

14 Indeed, Aristotle, as is often pointed out, was the first person to identify and discuss metaphors formally (in his *Poetics* and *Rhetoric*), and his conceptions are still of substantive value.

15 St. Augustine is generally credited with being the first to develop a systematic concept of will. This concept was necessary "in order to clarify which part of the human personality is concerned with freedom, sin, and divine grace" (Dihle, 1982, pp. 194–5). Whether Aristotle had previously formulated a theory of will is debatable and appears to depend on how one defines the will. Certainly Aristotle's discussion of agency laid the groundwork for an understanding of voluntary behavior, but it did not posit a separate faculty or part of the mind to serve this function. For general historical sources on the concept of will, see Bourke (1964) and Dihle (1982).

16 Nietzsche, in his *Will to Power* (1901/1968), refers to "weakness of the will" as a "metaphor that can prove misleading. For there is no will, and consequently neither a strong nor a weak will" (p. 28). But elsewhere (p. 52) he appears to accept weakness of will as a meaningful attribution.

17 John Locke (1690/1959), employing a metaphorical approach to emphasize his view that the question of freedom of will is meaningless, wrote that "it is as insignificant to ask whether man's *will* be free, as to ask whether his sleep will be swift, or his virtue square" (vol. 1, p. 319).

18 It is interesting that some authors, when they wish to make a metaphorical term appear more substantial, begin it with a capital letter. Note, for example,

Origin, Pawn, Plan. It may be observed that the term "origin" was also used to refer to human agency in the quotation from Aristotle given earlier in the text.

19 This phrase, "fabric of the heavens," later appeared in John Milton's *Paradise Lost* (1667/1968, bk. 7, l. 710; in later eds., bk. 8, l. 76) and is the title of a work by Toulmin and Goodfield (1961).

20 A later work by Bentham, *A Table of the Springs of Action* (1815/1969), was, I believe, the first volume devoted exclusively to the subject of motivation. The beautiful metaphor in its title, derived from the mainsprings of clocks, is still widely used as a dramatic synonym for motivation. As noted earlier, Bentham contributed significantly to the understanding of figurative language, and not surprisingly, we find a number of descriptive metaphors in his *Springs of Action*. These include references to motives as performing the "office" of a "spur" and, alternatively, the "office" of a "bridle" (p. 7). In another instance, Bentham posited that on some occasions certain motives may be substituted for others as "covering motives" (p. 30), employed as "fig leaves" (p. 32).

21 Berkeley (1713/1955) attributes the social impulse to divine implantation: "It is a principle originally engrafted in the very first formation of the soul by the Author of our nature" (p. 227). Further, he supposes that the impulse has a variety of manifestations: "As the attractive power in bodies is the most universal principle which produceth innumerable effects, and is a key to explain the various phenomena of nature; so the corresponding social appetite in human souls is the great spring and source of moral actions" (p. 227).

22 Though Thomasius employed the word *Grad* (degree) to indicate the units in his rating scales, this fact cannot be interpreted as strong evidence for a thermometer analog since *Grad* was used generically to express differences in intensity. It is interesting that Thomasius's younger colleague, Christian Wolff, was involved in the development of the thermometer (Bolton, 1900), though apparently only well after Thomasius completed his work on rating scales.

23 The translator (E. S. Forster) notes that "the marionettes seem to have been worked by means of cylinders round which weighted strings were wound, the cylinders being set in motion by the removal of pegs" (p. 463).

24 The fact that the word "neuron" derives from the Greek word for "string," as in the strings that operated the marionettes (Gregory, 1981, p. 69), neatly illustrates the role that metaphors play in the development of technical terms. It is interesting that Vesalius, the famous Renaissance anatomist, used the metaphor of "cords" in referring to nerves (Dampier, 1958, p. 122).

25 For a further discussion of hydraulic analogies in motivation, including additional examples, see Esper (1964, pp. 99–102). Some knowledge of hydraulics probably dates back to the ancient Mesopotamians since agricultural irrigation was central to their culture. It can also be conjectured that pneumatic principles may have become obvious through the observation of children playing with the bladders of butchered animals.

26 For stimulating discussions of the concepts of machines and mechanisms, see R. L. Gregory (1981) and Harré (1970). For general sources on the influence of the mechanistic world view on psychology, see Leahey (1980), especially "The Mechanization of the World Picture, 1600–1700" (chap. 3), and Lowry (1971).

27 Leary (Chapter 1, this volume) has called our attention to the interesting fact that whereas Newton evidently developed the concept of gravitation at least in part through analogy with the concept of sociability, Berkeley later argued for inherent human sociability by analogy with Newton's gravitation! This certainly illustrates both the ubiquity and adaptability of metaphors in scientific thought. Newton, it should be noted, lived in a transitional period and can be said to have had one foot in the mechanistic camp and the other still in the animistic camp (through alchemy). Though he attempted to eliminate all animistic notions from the *Principia,* the transitional nature of his period is reflected in his use of the psychological term "endeavor" (Latin, *conatus*) in the scholium following the definitions (Newton, 1687/1974, vol. 1, pp. 6–12; see Cohen, 1983, p. 82). It seems clear that the concept of "sociability" was meaningful to Newton through his studies of alchemy, which was heavily anthropomorphic. I am inclined to doubt Manuel's cautious suggestion that Newton's own personal isolation played a significant role in the development of his thought. For in-depth treatments of Newton's work in alchemy, see Dobbs (1975) and Westfall (1980, esp. chaps. 8 and 9).

28 The possible influence of the Parisian automata on Descartes's creative development is dramatically described by Jaynes (1970). For a 1615 pictorial sketch of these automata, see the frontispiece in Descartes (1662/1972). Tuchman (1978) provides a vivid picture of a fourteenth-century spectacle involving automata (p. 311).

29 Hobbes's theoretical emphasis on motion led Brandt (1928, p. 379) to suggest that he might better be termed a "motionalist" than a materialist. For further comments on the role of motion in Hobbes's conception of *conatus,* see Bernstein (1980).

30 For other sources on the role of the mechanical clock in the development of science, see the recent excellent treatments in part I of Mayr (1986), part II of Macey (1980), the first three chapters of Maurice and Mayr (1980), and the more popular but highly informative treatment by Landes (1983).

31 For example, the analog of the mill (as in a mill for grinding grain). Recall, for instance, these lines of Pope (1751/1942): "This subtle Thief of Life, this paltry Time,/What will it leave me, if it snatch my Rhime?/If ev'ry Wheel of that unweary'd Mill/That turn'd ten thousand Verses, now stands still" (p. 171).

32 Woodworth was not the first person to distinguish between the force and mechanism aspects of motivation. See the quotation from Paley in the text above.

33 See also Lundin (1972, pp. 220–33). The essential idea of Lewinian field theory was to relate behavior systematically to the overall environmental field in which the behavior occurs.

34 I have organized this chapter in terms of two levels of coverage of metaphors (MacCormac, 1985), and I consider this dichotomy valid and useful. In principle, however, one can conceptualize a continuum along which any metaphor could be assigned a place as a function of its range of application.

35 As a science progresses, metaphors that were formerly meaningful may become obsolete. For example, the telephone switchboard metaphor is no longer considered an adequate representation of brain functioning.

36 Bentham's reference to pain and pleasure as sovereign masters, noted early in this chapter, is an exception to this generalization.

37 The same metaphor may serve more than one of these functions.

38 The question can be raised as to whether *all* creative advances depend, in the final analysis, on analogical thought. An affirmative answer would presuppose that all new ideas are combinations of existent elements. Such a hypothesis is attractive, but it begs the issue of the *origin* of the elements. Further, it should be remembered that not all scientific advances are the result of new ideas. Many advances, in contrast, reflect new empirical discoveries. For example, our knowledge of the functions of the hypothalamus is based primarily on careful empirical examination, not on analogies.

39 I have in mind here the emphasis in ancient Greek culture on moderation and avoidance of excess.

References

Adkins, A. W. H. (1970). *From the one to the many*. Ithaca, NY: Cornell University Press.

Aristotle (1947). *The metaphysics* (bks. 1–9) (Loeb Classical Library: Aristotle, vol. 17; H. Tredennick, Trans.). Cambridge, MA: Harvard University Press. (Original work written ca. 330 B.C.)

(1968). *Movement of animals* (Loeb Classical Library: Aristotle, vol. 2, pp. 440–79; E. S. Forester, Trans.). Cambridge, MA: Harvard University Press. (Original work written ca. 340 B.C.)

(1975). *Nicomachean ethics* (Loeb Classical Library: Aristotle, vol. 19; H. Rackham, Trans.). Cambridge, MA: Harvard University Press. (Original work written ca. 335 B.C.)

Arkes, H. R., & Garske, J. P. (1977). *Psychological theories of motivation*. Monterey, CA: Brooks/Cole.

Barbu, Z. (1960). *Problems of historical psychology*. New York: Grove Press.

Bedini, S. A. (1964). The role of automata in the history of technology. *Technology and Culture, 5*, 24–42.

Bentham, J. (1948). *The principles of morals and legislation*. New York: Hafner. (Original work published 1789.)

(1969). *A table of the springs of actions*. In P. McReynolds (Ed.), *Four early works on motivation* (pp. 477–512). Gainesville, FL: Scholars' Facsimiles and Reprints. (Original work published 1815.)

Berkeley, G. (1955). The bond of society. In A. A. Luce & T. E. Jessup (Eds.), *The works of George Berkeley, Bishop of Cloyne* (vol. 7, pp. 225–8). London: Nelson. (Original work published 1713.)

Bernstein, H. R. (1980). Conatus, Hobbes, and the young Leibniz. *Studies in History and Philosophy of Science, 11*, 25–37.

Black, M. (1962). *Models and metaphors*. Ithaca, NY: Cornell University Press.

Bolton, H. C. (1900). *Evolution of the thermometer, 1592–1743*. Easton, PA: Chemical Publishing.

Bourke, V. J. (1964). *Will in Western thought*. New York: Sheed & Ward.

Boyd, R. (1979). Metaphor and theory change: What is "metaphor" a metaphor for? In A. Ortony (Ed.), *Metaphor and thought* (pp. 356–408). Cambridge University Press.

Brandt, F. (1928). *Thomas Hobbes' mechanical conception of nature* (V. Maxwell & A. I. Fausboll, Trans.). Copenhagen: Levin & Munsgaard.

Breuer, J., & Freud, S. (1955). Studies on hysteria. In J. Strachey (Ed. and

Trans.), *The standard edition of the complete psychological works of Sigmund Freud* (vol. 2, pp. 1–306). London: Hogarth Press. (Original work published 1895.)

Brumbaugh, R. S. (1966). *Ancient Greek gadgets and machines*. New York: Crowell.

Burke, K. (1969). *A grammar of motives*. Berkeley and Los Angeles: University of California Press. (Original work published 1945.)

Butterfield, H. (1957). *The origins of modern science* (rev. ed.). New York: Free Press.

Cannon, W. B. (1932). *The wisdom of the body*. New York: Norton.

Carnot, S. (1960). Reflections on the motive power of fire. In E. Mendoza (Ed.), *Reflections on the motive power of fire, by Sadi Carnot; and other papers on the second law of thermodynamics, by E. Clapeyron & R. Clausius* (pp. 1–69). New York: Dover. (Original work published 1824.)

Cattell, R. B., & Child, D. (1975). *Motivation and dynamic structure*. New York: Halstead.

Chapuis, A., & Droz. E. (1958). *Automata: A historical and technological study* (A. Reid, Trans.). New York: Central Book.

Charron, P. (1707). *Of wisdom* (vol. 1; G. Stanhope, Trans.). London: Bonwicke. (Original work published 1601.)

Coeffeteau, N. (1621). *A table of humane passions, with their causes and effects* (E. Grimeston, Trans.). London: Okes. (Original work published 1620.)

Cohen, I. B. (1983). The *Principia*, universal gravitation, and the "Newtonian style," in relation to the Newtonian revolution in science. In Z. Bechler (Ed.), *Contemporary Newtonian research* (pp. 21–108). Dordrecht: Reidel.

Comenius, J. A. (1910). *The great didactic* (M. W. Keatinge, Ed. and Trans.). London: Adam & Charles Black. (Original work published 1657.)

Dampier, W. C. (1958). *A history of science*. Cambridge University Press.

Darwin, C. (1859). *On the origin of species by means of natural selection*. London: Murray.

(1871). *The descent of man, and selection in relation to sex*. London: Murray.

de Charms, R. (1968). *Personal causation*. New York: Academic Press.

Descartes, R. (1972). *Treatise of man* (T. S. Hall, Trans.). Cambridge, MA: Harvard University Press. (Original work published posthumously 1662.)

Dihle, A. (1982). *The theory of will in classical antiquity*. Berkeley and Los Angeles: University of California Press.

Dijksterhuis, E. J. (1969). *The mechanization of the world picture* (C. Dikshoorn, Trans.). New York: Oxford University Press.

Dobbs, B. J. T. (1975). *The foundations of Newton's alchemy: The hunting of the greene lyon*. Cambridge University Press.

Dodds, E. R. (1951). *The Greeks and the irrational*. Berkeley and Los Angeles: University of California Press.

Eibl-Eibesfeldt, I. (1970). *Ethology, the biology of behavior* (E. Klinghammer, Trans.). New York: Holt, Rinehart & Winston.

Esper, E. A. (1964). *A history of psychology*. Philadelphia: Saunders.

Eysenck, H. (1967). *The biological basis of personality*. Springfield, IL: Thomas.

French, R. K. (1975). *Anatomical education in a Scottish university, 1620*. Aberdeen: Equipress.

Freud, S. (1963). Introductory lectures on psycho-analysis. In J. Strachey (Ed. and Trans.), *The standard edition of the complete psychological works of Sigmund Freud* (vols. 15 and 16). London: Hogarth Press. (Original work published 1917.)

(1964). New introductory lectures on psycho-analysis. In J. Strachey (Ed. and

Trans.), *The standard edition of the complete psychological works of Sigmund Freud* (vol. 22, pp. 5–182). London: Hogarth Press. (Original work published 1933.)

(1964). An outline of psycho-analysis. In J. Strachey (Ed. and Trans.), *The standard edition of the complete psychological works of Sigmund Freud* (vol. 23, pp. 141–207). London: Hogarth Press. (Original work published posthumously 1940.)

Gentner, D., & Grudin J. (1985). The evolution of mental metaphors in psychology: A 90-year retrospective. *American Psychologist, 40*, 181–92.

Gregory, J. C. (1927). The animate and mechanical models of reality. *Philosophy, 2*, 301–14.

Gregory, R. L. (1981). *Mind in science: A history of explanations in psychology and physics*. Cambridge University Press.

Griffin, A. K. (1931). *Aristotle's psychology of conduct*. London: Williams & Norgate.

Gruber, H. E. (1980). The evolving systems approach to creative scientific work: Charles Darwin's early thought. In T. Nickles (Ed.), *Scientific discovery: Case studies* (pp. 113–30). Dordrecht: Reidel.

Guerlac, H. (1983). Theological voluntarism and biological analogies in Newton's physical thought. *Journal of the History of Ideas, 44*, 219–29.

Hamilton, E., & Cairns, H. (Eds.). (1961). *The collected dialogues of Plato*. Princeton, NJ: Princeton University Press.

Harré, R. (1970). *The principles of scientific thinking*. Chicago: University of Chicago Press.

(1984). *Personal being*. Cambridge, MA: Harvard University Press.

Harré, R., & Secord, P. F. (1972). *The explanation of social behaviour*. Oxford: Blackwell Publisher.

Hero (1971). *The pneumatics of Hero of Alexandria* (facsimile of 1851 ed.). New York: Science History Publications. (Original work written ca. A.D. 62.)

Hesse, M. B. (1966). *Models and analogies in science*. Notre Dame, IN: University of Notre Dame Press.

Hester, M. B. (1967). *The meaning of poetic metaphor*. The Hague: Mouton.

Holt, R. R. (1968). Beyond vitalism and mechanism: Freud's concept of psychic energy. In B. B. Wolman (Ed.), *Historical roots of psychology* (pp. 196–226). New York: Harper & Row.

Hull, C. L. (1943). *Principles of behavior*. New York: Appleton-Century.

(1952). *Essentials of behavior*. New Haven, CT: Yale University Press.

(1962). Psychology of the scientist: IV. Passages from the 'Idea Books' of Clark L. Hull (R. Hays, Ed.). *Perceptual and Motor Skills, 15*, 807–82.

Hutcheson, F. (1725). *An inquiry into the origin of our ideas of beauty and virtue, in two treatises*. London: Darby.

Hurvich, L. M., & Jameson, D. (1957). An opponent-process theory of color vision. *Psychological Review, 64*, 384–404.

James, W. (1890). *The principles of psychology*. New York: Holt.

Jaspers, K. (1953). *The origin and goal of history* (M. Bullock, Trans.). New Haven, CT: Yale University Press.

Jaynes, J. (1970). The problem of animate motion in the seventeenth century. *Journal of the History of Ideas, 31*, 219–34.

(1976). *The origin of consciousness in the breakdown of the bicameral mind*. Boston: Houghton Mifflin.

Jung, C. G. (1960). On psychic energy. In *Collected works of C. G. Jung* (R. F. C. Hull, Trans.) (vol. 8, pp. 3–66). New York: Pantheon. (Original work published 1928.)

Klopfer, P. H., & Hailman, J. P. (1967). *An introduction to animal behavior: Ethology's first century.* Englewood Cliffs, NJ: Prentice-Hall.

Kramer, S. N. (1963). *The Sumerians: Their history, culture, and character.* Chicago: Unversity of Chicago Press.

Kuhn, T. S (1979). Metaphor in science. In A. Ortony (Ed.), *Metaphor and thought* (pp. 409–19). Cambridge University Press.

La Mettrie, J. O. (1912). *Man a machine* (G. C. Bussey & M. W. Calkins, Trans.). Chicago: Open Court. (Original work published 1748.)

Landes, D. S. (1983). *Revolution in time.* Cambridge, MA: Harvard University Press.

Lattimore, R. (Ed. and Trans.) (1962). *The Iliad of Homer.* Chicago: University of Chicago Press.

Leahey, T. H. (1980). *A history of psychology.* Englewood Cliffs, NJ: Prentice-Hall.

Leary, D. E. (1977). Berkeley's social theory: Context and development. *Journal of the History of Ideas, 38,* 635–49.

Leatherdale, W. H. (1974). *The role of analogy, model and metaphor in science.* Amsterdam: North-Holland.

Leonard, W. E. (Ed. and Trans.). (1908). *The fragments of Empedocles.* Chicago: Open Court.

Lewin, K. (1939). Field theory and experiment in social psychology: Concepts and methods. *American Journal of Sociology, 44,* 868–97.

Locke, J. (1877). Elements of natural philosophy. In J. A. St. John (Ed.), *The philosophical works of John Locke* (vol. 2, pp. 472–96). London: Bell. (Original work published posthumously 1720.)

(1959). *An essay concerning human understanding.* New York: Dover. (Original work published 1690.)

Lowry, R. (1971). *The evolution of psychological theory: 1650 to the present.* Chicago: Aldine.

Lundin, R. W. (1972). *Theories and systems of psychology.* Lexington, MA: Heath.

Macey, S. L. (1980). *Clocks and the cosmos.* Hamden, CT: Archon Books.

MacCormac, E. R. (1985). *A cognitive theory of metaphor.* Cambridge, MA: MIT Press.

Mair, M. (1977). Metaphors for living. In A. W. Landfield (Ed.), *Nebraska Symposium on Motivation* (pp. 243–90). Lincoln: University of Nebraska Press.

Manuel, F. E. (1968). *A portrait of Isaac Newton.* Cambridge, MA: Harvard University Press.

Maurice, K., & Mayr, O. (Eds.). (1980). *The clockwork universe.* New York: Neale Watson Academic Publications.

Mayr, O. (1986). *Authority, liberty, and automatic machinery in early modern Europe.* Baltimore, MD: Johns Hopkins University Press.

McDougall, W. (1933). *The energies of men.* New York: Scribner's.

McReynolds, P. (1970). Jeremy Bentham and the nature of psychological concepts. *Journal of General Psychology, 82,* 113–27.

(1971). Statues, clocks, and computers: On the history of models in psychology. *Proceedings of the 79th Annual Convention* (pp. 715–16). Washington, D.C.: American Psychological Association.

(1975). Changing conceptions of anxiety: A historical review and a proposed integration. In C. D. Spielberger & I. G. Sarason (Eds.), *Stress and anxiety* (vol. 2, pp. 3–26). New York: Halstead.

(1976). Anxiety and assimilation. In M. Zuckerman & C. D. Spielberger (Eds.), *Emotions and anxiety* (pp. 35–86). Hillsdale, NJ: Lawrence Erlbaum.

(1980). The clock metaphor in the history of psychology. In T. Nickles (Ed.), *Scientific discovery: Case studies* (pp. 97–112). Dordrecht: Reidel.

McReynolds, P., & Ludwig, K. (1984). Christian Thomasius and the origin of psychological rating scales. *Isis, 75,* 546–53.

Miller, G. A. (1979). Images and models, similes and metaphors. In A. Ortony (Ed.), *Metaphors and thought* (pp. 202–50). Cambridge University Press.

Miller, G. A., Galanter, E., & Pribram, K. H. (1960). *Plans and the structure of behavior.* New York: Holt.

Milton, J. (1968). *Paradise lost* (facsimile ed.). Menston: Scolar Press. (Original work published 1667.)

Mook, D. G. (1987). *Motivation: The organization of action.* New York: Norton.

Nash, H. (1962). Freud and metaphor. *Archives of General Psychiatry, 7,* 25–7.

Newton, I. (1974). *Mathematical principles of natural philosophy* (A. Motte, Trans.). Berkeley and Los Angeles: University of California Press. (Original work published 1687.)

Nietzsche, F. (1968). *The will to power* (W. Kaufmann & R. J. Hollingdale, Trans.). New York: Random House. (Original work published 1901.)

Nilsson, M. P. (1967). *A history of Greek religion* (2d ed., F. J. Fielden, Trans.). Oxford: Clarendon Press. (Original work published 1925.)

Ogden, C. K. (1959). *Bentham's theory of fictions.* Paterson, NJ: Littlefield, Adams.

Onians, R. B. (1951). *The origins of European thought.* Cambridge University Press.

Ortony, A. (Ed.). (1979). *Metaphor and thought.* Cambridge University Press.

Paley, W. (1825). *The works of William Paley.* Edinburgh: Brown, Nelson, & Allman.

Paprotte, W., & Dirven, R. (1985). *The ubiquity of metaphor.* Amsterdam: Benjamins.

Park, K., Daston, L. J., & Galison, P. L. (1984). Bacon, Galileo, and Descartes on imagination and analogy. *Isis, 75,* 287–326.

Parkes, H. B. (1959). *Gods and men: The origins of Western culture.* New York: Knopf.

Pepper, S. C. (1942). *World hypotheses.* Berkeley and Los Angeles: University of California Press.

Peters, R. S. (1967). *Hobbes.* Baltimore, MD: Penguin Books.

Pope, A. (1942). Imitations of Horace. In J. Butt (Ed.), *The poems of Alexander Pope* (vol. 4). New York: Oxford University Press. (Original work published 1751.)

Price, D. J. (1959). An ancient Greek computer. *Scientific American, 200,* 60–7.

(1964). Automata and the origins of mechanism and mechanistic philosophy. *Technology and Culture, 5,* 9–23.

Reynolds, E. (1971). *A treatise of the passions and faculties of the soule of man.* London: Bostock. (Original work published 1640.)

Rogers, R. (1978). *Metaphor: A psychoanalytic view.* Berkeley and Los Angeles: University of California Press.

Rotter, J. B. (1966). Generalized expectancies for internal versus external control of reinforcement. *Psychological Monographs, 80* (1, Whole No. 609).

Sandburg, C. (1916). *Chicago poems.* New York: Holt.

Sapir, J. D., & Crocker, J. C. (Eds.). (1977). *The social use of metaphor.* Philadelphia: University of Pennsylvania Press.

Sarbin, T. R. (1968). Ontology recapitulates philology: The mythic nature of anxiety. *American Psychologist, 23*, 411–18.

———. (1977). Contextualism: A world view for modern psychology. In A. W. Landfield (Ed.), *Nebraska Symposium on Motivation* (pp. 1–41). Lincoln: University of Nebraska Press.

———. (1982). A preface to a psychological theory of metaphor. In V. L. Allen & K. E. Scheibe (Eds.), *The social context of conduct* (pp. 223–49). New York: Praeger.

Siegel, R. E. (1970). *Galen's system of physiology and medicine.* Basel: Karger.

Simon, B., & Weiner, H. (1966). Models of mind and mental illness in ancient Greece: I. The Homeric model of mind. *Journal of the History of the Behavioral Sciences, 2,* 303–14.

Smith, N. W. (1974). The ancient background to Greek psychology and some implications for today. *Psychological Record, 24,* 309–24.

Snell, B. (1953). *The discovery of the mind* (T. G. Rosenmeyer, Trans.). Cambridge, MA: Harvard University Press.

Solomon, R. L., & Corbit, J. D. (1974). An opponent-process theory of motivation: I. Temporal dynamics of affect. *Psychological Review, 81,* 119–45.

Stagner, R. (1977). Homeostasis, discrepancy, dissonance. *Motivation and Emotion, 1,* 103–38.

Taylor, C. (1977). What is human agency? In T. Mischel (Ed.), *The self: Psychological and philosophical issues* (pp. 103–35). Oxford: Blackwell Publisher.

Thomä, H., & Kächele, H. (1987). *Psychoanalytic practice.* New York: Springer.

Toulmin, S., & Goodfield, J. (1961). *The fabric of the heavens.* New York: Harper & Row.

Tuchman, B. (1978). *A distant mirror.* New York: Ballantine Books.

Turbayne, C. M. (1962). *The myth of metaphor.* New Haven, CT: Yale University Press.

Westfall, R. S. (1980). *Never at rest: A biography of Isaac Newton.* Cambridge University Press.

Woodworth, R. S. (1918). *Dynamic psychology.* New York: Columbia University Press.

Worthen, T. D. (1970). Pneumatic action in the klepsydra and Empedocles' account of breathing. *Isis, 61,* 520–30.

Young, P. T. (1961). *Motivation and emotion.* New York: Wiley.

5

Cognitive metaphors in experimental psychology

ROBERT R. HOFFMAN, EDWARD L. COCHRAN,
and JAMES M. NEAD

In his classic article on reaction time research, Saul Sternberg (1969) began with the assumption that information is stored, retrieved, and operated on in a series of stages or mental operations between the stimulus and response. In his experiments, Sternberg had people learn lists of letters or digits and then indicate whether a given test letter or digit was in the learned list. The task is called "memory scanning" for a good reason: The metaphor relates to the phenomenal experience of remembering the list in the form of a mental image. The basic metaphor, a comparison of imaging to a beam scanner (Sternberg, 1969, p. 440), fits many participants' postexperimental reports of their experience at the task.

The scanner presupposes a mechanism that can look through the beam in order to carry out acts of recognition. Sternberg postulated a single homunculus that could either operate the scanner or examine the contents of memory but that could not do both at once. Furthermore, he assumed that it takes a fixed amount of time for the homunculus to switch from one operation to another. Each step of encoding and matching takes some amount of time for each item in the list. If the scanning were to go over the items one at a time, then one pattern in the reaction time data would be expected. If the scanning were to go over all the items at once, another pattern would be expected. Each assumption from the metaphor yielded further testable hypotheses.

This introductory example illustrates what we will do in this chapter: We will show how metaphors for various aspects of cognition relate to refined psychological theorizing and to ideas for experiments. The common metaphors that occur in ordinary language about cognition have been categorized in some detail (e.g., Lakoff & Johnson, 1980a; Reddy, 1979). Also amply documented is the use of metaphors in psychological theories (e.g., Gentner & Grudin, 1985; Hoffman & Nead, 1983; Kearns, 1987; Roediger, 1980; Romanyshyn, 1982). However, no one seems to have focused on the question of what roles metaphors play in actual psychological experimentation. It is one thing to demonstrate that both natural language about cognition and scientific theories of cognition are metaphorical, and quite another thing to show specifically how such metaphors articulate (if at all) with actual scientific practice. This is what we attempt to do in this chapter, following a lead given by Jerome Bruner (1965):

> It is my impression from observing myself and my colleagues that the forging of metaphoric hunch into testable hypothesis goes on all the time.... [But] our articles, submitted properly to the appropriate psychological journal, have about them an aseptic quality.... we may be concealing some of the most fruitful sources of our ideas. (p. 5)

In this chapter we hope to reveal some of the assumptions of experimental psychology by examining the use of cognitive metaphors in cognitive theories and research. We have three main reasons for our choice of this domain. First, the uses of metaphor and analogy in the physical sciences have been well documented and analyzed (e.g., Berggren, 1963; Black, 1962; Boyd, 1979; Gentner & Gentner, 1983; Hesse, 1953, 1966; Hoffman, 1980; Jones, 1982). Second, metaphor abounds in psychology – the domain is ripe for analysis (see R. H. Brown, 1976; de Man, 1978; Gentner & Grudin, 1985; Larsen, 1987; Pribram, Chapter 2, this volume; Smith, Chapter 7, this volume). Third, experimental psychology offers a challenge: It includes in its own domain the very phenomena (cognition and metaphor) that are being used in our descriptions. In other words, we are using cognitive concepts to analyze the cognition of cognitive scientists! This type of inquiry is one for which the results of the study could be used to justify the method of the study, but we trust that the circularity is not vicious. Any worthwhile hypotheses about cognition certainly should work when applied to the cognition of scientists. If the concept of metaphor helps us understand the mysteries of scientific problem solving, we shall be better off if we attend to it.

The organization and goals of this chapter

First, we will describe our view of the nature of metaphor. Next, we will describe the metaphors that appear in ordinary language about psychological phenomena as well as in the Western psychological tradition. Then we will present a series of "case studies" that describe the uses of metaphor in specific content areas: psychophysics, pattern recognition, the "ecological psychology" of James Gibson, motor skills, attention, and mental representation. After reviewing these case studies, we will consider the possible misuses of metaphor and some of the implications of metaphor for the philosophy of science. Finally, we will conclude with a call for a cognitive-experimental approach to understanding scientific practice.

Throughout this chapter we will be selective regarding historical details. We will use case studies to make particular points about the uses and contributions of metaphor in science, and we will analyze scientists' philosophical assumptions, their mental images, mechanistic models, and their metaphor-based analogies, as these are revealed by their rhetoric and the historical growth of their ideas. Weimer (1979, 1980) calls for such studies of the cognition and rhetoric of scientists with the goal of describing the psychological nature of inductive inference, creativity, and other aspects of science. We will not find out what science is by the mere philosophical analysis of details in the predicate calculus of theories (see also Estes, 1978, p. 15).

An unfortunate characteristic of some discussions of metaphor in science is the underlying attitude that metaphor makes for bad, illogical science. We have found that some experimental psychologists, upon being told that their theory is based on metaphor, become immediately defensive. Our aim in this chapter is not to caricature or lampoon experimental psychology by saying "It's only metaphor," although scientists sometimes do get away with that sort of criticism. Rather, our aim is to strengthen both experimental psychology and the philosophy of science by showing how useful metaphor can be.

We do not propose here that all uses of metaphor are necessarily beneficial or productive. In the main, however, each case study is intended to make positive comments about metaphor. Though we will point out some ways in which metaphors have been misused, we will claim that such "errors" can be attributed to scientists' reasoning rather than metaphor itself. We reserve most of our critical comments for the final case study, regarding mental representation, because this topic cuts across all the other domains of experimental psychology.

What is metaphor? – our point of view

Before starting our analysis, it behooves us to say something about the nature of metaphor and the literal–figurative distinction. In this chapter we will rely on an implicit notion of "literal" meaning in order to describe the role of figurative meaning in scientific theorizing and research. For us the distinction between literal and figurative meaning is an important one that offers descriptive and explanatory power in the analysis of science.

We assume that literal statements, such as "This chapter appears in an edited volume on metaphor," exist. We also assume that literal scientific statements exist. For example, some observation statements can be understood literally, even though metaphor can creep into them insofar as they are theory laden (MacCormac, 1976). We are not especially enamored of traditional definitions of "literal." In fact, traditional definitions of the literal are themselves metaphorical: They identify literal meaning as "logical truth values" and as what words "point" to (see Hoffman, 1988). By our interpretation, the significance of such theories of literal meaning is the obvious fact that social conventions and frequency-of-use factors (i.e., the pragmatics of referencing) play a role in judgments of "literalness." Certainly, one can find relatively clear cases of literal statements, but there are also cases about which people can reasonably disagree and cases in which literalness is only apparent.

Metaphor has been defined in many ways: as "saying one thing while meaning another," as "violating semantic rules," and as "making implicit comparisons of unlike things." A discussion of theories of metaphor would take us too far afield. For treatments of metaphor theory, see Black (1962), Hoffman, MacCormac, Lawler, and Carroll (1989), Levin (1977), Ortony (1979, 1980), or Ricoeur (1978). For recent reviews of psycholinguistic research on metaphor comprehension, see Hoffman (1984) and Hoffman and Kemper (1987). Though it is important to attempt to define the metaphor–literal distinction, the present investigation takes a broad approach in order to focus on the nature of scientific practice.

We are favorably inclined toward the "interaction theory" of metaphor (Black, 1962; Richards, 1936), which holds that metaphor involves the creation of new meanings, and not just logical comparisons or reduction to literal truth values. We try to avoid *a priori* notions about the nature of metaphors, such as the notion that metaphors are "only" analogies whereby the literal logic can be separated from the ornamental metaphor. We regard linguistic metaphor as a manifestation of complex processes of perceiving, acting, and remembering (Verbrugge, 1980). To emphasize our view that metaphor is not just a linguistic phenomenon, we will refer to comprehension in terms of the notion of "metaphoric understanding" (Lakoff & Johnson, 1980a,b,c).

In our analysis, we adopt standard terminology to describe the components of figures of speech – "topic" (the principal subject), "vehicle" (used to talk about the topic), and "ground" (the semantic basis of the figure). For example, in the simile *My love is like a red rose*, "my love" is the explicit topic (a particular beloved person is the implicit topic), "red rose" is the vehicle, and the ground is the variety of ways in which love can be related to red roses (e.g., it is beautiful, it grows, etc.).

Metaphor in science

In the context of the philosophy of science, metaphor stands out by virtue of its poetic and imagistic qualities. This sets it in contrast with literal logical language, which is traditionally regarded as the "real" basis of scientific reasoning. But metaphor abounds in science. For example, we pointed out above that formal definitions of metaphor in linguistics and psycholinguistics are themselves based on metaphorical notions about the nature of meaning (see Hoffman et al., 1989). This may seem doubly ironic to those who believe that all scientific thought must be literal.

Hanson (1958), Harré and Secord (1973), Simon (1973), and others have proposed that the "logic" of scientific discovery is psychological, that is, a matter of heuristics – and not just logical, that is, composed of deductions and predictions. Some philosophers of science who have realized this (e.g., Popper, 1959, pp. 31–2) argue that the topic of scientific discovery is therefore largely irrelevant to the philosophical-logical analysis of theories. The psychologist who follows Simon's lead need not view scientific discovery and theorizing as irreducibly intuitive or irrational. Rather, the creative process can be described, and metaphor seems to be one important way of describing it. Furthermore, the description could have implications for the philosophy of science.

For instance, theories in different disciplines have different domains to explain, and if human theorists understand the domains in different ways, the theories may have to differ in form and may have to be analyzed by different sorts of metatheoretic criteria (Deese, 1972). Theories of personality are written in words, may rely on some obvious metaphors, and should make sense to psychologists. Theories in physics should make intuitive sense to physicists, but will have to be partly, if not largely, mathematical, and the metaphorical concepts may be left largely implicit. Such differences, we feel, are matters of empirical investigation.

We are interested here in the process of theorizing, scientific creativity, and problem solving, rather than in static reconstructed theories. We are interested as much in the context of discovery as in the context of justification – these cannot be usefully characterized independently.

Having described our point of view regarding metaphor and science, we will now discuss and exemplify "cognitive metaphor," a central concept in this chapter.

Cognitive metaphor

A "cognitive metaphor" is created or used whenever some phenomenon of cognition is conceptualized or explained through the use of metaphor. Cognitive metaphors can refer to phenomena of language, learning, perception, motor skills, problem solving – indeed, to any phenomenon of cognition. Our purpose in this section is to illustrate the cognitive metaphors that occur in natural language and then to show briefly how similar cognitive metaphors form the core heritage of Western psychology. The discussion will set the stage for the subsequent case studies, in which we examine various domains of modern experimental psychology.

Cognitive metaphors in natural language

Natural language is laden with metaphors – not just novel metaphors, but also tens of thousands of common metaphors and idiomatic phrases (Becker, 1975; Pollio, Barlow, Fine, & Pollio, 1977). For example, people often compare war to insanity, surgeons to butchers, economic inflation to a disease, and marriages to prisons. Such common metaphors tend to fall into thematically related clusters or categories called "metaphor themes" (Black, 1962; Lakoff & Johnson, 1980c). For instance, according to the metaphor theme LOVE IS A JOURNEY, one can say such things as *Look how far we've come in our relationship, It's been a long, bumpy road, We can't turn back now, We're at a cross-roads, We have to go our separate ways, Our relationship isn't going anywhere*, and so on.[1]

Many metaphor themes are similar in terms of a general "orientational" function (Lakoff & Johnson, 1980a; Osgood, 1980; Rhodes & Lawler, 1981). For example, according to the theme CONSCIOUSNESS IS UP, THE UNCONSCIOUS IS DOWN, one can say *I fell asleep, He sank into a coma, It was a shallow trance, I woke up*, and *My consciousness was raised*. Similarly, the theme RATIONAL IS UP, EMOTIONAL IS DOWN relates such utterances as *I've thought this over, He fell in love*, and *The discussion was at a high level*. According to such orientational themes, our bodies are containers with boundaries and in–out, up–down, and front–back orientations.

Another set of cognitive metaphor themes uses the experiences of the senses as the vehicle of expression (Asch, 1958; Miller & Johnson-Laird, 1976; Romanyshyn, 1982). For instance, SEEING IS TOUCHING (*His eyes were glued to the task, I caught sight of it, She kept an eye on him*), UNDERSTANDING IS SEEING (*I saw what they meant, I got the whole picture, The theory was transparent*), and IDEAS ARE LIGHT SOURCES (*It was a bright idea, The concept was very illuminating, It was a flash of insight*) are all themes that utilize this comparison.

Metaphors are used to describe learning and the acquisition of knowledge (Scheffler, 1960; Schön, 1979; Skinner, 1968). One common theme is that KNOWLEDGE IS GROWTH (*The idea grew on me, A new idea was born today, It had a germ of truth in it*). According to this theme, the teacher is a gardener, and learning consists of stages or phases that emerge relatively independently of the teacher, although the teacher can help by providing optimal conditions that *nourish* the student and *culti-*

vate fertile minds. The relation of learning to organic growth processes is a very salient one (e.g., Piaget, 1971).

Many cognitive metaphors are variations on the theme that KNOWL-EDGE IS A STRUCTURE, which treats the mind as a container and ideas as contents (Jaynes, 1976; Lakoff & Johnson, 1980a; Reddy, 1979). Here are three variants of the structure theme:

WORDS AND IDEAS ARE OBJECTS OR ENTITIES

The words carried great weight, That thought has been around for centuries, The concepts buried him

WORDS CONTAIN MEANINGS OR INFORMATION

He put his ideas into words, The words held no meaning for me

MINDS ARE CONTAINERS

I didn't get anything out of it, Her mind is a sponge, That thought really sunk in

Ideas in the mental space are perceived in some sort of inner vision or perception: Ideas or memories can be *fuzzy, dim, obscure,* or *hidden.* Minds can be said to be *broad, open, closed, shallow,* or *narrow.* According to the structure themes, using language involves taking ideas from one mind and transferring them into another. Language becomes a "conduit" for the transmission of ideas:

COMMUNICATION IS THE TRANSFER OF OBJECTS

His meanings got across well, The ideas poured out, The words carried much information

The cognitive metaphor themes are often coherent with one another, in the sense that instances can be combined (Lakoff & Johnson, 1980c). For example, if ideas are light sources and the mind is a container and understanding is seeing, then the utterance *The idea was growing in the dim recesses of my mind* makes sense. As we will show, such mixing of metaphors occurs in cognitive theories as well as natural language.

Cognitive metaphors in the history of psychology: an overview of our Western heritage

Not only do cognitive metaphors and their themes abound in natural language about cognition; they also abound in the history of psychology. For example, the theme UNDERSTANDING IS SEEING was used by John Locke in his explanation of novelty and creativity in terms of a mental process of *reflection* on ideas and mental operations (Locke, 1690/1894, bk. 2, chap. 1). Most, if not all, of the key words that experimental psychologists use are of metaphoric origin. Here are some that came into English from Latin: "abstract" (to pull away from), "analysis" (to loosen), "comprehend" (to grasp), "induction" (to lead), "recollection" (to gather). Such etymological cognitive metaphors often go unnoticed – or, as some would say, these concepts have become literal in the language. In any event, their origin can be traced to metaphoric understanding.

A predominant metaphor theme in mentalistic psychologies of the 1700s and 1800s – and Western thought in general – is the *Vorstellung* theme. In German, the word *Vorstellung* means "presentation." In academic psychology, the word has also meant "image" (see Ebbinghaus, 1880/1971). According to the *Vorstellung* theme, MENTAL PHENOMENA ARE THEATRICAL EVENTS. Many common metaphorical expressions about social action, social cognition, and life's stages relate etymologically to the theater: *He played a silent role in the affair, They made a scene, I got upstaged.* In many cognitive theories, ideas or mental phenomena are regarded as presentations (*Vorstellungen*) that are *set before* the inner perception of thoughts, just as a work of art is set before an interpreter. Remembering is regarded as the having of *re-presentations* of knowledge. Conscious awareness can be likened to a spectator, who is only partially aware of the inferences going on "back stage" or below awareness. Also, conscious experience can be "on stage" actively perceiving rather than in the audience thinking about thoughts. The stage metaphor for mental life is a rich one, and was relied upon – and debated about – by many scholars: Goethe, Kant, Reid, Brentano, Ward, Freud, Titchener, and later phenomenologists (see Goffman, 1974). For example, here is a passage from David Hume (1739–40/1978):

> The mind is a kind of theatre, where several perceptions successively make their appearance; pass, re-pass, glide away, and mingle in an infinite variety of postures and situations. There is properly no *simplicity* in it at one time, nor *identity* in different; whatever natural propension we may have to imagine that simplicity and identity. The comparison of the theatre must not mislead us. They are the successive perceptions only, that constitute the mind; nor have we the most distant notion of the place, where these scenes are represented, or of the materials, of which it is compos'd. (vol. 1, pt. 4, sec. 6, p. 253)

Many of the metaphors on which experimental psychology is based can be attributed to René Descartes and the Cartesians (de Man, 1978; Johnson, 1981; Kearns, 1987; McReynolds, 1980; E. S. Reed, 1980). The Cartesians' use of metaphors and analogies was quite deliberate, out of recognition of their utility in hypothesis formation (Descartes, 1628/1911, p. 36; Kant, 1790/1951, pt. 2, sec. 61). Descartes's metaphors have left a formidable legacy of beliefs that are ingrained and implicit in much of psychology, philosophy of mind, and linguistics. Because the Cartesian legacy has had such a formative influence, we will survey some of the major Cartesian metaphors to set the stage for our case studies of some of modern experimental psychology's domains.

A central problem that Descartes tackled has to do with the foundations of physics and psychology: Perception is the ground for scientific judgments and knowledge, but how do people get from their subjective perceptual experience ("secondary qualities") to a knowledge of the objective properties of things ("primary qualities")? This is both a problem in physical ontology (What exists?) and a problem in epistemology (How can we have knowledge?). According to the theoretical system Descartes created, psychology should explain the phenomena and qualities that are not assumed to be real by physics. The specifics of Descartes's system are laden with metaphors for mental life, including the metaphor theme *MINDS ARE MACHINES*. Although Descartes himself (1662/1972) was inspired by hydraulic statues, for many others of the sixteenth and seventeenth centuries, such as Leibniz (1695/1912, p. 219) and La Mettrie (1748/1912), the machine of choice was clearly the clock. The human being was regarded as a "divine machine" to be explained by analogy to "artificial automata." Even Hobbes (1651/1950, p. 3), who rejected the notion that higher mental processes could be explained by the automation concept, relied on the clockwork metaphor in his explanation of behavior.

One of the things Descartes (1662/1972) wanted to explain is how visual images that are *painted* or *projected* onto the retinal *screen* come to be interpreted. To do this, he devised what we today would call a model of perception. He hypothesized that light rays impinge on a receptor surface that is like a *mosaic* or *rubber sheet*. Individual rays *prick* at points on the sheet. The geometry of the image will thus correspond with movements that are caused on the receptor surface. These motions are carried back to the brain hydraulically as if down a set of *tubes* or *channels*. Thus, the sensations will lead mechanically to brain events and their corresponding mind events. Awareness occurs when the movements arrive as ideas at certain places in the brain. The perceptual machine produces experience and memory; the acts of perception and reason are regarded as metrical reckoning, like the mathematical judgments of the geometer who is measuring angles and distances (see Descartes, 1638/1965).

As far as scientific hypotheses go, the Cartesian mechanistic approach has been very successful. With an additional boost from Locke, the British associationists continued the tradition of mechanistic and physicalistic theorizing (see Brett, 1965, chap. 12; Watson, 1979, chap. 11). For instance, Hume (1748/1955, essay 2) described the process of association as a form of *mental gravity* wherein ideas in the *mental space* are *attracted* and *repelled* by one another. Later, John Stuart Mill (1843, bk. 6, chap.

4, sec. 3) considered associations to result from a form of *mental chemistry*. About the same time, in the nineteenth century, the paradigms of psychophysiology and psychophysics arose when Müller, Weber, Lotze, Helmholtz, and others relied on such Cartesian concepts as the distinction between sensation and perception, the notion that sensations are conducted down sensory fibers, and the notion that consciousness or will is a "higher" or more "central" process. To provide just one more example of the Cartesian legacy, broadly conceived, Wundt (1911/1912, chap. 12) argued that thoughts consisted of *elemental sensations* put together into *psychical compounds*.

Memory metaphors

There is a long and venerable history of postulating hypothetical entities and processes to account for memory. Memory has been said to be like a *wax tablet,* a *dictionary*, an *encyclopedia*, a *muscle*, a *telephone switchboard*, a *computer*, and a *hologram*. Across the decades of modern psychology, theorists have proposed *core-context* units, *cognitive maps*, memory *tags, kernels, loops*, and so on (Underwood, 1972). In direct continuity with the Western psychological tradition, modern information-processing theories describe memories as contents that are *stored* and then either *recovered* or *lost*. Memory is regarded as an organized space, such as a *structure* of *networks* with *nodes* and *paths*, or *hierarchies* with *locations* and *classifications*. The nodes or locations represent verbal, perceptual, propositional, or other entities. *Shifts* of attention are regarded as passing at a definite rate through intermediate points in the *semantic space* (e.g., Lockhead, 1972).

Roediger (1980) described in detail many of the metaphorical ideas psychologists have used to describe memory, including Freud's (1917/1963) metaphor of memory as a *house full of rooms*, Murdock's (1974) metaphor of memory as a *conveyor belt*, and Neisser's (1967) metaphor of memory as an *archaeological reconstruction* process (see also Larsen, 1987). Roediger concluded that most theories of memory are variations of a metaphor theme of mental space, with recall generally regarded as a search through the contents of this space.

In addition to mental space and storage metaphors, another major metaphor theme for memory is the *trace* metaphor, which we referred to above as being a core concept in Descartes's theory of perception. According to this theme, memory is like a *riverbed* through which sensory impressions *flow*. The source of Descartes's hydraulic pores-and-channels metaphors was Harvey's (1628/1847, chap. 8) description of the circulatory system as a set of locks and canals. In the memory metaphor, memories can be said to be formed by the wearing of impressions into the riverbed, the laying down of *traces* that can be *strengthened* or can *decay*. Discussions of trace strength theory can be found in Hartley's theory of associations as "impressions" (1749/1966, chap. 1), in the *mental mechanics* of James Mill (1829/1967, chap. 3), the *mental chemistry* of J. S. Mill (1843, vol. 2, bk. 6, chap. 4), and the theorizing about memory in Ebbinghaus's classic monograph (1885/1964).

The metaphors of Western psychology, like those in natural language, conceive cognitive phenomena in terms of buildings, conduits, events, machines, object entities, containers, and orientations. The elements of conscious experience are reified as entities, projected into an inner mental container with orientations and transferred from one mind into another. Consider, for example, the modern "levels of processing" hypothesis about memory (Craik & Lockhart, 1972). It was intended to be an alternative to the hypothesis of separate memory stores (Waugh & Norman, 1965). According to the separate-stores hypothesis, different kinds of memory hold different types of information, have different storage capacities, and have different rates at which information can be processed. For example, sensory short-term memory briefly records perceptual appearances, whereas long-term memory records meaning. Craik and Lockhart (1972) proposed that memory involves a number of "levels." Preliminary levels deal with sensory and physical properties and pattern recognition; *deeper* levels deal with meaning and more elaborate processing. Craik and Lockhart held that their approach was a literal view – by virtue of its basis in information-processing notions and by virtue of its contrast with the more obviously metaphorical separate stores hypothesis (p. 681). Nevertheless, the levels-of-processing hypothesis is clearly based on orientational metaphor themes.

Cognitive metaphors have been used to generate not only hypotheses, but also full-fledged research domains and paradigms. Figure 5.1 presents a general information-processing diagram of the speech perception and production process (based on Liberman, 1970; Pisoni, 1978; Repp, 1981; and Studdert-Kennedy, 1976). Though theorists' views differ in details, many speech researchers have assumed that speech is a conduit that carries coded information from the speaker to the listener. In the listener's cognitive processing, the information is carried to the mind, where operations are performed on it by virtue of the memory containers. The containers involve the various levels of speech – auditory, articulatory, phonetic, lexical, syntactic, prosodic, pragmatic, and semantic. The processing leads to final awareness and recognition of the signal as meaningful speech.

Now the question arises: How are such cognitive metaphors related (if at all) to actual research? To address this question, we begin our case studies.

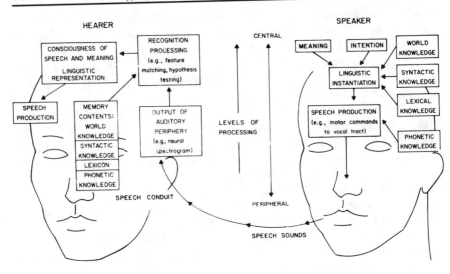

Figure 5.1. General information-processing diagram for speech perception and production. The diagram relies on the conduit, container, and orientational metaphor themes.

Case study 1: perception and psychophysics

The research literature on visual perception shows how abundant metaphor can be in a scientific domain. The field has many specific metaphorical labels for experimental tasks (e.g., binocular *rivalry*, perceptual *vigilance*), for psychological phenomena (e.g., perceptual *defense*), and for mental mechanisms or processes (e.g., feature *detectors*, perceptual *tuning*).

Even perception itself is defined using metaphors. For example, according to Attneave (1954), perception *predigests* information before it *reaches* consciousness. Perception *averages out* any redundancy to yield an *economical* representation. Although the variety of definitions of perception includes such uses of the theme IDEAS ARE FOOD, the orientational theme, and other metaphors, a basic metaphor – Cartesian in spirit – that appears in the work on perception of Attneave and others is a comparison of perception to a measuring process. According to this metaphor, reports about perceptual experience are references to central mental representations that are based on a classification of physical attributes and their values (Natsoulas, 1967; Triesman, 1962). Perception involves measuring the magnitudes of sensations or of excitations in places in the nervous system (Stevens, 1972; Warren, 1958). Perception is likened to the use of a set of instruments; the observers in psychophysical experiments are likened to physicists who are calibrating and using instruments to measure physical properties (Perkins, 1953).

Threshold metaphors

In order for a given stimulus to be perceivable – say, a dim light in an otherwise darkened room – the stimulus must be of a certain minimum intensity or duration. That degree of intensity or duration at which the stimulus becomes perceivable is called the "threshold." The very term "threshold" suggests that conscious contents enter the room of the mind by passing some sort of doorway or boundary. Freud (1917/1963) relied heavily on this type of metaphor:

> Let us compare the system of the unconscious to a large entrance hall, in which the mental impulses jostle one another like separate individuals. Adjoining this entrance hall there is a second, narrower, room – a kind of drawing-room – in which consciousness . . . resides. . . . The impulses in the entrance hall . . . are out of sight of the conscious. . . . If they have already pushed their way forward to the threshold and have been turned back by the watchman . . . , we speak of them as *repressed.* (vol. 16, pp. 295–6)

Perception researchers have conceived and measured perceptual thresholds in a number of ways. For example, Helson (1964) regarded thresholds as a *balance* or *weighted influence* of all the past stimuli that affected the organism. (Much of Helson's research involved weight judgments!) Historically, the concept of a threshold was supposed to refer to the inner mechanisms of perception, and not just to an externally or operationally defined independent variable. The general psychometrical function (or neural *quantum*) was believed to reflect the inner workings of the discrimination process (Corso, 1956). According to Fechner (1860/1965):

> The dependence, quantitatively considered, of sensation on stimulus, must finally be translated into one of sensation on the bodily processes which directly underlie the sensation – in short the psychophysical processes; and the sensation, instead of being measured by the movement of the stimulus, will be measured by the intensity of these processes. (p. 69)

According to Herbart (1816/1891, pt. 1, chaps. 2 and 3), the ways ideas influence one another can be described in terms of the mechanics of forces. Specifically, he (and many others) relied on a metaphor of ice floating on water. Ideas *float* near the surface of consciousness unless they *sink* or are *suppressed* by other ideas. As in the room metaphor, the ice metaphor postulates a boundary between conscious awareness and the mass of ideas and mental processes. In addition to the concept of the threshold, other concepts and phenomena in psychophysics are described metaphorically.

Backward masking

The concept of "backward masking" serves as an excellent example of how a metaphorical label for a phenomenon can generate research ideas. When two very brief stimuli (of the order of tens of milliseconds) are presented in close succession, the observer may be unable to perceive the first stimulus, even though it may be clearly perceivable when the second stimulus, the *mask*, is not shown (Dember & Warm, 1979, pp. 241–51). According to one hypothesis, the neural discharge from the second stimulus *catches up* with the first stimulus and *overtakes* it. This notion follows the conduit theme. According to another explanation (Averbach & Sperling, 1961), there are limits on the ability to extract and process information from brief visual displays. *Working* memory is capable of registering more information than can be read off during the duration of the memory – the memory *decays* or begins to *fade*. Masking is thus the erasure of information. Averbach and Sperling's hypothesis follows the container theme and the theme of minds as computers. Another explanation of masking relies on hypothetical neural networks, which undergo such processes as excitation, inhibition, and summation (Dember & Purcell, 1967; Weisstein, 1970). According to this view, neurons convey information messages from peripheral neurons to central *decision* neurons. Here we have an example of the orientational theme, with the addition of a fairly explicit "homunculus" (a hypothesized "little man" inside).

In the masking paradigm, it is possible to present a third stimulus. This can "mask the mask" and hence reveal the first stimulus! To explain this, Dember and Warm (1979) proposed a "fish model" of masking. The first stimulus, the target (a little fish), is swallowed by the mask (a bigger fish), but the little fish is not lost. If a second mask (an even bigger fish) comes along, it can frighten the mask into releasing the target back into the *perceptual stream*. Though admittedly whimsical, the formal counterpart to the fish model may help explain the differences among types of empirical masking functions.

Our point in this case study was to show how an area of experimental psychology can generate numerous and varied metaphors in definitions of its basic concepts and phenomena. The level of detail that can be achieved by a single metaphor-based theory is illustrated in our next case study.

Case study 2: pattern recognition

Historically, the key problem in the area of pattern recognition has been to specify and quantify the physical dimensions of patterns that are critically related to the perception of form. In this case study, we will explore the "pandemonium" model of Selfridge (1959/1966). However, we should begin by pointing out that metaphors are rampant in this domain, just as they are in psychophysics and the psychology of perception in general. For example, according to *neural network* theory (Uttal, 1973), the central nervous system is a *decoder* that recognizes patterns on the basis of inhibition and excitation processes. Points within the cortex that correspond to perceptual features – spots, edges, movements, orientations, and the like – have been named *feature detectors* (Hubel & Wiesel, 1962). The content of visual impressions consists of perceptual features arranged in a hierarchical classification of the perceptual forms in the world. Recognition of forms has also been said to rely on *templates* (e.g., Lindsay & Norman, 1977). A template is basically a stencil or outline cutout. If one shines a light through the cutout, the outline can be projected onto a surface, and one can look at the projected image for correspondences between the stencil and an input pattern (i.e., recognition).

Computer metaphors

Pattern recognition modeling with computers began about 1954 with attempts – none of them especially successful – to develop systems for recognizing printed texts. The work was not specifically tied to the question of how humans recognize patterns. However, the concepts that were used to describe programs, terms such as "image" and "idea," were clearly references to human perception. According to the general artificial intelligence view, pattern recognition is a process that analyzes signals from the senses and decides which class or type a given input pattern belongs to. The input is an array of discrete symbols, points, or brightnesses. The program must describe the transformations and other analyses that are needed to get from the input array to a class name that is stored in a set of representations of possible patterns (Uhr, 1965). To accomplish this there are a number of stages. There is a "preprocessing" of sensory inputs in order to "normalize" them (i.e., sharpen the contours, fill in irregularities, align orientations, etc.). Next comes the problem of efficient searching through the memories of alternative patterns. For instance, the search could be serial or parallel, exhaustive or self-terminating. Once alternatives are retrieved, they can be compared to the input in a matching or decision-making process.

The "pandemonium" model

In a sense, the early failures to get computers to "see" gave rise to the area of pattern recognition. One cannot simply hook up a camera to a computer, have it learn, search through an orderly set of alternatives, and thereby recognize patterns. One faces not just the tough problem of storing and processing complex data, but the tougher problem of representing knowledge.

Selfridge (1959/1966) proposed a metaphorical information-processing model for visual pattern recognition that stands as a good example of many of the basic components of information-processing theories of visual perception. Selfridge's main goal was to develop a system of perception that could be flexible and could learn – in order to represent in a better way how humans process visual information. In his "pandemonium" model, the mind is said to consist of a set of cognitive *demons*, each of which represents a possible pattern (type of form) or particular features (e.g., lines, angles, etc.). The demons are said to *look* for inputs that match their patterns, with the output of the demons depending on the degree of computed similarity. The demon *shrieks loudly* if the similarity is great. The *decision demon* responds to the loudest pattern demon, labeling the input pattern with the category of that loudest demon.

Selfridge wanted the system to *evolve* through *natural selection* of the demons. There were a number of ways that this could happen:

1. Through changes in the weightings of the features that make up the patterns. Across all possible instances of a pattern, a common weighting would emerge.
2. By selecting new feature subdemons that strongly affect the decisions and by eliminating inefficient subdemons. These processes were called *fission* and *conjugation* of demons.
3. By having decision demons that could change themselves. Ultimately, there would be one demon for efficiently classifying each of the input patterns.

One level of the pandemonium system is *data driven*, that is, based on the analysis of the incoming sensory signals. Another level is *conceptually driven*, such that *higher* mental processes add to the low-level processes (Lindsay & Norman, 1977). In conceptually driven processing, general knowledge guides the analysis: There are special demons for contextual information, for expectations, and for meanings.

Since the demons are organized into levels, and since they can change or learn, a given signal need not be completely analyzed. Rather, attention is guided according to the most pertinent features. Nevertheless, all the demons must be able to communicate with one another. To allow for this, Lindsay and Norman postulated a *mental blackboard*. The demons can take from or add to the blackboard any information they may need. Also, there is a *supervision demon*, who puts together a logical interpretation of the sensory inputs based on the information of the blackboard.

The pandemonium model is obviously metaphorical. It supposes homunculi (or, rather, diaboli) that recognize, compute, decide, and shout. The model relies on cognitive metaphor themes (i.e., orientations, conduits, memory contents). But despite the obvious metaphoricalness, the theorists who espouse this model often seem to believe that they are describing something literally true about human minds (e.g., Lindsay & Norman, 1977, p. 258). Theoretically, the demon processes correspond to hypothetical neural processes, supposedly making the theorizing more literal and the hypothetical processes more real.

This case study was intended primarily to show how an individual theoretical model can rely on a concatenation of metaphors. But must cognitive metaphors fit together as neatly as all the information-processing metaphors seem to, or can they sometimes be at odds with one another?

Case study 3: Gibson's ecological psychology of perception

The various "schools of thought" in psychology favor particular metaphors and metaphor themes (Gentner & Grudin, 1985; Hoffman & Nead, 1983). The perception theory of James J. Gibson provides an interesting case study of how one point of view (and its metaphors) can be at odds with another point of view (and its metaphors). In this instance, the contrast is between Gibson's "ecological psychology" and the approach to visual perception taken by traditional thinkers in Western psychology and typified by the works of such scholars as Descartes and Helmholtz. To those trained in this tradition, which is the majority of psychologists, Gibson's theory seems definitely curious. Analysis of the metaphors involved can clarify the two different theoretical positions and show how they are at odds.

The Cartesian–Helmholtzian tradition

As we pointed out in our illustrations of cognitive metaphors, Descartes and many of his intellectual ancestors took physical and geometrical optics to be a literal description of human vision. According to this view, light rays are converged by the eye to produce retinal pictures. These images are then carried along nerve fibers to the brain. By the early nineteenth century, the mathematics was so refined that all manner of optical projections could be described in geometrical terms. This tradition reached a climax with Helmholtz's *Handbook of Physiological Optics* (1867/1962). Following Helmholtz's reasoning, most psychologists still regard perception as a process of "unconscious inference" – because (it is said) the data for visual sensation are impoverished, two-dimensional retinal images. Perceptual experience is believed to be not of the world, but of an analogy to the world – the results of the operations that process sensations by adumbrating or supplementing them through inference and memory (Haber, 1968, p. 4; Helmholtz, 1867/1962, vol. 3, pp. 2–13). The bare sensations have no meaning; the nervous system uses them as *clues, cues, codes,* or *features.*

Gibson's ecological alternative

To Gibson (1979), the Cartesian–Helmholtzian notions are completely metaphorical – a confusion of an event with our words for describing it (p. 672), a confusion that leads to an endless philosophical debate about ontology and "what exists." There may be processes of sensation involved in perception, but these need not rely on the processing of hypothetical impoverished sensations or "clues." To Gibson, light itself is highly structured; the optic environment is a *sea* of optical energy that has a specific pattern in three spatial dimensions from any given point of view. Changes in the pattern over time will specify the invariant environmental relations and the changing ones.

To Gibson, psychology made a critical error when it assumed that the physics of stimuli is basic to sensations and that sensations are basic to perception. The information-processing view, a modern manifestation of the Cartesian–Helmholtzian tradition, led psychology to avoid its obligation to study the natural environment (Gibson, 1979, p. 699). What psychology needs is an "ecologically valid" optics, an optics of surfaces and objects, not of isolated spots viewed through a tachistoscope (see also Johansson, 1985).

What is perceived? To Gibson (1977), "affordances" are perceived. Affordances are things like the graspability of a stick, the supportability of surfaces, the liftability of objects, the fall-over-ability of slopes. An affordance is a combination of properties taken with respect to an organism. The notion of affordance cuts across the traditional Cartesian distinction between subjective and objective. Gibson wanted to reject the age-old distinction between primary and secondary qualities, especially insofar as the distinction postulates that secondary qualities are aroused in the brain as a result of sensations or primary qualities. To Gibson, this is so much mythic bosh. The ripeness of a banana, like its color and shape, is directly specified in the optic array.

"Direct" versus "indirect" perception

To Gibson, perceptions are not built bottom-up out of sensations. Rather, affordances are directly perceived via the invariants that are specified in the optic array. There need not be indirect perception, that is, the deductive inference of objects or information that is not present in the sensory impressions. One need not assume that stimuli are impoverished and have to be processed. One need not assume that phenomenal experience results from unconscious processing – some sort of mental mediator or representation. Gibson assumed that conscious experience resides a bit closer to the world in "direct" perception. Gibson did not claim that inference or other mental processes do not exist, nor did he claim that such processes are not involved in such things as language comprehension or the interpretation of pictures. His strategy was to avoid "taking out loans" by using cognitive-mediational mechanisms in order to explain perception (see Shaw, Turvey, & Mace, 1982).

The notion of direct versus indirect perception makes sense from the standpoint of an implicit metaphorical orientation or spatial relation of the mind to the world. The perplexing thing about Gibson's theory is not that he totally rejected our usual metaphoric understandings of the mind, but that he twisted them around. Gibson postulated that, rather than information *coming into* the mind, perceivers actively *reach out, sample*, and *pick up* information. He transformed the orientational metaphor theme CONSCIOUSNESS IS UP to CONSCIOUSNESS IS OUT.

Comparison of the Gibsonian and information-processing views

There are a number of points of similarity between the Gibsonian and information-processing views. Both direct and indirect perception are said to result in knowledge. Both are said to result in fallible or unreliable knowledge (e.g., invariants may be involved even when there is misperception). Both are said to rely on information that can be incomplete or misleading (e.g., illusions created in the laboratory). Both are said to rely on support from physiological systems that have been shaped by evolutionary and genetic factors. Both direct and indirect perception theories assume that perceptual acts can in some cases (e.g., language comprehension) rely on memory and inference as preparation or "material support" for phenomenal experience (Shaw & Bransford, 1977, pp. 35–8) or as support for judgments about past experience. Finally, both direct and indirect perception can involve "immediate" perception of significant events or properties. Immediate perception, a concept articulated by Bertrand Russell (1948, chap. 5), is not quite the same as direct perception. By "immediate," Russell meant rapid or automatic perception due to overlearning or strong perceptual expectations.

Such similarities should not be taken as evidence that Gibson's views do not really depart from those of the Cartesian–Helmholtzian tradition. For example, according to Gibson, perceptual acts produce new states of the system. This can be considered a variant of the Cartesian memory trace metaphor (Gibson, 1979, p. 254; Neisser, 1976, chap. 6). However, Gibson denies that memory, as it is usually conceived, is necessary for perception. To paraphrase Reed and Jones (1978), the perception of a persistence – an act that relies on memory in the traditional view – does not depend on some persistence in the organism (i.e., memory storage of copies of things in the world) since there is enough information available that specifies the persistences and changes. That is, do not "take out loans on intelligence" in order to explain perception (Turvey & Carello, 1981, p. 314).

By means of the hypothesis of direct perception, it is claimed that one need not postulate memories or mental representations in order to explain perception. Furthermore, Gibsonians claim that perceptual experience itself, even when mediated, is not equivalent to the memories or inferences that may provide material support for the percepts (see Reed & Jones, 1978; Shaw & Bransford, 1977). Perceptual experience is not the awareness of activated memory traces or memorial adumbrations of sensory messages. Thus, a key issue that separates the information-processing and Gibsonian views is whether hypothetical mediators are just causal supports for perception or are also representations of perceptual experience (epistemic mediators).

As with the other case studies, our discussion has been brief. It does not do justice to the original works, and certainly not to their associated research programs. The Gibsonian program of ecological psychology has been treated elsewhere at length (e.g., Hagen, 1985; Warren & Shaw, 1985; see also Gibson, 1985). We hope that this discussion of Gibson's metaphors has clarified the contrast between his theory and traditional views of perception: One reason that Gibson's theory may be hard for some to grasp is that he twists around our usual orientational metaphor theme. We have also shown how an epistemological problem, that of direct versus indirect perception, is based on an underlying metaphorical conception of the relation of the knowing agent to the world.

On a general level, this case study shows how rival theories can utilize contrasting metaphors. However, rival theories can also share metaphors, as shown in our next case study.

Case study 4: motor skills

Historically, motor skills theorists have borrowed metaphors that are popular in other areas of inquiry and applied them to the motor skills domain. Most theorists continue to invoke models in which cognitive metaphors play a central role. (For a review of the motor skills area, see Kelso, 1982a.) Our discussion revolves around a basic distinction between ways of storing *motor commands* (to muscles) in memory. This distinction is between *open-* and *closed-loop* theories of the nature of movement *feedback*.

Feedback

Theories of motor skills that involve *feedback* control can be divided into two types: those that claim that feedback involves a comparison of actions to a *stored copy* of the commands sent to the muscles and those that claim that feedback is compared to *stored expectations* of the consequences of a given planned act. According to the seminal theorizing by von Holst (1954), an image or copy of the impulses sent to the muscles (the "efferent copy") is used to modify or control incoming visual impressions. This hypothesis was intended to explain how we can distinguish movement of objects from self-movement on the basis of retinal images alone. There is some evidence that can be taken to support the efferent copy theory. However, efferent copy theories have been criticized for failing to explain how we can detect errors that are caused by environmental factors (Hershberger, 1976). Specifically, a movement that is executed exactly as planned but was inaccurately planned to begin with could not be determined to be erroneous. Such difficulties led to the conception of feedback as involving a comparison of the results of an act with stored expectations of the consequences of the act.

Loops

Motor theories differ in the way they conceptualize the feedback. There are two primary kinds of feedback theories: *open-loop* theories, in which feedback is used after an act is completed, and *closed-loop* theories, in which feedback is used in continuous monitoring of the system's performance. The most common example of the latter sort is the home thermostat. Closed-loop systems require that feedback from each segment of a movement be used in the execution of the task. Open-loop systems do not require feedback during performance since each act is preplanned. However, open-loop systems require explicit knowledge of the initial conditions in which an act occurs. They do not deny that feedback of some type occurs: Knowledge of results can play a role in the execution of subsequent acts.

The use of closed- and open-loop concepts to theorize about motor skills is not new. William James (1890) proposed that feedback from one part of a movement led to the initiation of the next and called this the reflex *chaining* hypothesis (vol. 1, p. 116). Bartlett (1932) proposed that a motor response is "not merely set off by receptor function, but is guided by it" (p. 31). Bernstein (1935/1967) distinguished between closed-loop control, which he called the *chain* hypothesis, and open-loop control, which he called the *comb* hypothesis: "The mechanism lies outside the engrams themselves and directs their order by an hierarchic principle" (p. 37). Similar distinctions have been pointed out by others since then, and closed-loop theories have become numerous (e.g., Chase, 1965; Craik, 1947; Lazlo, 1967).

The idea that the same metaphors can appear in rival theories is best illustrated by an analysis of two modern theories of motor behavior: Adams's trace theory, a closed-loop theory, and Schmidt's schema theory, an open-loop theory.

Adams's trace theory

A detailed closed-loop theory of motor skills was proposed by Adams (1971, 1976). Adams defined a *memory trace* as an agent responsible for selecting and initiating a movement, "a modest motor program that only chooses and initiates the response" (1971, p. 126). In addition, a hypothetical *perceptual trace* is the reference for determining whether a given response is accurate. The perceptual trace "is a motor image (not necessarily a conscious one) and the comparison of feedback stimuli with it is an act of recognition" (1976, p. 91). Traces of both types are laid down on each trial or repetition of an act. The effect of learning is a distribution of traces across repetitions, each trace leaving a small change in the memory substratum. Learning is the formation of new traces, and movements become automatic when strong traces have been laid down.

Adams had conducted some experiments on performance at a simple lever-positioning task. If each movement in such a task is really a series of corrected movements, more of the total movement time should be devoted to the final portions of the task as more corrections are made. A simple mathematical instantiation of the trace model, therefore, would have two components in the total reaction time: $RT = t + \Delta t$, with Δt representing the effect of the corrections. This equation was an important step toward explaining the empirical relation known as Fitts's law (Fitts, 1964; Keele, 1973). Adams's theorizing was also supported by research that showed that response time increases as a function of the amount of information processing demanded by a motor task (i.e., choice among a number of alternatives) and that response time increases as more mediational or processing stages are required (e.g., pressing a button in response to a simple light stimulus vs. in response to pictures or to words) (Fitts, 1964; Hick, 1952; Hyman, 1953).

A problem for closed-loop theories has to do with the limits on the rapidity with which movements can be executed. Lashley (1951) cited evidence that movements can be extremely rapid, such as the piano player's trilling of notes at a rate of sixteen or so per second. Such rates present a challenge to theories that rely on the closed-loop control of movements, since the theories may not allow enough time for feedback and error correction (Keele & Posner, 1968). An alternative is open-loop control, in which some acts are planned before execution and feedback is not necessary. This possibility was supported by work on surgical deaf-ferentiation (severing of sensory nerves) by Lashley and others (T. G. Brown, 1914; Ingebritzen, 1933; see Lashley, 1917), which showed that movements could be accurate and coordinated movements could be rhythmic, despite deafferentiation.

Schmidt's schema theory

There have been several instantiations of the open-loop metaphor that have in common the idea that feedback from an ongoing movement does not affect the execution of the movement, although it can be used to replan future actions of the same type. We will discuss one well-developed open-loop theory, that of Schmidt (1975, 1982a,b).

Schmidt based his theory on the idea of a memory *schema*. This theory was intended to allow for movements that are too rapid for sensory feedback and also to allow for novelty and variability – which is where schemata (or schemes) come in. Consider, for example, signing your name in large letters on a blackboard. When done for the first time, this would be a novel act as far as specific muscle movements are concerned, so trace storage would be of little help. To Schmidt, one's ordinary signature and the one done in large letters on a blackboard would rely on the same schema and should therefore be similar despite the dissimilarity of the muscle movements.

Like Adams, Schmidt draws a distinction between recall and recognition processes: Recall processes generate movements based on the initial conditions (e.g., the position of the hand in a grasping task); recognition processes evaluate feedback from the movement and generate error signals. Thus, Schmidt's theory incorporates a number of sources of information: (1) the initial conditions, (2) the sensory consequences of previous similar movements, (3) the outcomes of previous movements, and (4) the goals involved in the next movement. This information is captured in the recall and recognition schemata. The relationship between past response specifications and past outcomes produces the new response specifications. These are then used as parameters for a *motor program* that executes the response. At the same time, the expected consequences are generated by the recognition schema, and any mismatch with feedback is used to modify future responses. This is accomplished by means of an *error-labeling* schema. The full theory is depicted in Figure 5.2.

Like Adams, Schmidt relies on the memory trace metaphor to explain learning: Schemata can be strengthened with each repetition of a movement. However, according to Adams's model, which relies on memory traces only, skill acquisition depends on the precise repetition of acts. According to Schmidt's schema theory, learning also depends on the

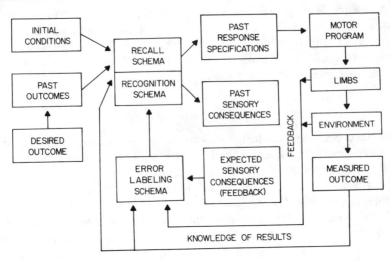

Figure 5.2.   Schema theory of motor skills. (After Schmidt, 1975.)

variability of the practice experience: The learning of a schema or overall pattern will be better if a person acquires experience through diverse instances of the task. A number of experiments using simple lever-positioning tasks have found increased transfer from practice to test trials if people are able to acquire experience through more variable training (Newell & Shapiro, 1976; Wrisberg & Rogsdale, 1979).

Schmidt's theory is simultaneously promising and frustrating. It is promising in that it goes further than other theories in providing answers to the question of spatial representation and frames of reference in motor control. But it is frustrating in that it depends critically on the functions and capabilities that are assigned to the hypothetical schemata. Historically, schematas have been regarded as holistic, abstract representations of patterns that underlie perception and action (Attneave, 1957; Bartlett, 1932; Keele & Posner, 1968; Northway, 1940; Paul, 1967). As defined by neurologist Henry Head (1920), they are "combined standard[s], against which all subsequent changes in posture are registered before they enter consciousness.... We are always building up a postural model of our-selves.... [Every change] is recorded on this plastic schema" (vol. 2, p. 605). The concept of the schema is an abstract conceptualization of mental representations – a dynamic pattern that may only be approxi-mated by individual instances. As abstract categories, schemata can contain whatever a theorist wishes – practice effects, spatiotemporal qualities, even intention. Indeed, to Schmidt (1975), a schema is a *rule* (p. 233), a set of *abstract information* (p. 235), and an *agent* that gener-ates responses (p. 236). The schema boxes are both memories and inten-tional agents that *coordinate, integrate,* and *generate.*

Schema theory holds that it is not necessary to store programs for all possible motor acts, or perceptual traces from all motor acts, or any other specific information necessary to initiate or monitor performance. Through the reliance on abstract schemata, considerable savings in memory storage requirements are achieved. But how general can a schema be? Obviously, the more general, the fewer the storage requirements, but it is not clear how general a schema can be before the concept begins to lose its theoretical justification. As the initiators of motor programs, schemata have many of the characteristics that entire organisms have in the simpler closed-loop formulations. Recognition schemata, for example, invoke all the metaphors of the pattern recognition models that were described in our second case study.

In essence, Schmidt has developed a theory that builds on the metaphorical qualities of many psychological theories and provides a domain-specific framework for integrating them.

Mixed metaphors

At times, the metaphors in science can be confusing. For instance, we find theorizing in the motor skills domain to be somewhat confusing. (We are not alone; see Kelso, 1982b.) For some reason, perhaps the influence of papers by Pew (1966, 1970) and especially Adams (1971), the concept of a *motor program* has been generally identified with linear (open-loop) sequences of commands and the concept of closed-loop (feedback-based) systems has been identified with efferent-copy or stored-expectation theories. These identifications make it necessary to invoke some kind of open-loop control mechanism in closed-loop systems in the initial stages of an act. Furthermore, it is possible to regard loops that involve motor programs as closed because an executive program triggers and monitors the chain. In fact, most open-loop theories make use of the metaphors used in closed-loop theories. Thus, there can arise some confusion about what "kind" of theory a particular theory is. The metaphors of loops, programs, feedback, and copies or traces are not mutually exclusive, but can be mixed and rearranged to develop new theories or to guide further research, as Schmidt has done in his theorizing and research.

Our next case study is intended to show how metaphors can "drive" research.

Case study 5: attention research

Modern research on attention shows clearly how metaphors can generate ideas for experiments. In addition, this case study illustrates how the experimental results can in turn suggest refinements of their root metaphorical theory.

The application of information theory and communication theory (Shannon, 1948; Shannon & Weaver, 1949; Wiener, 1948) to problems in psychology (Miller & Frick, 1949) had a profound impact on areas such as the psychology of attention. The original metaphor provided by the theory (Broadbent, 1952, 1954, 1958) was the likening of the components of the perception process to the components of a radio communications system: An information source (the transmitter) produces signals (stimuli) that are detected by a sensor system and passed on to some sort of central processor (the central nervous system), where they are filtered and decoded (recognition, categorization). Generalizing on the radio to include other types of information-processing systems (i.e., computers), humans were regarded as limited-capacity information-processing channels.

Many perceptual processes were described as involving computations of the information value of stimuli, and a great deal of research was generated by pursuing this approach (e.g., Attneave, 1954; Fitts & Posner, 1967; Garner, 1962; Miller, 1953). The information-processing notions were applied to the problem of explaining the phenomenon of selective attention. According to Broadbent (1958), the inputs (the ears, eyes, touch, etc.) would correspond to different channels with parallel input lines. Selective attention would be necessary to avoid *bottlenecks* or *overloads* of the system. There must be some sort of *sampling* of the inputs, some sort of selection or choice, some sort of *switch*. Broadbent (1954) conducted some research that relied on the switch metaphor. In his "split-span" experiment, people listened over headphones to a tape recording of spoken numbers. The participants heard a series of three numbers in one ear and, at the same time, another series of three numbers in the other ear. After listening, the participants were instructed to recall the numbers. People tended to recall the numbers by ear, that is, they would recall the three numbers heard in one ear and then recall the three heard in the other ear, with recall performance being better for the first set recalled. According to the switch theory of attention, the signal from one of the ears (i.e., one of the channels) was passed through the perceptual switch and processed. The message from the unattended channel was lost from short-term memory storage before it could be processed, and hence the poorer recall for the second set of three numbers.

One of Broadbent's manipulations involved instructing people to recall the numbers in an order that alternated ears (channels), for example, right ear, left ear, right ear, and so on. In this case, the listeners had great difficulty recalling the numbers, especially for brief presentation rates (of the order of a second or so per number). By manipulating presentation rate, Broadbent was able to estimate the "switching time" of selective attention.

Cherry (1953) reported the results of experiments on attention in which people listened over headphones to tape-recorded prose passages, a different passage in each of the two ear channels. The listeners' task was to "shadow" or repeat out loud whatever was heard in one of the two channels. A number of studies using the shadowing task have found that people can be so attentive to the content of the target message that they may be unable to remember much about the content of the unattended message. Not only that, they can fail to notice that the speech in the unattended signal is being played backward or has suddenly changed language. Messages can be repeated in the unattended channel many times and still not be recalled. Even an instruction to stop shadowing embedded in the unattended message can be missed (Moray, 1959).

Such results supported the switch model, in that it suggests that no aspect of the unattended message is analyzed beyond the point of the switch. However, listeners in the shadowing task can notice their own name if it occurs in the unattended channel (the "cocktail party phenomenon"), and they also sometimes notice when the voice in the unattended channel changes from male to female or vice versa (Cherry, 1953; Moray, 1959). Thus, one can notice certain salient aspects of the unattended channel. This result suggests that selective attention is based not on a simple switch, but on a *filter*: In some cases, the rejected information can "leak" through into perceptual analysis. Relying on the root metaphor of a radio communication system, Broadbent (1958) altered his earlier mechanical switch model and explained Cherry's results in terms of an electronic *filter*: "A practical analogy may be found in a radio receiver designed to eliminate input interference. [It would] make use of the fact that the interference possesses frequency components not present in the desired signal" (p. 41).

A next major development was the demonstration that the message in the unattended ear is analyzed for meaning. Triesman (1960) conducted a shadowing experiment in which the two prose messages were occasionally switched from ear to ear, so that the message that had been shadowed from one ear was suddenly coming to the ear that was supposed to be ignored. She found that listeners would continue to shadow the target message when the two channels were switched, only to notice moments later that they were suddenly listening to the "wrong" ear. In another study, Triesman (1964) showed that it is harder to shadow a prose passage if the unattended channel carries a prose passage with similar content. These results indicated that the filter may not screen out meaning. In a revision of Broadbent's theory, Triesman proposed a system in which filtering occurs on two levels. After an initial filter that selects according to physical features, there is a second set of filters, with variable thresholds, that select messages according to meaningfulness and semantic features. She conceived of this second set of filters as comprising a *perceptual dictionary*. Such a mechanism would explain the fact that the unattended message can be analyzed for meaning and the finding that contextual and instructional factors can bring about changes in the salience of the unattended message (Moray, 1969).

Since the work by Broadbent, Cherry, Triesman, and others, attention research has been dominated by the refinement of the basic metaphors on the basis of experimental results (e.g., Deutsch & Deutsch, 1963; Norman, 1968). For example, Kahneman (1973) sought a new type of conceptualization of attention, which he called the "effort" or "resource" theory. According to this theory, attention is likened to an economic trade-off of supply and demand, rather like a home electrical system with limited capacity to run appliances. Although relying on the concept of a channel, the theory does not involve a limitation of information-carrying capacity, but a limit on the capacity to do *mental work*, a metaphorical personification of attention. If the mental work capacity is limited, some way must be found to allocate strategically the resources according to task demands. The more work capacity devoted to one task, the better is the performance at that task; however, less capacity will be available for other tasks. In other words, selective attention was regarded as a post-perceptual phenomenon, having to do with the selection of information to respond to and having nothing to do with blocking signals from perceptual analysis.

Like the other attention theories, the effort theory has led to ideas about new experiments. A great deal of research has been conducted to test the differing predictions made by the filter and response selection models (Dember & Warm, 1979, chap. 5). Our description of attention theories and research is not detailed or complete, or even up to date. It is intended to show how metaphors play a role in the cycle whereby theories and experimental results are related. This is a cycle of mutual constraint – the metaphors and theories suggest particular experimental designs, and in turn the results support one or another of the hypotheses. It is also a cycle of mutual refinement – the results can lead to improvements in the theories and metaphors, which in turn can suggest further refinements and advances in research.

Looking across the case studies we have presented so far, we can see a common thread or two. In each of the research domains, researchers have the goal of discovering the cause–effect relations among mental processes and representations. To conceive of those processes and representations, they rely on cognitive metaphors. Having illustrated how the metaphors relate to ideas for research in specific domains, we turn now to the broad issue of mental representation.

Case study 6: the issue of representation in cognitive science

What is a representation?

The term "representation" derives from the Latin *esse*, which in turn has its roots in the Sanskrit *es* and *sat*, "to be real, present, or existing." The word "represent" comes directly from the Latin *praesse* and *representare*, "to be before the mind" or "to be in view." Something represents something else if it brings to mind the original experience – in other words, if it is a re-presentation of existence.

In their timely monograph on figurative language, Lakoff and Johnson (1980c) defined metaphor by saying that "the essence of metaphor is the understanding and experiencing of one kind of thing in terms of another" (p. 5). In his paper on representation, Palmer (1979) said that a representation "is something that stands for something else" (p. 262). In the literature on metaphor, metaphor has been defined as a comparison or analogy taken across domains or territories, as in the perception of the similarity of nonidentical things. So too have representations been defined as analogies between different domains. Just as there are semantic feature-mapping theories of representation, so too are there such theories of metaphor (e.g., Gentner, 1982). In the literature on representation it has been claimed that mental representations are "incomplete" in that they capture only some aspects of the represented world (Palmer, 1979). Also, some of the aspects of the represented world may be irrelevant. Similar points have been made about metaphors (e.g., Eberle, 1970, p. 230). Both metaphors and representations have been said to focus the user's attention on relevant or salient aspects or differences, at the expense of "hiding" or "losing" information.

What all these similarities suggest, of course, is that the psychological and philosophical problems involved in the issue of the nature of mental representations are problems with metaphors. Indeed, the taxonomic problem of defining the meanings of the term "representation" is not one of literal scientific meaning, but one of metaphorical scientific meaning. A number of metaphor themes have been relied upon in various discussions of the nature of representation and mental representation (Goodman, 1976). The following are some examples:

REPRESENTATIONS AS ESSENCES

According to this ancient theme, representations are regarded as *idealizations, essences,* or *essential properties.* It is true of much of language that words are taken to represent the essence of the things denoted. For example, the names of gods were once believed to be devices for invoking their particular powers and personalities, and the Greek words for "men" and "stones" were related, reflecting the belief that humans originally grew from stones (Cassirer, 1925/1946, pp. 4–10).

REPRESENTATIONS AS VISION

According to this theme, representations are regarded as *pictures* of the world, *mirrors* of the structure of the world, *portraits, depictions, likenesses,* or perspectival *ways of viewing* the world (see Romanyshyn, 1982, chap. 3).

REPRESENTATIONS AS THEATRICAL PERFORMANCES

According to the *Vorstellung* theme we referred to earlier, representations are things produced on a stage (see Goffman, 1974). As a role can represent a person, so too can a computer *simulate* people and *act* as if it were intelligent.

REPRESENTATIONS AS MAPPINGS

This theme regards representations as geometrical entities, and it concerns itself with correspondences between domains or *territories* (Parker, 1982). The mapping can be a one-to-one or isomorphic map or it can involve a many-to-one map, as in computer language interpretation programs and compliers.

REPRESENTATIONS AS LANGUAGE OR SYMBOLIC FORMS

Examples of this theme are the perception of a black cat as a symbol for evil or the perception of musical notation as abstract signs that represent music. In this theme, representations are compared to logic, which as a concept is itself understood metaphorically through a comparison with language (see Hoffman et al., 1989). Representations are believed to be *interpretations* or *translations* of the represented world, logical assessments involving propositions and inferences (e.g., Fodor, 1984).

Metaphors for mental representation in information-processing psychology

In information-processing psychology it has been widely assumed that mental representations are mental states that have a causal structure logically composed of names, predicates, quantifiers, concepts, or other elements (e.g., Dennett, 1978; Fodor, 1981, 1984; Harman, 1978; Haugeland, 1981; Martin, 1978; Oatley, 1978; Pylyshyn, 1984). It is assumed that inputs (sentences, percepts, etc.) have mental representations, that conscious experience is of mental representations, and that learning, language, and other skills depend on the acquisition and manipulation of mental representations.

A major distinction regarding mental representations that appears throughout the literature on cognition contrasts representations as formulas in notational systems with representations as things that preserve the perceptual form of the represented world (Goodman, 1976, chap. 6). Representations that preserve perceptual form are things like working models, diagrams, maps, and pictures. In contrast, symbolic representations "decouple" the representation from the world in terms of physical or perceptual resemblances (Shepard & Chipman, 1970). We could thus place things like three-dimensional motion holograms and color photographs nearer to one end of a continuum and abstract symbol systems nearer to the other end. Between the extremes would be such things as black-and-white photographs, outlines, caricatures, and other forms. At one extreme, the representation re-presents the perceptual form of the thing that is represented. At the other extreme, the perceptual form is not represented, but is somehow preserved in a symbolic manner. Information-processing psychology relies heavily on the metaphor of representations as logical symbolic systems. Since thoughts have the quality of being judgments (Brentano, 1874/1973; Pillsbury, 1908), predication, relation, and all sorts of abstract logical notions can be used to describe the mental representations that presumably underlie all thought, language, and imagery.

Information-processing theories usually combine the logic theme for representations with other metaphors that typify the mechanistic Cartesian heritage of psychology. Although Descartes himself did not extend mechanism to mind, in modern information-processing psychology the mind is regarded as a calculating engine that can do cognitive logic. As Craik (1947) put it, "My hypothesis is that thought models or parallels reality – that its essential feature is not 'the mind,' 'the self,' or 'sense data,' but symbolism of the same kind as in mechanical devices which aid thought and calculation" (p. 57). According to Neisser (1967), mental activity is the transformation of information, and the goal of cognitive psychology is to show the pattern of the transformations and operations. In terms of the computer metaphor, psychology seeks to understand the *program* of the mind as well as its *hard wiring* (or physiology).

Time and process

The metaphors for mental representation in information-processing psychology have implications for the way time and process are treated. For example, a main purpose of some modern linguistic rule systems (e.g., Chomsky, 1965) is to cope with the "infinity" problem, which has to do with the nature of creativity at syntactic and semantic levels (Brewer, 1974; Hoffman & Honeck, 1976; Schwartz, 1978). As linguists put it, the problem is how a finite set of syntactical rules can generate the infinite set of sentences in a language (Katz, 1973). Linguistic rules that generate phrase structures and transform sentences reflect an attempt to deal with some of the creative aspects of language as well as some of its regularities. But in phrasing the infinity problem the way they have, linguists are, of course, speaking metaphorically – they are treating language as a container of sentences and rules. (For reviews of the metaphors that linguists use in their theorizing, see Wilks, 1985; Zwicky, 1973.)

Rule systems such as Chomsky's evolved along with the general information-processing view and the metaphorical comparison of minds to computers. The generative linguistic rule systems can easily be taken to be hypothetical psychological process models. For example, although the *deep structure* of a sentence includes no indication of its lifetime, once an appropriate transformation rule is applied, the rule brings about a change. A great deal of research in the area of psycholinguistics consists of attempts to explore hypotheses about the psychological reality of linguistic rule systems and of such entities as deep structures. For example, transformation steps might be reflected in comprehension reaction time (see S. K. Reed, 1988, chap. 10).

According to the general information-processing view, some mental representations take the form of rules, procedures, or commands; some take the form of stored content or knowledge. In the operation of the cognitive engine, the continuous flow of time runs forward in steps – a series of transformations of stored contents, each transformation bringing about a new cognitive state. A new state might involve a change in contents; it might also involve the "calling up" of some other procedure.

Generative systems treat language as a process, but in the states-and-transformations theorizing, time itself is "frozen out" in that it becomes accidental to the process. In general, what we call structure is actually temporary, but is invariant relative to processes or events or relative to the ways it is measured or characterized (Newell, 1972). What we call process is of necessity dynamic, but processes themselves are represented statically as invariant rules or procedures. In other words, our conception of the dynamic involves a double metaphor – mental contents are assumed to be static, and mental processes are themselves represented as static forms.

Image representations

Perhaps nowhere in cognitive psychology are metaphors for representation more salient than in discussions of mental imagery. The concept of "image" is intimately related to the Cartesian metaphor theme PERCEPTION COPIES THE WORLD, which underlies most cognitive theories of visual perception. A common assumption of imagery theories is that images are *spatial* and *picture-like*. Imagery is said to rely on some of the same mechanisms as the perceptual system. For example, it is thought that visual images are anticipations of percepts (Neisser, 1976).

Images are described by a number of metaphors in the psychological literature (Paivio, 1979; Pylyshyn, 1973, 1984, chap. 8), both spatial ones (e.g., images are described as *drawings, working spaces, primal sketches, mental blackboards*, and *scratch pads*) and abstract ones (e.g., images are described as *possible worlds* and *abstract data structures*). It is said, both in psychology and in natural language, that images can be *dim, focused, vivid, sharp, fragmentary, constructed*, and *scanned*. In their classic experiments, Shepard and Metzler (1971) measured the time it took people to compare mentally two drawings of three-dimensional shapes that would appear in different orientations. The results implied that images undergo a smooth, continuous rotation, as if mental objects are being turned. Some reaction time data even suggest that images could be described as having inertia and showing deceleration (see Cooper & Shepard, 1973).

Critics of the picture metaphor have pointed out that images are not copies. The picture metaphor for visual images implies that images need analysis or interpretation, when in fact images already are interpretations, which is to say, they are not "raw" (Kosslyn & Pomerantz, 1977; Pylyshyn, 1973). The ways in which images are vague are not like the ways in which pictures are vague. Images are not reperceptions of pictures; they can show a loss of details, qualities, and relations. Images are not pictures in that they can be influenced by expectations and can contain nonpictorial aspects (e.g., perceived causation).

Anderson (1979), Kosslyn, Pinker, Smith, and Schwartz (1979), and others are willing to argue that the picture metaphor is a good one, a flexible one, one that can be profitably used to generate ideas for experiments. However, Field (1978), Kintsch (1974), Kosslyn and Pomerantz (1977), Palmer (1975), and Pylyshyn (1984) argue that images are represented in terms of propositions. In general, a proposition is considered to be a statement with two terms that are connected by some relation, an *atomic fact* having some truth value. Some authors consider associations (binary relations) and lists to be propositions (see Anderson & Bower, 1973, chap. 1). The notion of propositions was imported into cognitive psychology along with the notion that the rules of logic are the laws that govern the operation of the cognitive engine. According to this metaphor, intelligence is regarded as symbol manipulation (Pylyshyn, 1978). Forming and using a mental image is supposed to be the same as *accessing a node* and *retrieving* a perceptual description, or *assembling a structure* or a *semantic net* in some form of *workspace* (Kieras, 1978; Pylyshyn, 1973).

Since we can give a verbal description of our images and since verbal input can lead to the formation of images, there must be some common *format, code*, or *interlingua* (see Dennett, 1978, chap. 6). According to the proposition theory, images could be mentally represented in the same format as verbal information. With propositions, one format can be used to represent any type of well-specified information – whether it be verbal, perceptual, or imaginal. Mental rotation could be expressed as a series of small computations or changes. In addition to its contributions on a theoretical level, the proposition theory has also been relevant to the interpretation of research findings. According to the theory, the reason that images and concrete words are remembered more accurately in recall and recognition tasks than is less imageable information (i.e., abstract words or sentences) is not that imagery is a privileged format, or content, but that highly imageable materials are represented by richer, more elaborate propositional encodings (see Anderson & Bower, 1973, chap. 14; Kintsch, 1974, p. 216).

The claim with which we began this case study was that problems and debates about representations are largely problems with metaphors. In fact, the entire issue of the nature of mental representation is a morass of metaphorical relationships: Theories of perception provide analyses and representations of aspects of the real world, which must be linked to analyses and representations of the perception process, which in turn must be linked with analyses and representations of the phenomenal experience of percepts. Thus, the model of perceptual mechanisms and phenomenal experience is a representation of a representation of the world. This morass of relations rests on fundamental metaphoric assumptions, with different researchers invoking different representational metaphors to get at different aspects of psychological phenomena or research.

To determine that our analysis of cognitive psychologists' metaphors for representation is pertinent to cognitive science in general, we will now examine some literature in the artificial intelligence (AI) branch of cognitive science.

Metaphors for representation in artificial intelligence

A basic problem addressed by researchers in AI is that in order to have intelligence one needs to represent knowledge, as we pointed out in the case study on pattern recognition. Questions concerning representation therefore comprise a major area of AI and "expert systems" research (Hoffman, 1987). According to the general AI approach to knowledge representation (e.g., Palmer, 1979; Raphael, 1972), words are stored in computer memories as *contents* at locations that have *addresses* and *pointers* that inform the machine of the next step (i.e., some other location to "go" to). Representations are made up of lists or strings that express properties or processes. According to Raphael (1972), representations are *idealizations* that provide solutions that can be *translated* back into the original problem's language. The translation is not one-to-one, but is a complex mapping that preserves information by setting up correspondences with the represented world. Thus, according to

Palmer (1979), representations are to be compared in terms of their information content and computational efficiency. A number of mathematical notions can be used to describe the relation of a representation to the represented world – for example, asymmetry, transitivity, isomorphism, and homomorphism.

In the areas of cognitive simulation and AI, metaphors for representations are quite abundant. When taken out of their contexts and simply listed, the metaphoricalness of most technical terms in AI stands out quite clearly. There are *access skeletons, working memories, combinatorial explosions, systems hygiene,* and *canonical coreferents* that come in different *flavors.* In Table 5.1 we offer a glimpse of our classification of more than 350 metaphorical sentences and phrases that we identified in the "Special Issue on Knowledge Representation" of the newsletter of the Special Interest Research Group on Artificial Intelligence (Brachman & Smith, 1980). Illustrated in Table 5.1 are many of the metaphor themes that have been used in the history of Western psychology to talk about representations and many of the metaphors that have been used in the past few decades of information-processing psychology to talk about cognition.

The metaphorical interface

We close this case study with a conjecture about the relation of cognitive simulation work to cognitive psychology. People speak about computers as if they do what heads do, and they speak about heads as if they do what computers do: The computer metaphor goes both ways. As a challenge, we propose that it would be impossible to give a generally acceptable description of *either* computers or minds without using metaphorical language. But this raises an interesting possibility. If an intelligent computer were able to communicate effectively about its representations, it would need the language that people use to create, manipulate, and talk about representations – the cognitive metaphors that we mortals use to understand representations, language, memory, perception, meaning, and other cognitive phenomena.

Some researchers in AI have attempted to program computers to "comprehend" metaphors by reducing or transforming the metaphors into basic, literal-meaning elements (for a review see S. W. Russell, 1986). An alternative approach would be to arm a computer with the metaphor themes themselves as a part of the semantic base. This might enable the computer to comprehend novel metaphors by recognizing them as instances of the themes. Carbonell (1980) has had some success with this type of approach. Going even further, it is conceivable that a computer interface system could describe its own internal states with the same metaphors that we mortals use to refer to the mind. One need not

Table 5.1. *Classified examples of more than 350 metaphorical phrases and sentences found in Brachman and Smith (1980)*

Machines
Inference machinery, pattern-matching engine, mental apparatus, mechanical procedures; mechanisms simulate behaviors; tasks can be easy or difficult for machines

Entities
Ontological primitives, mental dictionaries, inference traps and triggers, servants and demons, pointers, atoms; relations and propositions can be formal objects; ideas get embodied in computers and minds

Buildings
Fixed skeletons, data bases, semantic structures, embedded structures, basic building blocks; computers build schemata and prototypes; representations are tools; thought is modeled with structures

Personification
Control strategies and structures; computers manipulate symbols; programs activate entities, focus attention, and guide inference; programs behave like experts; concepts guide thought

Paths and locations
Cognitive maps, surrogate path markers, associative paths, semantic networks and nodes, problem spaces, linkages, partitions, associative inheritance, topological freedom, chains of symbols; one can fetch information and have search problems; inferences follow patterns; memories are accessed

Mirrors and vision
Self-referential programs, reflexive interpreters, clear theories, illusory theories; systems can explain their own reasoning and modify their own behavior

Processes
Flow graphs, frozen processes, fixed meanings, network flow, future states; reasoning is a process; changes can be divorced from time; computers can reason backward in time; beliefs are updated

Languages
Primitive vocabulary, treelike syntax, layers of language, syntactic economy, graph grammars; languages can be computational, symbolic, universal, and equivalent; computers translate languages and generate interpretations; representations have a grammar and a syntax

Levels and orientations
Spaces of possible tokens, distances between concepts, linguistically deep ideas, surface properties; knowledge and structure can be of higher or lower levels; control can be global or local; programs can be concept centered

Logic
Encodings and decodings of concepts, fuzzy logic, rich encodings, conceptual hierarchies; representations are logical; representations capture essences; predicate logic represents knowledge; programs are formal representations; inferences can be systematic, hidden, obvious, or exposed

only ask how to make a computer more intelligent; one can also ask how to make a computer communicate about its internal states "as if" it were intelligent. That is, the use of natural-language cognitive metaphors might lead to more "user-friendly" programs, as well as "smarter" ones.

In this chapter we have sampled experimental psychology – speech perception, visual perception, pattern recognition, ecological psychology theory, motor skills, and attention. Looking across the case studies, we have shown how abundant cognitive metaphors are, how they lead to refined theorizing, how metaphors and theories can be at odds with one another, how contrasting theories can sometimes share metaphors, and how metaphors can play a role in the generation of ideas for experiments. Our final case study cut across the various domains and focused on the general issue of the nature of mental representations. Throughout our discussion we have tried to keep our illustrations of the uses of metaphor distinct from any criticisms regarding the potential misuse of metaphor. It is now time to turn to the latter topic.

On the "misuse" of metaphor

Representational imperialism

For some reason, cognitive scientists tend to believe that there is one true exclusive representational format – for example, that all knowledge takes the form of propositions or schemata. Psychologists and other cognitive scientists seem to operate with a somewhat distorted notion of parsimony. The point of Occam's razor is that the level of complexity of a theory should match the complexity of the phenomena, not that all theories should be simplistic. Yet cognitive scientists seem to feel that they are free to pick a favorite formalism and assume that it holds for all manner of mental phenomena and representations.

Mixed metaphors

In contrast to the tendency toward representational imperialism is the tendency to invent more – and more clever – combinations of metaphorical hypotheses. The various metaphors in cognitive science, from logical processes to memory boxes to levels of processing, are coherent for the most part. It usually makes sense when cognitive scientists mix them as they do. But theorists often operate as if they were completely free to invent any sort of metaphorical theory they want or completely free to pick and choose among possible hypothetical mental representations. Thus, one can find theories that combine propositional reckoning with schemata or combine feature hierarchies with templates, and so on. Anderson (1979) defines schemata as subsets of propositions. Schmidt

(1975) defines schemata as intentional agents with abstract structures. Sternberg, Tourangeau, and Nigro (1979) define comprehension as the computation of vectors in a semantic hyperspace. This sort of strategy might work in AI, where one is seeking clever ways of finding computational solutions to tough memory search or inference-making problems without necessarily being terribly concerned with how the human mind solves similar problems. But for the psychologist interested in cognitive simulation, some means has to be found to constrain the theorizing and to link it with research findings and, one would hope, the reality of cognition (Bahrick, 1987). Otherwise, cognitive psychology might just as well return to being a branch of the philosophy of mind. Metaphors can be elaborated and combined ad infinitum, and they certainly do tend to proliferate in experimental psychology (Roediger, 1980; Underwood, 1972). What strong experimental evidence or phenomenal experience warrants even simple compoundings of metaphors?

Reification

With propositions or schemata one can do all sorts of clever things, but is that a sufficient reason for believing that propositions or schemata are actual mental entities? What sort of justification should be given for explaining one set of data, say, by invoking schemata and another set by invoking templates? All too often in cognitive science, little justification is given for the metaphorical entities and processes that are postulated (Bahrick, 1987).

The notions of proposition, schema, template, and the others are all candidates for reification, but to validate a candidate for reification, we must be able to say more than "It is parsimonious." The theoretical representation of cognition is not necessarily what minds do when they cognize, although it may nonetheless provide a description that is adequate for particular purposes. (A similar distinction between description and representation was drawn by Goodman, 1976.) Given that cognitive science seems unconstrained in its theorizing, we should ask where the constraints are to come from. The issue is one of method and purpose: How should we use hypothetical mental representations, and what ontological status should we grant them? Converging evidence must be found that a given representation has something to do with actual intervening mental states or processes (Garner, Hake, & Eriksen, 1956; Paivio, 1975). This evidence must be different from the evidence, demonstration, or phenomenon that led to the postulation of the representation in the first place. Furthermore, the various types of representations require different sorts of justification and evidence. In any event, there must be some continued interaction of the theory with the data produced by new experiments. Otherwise, the modeling remains at the level of theorizing alone, and at that level it seems that anything goes.

One thing this chapter should make clear is that the information-processing view offers no free ticket for going from metaphors to a theory of what the mind is (see also Bahrick, 1987; Dennett, 1978; Roediger, 1980).

The myth of literalness

There seems to be some confusion in the images versus propositions literature about the relation of propositions to verbal information. Some researchers (e.g., Anderson & Bower, 1973, chap. 1) are careful to point out that propositions are supposedly nonverbal entities. Yet the fact remains that words are virtually invariably used to express and explain propositions, and if not words then some logical symbols that, to have any meaning at all, must be the objects of the mental acts of theorists. "Proposition" is no less a metaphor for thought than "picture" is a metaphor for imagery. Advocates of the proposition metaphor claim that the picture metaphor demands a homunculus that can interpret picture images. But their own computational metaphor demands a homunculus that can *call up* subroutines and *make* inferences. The fallacy at work here is the assumption (in its most extreme form) that any theory suspected of being metaphorical is necessarily bad or stupid, inviting replacement by some better (i.e., literal) theory. What is usually substituted, of course, is another metaphor.

Many examples can be found of theorists who criticize someone else's theory for being metaphorical – seemingly assuming that this alone is enough to brand the theory as false and unscientific – while they themselves propose an alternative theory that is just as metaphorical. Here, for example, is part of Chomsky's (1959) critique of Skinner's learning theory:

> [Skinner] utilizes experimental results as evidence for the scientific character of his system of behavior and analogical guesses (formulated in terms of metaphorical extension of the technical vocabulary of the laboratory) as evidence for its scope. This creates the illusion of a rigorous scientific theory ... although in fact the terms used in the description of real life and laboratory behavior may be mere homonyms.... With a literal reading ... the book covers almost no aspect of linguistic behavior, and with a metaphorical reading it is no more scientific than traditional approaches to its subject matter. (pp. 30–1)

In order to criticize Skinner's rats-and-reinforcements metaphors, Chomsky adopts the metaphor that heads compute. Well, if metaphoricalness is sufficient to condemn Skinner, then Chomsky is the sinner who cast a stone. Of course, both theories have their merits and failings, both led to some useful research, and both generated refinements through criticisms of their metaphors. At every turn, the metaphors were doing their job. The theorists were making errors when they presented their own theories as literal truth.

Some implications for the philosophy of science

Is metaphor necessary?

Occam's carefully worded advice (*Essentia praeter necessitatem non sunt multiplicanda*) implies that some phenomena, at least, may be complex enough that a complete explanation of them requires the use of multiple concepts. However, the operationalists and logical positivists latched onto the "razor" as a clarion call for a "linguistic hygienics" that would purge all scientific theories of the vagaries and metaphors of natural language (e.g., George, 1953; Kantor, 1938). (Ironically, operationalism and logical positivism, the epitome of literal, logical, rigorous scientific theorizing, were themselves based on metaphors; see Smith, Chapter 7, this volume.)

To counterbalance this warped approach to the nature of science, Hoffman (1979) proposed a specification of the other edge of the razor: *Essentia praeter fidem non sunt subtrahenda*. In other words, do not pretend to do without concepts you honestly cannot do without. In the case of experimental psychology (and "behavioral science" as a whole?), cognition is one such concept. In the case of the philosophy of science, metaphor is certainly such a concept.

The major fallacy we hope this chapter will help to dispell is the literalist idea that metaphor plays no role in the generation of ideas for experiments and in the refinement of theories and models. As it appears in the philosophy of science, the myth of literalism is the belief that proper theories are literal, logical constructs (which is itself an abstract metaphor). However, discovery is often the invention of new metaphorical ways of representing things, and choosing between theories is often a matter of choosing between more and less fruitful metaphors (Hesse, 1966; Kaplan, 1965; Simon, 1978).

The grand question, implicit in what we have said so far, is whether any theory can be completely devoid of metaphor. Can fundamental discoveries occur without some metaphorical extension of an idea or practice or without some metaphorical description of newly found phenomena? As we stated at the beginning of this chapter, we do assume the existence of literal statements, and literal scientific statements. Without some such assumption, the concept of metaphor would lose all its descriptive and explanatory power. Clearly, what counts as a literal statement varies according to the criteria used in different contexts. The means of specifying the "similarities" implied by a metaphor (or a "literal" statement of identity) are the critical considerations, and they vary across research communities. The issue of whether metaphor plays a necessary role in scientific theories and scientific discovery has been discussed at length (see Boyd, 1979; Hesse, 1966; Hoffman, 1980; MacCormac, 1976). At one extreme is the view that theories cannot be devoid of metaphor, even if they also include some literal statements. This has been claimed, for example, about theories of metaphor – that they necessarily rely on metaphorical notions of what meaning is (Nemetz, 1958).

At the other extreme is the view that metaphors are completely un-necessary – that any metaphorical components of a theory can be rewritten into a literal form. There are theories of metaphor which assume that figurative meaning can be reduced to literal meaning: Both the "substitution" and "comparison" theories of metaphor assert that the comprehension of metaphor relies on some sort of literal paraphrase (Johnson, 1981). The claim is sometimes made that metaphors can be reduced to underlying logical analogies or literal restatements (e.g., Davidson, 1978). We should perhaps be careful not to confuse analogy, as a metaphorical way of describing metaphor and cognition, with what people might actually be doing when they comprehend a metaphor (Hoffman et al., 1989). Granted, analogistic reasoning does sometimes play a role in science (see Gentner, 1982), but scientific analogies are almost always post hoc relative to root metaphors. That is, the scientist is thinking in terms of a metaphor or its basic image, and only after considerable thought might the relations be spelled out using an explicit analogy format (Hoffman, 1980, 1985).

Metaphor as process

A major reason the substitution, comparison, and analogy theories of metaphor are doomed to fail is not just because they assume that meaning, at its basic level, is literal. Rather, each of them runs into trouble because of its resistance to the idea that metaphor is a process. Take, for example, the literature on mental imagery. Some theorists (e.g., Kosslyn & Pomerantz, 1977; Pylyshyn, 1973) criticized the picture theory of imagery by saying, "It's only a metaphor." Other theorists seem some-times to have taken this criticism at face value. For example, Paivio (1976) said, "No imagery theorist accepts the metaphorical view as a working theory" (p. 2). But when one looks closely at how psychologists are using the picture metaphor, something very revealing appears. Some theorists use the metaphor of images as pictures to specify the ways in which images are like pictures (they can be *scanned*, they have degrees of *vividness*, etc.), while other theorists use the metaphor to show how images are *not* like pictures (they seem incomplete, they are fleeting, etc.). Pylyshyn (1973), for example, has claimed that the picture metaphor "hides" issues in the notion that images are perceived. And yet Pylyshyn used the picture metaphor to disclose systematically what the theorizing supposedly hid.

Note what is going on here: The metaphor is doing exactly what a scientific metaphor should do. It can be used to generate theoretical classification systems and ideas for experiments. It can also be used to specify the ways in which the phenomenon of interest demands further description and theorizing. It is no "fault" of a metaphor that it sometimes seems "wrong." In fact, that can be one of its virtues. It is just not proper to say that a metaphor is wrong – metaphor is a *process* of showing both similarities and dissimilarities, a process of generating new ideas.

Scientific meaning is not independent of literal meaning, but it is not reducible to it either. *Modification* of meaning occurs when a metaphor has worked as an explanation, and this is not only a form of literal deduction, but meaning change. In other words, there is no strict *a priori* rule for distinguishing between the literal and figurative meanings of scientific terms. One cannot say, "These things suggested by the metaphor are true and literally acceptable and these other things are metaphorical and false or irrelevant" without presupposing a static view of both science and metaphor.

At any given time, a scientist may not be sure what the important similarities and differences are. One is rarely offered a forced choice between mathematical models and poetic theories. (The question of whether mathematical descriptions are themselves metaphors would take us too far afield; see Jones, 1982; Lakoff, 1987, chap. 20.) Once a metaphor has been refined into a theory (or a model), it becomes easy to regard the theory as an isolated, literal, static entity that "has" a meaning independent of cognizing theorists. Though metaphors lead to the generation of refined hypotheses and mathematical theories, the metaphors on which they are based are not discarded like soiled linen. The grounding in the images and metaphors will remain and can be especially apparent in the process of generating ideas for new experiments and in the process of science education. As many people who have taken courses in basic chemistry and physics will attest, science textbooks are often short on prose and long on mathematical and other formalisms. Such texts can leave students with little or no sense of the historical growth of the concepts and of the research methods and results that led to the formalisms. As a contrast, see Feynman's (1965) physics text, which is at once very poetic and very mathematical.

Metaphor and model

In addition to relating theories to new ideas for experiments, metaphor connects all the major functional components of science. In this chapter we have given examples of metaphor themes, specific metaphorical hypotheses, metaphorical theories, mathematical models based on metaphors, and metaphorical "flow" diagrams. A model is technically a substantive thing. All other uses of the term "model" are metaphorical extensions of this basic meaning, including the abstract mathematical notions of a "mathematical model" and "model theory." Psychologists' cognitive theories are often regarded as models, as in the "attention models."

Two things are common to scientific products that are called models: (1) They have similar compositions, namely, physical or symbolic representations that preserve hypothetical correspondences or relations of things in the represented world (Palmer, 1979); and (2) they behave similarly, that is, they generate symbols or other outputs. To the literature on the relations of metaphors and models we would like to add a distinction, between physical models and "metaphorical diagrams." Physical models do things; they produce outputs (symbols, numbers, etc.). Most information-processing flow diagrams do not do this, although the programs they may represent can. A metaphorical diagram need not precisely specify the nature of the represented information, just as Figures 5.1 and 5.2 and similar "models" (metaphorical diagrams) only partially specify some of the factors and transformations involved in the hypothetical boxes. The more specific and generative a representation or diagram is, the more willing one might be to say that it presents a model. Adams's (1971) simple equation for motor skill reaction time is a good example. It can be represented as a metaphorical diagram (with the mathematical operations indicated by concept terms in the boxes) or as a physical model (i.e., it can be used to compute or generate temporal intervals).

Metaphor and the falsification of theories

Not all scientists are suckers; they are often painfully aware of metaphorical and literal aspects of their theorizing, aware of metaphoricalness in falsified theories that were retained for the sake of advances on both theoretical and research levels. Here, for example, is another passage from Freud (1917/1963):

> I know you will say that these ideas are both crude and fantastic and quite impermissible in a scientific account. . . . They are preliminary working hypotheses, like Ampère's manikin swimming in the elec-

tric current.... I should like to assure you that these crude hypotheses of the two rooms, the watchman at the threshold between them and consciousness as a spectator at the end of the second room, must nevertheless be very far-reaching approximations to the real facts. (vol. 16, p. 296)

What Freud was suggesting is that a fallacy is committed whenever a metaphor in a theory is blamed for any shortcomings of the theory, when in fact it is the depth or extent of the theorizing that may be insufficient. As we have shown, metaphor leads to advancement in more ways than providing ideas for new experiments. Metaphor leads to the refinement of theories by pointing out the theorist's assumptions. Metaphor can be used in falsification by pointing out the shortcomings of the theorizing of which the metaphor is one part. These are all positive contributions of metaphor, not failings.

Another fallacy is committed when it is assumed that metaphoricalness alone is sufficient to falsify a theory and sufficient to justify the abandonment of a theory. In actuality, metaphoricalness alone is not sufficient for falsification, and falsified theories should not necessarily be abandoned, since they may have some "truthlikeness." Even theories that are believed to be literal can need simplifying assumptions (e.g., "All other things being equal"), mathematical shortcuts, temporary hypotheses, incompletenesses, entities that are not "real," phenomena or properties that are not "directly sensible," and the like. So it is logically incorrect to abandon a theory on the assumption that its metaphoricalness detracts from its truthlikeness. Metaphors, like literal statements, can be regarded as falsified and yet be used creatively to generate experimental confirmations and disconfirmations. It is never necessarily a mistake to propose a metaphor in an attempt to explain or clarify something or to come up with new ideas. Any given metaphor might have payoffs if pursued. Scientific metaphors are embryonic theories: They can grow into precise hypotheses that can ultimately go beyond their root metaphors in descriptive or explanatory power.

One can certainly establish rules for deciding whether to accept (tentatively) a given theory on the basis of the occurrence of metaphors in the theory. One simple rule, often relied on in debates, is: If the theory contains metaphor, abandon it. Another such rule, perhaps a more reasonable one, would be: If the metaphor suggests more resemblances that are demonstrably incorrect than ones that are demonstrably correct, seek another metaphor. However, the question of when to know whether to apply any such rule (i.e., the rule's "decidability") is problematic. That is, in practice one can never be sure *a priori* that a decision to reject (or accept) a theory on the basis of a criterion of metaphoricalness is a sound one (Hoffman, 1980).

This conjecture – the undecidability of criteria for the rejection of scientific metaphors – is a variation on a claim made by Maxwell (1970) that there can be no strict inductive justification (i.e., *a priori* logical guidelines) for belief in scientific (here, metaphorical) principles. Hesse (1966) argued somewhat similarly that the postulation of new entities must involve metaphorical extensions since a strictly deductive (or "rational") method cannot make such postulations. One may not be able to determine which characteristics of a theory or model can be exploited and which are irrelevant. Hutten (1954) and Lachman (1960) argued that models can be evaluated *a priori*, that is, by rational rather than empirical means, according to their scope and precision. Yet, they maintained, there can be no sufficient rational grounds for determining beforehand how well a theory or model will work out. In terms of the present analysis, there is no deductive means for deciding which metaphor to introduce (or throw out) or for deciding which correspondence rules to use to fit the metaphor into a theory. As Berggren (1963) put it, this is because metaphors "partially create what in fact they reveal" (p. 462). The moral? Do not reject a theory offhand because it is metaphorical.

The cognitive-experimental approach to the philosophy of science

In his summary of various philosophical positions with regard to the nature of scientific knowledge, Lakatos (1970) wrote:

> Justificationists want scientific theories to be proved before they are published. Probabilists hope a machine can flash up the degree of confirmation of a theory given the evidence. Falsificationists hope that the elimination of a theory is the verdict of experiments. All these theories of instant rationality – and instant learning – fail. The constraints in science, the tenacity of some theorists, the rationality of a certain amount of dogmatism, can only be explained if we construe science as a battleground of research programs rather than of isolated theories. (pp. 174–5)

The cognitive-experimental perspective on science encourages the view that psychological factors – such as metaphor and the heuristics and biases that operate in problem solving – play just as important a role as logical factors. This is essentially the opposite of the view taken by logical positivists and empiricists. That view dominated the philosophy of science for many years but has been challenged in the past few decades. To philosophers of science such as the "instrumentalists" (e.g., Maxwell, 1970) and "fallibilists" (e.g., Weimer, 1979), knowledge does not come only from experience sifted through the rules of logic; there are other important and necessary components. The notion that science can be fully understood only through a naive view of observation and steadfast reliance on logical analyses leads to an impoverished philosophy of science, one that eschews empirical studies of actual scientists in favor of the predicate-calculus analysis of static, inhuman, context-free "theories."

Philosophers of science generally reify theories. A major goal of their discipline is to define what a "theory" is. But strictly speaking, there is no such thing as a theory with fixed meaning and independent of cognizing theorists. Most of the history of the philosophy of science and epistemology consists of repeated attempts to convince ourselves that theories exist, that bits of knowledge exist, and that they can be literal and true. In practice, it would be better to focus on the idea that theorizing exists, and not theories.

The analysis of scientists' cognition suggests that a collaboration of philosophers and psychologists in research programs on real domains of scientific practice could be more productive for philosophy (addressing questions such as "What is inductive inference?") and more productive for psychology (addressing questions such as "Does a given theory of cognition work for scientific problem solving?") than a philosophy of science that focuses on postulational theories and repeated attempts to salvage empiricism through refinements in logical calculi (Weimer, 1979). In what cases, if any, do metaphors appear to serve a necessary scientific function? How do scientists go from metaphors and images to mathematical equations? Would a knowledge of the different rhetorical forms of figurative language be of assistance in actual problem-solving situations? Must certain types of metaphors be used in the comprehension of certain domains?

Science is a kind of poetry in motion, under the multiple constraints of physical, conceptual, and methodological factors. The analysis of metaphor, its many uses in scientific theorizing and research, will not illuminate the entire truth. But by classifying cognitive metaphors, seeing their thematic coherence, and clarifying their role in experimental psychology, we somewhat nearsighted psychologists may be able to see the flickering shadow on the wall of the cave a bit more sharply.

Acknowledgments

This chapter stems from previous works (Hoffman, 1979, 1980) concerning metaphor in science. It actually began as a larger work that has now become a triad. Elsewhere (Hoffman & Nead, 1983) we explore the use of metaphor in general world views, including those in psychology and artificial intelligence. Hoffman (1985) goes into more detail on the implications of metaphor for the philosophy of science. Looking back over the triad, we see that a few points are repeated (briefly), but we feel that these points need repeating, especially in a review chapter such as this.

The preparation of a draft of this chapter was supported by a postdoctoral associateship to the first author and a predoctoral associateship to the second author under Grant HD-07151 from the National Institute of Child Health and Human Development to the Center for Research in Human Learning of the University of Minnesota. Many of the ideas expressed here first arose in a seminar on mental representation held at the center in 1979 and 1980. The seminar was attended by Joseph Blount, Edward Cochran, Stephen Chew, Grant Cioffi, Peter Eisenberg, Robert Hoffman, James Jenkins, Jeffrey Kreps, James Nead, Edward Reed, Mary Ann Records, Jan Wald, Jerry Wald, and Connie Wellen. The authors would like to thank Joseph Blount, Ben Bravermen, Russell Burrhus, Peter Eisenberg, Terry Gottfried, Lenief Heimstedt, Leah Larkey, Edward Reed, and Jan Wald for their helpful comments on drafts of sections of this chapter. David Leary deserves special thanks for his painstaking attention to historical details. Our thanks also go to Mary Wolf and Jim Becker for preparing the figures.

Note

1 Throughout this chapter, we follow the convention of putting metaphors in italics and metaphor themes in capitalized italics. In the following discussion, we give only a few examples of each metaphor theme, but we invite the reader to generate other examples.

References

Adams, J. A. (1971). A closed-loop theory of motor learning. *Journal of Motor Behavior, 3*, 111–50.

(1976). Issues for a closed-loop theory of motor learning. In G. E. Stelmach (Ed.), *Motor control* (pp. 87–107). New York: Academic Press.

Anderson, J. R. (1979). Arguments concerning representations for mental imagery. *Psychological Review, 85*, 249–77.

Anderson, J. R., & Bower, G. H. (1973). *Human associative memory*. Hillsdale, NJ: Erlbaum.

Asch, S. E. (1958). The metaphor: A psychological inquiry. In R. Taguiri & L. Petrullo (Eds.), *Person perception and interpersonal behavior* (pp. 86–94). Stanford, CA: Stanford University Press.

Attneave, F. (1954). Some informational aspects of visual perception. *Psychological Review, 61*, 183–93.

(1957). Physical determinants of the judged complexity of shapes. *Journal of Experimental Psychology, 53*, 221–7.

Averbach, E., & Sperling, G. (1961). Short-term storage of information in vision. In C. Cherry (Ed.), *Information theory* (pp. 196–201). London: Butterworth.

Bahrick, H. P. (1987). Functional and cognitive memory theory: An overview of some key issues. In D. S. Gorfein & R. R. Hoffman (Eds.), *Memory and learning: The Ebbinghaus Centennial Conference* (pp. 387–95). Hillsdale, NJ: Erlbaum.

Bartlett, F. (1932). *Remembering.* Cambridge University Press.

Becker, J. D. (1975). *The phrasal lexicon* (Rep. no. 3081). Bolt, Beranek & Newman, Inc., Cambridge, MA.

Berggren, D. (1963). The use and abuse of metaphor. *Review of Metaphysics, 16,* 450–72.

Bernstein, N. (1967). *The coordination and regulation of movements.* New York: Pergamon. (Original work published 1935.)

Black, M. (1962). *Models and metaphors.* Ithaca, NY: Cornell University Press.

Boyd, R. (1979). Metaphor and theory change: What is "metaphor" a metaphor for? In A. Ortony (Ed.), *Metaphor and thought* (pp. 356–408). Cambridge University Press.

Brachman, R. J., & Smith, B. C. (Eds.). (1980, February). Special Issue on knowledge representation. *SIGART Newsletter,* no. 70. New York: Association for Computing Machinery.

Brentano, F. (1973). *Psychology from an empirical standpoint* (A. C. Rancurello, D. B. Terrell, & L. L. McAlister, Trans.). New York: Humanities Press. (Original work published 1874.)

Brett, G. S. (1965). *A history of psychology* (rev. ed; R. S. Peters, Ed.). Cambridge, MA: MIT Press.

Brewer, W. F. (1974). The problem of meaning and the interrelations of the higher mental processes. In W. B. Weimer & D. S. Palermo (Eds.), *Cognition and the symbolic processes* (pp. 263–98). Hillsdale, NJ: Erlbaum.

Broadbent, D. (1952). Listening to one of two synchronous messages. *Journal of Experimental Psychology, 44,* 51–5.

(1954). The role of auditory localization in attention and memory span. *Journal of Experimental Psychology, 47,* 191–6.

(1958). *Perception and communication.* New York: Pergamon.

Brown, R. H. (1976). Social theory as metaphor. *Theory and Society, 3,* 169–97.

Brown, T. G. (1914). On the nature of the fundamental activity of the nervous centers. *Journal of Physiology, 48,* 18–46.

Bruner, J. (1965). *On knowing.* New York: Atheneum Press.

Carbonell, J. (1980). *Metaphor: A key to extensible semantic analysis.* In *Proceedings of the 18th annual meeting of the Association for Computational Linguistics* (pp. 17–21). New York: Association for Computational Linguistics.

Cassirer, E. (1946). *Language and myth* (S. K. Langer, Trans.). New York: Harper Bros. (Original work published 1925.)

Chase, R. (1965). An information-flow model of the organization of motor activity: I. Transduction, transmission, and central control of sensory information. *Journal of Nervous and Mental Disease, 140,* 239–51.

Cherry, E. C. (1953). Some experiments on the recognition of speech with one and two ears. *Journal of the Acoustical Society of America, 25,* 975–9.

Chomsky, N. (1959). Review of B. F. Skinner's *Verbal behavior. Language, 35,* 26–58.

(1965). *Aspects of a theory of syntax.* Cambridge, MA: MIT Press.

Cooper, L. A., & Shepard, R. N. (1973). Chronometric studies on the rotation of mental images. In W. G. Chase (Ed.), *Visual information processing* (pp. 75–176). New York: Academic Press.

Corso, J. F. (1956). The neural quantum theory of sensory discrimination. *Psychological Bulletin, 53,* 371–93.

Craik, F., & Lockhart, R. S. (1972). Levels of processing: A framework for memory research. *Journal of Verbal Learning and Verbal Behavior, 11,* 671–84.

Craik, K. (1947). A theory of the human operator in control systems. *British Journal of Psychology*, *38*, 56–61.

Davidson, D. (1978). What metaphors mean. In S. Sacks (Ed.), *On metaphor* (pp. 29–45). Chicago: University of Chicago Press.

Deese, J. (1972). *Psychology as science and art*. New York: Harcourt Brace Jovanovich.

de Man, P. (1978). The epistemology of metaphor. In S. Sacks (Ed.), *On metaphor* (pp. 11–28). Chicago: University of Chicago Press.

Dember, W. N., & Purcell, D. G. (1967). Recovery of masked visual targets by inhibition of the masking stimulus. *Science*, *159*, 1335–6.

Dember, W. N., & Warm, J. S. (1979). *Psychology of perception*. New York: Holt, Rinehart & Winston.

Dennett, D. C. (1978). *Brainstorms: Philosophical essays on mind and psychology*. Montgomery, VT: Bradford Books.

Descartes, R. (1911). Rules for the direction of mind. In E. S. Haldane & G. R. T. Ross (Eds. and Trans.), *The philosophical works of René Descartes* (vol. 1, pp. 1–77). Cambridge University Press. (Original work published 1628.)

(1965). Dioptrics (M. D. Boring, Trans.). In R. J. Herrnstein & E. G. Boring (Eds.), *A sourcebook in the history of psychology* (pp. 113–17). Cambridge, MA: Harvard University Press. (Original work published 1638.)

(1972). *Treatise of man* (T. S. Hall, Trans). Cambridge, MA: Harvard University Press. (Original work published posthumously 1662.)

Deutsch, J. A., & Deutsch, D. (1963). Attention: Some theoretical considerations. *Psychological Review*, *70*, 80–90.

Ebbinghaus, H. (1964). *On memory: A contribution to experimental psychology* (H. A. Ruger & C. E. Bussenius, Trans.). New York: Dover Press. (Original work published 1885.)

(1971). *Urmanuskript über das Gedächtnis* [Original manuscript on memory]. Passau: Passavia Universitatsverlag. (Original work written 1890.)

Eberle, R. (1970). Models, metaphors, and formal interpretations. In C. M. Turbayne, *The myth of metaphor* (rev. ed., pp. 219–33). Columbia: University of South Carolina Press.

Estes, W. K. (1978).The information processing approach to cognition: A confluence of metaphors and methods. In W. K. Estes (Ed.), *Handbook of learning and cognitive processes* (vol. 5, pp. 1–18). Hillsdale, NJ: Erlbaum.

Fechner, G. T. (1965). Elements of psychophysics (H. S. Langfeld, Trans.). In R. J. Herrnstein & E. G. Boring (Eds.), *A sourcebook in the history of psychology* (pp. 66–75). Cambridge, MA: Harvard University Press. (Original work published 1860.)

Feynman, R. (1965). *The character of physical law*. Cambridge, MA: MIT Press.

Field, H. (1978). Mental representation. *Erkenntnis*, *13*, 9–61.

Fitts, P. M. (1964). Perceptual-motor skill learning. In A. W. Melton (Ed.), *Categories of human learning* (pp. 244–85). New York: Academic Press.

Fitts, P. M., & Posner, M. I. (1967). *Human performance*. Monterey, CA: Brooks/Cole.

Fodor, J. A. (1981). *Representations: Philosophical essays on the foundations of cognitive science*. Cambridge, MA: MIT Press.

(1984). *The modularity of mind*. Cambridge, MA: MIT Press.

Freud, S. (1963). Introductory lectures on psycho-analysis. In J. Strachey (Ed. and Trans.), *The standard edition of the complete psychological works of Sigmund Freud* (vols. 15 and 16). London: Hogarth Press. (Original work published 1917.)

Garner, W. R. (1962). *Uncertainty and structure as psychological concepts*. New York: Wiley, 1962.

Garner, W. R., Hake, H. W., & Eriksen, C. W. (1956). Operationism and the concept of perception. *Psychological Review, 63*, 149–59.

Gentner, D. (1982). Are scientific analogies metaphors? In D. S. Miall (Ed.), *Metaphor: Problems and perspectives* (pp. 106–32). Brighton: Harvester Press.

Gentner, D., & Gentner, D. R. (1983). Flowing waters and teeming crowds: Mental models of electric circuits. In D. Gentner & A. Stevens (Eds.), *Mental models* (pp. 99–130). Hillsdale, NJ: Erlbaum.

Gentner, D., & Grudin, J. (1985). The evolution of mental metaphors in psychology: A 90-year retrospective. *American Psychologist, 40*, 181–92.

George, F. H. (1953). Logical constructs and psychological theory. *Psychological Review, 60*, 1–6.

Gibson, J. J. (1977). The theory of affordances. In R. Shaw & J. Bransford (Eds.), *Perceiving, acting, and knowing* (pp. 67–82). Hillsdale, NJ: Erlbaum.

(1979). *The ecological approach to visual perception*. Boston: Houghton Mifflin.

(1985). Conclusions from a century of research on sense perception. In S. Koch & D. E. Leary (Eds.), *A century of psychology as science* (pp. 224–30). New York: McGraw-Hill.

Goffman, E. (1974). *Frame analysis: An essay on the organization of experience*. New York: Harper & Row.

Goodman, N. (1976). *The languages of art*. Indianapolis, IN: Hackett.

Haber, R. N. (1968). Introduction. In R. N. Haber (Ed.), *Contemporary theory and research in visual perception* (pp. 1–5). New York: Holt, Rinehart & Winston.

Hagen, M. A. (1985). James J. Gibson's ecological approach to visual perception. In S. Koch & D. E. Leary (Eds.), *A century of psychology as science* (pp. 231–49). New York: McGraw-Hill.

Hanson, N. R. (1958). *Patterns of discovery*. Cambridge University Press.

Harman, G. (1978). Is there mental representation? In C. W. Savage (Ed.), *Minnesota studies in the philosophy of science* (vol. 9, pp. 57–64). Minneapolis: University of Minnesota Press.

Harré, R., & Secord, P. (1973). *The explanation of social behaviour*. Totowa, NJ: Littlefield, Adams.

Hartley, D. (1966). *Observations on man, his frame, his duty, and his expectations*. Delmar, NY: Scholars' Facsimiles and Reprints. (Original work published 1749.)

Harvey, W. (1847). An anatomical disquisition on the motion of the heart and the blood in animals. In R. Willis (Ed. and Trans.), *The works of William Harvey, M.D.* London: Sydenham Society. (Original work published 1628.)

Haugeland, J. (Ed.). (1981). *Mind design: Philosophy, psychology, artificial intelligence*. Montgomery, VT: Bradford Books.

Head, H. (1920). *Studies in neurology*. London: Frowde, Hudder & Stoughton.

Helmholtz, H. (1962). *Handbook of physiological optics* (J. P. C. Southall, Trans. and Ed.). New York: Dover Press. (Original work published 1867.)

Helson, H. (1964). *Adaptation level theory*. New York: Harper & Row.

Herbart, J. F. (1891). *A text-book of psychology* (W. T. Harris, Ed., and M. K. Smith, Trans.). New York: Appleton. (Original work published 1816.)

Hershberger, W. A. (1976, September). *Afference copy: The closed-loop analog of von Holst's efference copy*. Paper presented at the convention of the American Psychological Association, Washington, DC.

Hesse, M. B. (1953). Models in physics. *British Journal of the Philosophy of Science*, *4*, 198–214.

(1966). *Models and analogies in science*. Notre Dame, IN: University of Notre Dame Press.

Hick, W. E. (1952). On the rate of gain of information. *Quarterly Journal of Experimental Psychology*, *4*, 11–26.

Hobbes, T. (1950). The leviathan. In Sir W. Molesworth (Ed.), *The English works of Thomas Hobbes*. London: Bohn. (Original work published 1651.)

Hoffman, R. R. (1979). Metaphors, myths and mind. *Psychological Record*, *29*, 175–8.

(1980). Metaphor in science. In R. P. Honeck & R. R. Hoffman (Eds.), *Cognition and figurative language* (pp. 393–423). Hillsdale, NJ: Erlbaum.

(1984). Recent psycholinguistic research on figurative language. *Annals of the New York Academy of Sciences*, *433*, 137–66.

(1985). Some implications of metaphor for philosophy and psychology of science. In W. Paprotte & R. Dirven (Eds.), *The ubiquity of metaphor* (pp. 327–80). Amsterdam: Benjamins.

(1987). The problem of extracting the knowledge of experts from the perspective of experimental psychology. *AI Magazine*, *8*, 53–67.

(1988). *On the meanings of "literal."* Manuscript, Department of Psychology, Adelphi University, Garden City, NY.

Hoffman, R. R., & Honeck, R. P. (1976). Bidirectionality of judgements of synonymy. *Journal of Psycholinguistic Research*, *5*, 173–83.

Hoffman, R. R., & Kemper, S. (1987). What could reaction-time studies be telling us about metaphor comprehension? *Metaphor and Symbolic Activity*, *2*, 149–86.

Hoffman, R. R., MacCormac, E. R., Lawler, J. M., & Carroll, J. M. (1989). *The metaphors of semantics and the semantics of metaphors*. Manuscript, Department of Psychology, Adelphi University, Garden City, NY.

Hoffman, R. R., & Nead, J. M. (1983). General contextualism, ecological science, and cognitive research. *Journal of Mind and Behavior*, *4*, 507–60.

Hubel, D. H., & Wiesel, T. N. (1962). Receptive fields, binocular interaction, and functional architecture in the cat's visual cortex. *Journal of Physiology*, *160*, 106–54.

Hume, D. (1955). *Enquiries concerning human understanding and concerning the principles of morals* (L. A. Selby-Bigge, Ed.). Oxford: Clarendon Press. (Original work published 1748.)

(1978). *A treatise of human nature* (P. H. Nidditch, Ed.). Oxford: Clarendon Press. (Original work published 1739–40.)

Hutten, E. H. (1954). The role of models in science. *British Journal of the Philosophy of Science*, *4*, 284–301.

Hyman, R. (1953). Stimulus information as a determinant of reaction time. *Journal of Experimental Psychology*, *45*, 188–96.

Ingebritzen, O. C. (1933). Coordinating mechanisms of the spinal cord. *Genetic Psychology Monographs*, *13*, 483–555.

James, W. (1890). *The principles of psychology*. New York: Holt.

Jaynes, J. (1976). *The origin of consciousness in the breakdown of the bicameral mind*. Boston: Houghton Mifflin.

Johansson, G. (1985). About visual event perception. In W. H. Warren & R. E. Shaw (Eds.), *Persistence and change: Proceedings of the First International Conference on Event Perception* (pp. 29–54). Hillsdale, NJ: Erlbaum.

Johnson, M. (1981). Metaphor in the philosophical tradition. In M. Johnson

(Ed.), *Philosophical perspectives on metaphor* (pp. 3–47). Minneapolis: University of Minnesota Press.

Jones, R. S. (1982). *Physics as metaphor*. Minneapolis: University of Minnesota Press.

Kahneman, D. (1973). *Attention and effort*. Englewood Cliffs, NJ: Prentice-Hall.

Kant, I. (1951). *Critique of judgment* (J. H. Bernard, Trans.). New York: Hafner. (Original work published 1790.)

Kantor, J. R. (1938). The operational principle in the physical and psychological sciences. *Psychological Record, 2,* 3–32.

Kaplan, A. (1965). *The conduct of inquiry*. San Francisco: Chandler.

Katz, J. J. (1973). The realm of meaning. In G. A. Miller (Ed.), *Communication, language, and meaning* (pp. 36–48). New York: Basic Books.

Kearns, M. S. (1987). *Metaphors of mind in fiction and psychology*. Lexington: University Press of Kentucky.

Keele, S. W. (1973). *Attention and human performance*. Pacific Palisades, CA: Goodyear.

Keele, S. W., & Posner, M. I. (1968). Processing of visual feedback in rapid movements. *Journal of Experimental Psychology, 77,* 155–8.

Kelso, J. A. S. (Ed.). (1982a). *Human motor behavior: An introduction*. Hillsdale, NJ: Erlbaum.

   (1982b). Concepts and issues in human motor behavior: Coming to grips with the jargon. In J. A. S. Kelso (Ed.), *Human motor behavior: An introduction* (pp. 21–58). Hillsdale, NJ: Erlbaum.

Kieras, D. (1978). Beyond pictures and words: Alternative information processing models for imagery effects in verbal memory. *Psychological Bulletin, 85,* 532–54.

Kintsch, W. (1974). *The representation of meaning in memory*. Hillsdale, NJ: Erlbaum.

Kosslyn, S. M., Pinker, S., Smith, G. E., & Schwartz, S. P. (1979). On the demystification of mental imagery. *Behavioral and Brain Sciences, 2,* 535–81.

Kosslyn, S. M., & Pomerantz, J. (1977). Propositions and the form of internal representations. *Cognitive Psychology, 9,* 52–76.

Lachman, R. (1960). The model in theory construction. *Psychological Review, 67,* 113–29.

Lakatos, I. (1970). Falsification and the methodology of scientific research programmes. In I. Lakatos & C. Musgrave (Eds.), *Criticism and the growth of knowledge* (pp. 91–196). Cambridge University Press.

Lakoff, G. (1987). *Women, fire, and other dangerous things: What categories reveal about the mind*. Chicago: University of Chicago Press.

Lakoff, G., & Johnson, M. (1980a). The metaphorical structure of human conceptualization. *Cognitive Science, 4,* 195–208.

   (1980b). Conceptual metaphor in everyday language. *Journal of Philosophy, 77,* 453–86.

   (1980c). *Metaphors we live by*. Chicago: University of Chicago Press.

La Mettrie, J. O. (1912). *Man a machine* (G. C. Bussey, Trans.; revised by M. W. Calkins). Chicago: Open Court. (Original work published 1748.)

Larsen, S. F. (1987). Remembering and the archaeology metaphor. *Metaphor and Symbolic Activity, 2,* 187–200.

Lashley, K. S. (1917). The accuracy of movement in the absence of excitation from the moving organ. *American Journal of Psychology, 43,* 169–94.

   (1951). The problem of serial order in behavior. In L. Jeffress (Ed.), *Cerebral mechanisms in behavior* (pp. 112–36). New York: Wiley.

Lazlo, J. (1967). Training of fast tapping with reduction of kinesthetic, tactile, visual, and auditory sensations. *Quarterly Journal of Experimental Psychology, 19,* 344–9.

Leibniz, G. (1912). The monadology (R. Latta, Trans.). In B. Rand (Ed.), *The classical psychologists* (pp. 208–28). Boston: Houghton Mifflin. (Original work published 1695.)

Levin, S. R. (1977). *The semantics of metaphor.* Baltimore, MD: Johns Hopkins University Press.

Liberman, A. (1970). The grammars of speech and language. *Cognitive Psychology, 1,* 301–23.

Lindsay, P. H., & Norman, D. A. (1977). *Human information processing.* New York: Academic Press.

Locke, J. (1894). *An essay concerning human understanding* (A. C. Freeman, Ed.). New York: Oxford University Press. (Original work published 1690.)

Lockhead, G. R. (1972). Processing dimensional stimuli. *Psychological Review, 79,* 410–19.

MacCormac, E. R. (1976). *Metaphor and myth in science and religion.* Durham, NC: Duke University Press.

Martin, E. J. (1978). The psychological unreality of quantificational semantics. In C. W. Savage (Ed.), *Minnesota studies in the philosophy of science* (vol. 9, pp. 165–81). Minneapolis: University of Minnesota Press.

Maxwell, G. (1970). Theories, perception, and structural realism. In R. G. Colodny (Ed.), *The nature and function of scientific theories* (pp. 3–34). Pittsburgh, PA: University of Pittsburgh Press.

McReynolds, P. (1980). The clock metaphor in the history of psychology. In T. Nickles (Ed.), *Scientific discovery: Case studies* (pp. 97–112). Dordrecht: Reidel.

Mill, J. (1967). *Analysis of the phenomena of the human mind* (2d ed.; J. S. Mill, Ed.). New York: Kelley. (Original work published 1829.)

Mill, J. S. (1843). *A system of logic.* London: Parker.

Miller, G. A. (1953). What is information measurement? *American Psychologist, 8,* 3–11.

Miller, G. A., & Frick, F. C. (1949). Statistical behavioristics and sequences of responses. *Psychological Review, 56,* 311–24.

Miller, G. A., & Johnson-Laird, P. N. (1976). *Language and perception.* Cambridge, MA: Harvard University Press.

Moray, N. (1959). Attention in dichotic listening: Affective cues and the influence of instructions. *Quarterly Journal of Experimental Psychology, 11,* 56–60.

    (1969). *Attention: Selective processes in vision and hearing.* New York: Academic Press.

Murdock, B. B. (1974). *Human memory.* Hillsdale, NJ: Erlbaum.

Natsoulas, T. (1967). What are perceptual reports about? *Psychological Bulletin, 67,* 249–72.

Neisser, U. (1967). *Cognitive psychology.* New York: Appleton-Century-Crofts.

    (1976). *Cognition and reality.* San Francisco: Freeman.

Nemetz, A. (1958). Metaphor: The Daedalus of discourse. *Thought, 33,* 417–42.

Newell, A. (1972). A note on process–structure distinctions in developmental psychology. In S. Farnham-Diggory (Ed.), *Information processing in children* (pp. 126–39). New York: Academic Press.

Newell, K., & Shapiro, P. (1976). Variability of practice and transfer of training: Some evidence toward a schema view of motor learning. *Journal of Motor Behavior, 8,* 233–43.

Norman, D. A. (1968). Toward a theory of memory and attention. *Psychological Review, 75*, 522–36.

Northway, M. L. (1940). The concept of the "schema." *British Journal of Psychology, 30*, 316–25.

Oatley, K. (1978). *Perceptions and representations.* New York: Free Press.

Ortony, A. (Ed.) (1979). *Metaphor and thought.* Cambridge University Press.

(1980). Some psycholinguistic aspects of metaphor. In R. P. Honeck & R. R. Hoffman (Eds.), *Cognition and figurative language* (pp. 69–83). Hillsdale, NJ: Erlbaum.

Osgood, C. E. (1980). The cognitive dynamics of synaesthesia and metaphor. In R. P. Honeck & R. R. Hoffman (Eds.), *Cognition and figurative language* (pp. 203–38). Hillsdale, NJ: Erlbaum.

Paivio, A. (1975). Neomentalism. *Canadian Journal of Psychology, 29*, 263–91.

(1976). *Images, propositions and knowledge.* London, Ontario: University of Western Ontario Press.

(1979). Psychological processes in the comprehension of metaphor. In A. Ortony (Ed.), *Metaphor and thought* (pp. 150–71). Cambridge University Press.

Palmer, S. E. (1975). Visual perception and world knowledge: Notes on a model of sensory–cognitive interaction. In D. A. Norman & D. E. Rumelhart (Eds.), *Explorations in cognition* (pp. 279–307). San Francisco: Freeman.

(1979). Fundamental aspects of cognitive representation. In E. Rosch & B. Lloyd (Eds.), *Cognition and categorization* (pp. 259–303). Hillsdale, NJ: Erlbaum.

Parker, P. (1982). The metaphorical plot. In D. S. Miall (Ed.), *Metaphor: Problems and perspectives* (pp. 133–58). Brighton: Harvester Press.

Paul, I. M. (1967). The concept of a schema in memory theory. In R. R. Holt (Ed.), *Motives and thought: Psychoanalytic essays in honor of David Rapaport* (pp. 219–58). New York: International Universities Press.

Perkins, M. (1953). Intersubjectivity and Gestalt psychology. *Philosophy and Phenomenological Research, 13*, 437–51.

Pew, R. W. (1966). Acquisition of a hierarchical control over the temporal organization of a skill. *Journal of Experimental Psychology, 71*, 764–71.

(1970). Toward a process-oriented theory of human skilled performance. *Journal of Motor Behavior, 11*, 8–24.

Piaget, J. (1971). *Biology and knowledge: An essay on the relations between organic and cognitive processes* (B. Walsh, Trans.). Chicago: University of Chicago Press.

Pillsbury, W. B. (1908). *Attention.* New York: Macmillan.

Pisoni, D. B. (1978). Speech perception. In W. K. Estes (Ed.), *Handbook of learning and cognitive processes* (vol. 6, pp. 167–233). Hillsdale, NJ: Erlbaum.

Pollio, H. R., Barlow, J. M., Fine, H. J., & Pollio, M. R. (1977). *Psychology and the poetics of growth.* Hillsdale, NJ: Erlbaum.

Popper, K. (1959). *The logic of scientific discovery.* London: Hutchinson.

Pylyshyn, Z. W. (1973). What the mind's eye tells the mind's brain: A critique of mental imagery. *Psychological Bulletin, 80*, 1–24.

(1978). Computational models and empirical constraints. *Behavioral and Brain Sciences, 1*, 93–127.

(1984). *Computation and cognition: Toward a foundation for cognitive science.* Cambridge, MA: MIT Press.

Raphael, B. (1972). *The thinking computer.* San Francisco: Freeman.

Reddy, M. J. (1979). The conduit metaphor: A case of frame conflict in our language about language. In A. Ortony (Ed.), *Metaphor and thought* (pp. 284–324). Cambridge University Press.

Reed, E. S. (1980). *The corporeal ideas hypothesis and the origin of scientific psychology.* Doctoral dissertation, Department of Philosophy, Boston University.

Reed, E. S., & Jones, R. (1978). Gibson's theory of perception: A case of hasty epistemologizing? *Philosophy of Science, 45,* 519–30.

Reed, S. K. (1988). *Cognition: Theory and applications.* Monterey, CA: Brooks/Cole.

Repp, B. H. (1981). On levels of description in speech research. *Journal of the Acoustical Society of America, 69,* 1462–4.

Rhodes, R. A., & Lawler, J. M. (1981). Athematic metaphors. In R. A. Hendrik, C. S. Masek, & M. F. Miller (Eds.), *Papers from the seventeenth regional meeting of the Chicago Linguistic Society* (pp. 318–42). Chicago: Chicago Linguistic Society.

Richards, I. A. (1936). *The philosophy of rhetoric.* New York: Oxford University Press.

Ricoeur, P. (1978). The metaphorical process as cognition, imagination, and feeling. In S. Sacks (Ed.), *On metaphor* (pp. 141–50). Chicago: University of Chicago Press.

Roediger, H. L., III (1980). Memory metaphors in cognitive psychology. *Memory & Cognition, 8,* 231–46.

Romanyshyn, R. D. (1982). *Psychological life: From science to metaphor.* Austin: University of Texas Press.

Russell, B. (1948). *Human knowledge.* New York: Simon & Schuster.

Russell, S. W. (1986). Information and experience in metaphor: A perspective from computer analysis. *Metaphor and Symbolic Activity, 1,* 227–70.

Scheffler, I. (1960). *The language of education.* Springfield, IL: Thomas.

Schmidt, R. A. (1975). A schema theory of discrete motor skill learning. *Psychological Review, 82,* 225–60.

(1982a). More on motor programs. In J. A. S. Kelso (Ed.), *Human motor behavior: An introduction* (pp. 189–218). Hillsdale, NJ: Erlbaum.

(1982b). The schema concept. In J. A. S. Kelso (Ed.), *Human motor behavior: An introduction* (pp. 219–35). Hillsdale, NJ: Erlbaum.

Schön, D. A. (1979). Generative metaphor: A perspective on problem setting in social policy. In A. Ortony (Ed.), *Metaphor and thought* (pp. 254–83). Cambridge University Press.

Schwartz, R. (1978). Infinite sets, unbounded competence, and models of mind. In C. W. Savage (Ed.), *Minnesota studies in the philosophy of science* (vol. 9, pp. 183–200). Minneapolis: University of Minnesota Press.

Selfridge, O. (1966). Pandemonium: A paradigm for learning. In L. Uhr (Ed.), *Pattern recognition* (pp. 339–48). New York: Wiley. (Original work published 1959.)

Shannon, C. E. (1948). A mathematical theory of communication. *Bell System Technological Journal, 27,* 379–423, 623–56.

Shannon, C. E., & Weaver, W. (1949). *The mathematical theory of communication.* Urbana: University of Illinois Press.

Shaw, R., & Bransford, J. D. (1977). Psychological approaches to the problem of knowledge. In R. Shaw & J. D. Bransford (Eds.), *Perceiving, acting, and knowing* (pp. 1–39). Hillsdale, NJ: Erlbaum.

Shaw, R. E., Turvey, M. T., & Mace, W. (1982). Ecological psychology: The consequence of a commitment to realism. In W. B. Weimer & D. S. Palermo (Eds.), *Cognition and the symbolic processes* (vol. 2, pp. 159–226). Hillsdale, NJ: Erlbaum.

Shepard, R. N., & Chipman, S. (1970). Second-order isomorphism of internal representations: Shapes of states. *Cognitive Psychology, 1,* 1–17.

Shepard, R. N., & Metzler, J. (1971). Mental rotation of three-dimensional objects. *Science, 171,* 701–3.

Simon, H. A. (1973). Does scientific discovery have a logic? *Philosophy of Science, 40,* 471–80.

  (1978). On the forms of mental representation. In C. W. Savage (Ed.), *Minnesota studies in the philosophy of science* (vol. 9, pp. 3–18). Minneapolis: University of Minnesota Press.

Skinner, B. F. (1968). *The technology of teaching.* New York: Appleton-Century-Crofts.

Sternberg, R. J., Tourangeau, R., & Nigro, G. (1979). Metaphor, induction, and social policy: The convergence of macroscopic and microscopic views. In A. Ortony (Ed.), *Metaphor and thought* (pp. 325–53). Cambridge University Press.

Sternberg, S. (1969). Memory scanning: Mental processes revealed by reaction-time experiments. *American Scientist, 57,* 421–57.

Stevens, S. S. (1972). A neural quantum in sensory discrimination. *Science, 177,* 749–62.

Studdert-Kennedy, M. (1976). Speech perception. In N. J. Lass (Ed.), *Contemporary issues in experimental phonetics* (pp. 243–93). New York: Academic Press.

Triesman, A. F. (1960). Contextual cues in selective listening. *Quarterly Journal of Experimental Psychology, 12,* 242–8.

  (1962). Psychological explanation: The "private data" hypothesis. *British Journal of the Philosophy of Science, 13,* 130–43.

  (1964). Verbal cues, language, and meaning in selective attention. *American Journal of Psychology, 77,* 206–19.

Turvey, M. T., & Carello, C. (1981). Cognition: The view from ecological realism. *Cognition, 10,* 313–21.

Uhr, L. (1965). Pattern recognition. In L. Uhr (Ed.), *Pattern recognition* (pp. 365–81). New York: Wiley.

Underwood, B. J. (1972). Are we overloading memory? In A. W. Melton & E. Martin (Eds.), *Coding processes in human memory* (pp. 1–23). Washington, DC: Winston.

Uttal, W. R. (1973). *The psychology of sensory coding.* New York: Harper & Row.

Verbrugge, R. (1980). Transformations in knowing: A realist view of metaphor. In R. P. Honeck & R. R. Hoffman (Eds.), *Cognition and figurative language* (pp. 87–125). Hillsdale, NJ: Erlbaum.

von Holst, E. (1954). Relations between the central nervous system and the peripheral organs. *British Journal of Animal Behavior, 2,* 89–94.

Warren, R. M. (1958). A basis for judgments of sensory intensity. *American Journal of Psychology, 71,* 675–87.

Warren, W. H., & Shaw, R. E. (Eds.). (1985). *Persistence and change: Proceedings of the First International Conference on Event Perception.* Hillsdale, NJ: Erlbaum.

Watson, R. I. (1979). *Basic writings in the history of psychology.* New York: Oxford University Press.

Waugh, N. C., & Norman, D. A. (1965). Primary memory. *Psychological Review, 72,* 89–104.

Weisstein, N. (1970). Neural symbolic activity: A psychophysical measure. *Science, 168,* 1489–91.

Weimer, W. B. (1979). *Notes on the methodology of scientific research.* Hillsdale, NJ: Erlbaum.

(1980, August). *Psychology of science: Do we know what we are talking about?* Paper presented at the annual convention of the American Psychological Association, Montreal.

Wiener, N. (1948). *Cybernetics.* New York: Wiley.

Wilks, Y. (1985). *Bad metaphors: Chomsky and artificial intelligence* (Rep. MCCS-85-8). Computing Research Laboratory, New Mexico State University, Las Cruces.

Wrisberg, C., & Rogsdale, M. (1979). Further tests of Schmidt's schema theory. *Journal of Motor Behavior, 4,* 159–66.

Wundt, W. (1912). *An introduction to psychology* (R. Pinter, Trans.). London: Allen. (Original work published 1911.)

Zwicky, A. M. (1973). Linguistics as chemistry: The substance theory of semantic primes. In S. R. Anderson & P. Kiparsky (Eds.), *A Festschrift for Morris Halle* (pp. 467–85). New York: Holt, Rinehart & Winston.

6

Metaphors of consciousness and cognition in the history of psychology

JEROME BRUNER AND CAROL FLEISHER FELDMAN

It is mind boggling to review past and present theories of consciousness and cognition with an eye peeled for metaphor. Even on the shallowest inspection, it is apparent that there have been *nothing but* metaphors in the history of these two topics. And these metaphors have been so varied and so riotously luxuriant, at least where consciousness is concerned, that we can only stand back and wonder: Of what or of whom does one speak in such cascading metaphors? Consciousness as a spotlight, a footlight before which scenes are enacted, a flowing river, a stream of thoughts, a seamless web, a set of sets, a graph, a powerless rider, a recursive loop, an internalized running back and forth, a readout, a pandemonium, a stage or display – there is no end to this parade. Nor can we fail to note the elusive, chimera-like quality of the metaphors of consciousness. Sometimes it is viewed as a state, sometimes as an act; sometimes it is input, sometimes output; sometimes it enjoys a unity, sometimes a diversity, and often a *unitas multiplex*.

One may wonder, as we have, Why this heaping of metaphors? Why, after all of human history and speculation, should one school of deep thinkers (e.g., Dewey, 1910; James, 1890/1983) think of consciousness as a biological specialization for dealing with conflict, contradiction, surprise, irregularity, and difficult choice, whereas another (e.g., Huizinga, 1938/1949) conceives of it as the child of play?

Cognition, in contrast, is rather more sedate and generates a far more cultivated garden of metaphors. The principal divergence is between those metaphors that depict cognition as a cycle of reflecting and then

230

reproducing the world – a kind of selective, but order-preserving copying machine, with degrees of freedom at the registering, storing, and printout points – and those that depict it as a creator, imposing its categories on whatever it encounters, ending by making a world of its own. Each of these approaches – let us call them the "reproductive" and "productive" theories of cognition – is relatively uncommitted as to the centrality it assigns to consciousness. But each is committed to a different view of its function, one emphasizing how the *contents* of consciousness reflect, distort, or otherwise mirror the world, however much in a glass darkly; the other how *acts* of consciousness impose not only structure but direction on experience.

Basic metaphors of consciousness

Let us consider first how the contents of consciousness have been rendered into metaphor by theorists in the reproductive tradition. Nakedness has to be a crucial concept in this discussion: "bare consciousness" – consciousness as "mere sensing," as "freed of the stimulus error," and as "elementary" – has been the basic premise of their approach. Nakedness has a long tradition. Aristotle, in the *De sensu* (ca. 330 B.C./1957), contrasts the special senses with the "common sense," the *sensus communis*. The special senses, according to Aristotle, yield only the unique sensibilities of bare touch, bare vision, bare sound; the common sense puts these together into something that has reference and sense. Aristotle asks how we know that it is Cleon's son descending the steps of the Parthenon, when all we have is some visual sensation, the sound of a voice, a particular gait, and so on. He argues that there must be something beyond the special senses, something that is a common sense that must partake of *nous*, or "soul." If Aristotle were translated by a twentieth-century enthusiast of artificial intelligence, he would talk about the *sensus communis* as accessing semantic memory and being under the control of an executive routine, much like the "upstream editing demons" in Oliver Selfridge's (1959/1966) pandemonium model. Similarly, the British empiricists, although they would have resisted being tagged Aristotelians, wanted to make and maintain the distinction between bare sensory stuff – John Locke's (1690/1959) primary qualities – and the more fully interpreted and less naked secondary qualities of sensation, as well as the operations whereby these could be welded together to make Bishop Berkeley's coach.

Yet neither Aristotle nor the British empiricists were primarily interested in where consciousness started, whether naked sensing was an actual conscious process, or whether it was merely an abstract description. By the mid-nineteenth century, however, such issues had come into their own. What entered the discussion at that time was an old metaphor put to new uses. We are referring to the metaphor of the "threshold" of consciousness, which implied that to become conscious, something has to step across a threshold, or limen. In the work of Johann Friedrich Herbart (1816/1891), for example, forms of knowing or awareness were held to exist at some level below consciousness and to need some kind of impetus to be boosted above the threshold. This metaphor was doubtless born of the everyday experience of searching for things that one knows but cannot "bring into" consciousness – tip of the tongue phenomena, transient forgetting, and the like. But if something had to be brought into consciousness, like a dead mouse being brought into the house by a cat, who was the cat? And who demanded that he bring in *this* mouse just *now*?

This brings us to the issue of how things "get into" consciousness – a curious metaphor that supposes consciousness to be like a well-lit atrium at the center of the temple called mind. Here there is a great divide. For Herbart, the force that impels content from the unconscious "apperceptive mass" over the threshold into awareness is the strength of an "associative connection" with something already in consciousness, which is an accident of the historical circumstances that have led particular ideas to be contiguous in time or space. The spatial and temporal location of contents in the mind, so to speak, is supposed to make them candidates for threshold crossing. In much the same spirit, the German psychophysicists of that last quarter of the nineteenth century (e.g., Müller, 1878) had sensations impelled over the threshold to consciousness by virtue of their mere physical strength.

This very passive picture, portraying a warehouse of ideas or physical stimuli that are pushed or pulled into the lighted atrium of the mind, has been challenged by representatives of the productive approach to cognition, an approach (as we have noted) that is based on a very different metaphor of consciousness. To members of this tradition of thought, the mind is not passive, but rather is an active seeker and constructor of experience. Immanuel Kant (1781/1965), awakened from his dogmatic slumbers by David Hume's *Treatise* (1739–40/1978), might be seen as the first person who argued that the contents of consciousness are what mind creates, rather than what mind encounters – that the experiences of space, time, causation, and even the forms of order described by arithmetic are made by mind rather than found in the world. But even before Kant, Leibniz (1704/1981) had countered Locke's argument that what is in the mind is only what comes through the senses, by the famous quip that mind itself was there all along. And so, for those who espouse a productive theory of cognition, experience and awareness are not bare but clothed by mind itself.

At the turn of our century, the British philosopher-psychologist G. F.

Stout (1896) referred the issue right back to Aristotle, denying that there can ever be anoetic sentience (awareness free of *nous* or mind) and arguing instead that consciousness is continually "shaped" by acts of mind. A half-century later, R. S. Woodworth (1947), an American experimental psychologist steeped in the native tradition of functionalism, wrote a celebrated article denying that there can ever be seeing without looking, or hearing without listening.

So, at the outset, we should recognize that there has been a long history of battle between two basic metaphors, the one having consciousness develop from the outside in, the other from inside out – the first guided by rules of entry and principles of responsiveness, the second by acts of creation. However, we should not overlook that these two views have had at least one thing in common: Both have been preoccupied with the need to distinguish between an inside, where consciousness is supposed to dwell, and an outside, where it does not. This essentially metaphoric distinction between the "inside" and "outside" dimensions of consciousness has given rise to some of the most fulsome imagery ever produced in the service of natural philosophy.

Some of this imagery has to do with the underlying uses or functions of consciousness. Even in its most ancient common-sense form, consciousness was understood through the metaphor of "concentrating" the mind, sometimes alternatively expressed as the "sharpening" of awareness or the "removing" of distraction. Again, two basic explanations for this process of "concentration" have been postulated. One has to do with how something outside the mind can force it to concentrate. This approach is best symbolized, perhaps, by Samuel Johnson's famous witticism to the effect that nothing concentrates the mind like hanging, and it is beautifully illustrated by E. B. Titchener's (1908) discussion of "primary passive attention." Titchener, you may recall, assigned the cause of this sort of concentration to compelling states of the world that force us to attend to them. Examples would include sharp or preternatural changes of stimulation, such as bangs, snaps, crackles, and pops.

In contrast to this explanation of focused consciousness, Titchener described a second process of concentration, which he ascribed to "active attention" and which will illustrate the other mode of conscious focusing to which we just referred. According to Titchener, this kind of attention requires some sort of mental effort to bring into the focus of attention things that themselves do not have the vividness to get there from outside: glitches, humdrummery, and those ordinary phenomena that on their own power would dwell either in the periphery of consciousness or on the nether side of the threshold.

Interestingly, Titchener allowed for an overlap of these two processes in his postulation of a hybrid form of "secondary passive attention." According to this notion, once we "actively" develop the habit of attending to items that would not normally enter into our consciousness, these erstwhile inconspicuous things can become "passively" focal and be effortlessly apprehended.

Permeating both the "active" and "passive" approaches to concentration is the assumption that consciousness has both a focus and a periphery and that the two can be manipulated from either "outside" or "inside." And if from inside, then we might ask by what means and toward what ends the focus of consciousness is controlled. This kind of question points our discussion toward the work of Sigmund Freud, the author of one of the most extraordinary metaphorical documents on the function of consciousness. We have in mind his "Note upon a 'Mystic Writing-Pad'" (1925/1961), but this relatively obscure article simply treats in condensed and lively fashion matters that he had already discussed in much richer detail in the famous seventh chapter of his *Interpretation of Dreams* (1900/1953). In these and other works (see Erdelyi, 1985), Freud's argument was the same: Consciousness functions as a shield. Not only is it shaped by the sort of order-imposing categories of mind that Kant had proposed, but hidden beneath it are a host of things that an interposing mechanism refuses to allow into the light of consciousness, lest they disturb the uncertain peace we have managed to force on our warring instincts.

Finally, for yet another metaphoric view of consciousness, let us take a quick glance at the information-processing models of contemporary cognitive science. These models are based on the view that consciousness is the "readout" at the end of a series of "filtering" processes. The specification of the nature of these filters has depended on what we know – and what we think we know – about perceptual processes and on the machine analogs at our disposal. Thus, the filterings before the readout into consciousness have been conjectured to be "linear and serial," to operate "in parallel," and to involve "recursions" in which the output from one filter operates as input to a loop in which the same process that produced it then operates on it again (see Palmer & Kimchi, 1986). As time and experience have shown, however, information-processing systems of this kind cannot be made to appear humanoid unless they operate "top down" as well as "bottom up" (see, e.g., Bransford & McCarrell, 1974; Shanon, 1987). Something high up in the hierarchy has got to inform the "downstream" filters about what is wanted in the readout. This is particularly the case when one is dealing with such complicated nonfinite state phenomena as language. So what gets into consciousness is, in a much more technical sense than was ever dreamed of before, a matter not only of higher-order structural principles but also of intentions, conventions, and stylizations. As a good many of our ancestors – from Leibniz and Kant onward – have said, being aware always means being aware with something ulterior in mind, being aware relative to a purpose or intention.

Basic metaphors of cognition

We have already noted that both the theories and the metaphors of cognition divide themselves into those that emphasize how mind (reproductively) reflects the world and those that focus on how it (productively) constructs experience and knowledge. Now, on the first score, mind has been pictured as a "mirror of nature," as a "wax tablet" on which the world writes, and even as a set of "unit receptors" that send staccato "messages" about this or that feature of the environment to a putative assembly point. Some of the reproductive theories of consciousness are locus theories: They specify where the "ghost in the machine" (Ryle, 1949) is supposed to reside, locating consciousness in the cortex, in the frontal lobes, in the temporal–parietal area, or in some other part of the brain. Whatever its address, this locus is presumably the spot at which the output of the unit receptors is eventually dumped.

In contrast to such outside-to-inside metaphors of cognition are the metaphors of production, which are even richer. For instance, there are metaphors of illumination (expressed in the language of searchlights, spotlights, and footlights), creative synthesis (expressed in the language of masonry, mental chemistry, and construction), assignment of meaning (expressed in the language of semantic networks, encoding, and decoding), and topography (expressed in the language of cognitive maps, schemata, and topological representations), to name only a few of the major categories.

Perhaps the big bang that produced the fission of reproductive and productive theories of cognition occurred back in the eighteenth century with the invention of association theory. No metaphor in the history of psychology has had greater power – or done longer service and greater damage – than the trope of association. Its metonymic rendering is that the experienced world, here and now, is as it is because the world there and then was as it was. This proposition has engendered a language of copies, mirrors, and faithful renderings, and in the fancy dress of reinforcement theory it has led to the allegation that the likelihood of a response increases as a function of the frequency with which it has been made in the presence of a particular environmental state. In this and other forms, the metaphor of association continues to carry the assumption of a one-to-one mapping between a living being and its nonliving environment, often expressed metaphorically as the intersecting axes of a graph.

The associationist is in for some hard knocks if he or she adheres ardently to such a passive metaphor. A supplementary metaphor of cognition had to be added – one that recognized the astonishing capacity of even simians and rodents to go beyond the information given and to turn the received world of spatiotemporal contiguities into possible worlds having other principles of organization. E. G. Boring (1950), whose volumes on the history of psychology managed to obscure our intellectual history, described this cognitive appendage of the association-ists as "act psychology." The "acts" of the Bavarian and Austrian act psychologists did some higher-order fancy work on the contents of consciousness without changing its basic nature. What they added – comparisons, abstractions, and so on – was never as "real" as the basic sensory stuff on which these acts were performed (see Humphrey, 1951). Boring summed it all up with an economist's metaphor: The "raw material" of sensation and association had to be worked into the "finished product" of everyday phenomenology. From this tradition of thought we have inherited a metaphoric view of mental processes according to which the substrate of sensory organization and association (what today we would call the machine language) constitutes the hard scientific core, and all else is virtually epiphenomenal to it. The particular scientific metaphor that captured Boring's theoretical imagination was Mendeleev's table of the elements. Chairs, tables, and bricks were all well and good, but the business of science was the description of the raw sensory materials of which these compound objects were composed.

Even the opponents of associationism became enmeshed in the rami-fications of the associationist metaphor, which conveniently fit the needs and assumptions of the physical monism that dominated nineteenth-century scientific thought – and has continued to sway twentieth-century conceptions of psychology and its objects. Take Gestalt psychology as an example. For all of their opposition to associationism as a general approach and all their insistence on naive phenomenology as a starting point for the analysis of experience, the Gestaltists nevertheless claimed that their doctrine rested on a principle of isomorphism, that is, on the proposition that for every phenomenal configuration there is a corres-ponding isomorphic physical gestalt in the brain (see Köhler, Held, & O'Connell, 1952). This proposition is homologous to the associationists' claim that for every mental state or condition there is a corresponding physical state "out there."

But there was another metaphor of cognition that grew from issues quite outside the realm of physicalism, sense data theories, and the associationism of British and German psychology. It was the metaphor of symbolism, of humans as symbol-making, symbol-using creatures who read signs and create meaning – the metaphor of sense and reference rather than mere associations. Mastering the world, according to this view, does not involve mirroring it, but "reading" it through a system of signs and symbols that permit the construction of hypotheses, theories, and interpretations. It is now plain that the great innovator of the symbol metaphor was Charles Sanders Peirce (1931–58). His views provided the foundation metaphors – icons, indexes, and symbols. These were what he proposed in place of the physicalistic sensations that dominated the thinking of his time. In essence, he identified language rather than physics as the most appropriate source for metaphors of cognition.

The metaphors of today and tomorrow

In this new dispensation, consciousness is neither a state reflecting the sensory order nor a reproduction of past associations yielding Berkeleyan coaches. Rather it is a process of symbolic *activity*. Now we are beginning to ask what consciousness *does* instead of what it *is*, to ask about the possible *uses* to which it may be put in constructing meaning and in assigning interpretations, and to ask such questions as whether the conscious–unconscious distinction corresponds in our symbolic activity to the distinction between marked and unmarked, new and given, explicit and implicit, topic and comment.

This points us toward some future questions. A new set of concerns regarding consciousness and cognition have begun to beckon us – and we have begun to respond: We are going "meta." No longer are we satisfied with the study of mere cognition; we are now studying metacognition. What happens when we think about thought and when we talk about talk? From such questions it will be but a small step to asking what metaphors we use to understand metaphors, in the history of psychology as elsewhere. As we look forward to such investigations – investigations that should shed further light on the nature and processes of consciousness and cognition – we can already see that, at least where psychologists are concerned, it is indeed by their metaphors that we shall know them.

References

Aristotle (1957). On sense and sensible objects. In W. S. Hett (Ed. and Trans.), *Aristotle* (vol. 8, pp. 205–83). Cambridge, MA: Harvard University Press. (Original work written ca. 330 B.C.)

Boring, E. G. (1950). *A history of experimental psychology* (2d ed.). New York: Appleton-Century-Crofts.

Bransford, J. D., & McCarrell, N. S. (1974). A sketch of a cognitive approach to comprehension: Some thoughts about understanding what it means to comprehend. In W. B. Weimer & D. S. Palermo (Eds.), *Cognition and the symbolic processes* (pp. 189–229). Hillsdale, NJ: Erlbaum.

Dewey, J. (1910). *How we think: A restatement of the relation of reflective thinking to the educative process*. Boston: Heath.

Erdelyi, M. H. (1985). *Psychoanalysis: Freud's cognitive psychology*. New York: Freeman.

Freud, S. (1953). The interpretation of dreams. In J. Strachey (Ed. and Trans.), *The standard edition of the complete psychological works of Sigmund Freud* (vols. 4 and 5, pp. 1–627). London: Hogarth Press. (Original work published 1900.)

   (1961). A note upon the "mystic writing-pad." In J. Strachey (Ed. and Trans.), *The standard edition of the complete psychological works of Sigmund Freud* (vol. 19, pp. 227–32). London: Hogarth Press. (Original work published 1925.)

Herbart, J. F. (1891). *A textbook of psychology: An attempt to found the science of psychology on experience, metaphysics, and mathematics* (2d ed.; W. T. Harris, Ed.; M. K. Smith, Trans.). New York: Appleton. (Original work published 1816.)

Huizinga, J. (1949). *Homo ludens: A study of the play-element in culture* (R. F. C. Hull, Trans.). London: Routledge & Kegan Paul. (Original work published 1938.)

Hume, D. (1978). *A treatise of human nature* (L. A. Selby-Bigge & P. H. Nidditch, Eds.). New York: Oxford University Press. (Original work published 1739–40.)

Humphrey, R. (1951). *Thinking: An introduction to its experimental psychology.* New York: Wiley.

James, W. (1983). *The principles of psychology.* Cambridge, MA: Harvard University Press. (Original work published 1890.)

Kant, I. (1965). *Critique of pure reason* (N. K. Smith, Trans.). New York: St. Martin's Press. (Original work published 1781.)

Köhler, W., Held, R., & O'Connell, D. N. (1952). An investigation of cortical currents. *Proceedings of the American Philosophical Society, 96,* 290–330.

Leibniz, G. W. F. von. (1981). *New essays on human understanding* (R. Remnant & J. Bennett, Eds. and Trans.). Cambridge University Press. (Original work written 1704.)

Locke, J. (1959). *An essay concerning human understanding* (A. C. Fraser, Ed.). New York: Dover. (Original work published 1690.)

Müller, G. E. (1878). *Grundlegung der Psychophysik* [The foundations of psychophysics]. Berlin: Hoffman.

Palmer, S. E., & Kimchi, R. (1986). The information processing approach to cognition. In T. J. Knapp & L. C. Robertson (Eds.), *Approaches to cognition: Contrasts and controversies* (pp. 37–77). Hillsdale, NJ: Erlbaum.

Peirce, C. S. (1931–58). *The collected papers of Charles Sanders Peirce* (C. Hartshorne, P. Weiss, & A. Burks, Eds.). Cambridge, MA: Harvard University Press.

Ryle, G. (1949). *The concept of mind.* London: Hutchinson.

Selfridge, O. (1966). Pandemonium: A paradigm in learning. In L. Uhr (Ed.), *Pattern recognition* (pp. 339–48). New York: Wiley. (Original work published 1959.)

Shanon, B. (1987). On the place of representation in cognition. In D. N. Perkins, J. Lochhead, & J. Bishop (Eds.), *Thinking: The second international conference* (pp. 33–49). Hillsdale, NJ: Erlbaum.

Stout, G. F. (1896). *Analytic psychology.* London: Sonnenschein.

Titchener, E. B. (1908). *Lectures on the psychology of feeling and attention.* New York: Macmillan.

Woodworth, R. S. (1947). Reinforcement of perception. *American Journal of Psychology, 60,* 119–24.

7

Metaphors of knowledge and behavior in the behaviorist tradition

LAURENCE D. SMITH

Until very recently, metaphor has been looked upon with considerable disfavor in Western scientific and philosophical thought. From Plato and Aristotle to the empiricist philosophers of the Scientific Revolution and on down to the positivists of the nineteenth and twentieth centuries, metaphor has been variously denigrated as an implement of deceit, a cryptic and circuitous means of conveying thought, and no more than a mere literary or rhetorical device for evoking an emotional response in others. The standard view has been that whatever real content a metaphorical assertion may have, the content can and should be reformulated in literal language. But even a cursory examination of the anti-metaphor tradition reveals that this injunction has proved far easier to preach than to practice. Not only have the denouncers of metaphor made liberal use of metaphors in their own positive pronouncements about the nature of the world and our knowledge of it, but they have failed to avoid metaphors even in the act of denouncing them. To cite but one example of this recurrent failure, Pierre Duhem (1906/1962), the great turn-of-the-century champion of purely descriptive science, referred to the mechanical metaphors and models that have accompanied physical theories as "parasitic growths" that have "fastened themselves on a tree already robust and full of life" (p. 95).

Even if one were to suppose that such uses of metaphor are incidental rather than substantive (which, as I shall argue, is hardly the case), the ironic, if not downright hypocritical, use of metaphors in formulating positions hostile to metaphor is a remarkable phenomenon that has continued in various forms even to our own time. In the twentieth.

century, the major school representing the antimetaphor tradition has been logical positivism. As is widely known, the logical positivists divided all discourse into three mutually exclusive types: logical propositions, empirical (or factual) propositions, and nonsensical expressions. To the category of nonsense they assigned the assertions of traditional metaphysics as well as poetic and metaphorical assertions, the aim of which was said to be purely emotive. Meaningful discourse was confined to the realms of logical and empirical statements.

How did the logical positivists characterize these realms and their interrelation? Certainly not in wholly literal language. In the formal realm of logic, there was metaphorical talk of *logical atoms, molecular propositions*, a *picture theory of meaning*, and a *logical structure (Aufbau) of the world*. In the context of scientific theory, the purely formal component of a theory was sometimes characterized as a *postulate set* (to use a geometrical metaphor), sometimes as a *machine for grinding out theorems* (to use a mechanical metaphor), and even as a *nomological net* (to use a piscatorial metaphor). In the frequently used architectural mode, theories were said to be *erected* or *constructed* on an *empirical foundation*. And what about this empirical foundation? Sometimes it was referred to as the *plane of empirical facts*, sometimes as the *soil of observation*, and sometimes simply as the *given*. And what was the relation between the formal and empirical realms? The formal component of theory, which was said to *float* or *hover* over the plane of facts, needed to be *tied* to the observable realm by means of what were variously described as *links, anchorings, chains of reduction sentences, bridge principles, rootlets descending into the soil*, and even *pilings driven into the swamp of fallible observation statements*. These connecting links were then said to permit an *upward seepage of meaning* from the observation base to the theoretical concepts.[1]

Note that these metaphors for the purely empirical realm and its ties to the formal or theoretical realm are intended to express something about the capacity of science for literal description. In effect, these logical positivist proponents of literal description had great difficulty characterizing literalness itself in nonmetaphorical terms. Lest the reader think that the foregoing inventory of examples was adventitiously assembled to create that impression or that the logical positivists *could* have given literal translations of their metaphors for literalness, it should be pointed out that, even by the logical positivists' own admission, the decades-long search for a precise literal account of observation statements ended in failure (see Brown, 1977, p. 173; Popper, 1959, p. 43).

The difficulty of being literal about literalness has also proved to be a problem for thinkers other than professional philosophers. In psychology, perhaps the most positivistic school of thought has been the behaviorist tradition. How, then, have behaviorists fared in characterizing the connection between our most literal knowledge of the world and the world itself? Perhaps a few examples will again be instructive. Edward C. Tolman (1935) spoke metaphorically of immediate experience as a *tangible real* composed of *raw feels* or, alternatively, as an *initial matrix* out of which science *evolves*; but no sooner did he speak of immediate experience in these metaphorical terms than he conceded that immediate experience is ineffable, that is, incapable of being described and communicated (pp. 359, 363). Clark Hull (1930a) characterized immediate knowledge as a simple Pavlovian-conditioned chained response that parallels a simple sequence of events in the environment; this conditioned response was then said to be a *kind of replica* of part of the world (p. 514). B. F. Skinner (1935) tells us that our descriptions of behavior have made good contact with the world when we have discovered the "natural *lines of fracture* along which behavior and environment actually *break*" (p. 40, italics added). In each case, we see the familiar pattern of metaphors being used to talk about literal description. And the behaviorists were not the only positivistic psychologists who resorted to metaphors. Titchener and his followers, arguably the most positivistic psychologists of any nonbehaviorist tradition, spoke of *introspection* (a figurative looking inward) of the contents of mind, discerning there the *elements* (later *dimensions*) of consciousness. Furthermore, in their efforts to give the most literal introspective descriptions of feelings, they found themselves describing feelings in terms of *pressure*, a dimension borrowed metaphorically from the sense of touch (Evans, 1973, p. 88).

I will not try to claim that the difficulties revealed by the examples cited thus far are sufficient to discredit fully the traditional view of metaphor. After all, one cannot prove that literal translations for all this metaphorical talk cannot or will not eventually be supplied. But the persistence of metaphorical talk by those most opposed to it, together with the apparent difficulty of giving a literal account of the very notion of literal description, suggests that something may be seriously amiss with the standard antimetaphor tradition. This realization has, in recent years, stimulated a reappraisal of the role of metaphor in the scientific enterprise. The trend of this reappraisal has been toward concluding that metaphor may well be unavoidable and ubiquitous in science. Even so devout an empiricist as W. V. Quine (1978) has acknowledged that metaphor is "vital . . . at the growing edges of science" (p. 159). But we can ask whether this acknowledgment goes far enough. Is the livelihood of metaphor limited to the "growing edges" of science, where its value in extending terminology to new domains is readily apparent? Or does metaphor also play a more central role in science, perhaps an indispensable role in the formulation of the scientific world views from which theories and testable hypotheses are drawn?

These are, of course, issues too large to be settled easily. But we can begin to explore the dimensions of metaphor in science by examining the use of metaphors in specific scientific traditions and by specific scientists. To this end, the present chapter addresses the use of metaphors in the behaviorist tradition. Following a brief overview of metaphors in prebehaviorist and early behaviorist thought, the metaphors of the leading neobehaviorists – Tolman, Hull, and Skinner – will be discussed. I hope to show not only that all three of these psychologists made liberal use of metaphors in formulating their respective theories of learning, but also that their core metaphors underlay their views on human cognition and scientific epistemology. In other words, their uses of metaphor were not limited to rhetorical or even heuristic purposes; rather their metaphors were used to formulate their deepest conceptions of the natural world and our knowledge of it. Not surprisingly, this larger task called for the development of coherent systems of metaphors, rather than mere scattered figures of speech selected for particular occasions.

Following a relatively detailed treatment of the major neobehaviorists, I will conclude with some remarks about the implications of this story for the general issue of the role of metaphor in science. To anticipate the upshot of this discussion: If even highly positivistic behaviorists have used metaphors in a substantive way, then perhaps it is reasonable to suppose that metaphor has played a more central role in science than the traditional view has ascribed to it.

Metaphors in the behaviorist tradition

The early tradition

As is commonly recognized, behaviorism can be viewed as having grown out of two somewhat distinct traditions: the reflexological tradition dating back to Descartes and the Darwin-inspired tradition of comparative psychology. In the reflex tradition, we can note the metaphorical character of Descartes's (1649/1911) "reflected spirits" (*esprits réfléchis*), a kind of reflecting wave impulse appropriate to Descartes's conception of a vital fluid transmitted from the sensory organ and rebounding back to the effector organ (see Jaynes, 1973). As reflex terminology gradually became more entrenched in scientific thought down through the nineteenth century, its metaphorical character became less apparent. By the time of the great Russian physiologists, the reflex model was sufficiently shopworn and familiar to be extended, again metaphorically, to the realm of thought. Taking a step that would have dismayed Descartes, Ivan Sechenov (1863/1935), among others, asserted that thinking is an inhibited reflex. Vladimir Bechterev (1907/1928) seconded this extension, identifying thought as reflexive movements of the speech apparatus and additionally bringing the metaphorical framework of associationism to bear on reflexology. The great Ivan Pavlov (1897/1902), in turn, referred to his conditional reflexes as "psychic reflexes" (see Boakes, 1984), thereby cautiously marking his extension of the terminology to the psychological realm of which he was generally leery. The aptness of Pavlov's metaphor seemed guaranteed by the close analogy between the operations used to produce psychic reflexes and their nonpsychic analogs; but as Karl Zener (1937) was later to show, so small a change of operations as leaving the dog unrestrained produced such marked differences in the conditioned response that alternative metaphors of sign or perceptual learning seemed more appropriate to the phenomenon.

In America, John B. Watson (1916) picked up the reflex metaphor rather belatedly, but he applied it relentlessly to a wide range of psychological phenomena. Following Sechenov's lead, he identified thought with covert speech and speech with reflexes, a metaphorical extension that gained the enthusiastic endorsement of no less than Bertrand Russell before its appropriateness was finally discredited by experiments demonstrating that thinking is *not* prevented by the paralysis of the speech musculature. But in the climate of American pragmatism, such setbacks did not prevent the emergence of the more global metaphorical claim that "to know is to do." In one form or another, all behaviorists subscribed to this view, although (as we shall see) they developed the metaphor in different ways.

Out of the evolutionary tradition came comparative psychology with its own array of metaphors. In its earlier versions, comparative psychology relied heavily on anthropomorphism, that is, the metaphorical ascription of human characteristics to lower animals. Thus, G. J. Romanes (1883) extended the terminology of human psychology to other organisms when he attributed emotions to spiders and powers of reason to the crab. Of course, the anthropomorphic metaphors soon lost favor, but they were replaced not with literal language but rather with new preferred metaphors. Among these "progressive" metaphors was the metaphor of reinforcement, based on the analogy between the strengthening of a physical structure and the strengthening of psychological associations. This conception may be found in the writings of Lloyd Morgan, whose famous (1894) "canon" eventually brought the metaphor of parsimony to bear on interpretations of the animal mind. Morgan (1894) also helped popularize the metaphor of trial and error with its fruitful evocation of the parallel evolutionary notions of variation and selection. As an immediate forerunner of behaviorism, E. L. Thorndike (1898) conjoined the trial-and-error metaphor with a version of the metaphorical framework of associationism. Thorndike thus spoke of associations between ideas and impulses (later to become associations between stimuli and responses) as being *stamped out* and *stamped in* by the consequences of error and success. Thorndike also used metaphors of *compound* and *element* responses, as well as *forces* of trial outcomes that were said to be *absorbed* by response tendencies. Finally, it was Thorndike (1898) who exemplified in a single sentence the entire trend of replacing anthropomorphic metaphors with equally figurative but more scientific-sounding metaphors when he wrote that his learning curves "represent the wearing smooth of a path in the brain, not the decisions of a rational consciousness" (p. 45).

In sum, by the time behaviorism became established as a school, it had already inherited a lively stock of metaphors from both sides of its family tree. But the neobehaviorists did not rest content with the inheritance. As we shall see, they contrived, borrowed, and extended metaphors from sources both old and new in order to formulate their even more ambitious versions of behaviorism.

Tolman: mazes and maps

As is apparent to anyone who has so much as glanced through Edward C. Tolman's classic *Purposive Behavior in Animals and Men* (1932), Tolman was exceptionally fond of spatial diagrams and images. He once remarked: "I feel comfortable only when I have translated my explanatory arguments into diagrams. . . . I am very unhappy whenever I do not have a blackboard in my office" (1952, pp. 326–7). But Tolman's penchant for explanation by diagram involved much more than a preferred mode of expression; rather it sprang from his deep-seated view of the world as a spatially extended complex of alternative routes to goal states. As Tolman put it in the metaphor that lay at the root of all his other metaphors, the world is a maze.

To understand how Tolman arrived at this conception, it is necessary to consider his early training in the neorealist epistemology of his Harvard teachers, Ralph Barton Perry and Edwin B. Holt (Smith, 1982). In developing William James's functional theory of consciousness, the neorealists argued that the mind is not a private entity encased in an "impenetrable shell"; it reaches out into the environment, where it grasps the objects of its attention in a relation of functional "objective reference." What they referred to as the "mind abroad" was said to be *out there* operating on and adjusting to the environment. Tolman eagerly embraced this view of mind. He wrote that a mental characteristic such as an organism's purpose could be "pointed to," that it "is *out there in* the behavior; of its descriptive warp and woof" (Tolman, 1926, p. 355), and that it lies in the "*externals* of the situation" (Tolman, 1923, p. 217).

Given this conception of psychological phenomena as extended in space, it is not surprising that Tolman chose the maze as the apparatus ideally suited to his studies of animal learning. With the maze, animal psychologists were able to observe the spatial relations involved in behavior. The rat's purposes could be observed as its gettings away from the start box and its gettings toward the goal box. Its cognition could be observed as its pattern and sequence of turns to the goal box. In Tolman's maze-inspired version of the pragmatists' to-know-is-to-do metaphor, knowing became a matter of confronting choice points in a maze and selecting routes to desired ends.

In 1925, Tolman reported a set of experiments in which rats were rewarded indifferently for selecting either arm of a simple T-shaped maze. Under these conditions, rats showed stable strategies of responding, for example, always choosing the left arm or consistently alternating left and right. Tolman later came to refer metaphorically to these response patterns as hypotheses (Tolman & Krechevsky, 1933). Still later, working with more complex mazes, Tolman (1948) saw that rats could acquire a more global knowledge of a maze, so that when some feature of a complicated maze was suddenly altered the rats could select an efficient alternative route to the goal. The rats were, in effect, fitting together their specific hypotheses about the various possible maze routes into an overall picture of it. For this broader picture, Tolman adopted the famous metaphor of the cognitive map.

In an earlier use of spatial imagery, Tolman (1932) had asserted that what an animal learns in a maze is "probably never adequately represented by single lines, but always rather by some degree of *spreading, fanning,* or *networking* of the lines" (p. 171). With his notion of a map, he now had a powerful metaphor to express this point. By its very nature, a map represents a network of spatial relationships, coded in such a way as to serve the needs of a particular organism in a particular extended environment. The metaphor facilitated Tolman's thought in various ways. For one, it gave him a way to characterize his view of the central nervous system, especially in distinguishing it from other metaphorical views. Thus, he (1948) wrote that the "central office" of the nervous system "is far more like a map control room than it is like an old-fashioned telephone exchange," with incoming signals being "worked over and elaborated in the central control room" rather than being "connected by just simple one-to-one switches to the outgoing responses" (p. 192). For another, it allowed Tolman to distinguish between the "broad and comprehensive" maps that are formed under conditions of optimal motivation and the "narrow and strip-like" maps formed under excessively high levels of motivation or frustration (p. 193).

Tolman's use of the maze as a laboratory apparatus was initially suggested to him by his early neorealist epistemological views, but in time the maze took on additional significance both as a heuristic device and as a central metaphor for formulating and expressing his deepest views about the world. That it served as a heuristic device in the continual development of his research program is obvious enough. To address a research problem, Tolman and his students would routinely transform the problem into one of how to diagram, design, and construct a suitable maze; in turn, the maze would suggest new hypotheses and directions for research. That the maze served also as a fundamental metaphor may be less immediately obvious, especially to those who would view Tolman as a positivist of the typical antimetaphorical bent. Nonetheless, in his most serious pronouncements about the world, Tolman repeatedly turned to his family of maze metaphors. In addressing a group of philosophers, Tolman (1926) stated that "the world for philosophers, as for rats, is, in the last analysis, nothing but a maze of discrimination-manipulation possibilities, extended or narrow, complex or simple, universal or particular" (p. 369). Again, in one of his later classic articles, he concluded with a dramatic reference to "that great God-given maze which is our human world" (1948, p. 208). Clearly, Tolman took his maze metaphor seriously. When he spoke of issues that mattered most to him, he fell back on his extended metaphor. For example, Tolman, who was a lifelong pacifist, depicted one of the causes of war as the narrowness of people's maps of the world-maze (p. 208). All in all, it would be grossly underestimating Tolman's use of metaphor to say that it served only rhetorical or heuristic roles for him; rather, his metaphors appear to have played a crucial role in formulating the world view from which his testable ideas arose and within which they found their true significance.

To see more clearly the depth of Tolman's use of metaphors, let us consider another of his spatial metaphors and its relation to his general world view. In a vividly metaphorical statement, Tolman (1926) wrote:

> We may liken the environment to a multidimensional spider's web radiating out from the behaving organism in many directions. The far ends of the threads terminate in final to-be-sought-for quiescences, or final to-be-avoided disturbances. Environmental objects and situations are responded to and cognized only in their character of providing bridges or routes along these threads. (pp. 357–8)

This spider-web metaphor dovetailed neatly with Tolman's other metaphors of *warp and woof* and the *spreading, fanning*, and *networking* of lines. The behaving organism was always enmeshed in what Tolman and Brunswik (1935) would later call the *causal interweavings* or *causal texture* of the environment. In operating on such a complexly textured environment, an organism would need to employ maps and hypotheses about the various strands of causality (i.e., about what leads to what), simply because the ends of the strands were generally too remote to be known directly. Given this view of the world, cognition became for Tolman a kind of map-guided movement along various strands of a texture, a form of action based on expectancies.

As we have seen, Tolman's view of the world as a grand maze applied to the human world as well as to the rat's world. Significantly, Tolman considered rats and humans to lie on the same epistemological, as well as ontological, plane. As should be evident from the anthropomorphic character of Tolman's metaphors for cognition, he viewed human knowledge, like rat knowledge, as a kind of operating on environments under the guidance of hypotheses and maps. Perhaps more remarkable is the fact that Tolman applied his metaphors for cognition to the very paragon of human knowledge – science itself: According to Tolman, the scientist, like the rat, forms hypotheses that can undergo confirmation and disconfirmation by the environment (see Tolman, 1933, pp. 396–7). For him, the rat's map-based expectancies do not differ in principle from the scientist's predictions. In a related vein, Tolman (1936/1966) drew explicit parallels between operationism as a method practiced by the scientist and the operations of the rat in the maze (pp. 115–16). And at the core of Tolman's view of science was one last grand metaphorical claim: The theories of science are maps. Just as the well-trained, knowledgeable rat integrates its well-confirmed hypotheses into a composite map, so the successful scientist arrives at relatively global theory-maps of the world. In the final chapter of *Purposive Behavior*, Tolman (1932) defended this extension of the map metaphor in the course of explicating his "doctrine as to the ultimate methodology and status of science":

> All science presents, it seems to us, but a map and picture of reality. If it were to present reality in its whole concreteness, science would not be a map but a complete replica of reality. And then it would lose its usefulness. One of the first requisites of science is, in short, that it be a map, i.e., a short-hand for finding one's way about. . . . Our account of mind is, we hold, a map-account. And so also is the physicist's account of matter. (pp. 424–5)

Thus, we once again find Tolman's basic metaphors being applied equally to the human and the rat.

But surely, one might protest, Tolman's map metaphor cannot be taken seriously when applied to science. Map knowledge in the rat must perforce be limited by the rat's particular experiences and needs, whereas science provides universal knowledge that is independent of time-bound human desires and needs. Tolman, however, did not accept this argument against extending the map metaphor to scientific knowledge:

> All knowledge of the universe is always strained through the behavior-needs and behavior-possibilities of the particular organisms who are gathering that knowledge. That "map" knowledge is "true" which "works," given the particular behavior-needs and the particular behavior-capacities of the type of organism gathering such

knowledge. Physics and purposive behaviorism are both, therefore, but humanly conditioned "behavioral" maps. (1932, p. 430)

In other words, Tolman stood by his map metaphor and all its implications; he took it seriously as indicative of the "ultimate status of science." And he was, in this respect, no hypocrite: He freely admitted that his own system of psychology, like any other, was "obviously bound to be wrong" and was inevitably "twisted out of plumb by the special cultural lack of building materials inherent in the time and place of its origin" (p. 394). Tolman's approach to science was that of a thoroughgoing pragmatist, and he urged his readers to adopt the same attitude. Speaking of his own theory of psychology, he wrote, "May neither you nor we ever seek to hold up these propositions, save in a somewhat amused, a somewhat skeptical, and a wholly adventure-seeking and pragmatic behavior-attitude" (p. 394).

As a pragmatist, Tolman was naturally inclined to view science as a kind of exploratory activity, and this attitude carried over into his personal style as a scientist and into his views on methodology. In their famous studies on latent learning in rats, Tolman and Honzik (1930) had shown that the rat could learn useful things about its maze-world through mere exploratory activity. What the rat learns through exploring, said Tolman (1925), would depend on the "range, methodicalness, and flexibility of his exploratory impulses" (p. 290). And so it is for the human scientist: One needs to be methodical in science, but not at the expense of the range and flexibility of one's explorations. The science-as-exploration metaphor was, again, one that Tolman took seriously. Indeed, the loose, exploratory style of his own research and theorizing was widely recognized by the psychologists of his day, and not infrequently he was reviled for it. But in defending himself, Tolman put his spatial metaphors to good use. In reference to what he called the "psychological landscape" (Tolman, 1932, p. 394), he reminded his detractors that psychology was still a "vast continent of unknowns" (Tolman, 1959, p. 98) and proudly referred to his own scientific work as "theoretical meanderings" (Tolman, 1952, p. 335). These spatial, even geographical, metaphors so neatly captured Tolman's attitudes toward science that it was quite natural for him to reprise them in his 1937 presidential address to the American Psychological Association (APA). At the close of that address (p. 34), he (1938) recited the following poem:

> To my ratiocinations
> I hope you will be kind
> As you follow up the wanderings
> Of my amazed mind.

With its reference to "wanderings" and its pun on "amazed," the verse cleverly epitomized his view of scientific activity as a loosely guided wandering through the world-maze. Tolman's mind was certainly amazed in the sense that he approached the natural world with a sense of wonder and respect for its complexity; but it was also "amazed" in the deep metaphorical sense of being thoroughly suffused with maze-thinking. For Tolman, the extended metaphor of mazes and maps was more than a manner of expression – it was the very language of his deepest thoughts and beliefs.

Hull: the organism in the world machine

Although Clark Hull is known chiefly as a behaviorist, his earliest interests in psychology grew out of an interest in epistemology. While still a graduate student, Hull decided that the "greatest need" in psychology was for a "*scientific* knowledge of the higher mental processes" (Hull, 1962, p. 814). In fact, it was toward this end that Hull devoted his dissertation research to the problem of concept formation in humans. But Hull felt that all of the extant theories of knowledge and thought were flawed by their assumption of incorporeal entities or processes. Convinced that the principle of conservation of energy ruled out the possibility of nonmaterial ideas producing physical action, Hull believed that any genuinely *scientific* account of knowledge and thinking would have to be a strictly materialistic account. He was firmly committed to a materialist world view and had no doubts as to its adequacy for psychology as well as physics. As he wrote in his intellectual diary (the "Idea Books," 1927–8), "I feel quite sure that all kinds of action, including the highest forms of intelligent and reflective action and thought, can be handled from the purely materialistic and mechanistic standpoints" (p. 206).

Of considerable significance in the development of Hull's thought is the fact that he was highly adept at the design and construction of machines. While studying engineering as an undergraduate at the University of Michigan, Hull had built a logic machine that, at the turn of a crank, would generate the valid implications of syllogistic reasoning (Gardner, 1958, p. 124; Hull, 1952, p. 146). During the mid-1920s, he devised and assembled a machine (now housed at the Smithsonian Institution) that automatically computed correlation coefficients (Hull, 1952, p. 151). The capacity of these machines to perform what might be called "mental work" was taken by Hull to be a convincing demonstration that even the most abstract forms of intelligence are manifestations of activity within material bodies. As Hull himself recognized, there was nothing inherently novel in this conclusion. Indeed, he had read and admired the mechanical philosophy of Thomas Hobbes, but believed that Hobbes's efforts to extend the mechanical world view to psychology had been impaired by his lack of knowledge of the actual workings of machines. Hull now believed that his own proven competence with complex machinery removed any such limitation and made him uniquely qualified to apply the mechanical world view to psychological phenomena.

By 1926, Hull had arrived at his central metaphor and guiding vision for psychology. In that year he wrote, "It has struck me many times of late that the human organism is an extraordinary machine – and yet a machine." In Hull's view, Newton had shown the inanimate world to be an elaborate machine, and Darwin had shown humans, like other organisms, to be a part of the world machine. It remained only for an adroit mechanist, like Hull himself, to complete the vision by actually devising intelligent mechanisms. Formulating what he would later call the "robot approach," Hull continued his statement of 1926 as follows:

> So far as the thinking processes go, a machine could be built which would do every essential thing that the body does.... to think through the essentials of such a mechanism would probably be the best way of analyzing out the essential requirements of thinking, responding to abstract relations among things, and so on. (Hull, 1962, p. 820)

In effect, Hull was giving a clear and early statement of the rationale for machine simulations of psychological processes, thereby anticipating the founding of the modern science of cybernetics by more than a decade (see Gunderson, 1967). Significantly, Hull's statement went on to specify as one of the properties of good simulations that they be designed with "hierarchies of control" to govern their various submechanisms (p. 821). The notion of the hierarchy was to become an important aspect of Hull's machine metaphor.

In 1927, Pavlov's *Conditioned Reflexes* became available in English translation, and Hull avidly seized on it as the basis for his mechanistic psychology. Pavlov's simple conditioned reflexes would serve as the raw material – or, more precisely, the computational units – of Hull's simulations, and the basic laws of conditioning would serve as the rules of computation. Hull set out immediately to design and build a simple conditioned-reflex machine, a machine that would learn and thus exhibit intelligence simply by coming into contact with the environment. The first of these so-called psychic machines, built while Hull was at the University of Wisconsin, was described in an article in *Science* (Hull & Baernstein, 1929). After Hull moved to Yale in 1929, he and his co-workers devised and published papers on several other automata (Baernstein & Hull, 1931; Ellson, 1935; Hull & Krueger, 1931). Although the details of construction varied from case to case, all of these conditioning machines were designed according to a similar pattern. Some mechanical or electrochemical analog of Pavlovian or trial-and-error conditioning was constructed such that when the device was subjected to suitable combinations of excitatory and inhibitory procedures, it would exhibit an array of known conditioning phenomena (e.g., generalization, higher-order conditioning, persistence of responding until the attainment of a goal object).

In the 1930s, Hull turned to research on conditioning theory in order to demonstrate the adequacy of simple learned habits as a basis for his larger materialist theory of thought and knowledge. This research was to be guided throughout by the machine metaphor. Before embarking on his famous series of theoretical papers in the early 1930s, he expressed the hope that his work would be a "sufficiently original performance in what really amounts to mechanical design to be fairly impressive" (Hull, 1962, p. 833). Impressive it was. One by one, Hull analyzed phenomena that appeared to be instances of purpose, insight, and the like and showed how they could be "derived" from relatively simple interactions of elementary conditioned habits. Although Hull did not construct an actual machine for each of these theoretical analyses, he did point out in each case that such a machine could be built. Thus, after analyzing a type of what might be called purposive behavior, he (1930b) wrote, "If the type of explanation put forward above be really a sound deduction, it should be a matter of no great difficulty to construct parallel inanimate mechanisms . . . which will genuinely manifest the qualities of intelligence, insight, and purpose, and which will insofar be truly psychic" (p. 256). In other words, Hull was asserting that machine design was translatable into psychological theory, and vice versa.

An important implication of this intertranslatability of theory and design was that, if machine design is expressed in hierarchical systems of control, then psychological theory should also be cast in a hierarchical form. In this way, the hierarchical and deterministic structure of organismic behavior could be captured in a parallel hierarchical and logical structure of theory. Today's proponents of the organism-as-machine metaphor work with modern programming languages in which hierarchical control is expressed as subroutines, iterative loops, and the like. But given that no such language was available to Hull, he made use of the deductive, hierarchical systems of geometry and symbolic logic in formulating his mechanistic theories of behavior. Hull's use of logic in his theorizing has often been attributed to the influence of logical positivism, but by the time Hull encountered logical positivism he had already arrived at his deductive approach to psychological theory as a consequence of his fundamental machine metaphor (Smith, 1986, chaps. 6–8).

In a real sense, Hull's mechanical world view was prior to his behaviorism, both chronologically and logically. He took his machine metaphor quite seriously. The conditioning machine played the role for Hull that the maze played for Tolman: It was a centerpiece of laboratory activity, a heuristic source of concepts and hypotheses, and a general metaphor for psychological phenomena. Just how seriously he took the metaphor is indicated by the fact that his "Idea Books" of the early period were full of drawings of machine parts, by the fact that he once drew up plans to establish a museum of "psychic machines" at Yale, by the fact that he concluded his 1936 APA presidential address (Hull, 1937) with a demonstration of one of his automata (see Chapanis, 1963, p. 120), and by the fact that he once considered titling his magnum opus (eventually *Principles of Behavior*) "Psychology from the Standpoint of a Mechanist."

Yet despite the importance of the mechanical metaphor in Hull's thought, it gradually receded from prominence in his published writings. This curious development may be attributed to two sorts of events that suppressed his public displays of allegiance to the metaphor. First, there are indications that during the 1930s certain authorities at Yale took a dim view of his robot approach to psychology (Hull, 1962, p. 852). Hull had earlier voiced fears that the approach would be viewed as "grotesque" and that he would be "criticized" and "called a trifle insane" for pursuing it (Hull, 1962, pp. 828, 829). When the threat of suppression did arise, he noted to himself that his work with "psychic machines" would have to be "handled discreetly with an avoidance of newspaper publicity" and that he "should not take the models too seriously, at least in the eyes of the public" (Hull, 1927–8, pp. 179–80, 181). Second, and more important, Hull's mechanical metaphor was suppressed in his published works as a consequence of the rising popularity of positivist philosophy among his psychological peers. In the late 1930s and 1940s, an increasing number of psychologists were being won over by the logical positivist philosophy of science, a philosophy that actively discouraged the use of metaphor in science. Hull bowed to this trend by publicly downplaying the mechanical metaphor while calling attention to those deductive aspects of his theorizing that *did* harmonize with the logical positivist schema of science. Hull was persuaded by his own disciple Kenneth Spence, who was closely allied to logical positivism, to delete some of his talk of behavioral mechanisms from an early draft of *Principles of Behavior*. When the book finally appeared in 1943, it contained only a brief passage on the robot approach (pp. 27–8), whereas earlier drafts had devoted an entire chapter to it (see Koch, 1954, p. 16). Still, Hull's robot approach did not slip from view without exerting some influence on other, more seminal articulations of the metaphor: During the 1940s Kenneth Craik, one of the founders of British cybernetics, approvingly cited Hull's conception of the robot (see Craik, 1966, pp. 81–3); and Warren McCulloch, one of the participants in Hull's seminars of the 1930s (see Northrop, 1960, p. 46), would later become well known for his treatment of the brain as a kind of logic machine.

Hull had originally regarded his research on conditioning theory as preliminary groundwork for his more important work on a scientific epistemology. However, conditioned habits turned out to be a more complex and controversial topic than he had anticipated. Consequently, as he became more and more embroiled in protracted debates about animal learning, he was increasingly sidetracked from his earlier goal of establishing what he called a "purely physical theory of knowledge" (1934, p. 40). Faced with advancing age, poor health, and unresolved problems in his learning theory, Hull eventually abandoned his aim of writing an entire book on his mechanistic theory of knowledge, and even his more modest plan to write a series of short papers on the topic was scrapped. Nonetheless, it is apparent from his "Idea Books" and from scattered passages in his published works that Hull did formulate a mechanical theory of knowledge. Hull believed that the theory, though never worked out in full detail, could account for the entire range of epistemic phenomena, including the theories of science; and in fact, the theory continued to underlie his own views on science.

In Hull's account, the basic mechanism of knowledge was a kind of serially conditioned response chain. Consider an organism that is exposed to some sequence of events in the world. Initially, each stimulus event simply evokes a corresponding response. However, each response in the response sequence produces proprioceptive stimuli, which by virtue of being paired with the next event in the world sequence come to evoke on their own the succeeding response. As a result, the entire response sequence, once triggered by the first stimulus event, can eventually run its course independently of the world. As Hull (1930a) stated it: "Henceforth the organism will carry about continuously a kind of replica of this world segment. In this very intimate and biologically significant sense the organism may be said to know the world" (p. 514). Thus, for Hull, to know is to do in the sense of acquiring a serial conditioned response that replicates a relevant part of the world. The adaptive value of such knowing is readily apparent: Once the response chain achieves independence of the world sequence, it can run off more rapidly than the world sequence, allowing the organism to prepare for significant events. Hull referred to this phenomenon as foresight or foreknowledge. Furthermore, Hull pointed out, the intervening responses in the chain can undergo a reduction in magnitude as long as they remain just strong enough to mediate the sequence. Hull (1930a) referred to responses that are so reduced as to become covert responses as "pure stimulus acts" or "pure symbolic acts" (p. 515). These became his material equivalent of ideas. "While indubitably physical," he (1931) wrote with a metaphorical flourish, "they occupy at the same time the very citadel of the mental" (p. 502).

Hull considered all higher knowledge to be, in one form or another, a complex machinery of pure stimulus acts. Scientific laws differed from more basic forms of knowledge only in that they were abstract replicas of broad classes of causal sequences in the world, rather than specific replicas of specific sequences. A theory, in turn, was an intricate machinery of symbolic habits that paralleled an even more abstract causal structure of the world. By encompassing various laws within its deductive hierarchy, a theory could mirror the *hierarchical* structure of the world as well. As we have seen, when the deductive theory happens to be a theory of behavior, it runs parallel to the hierarchical structure of an organism machine. And any theory, according to Hull, is predictive by virtue of the capacity of its symbolic machinery to operate more rapidly than the relevant part of the world machine that it parallels. In sum, Hull viewed organismic adaptation (i.e., knowledge) as a kind of parallel operation of an organism machine and a world machine. In the case of human science, adaptation meant the closely parallel operation of the conceptual machinery of theory and the machinery of the world (Smith, 1986, chap. 8).

Just as Tolman applied his metaphors for science to his own scientific activities and attitudes toward method, so too did Hull. For example, after getting settled into a work routine following his disruptive move from Wisconsin to Yale, he wrote, "I seem to have gotten my life sufficiently mechanized in this new environment so that I can work really effectively" (Hull, 1962, p. 832). But efficient scientific practice was not just a matter of *individual* workers becoming mechanized. Hull projected his metaphor of the hierarchical machine onto the *social* structure of science as well. Thus, in the 1930s when Hull was attempting to integrate the research activities of Yale's Institute of Human Relations, he informed a research group there that "the integrative medium is a structure of implicative pure stimulus acts" – in other words, a theoretical machinery (Hull, 1936, p. 150). In the social hierarchy that was to parallel this theoretical machinery, the highest positions would be occupied by the postulate makers, a select group of theoretical scientists among whose members Hull, of course, counted himself. At the next level were the deducers or logic grinders, a group of mathematicians and logicians who would derive from the postulates a variety of theorems that could then be checked by observation. At the bottom of the hierarchy was a large group of experimentalists (composed mainly of graduate students) who would subject the theorems to experimental tests. The postulate–deduce–test method of science was thus transformed into a social mechanism in which each scientist became a gear or cog wheel in the great machine of science. Whereas Tolman's metaphors led him to view science as an adventurous, multiple-tracked exploration of the world, Hull's metaphors led him to conceive of science as a "long and grinding labor" required by a "grim and inflexible" adherence to the rules of scientific method (Hull, 1937, p. 31; 1943, p. 24).

Skinner: selection by consequences and the concept of biological economy

B. F. Skinner has been called "America's most brilliantly and consistently positivistic psychologist" (Feigl, 1981, p. 41). Indeed, Skinner has held an unswerving positivistic stance throughout his long and productive career. The mainstays of his descriptive positivism are well known: his denial of the value of theories, his eschewal of unobservable constructs, and his rejection of causes in favor of functional relations between independent and dependent variables. On the face of it, Skinner would seem to be the psychologist who comes closest to achieving the traditional positivist aim of eliminating metaphorical discourse from science. But *has* he managed to formulate his descriptive psychology in purely descriptive and literal terms? In this section, it will be argued that Skinner has often employed metaphors in advancing his scientific views and furthermore that Skinner's metaphors, like those of Tolman and Hull, arise out of and reveal a deeply held set of beliefs about the world. In Skinner's case, the world view in question is that of Darwinian biology.

Skinner's psychology is based on operant conditioning, a phenomenon that he metaphorically characterizes as a process of "selection by consequences" or "selection by contingencies of reinforcement." The behavior of an individual is said to be emitted and then selected upon by environmental contingencies in much the same way that variations among individuals are selected upon by an environment in the course of evolution. The notion of selection by an environment may not strike us as highly metaphorical because it is based on the now-familiar Darwinian metaphor of natural selection. But the anthropomorphic imputation of a selecting action to the environment was recognized by Darwin himself as metaphorical (Young, 1971, pp. 465–6), and it remains so today. In fact, in Skinner's use, it is a twice-extended metaphor in that he has brought it from its original context of phylogenetic adaptation into the realm of ontogenetic adaptation.

Along with the Darwinian selection metaphor come several related metaphors. First, and perhaps most obvious, is the widespread metaphor of "shaping." Skinner speaks of behavior being "shaped," sometimes by an experimenter in a laboratory and sometimes by contingencies in the environment (see, e.g., Skinner, 1969, p. 176). Deliberate "shaping" in the laboratory is, of course, an apt metaphorical extension of the literal shaping that one might perform on a piece of clay; but the notion of shaping by an *environment*, like that of selection, involves an additional metaphorical dimension in its anthropomorphizing of nature. More recently, Skinner (1975) has even spoken of phylogenetic shaping by environmental contingencies in the case of the migratory behavior of marine animals. In another Darwinian-inspired metaphor, Skinner (1974) has referred to "accidental variations" in behavior, which are then selected upon by the environment (p. 114). The obvious parallel here is to the so-called accidental variations that have played an important role in evolutionary theory. In yet another related metaphor, Skinner (1969) refers to behaviors that are selected by adventitious contingencies as "superstitious" behaviors, noting that these behaviors find their phylogenetic parallel in evolved characteristics that do not contribute to survival (p. 177). Another metaphor having evolutionary origins and extensively employed by Skinner (though not original with him) is that of "extinction" – the decline and eventual elimination of a learned response in the absence of selection by favorable consequences, a phenomenon parallel to the decline and demise of a species under analogous conditions.[2]

Now it is to be admitted that Skinner's metaphors are neither as conspicuous nor as fully elaborated as those of Tolman and Hull. It should also be pointed out that Skinner has warned against inappropriate interpretations of his various selectionist metaphors (see, e.g., Skinner, 1974, p. 37) and that he has occasionally placed quotation marks around them, apparently as a warning to readers. But he nonetheless continues to use metaphorical expressions, and to use them systematically. Skinner's metaphors are not just assorted figures of speech, employed for their economy of expression or for their effect on the reader in a given context. Rather they represent a coherent – and consistently used – family of metaphors, united by their common origins in Skinner's Darwinian world view.

Skinner acquired his Darwinian conception of nature both through his early reading of Darwin and, more important, through the Darwinian epistemological writings of Ernst Mach, one philosopher whom Skinner credits with having exerted a profound influence on him (Smith, 1986, chap. 9). It was Mach who repeatedly insisted that the evolution of science is strictly continuous with biological evolution. According to Mach, science is an adaptive human activity that promotes preservation of the human species. Its historical roots lie in the adaptation of animals to their environments and, more proximally, in the practical commerce of humans – hunters, farmers, and artisans – with their environments (Mach, 1905/1976). As Mach put it, "Knowledge, too, is a product of organic nature," or more forcefully, "The ways even of science still lead to the mouth" (Mach, 1894/1943, p. 217; 1886/1959, p. 23). For Mach, these views implied that science is subject to the demands of what he called "biological economy," a striking metaphor in its own right. If science is to serve its biological function, it must exhibit a corresponding intellectual economy. The scientist must make efficient, direct contact with the subject matter; economical descriptive laws must be substituted for uneconomical theories and unobservable constructs; and the notion of cause must be replaced with the more economical notion of functional relations between observable variables.

As may already be apparent, Skinner has followed Mach in all of these respects. For Skinner, as for Mach, science contributes to the survival value of a culture (see Skinner, 1971, pp. 129, 136). Just as animal behavior is selected by environmental contingencies, so human knowledge is a form of adaptation to the world. Skinner (1969) has written: "The world which establishes contingencies of reinforcement of the sort studied in an operant analysis is presumably 'what knowledge is about.' A person comes to know that world and how to behave in it in the sense that he acquires behavior which satisfies the contingencies it maintains" (p. 156). Scientific knowledge differs from ordinary human knowledge in that it consists of verbal operants that are generated and transmitted under the control of a specialized scientific community (Skinner, 1957, chap. 18). The verbal operants composing scientific knowledge are selected because they lead to favorable outcomes. Scientific laws are said to be concise economical descriptions of contingencies in the environment and can thus serve as "rules for effective action" (Skinner, 1974, p. 235). In Skinner's (1969) words, the laws of science are "not . . . obeyed by nature but by men who effectively deal with nature" (p. 141). Like other neobehaviorists, Skinner extends his theory of learned behavior to the activity of scientists, and he clearly adheres to the general pragmatist metaphor that "to know is to do."[3]

Given his Machian-evolutionist perspective on science, Skinner's metaphors can be seen to arise quite naturally. Belief in the continuity of science with more primitive forms of organic adaptation has licensed Skinner to apply the metaphor of "selection by consequences" to scientific knowing as well as to the behavior of rats. The behavioral scientist who "shapes" behavior, in or out of the laboratory, is making a kind of direct contact with the behavioral subject matter, much as the artisan shapes something useful out of the relevant raw material. When Skinner asserts metaphorically that "no one steps outside the causal stream" or that a person is a "locus of a system of variables," we can see the basis of these metaphors in his Machian view of cause as functional relation between observables (Skinner, 1974, p. 206; 1947/1961, p. 236). And the Machian metaphor of intellectual, and ultimately biological, economy is echoed throughout Skinner's writings. The criteria for evaluating a scientific system, says Skinner (1938), are supplied by the "usefulness and economy of the system with respect to the data at hand" (p. 438). Scientific practices and formulations that are unacceptable to Skinner are said to be "wasteful," "useless," "unpractical," and even "clumsy and obese" – a metaphor that vividly connotes unfitness in a biological sense. In other words, Skinner's positivism is a biologicoeconomical positivism, stemming from the demands of expedient adaptation in a Darwinian world.

As was the case with Tolman and Hull, Skinner's metaphors reveal a deeply held set of beliefs about the world and about the behavior of organisms in it. Also like them, Skinner has been remarkably consistent in applying his world view to the entire spectrum of organismic behavior – from the laboratory rat to the highest forms of human cognition and scientific knowing. In his emphatically positivistic views of science, Skinner has perhaps been the most insistent of the three neobehaviorists discussed here in laying out the implications of his world view for the actual practice of science. One marvels at the consistency with which he has pursued his vision. Yet if there is an inconsistency to be found in his systematic approach, it is that he rejects metaphors in science on the grounds of intellectual economy, which is itself a metaphorical criterion of science. Skinner would undoubtedly deny that his notions of biological and intellectual economy are inherently metaphorical, arguing instead (as did Mach) that such notions are but descriptive extensions of evolutionary theory. As will be suggested in the following section, however, such a position grossly underestimates the constitutive role of metaphor in formulating world views of the sort that make "descriptive" generalizations possible.[4]

The place of metaphor in science: growing edges or metaphysical core?

In summary, the following points can be made: First, thinkers who have been hostile to the use of metaphors have themselves had difficulty doing without figures of speech, even in the process of denigrating them. Second, behaviorism, a school of thought commonly associated with the antimetaphorical positivist tradition, has often relied on metaphorical formulations, both in its prehistory and in its early history. Third, each of the major neobehaviorists discussed here has made extensive use of metaphors. Fourth, each of these thinkers has used metaphors not merely as rhetorical devices, but in systematic ways that reveal a pattern of deep-seated commitments amounting to the formulation of a world view. And, fifth, each of these neobehaviorists began his career with serious interests in epistemology and eventually extended his coherent metaphor system to the roots of human epistemology as well as to cases of animal "knowing." Thus, each of their metaphor systems can be said to be coherent both in the sense of stemming from a cohesive metaphysical world view and in the sense of being applied consistently to a wide range of intelligent organismic functioning.

To refer to the world views of the major neobehaviorists as "metaphysical" is perhaps to raise a red flag – or at least it would have been twenty years ago, and probably still is in some circles today. After all, the behaviorists have routinely been thought of as positivists, and they certainly formulated many of the views in question during the ascendancy of the vigorously antimetaphysical school of logical positivism. Yet the ascription of metaphysical views to quasi-positivistic behaviorists will surprise no one familiar with the actual development of their thought or with the history of positivism in this century. In the first place, it is by now fairly widely accepted that not even the logical positivists managed to avoid metaphysical commitments (see, e.g., Bergmann, 1954; Brown, 1977). Furthermore, despite frequent claims to the contrary, the neobehaviorists (with the exception of Kenneth Spence) were *not* closely allied with logical positivism (Amundson, 1983; Amundson & Smith, 1984; Smith, 1986). And most important, the neobehaviorists did in fact advance blatantly metaphysical assertions, even in the face of the positivist climate of their time. When Tolman asserted that the world is a complex maze, or Hull that organisms are machines, or Skinner that the known world is a set of contingencies, we see in these assertions the expression of deeply held beliefs about the world, not just colorful expressions of straightforward positivistic facts.

Though it may be unorthodox to accuse these neobehaviorists of engaging in metaphysics, to do so is far from accusing them of being unscientific. The old positivist equation of the metaphysical with the meaningless or the unscientific has long since been laid to rest (see, e.g., Wartofsky, 1979, chap. 4). As historians of science have been aware for some time (and philosophers of science only more recently), many of the great scientific issues and achievements through the ages have been metaphysical in character – a generalization that holds just as well for physics as for the "less mature" sciences. As one philosopher has put it, the scientist "is, most often, *métaphysicien malgré lui*, in proposing and examining conceptual models in his domain" (Wartofsky, 1979, p. 86).

Far from being irrelevant or antithetical to scientific practice, the metaphysical views of scientists are often closely connected with their productivity as scientists. What matters from the standpoint of conducting science is how the implications of one's metaphysics are drawn out and applied to the world of observable phenomena – how, in the long run, one's underlying vision of the world is put to use in generating empirical research and conceptual insights. On this score, the major neobehaviorists have fared reasonably well, a conclusion attested to by their own records of productivity and by the fruitful research traditions they fostered (see Smith, 1986, pp. 334–5, and the discussion below). But it would be a mistake to try to understand their work by focusing on their explicit theoretical stances to the exclusion of the metaphysical views that generated them. As Howard Gruber (1980) has stated, "The testing of hypotheses has been the glory of methodologists, but it remains a sterile glory so long as little or nothing is said about the primitive roots – both imaginal and ideological – from which testable ideas spring" (p. 155). It is these roots, these metaphysical underpinnings, that lend power and coherence to the neobehaviorists' theories and to those of any scientist.

The general conclusion I wish to draw here is that for the major neo-behaviorists – and I suspect for many scientists who have attempted broad conceptualizations – the means of formulating their all-important world views was metaphor itself. That is, metaphorical language, far from serving only as an instrument of rhetoric, provided the very language of their deepest metaphysical beliefs. To be sure, the metaphor systems of these figures played an important *linguistic* role in extending their terminology to new phenomena, and they clearly played an important *heuristic* role in generating novel concepts and productive lines of research. But I would suggest that they also played a deeper *constitutive* role in framing the world views from which their theoretical concepts, their research programs, and their empirical discoveries arose. In short, the role of metaphor in their work was not confined to the "growing edges" of their systematic thought, to use Quine's (1978) metaphor, but rather was centrally located at its metaphysical core. In a real sense, the visions for psychology created by Tolman, Hull, and Skinner were *constituted* by their characteristically metaphorical ways of viewing organismic activity in the natural world. This claim accords with the view of Nelson Goodman (1978) that metaphor serves many functions, including the essentially metaphysical function of "worldmaking." As Goodman (1979) has stated, "Far from being a mere matter of ornament, [metaphor] participates fully in the progress of knowledge: in replacing some stale 'natural' kinds with novel and illuminating categories, in contriving facts, in revising theory, and in bringing us new worlds" (p. 175).

The idea proposed here that the use of metaphors in science is intimately linked with the articulation of a scientific metaphysics obviously calls for further investigation of its generality and adequacy. But some suggestive parallels between metaphor systems and metaphysics in science are already apparent. In particular, I would assert (lacking space to argue in detail) that the following interrelated parallels hold: (1) Although the metaphors/metaphysics underlying a particular line of scientific thought may not be immediately obvious, they are always there even if only implicitly. (2) The pretense to do without metaphors/metaphysics is, to use I. A. Richards's (1936/1965) words, "never more than a bluff waiting to be called" (p. 92). (3) An antimetaphorical/antimetaphysical position cannot even be formulated without engaging in metaphorical/metaphysical discourse. (4) Scientists can criticize the metaphor systems/metaphysics of other scientists only from the perspective of a metaphor systems/metaphysics of their own. (5) To abandon one system of metaphors/metaphysics is to adopt another. (6) Even though metaphors/metaphysics are far from irrelevant to science, the assessment of their scientific fertility is not a quick or simple matter; their fruitfulness can be gauged only in the long run, through extended efforts at drawing out their implications.

In retrospect, perhaps the most remarkable aspect of the neobehaviorists' development of metaphysical metaphor systems is that these systems were formulated during an era in which positivist aims were held in high repute. Through much of the twentieth century, the literature of philosophy and theoretical psychology contained an abundance of endorsements of logical positivism and numerous proposals for the reduction of theoretical science to the level of pure description. Had the neobehaviorists seriously attempted to act in accordance with positivist prescriptions for science, it is doubtful whether their systematic approaches to psychology would have survived for long or even been formulated. As it turned out, they sufficiently withstood the positivistic currents of their time to be able to produce fruitful metaphors for knowledge and behavior – metaphors, in fact, that are still in use today. Tolman's anthropomorphic metaphor of "expectancy" has become a central concept in recent theories of animal learning (e.g., Mackintosh, 1974), while his metaphor of the "cognitive map" has proved to be a fertile one both in animal psychology (e.g., Hulse, Fowler, & Honig, 1978) and in human geography (e.g., Downs & Stea, 1973). The Hullian metaphor of organism as machine is so widely current in modern cognitive science as to require no further comment. And Skinner's various evolutionary metaphors, especially those of variation and selection, have been employed and extended in recent influential formulations within the Skinnerian tradition (e.g., Staddon & Simmelhag, 1971). If those who use such metaphors today are largely uncognizant of the metaphysical background of their concepts, their lack of awareness evinces the continuing sway of positivism and constitutes a situation that may well be to their detriment as scientists.

Notes

1 I have focused only on metaphors for theories and their relations to observation, but it is tempting to conclude more generally that all global accounts of human knowledge are metaphorical. From Neurath's (1932–3/1959) *ship-at-sea* metaphor to Quine and Ullian's (1970) notion of a *web of belief* and from Kuhn's (1970) *revolutionary* view to Toulmin's (1972) *evolutionary* view, we see the same pattern repeating itself.

2 Further parallels between operant conditioning and evolutionary phenomena are discussed from a Skinnerian standpoint by Staddon (1973, 1975).

3 Skinner's interests in developing an empirical psychology of science were formed while he was in graduate school, partly under the influence of Mach's (1905/1976) efforts to do the same. In fact, Skinner's first book, begun in the early 1930s, was his *Sketch for an Epistemology* (see Skinner, 1979, pp. 115, 146, 159), only one chapter of which was ever published (1935). Among his later writings on the psychology of science, the most important are "The Operational Analysis of Psychological Terms" (1945) and *Verbal Behavior*

(1957). Discussions of his psychology of science may be found in Burton (1980), Smith (1986, chap. 9), and Zuriff (1980).

4 Skinner is unique among the behaviorists discussed here in having given an explicit treatment of the nature of metaphorical language. In his account, which expresses by and large a traditional empiricist view of metaphors, Skinner (1957) makes the following claims: (1) Metaphor is appropriate in literature but to be avoided in science (pp. 98, 99); (2) the use of metaphor involves the extension of terms to new entities in a way that is not ordinarily reinforced by the speaker's verbal community (p. 92); (3) as opposed to metaphorical extension, the process of generic extension involves applying old terminology to new domains in a way that *is* respected by the verbal community, largely as a result of being consonant with the community's consensual modes of categorizing entities (p. 91); (4) generic extension is accepted in science because of its practical consequences, whereas metaphorical extension is punished or extinguished by a scientific community because of its disadvantageous consequences (pp. 99, 419–20); and (5) when metaphorical extension *is* used in science, the metaphor is quickly "robbed of its metaphorical nature through the advent of additional stimulus control" – in effect through empirical definition (p. 419). Now it should be obvious, even on Skinner's own grounds, that what might count as generic extension for one scientific verbal community might well count as metaphorical extension for another scientific verbal community or even the community of scientists as a whole. If Skinnerians reinforce each other's "descriptive" (i.e., ostensibly generic) extensions of evolutionary theory, such a practice says more about their verbal habits as a community than it does about the nature of the world. (Presumably if Skinner had spent an appreciable amount of time observing communities of Tolmanians or Hullians, he would have been forced to the realization that very different sets of extensions were being reinforced and punished in those communities.) And, of course, the "advent of stimulus control" can hardly be expected to provide univocal reductions of metaphor to literal description, given that any such process would be carried out differently in different verbal communities. I would assert that a given scientific community's modes of categorization and means of deciding which uses of language are beneficial or disadvantageous will themselves typically be determined by its preferred fundamental metaphors. Scientists do not punish or extinguish metaphors as a matter of general course; rather, they selectively punish the metaphors favored by competing scientific traditions.

References

Amundson, R. (1983). E. C. Tolman and the intervening variable: A study in the epistemological history of psychology. *Philosophy of Science, 50*, 268–82.

Amundson, R., & Smith, L. D. (1984). Clark Hull, Robert Cummins, and functional analysis. *Philosophy of Science, 51*, 657–66.

Baernstein, H. D., & Hull, C. L. (1931). A mechanical model of the conditioned reflex. *Journal of General Psychology, 5*, 99–106.

Bechterev, V. M. (1928). *General principles of human reflexology* (4th ed., E. Murphy & W. Murphy, Trans.). New York: International. (Original work published 1907.)

Bergmann, G. (1954). *The metaphysics of logical positivism*. Madison: University of Wisconsin Press.

Boakes, R. (1984). *From Darwin to behaviorism: Psychology and the minds of animals*. Cambridge University Press.

Brown, H. I. (1977). *Perception, theory and commitment: The new philosophy of science*. Chicago: University of Chicago Press.

Burton, M. (1980). Determinism, relativism and the behavior of scientists. *Behaviorism, 8*, 113–22.

Chapanis, A. (1963). Men, machines, and models. In M. Marx (Ed.), *Theories in contemporary psychology* (pp. 104–29). New York: Macmillan.

Craik, K. (1966). *The nature of psychology* (S. L. Sherwood, Ed.). Cambridge University Press.

Descartes, R. (1911). The passions of the soul. In E. S. Haldane & G. R. T. Ross (Eds. and Trans.), *The philosophical works of Descartes* (vol. 1, pp. 329–427). Cambridge University Press. (Original work published 1649.)

Downs, R. M., & Stea, D. (Eds.). (1973). *Image and environment*. Chicago: Aldine.

Duhem, P. (1962). *The aim and structure of physical theory* (P. P. Wiener, Trans.). New York: Atheneum. (Original work published 1906.)

Ellson, D. G. (1935). A mechanical synthesis of trial-and-error learning. *Journal of General Psychology, 13*, 212–18.

Evans, R. B. (1973). E. B. Titchener and his lost system. In M. Henle, J. Jaynes, & J. J. Sullivan (Eds.), *Historical conceptions of psychology* (pp. 83–97). New York: Springer.

Feigl, H. (1981). *Inquiries and provocations: Selected writings, 1929–1974* (R. S. Cohen, Ed.). Dordrecht: Reidel.

Gardner, M. (1958). *Logic machines, diagrams, and Boolean algebra*. New York: Dover.

Goodman, N. (1978). *Ways of worldmaking*. Indianapolis, IN: Hackett.

  (1979). Metaphor as moonlighting. In S. Sacks (Ed.), *On metaphor* (pp. 175–80). Chicago: University of Chicago Press.

Gruber, H. E. (1980). Darwin on psychology and its relation to evolutionary thought. In R. W. Rieber & K. Salzinger (Eds.), *Psychology: Theoretical-historical perspectives* (pp. 145–74). New York: Academic Press.

Gunderson, K. (1967). Cybernetics. In P. Edwards (Ed.), *Encyclopedia of philosophy* (vol. 2, pp. 280–4). New York: Macmillan.

Hull, C. L. (1927–8). *Idea Books* (Unpublished diaries, vol. 11). Clark L. Hull Papers, Yale University Library, New Haven, CT.

  (1930a). Knowledge and purpose as habit mechanisms. *Psychological Review, 37*, 511–25.

  (1930b). Simple trial-and-error learning: A study in psychological theory. *Psychological Review, 37*, 241–56.

  (1931). Goal attraction and directing ideas conceived as habit phenomena. *Psychological Review, 38*, 487–506.

  (1934). The concept of the habit–family hierarchy and maze learning. *Psychological Review, 41*, 33–52, 134–52.

  (1936). *Seminar notes: Institute of human relations*. Clark L. Hull Papers, Yale University Library, New Haven, CT.

  (1937). Mind, mechanism, and adaptive behavior. *Psychological Review, 44*, 1–32.

  (1943). *Principles of behavior: An introduction to behavior theory*. New York: Appleton-Century.

  (1952). Clark L. Hull. In E. G. Boring, H. S. Langfeld, H. Werner, & R. M. Yerkes (Eds.), *A history of psychology in autobiography* (vol. 4, pp. 143–62). Worcester, MA: Clark University Press.

(1962). Psychology of the scientist: IV. Passages from the "Idea Books" of Clark L. Hull (R. Hays, Ed.). *Perceptual and Motor Skills, 15*, 807–82.

Hull, C. L., & Baernstein, H. D. (1929). A mechanical parallel to the conditioned reflex. *Science, 70*, 14–15.

Hull, C. L., & Krueger, R. G. (1931). An electro-chemical parallel to the conditioned reflex. *Journal of General Psychology, 5*, 262–9.

Hulse, S. H., Fowler, H., & Honig, W. K. (Eds.) (1978). *Cognitive processes in animal behavior*. Hillsdale, NJ: Erlbaum.

Jaynes, J. (1973). The problem of animate motion in the seventeenth century. In M. Henle, J. Jaynes, & J. J. Sullivan (Eds.), *Historical conceptions of psychology* (pp. 166–79). New York: Springer.

Koch, S. (1954). Clark L. Hull. In W. K. Estes, S. Koch, K. MacCorquodale, P. E. Meehl, C. G. Mueller, Jr., W. M. Schoenfeld, & W. S. Verplanck (Eds.), *Modern learning theory* (pp. 1–176). New York: Appleton-Century-Crofts.

Kuhn, T. S. (1970). *The structure of scientific revolutions* (2d enl. ed.). Chicago: University of Chicago Press.

Mach, E. (1943). *Popular scientific lectures* (5th ed., T. J. MacCormack, Trans.). La Salle, IL: Open Court. (Original work published 1894.)

(1959). *The analysis of sensations* (5th ed., C. M. Williams & S. Waterlow, Trans.). New York: Dover. (Original work published 1886.)

(1976). *Knowledge and error: Sketches on the psychology of inquiry* (5th ed., T. J. McCormack & P. Foulkes, Trans.). Dordrecht: Reidel. (Original work published 1905.)

Mackintosh, N. J. (1974). *The psychology of animal learning*. New York: Academic Press.

Morgan, C. L. (1894). *An introduction to comparative psychology*. London: Scott.

Neurath, O. (1959). Protocol sentences. In A. J. Ayer (Ed.), *Logical positivism* (pp. 199–208). Glencoe, IL: Free Press. (Original work published 1932–3.)

Northrop, F. S. C. (1960). *Philosophical anthropology and practical politics*. New York: Macmillan.

Pavlov, I. P. (1902). *Lectures on the work of the digestive glands* (W. H. Thompson, Trans.). London: Griffin. (Original work published 1897.)

(1927). *Conditioned reflexes* (G. V. Anrep, Trans.). New York: Oxford University Press.

Popper, K. R. (1959). *The logic of scientific discovery*. New York: Harper & Row.

Quine, W. V. O. (1978). A postscript on metaphor. In S. Sacks (Ed.), *On metaphor* (pp. 159–60). Chicago: University of Chicago Press.

Quine, W. V. O., & Ullian, J. S. (1970). *The web of belief*. New York: Random House.

Richards, I. A. (1965). *The philosophy of rhetoric*. New York: Oxford University Press. (Original work published 1936.)

Romanes, G. J. (1883). *Mental evolution in animals*. London: Kegan Paul, Trench.

Sechenov, I. M. (1935). Reflexes of the brain (A. A. Subkov, Trans.). In I. M. Sechenov, *Selected works* (pp. 264–322). Moscow: Gozmedizdat. (Original work published 1863.)

Skinner, B. F. (1935). The generic nature of the concepts of stimulus and response. *Journal of General Psychology, 12*, 40–65.

(1938). *The behavior of organisms: An experimental analysis*. New York: Appleton-Century.

(1945). The operational analysis of psychological terms. *Psychological Review, 52*, 270–7, 291–4.

(1957). *Verbal behavior.* New York: Appleton-Century-Crofts.

(1961). Current trends in experimental psychology. In *Cumulative record* (enl. ed., pp. 223–41). New York: Appleton-Century-Crofts. (Original work published 1947.)

(1969). *Contingencies of reinforcement: A theoretical analysis.* New York: Appleton-Century-Crofts.

(1971). *Beyond freedom and dignity.* New York: Knopf.

(1974). *About behaviorism.* New York: Knopf.

(1975). The shaping of phylogenetic behavior. *Journal of the Experimental Analysis of Behavior, 24*, 117–20.

(1979). *The shaping of a behaviorist: Part Two of an autobiography.* New York: Knopf.

Smith, L. D. (1982). Purpose and cognition: The limits of neorealist influence on Tolman's psychology. *Behaviorism, 10*, 151–63.

(1986). *Behaviorism and logical positivism: A reassessment of the alliance.* Stanford, CA: Stanford University Press.

Staddon, J. E. R. (1973). On the notion of cause, with applications to behaviorism. *Behaviorism, 1*, 25–63.

(1975). A note on the evolutionary significance of supernormal stimuli. *American Naturalist, 109*, 541–5.

Staddon, J. E. R., & Simmelhag, V. L. (1971). The "superstition" experiment: A reexamination of its implications for the principles of adaptive behavior. *Psychological Review, 78*, 3–43.

Thorndike, E. L. (1898). Animal intelligence: An experimental study of the associative processes in animals. *Psychological Review Monograph Supplement, 2* (Whole No. 8).

Tolman, E. C. (1923). A behavioristic account of the emotions. *Psychological Review, 30*, 217–27.

(1925). Purpose and cognition: The determiners of animal learning. *Psychological Review, 32*, 285–97.

(1926). A behavioristic theory of ideas. *Psychological Review, 33*, 352–69.

(1932). *Purposive behavior in animals and men.* New York: Century.

(1933). Gestalt and sign-gestalt. *Psychological Review, 40*, 391–411.

(1935). Psychology versus immediate experience. *Philosophy of Science, 2*, 356–80.

(1938). The determiners of behavior at a choice point. *Psychological Review, 45*, 1–41.

(1948). Cognitive maps in rats and men. *Psychological Review, 55*, 189–208.

(1952). Edward Chace Tolman. In E. G. Boring, H. S. Langfeld, H. Werner, & R. M. Yerkes (Eds.), *A history of psychology in autobiography* (vol. 4, pp. 323–39). Worcester, MA: Clark University Press.

(1959). Principles of purposive behavior. In S. Koch (Ed.), *Psychology: A study of a science* (vol. 2, pp. 92–157). New York: McGraw-Hill.

(1966). Operational behaviorism and current trends in psychology. In *Behavior and psychological man: Essays in motivation and learning* (pp. 115–29). Berkeley and Los Angeles: University of California Press. (Original work published 1936.)

Tolman, E. C., & Brunswik, E. (1935). The organism and the causal texture of the environment. *Psychological Review, 42*, 43–77.

Tolman, E. C., & Honzik, C. H. (1930). Introduction and removal of reward, and maze performance in rats. *University of California Publications in Psychology, 4*, 257–75.

Tolman, E. C., & Krechevsky, I. (1933). Means-and-readiness and hypothesis: A contribution to comparative psychology. *Psychological Review, 40*, 60–70.

Toulmin, S. E. (1972). *Human understanding: The collective use and evolution of concepts*. Princeton, NJ: Princeton University Press.

Wartofsky, M. (1979). *Models: Representation and the scientific understanding*. Dordrecht: Reidel.

Watson, J. B. (1916). The place of the conditioned-reflex in psychology. *Psychological Review, 23*, 89–117.

Young, R. M. (1971). Darwin's metaphor: Does nature select? *Monist, 55*, 442–503.

Zener, K. (1937). The significance of behavior accompanying conditioned salivary secretion for theories of the conditioned response. *American Journal of Psychology, 50*, 384–403.

Zuriff, G. E. (1980). Radical behaviorist epistemology. *Psychological Bulletin, 87*, 337–50.

8

Metaphor, metatheory, and the social world

KENNETH J. GERGEN

Metaphor is the chief vehicle through which we advance our understanding of social life. Indeed, without metaphor, scientific thinking as a whole would remain paralyzed. To explore these claims, I shall focus in this chapter on some of the major theoretical developments in social psychology – and, more particularly, on the dominant metaphors that have generated these theoretical developments. Within this context, I shall propose that the metaphors used to build scientific theories of human action should be consonant with one's conceptions of scientific conduct itself. In other words, one's conception of what it is to carry out proper behavioral science should mesh with the theories of human conduct (including the conduct of scientists) that one constructs.

This proposal suggests that a special tension may exist, at any given time, between the current philosophy of science and particular conceptualizations of the social world: One's theoretical metaphors may be more or less compatible with the root metaphor underlying one's account of science itself. Indeed, I shall argue that in recent decades the tension between social psychology and the typical understanding of the nature of science has become unusually acute – and has even reached a breaking point. The family of metaphors underlying major theories in contemporary social psychology – not to mention emerging strands of social inquiry – form essential challenges to the traditional concept of science. As a result, a new conception of science seems to be demanded.

The metaphoric and the literal in social theory

Before we can appreciate the critical functions played by metaphor in the construction of scientific theory, it is necessary to focus on the nature of metaphor itself. How are we to understand metaphor? Traditionally, it has been defined in opposition to *literal* discourse. Whereas literal language has been viewed as directly representing the objects to which it refers, and thus as being essentially "true to fact," metaphoric language has been said to be suffused with imagination, to be merely figurative, and to be exaggerated. Not surprisingly, given this opposition, it has also been said that proper science should renounce the metaphoric and strive assiduously toward the achievement of a pure, literal language. Scientists, in other words, have been urged to leave metaphor to poets, novelists, and ideologues and to let their own language simply "carve nature at the joint."

Within this traditional context, the thesis that metaphor plays a key role in the advancement of scientific thinking may seem perverse. How could metaphor be accorded such importance? To appreciate the argument, consider first the attempt by logical positivists to establish the grounds for a scientific language. As they initially agreed, the theoretical language of an empiricial science should be tied closely to particulars in the real world. Ideally, as Russell (1918–19) reasoned, each term within the theoretical network should stand in one-to-one correspondence with real-world particulars. If this were accomplished, the meaning of theory within an empirical science would be derived from its relationship with observables. For psychologists this line of thinking gave rise to the long-standing attempt to furnish operational definitions for conceptual terms (see, e.g., Boring et al., 1945). Yet despite the attraction of such a proposal, the means by which empirical anchoring was to be achieved was never satisfactorily rendered. Should real-world particulars be related to individual words at the theoretical level, or to phrases, or to entire sentences? What was to be made of the many theoretical terms in the advanced sciences, terms essential to understanding but for which there were no observables? If operational definitions were also described in words, didn't these words require objective anchoring? And if such anchoring was similarly brought about by means of words that needed their own anchoring, had we not entered an infinite regress of definition?

These and many other questions left the logical empiricist attempt to justify a literal language vulnerable to attack. Such attack came along different fronts. For instance, Quine's (1960) analysis of radical translation was lethal to any attempt at a simple, mimetic theory of reference. As Quine demonstrated, there are no ultimate means by which a visitor to a primitive tribe could determine whether their term *gavagai* could properly be translated into the English term "rabbit." Looking at all the contexts in which *gavagai* was applied to real-world events would lead only to perplexity in this respect. Even if capable of substituting the term "rabbit" on each occasion, the visitor could never know whether the native was using the term to refer, for example, to a set of attached rabbit parts whereas he himself used it to refer to the rabbit as a whole. By extrapolation, when two members of the same language community use the same term on the same occasion, we cannot ultimately determine the precise thing, event, or property to which the term refers – all the more so since attempts to sort out possible disagreements must themselves be framed in a language in which the precise particulars remain unknown, and so on.

Wittgenstein's (1953) work provided another major antidote to literalism. As he demonstrated, descriptive terms appear in multiple linguistic configurations, which he called "language games." The limits on how a descriptive term can be employed are thus to be traced primarily to the linguistic context. What can be said, for example, about "rabbit" depends on whether one is a zoologist, a hunter, a writer of children's books, or a cook. Descriptive terms gain their meaning not from objects in the real world, but from their use in the various "games" of language.

When extended, such forms of criticism suggest that the traditional distinction between a literal and a metaphoric language is specious. If language cannot provide a mirror or map to the world, then the very concept of a literal language becomes dubious. At the same time, without a viable concept of literal language the concept of metaphor also perishes; for if all theoretical description is metaphoric, the latter term is simply redundant with what we mean by theoretical description, and we are thus left with the unchallenging conclusion that theoretical description is simply what it is.

How, then, is the meaning of metaphor to be rescued? The critical turn, in this case, has been prepared by Wittgenstein's attack on the assumption of linguistic mapping. Wittgenstein's demonstrations of the constraining power of linguistic context over descriptive terminology are fully convincing. However, it would be a mistake to delimit the constraining context to the level of language alone. There is little reason to suppose that a person's linguistic activities (e.g., speaking and writing) should alone constrain word usage, while other activities (e.g., pointing, lifting, and running) should not. Let us then expand the concept of context to include the entire range of social practices (linguistic and otherwise) in which words are ensconced. Let us expand it further to include the various objects, paraphernalia, physical settings, and so on, in which these social practices are embedded. A fully developed theory of word meaning might thus include words, movements, objects, and so on. Now to draw again from the Wittgensteinian perspective, it may be said that the "meaning" of each constituent – word, action, or object –

depends on its place within the entire array. From this vantage point the meaning of a word is not derived from the empirical world that it is said to represent (as the logical empiricists would have it), nor is it dependent on the speaker's underlying intention (as most hermeneuticists and speech act philosophers would claim). Rather, meaning is derived from an array of patterned practices within varying contexts. To inquire into the meaning of a term is to ask neither for its observable referents nor for the speaker's intention; it is to request from the interlocutor a display of the fuller set of practices in which the term is embedded on a particular occasion.

On this view there is no literal language in the traditional sense of a language that simply "fits the world," perfectly and without remainder; nor is there metaphoric language that we can define once and for all, in Aristotelian fashion, as language that talks about something as if it were something else. However, denying these alternatives does not imply that the distinction between the literal and metaphoric is itself vacuous. Rather, within the present analysis we may view literal language as essentially any constituent of an established or reiterative pattern (word–action–object). In other words, literal words are simply those that occupy an established position in a language game that is repeated with some kind of regularity. Such words "feel right" – they seem to "reflect" the world or to "call a spade a spade." In contrast, what we call metaphoric language would emerge, from this perspective, in cases where the established pattern is altered. Metaphoric words are replacements or substitutes for culturally sedimented vocabulary. The capacity of these substitutes to innervate the writer or reader is derived from the associated practices that they import into the established context. Novel uses of words invite alternative practices, both linguistic and otherwise.

As we discern from this analysis, the distinction between literal and metaphoric language is graduated or dimensional rather than categorical. A new term thrust into an alien context will seem metaphoric at the outset. However, as it gradually becomes incorporated into the communal practices and as the new patterns become solidified, the term will become increasingly literal. For example, as MacCormac (1976) has pointed out, in 1755 the term "chaff" was defined by Samuel Johnson as "refuse left after the process of threshing grain." By 1966, however, dictionaries included another literal entry for the word: "thin metallic strips that are dropped from an aircraft to create confusing signals on radarscopes" (p. 77). The change occurred when the term "chaff" became commonly used for metal scraps left from the milling process and when these scraps were subsequently found to be useful in confusing radar detection devices. For many air personnel, at least, chaff has thus shifted from the metaphoric to the literal. In the same way we use "inspiration" as a literal term today. People do in fact seem to us to be "inspired." Yet if we consider the origins of the term, with its reference to the spirit entering the body, we will realize its original metaphorical dimension.

Metaphor in the construction of social understanding

Thus far, I have argued against the traditional mode of defining metaphor in opposition to literal description. However, if we view the distinction between metaphor and literal language as reflecting degrees of normative acceptability, the concept of metaphor is revitalized in important ways. At the outset, we find that literal language is the anticipated outcome of ongoing interchange among persons, including scientists. That is, as people attempt to coordinate their actions with one another, they find it necessary and useful to develop a common language that remains stable across time. In effect, this creates a strong tendency toward normalization – or "literalization" – of discourse. "Please pass the salt" is functional as an illocutionary device in English-speaking culture precisely because words such as "pass" and "salt" – when uttered in the mealtime setting – have acquired the status of literal language. In the same way, scientific terms such as "gravity" and "classical conditioning" have bcome literal in the scientific community. They are useful not because they necessarily reflect what is the case, but because they enable certain scientists to coordinate their activities across time and circumstance.

At the same time, we see that the achievement of a literal language within a community carries the threat of social stasis. To accept a literal language is to sustain the broad range of practices in which this language is embedded. Thus, within the scientific community, the extent to which participants acquiesce to the standard linguistic practices is a reliable measure of the extent to which science will remain static, its outcomes will be increasingly diminished, and the productivity of the scientific paradigm will approach asymptote. For example, biological theories of reproduction have traditionally characterized the process of fertilization as one in which the sperm is the active agent and the egg a passive receptacle. Biological theory has thus relied on the metaphor of traditional heterosexual relations to comprehend the process of biological reproduction. Over time, the metaphor has been transformed into literal language. Yet as various feminist critics (Fausto-Sterling, 1985; Martin, 1987) have pointed out, the use of the metaphor in this case not only sustains oppressive social patterns, but places limits on biological theory and research. By employing a different metaphor – by granting, for example, that the egg may have a more active role in the process of reproduction – new predictions can be made and new "findings" generated. In other words, new metaphors enable investigators to see the phenomenon in a different light, to formulate novel predictions, and to search for new forms of evidence.

In this context, we find that scientific advances depend vitally on pressing against the boundaries of existing forms of understanding. New types of interpretation constitute the necessary foundation of new ranges of exploration.

Yet how is the scientist to break with traditional forms of understanding? One cannot simply introduce a form of private language – in effect, a language composed of "nonsense syllables" – into the community. Such a language would have no meaning, which is to say, it would not be embedded within existing patterns of interchange in such a way that anyone would know how to respond. The critical question, then, is how the theorist can break with traditional, sedimented forms of language and at the same time continue to make sense in the scientific culture. In other words, the question is how new forms of understanding can ever be achieved if understanding depends on commonly accepted forms of discourse. It is at this point that we can begin to appreciate the critical role that metaphors play in the sciences, for as we have seen, when we shift from the literal to the metaphoric we are moving from an *accepted* use of language to a *partially acceptable* use of language. Metaphors hover at the edge of intelligibility; they rely on certain conventions while violating others; they are sufficiently reasonable that they communicate, but sufficiently novel that they threaten the status quo.

As an illustration, suppose someone says that the traditional family operates like a machine. Clearly, this statement is metaphoric. By current standards of literal language usage, families are not identical to machines. However, the metaphor makes sense by virtue of the fact that certain definitional components of the machine are also definitional components of the traditional family. For example, both the machine and the family are (or should be) smooth running, dependable, solid, and so on. At the same time the machine metaphor invites one to consider a new range of terms for speaking of the traditional family, terms that are not now part of the literal language. For example, the metaphor invites one to think of the family as a structured set of interdependencies, the functioning of which depends on certain inputs into the system. In effect, the metaphor opens up new departures for understanding and research. Over time, if the new language is elaborated and extended within various research practices, its metaphoric character will recede. Indeed, for many researchers, "family structure" has already become a literal reality.

In summary, metaphor serves as the critical device by which theoretical forms of understanding are generated and transformed in the sciences – and more informally in the culture at large. Metaphor, in other words, furnishes the essential foundation for new avenues of investigation. Yet even this analysis is limiting, for as we explore various metaphors in the history of social inquiry, we find that metaphor serves other functions as well. Four of these deserve special mention.

Metaphor and conceptual problem solving

At the outset metaphors enable the social theorist to solve theoretical problems created by existing forms of understanding. With a properly selected metaphor one can reorganize conceptions of social life and transcend antinomies or conflicts of long standing. The concept of the Great Chain of Being illustrates the point. Consider the problem of classifying forms of living beings. Merely to group such beings according to physical differences leaves one with only a series of isolated labels and fails to furnish a sense of organization or relatedness. Thus, for Aristotle and many subsequent thinkers, it proved useful to think of all creatures as related on a continuum from the lesser to the greater. In the eighteenth century the metaphor of the Great Chain of Being formalized this possibility (see Lovejoy, 1936). For many thinkers of that time, the concept also solved new problems. With the continuing emergence of a science of biology, the place of religious understanding was threatened. From the theological perspective (and for many biologists) there was a need for a concept that would demonstrate the unity among different species. The Great Chain of Being solved the problem. If living creatures could be grouped from the lesser to the greater, and humans (the greatest of the creatures) were created in the image of God, then God acquired a place at the head of the chain, and a natural continuity was established between the biological and the spiritual. In this as in other ways, the chain metaphor played a valuable conceptual role.

Metaphor as agency of social change

To the extent that metaphors are associated with new forms of social practice, they can serve a powerful function in the process of social change. Like a banner, emblem, or anthem, they come to serve as symbols of collective goals. Yet they can often be used with greater efficacy than such symbols because of their capacity to confer meaning, rationality, and a sense of justice upon given forms of society. Some of the most dramatic illustrations of this point may be found in the past century. Consider, for instance, the metaphor of social change as a form of "natural growth." Just as all living organisms go through predetermined stages of development, as the earth moves in its natural orbit, and as species emerge and disappear according to natural conditions, so too, it is said, societies possess a naturally determined trajectory (according to which they rise, fall, etc.). In effect, the "natural growth" metaphor recommends, invites, and justifies social change. Darwinian accounts of social change ("social Darwinism") made explicit use of this metaphor. There is also an important sense in which Marxist theory relies on the same view. To be sure, Marx also employed the Hegelian concept of dialectic change. However, when Hegelian idealism was materialized, with being and negation recast as antagonistic social classes, Marxist theory acquired all the rhetorical value of the Darwinian account. Not only is bourgeois society competitive and divided, according to Marx (1867/1954); it has created devastating weapons and placed them in the hands of the proletariat. In effect, the ruling class has become an unfit species and its demise is a natural and predictable outcome. For many, this metaphor has been compelling, and the result has been social change of enormous magnitude.

Metaphor and legitimation

In the same way that metaphors can serve as implements of social change, they may also be used to legitimate or rationalize social orders. To illustrate, the mechanistic metaphor has played a critical role in sanctioning a variety of social endeavors. As political scientist Martin Landau (1961) proposes, it was this metaphor – the metaphor of the machine – that dominated the thoughts of those who penned the American Constitution. John Adams, for instance, wrote in his 1787 defense of the Constitution that the three branches of government have an "unalterable foundation in nature." To invest a single political body with all power, without "balance" or "equilibrium," said Adams, is to violate nature's laws (quoted by Landau, 1961, p. 341). Thomas Jefferson added that the states "as well as their central government, like the planets revolving around their common sun, acting and acted upon according to their respective weights and distances, will produce that beautiful equilibrium on which our Constitution is founded" (quoted by Landau, 1961, pp. 341–2). In effect, the mechanistic metaphor lent to governmental institutions a solidity, permanence, and God-given propriety.

Metaphor as collective expression

In certain historical periods metaphors serve to express commonly held but imperfectly articulated feelings. People often share certain sentiments, fears, or hopes that have failed to reach expression for lack of adequate means. At such times a well-chosen metaphor may be taken up quite eagerly. Such popular metaphors serve as a medium of common understanding, giving people a sense of commonality and possible direction. Consider early explanations of crowd phenomena. Especially during the nineteenth century, many theorists viewed the crowd essentially as a demon force, capable of unleashing ferocious actions that individuals would never dream of committing on their own. This metaphor was elaborated most effectively by Gustave Le Bon (1896). As he wrote, the person in a crowd is no longer conscious of his acts. In his case, as in the case of the hypnotized subject, at the same time that certain faculties are destroyed, others may be brought to a high degree of exaltation. Under the influence of suggestion, he will undertake the accomplishment of certain acts with irresistible impetuosity. (p. 35)

There is reason to believe that Le Bon's work gave vent to widely shared but ill-expressed sentiments in French culture. First, his was but one of a notably large number of attempts to understand the actions of mobs. Already in 1837 George Craik had published his *Sketches of Popular Tumults*. Other treatments, more contemporary to Le Bon but similar to Craik in perspective, were offered by Tarde (1890/1903), Sighele (1892), and Sidis (1898), among others. The "problem" of crowds was thus widely apparent. Furthermore, since the majority of this work was the product of French intellectuals, one suspects that much of it was attempting to render intelligible the irascible and often bloody incursion of demonstrating crowds on the French political scene. Not fifty years before Le Bon's birth, the nation had witnessed thousands of crowd-pleasing executions (in one three-month period, more than seven thousand executions). Since then the government had changed hands numerous times, and surging, angry, and often armed groups frequently roamed the city streets. One can only imagine the public anxiety over "the group" and its unpredictable violence. In this context it is more than credible to suppose, as Moscovici (1985) suggests, that Le Bon's work was motivated largely by the fear of crowds.

It should also be noted that this metaphor – the crowd as demonic force – has not completely run its course. It is evident in Solomon Asch's (1956) work on conformity, in the "risky shift" literature (Cartwright, 1973), and in Irving Janis's (1972) thesis of "group think." All convey a basic mistrust of the effects of social groups on individuals, lending expression to a continuing, widespread, but still only indirectly articulated fear.

The historical legacy

Having inquired into the nature of metaphor and its uses in social thought, we are in a position to examine the metaphors on which social psychological theory has been constructed. This review will first consider a range of metaphors used in prescientific thought and then turn to the primary metaphors of the twentieth century. As we shall see, a brief discussion of the dominant metaphors underlying prescientific theories will help us appreciate the conceptual legacy of the past. Such theories furnish a rich set of cultural resources that are still being drawn upon in the construction of social theory. At the same time, insofar as the metaphors in prescientific discourse seem inadequate, they will provide a series of benchmarks against which subsequent conceptual progress can be charted. Even though a review of the full range of these early metaphors is beyond the scope of this chapter, it will be useful to touch on a number of metaphors that have played, and continue to play, a significant role in social thought.

In considering metaphors generated in earlier times it is useful to distinguish first between metaphors of the animate and metaphors of the inanimate. Whereas some theorists encounter the social world as fluctuating, transient, or unstable, others are led by the same experiences to conclude, "The more things change, the more they stay the same." In the former case, theorists are likely to draw on metaphors from the animate world; in the latter, metaphors of the inanimate often prove more compelling. Let us first consider several dominant metaphors from the animate domain.

The group as human organism

It seems probable that in the history of humankind the attempt to describe and explain individuals preceded attempts to account for group behavior. The coordination of face-to-face interaction among single individuals would appear to be a prerequisite to the coordination of large social units. In any case, the vast, ever-expanding body of terms for individual actors has served as a ready reserve of descriptive terms for making group life intelligible. Few descriptive repositories offer such an enormous, differentiated, flexible, and commonly comprehensible set of terms as that employed in accounts of individual action.

It is difficult to ascertain the first usage of the person metaphor in understanding social life. Perhaps it was similar to St. Paul's limited, but effective use of it in his early epistles, where his intention was to develop a sense of unity among otherwise disparate bands of Christian believers. In his letters to both the Corinthians and the Romans, he suggests that their unity should be like that of a body. "Each of us," he wrote, "has one body, with many different parts, and not all these parts have the same function; just so we, though many in number, form one body in Christ, and each acts as the counterpart of another" (Rom. 12:4, 5; 1 Cor. 12:11). For Christians the sacrament of the Eucharist, in which the body and blood of Christ are symbolically ingested, serves as a continuous "realization" of this metaphor. A similar metaphor was offered earlier by Plato, who, in *The Republic* (ca. 375 B.C./1961), compared the relationship among classes in society with the relationship among parts of the body. The ruling class of a society, in his estimate, was equivalent to the head, the warrior class to the breast, and the slave class to the abdomen. Each class was as essential to the life of society as each part of the body is essential to its continuing vitality.

A less differentiated but compelling treatment of the state as an individual organism was proposed by Thomas Hobbes in the seventeenth century. The collectivity, as a collective organism, was to give superordinate strength and protection to the single individuals who comprised it. The well-known frontispiece of the first edition of Hobbes's *Leviathan* (1651), in which the social commonwealth is represented as a large kingly figure composed of many smaller individuals, powerfully illustrates this contention. The same metaphor surfaces again in Herbert Spencer's *Principles of Sociology* (1876). Like Plato, Spencer views the ruling body as a form of brain. The communications and traffic systems along with the stock exchange are said to operate like a circulatory system, and the agricultural and industrial spheres are equated with the nutritive processes. Similar views are apparent in Hegel's (1807/1910) concept of the *objektiver Geist* (a superordinate social entity with the characteristics of a single person), in Espinas's (1877) concept of the "collective consciousness" of social groups, and in Durkheim's (1898) argument for "collective representation." The metaphor of the social world as person recurs in the present century. Though roundly criticized, the first edition of William McDougall's *Group Mind* (1920) posited a superordinate entity, the group, which outlived its individual constituents but depended on their consciousness for its vitality. More recently, George Homans's *Human Group* (1950) made use of the same metaphor.

The human as animal

Although not as well elaborated, early attempts to explain human social conduct have frequently made use of animal metaphors. Aristotle was among the first to do so. When faced with the question of why people develop organized social groups, Aristotle answered in his *Politics* (ca. 330 B.C./1947) that people are instinctively gregarious, that humans are by nature "political animals" (p. 556). However, whether for lack of a well-developed zoological vocabulary or because of the deeply rooted assumption that nonhuman creatures are somehow different and inferior, the animal metaphor was not employed extensively until the nineteenth century.

In early social psychology, it was William McDougall (1908) who made the most extensive use of the animal metaphor, based on the Darwinian assumption that, in given environmental conditions, species survival depends on inherent or genetic dispositions. Since humans are a species of animal whose actions must contribute to survival, it seemed sensible to view basic action patterns as genetic in origin, and McDougall accordingly posited the existence of instincts for procreation, pugnacity, curiosity, self-abasement, repulsion, and flight. In addition, he viewed more complex social behaviors as emergent combinations of instinctual tendencies. For example, he supposed that religious activity resulted from the combination of curiosity, self-abasement, flight (fear), and the tender emotion accompanying the parental instinct.

Although criticized for this as well as other aspects of his work, McDougall's orientation continued in one form or another to capture the social psychological imagination. For instance, Bernard (1924) built an entire theory of social psychology around the instinct concept, and in more recent times the concept has resurfaced in sociobiological studies of human conduct (see Cunningham, 1981). Although the genes of the animal have replaced animal instincts in sociobiological theory, the metaphoric form and result are similar. We will have more to say about the animal metaphor when we discuss the dominant trends of the scientific era.

As we have seen, when focusing on the animated quality of human action, theorists have often employed the characteristics of humans and animals to understand human actions. One may also view argumentation and enlightenment as forms of animated activity. Plato viewed these processes as dialectical – as processes in which thesis and antithesis lead to higher-order synthesis. This form of account was later deployed metaphorically by Hegel (1861/1956) and Marx (1867/1954) to explain historical change in society. More recently the dialectical metaphor has been used by numerous social psychologists (e.g., Altman, Vinsel, & Brown, 1981; Georgoudi, 1984; Israel, 1979) to account for personal and social change.

As noted, the use of animate metaphors is more common when theorists are focusing on the instability or changes in social phenomena. However, many theorists have been inclined to search for that which is stable in social life – for underlying characteristics that persist beneath the transitory. In such instances it is not metaphors of the animate but metaphors of the inanimate that tend to be most useful. Let us consider several manifestations.

Social life as physical structure

In the same way that the image of the human organism has served as a useful repository of terms for accounts of social groups, so too has the language of material construction, particularly the construction of public edifices. Although less elaborate than person language, architectural metaphors have obvious potency owing to the stable and sometimes central place that physical constructions occupy in community life. Their use has been widespread. For instance, both Plato in his *Republic* and Aristotle in his *Politics* make extensive use of the concept of "levels" of governance; in Matthew's Gospel, Jesus says to Peter, "You are a rock, and on this rock foundation I will build my church" (Matt. 16:18); and early in the fourteenth century Dante (ca. 1320/1932) gave full expression to these images in his vision of Purgatory and of Hell, which he depicted as being composed of many different architectural levels that paralleled both the relative evil of the person's lifetime actions and the social organization of the afterlife.

The concept of levels, often instantiated in architectural metaphors, later corroborated another important physical metaphor – the Great Chain of Being. This concept, before it was elaborated in the eighteenth century, was proposed three centuries earlier by Nicolas of Cusa, who held that there is a regular gradation of created beings from humans down to the most simple living organisms. All levels of the chain are similar; that is, they share such attributes as joy, grief, and spirituality. Furthermore, because all links in the chain are products of God, they all share in the divine, though to lesser degrees (see Lovejoy, 1936). These concepts were still reflected in the work of nineteenth-century theorists who believed that the laws governing social life were reflections of God's moral attributes. Thus, these theorists viewed social organization as morally ordained. Much the same idea was carried into the twentieth century by various religious theorists; the notion was also reflected in the formalized concept of species levels, and even now plays a muted but significant role in research and debates on primate language. Such debates often suggest a fear that if nonhuman primates can be shown to possess the ability to communicate linguistically, the sacred belief in the superior level of human functioning will be called into serious question.

Later, Newtonian mechanics largely replaced architectural structure and the chain as the chief source of metaphors drawn from the inanimate realm. A system is mechanical in the Newtonian sense if it consists of discrete bodies, each possessing a specific set of properties (such as mass or weight) that act over space and time according to fixed laws. It was this metaphor that prompted David Hume (1739–40/1978) and others to propose that the world is but one great machine and to draw some historically significant conclusions from this proposition. Indeed, so many corollaries have been extrapolated from the machine metaphor that there is an important sense in which much contemporary social science owes its beginnings to Newtonian mechanics. If the universe is one great machine, with lawful interdependence among its parts, then a certain form of social inquiry is clearly invited. Specifically, it becomes the task of the social sciences to isolate and identify the parts of the social world and to discover the lawful relations among them, and between them and the other parts of the universe. This was the task to which such social thinkers as Adam Smith (1776/1970), Thomas Malthus (1798/1970), and Herbert Spencer (1851) devoted themselves before the emergence of systematic social science. It remains the task that many professionals set before themselves today. We shall have more to say shortly about contemporary manifestations of the mechanistic metaphor.

It should finally be noted that the distinction between metaphors of the animate and inanimate has recently surfaced in an important discussion of mechanistic versus organismic theories of human development (Overton & Reese, 1973). In this case an attack has been made on the machine metaphor of human development on grounds that it renders the organism's actions entirely dependent on input conditions. In contrast, Overton, Reese, and others presume that personal development is under a high degree of autonomous power. People develop in intrinsically programmed ways. The animate metaphor in this case is typically the growing plant or flower, which is said to possess its own directionality. This debate has now begun to stimulate dialogue in social psychology, particularly with regard to cross-time alterations in social patterns (Gergen & Gergen, 1984). Forms of relationship appear to have their own patterns of unfolding development, not dependent on stimulus inputs.

We have now glimpsed a number of metaphors from the prescientific era that helped to make social life intelligible. They have been singled out because of their historic importance in the description and explanation of social change and stability. Of course, many other metaphors have played an important role in social theorizing. For instance, Jean Jacques Rousseau (1762/1968) and Sir Henry James Sumner Maine (1885), among others, used the concept of the "legal contract" to describe the necessary form of interdependence in society. Giambattista Vico (1744/1948) used the concepts of "ages" and "cycles" to account for social change. Thomas Hobbes (1651) made use of the concept of "family," in addition to the notion of the "leviathan," in speaking about the ways in which entire peoples, for purposes of mutual protection, agree to serve a sovereign power. And in his *Future of an Illusion* (1927/1961), Freud made use of much the same "family" metaphor in describing religious institutions. Even today we continue to speak of the "family of man."

Social metaphors in the scientific era

As we have seen, prescientific history furnishes a rich array of social metaphors and informs contemporary scientists of various ends they may serve. We have also seen how certain of these metaphors have threaded their way into contemporary scientific discourse. However, it may fairly be said that the "age of scientific social psychology" has not relied heavily on the specific metaphors discussed thus far. To be sure, a vast debt is owed to prescientific analyses, but because of new problems and prospects, the dominating metaphors of the present century have made use of other imagery. We shall consider six of these metaphors along with some of their selected uses and limitations.

Of particular concern will be the relationship of these metaphors to the traditional account of scientific behavior; for as I suggested in the introduction to this chapter, a theory of scientific conduct is perforce a theory about human activity. It contains assumptions about the nature of human knowledge, how it is acquired, and how it may be subverted. In many respects, the theory of scientific conduct is normative; it informs the investigator and society of the nature of the good and proper way of life and thought. Once a commitment has been made to the theory, the investigator is no longer free to pursue any metaphor that he or she wishes. Accounts of social activity must be consistent with the premises of the scientific metaphor, or else the theory of scientific conduct will be threatened. Indeed, if a theory of human activity is grounded on a metaphor that is uncongenial to accepted assumptions about scientific conduct, and if this theory comes to be accepted as a literal ("true") or even quasi-literal ("truthful"), this theoretical account of human activity would invalidate the assumptions built into the traditional theory of science.

The logical empiricist theory of scientific activity needs little introduction. Its contours are widely known (and frequently invoked) by most contemporary psychologists. In general, it is an account that views the goal of science to be the generation of theories that correspond to the nature of an independent reality. The efficacy of such theories is demonstrated by the degree to which they enable successful predictions to be made about events in nature. To be effective, the scientist, according to this theory, is supposed to remain sensitive or open to the causal relations among events in nature, develop propositions about these relations, test these propositions against nature, and then revise them according to the outcomes of such tests. The most appropriate method for testing propositions is assumed to be the controlled experiment. If this hypotheticodeductive procedure is consistently followed, the scientist is supposed to accumulate an effective repository of knowledge.

As our review will show, the early metaphors of the scientific discipline tended to be in harmony with this metatheory. However, as decades have passed, theorists have become increasingly insensitive to the demands of the metatheory, and their central metaphors have become increasingly antithetical to the traditional view of scientific activity. As a result, we have now reached the stage at which critical questions must be raised concerning the viability of this scientific metatheory.

Social life as animal laboratory

Two textbooks in social psychology appeared in 1908, one by William McDougall and the other by E. A. Ross. As we have seen, the former made abundant use of the metaphor of humans as animals. The other was strongly sociological in its orientation. At this point there simply was no identifiable tradition of social psychology available for explication. By 1924, however, Floyd Allport could confidently presume in his text the existence of an identifiable and interconnected corpus of social psychological inquiry. To be sure, Allport's view of the field was crafted with visionary goals in mind. His volume was more a template for future undertakings than a record of accomplishments, but judging by the dominant trends of the next thirty years, one might credit Allport with prophetic powers. His view of human action was essentially one of stimulus–response. Such language may no longer appear metaphoric to a contemporary trained experimentalist, since it has by now become virtually literal. Yet for early social psychologists, who had no literal language on which to draw, the stimulus–response paradigm was initially seen for what it was, a metaphor for understanding social life – a metaphor drawn from the world of animal experimentation, and chiefly from the reflexological work of Ivan Pavlov (1928). In the decades before and after the publication of Allport's text, Pavlov and other animal experimentalists had made great strides in bringing the behavior of dogs and rats under a degree of systematic control, and so there was good reason for the growing optimism that this success could be extended to the case of human activity.

What occurred, then, was the importation into the social realm of the argot of animal experimentation. "Persons" became "organisms"; their activities became "responses"; their life situations were transformed into "stimulus conditions." The stimulus–response metaphor and the associated practices of laboratory manipulation and control became most pronounced at the Institute for Human Relations at Yale University. Clark Hull, around whom the institute largely revolved, was primarily an animal experimentalist. Yet he and his colleagues extended the language of the learning laboratory to treatments of human aggression (Dollard, Doob, Miller, Mowrer, & Sears, 1939), personality formation (Dollard & Miller, 1950), communication and persuasion (Hovland, Janis, & Kelley, 1953), and other domains.

Although it has declined in influence, the animal experimentation metaphor continues to play a robust role in social psychology. It is prominent, for example, in Zajonc's (1965, 1980) work on social facilitation, in which the mere presence of another member of the same species (the stimulus) is presumed to arouse an organism. Such arousal, Zajonc tries to demonstrate, will facilitate problem solving in the case of simple tasks but impair it when tasks are difficult. To support the general validity of his argument, Zajonc juxtaposes the results of laboratory experiments with cockroaches and humans.

Before considering two important variations on the stimulus–response themes, it is useful to consider ways in which the metaphor has functioned within the profession. At the outset, it is apparent that the metaphor championed a form of what Sampson (1978) and others have termed "self-contained individualism." As is often noted, American culture has long been committed to the view that society is made up of self-contained units, individuals responding to or acting within particular circumstances. It is the individual who makes decisions to act, who is held responsible for actions both good and ill, and on whom society must depend for its welfare. Although the ideology of the self-contained individual has come under increasing attack in recent years, it is far from dead, and the metaphor of animal experimentation, which is clearly consistent with its major thrust, has served to sustain its power as a cultural ideology.

More important to our present thesis, the animal experimentation metaphor has served to legitimate and extend the empiricist metatheory on which the psychological sciences were supposed to be established. As we have seen, the metatheory placed a strong demand on tying theoretical terms to observables and tracing phenomena to antecedent conditions. It also espoused the framing of theoretical propositions in an "if . . . then" format. Each of these demands could be realized in the metaphor of animal experimentation, where both stimulus and response were held to be observable, responses were held to be a function of antecedent stimulus conditions, and the experimental method was used to demonstrate the validity of "if . . . then" propositions. Thus, by contextualizing their work in this metaphoric language, social psychologists established their discipline as a foundational science and legitimated a view of knowledge that granted them voice (including position, material support, etc.) within the sciences and the wider culture alike.

Neobehaviorism: the machina ex deo

Perhaps the major shortcoming of the animal laboratory as a source of constitutive metaphors was that it prevented psychologists from realizing what for many of them was a deeply cherished goal – that of elaborating uniquely psychological accounts of human conduct. Not only did the strong emphasis on observables militate against psychological speculation, but the metaphor of the laboratory frustrated those who, following an intellectual tradition from the Great Chain of Being through Darwin, believed that humans were inherently different from and superior to animals, even if continuous with them along a hierarchy of organisms. Somehow people possessed superior capacities for self-reflection and more complex emotional and motivational states than could easily be framed in the language of the animal experiment. Modification of the metaphor thus became essential.

Yet what form could this humanization take? Few wished to abandon the logical empiricist scaffolding, especially when the status of psychology within the academic sphere was prospering in its wake. Nor did it seem necessary to abandon this framework, since empiricist philosophers themselves had begun to justify the use of theoretical terms that had no direct correspondence with observables (see Carnap, 1966). What was required were metaphors of the psychological world that would preserve the status of psychology as an empirical science and the related promise of increasingly precise predictions. These ends, it seemed, could be achieved by a return to the repository of metaphors forming the Western intellectual heritage – more specifically, by the use of updated mechanical metaphors. Once again it seemed that the mechanical world possessed the kind of stability and reliability of operation that suited the theoretical needs of social theory while also promising to make psychological science capable of offering ever more dependable predictions. Further, since the output of mechanical processes (behavior) was to be understood as systematically dependent on environmental inputs (stimuli), the use of mechanical metaphors would make it easy for psychologists to retain the empiricist emphasis on observables linked by "if . . . then" propositions.

In social psychology the mechanics of the inner region have tended to be drawn from either physics or biology. In certain respects, the captivating quality of Kurt Lewin's (1935, 1951) theorizing can be attributed to its type of mental mechanics. Lewin's late arrival in the United States, in 1933, insulated him against much of the "S–R" (stimulus–response) emphasis on observable "inputs" and "outputs." Further, Lewin was aware of the generative significance of the chemical metaphor (e.g., "mental chemistry") in earlier German mentalist theorizing. Thus, he was free to take advantage of developments in post-Newtonian physics, including electromagnetic theory and Einstein's theory of relativity. Concepts of field, force, tension, valence, and so on were all incorporated in his theories to explain social conduct.

Although the insertion of mental mechanics between the stimulus world and organismic responses placed Lewin within the neobehaviorist mold, there is an important contrast to be made between his theories and the prevailing neobehaviorist accounts: Lewin occasionally emphasized the self-activating character of inner processes, in effect distinguishing his theoretical stance from the stimulus dependency views of his contemporaries. In this respect, Lewin was a precursor of the cognitive revolution in social psychology, about which we shall be concerned shortly.

From the standpoint of the empiricist psychology of the period, Lewin's major failing was his lack of concern about tying his psychological mechanics to observables – either stimuli or responses. In other words, his field theory formulations were too self-contained. His students were more sensitive to such problems and generally avoided the physical field metaphor. In its place, they tended to substitute a biological metaphor – that of the homeostatic process. The advantages of this metaphor were that (1) it suggested a close relationship between the psychological and biological strata, thus advancing psychology's status as a natural science, and (2) homeostatic processes could be translated into inputs (which were supposed to deflect the internal mechanism from its preferred state) and outputs (social conduct). To illustrate, Festinger's (1957) theory of cognitive dissonance and a host of cognitive balance models (see Abelson et al., 1968) were all based on a homeostatic principle of preferred state. People were said to have a natural preference for a state of cognitive consonance (where mental elements imply one another) or for a state of cognitive balance (where clearly adjudicated relations obtain among cognitive elements), and any deviation from the preferred state was supposed to set in motion counterforces that would return the organism to the initial state. Schachter's (1959) theory of affiliation, Brehm's (1966) reactance theory, and Duval and Wicklund's (1972) objective self-awareness theory are based on morphologically similar metaphors.

Yet with the emergence of the computer revolution, these physical and biological metaphors have been muted. Over the past few decades, cognitive psychologists have taken thorough advantage of the computer metaphor, with its well-elaborated descriptive terminology and its commonplace association with reason and logic. Aided by the widespread availability of actual machines to help vivify the metaphor, they have spread the computational gospel far and wide. Indeed, contemporary cognitive science may generally be viewed as a discipline built on the explication and elaboration of an existing machine. The impact of such developments on social psychology is readily apparent from the fact that "information processing," "information storage and retrieval," "schemata," and "heuristics" have become standard terms in the explanation of social action (e.g., see Fiske & Taylor, 1984).

Interestingly, as the computer has become the favored source of mechanistic metaphors, the computational metaphor has also begun to pose a threat to the empiricist theory of science, which it was designed to defend. As we have seen, the metaphor of the animal laboratory gave way to analyses in which mechanistic metaphors became focal. Until recently, these metaphors have generally been consistent with the empiricist canons for positivistic science: They assumed that individual action is a byproduct of antecedent conditions. Such a view is compatible with the notion of science as a systematic byproduct of real-world inputs. The rub is that the computer has come to be seen as an agent in its own right – a system capable of generating its own inputs. It can function without the presence of humans and with seemingly little reliance on human input. (Films such as *2001: A Space Odyssey* and *The Terminator* have given expression to the common suspicions of such autonomy.) In psychology this kind of autonomy is captured by the concept of "top-down" processes – processes that presumably direct the organism to search, categorize, and absorb information according to internal or machine demands. Interest in such processes has come to eclipse concern with so-called bottom-up processes, in which machine states are dependent on environmental conditions. This shift of concern to top-down processing is a major threat to the empiricist model on which scientific psychology was originally constructed. To the extent that the organism dictates its own course of action independent of stimuli – to the extent, in other words, that it fails to be reality driven – the stimulus–response model fails to be compelling and the empiricist philosophy of science fails as a justificatory device. If people, including scientists, are "reality makers" and do not act simply as faithful recorders of – and responders to – the physical world, then the possibility of a completely objective basis for scientific knowledge is seriously jeopardized.

Symbolic interaction: society as meaningful relations

A further line of social thought must be distinguished, one that was neither nurtured by the soil of the animal learning laboratory nor strongly wedded to the empiricist theory of science. Although this line of thought bears a certain resemblance to neobehaviorism, it provides a distinct and important contrast. As we have seen, neobehaviorist theory is generally identified by its use of mechanistic metaphors, which it has applied to both mental and behavioral functioning. Clearly, it is possible to comprehend the mental world with other images, these alternate images being of substantial consequence. What is known as symbolic interactionist theory is similar to neobehaviorism in its special concern with elaborating a metaphor of the mental world and with connecting the mental and physical (environment and action) domains. However, rather than assuming that the mental world is structured like a machine, the symbolic interactionists understand it to be composed of symbols.

The concept of the symbol can be traced to a variety of contexts. The term has played a lively part in theological discourse and may be traced in this context all the way back to pre-Christian debates over the ways in which the gods expressed divine intent through worldly symbols. Theories of stagecraft – including treatments of the symbolic value of facial expressions, gestures, and props – have also been available to twentieth-century scientists. And significantly, the concept of the symbol has figured prominently in aesthetic dialogue. Indeed, given the vitality of symbolist movements in both literature and the fine arts during the nineteenth century, symbolic interactionist theory seems scarcely a historical accident.

These various streams have insinuated themselves into social theories in a variety of ways. For instance, Mead's (1934) pivotal use of the concepts of gesture, imitation, and role taking links his work significantly to the literature of the stage. The "generalized other," from whom the concept of self is acquired, functions primarily according to Mead as an audience that evaluates the actor through applause, laughter, and so on. Drawing from the literary realm, Mead also presumes that private experience reflects the characteristics of authorship. As he writes, "One individual has one experience and another has another experience, and both are stated in terms of their biographies" (Mead, 1934, p. 33). A similar theory is that of Cooley (1902/1922), which is based largely on the concept of imagination. Like the actor or the author, the social being according to Cooley must imagine other worlds, including the views of other individuals, in order to adapt. Cooley's emphasis on disinterested and contemplative love, and the importance attached to it in organized society, links his symbolic realm to the Judaeo-Christian heritage.

As we can see, symbolic interactionism shares with neobehaviorism a central concern with the workings of the mind. In its reliance on the mind as the major vehicle for explaining social life, it also shares with neobehaviorism a primary focus on the individual rather than the group per se. However, its replacement of the machine by the symbol leads to certain important consequences. With the exception of top-down computeristics, the neobehaviorists' use of mechanical metaphors has generally enabled them to retain a strong interest in environmental inputs and simultaneously vindicated the view of science on which they have stood. However, when the metaphor of the symbol replaces that of the machine, the environment as given (or as constituted by "brute facts") ceases to be critical. It is not the objective environment that determines the contours of social life, but what this environment symbolizes: It is the "meaning" of the environment that is all-important. It is partly for this reason that many symbolic interactionists have demonstrated little interest in laboratory research. From their standpoint, laboratories do not control stimuli; they only communicate symbolically to the subject. And, they argue, it is the symbolic communication (with its implied requests, expectations, or commands) that subtly engenders what appear to be stimulus-driven results in the laboratory.

Further, although the metaphor of symbolism focuses attention on individual actors, it lends itself far more than the mechanical metaphor to a concern with social wholes and extraindividual issues. The environmentalism to which the mechanical metaphor has (until the advent of the computer) been largely wedded turned the investigator's eyes toward person–environment relations – toward single individuals acting in an impinging environment. In contrast, the symbolist framework encourages the investigator to think in terms of the relation of one person's symbol system to that of others – in effect, to think in terms of social interdependence. From this vantage point, societies and social groups are not the simple sum of individual actors, but include relationships created by shared systems of meaning. By implication, social networks can be expanded to include communities or entire cultures, defined as groups of people whose shared symbol systems unite them in unique ways.

The social world as marketplace

As we have seen, the animal laboratory has served as a source of compelling metaphors for many social analysts. However, much social theory has also employed secondary metaphors in accounting for the environmental conditions said to "produce" the individual's responses. One of these metaphors, that of "behavioral rewards," has had a marked impact of its own, especially among operant conditioning enthusiasts. Its effects have been favored by the semantic ambiguity of the term "reward." Over and above its meanings as a form of reinforcer and as an incentive, the term is also a constituent of economic discourse. Payment for work is commonly termed an "economic reward," and economic theorists have long made use of a model of economic behavior in which the individual's rational calculation of rewards and costs is central. It thus became increasingly apparent to social theorists that operant theory could set the stage for adopting some form of homo economicus as the guiding metaphor for social life.

George Homans's (1961) work was seminal in this respect: Homans drew a distinct parallel between the behavior of pigeons in the operant conditioning paradigm and people's behavioral responses to their mates (chap. 2). In effect, Homans began his analysis with the metaphor of the animal laboratory firmly in place. Yet as his work progressed, he expanded the concept of "reward," placing it in an economic context and contrasting it with "cost." He then developed the concept of psychological "profit," which he defined as rewards minus costs. Along the same line, Thibaut and Kelley (1959) were equally influential in contrasting reward with cost and in establishing "exchange theory" as a central mode of social analysis. Besides the notion of exchange, they added to their analysis the decision matrix, familiar to many from contemporary discussions of economic bargaining. With the publication of Blau's *Exchange and Power in Social Life* (1964), the appropriation of the concept of reward from the economic sphere was complete.

One major use to which the marketplace has been put is that of legitimation. From the outset there was a particular political advantage to be gained by adopting the metaphor. Operant conditioners had developed a series of what appeared to be well-substantiated grounding suppositions. Homans (1961) itemized these in the second chapter of his volume. With the objective solidity of their basic suppositions apparently established in a separate, well-respected (though exotic) tradition, exchange theorists gained considerable advantage in the competitive arena of social theorizing. Few alternative accounts could claim such a strong, empirical foundation. Furthermore, exchange theorists acquired the colleagueship and support of members of the economic establishment, many of whom realized the lack of substantive grounds for the psychological suppositions on which economic theory largely rests. This relationship continues to be employed to mutual advantage, both politically and conceptually (Stroebe & Frey, 1982).

With respect to its implications for scientific metatheory, the economic exchange metaphor contains mixed signals. Its legacy from the animal laboratory places it on the side of empiricist science. In addition, if the exchange theorist is committed to a belief in fundamental principles of exchange (e.g., maximization of reward, reciprocity, equity, etc.), the orientation articulates well with the empiricist view of science. However, to the extent that one views economic rationality as a *prescription* for adequate or adaptive behavior, the metaphor poses problems for this view of science; for if one holds – as do economists, decision theorists, and game theorists – that rationality is manifest in particular strategies or heuristics, the strong implication is that the individual retains the choice to act rationally or not. In effect, exchange theory will provide an adequate account of human conduct if and only if – when and only when – people choose to adopt its strategies or heuristics. People may choose to do so in any given situation; but then again, they may not choose to do so, thus violating the predicted, lawful pattern. To write the conclusion in broader terms, an elaboration of the premises of exchange theory suggests that scientific lawfulness is possible only when people choose to act lawfully. This state of affairs is hardly a sanguine one for empiricist foundationalists.

It should finally be noted that some of the most effective criticism of the exchange metaphor has been mounted by those who are concerned about its implications for social change. After all, what if people really came to think of the social world as a marketplace where everyone was out to profit from others? Wouldn't social life be transformed for the worse? Wouldn't the market metaphor, acting as a normative concept, lend itself to a deteriorated form of cultural life? In particular, doesn't the metaphor reduce people to market commodities, denigrate trust and humane concern, promote capitalistic values, and reduce intrinsic motivation, as critics (Plon, 1974; Schwartz, Lacey, & Schuldenfrei, 1978; Wexler, 1983) claim? And going even further, doesn't the metaphor negate many of the phenomena it is intended to explain? If intimate relations really are a form of social exchange, as exchange theorists have asserted, this contradicts the very concept of intimacy as an interpersonal relationship in which the participants do not believe the others to be operating on a "minimax strategy" (minimizing cost and maximizing reward). As Davis and Todd (1982) have pointed out, if people were to believe that others were consistently and at all times attempting to maximize their own gain, there would be no intimate relations as we now understand them. An adequate defense of the metaphor against such criticism has not been forthcoming.

The social world as stage

The possibilities of viewing the social world as theater can be traced to at least the sixteenth century, when there was a well-developed tradition of theater that depicted common life. If theater can imitate life, the opposite possibility seems inescapable. It was left to Shakespeare to draw the full implications of this possibility. As Jaques announces in *As You Like It*, "All the world's a stage, and all the men and women merely players: They have their exits and their entrances; and one man in his time plays many parts" (II.vii.139; Wright, 1936, p. 677). Three centuries later this metaphor was to gain sufficient momentum that the issue of whether daily life was but an imitation of theater or vice versa was to occupy some of the best intellects of the era.

In the twentieth century, Vaihinger's *Philosophy of 'As If'* (1911/1924), although written for quite different purposes, made an early contribution to the dramaturgic mode of thought, and Jung's (1928–1943/1956) concept of the *persona* provided an early illustration of its implementation in psychological theory. Still, the dramaturgical metaphor was slow to develop in social psychology. At least one major reason for this was that the pivotal concept of "role" was semantically ambiguous. It had a critical function in at least two central lines of discourse: the theatrical and the structural. In the latter instance the concept had become virtually literal: One could speak with seeming objectivity about the role of this or that object in a given structure or machine (e.g., the role of the keystone in the structure of an arch, the role of the sparkplug in the functioning of a motor, etc.). As structural metaphors pervaded social theory from the 1930s to the 1960s, the structural usage of the concept of role tended to obscure its dramaturgic potential. At the same time, the structural usage played an important sustaining function: The concept of role was retained in the vernacular of social theory until the context became congenial for its dramaturgic elaboration.

Moreno's (1946) development of psychodramatic techniques of personal change, along with Kelly's (1955) development of role-playing therapy, prepared the way for the dramaturgic turn. However, it was Sarbin's (1954) contribution to the first *Handbook of Social Psychology* that began to explore the dramaturgical potential in a serious way. His concepts of role enactment, role-taking ability, and role involvement all began to realize the potential. Later, the works of Goffman (1959) and

Berne (1964) brought the dramaturgic metaphor into broad public view. Today the orientation figures heavily in the ethogenic movement (Harré & Secord, 1972), the social psychology of self-presentation (Schlenker, 1980), and social accounting processes (Semin & Manstead, 1983; Shotter, 1984).

The dramaturgic metaphor has served a variety of functions for social theorists. For some the metaphor has been an expressive one, giving form to the suspicion that social relationships are constituted by artifice or pretense (a suspicion especially characteristic of Goffman, 1959, 1963) and sometimes articulating the ludic or playful aspects of human relations. But more important for present purposes is the fact that the dramaturgic metaphor has been used by theorists to facilitate social change, including change within psychological science itself. More specifically, the elaboration of the metaphor has been used as a means of questioning the empiricist metatheory of science that is so closely wedded to the animal, machine, and economic metaphors previously described. If humans are actors, actively playing out their parts, then stimuli – whether environmental inputs or payoffs – cease to be the essential and only causes of human actions. Rather, they are reduced to accessories, props, or cues; they set the context for action but do not determine its character. And if stimulus events are not causal in the traditional sense, then the attempt to transform the world into an array of antecedent-consequent relations ceases to be compelling.

In addition, the dramaturgic metaphor flies in the face of the scientific promise of cumulative knowledge (Schlenker, 1977). If social life is the playing out of roles or scripts, one must also assume that such patterns are free to change across history. If this is the case, contemporary patterns would indeed be contemporary, and it should be anticipated that as history moves on, so will the nature of the human drama. The empiricist promise of increasingly precise predictions thus ceases to be compelling. This use of the dramaturgic metaphor, for the purpose of establishing and justifying a new form of social science, is most prominent in the work of ethogenicists (see Harré & Secord, 1972).

From the individual to the social unit

Thus far, our review has emphasized metaphors for understanding social life as derived from individual actions rather than as a distinctive and autonomous realm of existence. It is the individual who is animal-like, machine-like, an economic bargainer, a symbol user, a dramatic actor, and so on. We have seen, however, that when extended, certain of these metaphors invite one to move from the intrapersonal to the interpersonal domain. The metaphors of the economic bargainer and symbol user, for example, are more inviting in this sense than those derived from the animal laboratory or machine. Yet even in the dramaturgic case the individual remains the fundamental unit of concern, and social wholes are ultimately seen as derivative. It is safe to say that, in terms of its emphasis, the preceding review has been generally reflective of the dominant interests and approaches in twentieth-century psychology. The work of most psychologists has been, and continues to be, centered on the individual. It is also the case that the empiricist theory of knowledge is based on an individualist premise: It is the individual scientist who observes and reasons; it is the individual who serves as the locus of knowledge. For these reasons, the use of metaphor in rendering intelligible the social unit as the basis of explanation warrants special attention.

Much holistic theory in psychology has sprung from the study of organizational life, and as Weick (1979) has noted, the literature in this area is rich in metaphoric variation. Organizations have been likened to anarchies, seesaws, space stations, garbage cans, savage tribes, octopoids, marketplaces, data-processing schedules, athletic teams, ladders, and pyramids, to name but a few of the relevant metaphors. Within recent years, however, there has been a steadily increasing interest in analyzing relational processes as "systems." Systems notation is clearly metaphoric, and like many of the metaphors discussed so far, the systems metaphor is also polysemic. That is, it draws its meaning from a variety of contexts. Rather than rely on a specific domain of related discourse, it conjoins meanings from a variety of domains. Systems theories can be traced, more generally, to the mechanistic tradition in which one assumed a reliable, determinative relationship among elements. More proximally, however, computer language has played perhaps the single most influential role in determining how systems have come to be characterized. After computer theorists furnished a vocabulary of inputs, outputs, bits of information, storage functions, and so on, this language was applied to human communication and then to social organizations more generally. Another influence came from the field of cybernetics, which is concerned with the nature of control systems in machines, organisms, and (more recently) social systems. At the same time that it absorbed computer technology, cybernetics evolved its own language of description and explanation – an independent discourse that features servomechanisms, feedback loops, and self-regulation. Much of this terminology has had an impact on developing theories of group life. Finally, biological theorists from von Bertalanffy (1968) to Maturana and Varela (1980) also contributed to the emergence of holistic theory in psychology, by furnishing systems accounts of living organisms. Though such accounts have borrowed heavily from the computer and cybernetics spheres, they have also added a range of new concepts such as systems boundaries, homeostasis, open systems, and self-organization. And to these contributions one must add those of economists (Boulding, 1967), mathematicians (Rapaport, 1956), bacteriologists (Ashby, 1962), and family therapists (Keeney & Ross, 1985), to name but a few.

This mixing and blending of metaphors has been a potent stimulus for social theorists. Partly because of the holistic emphasis of systems accounts, sociologists were among the first to find the systems metaphor useful. Foremost in this case was the work of Talcott Parsons (1951). In a set of bold theoretical strokes, Parsons attempted to extend the systems motif across different domains, ranging from society to the single cell. Regardless of level of analysis – society, community, family, personality, and so on – systems concepts were shown to be applicable. On the individual level, the work of Miller, Galanter, and Pribram (1960) in psychology was also a seminal influence. On the basis of their largely cybernetic model of how individuals plan and execute actions, other theorists have rapidly moved on to develop so-called action theories that have broad social application (Carver & Scheier, 1981). Equally stimulated by the systems metaphor have been organizational theorists wishing to focus on the large organization rather than the individual as the critical unit of analysis (Malik & Probst, 1982).

The systems metaphor shares with the dramaturgic metaphor revolutionary implications with regard to the character of science. Traditional empiricist metatheory is built on a distinction between the observing subject and an independent, external world. Only when the scientist (or his or her surrogate) experiences this world under systematically controlled conditions is knowledge said to be properly and securely generated. However, when extended, the systems metaphor undermines the subject–object dichotomy (Krippendorff, 1984). From the systems perspective one is invited to view subject and object as part of the same system – as a configurational whole rather than as separate entities. Similar implications emerge when one applies systems thinking to the community of scientists. In this case one is invited to see the scientific community operating as a single organizational unit. Thus, the autonomy of the single scientist, and his or her capacities to make observations unrelated to organizational requirements, are called into question. As a result, the products of science (books, papers, technology, etc.) come to be seen as products of the system, and thus subject to the needs and constraints of the system. Rather than being data driven, as traditional empiricist doctrine would have it, scientific theories are understood to be system driven. The force of this position has been most compellingly demonstrated by sociologists of science (e.g., Knorr-Cetina, 1981; Latour & Woolgar, 1979).

Concluding thoughts

As we have seen, the metaphors pervading social psychological theories over the past few decades have become increasingly at variance with the logical empiricist metatheory to which the discipline has been traditionally committed. What conclusion is to be drawn from this growing antinomy? At the outset, one might argue that the field has simply gone astray, that these more recent departures are only of local interest, and that they will eventually be replaced by social theory that is coherent with the traditional view of science. From this perspective, retrenchment is ultimately necessary and inevitable. But such a view seems deeply problematic. For one thing, it is clear that the era of foundationalist pursuits is nearing an end. Few philosophers of science continue to pursue the task of justification, and most of the major debates in this domain have turned on issues arising from the history and sociology of science. As it is frequently said, the intellectual climate is now postempiricist. What form of alternative (if any) to logical empiricism will emerge over the next few decades remains unclear. Consistent with the demise of logical empiricism are a number of arguments raised in the opening sections of this chapter against the picture theory of language. In undermining the traditional distinction between literal and metaphoric language, we were also laying siege to the view that scientific theories can operate as pictures or mirrors of an independent reality. It seems, then, that attempts to realign present theory so that it will be more consistent with logical empiricist metatheory are ill advised.

More promising at this juncture are attempts toward devising metatheories that offer greater latitude of development at the theoretical level. What seems to be required is a view of scientific activity that invites a multiplicity of perspectives on human action. In previous writings (e.g., Gergen, 1982, 1985a,b, 1986), I have attempted to spell out the contours of a social constructionist metatheory for the human sciences. Although the orientation is far from complete, it argues against the view that science is a product of individual minds, each bent on locating some singular truth. Rather, this approach replaces individuals with communities of scientists, working together to hammer out forms of discourse that will service their localized ends. From this vantage point, the aim of science becomes not a single, generalizable truth, but different forms of intelligibility or understanding, each with restricted, practical value. In this respect, we may welcome the multiplicity of metaphors that have come to characterize social inquiry; for as the range and forms of theoretical understanding have expanded and multiplied, so have our potentials for action – both within science and without. And as some of these forms of understanding are converted from the metaphoric to the literal, some of these potentials will become the realities of tomorrow.

The moral is simple: Metaphors are important, not only for the construction of our theories and metatheories, but for the reconstruction of our social world.

References

Abelson, R. P., Aronson, E., McGuire, W. J., Newcomb, T. M., Rosenberg, M. J., & Tannenbaum, P. H. (Eds.). (1968). *Theories of cognitive consistency: A sourcebook*. Chicago: Rand McNally.

Allport, F. (1924). *Social psychology*. Boston: Houghton Mifflin.

Altman, I., Vinsel, A., & Brown, B. B. (1981). Dialectic conceptions in social psychology: An application to social penetration and privacy regulation. In L. Berkowitz (Ed.), *Advances in experimental social psychology* (vol. 14, pp. 108–60). New York: Academic Press.

Aristotle (1947). Politics (W. D. Ross, Trans.). In R. McKeon (Ed.), *Introduction to Aristotle* (pp. 545–617). New York: Modern Library. (Original work written ca. 330 B.C.)

Asch, S. E. (1956). Studies of independence and conformity: A minority of one against a unanimous majority. *Psychological Monographs, 70* (Whole No. 416).

Ashby, R. W. (1962). Principles of the self-organizing system. In H. Von Foerster & G. W. Zopf, Jr. (Eds.), *Principles of self-organization* (pp. 255–78). New York: Pergamon.

Bernard, L. L. (1924). *Instinct: A study in social psychology*. New York: Holt.

Berne, E. (1964). *Games people play*. New York: Random House.

Bertalanffy, L. V. (1968). *General systems theory*. New York: Braziller.

Blau, P. (1964). *Exchange and power in social life*. New York: Wiley.

Boring, E. G., Bridgman, P. W., Feigl, H., Israel, H., Pratt, C. C., & Skinner, B. F. (1945). Symposium on operationism. *Psychological Review, 52*, 241–94.

Boulding, K. E. (1967). Dare we take the social sciences seriously? *American Psychologist, 22*, 879–87.

Brehm, J. W. (1966). *A theory of psychological reactance*. New York: Academic Press.

Carnap, R. (1966). *Philosophical foundations of physics: An introduction to the philosophy of science* (M. Gardner, Ed.). New York: Basic Books.

Cartwright, D. (1973). Determinants of scientific progress: The case of research on the risky shift. *American Psychologist, 28*, 222–31.

Carver, C. S., & Scheier, M. F. (1981). *Attention and self-regulation: A control-theory approach to human behavior*. New York: Springer.

Cooley, C. H. (1922). *Human nature and the social order*. New York: Scribner's. (Original work published 1902.)

Craik, G. L. (1837). *Sketches of popular tumults*. London: Knight.

Cunningham, M. R. (1981). Sociobiology as a supplementary paradigm for social psychological research. In L. Wheeler (Ed.), *Review of personality and social psychology* (vol. 2, pp. 69–106). Beverly Hills, CA: Sage.

Dante (1932). *The divine comedy* (M. B. Anderson, Trans.). New York: Oxford University Press. (Original work written ca. 1320.)

Davis, K. E., & Todd, M. J. (1982). Friendship and love relationships. In K. E. Davis & T. O. Mitchell (Eds.), *Advances in descriptive psychology* (vol. 2, pp. 79–122). Greenwich, CT: JAI.

Dollard, J., Doob, L. W., Miller, N. E., Mowrer, O. H., & Sears, R. R. (1939). *Frustration and aggression.* New Haven, CT: Yale University Press.

Dollard, J., & Miller, N. E. (1950). *Personality and psychotherapy.* New York: McGraw-Hill.

Durkheim, E. (1898). Représentations individuelles et représentations collectives [Individual and collective representations]. *Revue de Métaphysique et de Morale, 6,* 273–302.

Duval, S., & Wicklund, R. A. (1972). *A theory of objective self-awareness.* New York: Academic Press.

Espinas, A. V. (1877). *Des sociétés animales* [Animal societies]. Paris: Baillière.

Fausto-Sterling, A. (1985). *Myths of gender.* New York: Basic Books.

Festinger, L. (1957). *A theory in cognitive dissonance.* Stanford, CA: Stanford University Press.

Fiske, S. T., & Taylor, S. E. (1984). *Social cognition.* New York: Random House.

Freud, S. (1961). The future of an illusion. In J. Strachey (Ed. and Trans.), *The standard edition of the complete psychological works of Sigmund Freud* (vol. 21, pp. 1–56). London: Hogarth Press. (Original work published 1927.)

Georgoudi, M. (1984). Modern dialectics in social psychology. In K. J. Gergen & M. M. Gergen (Eds.), *Historical social psychology* (pp. 83–101). Hillsdale, NJ: Erlbaum.

Gergen, K. J. (1982). *Toward transformation in social knowledge.* New York: Springer.

(1985a). Social psychology and the phoenix of unreality. In S. Koch & D. E. Leary (Eds.), *A century of psychology as science* (pp. 528–57). New York: McGraw-Hill.

(1985b). The social constructionist movement in modern psychology. *American Psychologist, 40,* 266–75.

(1986). Correspondence versus autonomy in the language of understanding human action. In D. W. Fiske & R. A. Shweder (Eds.), *Metatheory in social science* (pp. 136–62). Chicago: University of Chicago Press.

Gergen, K. J., & Gergen, M. M. (Eds.). (1984). *Historical social psychology.* Hillsdale, NJ: Erlbaum.

Goffman, E. (1959). *The presentation of self in everyday life.* Garden City, NY: Doubleday.

(1963). *Behavior in public places.* New York: Free Press.

Harré, R., & Secord, P. F. (1972). *The explanation of social behaviour.* Oxford: Blackwell Publisher.

Hegel, G. W. F. (1910). *The phenomenology of mind* (J. B. Baillie, Trans.). London: Macmillan. (Original work published 1807.)

(1956). *The philosophy of history* (J. Sibree, Trans.). New York: Dover. (Original work published posthumously in 1861.)

Hobbes, T. (1651). *Leviathan, or the matter, forme, & power of common-wealth ecclesiasticall and civill.* London: Crooke.

Homans, G. W. (1950). *The human group.* New York: Harcourt Brace.

(1961). *Social behavior: Its elementary forms.* New York: Harcourt, Brace, & World.

Hovland, C., Janis, I. L., & Kelley, H. H. (1953). *Communication and persuasion.* New Haven, CT: Yale University Press.

Hume, D. (1978). *A treatise of human nature* (P. H. Nidditch, Ed.). Oxford: Clarendon Press. (Original work published 1739–40.)

Israel, J. (1979). *The language of dialectics and the dialectics of language.* Atlantic Highlands, NJ: Humanities Press.

Janis, I. L. (1972). *Victims of groupthink: A psychological study of foreign policy decisions and fiascos.* New York: Free Press.

Jung, C. G. (1956). *Two essays on analytical psychology* (R. F. C. Hull, Trans.). New York: Meridian Books. (Original works published 1928 and 1943.)

Keeney, B. P., & Ross, J. M. (1985). *Mind in therapy: Constructing systemic family therapies.* New York: Basic Books.

Kelly, G. (1955). *The psychology of personal constructs* (vol. 1). New York: Norton.

Knorr-Cetina, K. D. (1981). *The manufacture of knowledge.* New York: Pergamon.

Krippendorff, K. (1984). Paradox and information. In B. Dervin & M. J. Voigt (Eds.), *Progress in communication sciences* (vol. 5, pp. 45–71). Norwood, NJ: Ablex.

Landau, M. (1961). On the use of metaphor in political analysis. *Social Research, 28,* 331–53.

Latour, B., & Woolgar, S. (1979). *Laboratory life, the social construction of scientific facts.* Beverly Hills, CA: Sage.

Le Bon, G. (1896). *The crowd* (no translator given). London: Unwin.

Lewin, K. (1935). *A dynamic theory of personality* (D. K. Adams & K. E. Zener, Trans.). New York: McGraw-Hill.

   (1951). *Field theory in social science* (D. Cartwright, Ed.). New York: Harper & Row.

Lovejoy, A. O. (1936). *The Great Chain of Being: A study of the history of an idea.* Cambridge, MA: Harvard University Press.

MacCormac, E. R. (1976). *Metaphor and myth in science and religion.* Durham, NC: Duke University Press.

Maine, H. J. S. (1885). *Popular government: Four essays.* London: Murray.

Malik, J., & Probst, G. (1982). *Self-organization and management of social systems.* St. Gallen: University Press.

Malthus, T. R. (1970). *An essay on the principle of population* (A. Flew, Ed.). Harmondsworth: Penguin Books. (Original work published 1798.)

Martin, E. (1987). *The woman in the body: A cultural analysis of reproduction.* Boston: Beacon Press.

Marx, K. (1954). *Capital, a critical analysis of capitalistic production.* Moscow: Foreign Languages Publishing. (Original work published 1867.)

Maturana, H. R., & Varela, F. J. (1980). *Autopoiesis and cognition: The realization of the living.* Dordrecht: Reidel.

McDougall, W. (1908). *Introduction to social psychology.* London: Methuen.

McDougall, W. (1920). *The group mind: A sketch of the principles of collective psychology.* New York: Putnam's.

Mead, G. H. (1934). *Mind, self, and society from the standpoint of a social behaviorist* (C. W. Morris, Ed.). Chicago: University of Chicago Press.

Miller, G. A., Galanter, E., & Pribram, K. H. (1960). *Plans and the structure of behavior.* New York: Holt.

Moreno, J. L. (1946). *Psychodrama.* New York: Beacon House.

Moscovici, S. (1985). *The age of the crowd: A historical treatise on mass psychology* (J. C. Whitehouse, Trans.). Cambridge University Press.

Overton, W. F., & Reese, H. W. (1973). Models of development: Methodological implications. In J. R. Nesselroade & H. W. Reese (Eds.), *Life-span developmental psychology: Methodological issues* (pp. 65–86). New York: Academic Press.

Parsons, T. (1951). *The social system.* New York: Free Press.

Pavlov, I. (1928). *Lectures on conditional reflexes: Twenty-five years of objective study of the higher nervous activity (behaviour) of animals* (W. H. Gantt, Ed. and Trans.). New York: International.

Plato (1961). The republic (P. Shorey, Trans.). In E. Hamilton & H. Cairns (Eds.), *The collected dialogues of Plato* (pp. 575–844). Princeton, NJ: Princeton University Press. (Original work written ca. 375 B.C.)

Plon, M. (1974). On the meaning of the notion of conflict and its study in social psychology. *European Journal of Social Psychology, 4,* 389–436.

Quine, W. V. O. (1960). *Word and object.* Cambridge, MA: MIT Press.

Rapaport, F. A. (1956). The promise and pitfalls of information theory. *Behavioral Science, 1,* 303–9.

Ross, E. A. (1908). *Social psychology.* New York: Macmillan.

Rousseau, J. J. (1968). *The social contract* (M. Cranston, Ed.). Harmondsworth: Penguin Books. (Original work published 1762.)

Russell, B. (1918–19). The philosophy of logical atomism. *Monist, 28,* 495–527; *29,* 32–63, 190–222, 345–80.

Sampson, E. E. (1978). Scientific paradigms and social values: Wanted – a scientific revolution. *Journal of Personality and Social Psychology, 36,* 1332–43.

Sarbin, T. R. (1954). Role theory. In G. Lindzey (Ed.), *Handbook of social psychology* (vol. 1, pp. 223–58). Cambridge, MA: Addison-Wesley.

Schachter, S. (1959). *The psychology of affiliation.* Stanford, CA: Stanford University Press.

Schlenker, B. R. (1977). On the ethogenic approach: Etiquette and revolution. In L. Berkowitz (Ed.), *Advances in experimental social psychology* (vol. 10, pp. 315–30). New York: Academic Press.

(1980). *Impression management: The self-concept, social identity, and interpersonal relations.* Monterey, CA: Brooks/Cole.

Schwartz, B., Lacey, H., & Schuldenfrei, R. (1978). Operant psychology as factory psychology. *Behaviorism, 6,* 229–54.

Semin, G. R., & Manstead, A. S. R. (1983). *The accountability of conduct.* New York: Academic Press.

Shotter, J. (1984). *Social accountability and selfhood.* Oxford: Blackwell Publisher.

Sidis, B. (1898). *The psychology of suggestion.* New York: Appleton.

Sighele, S. (1892). *La foule criminelle* [The criminal mob] (P. Vigny, Trans.). Paris: Alcan.

Smith, A. (1970). *The wealth of nations* (A. Skinner, Ed.). Harmondsworth: Penguin Books. (Original work published 1776.)

Spencer, H. (1851). *Social statics.* London: Chapman.

(1876). *The principles of sociology* (vol. 1). London: Williams & Norgate.

Stroebe, W., & Frey, B. S. (1982). Self-interest and collective action: The economics and psychology of public goods. *British Journal of Social Psychology, 21,* 121–37.

Tarde, G. (1903). *The laws of imitation* (E. C. Parsons, Trans.). New York: Holt. (Original work published 1890.)

Thibaut, J. W., & Kelley, H. H. (1959). *The social psychology of groups.* New York: Wiley.

Vaihinger, H. (1924). *The philosophy of 'as if'* (C. K. Ogden, Trans.). New York: Harcourt, Brace. (Original work published 1911.)

Vico, G. (1948). *The new science of Giambattista Vico* (T. G. Bergin & M. H. Fisch, Eds. and Trans.). Ithaca, NY: Cornell University Press. (Original work published 1744.)

Weick, K. E. (1979). *The social psychology of organizing* (2d ed.). Reading, MA: Addison-Wesley.

Wexler, P. (1983). *Critical social psychology*. London: Routledge & Kegan Paul.

Wittgenstein, L. (1953). *Philosophical investigations* (G. E. M. Anscombe, Trans.). Oxford: Blackwell Publisher.

Wright, W. A. (1936). *The complete works of William Shakespeare*. Garden City, NY: Garden City Books.

Zajonc, R. B. (1965). Social facilitation. *Science, 149*, 269–74.

(1980). Compresence. In P. B. Paulus (Ed.), *Psychology of group influence* (pp. 35–60). Hillsdale, NJ: Erlbaum.

9

Metaphors of unwanted conduct: a historical sketch

THEODORE R. SARBIN

In every age and in every society, rules of propriety are laid down. When a person engages in conduct that others perceive to be rule breaking, those persons responsible for the maintenance of order within the group make efforts to understand and control the rule breaker. If the violated rule is an explicit one, such as a law of property, the social group (or its designated officers) apply the sanctions that have been legislated for the particular norm violation. If the rule is not explicit, as, for example, the norms governing reciprocal talk, the problem is more complex, since neither the law nor the lore provides reliable sanctions. A convenient way of referring to such noncodified rule breaking is "unwanted conduct." In this essay, I shall sketch a historical account of the metaphors that have guided the search for the understanding and control of unwanted conduct. For the past century, such conduct has been the concern of the subdiscipline of medicine called psychopathology. Later in the essay, I shall point to some of the historical contexts leading to the coinage of that term.

A complete history would consider the metaphors employed in earlier times when devils and demons, good and evil spirits, and other occult entities provided the ground for theory building as well as the rationale for managing deviant persons. My selective historical account begins with the introduction of a novel metaphor that displaced demonological concepts and paved the way for the classification of unwanted conduct as forms of illness.

The mental illness metaphor

Clearly, metaphors do not arise out of the blue. They are forged in the course of attempts to communicate events for which no satisfactory vocabulary is available. Like all communicative acts, metaphors occur in social contexts, and they are intended to solve concurrent problems. Teresa of Avila (1515–81), an important figure in church history, was one of the first influential leaders to shift the burden of the social control of norm violators from religious authorities to practitioners of Renaissance medicine. The norm violations under consideration were perplexing and unpopular imaginings that were reported by some members of a cloister of nuns. At a later time, the reported "visions" would have been labeled "hallucinations," and the nuns would have been identified as "hysterics." In a humane act calculated to save the nuns from the Inquisitors, Teresa declared that the unwanted conduct, the reported visions, should be treated *as if* they were symptoms of illness – *como enfermas* (Teresa of Jesus, 1573/1946, pp. 36–40).

Leaning partly on the recently recovered humoral theory of Galen, Teresa argued that the unwanted conduct of the nuns could be accounted for by natural causes – by melancholy (an excess of black bile), a feeble imagination (lack of skill in assigning causes to imaginings), and drowsiness or sleeplike states. Spiritual causes, she contended, need not be invoked.

Teresa's strategy for saving the nuns was based on arguments that were difficult to refute. Before her time it had been established that sickness or infirmity (*enfermas*) is something that happens *to* a person. Since the person is not the agent of action in sickness, he or she cannot be held responsible. Sickness is a happening and not a doing. By invoking these assumptions, Teresa effectively sidetracked the Inquisitors from their usual practice of locating the cause of unauthorized visions in the visionary's intentional commerce with the devil. She thus contributed to the trend, already begun, by which religious authority slowly gave way to science (at least in areas relating to material things) and came to recognize the relative importance of science in practical affairs.

The introduction of the "illness" metaphor reflected an important change in the construction of reality. From an earlier conception of reality that maintained a strict partition between spiritual, atemporal things and earthly, material things, a new conception that allowed a merger of spiritual and material events had begun to take shape. The accommodation was apparent, in Teresa's time, in the revised system of Galenic medicine offered by the practitioners of physik, the science of the body and its afflictions. In this system, the sort of "as if" diseases that were later subsumed under the generic label "mental illness" required diagnosis and treatment no less than did somatic illness. As a result, these forerunners of contemporary physicians turned their attention to the new category of "as if" diseases. As they did so, the metaphoric marker employed by St. Teresa, *como* ("as if"), was perhaps inevitably dropped. Thus, it happened that the doctors incorporated into their theories of bodily diseases the performances of persons whose bodies could be healthy but whose public conduct was disturbing, nonconforming, perplexing, embarrassing, or bothersome.

Teresa was not the only one to institute the "illness" metaphor. Johann Weyer (1515–88), a Dutch physician working within the constraints of contemporary theology, also argued for the validity of "illness" as a metaphor for disordered or disturbing conduct. Because physicians of this period were frequently called upon to help establish whether a behavioral symptom was caused by commerce with the devil or by disease processes, the differential diagnosis was witchcraft or disease. Under these circumstances, physicians made no effort to examine the fine points of metaphor making and reification. In rejecting the diagnosis of witchcraft, it would have been counterproductive for them to undress the illness metaphor, distancing unwanted conduct from the class anchored by familiar bodily disease concepts (Veith, 1965).

Physicians were not always as persuasive as Teresa or Weyer in convincing church or civil authorities of the appropriateness of the illness metaphor for unwanted conduct. In 1602, Edward Jorden, an English physician, was called upon to diagnose a woman accused of witchcraft. After his examination, he reported that the unwanted behavior was the product of natural causes, and illness was the appropriate diagnosis. The court rejected his expert testimony, and the accused was punished as a witch (Jorden, 1603). Clearly, the transition from theological to medical explanations for crazy or problematic behavior was not accomplished in a single century. Still, by the time of the Enlightenment, naturalistic explanations had for the most part replaced theological doctrine in the effort to understand crazy behavior, and physicians were routinely assigned the specialist role of diagnosing illness, whether somatic or "mental" (Zilboorg & Henry, 1941).

As this historical sketch suggests, the term "mental illness" reflects the combining of two unrelated concepts: "illness" and the qualifier "mental." Understanding the semantic features of "illness" is a prerequisite for comprehending the act of inserting "mental" into the now popular "mental illness" concept. The basic referents for illness and its synonyms, sickness and disease, have been relatively stable over the centuries. To our progenitors, no less than to our contemporaries, the referent for illness or disease was discomfort of some kind (i.e., chills, fevers, trembling, cramps, itchings, etc.). Indeed, disease was originally a near synonym of discomfort (dis + ease), although only "malaise" has been retained as a term for subjective discomfort. The original referents for the terms "disease" and "malaise" were self-assessments made with regard to compelling stimuli arising within the body. When these internal events occur simultaneously with dysfunction or incapacity of the body, they are interpreted as signs or symptoms of disease. Sometimes an explicit causal connection is inferred: The subjective discomfort is supposed to be caused by the somatic dysfunction. A diagnosis of illness or disease means not only that a person is suffering discomfort, but that he or she is incapable of performing some, if not all, customary roles. This general description of illness is widespread and is found in ancient writings, in the reports of ethnologists, and in contemporary parlance.

Of special interest to historians of psychology are the following questions: What were the conditions that influenced the inclusion of misconduct in the semantic matrix of illness or disease? What events made it possible to mix intentional behavior with chills, tumors, nausea, fever, pain, and other somatic complaints? What other conditions influenced the assimilation of unwanted conduct into the illness concept?

When employing metaphors, there is a common human tendency to drop the "as if" or to elide the contextual features that mark the expression as figurative rather than literal (Chun & Sarbin, 1970). Galenic practitioners shared this common tendency. Although Teresa introduced the metaphor with the "as if" marker *como* to identify conditions that did not meet the criteria for somatic illness, the doctors could not readily perform their diagnoses and treatments on "as if" or imaginary illnesses. Through the expedient of dropping the metaphoric marker, the practitioners of physik were relieved of the task of differentiating "as if" illnesses from somatic illnesses. Nonconforming or perplexing behaviors – that is, unwanted conduct – could then be interpreted as "symptoms" of underlying humoral imbalances in much the same way that fever was interpreted as a "symptom" of distempered humors.

A review of sixteenth- and seventeenth-century treatises on physik makes plain that the prevailing paradigm for the diagnosis and treatment of sickness made liberal and often exclusive use of Galen's humoral theories. Writers copied from Galen and other Greco-Roman authorities. Hunter and Macalpine (1963), historians of psychiatry, point out that post-Renaissance doctors continued to use Galen's classifications and that the presence or absence of fever was their main diagnostic guide.[1]

An excerpt from a sixteenth-century writer on physik illustrates the extensive use of Galenic ideas. Barrough (1583/1963) described one of a dozen disorders, "madness," in terms of humoral pathology:

Mania in Greeke is a disease which the Latines do call *Insania* and *furor*.... They that have this disease be wood and unruly like wild beastes. It differeth from the frenesie, because in that there is a fever.... It is caused of much bloud, flowing up to the braine,

sometime the bloud is temperate, and sometime only the abound-
ance of it doth hurt, sometime of sharpe and hote cholericke
humours, or of a hote distempure of the braine. There goeth before
madnes debility of the head, tinckling of the eares, & shinings come
before there eies, great watchings, thoughtes, and straunge things
approach his mind, and heaviness with trembling of the head. . . .
But madnes caused of bloud only, there followeth continuall laughing, there commeth before the sight (as the sicke thinketh) things to
laugh at. But when choler is mixed with bloud, then the pricking
and fervent moving in the braine maketh them irefull, moving,
angry, and bold. But if the choler do waxe grosse and doth pricke
and pull the brain and his other members, it make them wood, wild,
and furious, and therefore they are worst to cure. (p. 27)

The traditional concept of illness had depended on a conjunctive criterion: An ill person had to exhibit complaints *and* observable somatic
symptoms. The concept of illness was reformulated, however, as a result
of the introduction of "as if" diseases and the subsequent dropping of the
metaphoric marker. The concept of illness now rested on a disjunctive
criterion: Illness was demonstrated by complaints and somatic symptoms
or simply by complaints by others of unwanted conduct. The uncritical
acceptance of Galen's humoral pathology as the only scientific framework
within which to view both somatic and conduct disorders facilitated the
incorporation of disordered behavior into the domain of medical practice.
To meet the basic requirements of the medical model, "symptoms" of
disease had to be observed. The report of a vision, for example, was
treated as equivalent to fever or boils; both were symptoms of humoral
pathology. As a result of the shift from a metaphorical to a literal
interpretation of a behavioral act as "symptom," humoral medicine came
to embrace not only every aspect of the body but also all intentional
actions. This linguistic transformation made it possible for every human
action – laughing, crying, shouting, praying, lying, and believing – to be
perceived as a symptom of underlying humoral imbalances.

Although Galen's system began to decline in influence after the Renaissance, the basic Galenic model served medical practitioners well into
the nineteenth century (Temkin, 1973, chap. 4). Then, under the influence of a new set of metaphors (see Pribram, Chapter 2, this volume),
neurologists began to revise and refine the concepts traditionally tied to
the humors. In their observations, they found that some conduct disorders could be traced to neuropathology, for example, to cerebral
trauma. Other disorders appeared to have no somatic antecedents. Thus
was born the distinction between "organic" and "functional" disorders.
(For early antecedents of this distinction, see Langermann, 1797; Pinel,
1813; Stahl, 1702.) The use of the metaphor "organic" for a range of

disease processes followed from the increasing knowledge of anatomy: Affected organs could cause certain behavioral effects. The use of "functional" was not so clear-cut. The term was supposed to direct attention to the disturbed functioning of the organic system in the absence of demonstrable organic pathology. Within the prevailing medical framework, the specialists were confronted with the problem of locating causal agents for these "functional disorders." Since the neuropathologists had preempted the body and its organs as the causal agents for "organic disorders," those who had accepted the mission of finding the causes of "functional disorders" had to look elsewhere. As they looked, they developed the explicit concept, term, and myth of "mental illness" (see Szasz, 1961).[2]

Having described some of the relevant semantic and pragmatic features of the concept of illness up to the time of the emergence of the "mental illness" metaphor, I can now address the following question: What influenced nineteenth- and twentieth-century writers to join together the materialist concept "illness" and the nonmaterialist concept "mental"? Surely one significant factor was the presumption of mind–body duality by those scientists who undertook the diagnosis and treatment of "functional disorders." No prolonged exegesis is necessary to claim that, for most European and American scientists, the concept of mind was a given, not unlike the concept of soul for generations of Western theologians.

"Mind" as a term parallel to "body" has a long history. Mind is supposed to be immaterial and invisible, like its predecessor "soul." Yet it is located within the body like more visible and palpable organs such as the heart, the stomach, and the lungs. Early theorists asked the obvious question: If the body was subject to sickness, why not the mind, even though sicknesses of the mind had to be of a different order than bodily disease? As a result of such questioning, the previously cryptic "functional disorders" were eventually renamed "mental disease" or "mental illness."

In one sense, combining the materialist word "illness" with the spiritualist "mind" is illicit. The effect of the complex metaphor is to assign qualities to the mind that are associated with the body. The meanings of mind are all too abstract – and the experiences of the mind too ephemeral – to be serviceable to the practitioners of the healing arts. In the same way that bodily organs had identifiable properties, the mind was said to have specific properties. The differentiating characteristics of the ephemeral mind were reified and expressed as "states of mind." States of love, anxiety, joy, fear, anger, apathy, lucidity, and so on were postulated to account for observed conduct, normal and abnormal. The practitioner now had the task of determining through chains of inference – sometimes tortured – which mental states were the causes of observed conduct (Baillarger, 1853; Falret, 1890).[3]

One of the reasons that mind has been given an ontological status by writers in the mental illness tradition is its grammatical form. "Mind" is a noun. Many nouns refer to entities that have substance. Hence, mind has been associated with, and assumed to be, a substantive entity. It is treated as if it were a thing. Originally, however, "mind" stood for acts, rather than states or entities. "Minding" – that is, remembering, thinking, imagining, and perceiving – concerned actions performed in social contexts. We still have some residues of the earlier usage of the verb: "Mind the step!" "Mind your manners!" "Remind me."

Like most words, "mind" at one time was a metaphor. It was coined to identify actions often carried out privately, silently, and covertly, in contradistinction to acts that were more overt, public, and noisy. As happens with other metaphors, the continued use of "mind" as a substantive in the absence of reminders of its metaphoric status led to a radical shift in meaning. Such a phenomenon has been identified as the metaphor-to-myth transformation (Sarbin, 1964, 1968). What was once a figure of speech was transformed into a believed-in entity, a thing with properties and powers.[4]

The implications of the metaphor-to-myth transformation are manifold. Most significant is the problem of uncovering the causes of unwanted conduct. How and where were researchers to probe for the mythical organ responsible for behavior judged to be unacceptable by others? During the past century, the search has been directed toward uncovering complexes, neuropsychic dispositions, mental states, traits, psychic flaws, and other entities and characteristics that presumably reside within the mind. A moment's reflection on these "states of mind" leads to the conclusion that the identification of internal "mental" causal entities can be carried out only through chains of inference, premised on self-reports or the reports of complainants. The development of such chains of inference, following the canons of contemporary science, helped create a science of abnormal conduct. Nineteenth-century scientists were committed to the mechanistic world view. They were also expected to avoid the vernacular and to make use of Greek roots and affixes in naming their discoveries and inventions. Thus, in their attempt to make the study of "mental illness" more scientific, nineteenth-century scientists created a new metaphor: psychopathology.

Psychopathology

The new metaphor and science of psychopathology depended on a combination of two root metaphors.[5] The first was a particular concept of "mind" as an autonomous "thing" that operated according to its own norms and regulations. This metaphorical concept, according to Pepper's

(1942) analysis, is associated with "formism," a world view that assigns to each phenomenon in the universe its own formal characteristics and essence. When medically oriented scientists turned to Greek for a scientific label to represent this thing called mind, they selected "psyche," a term that originally referred to one of the forces posited by post-Homeric Greeks as a source of action (Adkins, 1970).

The second root metaphor underlying the modern conception of psychopathology – the metaphor of the universal transmittal of force – was derived from the mechanistic rather than the formistic world view. According to this world view, objects are to be conceived as parts of a ubiquitous mechanical apparatus that transmits forces from one place to another. As a result, the science of pathology should have as its mission the uncovering of causes along mechanistic lines.

As a fitting consequence of these conceptual underpinnings, "psychopathology" was an outgrowth of the successful development of biology as a scientific discipline, a development that owed its success to the application of the root metaphor of mechanism. The mechanization of biology reached its apex in the latter half of the nineteenth century (Coleman, 1971; Singer, 1959). The mechanistic conception of life was the starting point for research and theory in the various biological disciplines, including pathology. It had an ideological cast and was taken seriously by significant members of the scientific community. Its importance is reflected in the oath and careers of Ernst von Brücke, Emil du Bois-Reymond, Hermann von Helmholz, and Carl Ludwig. In 1848 these soon to be famous biologists swore to account for all bodily processes in physicochemical terms, and they spent their lives in the service of this goal (Cranefield, 1957).

The word "psychopathology" reveals its medical roots, even to those ignorant of Greek. "Pathology" came into use as early as the seventeenth century to denote the study of somatic disease. It was not until the middle of the nineteenth century that it was used to denote conditions other than the effects of tumors, toxins, parasites, and microbes. In combining "psyche" with "pathology," psychopathology stimulated imagery that was faithful to its medical context. At the same time users of the term had to incorporate images that were consistent with the formist abstraction "psyche." Taking for granted that the human body is a complex biological machine, the psychopathologists undertook the study of the psyche as another complicated piece of machinery, subject to nature's causal laws.

The mechanization of biology was the framework within which the psychopathologists conducted their work. A relevant example of the use of the root metaphor of mechanism is found in the mechanistic conception of hysteria.

The mechanization of hysteria

The psychopathologists attempted to validate their professional calling by solving the puzzle of hysteria. The metaphorical history of hysteria provides yet another example of the metaphor-to-myth transformation. The early Greeks traced the source of unwanted, perplexing conduct in women to the most obvious internal organ that differentiated women from men: the uterus. They explained conduct that violated role expectations as the behavioral effect of a wandering uterus. The treatments they recommended were reasonable, given the premises embedded in their theory. To coax the uterus into its proper position, Greek doctors would apply substances that emitted foul odors to the genital region and sweet fragrances to the nose, or vice versa, depending on the assumed misplacement of the uterus (Veith, 1965).

Although the wandering-uterus theory faded into oblivion, the label "hysteria" (from the Greek word for uterus) was retained and served as the focus for a vast amount of speculation and clinical work in the eighteenth and nineteenth centuries. The focus of the work was the behavior of women (and some men) that violated role expectations and bore some minimal resemblance to "symptoms" of established somatic disease: contractures, paralyses, paresthesias, "fits," uncontrolled weeping or laughing, bizarre posturing, sensory anomalies, and even so-called delusions and hallucinations.

The most prominent contributors to the new science of psychopathology were physicians. Jean-Martin Charcot (1825–93), Sigmund Freud (1856–1939), and Pierre Janet (1859–1947), among others, brought their training in medicine and the taken-for-granted mechanistic ethos to the study of abnormal conduct. However they differed in particulars, they all embraced the search for causality, if not in the brain or central nervous system, then in the psyche, mental processes, or various states of consciousness.

Hysteria, once a metaphor for unwanted conduct among women, became a wastebasket term and, depending on the particular author, could include any deviation from the norm. From her historical account of the use of the diagnostic term "hysteria," Veith (1977) concluded that, before the age of the psychopathologists, physicians were reluctant to treat women whose complaints could not be corroborated by physical and neurological examination. Such women were regarded as nuisances, malingerers, liars, and childish attention getters. Charcot was among the first to take seriously the conduct of patients whose "symptoms" did not fit into the current nosological schemes. However, he redefined hysteria as illness (Szasz, 1961).

The historical influence of Charcot's reconceptualization of hysteria is at least partially due to the fact that he had already established his reputation as a leader in the rapidly developing field of neuropathology before his work on hysteria. His observations on multiple sclerosis and on localization of spinal chord lesions, among other discoveries, had made him famous. These observations exemplified the transmittal-of-force notion that was the root metaphor of the mechanistic world view. Damage or disease to the nerve fibers interrupted the flow of force or energy to or from the brain. The problem for Charcot was to account for conduct for which the physical examination revealed no known type of neurological disease or damage – no abnormal reflexes or atypical sensorimotor signs. At first, he assimilated hysteria to neurological disease. The symptoms, he claimed, were produced by nonobvious blockages of the nerve fibers. Later, he modified his position by making use of mentalistic constructs: He treated the mind as if it were an organ that could participate in the transmittal of physicochemical energy along nerve trunks, and he couched his scientific account of disordered or unacceptable conduct in mechanistic language. The patient's symptoms, he proposed, were the inevitable consequence of the excitation and inhibition of the flow of impulses through the networks of nerve fibers (see Ellenberger, 1970).

The imagery of the anatomy and physiology of the nervous system was to a large extent influenced by the development of telephone technology (see Pribram, Chapter 2, this volume). "Messages" were supposed to travel up and down the nerve trunks as "messages" travel through telephone wires. The same imagery was instrumental in fashioning a model of the mind. The conceptual nervous system became a fount for metaphors to account for all kinds of performances, especially those that had surface similarities to the symptoms of neurological disease.

Other psychopathologists followed the same course. They relied on the central nervous system as the source of metaphors to account for the actions of so-called hystericals. Freud's clinical and theoretical writings can be traced to the time in his career when he shifted from the search for cause-and-effect relations in the nervous system to the search for causal relations in the psyche. To understand the actions and the talk of his hysterical patients, he had to reinvent the unconscious. In this connection, it is worth remembering that the nineteenth century witnessed a number of attempts besides Freud's to fashion metaphors that would convey the imagery of a mind that could operate independently of the person as agent. Unconscious cerebration, unconscious inference, instantaneous ratiocination, among other metaphors, were coined to help explain what Freud and others saw as the dynamics of hysterical actions. Freud's own metaphor of a three-part mind composed of id, ego, and superego was undoubtedly influenced by his knowledge of the morphology of the brain.

It is interesting that "hysteria" is no longer part of the official nomenclature (American Psychiatric Association, 1987). Some of the abnormal conduct that previously would have been labeled "hysterical" is now subsumed under "conversion reaction." This is a carryover of Freud's metaphoric explanation of hysteria as a *conversion* of psychic energy into disabling symptoms. "Psychic energy," in turn, is still widely used in psychoanalytic writings and is another case of metaphor turned myth. At one time, it may have been a convenient figure to help describe a complex phenomenon, but for many writers "psychic energy" has become reified and is treated as if it were of the same order as solar energy.

Another metaphor that has become popular in recent times to describe the same kinds of unacceptable conduct is "histrionic personality disorder." This metaphor departs from the imagery of a person being at the mercy of disordered nerves or disordered mental machinery. Instead it evokes an image of a person being the author of his or her actions in efforts to solve identity or existential crises. That the "histrionics" may create interpersonal problems and lead to negative valuations by significant others points to the necessity for looking at unwanted conduct as involving a social judgment process.

In view of these recent conceptualizations, an interesting question can be posed. Did hysteria, like smallpox, just disappear? Or did scientists recognize that the reified metaphor no longer had referential utility?

Schizophrenia: an exercise in metaphor

The mechanization of hysteria occurred in parallel with the design of nosological systems to aid physicians and medical psychologists in the scientific job of classifying diseases of the mind. The usual pattern was to make systematic observations of persons brought to clinics and hospitals and to distill the observed and reported "signs and symptoms" into a single word or phrase. The convention among medical scientists and practitioners, as we have already seen, was to use Greek roots and affixes to construct names for the discovered (or invented) syndrome or disease. From our present perspective, these scientists engaged in the fashioning of metaphors that frequently implied that the esoteric Greek terms were packed with causal implications. "The patient suffers from kleptomania" could be interpreted as a statement that the patient suffers from a disease, rather than as an opaque restatement of the presenting symptom, "He stole something for no apparent reason."

In the absence of physical trauma or known pathogens, medical practitioners assigned various Greek-inspired labels to serious violations of propriety norms. Among these labels were moral insanity, psychosis, dementia praecox, and schizophrenia. At one time, each of these terms was a metaphor. With continued and uncritical use, they were reified and treated as if they had the same sort of referents as pneumonia, arteriosclerosis, or cancer. Although each of the metaphors coined in the past century has an interesting story, I will center my discussion on schizophrenia.

The term "schizophrenia" was introduced by the Swiss psychiatrist Eugen Bleuler (1857–1939). Bleuler conducted intensive clinical investigations with patients who were labeled as suffering "dementia praecox" (see Bleuler, 1911/1950). Because many persons who were sent to clinics and hospitals for exhibiting crazy (norm-violating) behavior were in their postpubertal years, mid-nineteenth-century physicians described the conduct by borrowing "dementia" (absence of mind) from "senile dementia" and adding the qualifier "praecox" (precocious). The brain was said to deteriorate prematurely, and the patient was generally evaluated as suffering from the effects of moral degeneration. The metaphor had a life well into the twentieth century in spite of Bleuler's detailed studies that showed that the symptoms of so-called dementia praecox could be observed among people of all ages.

Bleuler's work on schizophrenia was continuous with that of Emil Kraepelin (1855–1926) on dementia praecox. Kraepelin is credited with having created a nosological system for psychiatry – a system that followed the principles of organic medicine. He was the force behind the movement to incorporate the new discipline of psychiatry into the practice of medicine, and his basic ideas continue to serve as the metaphorical foundation of the diagnostic manuals sponsored by official psychiatry.

Kraepelin's *Textbook of Psychiatry* went through nine editions. The fifth (1896) edition provided a relatively full account of his justifications for the diagnosis of dementia praecox. To understand the ready acceptance of the concept of dementia praecox, the concurrent climate of medical practice must be taken into account. Medical professionals of the later nineteenth century properly looked upon neurology as a legitimate branch of medicine. It was to neurologists that they directed patients whose perplexing and/or deviant conduct might be caused by pathology of the nervous system. Presenting symptoms were many and varied, some clearly related to neuropathology caused by tumors, traumas, and toxins. Other presenting symptoms, such as atypical imaginings, nonconforming beliefs, and bizarre acts, were less clearly related to neuropathology. In the medical clinics and hospital wards, no fine distinctions were drawn. Disease was disease, whether the symptoms were obviously connected to neurological damage or were assumed to have neurological origins.

Patients diagnosed as suffering from dementia praecox were all regarded as neurologically and somatically defective. Kraepelin advanced the notion that, like all organic diseases, dementia praecox had a typical onset, course, and outcome. No cure was to be expected, only degeneration into feeblemindedness and death. If a patient recovered, the diagnosis had been incorrect.

Mary Boyle (in press) has recently unearthed some startling facts that help account for Kraepelin's (and Bleuler's) pessimistic diagnosis and, more important, for the initial observations that led to the hardening of dementia praecox into an irresistible diagnostic entity. Kraepelin discovered clear-cut somatic signs to support his claim to having identified a class of somatically flawed human beings. For some patients, Boyle reports, Kraepelin recorded signs and symptoms such as "marked peculiarities of gait . . .; excess production of saliva, and urine; dramatic weight fluctuations; tremor; cyanosis of the hands and feet; constraint of movement and the inability, in spite of effort, to complete 'willed' acts." Kraepelin also wrote of "severe structural brain damage which was revealed microscopically at post-mortem" (Boyle, in press). The brain damage noted at postmortem was similar to the brain damage of patients who had been victims of encephalitis lethargica. Such structural damage is absent from postmortem examinations of present-day patients who are diagnosed as schizophrenic.

In her reconstruction of the dementia praecox concept, Boyle shows that Kraepelin assimilated the perplexing and deviant conduct of *all* patients who appeared to be withdrawn and noncommunicative to a subclass of patients whose behavior matched the diagnosis of encephalitis lethargica. Thus, Kraepelin created a model for dementia praecox: the public behavior of patients suffering from encephalitis lethargica. Flattened affect, loosening of associations, ambivalence, and autism – the presumed psychological criteria of dementia praecox (later schizophrenia) – were actually the behavioral effects of an infectious brain disease.

It is interesting that contemporary practitioners do not encounter patients who match Kraepelin's description. Encephalitic patients are no longer housed with patients who employ deviant epistemic and behavioral strategies to solve their life problems. Nevertheless, Kraepelin's confounding of dementia praecox with encephalitis lethargica has continuing, and not merely historical, import: Bleuler's revision of the dementia praecox concept – the basis for current beliefs about schizophrenia – absorbed Kraepelin's description of the psychological concomitants of encephalitis.

Bleuler made this revision, seeking to establish a psychological diagnosis of dementia praecox, because he became dissatisfied with the notion of a biologically produced moral degeneration. From clinical observations, he had concluded that the people who were brought into his clinic and hospital suffered from a pathology of mind in which the various departments or faculties of the mental apparatus did not function in unison. In other words, the faculties were "split off" from each other (see Bleuler, 1916/1924). In keeping with the medical tradition, he created a diagnostic category by using Greek roots, to wit, "schizophrenia." It is instructive to reconstruct the context for the fashioning of this diagnostic label. For a long time, it has been customary to divide psychological processes into a threefold system: the intellect, will, and emotion. Bleuler noted that many of his patients showed a discrepancy between the intellectual recognition of a fact (e.g., the recently announced death of one's parents) and the emotional response to it (e.g., laughter or apathy).

I underscore the fact that Bleuler made detailed observations of the overt conduct of patients. He then classified the observed behaviors according to the traditional tripartite classification. This classifying activity was dependent on certain metaphysical assumptions, the first being that the mind or psyche is an existent reality. The second assumption was that the mind could be divided into three distinct regions. When Bleuler declared that a certain type of crazy conduct was due to the splitting of the mind, there was an "as if" lurking in the epistemological shadows: It was *as if* the parts of the mind were not functioning in unison. The "as if" formula was invoked inasmuch as the intellect, the will, and the emotions were speculative, not empirically established entities.[6]

Another popular concept aided the formation of the schizophrenia metaphor. The concept of the association of ideas had been well received in medical circles. Although connected primarily to the writings of British philosophers, the concept of association was congenial with the known facts of neurology. A metaphoric leap from connections observed in anatomical studies to connections or associations in the mind helped to form the premise from which Bleuler created the schizophrenia doctrine. If ideas could be "associated," they could also be "dissociated."

"Schizophrenia" is a compound metaphor. *Schizo* (split, dissociated) is one feature. The second root, *phrenia*, is an interesting choice. The ancient Greeks believed that the seat of the soul was the phrenos, the diaphragm. The root continued to be used to connote mind or mental, even though Bleuler and his contemporaries located the mind in the brain rather than in the midriff.

Unlike an ordinary-language description of unwanted conduct (using such terms as mad, crazy, loco, nutty, weird, odd, bizarre, far out, flaky, etc.), the use of a scientific-sounding, albeit opaque term of Greek origin suggests that the term has causal implications. Although "schizophrenia" has been the object of research for three-quarters of a century, no unequivocal criterion of its existence has been discovered or invented. It is another example of a metaphor-to-myth transformation. Schizophrenia, originally a metaphor created to help communicate about crazy behavior, is now regarded as a disease entity by most medical practitioners. A review of current research makes clear that many scientists have revived the Kraepelinian model and devote their lives to searching for the microbe, the parasite, the chemical compound, the gene, or the brain anomaly that causes this "disease" (M. Bleuler, 1968; Sarbin & Mancuso, 1980).

Hallucination: the psychology of believed-in imaginings

In the preceding pages, I have presented a historical sketch of metaphors invented as class names to give form to certain kinds of disvalued, disturbing norm violations. "Mental illness," "psychopathology," and "schizophrenia" are class names employed by professionals and laypersons to identify people whose public behavior fails to meet normative prescriptions. The items of conduct that have been subsumed under these class labels are legion. Each of these items, often called symptoms, can be better understood if its metaphoric origins are traced. In the following pages, I will trace the history of one such "symptom," hallucination.

What are the raw observations for which the term "hallucination" is employed? A person may publicly report hearing the voice of a long-dead parent, seeing an absent historical figure (such as Napoleon), seeing and hearing a religious figure (perhaps the Virgin Mary), or experiencing his or her head expanding and deforming to the size of a twenty-foot doughnut. The test for hallucination is consensus: If the audience does not confirm the claimed perception of the long-dead parent, Napoleon, the Virgin Mary, and so on, then "hallucination" is generally used to describe the person's experience.

The word "hallucination" originated in a world that was witnessing a shift in authority from churchmen to scientists. Remnants of the views of mystics and scholastics, however, continued to influence the meanings and valuations of publicly uttered nonconsensual claims of seeing persons or objects and hearing voices of people or gods. The first use of "hallucination" in English occurred in a translation of a tract by Ludwig Lavater (1570/1572), who wrote of "ghostes and spirites walking by nyght, and of strange noyses, crackes, and sundry forwarnynges, whiche commonly happen before the death of menne, great slaughters & alterations of kyngdomes" (p. 1). It is clear that Lavater was referring in this passage to apparitions and that he used the word "hallucination" (an anglicized form of the Latin word *allucinatio*, which carried the meaning of "idle talk," "prating," "a wandering of the mind") as a synonym for "illusion," the Latin root of which (*illusio*) is equivalent to "mocking," "jeering," or "bantering." The *Oxford English Dictionary* informs us that "hallucination" was synonymous with "illusion" and was used to indicate the "mental condition of being deceived or mistaken, or of entertaining unfounded notions," and furthermore that a hallucination was an "idea or belief to which nothing real corresponds." Thus, a sixteenth-century physician, whose chief authority was Galen, would interpret the public avowal of imaginings-as-perceptions as erroneous images, as possible symptoms of insanity, or as an illness caused by an excessive amount of black bile or melancholia, but *not* as signs of goodness or evil, of possible sainthood or devil possession.

It will be instructive to consider how the metaphor of hallucination, originally referring to "idle talk," was employed by neo-Galenic practitioners. In the first place, we should recall the context of neo-Galenic medical practice, in which the physician was called upon by patients or by citizens or officials to render a diagnosis and to prescribe treatment. Thus, the physician examined persons who believed they were sick or who were thought to be sick by interested, nonprofessional laypersons. There was an assumption of sickness, else why consult a physician? Let us suppose that a putative patient was brought to a physician by relatives because he declared that he had seen and spoken with St. Peter. The practitioner of neo-Galenic medicine would first set out to determine the intention of the patient when he said, "I have seen St. Peter." Was it the intention of the patient to seek help from a knowledgeable professional? (In current practice, this step would be equivalent to identifying the "chief complaints.") The doctor would then focus on the following question: Was the image of St. Peter erroneous? To answer this question a complex series of inferences would be required, calling for considerable linguistic sophistication and a number of concepts shared by both the patient and the physician.

Because of the existence of the newly coined diagnostic label "hallucination," the practitioner could simplify his work and use whatever cues were available to confirm the hypothesis of error in image making, the criterion for declaring a person to be a hallucinator. If the doctor deduced that the patient's locution referred to a memory image of a statue of St. Peter that the patient had seen, the inference of an erroneous image would not have been drawn. If, however, a memory image of the village barber served as the basis for the patient's claim that he saw St. Peter, the doctor would have declared that the image was erroneous, and "hallucination" would have been the preferred label.

The neo-Galenic practitioner faced another problem, a problem that still confronts contemporary professionals: When a patient says, "I have seen St. Peter" (or any mythical or nonpresent person), the listener must determine the intention behind the use of the verb "to see." In the concrete case, is "see" to be taken literally ("I actually, corporally, have seen the disciple known as St. Peter"), or is "see" to be taken figuratively ("It is *as if* I have seen St. Peter")? Whether to assign the label "hallucination" or an alternative label, "poetic expression," depends to an extent on the doctor's knowledge of the patient's reputation. If the referring agent had already declared that the patient was a lunatic, an outcast, or a public nuisance, the doctor's job would be an easy one: His diagnosis would be hallucination. If the doctor, after considering all the evidence, including the reputation of the patient, inferred that the person was merely using poetic speech, he would be likely to cast about for a nonpejorative label: fancy, daydream, fantasy, or even metaphor.

A more complete understanding of the phenomena for which physicians had employed the label "hallucination" was initiated in the nineteenth century with the beginnings of the empirical study of psychology. Avoiding the clinic, madhouse, and hospital, philosophically oriented psychologists adopted a naturalistic mode of investigating "erroneous images." Their investigations led to the conclusion that such phenomena were common events and were not signs of madness. Notwithstanding, most medical practitioners working in clinical settings operated from the belief that "erroneous images" were symptoms of underlying cerebral or psychic pathology.

The medical model contained two conceptions that, when conjoined, formed a circular argument: (1) Hallucinations are imaginings reported by crazy people; and (2) certain forms of madness are characterized by hallucinations. The confounding of these conceptions was ignored by medical practitioners, notwithstanding the observation that erroneous images occurred with great frequency among people who had not been diagnosed as mad or melancholic.

It was in the nineteenth century that the medical model was consolidated. Jean-Etienne Dominique Esquirol (1833), the acknowledged medical authority, was certain that hallucinations and illusions were pathological phenomena:

> In hallucinations everything happens in the brain. The visionaries, the ecstatics, are people who suffer from hallucinations, dreamers while they are awake. The activity of the brain is so energetic that the visionary, the person hallucinating, ascribes a body and an actuality to images that the memory recalls without the intervention of the senses. In illusions, on the other hand, the sensibility of the nervous extremities is excited, the senses are active, the present impressions call into action the reactions of the brain. This reaction, being under the influence of ideas and passions, dominates the insane; these sick people are mistaken about the nature and use of their present sensations. (p. 7)

Bringing the study of "erroneous images" into contemporary times, the psychological and medical orientations remain with us. William James (1890) was aware of the studies reported by psychologists that made it abundantly clear that so-called hallucinations were part and parcel of the cognitive activity of normal people. Freud, in contrast, regarded hallucinations as wakeful dreams, both regressive and primitive. Hallucinations were normal during dreaming but abnormal during wakefulness (Freud, 1900/1953a, 1940/1964).

It is important to remind ourselves that the unexamined metaphor can play havoc with logic. The early forms of the word "hallucination" denoted idle talk. When employed in the medical context, the term was transformed into a defining criterion for madness and/or an effect of madness. A review of contemporary textbooks of psychology makes clear that both uses of "hallucination" – the medical and the psychological – have been uncritically retained. For example, in their chapter on behavioral pathology, Kimble and Garmezy (1963) write: "Hallucinations are false sensory impressions. The schizophrenic may see things that aren't there or voices that don't exist, except for him" (p. 539). In another chapter on the detection and interpretation of stimulation, they define illusions as "false perceptions that produce various sorts of distortion in the world" (p. 324). A clinical practitioner using the Kimble–Garmezy book as a guide would have the impossible task of differentiating between "false sensory impressions" and "false perceptions." The reification of hallucination has created conditions for diagnostic confusion. In what way could a sensory impression be "false"?

In summary, an examination of the use of "hallucination" in modern times reveals that this once-lively descriptive metaphor, in the hands of mechanistically inclined physicians and mental health practitioners, became reified. A careful look at the semantics and pragmatics of the professional employment of the label "hallucination" leads us to the recognition of the Alice in Wonderland transfiguration of the "idle talk" metaphor: The erroneous images reported by mad or crazy people are hallucinations; if a person "has" hallucinations, he or she must be mad or crazy.[7]

Metaphors of intervention

A discussion of metaphors of unwanted conduct would be incomplete without a parallel discussion of the metaphors of intervention. In any historical period and in any culture, intervention by societal agents is tacitly called for – and legitimated – when a person is identified as a deviant for displaying contranormative conduct. The intervention may be legal or quasi-legal (such as exile, imprisonment, capital punishment, or public flogging) or educational (such as habit training, religious practice, or various forms of psychotherapy). When a man or woman violates the norms for an ascribed role, theorists and ordinary folk seek causal explanations. The metaphor chosen to connote the assumed causal agency influences the form of intervention. Exorcism, for example, became the intervention of choice when the assumed cause was Satanic influence. Religious doctrine provided the underlying causal metaphor, and the choice of intervention followed logically from the assumed cause. Similarly, when societal agents employ the illness metaphor, it follows logically that concurrently acceptable medical treatments will be the intervention of choice.

The central point is that specific modes of intervention flow at any given time from the regnant world views about human nature. When the dominant world view was a mixture of medieval formism and mysticism, intervention techniques followed logically from the belief in witchcraft as a causal theory. The draconian interventions intended to control alleged witches (including burning them at the stake) were consistent with the underlying belief that the devil would be responsive only to the most violent forms of intervention. By the end of the eighteenth century, the belief in witchcraft as a causal theory had been assigned to the dustbin of psychological theory: superstition. Burning at the stake was no longer practiced, but other draconian methods were still in favor (floggings, chains, sequestration, etc.). As scientific metaphors displaced religious metaphors for understanding natural phenomena, the claim that madness (unwanted conduct) had supernatural origins was repudiated. Human beings were subject to scientific laws no less than were other objects in the universe. Despite their commitment to empirical science, eighteenth-century physicians for the most part regarded madness as incurable, and their prescribed interventions were no different from those of jailers, almshouse keepers, and madhouse proprietors (physical restraint, bleeding, induced vomiting, cathartics, control by fear of punishment, and flogging). Some doctors advised the keepers to avoid violence, but in practice these draconian methods were continuous with eighteenth-century medical and penological practice (Dain, 1964).

The beginning of the nineteenth century witnessed the emergence of a radically different metaphor for understanding human conduct, a metaphor that dictated *moral* management as the appropriate intervention. The creation of asylums and colonies for the care of persons who were unable to look after themselves was a reaction against the cruelties of the earlier period. Moral treatment – kindness, wholesome food, sanitary living conditions, prayer, moderate work, and recreation – arose concomitantly with the interest in formulating scientific theories about unwanted conduct. Still largely dependent on a paradigm inherited from Galen, early-nineteenth-century physicians constructed physiological theories about the etiology of madness. Locating the cause of insanity in the workings of the body made it possible – indeed reasonable – to shift from a free will to a determinist position. The mad person, then, was no longer responsible for his or her plight. Thus, moral treatment, rather than cruel punishment and violent medical practices, was the logical, humane prescription (see Bockoven, 1963).

A paradox emerged. At the same time that they adopted nonphysiological interventions, doctors leaned more and more on physiological metaphors of causality. To understand how this could be, we need to consider the time frame of these developments – the turn of the century, shortly after the American Revolution. Among the ideological origins of the Revolution were resolute stances on freedom of religion and the priority of civil liberty. The first of these was based on a belief in the dignity of the person (Bailyn, 1967). A prevailing optimism, perhaps asscciated with extending national frontiers and with general prosperity, influenced a choice of intervention that most closely resembled the Christian ideal. The civil libertarian premise, metaphorized by Bailyn as the "contagion of liberty," pushed aside the repressiveness of the eighteenth century. The older attitudes faded out with the acceptance of the moral metaphors of democracy.

Nineteenth-century physicians took pride in the more humane methods of moral management. Moral treatment, however, bore an interesting similarity to the older treatment methods. Both were concerned with social control:

> In abandoning the methods of the eighteenth century, nineteenth century physicians were not abandoning their roles as guardians of the moral order and agents of social control. Physical restraint, coercion, and exile are replaced by the philosophy of the self which emphasizes the dual nature of man, the power of the will to prevent and control insanity and which elaborated the arts of self government. (Skultans, 1975, p. 9)

In this regard, we should pay particular attention to the choice of the term "moral" in "moral treatment" and "moral management." Two hundred years ago, the descriptor "psychological" had little currency. Writers employed "moral" as an adjective in somewhat the same manner as "psychological" would be employed today. As is clear in the quotation preceding this paragraph, however, the ethical and religious connotations of "moral" remained part of its semantic structure.

Meanwhile, Esquirol's influential treatise on insanity (1838/1845) was instrumental in promoting explanatory metaphors that made sense in terms of the increasing interest in anatomy and physiology. Madness could be accounted for by invoking the notions of flawed biological development and regression to childhood. If adult norm violators were to be regarded as partially developed humans or as children, then it followed that societal agents had the duty to guide them toward the goal of becoming mature, responsible, self-reliant adults. It is more than a coincidence that this was the period of European expansionism and imperialism: These contemporary political and economic policies supported the moral theory that firm, consistent, moral treatment would elevate inferior races – as it did inferior individuals – from the darkness of superstition to enlightened self-control (Sarbin & Juhasz, 1982).

Esquirol reflected the increasingly popular belief in the power of education to overcome differences in people; it did not matter whether the differences were the consequences of age, culture, heredity, or other conditions. Equally important to the belief in the power of education was the image of the educated European adult as a man of reason, as the model for all other persons to follow. Because of his assumed superior biological and intellectual endowment, it was no less than his duty (later epitomized as the "white man's burden") to educate the less fortunate and to bring them to his level of intellect and self-governance. The earlier enthusiasm for saving the fallen souls of savages was displaced by a missionary zeal for upgrading the retarded development of children, colonials, peasants, immigrants, women, and even the insane. Among the outcomes of this philanthropic zeal was the creation of asylums for those unfortunates whose conduct could not be assimilated to prevailing norms.[8]

In the political ideology of the nineteenth century, the maintenance of order was an equally important consideration. The asylum, besides being a response to one of the domestic burdens of the white man, was one of several innovations designed in the interest of maintaining public order (Rothman, 1971).

A reading of tracts on moral management makes clear that order, regularity, and predictability were explicit goals. A submerged metaphor provided the motivation for supporting the asylum as a societal invention for the maintenance of public order. In the political and economic expansion of the nineteenth century, public order was dependent on containing "dangerous persons" and "dangerous classes." The word "danger" is derived from "dominium," the power relationship of lord to vassal. "Danger" was used to signify the possibility of inverting the relationship of lord and vassal, master and slave, controller and controllee (Sarbin, 1967). Even today the phrases "dangerous to self" and "dangerous to others" are employed as criterial attributes of madness. They are found in abundance in legislative acts and in police and juristic procedures for depriving potential harmdoers of their liberty (see, e.g., Dershowitz, 1973; Morse, 1978). When a person or class is declared "dangerous," the constitutional guarantee of due process is put aside on the grounds that the labeled norm violator might in the future engage in offensive conduct.

Not every nonconformist was (and is) perceived as dangerous, as harboring the potential for violence. A social policy evolved for the differential recruitment of candidates who would benefit from the ordered life of the asylum. Social class became an important criterion in the selection process (Rothman, 1971). Immigrants, impoverished men and women, ghetto dwellers, and other social failures were the people for whom the abstraction "dangerous classes" was disproportionately used in political tracts arguing for social control legislation.[9]

To support the epistemic connection between being "dangerous" and being foreign-born, poverty-stricken, or otherwise stigmatized required a firm, if tacit, major premise. The metaphor of the "wild man within" served as the basis for nineteenth-century theories of human nature. (It was implicit, e.g., in the theories of Lombroso and Freud.) In his account of the origins of the myth, White (1972) has shown how Europeans nurtured and reified the metaphor in the preceding centuries. Large areas of the globe had not yet been explored, and most Europeans believed that the inhabitants of unknown worlds were wild and uncontrolled savages. The belief was contingent on naive ethnocentric assumptions regarding how human beings would act if they had no opportunity to receive the benefits of (European) civilization. The remote origins of the linkage between the diagnosed deviant and the "wild man within" are obscure, but observation of the conduct of inmates in eighteenth-century madhouses undoubtedly conferred credibility on the literalized "wild man" metaphor. Before the intervention of moral management, the brutality inflicted by the keepers and spectators at La Bicêtre, the Salpêtrière, and Bedlam shaped the inmates into creatures that could hardly be identified as human. Caged, chained, harassed, and otherwise treated as if they were wild animals, they had no options but to express their frustration and hopelessness through "wild" actions. Parenthetically, the reified metaphor continues to receive support in the "wild beast" theory of insanity drawn from early English law (Platt & Diamond, 1965).

The uneasy alliance between physicalistic (medical) theories and moral treatment could not be maintained. The image of the asylum as advocated by early nineteenth-century reformers such as Samuel Tuke (1813/1964) in England and Philippe Pinel (1802) in France was a quiet, secluded, pastoral dwelling that housed a small number of persons who had failed to meet the demands of everyday life. With the increasing growth of industrial and urban populations, such an ideal could not be realized. The middle of the nineteenth century witnessed the change from small asylums to vast, overcrowded, and understaffed warehouses for society's rejects. At the same time, the prestige given to practitioners of science and technology reflected on the practitioners of medical science. The superintendents of asylums, by fiat, became medical superintendents of mental hospitals. Moral management practices eroded under the authority of the physicians, and the illness metaphor was revived and given ontological status.[10] The newer causal metaphors were borrowed from the fast-developing sciences of neurology and pathology, as described in an earlier section of this chapter. By the end of the nineteenth century, physicians were acknowledged as appropriate professionals for diagnosing and treating "mental illness." The illness metaphor was so powerful that few alternatives to tumors, toxins, crazy ancestors, and microbes were considered. Except in rare instances (e.g., paresis), hypotheses that located the cause of abnormal behavior in pathological organic processes remained speculative. As I argued earlier, Cartesian dualism made possible the consolidation of organic sickness with mental sickness. The objects of medical treatment included not only the more obvious organs, such as the heart and liver, but also that inferred entity, the mind. Advances in neurology helped sustain the notion that mind and brain were intimately connected. Psychotherapy had its beginnings, as already noted, in the efforts of physicians to treat "sick" or "flawed" minds.

Since these early beginnings, the development of the behavioral sciences has broadened the conception of psychotherapy. At the same time, however, the belief in organic causality persists, reflected in the widespread use of "psychomimetic" drugs and in the hypothesis that "mental illness" (e.g., schizophrenia) is caused by biochemical and genetic abnormalities.

Although still a powerful force, organic causal metaphors are not so commonly implicated in psychotherapeutic interventions. In addition, the objects of psychotherapy are no longer exclusively the certified social failures for whom the asylums were conceived. The clients of psychotherapists are for the most part self-referred. They seek help in solving existential, identity, or interpersonal problems.

Psychotherapy is not a monolithic profession. Scores of psychotherapy and behavior change systems have been promulgated, each originating from the implicit or explicit use of a root metaphor, or world view, concerning the human condition. For our present purposes, psychotherapeutic systems can be sorted into four classes: the behavioral, psychodynamic, existential, and social systems approaches. Even though the guiding metaphors are blurred in practice, their constraints are clearly perceptible.

Behaviorist therapy

The prevailing root metaphor of science – mechanism – is reflected in the various forms of behavior modification. The origin of behavior theory is lost in antiquity, but the distinguishing feature is the recognition that environmental stimuli have cue properties and reinforcement properties. Habits may be fixed or modified by the effects of externally instigated actions, which presumably satisfy needs and reduce tension, or by the reinforcing effects of the linguistic acts of relevant others. The imagery of the underlying metaphor has traditionally been expressed as "man the machine," but the major supporting metaphors of contemporary behavior theorists have their origins in the physiological laboratory: Complex conduct is reduced to "stimuli" and "responses." The client or patient is perceived according to the constraints of the mechanistic root metaphor: He or she is assumed to be a neutral, passive organism, not a sentient, construing person (see, e.g., Thorndike, 1913; Watson & Rayner, 1920; Wolpe, 1958).

Psychodynamic therapy

The originators of psychodynamic theories began from mechanistic postulates (e.g., Freud's hydraulic metaphor), but when the explanatory powers of mechanism were exhausted, they turned to an essentialistic – or in Pepper's (1942) felicitous term, a formistic – conception of mind or psyche. The duality of mechanism and formism required no great postulational leap. Cartesian dualism was readily accepted: There were bodies and there were minds. The dualistic perspective, colorfully represented as the "ghost in the machine" (Ryle, 1949), was consonant with widely held religious beliefs. The reified metaphor – mind – became the object of attention. Disordered conduct, uncontrolled feelings, and personal discomfort, on this view, follow from imbalances among or accidents to the hypothesized structures of the mind.

The task for the formistic therapist is to adjust or rearrange the metaphorized mental structures. Not available to direct observation, mental structures are construed from analyses of verbal behavior and other "expressions" of the mind. It is assumed that the therapist can penetrate the mysteries of the mind by careful attention to clues embedded in talk and gesture. In endorsing the position that, in principle, a person can alter the structure of mind (the causal entity) through guided self-analysis, psychodynamic therapists imply that the client is responsible for his or her own misery. In assuming that clients must accept responsibility for their unhappiness and discomfort, they have become moralists (Rieff, 1979). Their claimed neutrality and objectivity conceal a normative moral posture that directs them to communicate that a person is ultimately responsible for his or her actions and feelings.[11]

Existential therapy

Sometimes associated with the so-called third force in psychology, the framework of existential therapy makes use of such concepts as being, awareness, experience, authenticity, existential crisis, and self-actualization. The underlying metaphor – the self – is an abstraction, understood in relation to other abstractions. The relationship of self to God, to the universe, to nature, to humankind – these are the foci of interest for the existential therapist. Phenomenological work helps to uncover meanings that have been disguised through metaphor and other figures of speech. As the behavioral perspective had its origins in the science laboratory and the psychodynamic perspective had its origins in Cartesian doctrine, the existential perspective had its origins in humanistic philosophy and theology. The failure to find an acceptable answer to the question "What am I in relation to the rest of reality?" may lead a person into conduct judged unacceptable by societal agents. Intervention by a therapist may be supplemented or replaced by meditation, prayer, aesthetic experience, or pain and suffering. The aim of existential therapy is to reorganize one's relationship to transcendental objects and events, thereby effecting change in the self (see, e.g., Frankl, 1965; May, 1969; Rogers, 1961).

Social systems therapy

The root metaphor underlying the social systems approach is the same as the root metaphor of the contextualist world view: the historical act (see Pepper, 1942). The focus is not on the isolated organism, nor on the ghost in the machine, nor on the self, but on the person in social context. Social science practitioners perceive unwanted conduct from a vantage point that includes not only the target person but also the persons who pass judgment on the target person's conduct. The notion of social systems contains an assumption that the actions of any member of the system will influence the conduct of other members. There is no recognition of "man alone" or "woman alone." In recent years, the adoption of the root metaphor of the historical act has influenced practitioners to take into account cultural and institutional factors as well as interpersonal factors. A number of intervention programs, among them community psychology, family therapy, and self-help and mutual help groups, have come into being as the result of psychologists adopting the historical act as the root metaphor (see, e.g., Denner & Price, 1973; Fairweather, 1964; Lieberman & Borman, 1979; Morrison, 1979; Satir, 1964).

Coda

This essay purports to be a historical sketch of the development of metaphors central to understanding and dealing with unwanted conduct. I should acknowledge, however, that like all historians I am not free of epistemological bias. To help control for the more typical and less warranted sorts of bias, I have tried to avoid such loaded terms as "abnormal," "aberrant," "disordered," "pathological," and "insane," and I have striven to employ terms that are more theoretically neutral. Among the latter is the label that I have selected for the phenomena of interest: unwanted conduct. But even "unwanted conduct" retains the rockbottom implication that is embedded (though usually disguised) in the former, more heavily loaded terms: It implies that the labeling of certain types of human action (as abnormal, or aberrant, or disordered, etc.) involves a value judgment regarding what is wanted and what is not wanted. I believe that this implication is entirely warranted and that its recognition is extremely important.

Furthermore, on evidence like that provided in my historical account, I believe that the judgments involved in designating certain behaviors as unwanted have typically been made, and continue to be made, by persons who possess more power and authority than the persons whose behavior is being judged and that these relatively more powerful authorities make their declarations against a background of beliefs, mores, and folkways that constitute a particular culture's moral code. In the end, then, I believe that the generation of policies and prescriptions for labeling and dealing with unwanted conduct is, inevitably, a moral enterprise.

This historical sketch of selected topics has taken the period of the Renaissance as its point of departure. To be sure, early Greek and Roman authorities coined metaphors to help communicate about perplexing and unwanted conduct. In fact, some of these metaphors entered into Renaissance and later formulations. I began with the Renaissance, however, because I wanted to discuss the more immediate historical background of Western culture's critical shift from demonism and witchcraft to the belief in sickness as a causal entity. It is the literalization of the metaphor of illness, I am convinced, that has been the major source of the psychiatric myths of our time, myths that have stood in the way of the creation and acceptance of more apt and more humane metaphors of unwanted conduct.

A review of the history of metaphors underlying theories of unwanted conduct reveals a fact of great importance – that under subtle or open ideological pressure, descriptive metaphors become myths. Once a myth becomes part of the fabric of a civilization's system of beliefs, it guides thought and action, and thus it inevitably militates against the introduction of alternative metaphors. In the same way that Renaissance figures created new descriptive metaphors to attenuate the excesses that followed the adoption of the mythology of demonism, some contemporary scholars, through research and semiotic analysis, have tried to demonstrate the mythic nature of the successor to demonism: the mental illness doctrine. Szasz (1961), in particular, has argued persuasively for an alternative metaphor – "problems in living." This metaphor requires no adherence to mechanistic ideology, and it fits well with the requirements of contextualist modes of thought. In addition, it accords with the central fact that the identification of an episode of conduct as "unwanted" requires not only overt conduct by a target person, but also a moral judgment by another (see Sarbin & Mancuso, 1980). I hope that readers of this essay will see the value and promise of this alternative metaphor.

Notes

1 Since Galen (ca. A.D. 130–200) and Galenic medicine are often mentioned in this essay, I should note that Riese (1963) has published translations of some of Galen's lesser known writings on moral philosophy and psychotherapy and that Siegel (1973) has provided a thorough and authoritative review and

analysis of those aspects of Galen's thought that are most relevant to the concerns of this essay. Temkin (1973) has documented the history of "Galenism" from the time of Galen to the nineteenth century.

2 Of course, there were some precedents for this development. For example, Rush (1812) had already discussed the "diseases of the mind," and Brigham (1844) had construed insanity as a "chronic disease of the brain." But the full-blown, systematic construction and use of the "mental illness" metaphor occurred only in the latter part of the nineteenth century.

3 The issues at stake here were as relevant to the legal profession as to the medical and psychiatric communities. For a collection of the seminal legal cases pertaining to insanity and jurisprudence, see Robinson (1978–80).

4 A perusal of the *Oxford English Dictionary* supports the assertion that "mind" entered the language as a verb to denote actions for which the contemporary speaker of English would use "remembering" and "attending." "Mind" and "memory" are derived from the same root. The transformation to substantive status took place when concurrent epistemology required speakers to invent a locus for the action. The mind then became the seat of remembering and attending. The location of mind was not always considered to be the head. Before our ancestors discovered that the brain was a powerful coordinating organ, the heart was sometimes assumed to be the seat of remembering. Vestiges of the heart-as-mind premise can be found in colloquial speech: "I learned the poem by heart" is equivalent to "I memorized the poem." On the theory that vocabulary arises from the literalization of figures of speech, see Sarbin (1967) and Turbayne (1962).

5 On the concept of root metaphors and world views (or "world hypotheses"), see Pepper's (1942) classic work, in which he specifies and discusses four major "world hypotheses" that are related, he argues, to four major "root metaphors" (formism, mechanism, contextualism, and organicism). According to Pepper, these different conceptual viewpoints are the major "relatively adequate" orientations that have been developed in the Western tradition of metaphysical speculation. For discussions and amplifications of Pepper's concepts and thesis, see Efron (1982).

6 For further discussion of Kraepelin, Bleuler, and the development of modern psychiatry, see Ellenberger (1970).

7 For further discussion of the historical background of the concept of hallucination, see Sarbin and Juhasz (1967).

8 For an idiosyncratic, but stimulating and suggestive discussion of the "birth of the asylum," see Foucault (1961/1965).

9 The tract writers embraced the notion of the "manifest destiny of the Anglo-Saxon race." Ethnocentric arguments were advanced to support the claim that all forms of societal disorder were traceable to the "dangerous classes." See, e.g., Brace (1872), Brown (1867), and Strong (1885).

10 On the downfall of the moral treatment movement and attempts to revive it in this century (e.g., in the community mental health movement), see Bockoven (1963).

11 The magnitude of the literature on psychodynamic therapies is such that one or two bibliographical references would hardly do justice to the subject. The flavor of this mode of intervention is reflected in Freud's paper "On Psychotherapy" (1905/1953b).

References

Adkins, A. W. H. (1970). *From the many to the one: A study of personality and views of human nature in the context of ancient Greek society, values, and beliefs.* Ithaca, NY: Cornell University Press.

American Psychiatric Association (1987). *Diagnostic and statistical manual of mental disorders: DSM III-R* (rev. 3d ed.). Washington, DC: Author.

Baillarger, J. G. F. (1853). *Recherches sur les maladies mentales et sur quelques points d'anatomie et de physiologie du système nerveux* [Studies of mental illnesses and of the anatomy and physiology of the nervous system]. Paris: Masson.

Bailyn, B. (1967). *The ideological origins of the American Revolution.* Cambridge, MA: Harvard University Press.

Barrough, P. (1963). Of the frenisie, lethargy, apoplexy, epilepsia, madnes and melancholie. In R. Hunter & I. Macalpine (Eds.), *Three hundred years of psychiatry, 1535–1860* (pp. 24–8). New York: Oxford University Press. (Excerpted from original work published 1583.)

Bleuler, E. (1924). *Textbook of psychiatry* (A. A. Brill, Trans.). New York: Macmillan. (Original work published 1916.)

   (1950). *Dementia praecox, or the group of schizophrenias* (J. Zinkin, Trans.). New York: International Universities Press. (Original work published 1911.)

Bleuler, M. (1968). A 23 year longitudinal study of schizophrenics, and impressions in regard to the nature of schizophrenia. In D. Rosenthal & S. Kety (Eds.), *The transmission of schizophrenia* (pp. 3–12). New York: Pergamon.

Bockoven, J. S. (1963). *Moral treatment in American psychiatry.* New York: Springer.

Brace, C. L. (1872). *The dangerous classes of New York.* New York: Wynkoop & Hallenback.

Brigham, A. (1844). Definition of insanity. *American Journal of Insanity, 1,* 97.

Brown, J. E. (1867). The increase of crime in the United States. *The Independent,* pp. 832–3.

Boyle, M. (in press). The nondiscovery of schizophrenia: Kraepelin and Bleuler reconsidered. In R. P. Bentall (Ed.), *Reconstructing schizophrenia.* London: Methuen.

Chun, K., & Sarbin, T. R. (1970). The metaphor-to-myth transformation. *Philosophical Psychology, 1,* 27–33.

Coleman, W. (1971). *Biology in the nineteenth century: Problems of form, function, and transformation.* New York: Wiley.

Cranefield, P. F. (1957). The organic physics of 1847 and the biophysics of today. *Journal of the History of Medicine and Allied Sciences, 12,* 407–23.

Dain, N. (1964). *Concepts of insanity in the United States, 1789–1865.* New Brunswick, NJ: Rutgers University Press.

Denner, B., & Price, R. H. (Eds.). (1973). *Community mental health: Social action and community reaction.* New York: Holt, Rinehart & Winston.

Dershowitz, A. M. (1973). Preventive confinement: A suggestive framework for constitutional analysis. *Texas Law Review, 51,* 1277–1324.

Efron, A. (Ed.). (1982). The Pepper papers. Special issue of the *Journal of Mind and Behavior, 3,* nos. 3 and 4.

Ellenberger, H. F. (1970). *The discovery of the unconscious: The history and evolution of dynamic psychiatry.* New York: Basic.

Esquirol, J. E. D. (1833). Sur les illusions des sens chez les aliénés [On the sensory illusions of the insane]. *Archives Générales de Medicine*, Ser. 2, *1*, 5–23.

(1845). *Mental maladies: A treatise on insanity* (E. K. Hunt, Trans.). Philadelphia: Lea & Blanchard. (Original work published 1838.)

Fairweather, G. W. (Ed.). (1964). *Social psychology in treating mental illness: An experimental approach*. New York: Wiley.

Falret, J. P. (1890). *Etudes cliniques sur les maladies mentales et nerveuses* [Clinical studies of mental and nervous illnesses]. Paris: Baillière.

Foucault, M. (1965). *Madness and civilization: A history of insanity in the age of reason* (R. Howard, Trans.). New York: Random House. (Original work published 1961.)

Frankl, V. (1965). *The doctor and the soul: From psychotherapy to logotherapy*. New York: Knopf.

Freud, S. (1953a). The interpretation of dreams. In J. Strachey (Ed. and Trans.), *The standard edition of the complete psychological works of Sigmund Freud* (vols. 4 and 5, pp. 1–621). London: Hogarth Press. (Original work published 1900.)

(1953b). On psychotherapy. In J. Strachey (Ed. and Trans.), *The standard edition of the complete psychological works of Sigmund Freud* (vol. 7, pp. 255–68). London: Hogarth Press. (Original work published 1905.)

(1964). An outline of psycho-analysis. In J. Strachey (Ed. and Trans.), *The standard edition of the complete psychological works of Sigmund Freud* (vol. 23, pp. 141–207). London: Hogarth Press. (Original work published 1940.)

Hunter, R., & Macalpine, I. (Eds.) (1963). *Three hundred years of psychiatry, 1535–1860*. New York: Oxford University Press.

James, W. (1890). *The principles of psychology* (2 vols.). New York: Holt.

Jorden, E. (1603). *A brief discourse of a disease called the suffocation of the mother*. London: Windet.

Kimble, G. A., & Garmezy, N. (1963). *Principles of general psychology* (2d ed.). New York: Ronald.

Kraepelin, E. (1896). *Lehrbuch der psychiatrie* [Textbook of psychiatry] (5th ed.). Leipzig: Barth.

Langermann, J. G. (1797). *De methodo cognoscendi curandique animi morbos stabilienda* [On establishing a method of identifying and curing mental disorders]. Jena: Maukianis.

Lavater, L. (1572). *Of ghostes and spirites walking by nyght* (R. H., Trans.). London: Watkyns. (Original work published 1570.)

Lieberman, M. A., & Borman, L. D. (Eds.). (1979). *Self-help groups for coping with crisis: Origins, members, processes, and impact*. San Francisco: Jossey-Bass.

May, R. (1969). *Existential psychology* (2d ed.). New York: Random House.

Morrison, J. K. (Ed.). (1979). *A consumer approach to community psychology*. Chicago: Nelson-Hall.

Morse, S. J. (1978). Crazy behavior, morals, and science: An analysis of mental health law. *Southern California Law Review*, *51*, 524–654.

Pepper, S. C. (1942). *World hypotheses: A study in evidence*. Berkeley and Los Angeles: University of California Press.

Pinel, P. (1802). *La médicine clinique rendue plus précise et plus exacte par l'application de l'analyse* [Clinical medicine made more precise and exact through the use of analysis]. Paris: Brosson, Gabon.

(1813). *Nosographie philosophique, ou la méthode de l'analyse appliquée à la médicine* [Philosophical description of diseases, or the analytic method applied to medicine] (5th ed., 3 vols.). Paris: Brosson.

Platt, A. M., & Diamond, B. L. (1965). The origins and development of the wild beast concept of mental illness and its relations to theories of criminal responsibility. *Journal of the History of the Behavioral Sciences, 1*, 355–67.

Rieff, P. (1979). *Freud: The mind of the moralist* (3d ed.). Chicago: University of Chicago Press.

Riese, W. (Ed.) (1963). *Galen on the passions and errors of the soul* (P. W. Harkins, Trans.). Columbus: Ohio State University Press.

Robinson, D. N. (Ed.) (1978–80). *Significant contributions to the history of psychology – Series F: Insanity and Jurisprudence* (6 vols.). Washington, DC: University Publications of America.

Rogers, C. R. (1961). *On becoming a person.* Boston: Houghton Mifflin.

Rothman, D. J. (1971). *The discovery of the asylum: Social order and disorder in the new republic.* Boston: Little, Brown.

Rush, B. (1812). *Medical inquiries and observations, upon the diseases of the mind.* Philadelphia: Kimber & Richardson.

Ryle, G. (1949). *The concept of mind.* London: Hutchinson.

Sarbin, T. R. (1964). Anxiety: Reification of a metaphor. *Archives of General Psychiatry, 10*, 630–8.

(1967). The dangerous individual: An outcome of social identification transformations. *British Journal of Criminology, 7*, 285–95.

(1968). Ontology recapitulates philology: The mythic nature of anxiety. *American Psychologist, 23*, 411–18.

Sarbin, T. R., & Juhasz, J. B. (1967). The historical background of the concept of hallucination. *Journal of the History of the Behavioral Sciences, 3*, 339–58.

(1982). The concept of mental illness: A historical perspective. In I. Al-Issa (Ed.), *Culture and psychopathology* (pp. 71–110). Baltimore, MD: University Park Press.

Sarbin, T. R., & Mancuso, J. C. (1980). *Schizophrenia: Medical diagnosis or moral verdict?* New York: Pergamon.

Satir, V. (1964). *Conjoint family therapy: A guide to therapy and technique.* Palo Alto, CA: Science & Behavior Books.

Siegel, R. E. (1973). *Galen on psychology, psychotherapy, and function and diseases of the nervous system: An analysis of his doctrines, observations and experiments.* New York: Karger.

Singer, C. (1959). *A short history of scientific ideas to 1900.* Oxford: Clarendon Press.

Skultans, V. (1975). *Madness and morals.* London: Routledge & Kegan Paul.

Stahl, G. E. (1702). *De medicina medicinae necessaria* [On the necessities of medicine]. Magdeburg: Henckelii.

Strong, J. (1885). *Our country: Its possible future and its present crisis.* New York: Baker & Taylor.

Szasz, T. (1961). *The myth of mental illness.* New York: Harper & Row.

Temkin, O. (1973). *Galenism: Rise and decline of a medical philosophy.* Ithaca, NY: Cornell University Press.

Teresa of Jesus [Teresa of Avila] (1946). Book of the foundations. In E. A. Peers (Ed. and Trans.), *The complete works of Saint Teresa of Jesus* (vol. 3, pp. 1–206). New York: Sheed & Ward. (Original work written 1573.)

Thorndike, E. L. (1913). *Educational psychology* (3 vols.). New York: Columbia University Teachers College.

Tuke, S. (1964). *Description of the retreat, an institution near York for the insane persons of the Society of Friends.* London: Dawson's of Pall Mall. (Original work published 1813.)

Turbayne, C. M. (1962). *The myth of metaphor*. New Haven, CT: Yale University Press.

Veith, I. (1965). *Hysteria: The history of a disease*. Chicago: University of Chicago Press.

—— (1977). Four thousand years of hysteria. In M. J. Horowitz (Ed.), *Hysterical personality* (pp. 7–94). New York: Aronson.

Watson, J. B., & Rayner, R. (1920). Conditioned emotional reactions. *Journal of Experimental Psychology, 3*, 1–14.

White, H. (1972). The forms of wildness: Archeology of an idea. In E. Dudley & M. E. Novak (Eds.), *The wild man within: An image in Western thought from the Renaissance to Romanticism* (pp. 3–38). Pittsburgh, PA: University of Pittsburgh Press.

Wolpe, J. (1958). *Psychotherapy by reciprocal inhibition*. Stanford, CA: Stanford University Press.

Zilboorg, G., & Henry, G. W. (1941). *History of medical psychology*. New York: Norton.

10

Generative metaphor and the history of psychological discourse

KURT DANZIGER

Just how does the topic of metaphor help us to understand the history of psychological discourse? What is it that this topic contributes to our analysis of past attempts at addressing psychological issues? Is the topic of metaphor compatible with a sober account of historical facts? I would like to suggest some preliminary answers to these questions before moving on to a consideration of the relevance of the analysis of discourse to the historiography of psychology.

First I should clarify what is entailed by the "topic of metaphor" in this context. The role that we attribute to metaphor in historical understanding will obviously depend on our conception of what metaphor is and how it functions. If the topic of metaphor is taken to involve no more than figures of speech with purely rhetorical functions, then its relevance in the present context will clearly be quite limited. However, it needs no elaborate analysis to recognize that metaphor is a phenomenon of thought as well as of speech. Metaphorical turns of speech are interesting because of what they indicate about the thoughts they express.

Discourse about psychological topics has long been replete with metaphorical allusions. More often than not, these allusions do not occur in an isolated fashion but have a repetitive, recursive quality. A particular theorist, we often find, is inclined to sustain the same metaphorical descriptions over much of his or her work. More significantly, a number of individuals often share the same metaphorical forms in their accounts of psychological processes. In such instances the analysis of metaphor becomes historically interesting, for we can use it to improve our under-

331

standing of patterns of psychological thought that were characteristic of a period, or a culture, or a particular intellectual community.

More particularly, an analysis of its metaphorical aspects allows us to go beyond the literal surface of psychological discourse to uncover its underlying assumptions and preoccupations. The literature of psychology certainly contains some metaphors that are little more than rhetorical flourishes. But it also contains others that seem to provide one of the important conditions for the very coherence of psychological discourse. Such metaphors are used pervasively over relatively long periods, and typically their users do not seem to regard them as "mere" metaphors but as expressing some kind of literal truth.

So when Alexander Bain (1873), for example, describes the learning process in terms of "tracks" and "turning off steam," or when William McDougall (1908) tells us that an organism without instincts would be like a "steam engine whose fires had been drawn," they are not simply indulging in picturesque and inaccurate language. Those images seem to fit their psychological theories in some quite fundamental ways. Bain really does believe that the mind is essentially tracked energy, and McDougall is convinced that it is an inert apparatus brought to life by the energy of the instincts. These images are not just literary devices for getting a point across; they actually seem to have a theory-constitutive function. As a result, they can give us an insight into some of the underlying assumptions and concerns that received expression in Bain's and McDougall's psychological theories.

If we are sensitive to this level of psychological discourse, we will also notice that Bain and McDougall, although they belong to different generations, are employing a similar basic image of the mind as an energy system. At the same time we will note that they emphasize different aspects of this image. Where Bain's main concern is with the harnessing or control of mental energy, McDougall is much more interested in the sources that guarantee its continued supply. What is taken for granted by the one becomes problematic for the other. This illustrates an important characteristic of fundamental psychological metaphors. They provide a basic common framework within which communication is possible, while at the same time providing scope for differences of emphasis. Basic metaphors, like that of psychological energy, provide a kind of rough schema that, when held in common, can constitute one of the minimal conditions for effective human communication. But because metaphors link two domains (such as mind and energy) in rather undefined ways, these schemata leave open the issue of precisely which assumptions and questions are to be transferred from the one domain to the other. So metaphorical schemata not only provide a framework for shared discourse, but encourage differences of emphasis and therefore provide conditions favorable for theoretical development.

In going below the surface of psychological discourse to examine some of its underlying metaphors, we are therefore doing more than uncovering buried archaeological strata. That fairly static image is not what I want to convey here. Rather, I am suggesting that underlying metaphorical systems have *generative* properties that give a certain cast to surface discourse while facilitating the appearance of novel features. Shared metaphorical images make it possible for people to exchange information about what they feel to be the same subject matter. But as long as the interpretation of these images remains open, those who share them are in a position to emphasize different sets of implications, any one of which could be suggested by the original metaphorical schema. The identification of such schemata is therefore important from the point of view of understanding the cognitive factors that provide some of the conditions of both coherence and novelty in the historical development of psychological discourse.

Applying such an analysis implies a certain view of metaphor as well as a certain view of psychological discourse. It means that we do not treat the latter as a set of more or less isolated propositions formulated by a succession of virtually independent individuals. As long as that was the prevailing norm in the historiography of psychology, questions about the conditions of coherence for shared discourse hardly arose and the appearance of novelty within a continuing tradition was unproblematic. But if we think of the history of psychological thought as a discourse with many contributors that is often locally and temporally coherent, then the analysis of metaphorical schemata becomes illuminating.

Of course, it is possible to talk in terms of a metaphorical schema only if one no longer regards metaphors as isolated figures of speech but recognizes their extended nature. On this point there appears to be virtual unanimity among a variety of modern writers on the topic of metaphor and theory. Black (1962) sees the subjects of metaphor as "systems of things rather than things." Berggren (1963) speaks of the "presiding schema" of a scientific theory, which he likens to the presiding image of a poem – not, one might note, to a specific metaphorical expression within the poem. Ricoeur (1977) similarly contrasts the "metaphoric network" of a theoretical model to the isolated metaphor as literary device. Perhaps the best way of conveying the meaning of this way of looking at what metaphor can do is in terms of Kenneth Burke's (1966) notion of "entitlement." When a major psychological domain is characterized metaphorically, as an energy system or perhaps as an information-processing system, what happens is not a matter of specific words describing specific features of the world. It is much more like giving a title to a novel. The basic metaphor functions as a title for a complex set of events, defining something essential about their nature and focusing on what is felt to be crucial about their structure. This does not involve an inferential process but an analogical "projection of meaning" (Cua, 1982, p. 253).

More than anything else, it is the recognition of this holistic aspect of metaphor (or more accurately of metaphorical networks) that has characterized the reversal in the evaluation of metaphor in recent times. It used to be believed that metaphor had no place in science because science was limited to giving a literal account of elements of the world. But before such a literal account can be undertaken, it is first necessary to agree on the terms of discourse and on the kind of domain the account is to be about. If it becomes possible to attach specific labels to bits of prepackaged information about parts of the world, this is only because those parts have already been identified in terms of an overall pattern. That such pervasive patterns are often based on a "root metaphor" was first suggested by Pepper (1942).

A further extension of this view of the role of metaphor leads to a recognition of those *generative* functions that I wish to emphasize here. If the metaphorical assertion does not simply claim that there is a similarity between two specific subjects but rather brings together two *systems* of implications, then it clearly entails the likely formation of new connections. In this "interaction" view of metaphor (Black, 1962), what is involved is not simply a comparison of two units, which could be reduced to a literal statement, but an application to the one subject of a whole set of implications previously linked with the other subject. Once such an application is made, it "*incites* the hearer to select some of the secondary subject's properties" and "*invites* him to construct a parallel implication-complex" (Black, 1979, p. 29). (I have italicized "incites" and "invites" in order to draw attention to the generative implications of this view.)

Thus, when the human mind is metaphorically characterized as an energy system or an information-processing system, a whole complex of knowledge and belief about energy systems or information-processing systems is potentially brought to bear on mental events and processes. As this potential is exploited, new perspectives and interpretations are very likely to emerge (Schön, 1963). Incidentally, the interaction between the two domains is not unidirectional. Thus, once the information-processing metaphor is used, it becomes quite natural to raise questions about the mentality of computers. In the case of the physical energy metaphor, the bidirectionality is just as striking. In fact, the interaction was historically recursive. Such concepts as "force," "power," and in part "energy" had strong psychological connotations before they were metaphorically extended to the physical world.

The implications of such a generative view of metaphor run counter to a long tradition of naturalism in the historiography of psychology. By naturalism I mean the approach that proceeds from the assumption that those objects, processes, or events to which our theoretical concepts refer have a natural existence before the act of discovery that leads to their labeling and their symbolic representation in our theories. Naturalism is a variant of what is sometimes referred to as "objectivism" (Lakoff, 1987). In both naturalism and objectivism there is an assumption that psychological events have fixed natural forms, which a few lucky philosophers and an army of systematic investigators have found and labeled. Thus, to each label there corresponds a fixed natural form. Almost inevitably, it turns out that such fixed natural forms correspond to the objects posited by the theories in which the psychologist-historian believes. Where it is not simply secondhand repetition, naturalistic history tends to be "justificationist" (Agassi, 1963) – it tends to suggest that the terms of current discourse have been determined by nature and not by art.

Clearly, the notion of generative metaphor points in a very different direction. It suggests that we treat the objects of psychological discourse not as things that were lying around waiting to be discovered, but as the product of generative schemata applied across various domains (Danziger, 1983, 1984). From this point of view the surface of past psychological discourse does not consist of a series of elements, each of which can be judged in terms of its literal correspondence with elements that appear in currently accepted discourse. Questions of historical continuity and discontinuity cannot be resolved by comparing elements in psychological discourse out of context. In fact, any phenotypical similarities and dissimilarities that emerge from such comparisons are apt to be quite misleading. Rather, what is needed is the uncovering and analysis of the different kinds of generative schemata that have resulted in various sorts of psychological discourse in the past. Such historical investigations, focusing on the underlying schemata that generate the elements that appear on the surface of discourse, are much more likely to contribute to our understanding of psychological discourse, including current discourse.

Problems in the historiography of psychology

My plea for the relevance of generative metaphor to the analysis of psychological discourse involves a (metaphorical) distinction between the surface and deeper layers of discourse. I would now like to consider the more specific significance of this distinction for the historiography of psychology.

The question is, How is an account of past psychological discourse to be structured? This question must be faced in a very concrete way by the authors of history texts and their readers. There have to be some principles of organization that determine the way in which the historical material is arranged and presented. Typically, authors will use a framework whose organization depends on some combination of chronology, individuals, and topic. All these aspects have far-reaching implications, but it is the last one that is the most problematic, for how does one determine that two (or ten) individuals, living several centuries (or two millennia) apart and writing in different languages, are talking about the same topic? The specific terms they use are obviously a poor guide, for the meanings of terms can – and indeed do – change quite radically over short periods of time, let alone centuries. In any case, psychological terms seldom have exact equivalents in different languages. Yet one wants to be able to identify those cases in which a difference of language is just that and nothing more.

Those volumes of historical readings that present brief extracts from various writers grouped by topic sometimes provide a transparent illustration of this problem. There we may find pages from a variety of texts assembled under section or chapter headings that refer to such categories as "intelligence," "motivation," "personality," "associative thinking," and so on. The selected excerpts are meant to illustrate different points of view or contributions regarding these topics. But the clear implication of such a scheme is that, while various authors have had different opinions *about* these topics, each topic as such corresponds to some fixed objective entity that is identified by the key term in the title of the selection. Almost invariably, those key terms are taken from the accepted vocabulary of twentieth-century (American) psychology and not from the vocabularies of the authors of the selected pre-twentieth-century texts. The use of contemporary terms strongly suggests that the objects of current psychological discourse are the real, natural objects and that past discourse necessarily referred to the same objects in its own quaint and subscientific way. What this organization of historical material overlooks is the possibility that the very objects of psychological discourse, and not just opinions about them, have changed radically in the course of history.

Naturalistic histories often proceed by taking elements of past psychological discourse out of their original context and placing them in the context of current discourse. It is the latter that supplies the titles by which the referents of discourse are identified, the implication being that those referents are what psychological discourse has always been about, even when the language was quite different. Of course, in many instances this may be correct, especially when we restrict ourselves to relatively recent times. My point is not that the assimilation of past to present discourse is necessarily wrong but that it is highly problematic. The disentangling of the genuine continuities and discontinuities of psychological discourse is a major task of historical analysis. When certain categories are effectively removed from this analysis because they are not thought to be theoretical categories but simply the names of natural objects, the result is likely to be an artificially imposed continuity that distorts historical realities. At least one historian (Smith, 1988) has been sufficiently surprised by the strange continuities assumed by psychologists to ask whether the history of psychology can be said to have a subject at all – and to give an essentially negative answer for the premodern period.

The fundamental distinction to be respected here is that between the symbolic objects that appear in psychological discourse and whatever it is outside this discourse that these symbols in some way signify. Psychological concepts like "intelligence" or "will" exist as such only on the level of discourse. The question of whether they refer to anything outside this discourse is a perfectly legitimate one, but it is not one to be prejudged and not one that should be confused with their analysis as discursive objects. When we study any kind of text, including modern research reports, the only objects we encounter are symbolic objects, and it is as such that we have to treat them.

Clearly, then, there are two kinds of question that we can raise about discursive objects. One concerns their relationship to some reality outside of discourse; the other involves their relationship to other discursive objects. In most cases the second question is logically prior to the first, for in order to make any judgments about the extradiscursive reference of anything that appears in discourse, we have to compare it with other information we have about that reference. But that information is generally available to us only in the form given to it by other discursive categories. So questions of reference cannot generally be decided rationally without the establishment of some kind of identity relationship between a number of discursive objects. In other words, we have to be sure that A and B are talking about the same thing X before we can use A's statement about X to correct, falsify, or reinforce B's statement about X. In many practical situations, within a short time span this may not raise many problems, but in the context of historical analysis it becomes the major problem.

Thus, before making assumptions about what a particular discursive object refers to, we ought to be clear about what exactly it is. But we can discover what it is only by examining its discursive context, its relationship to other symbolic objects. For instance, if a particular writer identifies intelligence with mental energy, that immediately provides us with an important clue about what sort of symbolic object his concept of intelligence is. Now, the identifying relationships that occur in psychological discourse are of two kinds: There are explicit literal definitions, and there are relationships of metaphorical analogy. On the whole, the latter tend to be more pervasive than the former. Therefore, the historical study of psychological discourse cannot afford to neglect the analysis of metaphorical relationships. If one is to avoid misidentifying the conceptual objects with which this discourse presents us, an understanding of any relevant metaphorical relationships seems to be indispensable.

Whereas discursive relationships of literal identity are generally quite explicit, those of metaphorical analogy are often more deeply hidden.

There are a variety of reasons why this should be so. In the modern period the authors of discourse are sometimes embarrassed by their reliance on metaphor. Because metaphors are not supposed to have a place in scientific discourse, they take care to bury their metaphors where they are less likely to arouse critical attention. But more often the metaphorical nature of many discursive relationships remains hidden and without an identifying label because they are taken to be self-evident or natural by the authors of discourse. When those hidden metaphors are similarly taken for granted by later students of such discourse, they tend to remain unrecognized and to function as unquestioned natural truths.

Metaphors may also remain hidden because they are not explicitly expressed in any single element of discourse, though they underlie the discourse as a whole. Thus, in certain instances an author may not inform us in so many words that he or she is using a mechanical metaphor, yet we are able to conclude with good reason that such a metaphor provides one of the conditions for the consistency and coherence of the discourse as a whole. In these cases what appears on the surface are the implications and consequences of a basic metaphor that itself is never summed up in so many words.

Confusion about identifying the appropriate categories of past discourse generally arises from two somewhat related sources of distortion. The one involves a failure to go beyond the surface of discourse to an analysis of its underlying cognitive schemata. This results in a kind of conceptual looseness that actually blocks any real analysis of the topic. Thus, a term like "association of ideas" may come to refer to the general conditions of coherent thought or to any influence of experience on cognition. In this situation an analysis of the metaphors used by different writers when treating such topics can help to bring some precision to an otherwise nebulous topic.

Another source of distortion in identifying the categories of historical discourse derives from the naturalistic attitude that I have already discussed. When one starts with the assumption that the natural facts are now known and that one's current discourse correctly represents those facts, it becomes fatally easy to see all kinds of references to the same natural facts in past discourse. For example, if one accepts a term like "associative thinking," not as an element in a particular kind of discourse, but as a label for a natural phenomenon whose existence is indubitable, then it is no longer necessary for an author to use the term for its meaning to be imputed to him. On this basis there is no limit to the "anticipations" of current discourse that history can offer to the undiscriminating reader. Sometimes this kind of approach serves the function of diminishing later developments, but more often it is used to legitimate current perspectives, which can then be seen as representing the real truth that earlier writers were straining to reach.

The history of associationism and the metaphor
of aggregation

To illustrate these rather general observations, I would like to turn to the history of associationism, a topic that can boast of a more extensive literature than most other topics in the historiography of psychology. I will not provide a comprehensive review of this literature, but will merely touch on certain aspects that are relevant in the present context.

In particular, I want to point to certain difficulties that arise when one tries to decide what properly belongs to the topic of associationism and what does not. Plainly, the doctrines of David Hartley, David Hume, James Mill, John Stuart Mill, and Bain must be included. But what of John Locke (1700/1959), who only mentions the association of ideas as an afterthought in the fourth edition of his major work, and then only as a way of accounting for mental connections that are not natural? Or Thomas Brown (1820), whose rejection of the term "association" is not just a matter of terminology, as is sometimes suggested, but the product of extensive critical analysis of fundamental issues? By what criteria would one decide whether the doctrines of Locke and of Brown are "really" to be grouped with those of the associationists? Presumably, one would need to identify some fundamental similarity that can be discerned below the surface of their writings. But what is the nature of this similarity?

The problem gets worse when we turn to other writers who do not even mention the association of ideas. Hobbes and Berkeley are the most obvious cases, but once it is no longer necessary to talk about associations in order to be included under the rubric of associationism, there is virtually no limit to what the historical imagination can accomplish. Leibniz and Spinoza have been enrolled in this club (Rapaport, 1974), as has Aristotle, the biggest catch of all.

The eighteenth-century founders of modern associationism were clearly aware of the novelty of their intellectual construction and did not refer to any predecessors. But as the "association of ideas" became a common element in the discourse of British empiricism, it was increasingly accepted as a natural fact, even by those who did not regard it as the sole principle of mental organization. This eventually led to a new reading of some very old texts that could now be interpreted as "anticipations" of currently accepted beliefs about the nature of the human mind.[1]

Typical of this kind of historiography is the awarding of good and bad marks to past authors, using current beliefs as criteria of truth: "In his account of Memory and Reminiscence, Aristotle displays an acute and penetrating intelligence of the great principles of the Association of Ideas."[2] Unfortunately, the key passage on which this praise is based occurs in Aristotle's treatment of reminiscence or recollection, which he distinguishes quite fundamentally from memory. Consequently, his

nineteenth-century interpreter proceeds to rap him over the knuckles for
the "exaggerated prominence that he has given to the distinction between
the two" since this "tends to perplex his description of the associative
process" (Grote, 1880/1973, p. 478). By the time this particular "origin
myth" (Samelson, 1974) enters the historical canon of twentieth-century
psychology, such subtleties have been lost and Aristotle's comments on
recollection are simply categorized with those of such authors as Hume,
Hartley, and Mill as dealing with the "associative nature of memory"
(see, e.g., Herrnstein & Boring, 1965). Past discourse is no longer permitted to speak in its own terms but is forced into categories of contemporary psychology that are quite alien to it.

Such an approach implies, of course, that nothing essentially new can
ever emerge from the study of past discourse. What is actually accomplished here is the reinforcement of an uncritical and unreflective acceptance of currently popular concepts that are confused with the order of
nature. Approached in this way the study of past psychological discourse
becomes a rather trivial activity, totally subservient to the prejudices of
the present. Once we stop automatically identifying the objects of past
discourse with the objects of *our* discourse, however, it becomes possible
for comparative historical studies to throw some light, by way of contrast,
on the categories of our own thinking, which we are too apt to take for
granted. There is an obvious analogy here with cross-cultural studies,
which, as is well known, often help to sharpen one's perspective on one's
own culture.

It is in the context of such comparative historical studies that an
analysis of metaphor can be particularly illuminating. One way of taking
past discourse seriously and actually allowing it to speak to us on its own
terms is to pay careful attention to its metaphors. Its metaphors identify
the kinds of objects it is speaking about, and the better we understand its
metaphors, the clearer we will be about the essential nature of its objects.

For instance, following our example of the association of ideas, let
us juxtapose what are probably the two most famous statements often
grouped under this topic:

> These are therefore the principles of union or cohesion among our
> simple ideas, and in the imagination supply the place of that in-
> separable connexion, by which they are united in our memory. Here
> is a kind of *Attraction*, which in the mental world will be found to
> have as extraordinary effects as in the natural, and to shew itself in
> as many and as varied forms. (Herrnstein & Boring, 1965, p. 348)

> Whenever, therefore, we are recollecting, we are experiencing cer-
> tain of the antecedent movements until finally we experience the
> one after which customarily comes that which we seek. This explains
> why we hunt up the series, having started in thought either from a

present intuition or some other, or from something either similar, or contrary, to what we seek, or else from that which is contiguous with it. (Herrnstein & Boring, 1965, p. 328)

The first statement is Hume's, the second Aristotle's.[3] Both accounts are strikingly metaphorical. But the contrast between their metaphors is profound. Aristotle's metaphor is that of the thinker as hunter; Hume's metaphor is based on an analogy between mental association and the attraction of physical bodies. Aristotle's account is completely agentic – it is we who "hunt" and "seek" – while Hume's account deals in impersonal forces of nature.[4] Now, if we take the so-called laws of association for what they are, namely, discursive rather than natural objects, it is clear that they are a product of Humean but not of Aristotelian discourse. Although the notion of "laws of association" is even more recent than Hume's own writings, its meaning depends entirely on the presuppositions expressed in Hume's analogy between the elements of the physical world and the elements of the mental world. The *metaphor* of association had to be constructed before the *conditions* of association could become an object of naturalistic investigation. In other words, the notion of "laws of association" as analogous to "laws of nature" is generated by a prior metaphorical identification of mental organization with physical elements and the forces of (gravitational) attraction they exert on one another.

By contrast, "laws of association" did not and could not become an object for Aristotelian discourse because the basic metaphorical framework that gives meaning to such a notion was absent. Instead, we get a completely different metaphorical framework that generates another set of discursive objects altogether.[5] Underlying the naturalistic assumption that Aristotle's mention of similarity or contiguity (in the crucial passage just quoted) ultimately must refer to the same thing as nineteenth-century "laws of association" is a primitive objectivist epistemology, according to which the basis of human discourse consists of neutral labels attached to preformed natural elements. The implication is that such terms as "contiguity" or "similarity" form part of a theory-neutral "observation language" on which various theories are subsequently superimposed. However, if we do not accept the axiomatic truth of this view and allow past psychological discourse to speak to us on its own terms, what we find are elements that change their meaning and significance as the generative metaphors in which they are embedded change. Thus, if the history of psychology is to do more than provide a justification for currently popular beliefs and categories, it will have to concern itself much more seriously with the analysis of basic cognitive schemata, metaphorical and otherwise, and with the factors involved in the change of such schemata.

For example, further analysis of Hume's analogy between mental association and physical attraction shows that it entails a highly distinctive model of psychological events. Talk about mental association as a quasi-Newtonian force is based on the assumption that the mental world is divisible into simple elements that are analogous to the ultimate corpuscular constituents of the Newtonian universe. Hume's analogy between mental and physical forces of attraction is an expression of a deeper, truly metaphorical identification of the structure of the mental world with the structure of a specific physical model. The essential features of this structure depend on the assumption that it functions as though it were composed of irreducible elements that retain their individual identity when they cohere to form compounds. The compounds can then be regarded as aggregates of such elements, and the relations among these elements are seen as external in the sense that the identity of the elements does not depend on the relations among them.

Although Hume does not employ this model with perfect consistency, it is quite pervasive in his treatment of psychological phenomena and leads to some very characteristic results. The best known and most radical of these is, of course, his reduction of the self to a collection of specific impressions. In other words, the association of ideas in the case of this author is not some limited theory of specific application to the phenomena of memory. Rather, it is a particularly direct expression of a very general structural schema or model that he considers applicable to all psychological phenomena. Hume's analogy between mental association and forces of physical attraction not only suggests that mental phenomena are explicable by "laws" that are analogous to the laws of Newtonian natural philosophy; it also implies that the mind and the Newtonian cosmos have analogous structures.

The relevant feature common to these structures is the particular type of part–whole relationship to which I have already alluded. It is characterized and constituted by the metaphor of aggregation, which operates as a master model, prescribing the formal characteristics of a vast range of phenomena. When this metaphor predominates, it predetermines the structure that objects have when they appear in psychological discourse. Whether the discourse deals with phenomena of memory, perception, motivation, or the self, its objects are presented as though they were compounded of elements whose identity is independent of the compound. Rather than functioning as a theory that could be tested against phenomena, the metaphor of aggregation serves as a blueprint that predetermines the presentation of the phenomena themselves. In this sense it generates the objects that exemplify it. Obviously, the metaphor of aggregation involves not a single metaphorical equation but an extended network of metaphorical relationships among a wide range of domains. As was indicated in the introductory section of this chapter, it is the existence of this kind of network that makes the analysis of metaphorical relationships an important aid in the understanding of the presuppositions of psychological discourse.

The importance of the metaphor of aggregation is significantly increased by the fact that it was not by any means the private property of a single author – even though that author be David Hume – but was a common basic feature of the psychological discourse of mature philosophical empiricism. Hartley's (1749/1967) associationism was based on it, as was the discourse of nineteenth-century associationism. When the philosophy of empiricism switched from taking sensations and ideas as its units to taking organism–environment (i.e., stimulus–response) units as basic, the metaphor of aggregation did not disappear. On the contrary, it became firmly embedded in that version of experimental methodology which assumed – and still assumes – that the structure of individual–environment relationships is a compound of elements whose identity and relation to one another is unaffected by the structure as a whole and their place in it.[6]

In the present context it is not possible to do more than hint at the importance of the metaphor of aggregation for modern psychology. The focus here is on the uses of metaphor, and reference to the metaphor of aggregation is intended merely to supply an example of one of the extended metaphors that have helped to shape modern psychological discourse. Such extended metaphors involve an "implicit or submerged model" of wide generality, and if one prefers one can refer to them as "archetypes" rather than metaphors, as Black (1962) suggests. The points to recognize are that metaphorical relationships may not be deliberately imposed but may remain implicit and that the relationship may link not just two domains but a whole series of domains. In other words, various domains may exhibit a certain identifiable homology of structure, and this homology would then constitute a major condition for the coherence of the discourse that contains these domains. When this occurs, it is as though the different sectors of the discourse reflect the same form, each in its own way, but the form itself never emerges except through the medium of these reflected images. Inside this hall of mirrors each image may be felt to "confirm" the others (Harrell, 1982, p. 229). This sense of "confirmation" may be particularly strong when the reflected images are experienced as extended backward in time, as in the naturalistic historiography I have criticized above. It may be even stronger when the structure is embedded in one's research practices whose products are then experienced as features of the world (Danziger, 1985; see also Gadlin & Ingle, 1975).

In any case, it is clear that root metaphors or archetypes are theory-constitutive. They predefine certain general features that are replicated in specific theories developed in various domains. Thus, the theory of the association of ideas was based on the metaphor of aggregation, though it was not the only form in which this metaphor found expression. Where this metaphor is absent, one cannot legitimately speak of an associationistic theory. At the same time, one cannot equate the overt theory with the presupposed form that it expresses. Classical associationism came close to being a pure representation of the underlying metaphor of aggregation, and yet it was not identical with it, for historically, archetypes (in Black's sense) have a life of their own that usually extends beyond the life of any of their specific theoretical expressions. Thus, the metaphor of aggregation survived the historical demise of classical associationism. Specific scientific theories may be put in jeopardy by empirical evidence, but underlying images of the nature of the world owe their life and death to factors of an altogether different order.

The example of associationism and the metaphor of aggregation illustrate how an analysis of underlying metaphorical schemata can provide a guide to genuine historical continuities and discontinuities. Without this level of analysis one runs the risk of ending up either with false continuities that amount to the construction of origin myths or with false discontinuities that break up into isolated contributions what is in fact a continuous discourse extended through time.

The multiple reference of extended metaphors

It is time to take the criticism of naturalism in the historiography of psychology one step further. Up to this point I have limited myself to questioning the appropriateness of applying *specific* modern psychological categories to discourse that is quite alien to them. However, I have continued to use the term "psychological discourse" itself as though this were an unproblematic category that could be applied in an abstract, ahistorical way. Of course, if I really believed this, I would be guilty of a gross form of that very naturalism I have been criticizing, for the notion of psychology as a separate subject matter, with its own quite distinctive concepts and categories, is surely a very recent one (Smith, 1988). The clear demarcation between psychological discourse and equally demarcated discourses that are philosophical, physiological, sociological, biological, and so on, is very largely a phenomenon that accompanies the institutional separation of these disciplines in historically recent times. To imagine that current conventions about dividing up university departments (and even subdepartments) are a reflection of the eternal natural divisions of the world virtually represents a *reductio ad absurdum* of the naturalistic attitude to intellectual history. I must therefore be explicit about the fact that my reference to "psychological discourse" is merely a shorthand notation resorted to as a matter of expository convenience. Some of the problems of this notation must now be unpacked.

In our own day we take for granted the existence of disciplinary languages that define their own objects in whatever ways are convenient to the various disciplinary language communities. Such languages, at least on the surface, are purely technical languages that are part of the constantly proliferating division of scientific labor. We do not expect the terms of such languages to have any intrinsic reference to objects other than those that are conventionally claimed by the discipline using the language. Thus, we expect psychological discourse to refer to psychological objects, sociological discourse to refer to sociological objects, and so on. However, we also know very well that real-world relationships do not respect disciplinary boundaries. In this situation, relationships that run counter to the way our disciplines have divided up the world have to be conceived in terms of the action of various kinds of disciplinary objects on each other. Thus, we think in terms of the reciprocal or unidirectional influence of psychological, sociological, and physiological "factors." What is not a regular part of a particular disciplinary or subdisciplinary discourse enters it in the form of *external* objects that act together with, or act on, the disciplinary objects but do not define their identity.

Though this may be the best way to proceed under present circumstances, we have to be careful about projecting our own disciplinary divisions backward in time. The boundaries of twentieth-century psychological discourse are twentieth-century boundaries. If we impose them on past discourse, we run the risk of confusing the reference of our own terms with the reference of analogous terms in a discourse that is not our own. For instance, the mixture of "psychological" and "physiological" references in the works of Aristotle leads to insoluble problems of interpretation unless we keep in mind that Aristotle "does not divide up the world at the same points" (see note 5) and that our post-Cartesian distinction between psychological and physiological discourse is not operative in this case.

But the same strictures apply to the interpretation of psychological discourse that is more directly linked with our own – for instance, the discourse of eighteenth-century empiricism. The reason historians of psychology have a legitimate interest in this discourse is that so many of the fundamental categories of subsequent psychological discourse originate there. Such categories as sensation, association, motivation, and stimulation began to be used in a recognizably modern way in the eighteenth century, and a study of their origins can throw considerable light on the way in which modern psychological discourse has come to organize its world. But this should not lead one to assume that such categories immediately take on the restricted technical reference they have for us. That restriction was the result of a fairly lengthy historical process. Originally, these categories were not part of the discourse of a segregated discipline of psychology, but were embedded in a much more general discourse on "human nature." This included much of what was later to be identified as the specific concern of fields like moral and political philosophy, political economy, and ultimately sociology and economics, as well as psychology per se. The process by which our modern disciplines were formed was a process of historical differentiation of older and more encompassing forms of discourse. In this process the specific objects of psychology, economics, and so on emerged, though the element of continuity with the parent discourse should not be overlooked.[7]

This early embedding of what to us are psychological categories in discourse that is not specifically psychological has one very important consequence. The real-world relationships, which in current specialized discourse are represented in terms of the influence or coaction of various discipline-defined "factors" that are external to one another, often appear in older, less differentiated discourse as metaphorical relationships among its objects. The early history of associationism once more provides us with a significant illustration of what is involved here. The classical associationists, without exception, developed their psychological theories in the context of a discourse that was directed primarily by social, moral, and political concerns.[8] Nowhere is this more apparent than in the major work of David Hartley (1749/1967), the most systematic and most "scientific" of the early associationists. Only by the most drastic surgery[9] was it ever possible to represent Hartley's work as that of some sort of precursor of a later "value-free" physiological psychology. However, modern scholarship has redressed the balance here and allowed us to see the moral context of his psychological ideas (Oberg, 1976; Verhave, 1973). But the situation is no different in the case of David Hume, whose very important conceptualization of psychological processes remains completely in the service of concerns that are not intrinsically psychological. That the transformation of the concept of the association of ideas into a general principle of mental functioning was motivated by the demands of empiricist moral philosophy emerges equally clearly in the contributions of less well known writers of this period (see Gay, 1731/1969; Long, 1747/1969).

As is well known, the crucial psychological contribution of this group of authors was the transformation of the concept of association from a principle that was invoked to explain "unnatural" reactions to one that became the foundation for a general psychology that sought to explain all of mental life. What was behind this transformation? Clearly, what had begun as a model of how certain psychological results might come about was being changed into a model of the structure of the mind as such. Both Hume (1739/1911) and Hartley (1749/1967) were aware of the homology of this model with the structure of the Newtonian physical universe. But there was another homology involved here that had already become incorporated into the language of association. In Warren's (1921) standard history of associationism there is a remarkable passage in which he observes that "the social contract theory...led to views regarding society which were quite favorable to the association psychology." The social theory and the psychological theory, he notes, have a similar "world view." More specifically,

> according to the social contract view, society...is an artificial union of human elements. And according to the earlier association theory ...the association of experiences is rather a mechanical reconstruction of elements into somewhat more intricate and complicated forms. Thus the two theories harmonized with each other and together constituted a tendency of thought during this period. (p. 162)

Had Warren pursued the matter, he might have discovered that the original psychological application of the term "association" did not constitute an arbitrary choice of a neutral term. Rather it represented a transfer of meaning from the social to the psychological level. This is documented in the first edition of Chambers's (1728) *Cyclopaedia*, which notes the derivation of "associate" from the Latin *socius*, a "fellow" or "companion," and then defines association as the "Act of associating or forming a Society or Company. Association is a Contract or Treaty of Partnership" (p. 161). After defining this primary meaning, it goes on to discuss the association of ideas, which was then a rather novel concept. More detailed documentation of the earlier, purely social meaning of "association" is provided by modern sources.[10] It seems likely that in the first half of the eighteenth century, when the purely psychological use of "association" was not yet something to be taken for granted, the social connotations of the term were inescapable.

Thus, it would appear that the introduction and popularization of the term "association of ideas" involved a metaphorical transfer of meaning from the social to the psychological level. Just as societies were considered to be formed by the combination of separate and independent persons, so individual minds could be thought of as formed by the association of separate mental elements. At first, the psychological application of the metaphor of association was limited, but fairly soon there was a recognition of the potential explanatory value to be derived from the extension of a model that had demonstrated its power in the social sphere to the essential functioning of the mind as a whole. What classical associationism accomplished was the establishment of a metaphorical homology among three levels of discourse, dealing respectively with the structure of society, the structure of the physical world, and the structure of the human mind. It was not just a technical psychological theory but implied an entire cosmology.

The cosmology itself was not the invention of the classical associationists, nor did they initiate the metaphorical extension of its archetypical schema to different kinds of discourse. On the level of social theory, the model of society as a combination of individuals – individuals whose essential attributes are independent of the social system whose elements they are – was already prominent in the work of Thomas Hobbes (1651/ 1958; see Macpherson, 1962). Subsequently, we meet an analogous model, applied to the physical world, in Newtonian natural philosophy. This philosophy, as Freudenthal (1986) has shown, is based on the presupposition that "the system of the world is composed of particles whose essential properties are attributable to them independently of their existence in this system" (p. 167). On the basis of his comparison between the Newtonian system and the rival system of Leibniz, Freudenthal concludes that there was an intimate link between the presuppositions of natural and political philosophy at the time. From the textual evidence it appears to me that this link was originally based on analogical extension rather than on logical inference. Against this background the classical associationists can be regarded as having systematically extended to the mental level an analogy that already existed between the system of nature and the social system. The link between an individualistic social theory and an elementaristic model of the individual mind proved to be extremely stable (Unger, 1975).

The cultural embeddedness of metaphors

The historical background of the metaphor of aggregation throws light on a more general issue, namely, the sociocultural embeddedness of psychological theory. Part of that embeddedness involves certain fundamental assumptions about the nature of the objects with which psychology is concerned. Where these objects are construed in terms of metaphorical homologies between the social order and the psychological order, the shape of the latter may come to be governed by the constraints imposed by the former. In other words, the structure of psychological objects is assumed to be such as to articulate with the structure of a certain kind of social order. Thus, to revert to the previous example, an individualistic image of society as an aggregate of elements, whose separate identities do not depend on the whole, may be structurally duplicated on the level of individual minds.

This kind of symbolic duplication has been documented for cultures that are remote from our own, but there is no good reason to exempt cultures closer to our own from this process. For instance, the anthropologist Mary Douglas (1973) has pointed out that "there are pressures to create consonance between the perception of social and physiological levels of experience." This means that culturally the human body is generally "treated as an image of society" (p. 98). Social boundaries, social hierarchies, and processes of social control tend to have their physiological counterparts. But if this kind of homology often obtains between social and physiological symbols, it is not really surprising to find that it also links social and psychological symbols. What happens here is a kind of mutual or reciprocal confirmation of the symbolic structure as incorporated in different levels of discourse. The structure of the body, or the mind, confirms the consonant structure of the social order, and vice versa. In this way some of the basic categories of psychology can be seen as being part of a culturally based cosmology. The structure of such a cosmology would be defined by a set of metaphorical relationships operating among various levels of discourse. It may well be that the sense of absolute conviction that generally characterizes belief in such a cosmology derives from the fact that, once inside the hall of mirrors, the same basic structure of the world seems to be reconfirmed over and over again wherever one looks.[11]

At this point it is appropriate to note that the effectiveness of archetypical metaphorical constructions depends quite crucially on their unintentional and taken-for-granted nature. In this way they are very different from novel literary metaphors that are intentionally invented by specific individuals for relatively short-term quasi-rhetorical purposes. By contrast, the origin of root metaphors cannot be traced to any single author; they are effectively "collective representations." Their life typically extends over long periods, and rather than being deliberately invented, the recognition of their metaphorical nature would probably destroy their effectiveness. Associationistic psychology, for example, could play a serious role, either as psychological theory or as a buttress for certain sociopolitical doctrines, only so long as it was taken literally. The recognition of its metaphorical kernel would have destroyed its credibility in both areas. To use a familiar analogy, the case is similar to that of repression. This too is a process that can do its work effectively only so long as there is no awareness that it is occurring.[12]

In the history of modern psychology one device in particular has tended to hide and to obscure the sociocultural basis of theoretical models. This involves the very common preoccupation with mechanical metaphors. From the hydraulically operated automata of Descartes and the mechanical clocks of the eighteenth century (McReynolds, 1980) to the computers of our own day, a succession of human artifacts has been appealed to as a source of psychologically relevant metaphors. It is these artifacts, rather than the social order that produced and utilized them, that have seemed to inspire some of the best known psychological metaphors of the past three centuries. But here one has to be careful to avoid the familiar naturalistic error that we have already had occasion to criticize. Certainly, one needs to understand on their own terms the mechanical metaphors that the history of psychology offers in such abundance. But one must also go beyond this, for the machine-like devices involved here are not simply found in nature; they do not stand on their own but are completely embedded in human social practice. Not only do mechanical clocks and electronic computers incorporate certain abstract design principles; they are also social artifacts, and as such they incorporate significant features of the social practices that produce and utilize them.

Clocks, steam engines, railways, hydraulic systems, telephone exchanges, computers, and so on, when they have been used as sources of psychological metaphors, have not been thought of as inert hardware, but as functioning systems. As functioning systems, they necessarily take their place within a certain social organization. Many kinds of society had and have no use for one or more of these devices, and if they adopt them they have to make the corresponding changes in their social organization. Thus, as functioning systems, these artifacts are also social elements that reflect certain social priorities and, above all, a certain organization of social activity.

So when the functioning of such artifacts is taken as prototypical for the functioning of aspects of the human mind or human behavior, this suggests, among other things, that a certain way of organizing social life is in accordance with human nature. Now, in a relative, historical sense this must be true, or the organization in which the artifacts are embedded would not be viable. What is misleading is the ahistorical nature of the claim that is implied. Perhaps, if we remember the essentially metaphorical nature of *all* artifactual analogies in psychology, we will be less inclined to apply inappropriate standards of universal literal truth to them (Lakoff, 1987, pp. 183–4). And perhaps, if we remember the social nature of all artifacts, we will be able to detect the limited, historical truth they represent, without turning them into fetishes from which we expect the final revelation about ourselves.

In order to prepare the way for such an approach, one crucial extension of our perspective on metaphor is necessary. I have been using a mirror analogy in order to convey certain aspects of metaphorical networks. But it is time for those mirrors to be broken, or else they will mislead us. The trouble with the mirror analogy is that it suggests a merely contemplative relationship to the world, and that, of course, is not how things are. The involvement of people in the various orders of reality that they represent to themselves is not just contemplative but practical and active. So their representations are not simply idle fancies but express particular concerns and goals. A metaphorical depiction of a particular subject matter is necessarily a partial depiction, and of course this is true whether it is conscious or unconscious. Out of the infinity of possible ways of construing the subject matter, one is picked out and given a privileged status. But which one is chosen depends on the preoccupations and special interests of those to whom the metaphor appeals.

One brief illustration of what is involved here must suffice. The notion of psychic energy was a dominant metaphor in psychological theory for nearly a century, not only in its Freudian version, but also in its Anglo-Saxon version, which goes back to the formulations of Carpenter (1850) and Bain (1873) and extends forward into twentieth-century American psychology. This metaphor was never just an intellectual exercise. In setting up an analogy between psychological processes and certain conceptions of physical energy, it also had certain practical implications. A fundamental property of physical energy was that it could not be created or destroyed, only transformed or made to flow along different paths. The transfer of this image to the psychological level was matched by the development of a tremendous concern with problems of psychological control. To see each individual as being subject to a force that is as blind as it is indestructible is necessarily to place on the agenda the question of psychological control mechanisms. Whether these control mechanisms were conceptualized in terms of habit mechanisms or in terms of Freudian mechanisms, there was a practical, programmatic aspect that was inseparable from the cognitive aspects of the metaphor of psychic energy.

When we remember that metaphors are not only cognitive constructions but are a part of communicative discourse, we recognize that they also have a programmatic aspect. When we define a certain part of the world metaphorically, this is not just an invitation to *think* about it in a certain way, it is also an invitation to *act* in terms of certain implied assumptions (Schön, 1979). By defining a particular object metaphorically we arouse certain expectations, focus attention on certain features, and thereby indicate certain priorities for practical action. Preferred metaphors tend to express particular concerns and interests that they translate into claims about the nature of the target of those concerns. When metaphors become extended and elaborated, they are transformed into models. This means that their programmatic aspects become more specific and technical. But it does not mean that they cease to express certain underlying concerns and interests. The elaboration of metaphors into models brings about a union of *telos* and technique (Wartofsky, 1968), which allows us to express problems in a way that already suggests the general nature of their solution.

The metaphorical networks of psychological discourse owe their significance to the work they do. Part of that work is performed on the level of cognition. By redefining and redescribing the subject matter, the use of such networks in effect makes available new objects for psychological scrutiny (Black, 1979). However, metaphors can be considered to have a generative function on yet another level. Undoubtedly, they take their place in what Wittgenstein (1953/1967) called "language games." But language games, as he also noted, must be seen in terms of broader constellations of activities, which he called "forms of life" (p. 23). The latter are not intellectual abstractions but "practical actualities" that depend on sociocultural forms. Stephen Toulmin (1969) has extended this line of analysis to suggest that the explanation of human actions involves placing them in the context of forms of life "whose significance goes without saying." One consequence of this insight is that descriptions of psychological characteristics should not be taken to refer to distinct entities and processes that inhabit the individual. Rather, as Toulmin notes, "they reflect our alternative ways of characterizing an agent, when we look at him from different standpoints and with different questions in mind" (p. 96).

Metaphorical definitions of psychological subject matter do not owe their importance to the fact that they may on occasion have private cognitive-heuristic functions (Hesse, 1980, p. 116). They become historically significant as a constituent of a public discourse that facilitates collective epistemic access (Boyd, 1979) to aspects of life that are experienced as problematic. In this function they are most effective when they describe the problematic features in terms of a framework that is grounded in understandings that are accepted without question within the community. But what is accepted without question changes culturally and also historically, a reflection that leads one to appreciate the dangers of misplaced arrogance with respect to currently fashionable explanatory metaphors.

Notes

1 The historiography of associationism makes a fascinating case study of the various ways in which the battles of the present are fought on the soil of the past. Ironically, it was the opponents of the "mechanical philosophy" of Hartley and Hume who first invented an ancient pedigree for associationism, the purpose being to discredit the new approach by showing that Aristotle and others had given a much better account of the key phenomena. In Britain, this argument begins with Coleridge (1817). Although Coleridge's fanciful scholarship was an easy target (Burton, 1846; Hamilton, 1846/1967; Mackintosh, 1830), the idea of a pedigree began to appeal to those who regarded the laws of association as obvious natural facts that must have been noticed by wise men of old. However, this meant that each version of nineteenth-century associationism interpreted the ancient texts in its own image. Compare, for instance, Hamilton's (1846/1967) Aristotle with Grote's (1880/1973).

2 On the significance of the awarding of marks by historians, see Agassi (1963) and Young (1966). The examples quoted here are from a work by Grote that was posthumously edited by his close associate, Alexander Bain, and by G. Croom Robertson. Part of Grote's (1880/1973) work on Aristotle was originally intended to form an appendix to the third edition of Bain's *The Senses and the Intellect* (1855/1872). In general, Grote wanted to show that what Aristotle

anticipated was not Scottish philosophy, as Hamilton had claimed, but something closer to the associationistic psychology of his friend, Bain. In spite of its dubious nature, the historical game of "anticipations" continues to attract both players and fans.

3 The passage from Aristotle is the one from which the fictional account of his "anticipation" of the laws of association takes off. It occurs in one of the minor works traditionally grouped together as the *Parva naturalia*, not in *De anima*. As several commentators (e.g., Ross, 1906/1973, pp. 260, 266) have noticed, one could just as well interpret a passage in Plato's *Phaedo* this way. I have quoted the Beare translation of Aristotle's statement that is used by Herrnstein and Boring (1965). The straightforward "hunt" is the usual English rendering, though the Hett translation used by Diamond (1974) has "follow the trail" (p. 251), which hardly affects the nature of the metaphor.

4 Of course, Hume drops into more agentic language at times, but this does not affect the contrast between different discursive objects that is being illustrated here. On Hume's "mental mechanism," see Lowry (1971, chap. 2).

5 See Sorabji (1979) on the futility of trying to force Aristotle into the categories of post-Cartesian philosophy: "He does not divide up the world at the same points" (p. 50).

6 Contemporary criticism of conventional experimental social psychology often takes the form of questioning the appropriateness of the metaphor of aggregation, Harré and Secord's (1972) being the already classical statement of this criticism. However, the operation of the metaphor of aggregation is not limited to this area but is likely to be manifest whenever an essentially additive view of psychological relationships prevails.

7 The emergence of specifically economic categories out of the older discourse, which did not clearly differentiate between them and moral, political, and psychological categories, has been traced in a particularly insightful way by Dumont (1977).

8 This was, of course, equally true of their nonassociationist contemporaries and immediate predecessors. On the moral basis of the psychological speculation of this period, see Leary (1980).

9 This involved physically or cognitively excising the entire second volume of his two-volume work – and a good part of the first volume as well.

10 For example, the *Oxford English Dictionary* notes such uses as "union in companionship on terms of social equality" (1660) and "a body of persons who have combined to execute a common purpose or advance a common cause" (1659).

11 It should be noted that there are at least two influential theoretical traditions that stress the primacy of social relations in the construction of such cosmologies. One of these derives from Marx, the other from Durkheim. For a radical development of the latter, applied to scientific concepts, see Bloor (1976). This issue is much too complex to be pursued here.

12 To avoid misunderstanding I should perhaps state explicitly that I am not suggesting that the operation of root metaphors literally depends on the psychological process of repression. What is possible, and may repay further investigation, is that both phenomena are instances of a broader, as yet unnamed category of psychological processes whose defining feature is that their effectiveness depends on their remaining inaccessible to metacognition.

References

Agassi, J. (1963). Towards an historiography of science. *History and Theory*, Beiheft 2.

Bain, A. (1872). *The senses and the intellect* (3rd ed.). New York: Appleton. (Original work published 1855.)
  (1873). *Mind and body: The theories of their relation*. New York: Appleton.

Berggren, D. (1963). The use and abuse of metaphor: II. *Review of Metaphysics, 16*, 450–72.

Black, M. (1962). *Models and metaphors*. Ithaca, NY: Cornell University Press.
  (1979). More about metaphor. In A. Ortony (Ed.), *Metaphor and thought* (pp. 19–43). Cambridge University Press.

Bloor, D. (1976). *Knowledge and social imagery*. London: Routledge & Kegan Paul.

Boyd, R. (1979). Metaphor and theory change: What is "metaphor" a metaphor for? In A. Ortony (Ed.), *Metaphor and thought* (pp. 356–408). Cambridge University Press.

Brown, T. (1820). *Lectures on the philosophy of the human mind* (vol. 1). Edinburgh: Tait.

Burke, K. (1966). *Language as symbolic action*. Berkeley and Los Angeles: University of California Press.

Burton, J. H. (1846). *Life and correspondence of David Hume* (vol. 1, pp. 286–8). Edinburgh: Tait.

Carpenter, W. B. (1850). On the mutual relations of the vital and physical forces. *Philosophical Transactions, 140*, 727–57.

Chambers, E. (1728). *Cyclopaedia: Or, an universal dictionary of arts and sciences* (vol. 1). London: Knapton.

Coleridge, S. T. (1817). *Biographia literaria*. London: Fenner.

Cua, A. S. (1982). Basic metaphors and the emergence of root metaphors. *Journal of Mind and Behavior, 3*, 251–8.

Danziger, K. (1983). Origins of the schema of stimulated motion: Towards a pre-history of modern psychology. *History of Science, 21*, 182–210.
  (1984). Towards a conceptual framework for a critical history of psychology. In H. Carpintero & J. M. Peiró (Eds.), *Psychology in its historical context: Essays in honour of Prof. Josef Brožek* (pp. 99–107). Valencia: Monografías de la Revista de Historia de la Psicología.
  (1985). The methodological imperative in psychology. *Philosophy of the Social Sciences, 15*, 1–13.

Diamond, S. (Ed.). (1974). *The roots of psychology: A sourcebook in the history of ideas*. New York: Basic Books.

Douglas, M. (1973). *Natural symbols*. Harmondsworth: Penguin Books.

Dumont, L. (1977). *From Mandeville to Marx: The genesis and triumph of economic ideology*. Chicago: University of Chicago Press.

Freudenthal, G. (1986). *Atom and individual in the age of Newton*. Dordrecht: Reidel.

Gadlin, H., & Ingle, G. (1975). Through the one-way mirror: The limits of experimental self-reflection. *American Psychologist, 30*, 1003–9.

Gay, J. (1969). Concerning the fundamental principle of virtue or morality. In D. D. Raphael (Ed.), *British moralists, 1650–1800* (vol. 1, pp. 411–21). Oxford: Clarendon Press. (Original work published 1731.)

Grote, G. (1973). *Aristotle* (2d ed.; A. Bain & G. C. Robertson, Eds.). New York: Arno Press. (Original work published 1880.)

Hamilton, W. (1967). Contribution towards a history of mental suggestion or association. In W. Hamilton (Ed.), *Thomas Reid: Philosophical works* (vol. 2, pp. 889–910). Hildesheim: Olms. (Original work published 1846.)

Harré, R., & Secord, P. (1972). *The explanation of social behaviour*. Oxford: Blackwell Publisher.

Harrell, B. J. (1982). The social basis of root metaphor: An application to *Apocalypse Now* and *The Heart of Darkness. Journal of Mind and Behavior, 3*, 221–40.

Hartley, D. (1967). *Observations on man*. Hildesheim: Olms. (Original work published 1749.)

Herrnstein, R. J., & Boring, E. G. (Eds.). (1965). *A source book in the history of psychology*. Cambridge, MA: Harvard University Press.

Hesse, M. (1980). The explanatory function of metaphor. In *Revolutions and reconstructions in the philosophy of science* (pp. 111–24). Bloomington: Indiana University Press.

Hobbes, T. (1958). *Leviathan*. Indianapolis, IN: Bobbs-Merrill. (Original work published 1651.)

Hume, D. (1911). *A treatise of human nature* (vol. 1). London: Dent. (Original work published 1739.)

Lakoff, G. (1987). *Women, fire, and dangerous things: What categories reveal about the mind*. Chicago: University of Chicago Press.

Leary, D. E. (1980). The intentions and heritage of Descartes and Locke: Toward a recognition of the moral basis of modern psychology. *Journal of General Psychology, 102*, 283–310.

Locke, J. (1959). Of the association of ideas. In *An essay concerning human understanding* (vol. 1, pp. 527–35; A. C. Fraser, Ed.). New York: Dover. (First published in 4th ed., 1700.)

Long, J. (1969). An inquiry into the origin of the human appetites and affections. In P. McReynolds (Ed.), *Four early works on motivation* (pp. 281–476). Gainesville, FL: Scholars' Facsimiles and Reprints. (Original work published 1747; Long's authorship uncertain.)

Lowry, R. (1971). *The evolution of psychological theory*. Chicago: Aldine.

Mackintosh, J. (1830). *Dissertation on the progress of ethical philosophy*. Edinburgh: Privately published.

Macpherson, C. B. (1962). *The political theory of possessive individualism*. New York: Oxford University Press.

McDougall, W. (1908). *An introduction to social psychology*. London: Methuen.

McReynolds, P. (1980). The clock metaphor in the history of psychology. In T. Nickles (Ed.), *Scientific discovery: Case studies* (pp. 97–112). Dordrecht: Reidel.

Oberg, B. B. (1976). David Hartley and the association of ideas. *Journal of the History of Ideas, 37*, 441–54.

Pepper, S. C. (1942). *World hypotheses*. Berkeley and Los Angeles: University of California Press.

Rapaport, D. (1974). *The history of the concept of association of ideas*. New York: International Universities Press.

Ricoeur, P. (1977). *The rule of metaphor* (R. Czerny, Trans.). Toronto: University of Toronto Press.

Ross, G. R. T. (1973). *Aristotle: "De sensu" and "De memoria."* New York: Arno Press. (Original work published 1906.)

Samelson, F. (1974). History, origin myth, and ideology: Comte's "discovery" of social psychology. *Journal for the Theory of Social Behavior, 4*, 217–31.

Schön, D. A. (1963). *Displacement of concepts*. New York: Humanities Press.
   (1979). Generative metaphor: A perspective on problem setting in social policy. In A. Ortony (Ed.), *Metaphor and thought* (pp. 254–83). Cambridge University Press.

Smith, R. (1988). Does the history of psychology have a subject? *History of the Human Sciences, 1*, 147–77.

Sorabji, R. (1979). Body and soul in Aristotle. In J. Barnes, M. Schofield, & R. Sorabji (Eds.), *Articles on Aristotle* (pp. 42–64). London: Duckworth.

Toulmin, S. (1969). Concepts and the explanation of human behavior. In T. Mischel (Ed.), *Human action: Conceptual and empirical issues* (pp. 25–60). New York: Academic Press.

Unger, R. M. (1975). *Knowledge and politics*. New York: Free Press.

Verhave, T. (1973). David Hartley: The mind's road to God. In T. Verhave (Ed.), *Hartley's theory of human mind*. New York: Johnson Reprint.

Warren, H. C. (1921). *A history of the association psychology*. New York: Scribner's.

Wartofsky, M. (1968). Telos and technique: Models as modes of action. In S. Anderson (Ed.), *Planning for diversity and choice: Possible futures and their relation to man-controlled environment* (pp. 140–8). Cambridge, MA: MIT Press.

Wittgenstein, L. (1967). *Philosophical investigations* (G. Anscombe, Ed.). Oxford: Blackwell Publisher. (Original work published 1953.)

Young, R. M. (1966). Scholarship and the history of the behavioural sciences. *History of Science, 5*, 1–51.

11

Metaphor, theory, and practice in the history of psychology

DAVID E. LEARY

The chapters of this volume provide more than ample illustration of the claim that "metaphor permeates all discourse, ordinary and special" (Goodman, 1976, p. 80), and they also demonstrate that metaphor is particularly vital "at the growing edges of science" (Quine, 1979, p. 159).

In these chapters we have seen that neuropsychological discourse has been advanced by the use of metaphors from telecommunications, control systems engineering, computer science, holography, and other developments in parallel distributed processing (Pribram, Chapter 2); that theoretical discussions of the emotions have revolved around metaphors of inner feelings, physiological responses, vestiges of animal nature, diseases of the mind, driving forces, and social roles (Averill, Chapter 3); that treatments of motivation have portrayed the human person as a pawn, an agent, a natural entity, an organism, or a machine (McReynolds, Chapter 4); that a vast array of cognitive metaphors have been insinuated into a variety of domains in psychology and related sciences, ranging from the metaphors of "vigilance" and "defense" in the field of perception through the "access skeletons" and "flavors" of artificial intelligence (Hoffman, Cochran, & Nead, Chapter 5); that separate traditions proposing "reproductive" versus "productive" theories of cognition have evolved from diverse views of consciousness as either a passive *mirror* of reality or an active *molder* of experience (Bruner & Feldman, Chapter 6); that there is a rich history of behaviorist metaphors, extending from Descartes's reflected spirits and Pavlov's psychic reflexes through Tolman's mazes, Hull's machines, and Skinner's selection by consequences (Smith, Chapter 7); that whereas traditional discussions of social groups have typically utilized organismic, animalistic, and physicalistic metaphors, recent social scientific discourse has tended to view social life from the metaphoric perspectives of the animal laboratory, mechanistic regulation, meaningful relations, and systems theory (Gergen, Chapter 8); that there is a long history of categorizing and reifying unwanted conduct through the use of "mental illness," "hysteria," "schizophrenia," "hallucination," and other such loosely warranted metaphors (Sarbin, Chapter 9); and that an analysis of the historical roots of modern associationism, besides revealing the importance of cultural context in the articulation of basic psychological metaphors, suggests that a fuller understanding of the role of metaphor will involve a broader consideration of metaphor's place within psychological discourse as a whole (Danziger, Chapter 10).

What may not have been so amply highlighted in the foregoing chapters, simply by virtue of their preordinate emphasis on the role of metaphor in the construction of psychological *theory*, is the extent to which metaphors are associated with the *practical routines* of day-to-day behavior – with the "dramas," "rituals," and "performances" that fill the lives of psychologists and their public.[1] As psychologists learn through metaphorical comparisons to see certain "commonalities in objects or situations," they rather naturally come to behave in a similar fashion toward these objects or situations (see Gardner, 1982, p. 166). Thus, if some psychologists conceptualize the mind as a computational device whose instrumentalities and procedures can be specified once and for all, whereas others think of the mind as an organic entity that changes both structurally and functionally over the course of a lifetime, they will adopt very different methodological practices in their psychological investigations. Similarly, if clinical or counseling psychologists consider members of the public to be their "clients" rather than their "patients," they are likely to orient their professional interactions in distinctive ways. In other words, the metaphors psychologists use to construe the objects and subjects of their concern are related – often in fundamental ways – to the methodological and social practices in which they engage.[2]

The commerce between metaphor and practice, like that between theory and practice, can be conducted in both directions. Metaphors can be drawn from the realm of the practical just as practical routines can be derived from the metaphorical conceptions underlying theoretical discourse. Furthermore, just as practice can be shaped by metaphor, so too can the creative extension or amendment of metaphors be facilitated or constrained by various practical factors and considerations.[3] For this reason, metaphorical thinking, in science as elsewhere, can hardly be treated, in its fullness, as some sort of disembodied or radically free play of the mind, limited (if at all) only by the past experiences, cognitive habits, and biases of individuals. That such treatments are sometimes proposed is sufficient cause for Knorr-Cetina's (1981, chap. 3) repeated insistence that metaphorical or analogical theories of scientific innovation are incomplete. It is certainly true, as she argues, that scientists must "work out" or "realize" metaphorical concepts in the tangible, nitty-gritty process of "knowledge production" that takes place in the labora- tory or clinic before any truly consequential innovations can be brought about. It is also true that the theoretical articulation of a metaphor often occurs closer to the end than to the beginning of the research process. Clearly, as Knorr-Cetina (1981) says, "the process of research production and reproduction is more complex than the equation of metaphor and innovation suggests" (p. 66).[4]

Furthermore, in addition to the social norms, institutional structures, and practical routines that may seem more immediately indigenous to scientific workplaces, the context of the production *and selective con-sumption* of research is composed of cultural values and constructs. As Durkheim (1912/1965) said long ago:

> It is not at all true that concepts, even when constructed according to the rules of science, get their authority uniquely from their objective value. It is not enough that they be true to be believed. If they are not in harmony with the other beliefs and opinions, or, in a word, with the mass of the other collective representations [the concepts taken for granted by most people in a given time and place], they will be denied; minds will be closed to them; conse- quently it will be as though they did not exist. (p. 486)

Investigating the social historical context as well as the social historical influence of any given metaphor will prove essential if we are to know not just that metaphors play an important role in the history of science, but why *this* or *that* particular metaphor plays *this* or *that* role at *this* or *that* time and in *this* or *that* place. In this regard, Kurt Danziger's call (in this volume) for careful attention to the sociocognitive or cultural setting of psychological theory and practice is very well justified. It is critical that we heed such calls if we are to carry the program of research initiated in this volume to its completion – or if we are, at the very least, to start down the path that future research must take. I would characterize this path by saying that it leads through the newly emerging field of the *rhetoric of science* toward an even wider concern with what might be called the *pragmatics of science*.

To situate these new and prospective fields, with special reference to the history of psychology, I would begin by noting that the practice of psychology is clearly framed and supported by the kind of social and institutional structures studied by sociologists of science. Beyond that, it is held together by the finer webs of cultural, historical, linguistic, and personal relations that anthropologists, historians, psychologists, *and rhetoricians* like to investigate. The subject matters of these various disciplines may be said to revolve around the problems and processes of community and communication. Science, as one of these subject matters, may seem to begin with the attempt to specify and clarify the products of perception, but as David Bohm (1977) has put it:

> the very act of perception is shaped and formed by the intention to communicate, as well as by a general awareness of what has been communicated in the past, by oneself and others. Even now, it is generally only in communication that we deeply understand, that is, perceive the whole meaning of, what has been observed. So there is no point in considering any kind of separation of perception and communication. (p. 374)

A similar awareness of the social context of perception – and of all that follows *after* perception in the standard conceptualization of scientific "knowledge production" – has been at the root of the recent "rhetorical turn" in historical and philosophical studies of science.[5] The investigation of the role of metaphor in the history of science is both a cause and an effect of this turn, and it invites the next step into a full-blown rhetoric of science.

To speak of the rhetoric of science is not to imply that science is some kind of mere word play, any more than speaking of metaphorical thinking in science commits one to such a view. To attend to the rhetoric of science is simply to acknowledge the potential significance of the fact that science – like all knowledge – is achieved *through* and *by means of* symbolic activity, especially linguistic activity. This linguistic activity includes the use of alternative sign systems (such as those composed of numbers) as well as the use of various distinctive means of argumentation and persuasion (such as standardized publication formats) that are intended both to capture and to communicate a particular sort of "grasp" on reality.[6]

An understanding of the pragmatics of science – the all-inclusive set of tangible practices that constitute how science actually *works* – lies on the other side of, and will encompass, an understanding of the rhetoric of science. Since we are presently far from enjoying a complete understanding of the latter, the pragmatics of science can be seen, for now, only as a heuristic goal toward which current and future research should aim. Still, it should prove useful to keep this goal in mind and to strive to reach it, all the more so because a complete understanding of the actual workings of science would be extraordinarily valuable.

Why is this so? Why would an understanding of the pragmatics of science be so important? Because *for better and worse*, science, including psychology and its many professional offshoots, has been woven into the very fiber of our culture. It has become an essential source of our culture's material goods, social practices, emotional comforts, and spiritual values – as it has also become associated with many of our culture's significant tensions, material dangers, social inequities, emotional distresses, and spiritual crises.

If the metaphors of science can "make one feel at home," as Freud (1933/1964, p. 77) once put it, they can also serve – and have served – to dislocate humans from their once taken-for-granted position in the world. If we are to "figure out" not only the nature and history of science and psychology, but also the contours and relations of a future world that would be more worthy and supportive of habitation, our metaphors and their encompassing rhetoric must be carefully selected, thoughtfully crafted, and judiciously used.

This volume marks only a beginning. Its individual chapters provide initial forays into largely uncharted territories, and they raise a number of issues that deserve further consideration.[7] As first steps go, this volume seems to be a good, solid one. Nonetheless, it begs for a sequel, for additional steps toward an understanding of the role of metaphor in the theory and practice of psychology – and toward a future that we can only imagine at the present time.

Notes

1 These term – "dramas," "rituals," and "performances" – are drawn from the work of Victor Turner (1974) and James Fernandez (1986). For other discussions of the "social use of metaphors" or the instantiation of metaphors in everyday life, see Sapir and Crocker (1977). For related discussions, see Edge (1974), Gouldner (1974), and Schön (1979). Some recognition was given to the practical import of psychological metaphors in Chapter 1 (e.g., in notes 52 and 53) as well as in other chapters (e.g., Chapter 8, by Gergen; Chapter 9, by Sarbin; and Chapter 10, by Danziger), but much more remains to be said.

2 Sarbin (Chapter 9) has pointed out the relation between the conceptual metaphors and therapeutic practices of behavioral therapists, psychodynamic therapists, existential therapists, and social systems therapists. Besides implicitly structuring the therapeutic situation, metaphors can also be used explicitly within the psychotherapeutic interchange, as the means by which both inner states and external problems can be identified, communicated, and resolved. See Barker (1985), Cox and Theilgaard (1987), Haley (1976), and Mills and Crowley (1986) for examples of such uses. For related discussions of "metaphors we live by" and "metaphors of living," see Lakoff and Johnson (1980) and Mair (1977), respectively. Also see White (1987) for an analysis of the folk wisdom embodied in proverbs, which appear to be a "special case of the more general process of metaphorical understanding" (p. 153). At the other end of the spectrum, see Sontag (1978, 1988) for discussions of metaphors of disease and dying. Although she admits that there can be no thinking without metaphors, Sontag has castigated the use of the metaphors that have come to be associated with cancer and AIDS, precisely because of the devastating effects they have on the victims of these diseases – on their hopes and fears, their self-images, and the ways they are considered and treated by others.

Insofar as she is correct about these effects of metaphorical thinking (and it is only the degree and not the influence itself that seems to me to be at issue), her examples provide a poignant demonstration of the impact of metaphors on the practical conduct of day-to-day lives. An awareness of such practical impact should increase the perceived need for the "management of metaphor" (Simons, 1981).

3 For instance, Danziger's treatment of associationism (Chapter 10, this volume) illustrates the reshaping of an old metaphor that can take place in a new cultural context. Similarly, Hoffman, Cochran, and Nead's essay (Chapter 5) is full of examples of conceptual and theoretical developments that had to await the creation of appropriate technological analogs. Indeed, each chapter in this volume offers examples that similarly reflect the influence of practical reality on theoretical formulation.

4 On the social practices associated with the production of research, see Latour and Woolgar (1979) and Star (1983) as well as Knorr-Cetina (1981). Morawski (1988) has discussed the "social bases of psychologists' work." With regard to the broader social context of scientific work, Brannigan (1981), Csikszentmihalyi (1988), Gruber and Davis (1988), and Rosenberg (1976), among many others, have begun to clarify the social origins and environment of scientific innovation, and O'Donnell (1985) has mapped out some of the social dimensions of the rise of American psychology around the turn of the century. The latter treatments of the encompassing social context are relevant to, but not equivalent to, the "closer" analyses of the social processes at work *within* the research environment to which I referred in the first sentence of this note.

5 Rhetoric, of course, is the art or science of spoken or written discourse, of the use of figures of speech and grammatical forms in the composition and communication of thought and feeling, of the effective use of speech and writing, with the particular aim to influence and persuade. The "rhetorical turn" in the study of science can be traced along one line to Toulmin's (1958) work on the "uses of argument," which helped to set the scene for the subsequent shift from the study of the rational logic of science to the study of the reasonable modes of argumentation in science, and along another line to Perelman and Olbrechts-Tyteca (1959/1969), who are frequently credited with reviving interest in rhetoric and its applications. Kuhn's (1970) work must also be cited as an important predecessor. Earlier predecessors, not directly influential on this shift, include Giambattista Vico (1744/1948; see Berlin, 1977; Mooney, 1985) and John Dewey. Dewey (1929/1960), following a line established by William James, argued for a distinction between old-fashioned "reason" and now-preferable "intelligence." According to this distinction, the strictly logical implementation of reason (in deducing necessary consequences of indubitable facts and assumptions) is associated with the old and unattainable ideal of achieving certain knowledge that exactly "mirrors" a presumably static world, whereas the instrumental use of intelligence (in making and continually revising contingent judgments) is associated (in Dewey's scheme) with an acceptance of the uncertainty inherent in a world in which the practical activity of coming-to-know helps to shape the reality-that-is-known. (For the essays of a contemporary Deweyan, see Rorty, 1982.) Like Toulmin, Dewey (1929/1960) used the *practicing* physician as the model of knowledge-in-action: The physician "draws upon a store of general principles of physiology, etc., already at command. Without this store of conceptual material he is helpless. But he does not attempt to reduce the case to an exact specimen of certain laws of physiology and patholo-

gy, or do away with its unique individuality. Rather he uses general statements as aids to direct his observation of the particular case, so as to discover what it is *like*. They function as intellectual tools or instrumentalities" (p. 207).

This shift of focus from rationality to reasonableness, from logic to argumentation, from the suppression to the recognition of the role and importance of rhetoric and practice reflects a "revolution" from theoretical ways of *knowing* to practical ways of *understanding*. Despite the fact that his own work preceded the recent shift by more than two centuries, Vico's emphasis on practical wisdom – on *sapientia* or *prudentia* rather than *scientia* – is a useful emblem of this "turn," especially insofar as this recent shift toward "postrational reasonableness" (as Pepper, 1942, christened it from afar) has raised long-overlooked issues regarding the value dimensions and practical import of knowledge and science. (For a related discussion of the "recovery" of practical concerns in philosophy, see Toulmin, 1988.)

Recent works on the rhetoric of science include Benjamin, Cantor, and Christie (1987), Knorr-Cetina (1981, chaps. 5 and 6), Leary (1987), McCloskey (1985), Nelson and Megill (1986), Nelson, Megill, and McCloskey (1987), Overington (1977), Schuster and Yeo (1986), Simons (1989), Weimer (1977, 1979), and Yearley (1981). For some reason, anthropologists have been particularly sensitive to the rhetorical dimension of their discipline. Clifford and Marcus (1986), Geertz (1988), Landau (1984), and Payne (1981) are but a few of many examples. On the relationship between rhetoric and moral action, see Jonsen and Toulmin (1988). Of the many works and developments in contemporary psychology that are consonant with the new interest in rhetoric, see Billig (1987), Bronfenbrenner, Kessel, Kessen, and White (1986), Bruner (1986), Gergen (1985), Gergen and Gergen (1983), Harré (1980), Kessen (1979), Polkinghorne (1988), Sarbin (1986), Scarr (1985), Schank and Abelson (1977), and Spence (1982). Brinton (1982) has addressed the relationship between William James's thought and the "epistemic view of rhetoric."

I have discussed the responsiveness of psychologists to their audience elsewhere (Leary, 1987). An additional illustration is provided by William James's statement: "I have found by experience that what my hearers seem least to relish is analytical technicality, and what they care for is concrete practical application. So I have gradually weeded out the former, and left the latter unreduced. ... In taking my cue from what has seemed to me to be the feeling of the audiences, I believe that I am shaping my books so as to satisfy the more genuine public need" (quoted in Vidich & Lyman, 1985, p. 68). Compare this statement with the definition of rhetoric at the beginning of this note.

6 Contrary to frequent denials, such as Clark Hull's (1943) strenuous (and ironic) argument against argumentation in science (pp. 7–9), science obviously *does* aim to persuade. Despite his own "mechanomorphic" metaphors (e.g., pp. 27–8), Hull, like so many other scientists, suffered from "tropophobia" as well as "rhetorophobia." (The poet Donald Hall, 1985, defined "tropophobia" as the "fear and loathing of metaphors.") However acute and misplaced, Hull's concern about rhetoric in science was not completely without cause. There are, in fact, a variety of ways of arguing and trying to persuade, and surely many types of discourse have less precise and less exacting standards and procedures than does science. Still, argument or persuasion is nonetheless what the scientific process aims toward. Even Rudolf Carnap, the premier logical empiricist philosopher of science, had no problem accepting this: He began his classic work on *The Logical Structure of the World* (1928/1967) with an unapologetic acknowledgment that the purpose of a scientific work is "to persuade the reader

of the validity of the thoughts which it presents" (p. xv). To clarify the forms
and means of scientific persuasion is what the rhetoric of science is all about.

7 As mentioned in my earlier chapter, one of the issues worthy of further study is
the following: What might be gained by making finer discriminations between
metaphor and other figures of speech and thought in the analysis of the ways in
which such figures have constituted, supported, and influenced psychological
theory and practice? It would also be useful to pursue more detailed analyses of
the different functions that metaphors can and have performed in the history of
psychology. To name only a few of these functions, some of which have been
noted in the preceding chapters, metaphors can be descriptive or explanatory,
illustrative or constitutive, informative or evaluative, revealing or masking,
enriching or deforming. This list of functions should not be taken as even
approximately definitive, nor should the *or* in these pairings be taken as
indicative of categorical or absolute distinctions. Seemingly "descriptive" or
"illustrative" metaphors, for instance, need not be simply (i.e., neutrally or
passively) "communicative" – they may actually help to *constitute* the "object"
or "event" to which they refer and/or imply (i.e., tilt the balance toward) a
certain type of explanation or a particular form of practical intervention.
Nineteenth-century analyses of the "irrational mob" and twentieth-century
discussions of "hyperactivity" may serve as examples.

Other important issues for future study revolve around the classic "Kantian,"
"Peircean," and "Jamesian" questions: How is metaphor possible *at all*? What
makes a particular metaphor more *apt* – and more *probable* to occur – in any
given context? And how are the *multiple dimensions* of rationality, including
the aesthetic, moral, and practical as well as intellectual dimensions, brought
to bear on the assessment of the truthfulness of metaphors? How metaphor
works, the nature of the constraints delimiting its operation, and the entire set
of issues related to the nature and attribution of "truth" are all relevant to
future inquiry along the lines established in this volume. Fortunately, contemporary researchers from many disciplines – from linguistics, psychology, and
philosophy, among others – are advancing our understanding of these matters
and thus preparing the way for a fuller understanding of the role of metaphor in
the history of psychology.

References

Barker, P. (1985). *Using metaphors in psychotherapy*. New York: Brunner-Mazel.
Benjamin, A. E., Cantor, G. N., & Christie, J. R. R. (Eds.). (1987). *The figural
    and the literal: Problems of language in the history of science and philosophy*.
    Manchester: Manchester University Press.
Berlin, I. (1977). The philosophical ideas of Giambattista Vico. In *Vico and
    Herder: Two studies in the history of ideas* (pp. 1–142). New York: Random
    House.
Billig, M. (1987). *Arguing and thinking: A rhetorical approach to social psychol-
    ogy*. Cambridge University Press.
Bohm, D. (1977). Science as perception-communication. In F. Suppe (Ed.), *The
    structure of scientific theories* (2d enl. ed., pp. 374–91). Urbana: University of
    Illinois Press.
Brannigan, A. (1981). *The social basis of scientific discoveries*. Cambridge Uni-
    versity Press.
Brinton, A. (1982). William James and the epistemic view of rhetoric. *Quarterly
    Journal of Speech, 68*, 158–69.

Bronfenbrenner, U., Kessel, F., Kessen, W., & White, S. (1986). Toward a critical social history of developmental psychology: A propaedeutic discussion. *American Psychologist, 41*, 1218–30.

Bruner, J. (1986). *Actual minds, possible worlds*. Cambridge, MA: Harvard University Press.

Carnap, R. (1967). *The logical structure of the world* (R. A. George, Trans.). Berkeley and Los Angeles: University of California Press. (Original work published 1928.)

Clifford, J., & Marcus, G. E. (Eds.). (1986). *Writing culture: The poetics and politics of ethnography*. Berkeley and Los Angeles: University of California Press.

Cox, M., & Theilgaard, A. (1987). *Mutative metaphors in psychotherapy: The aeolian mode*. London: Tavistock.

Csikszentmihalyi, M. (1988). Society, culture, and person: A systems view of creativity. In R. J. Sternberg (Ed.), *The nature of creativity: Contemporary psychological perspectives* (pp. 325–39). Cambridge University Press.

Dewey, J. (1960). *The quest for certainty: A study of the relation of knowledge and action*. New York: Putnam's. (Original work published 1929.)

Durkheim, E. (1965). *The elementary forms of the religious life* (J. W. Swain, Trans.). New York: Free Press. (Original work published 1912.)

Edge, D. (1974). Technological metaphor and social control. *New Literary History, 6*, 135–47.

Fernandez, J. W. (1986). *Persuasions and performances: The play of tropes in culture*. Bloomington: Indiana University Press.

Freud, S. (1964). New introductory lectures on psycho-analysis. In J. Strachey (Ed. and Trans.), *The standard edition of the complete psychological works of Sigmund Freud* (vol. 22, pp. 1–182). London: Hogarth Press. (Original work published 1933.)

Gardner, H. (1982). *Art, mind, and brain: A cognitive approach to creativity*. New York: Basic Books.

Geertz, C. (1988). *Works and lives: The anthropologist as author*. Stanford, CA: Stanford University Press.

Gergen, K. J. (1985). The social constructionist movement in modern psychology. *American Psychologist, 40*, 266–75.

Gergen, K. J., & Gergen, M. M. (1983). Narratives of the self. In T. R. Sarbin & K. E. Scheibe (Eds.), *Studies in social identity* (pp. 254–73). New York: Praeger.

Goodman, N. (1976). *Languages of art: An approach to a theory of symbols*. Indianapolis, IN: Hackett.

Gouldner, A. W. (1974). The metaphoricity of Marxism and the context-freeing grammar of socialism. *Theory and Society, 1*, 387–414.

Gruber, H. E., & Davis, S. N. (1988). Inching our way up Mount Olympus: The evolving systems approach to creative thinking. In R. J. Sternberg (Ed.), *The nature of creativity: Contemporary psychological perspectives* (pp. 243–70). Cambridge University Press.

Haley, J. (1976). Communication as bits and metaphor. In *Problem-solving therapy* (pp. 81–99). San Francisco: Jossey-Bass.

Hall, D. (1985, July 14). A fear of metaphors. *New York Times Magazine*, pp. 6–8.

Harré, R. (1980). Man as rhetorician. In A. J. Chapman & D. M. Jones (Eds.), *Models of man* (pp. 201–13). Leicester: British Psychological Society.

Hull, C. L. (1943). *Principles of behavior: An introduction to behavior theory*. New York: Appleton-Century-Crofts.

Jonsen, A. R., & Toulmin, S. (1988). Rhetoric and the springs of moral action. In *The abuse of casuistry: A history of moral reasoning* (pp. 293–303). Berkeley and Los Angeles: University of California Press.

Kessen, W. (1979). The American child and other cultural inventions. *American Psychologist, 34*, 815–20.

Knorr-Cetina, K. D. (1981). *The manufacture of knowledge: An essay on the constructivist and contextualist nature of science.* New York: Pergamon.

Kuhn, T. S. (1970). *The structure of scientific revolutions* (2d enl. ed.). Chicago: University of Chicago Press.

Lakoff, G., & Johnson, M. (1980). *Metaphors we live by.* Chicago: University of Chicago Press.

Landau, M. (1984). Human evolution as narrative. *American Scientist, 72*, 262–8.

Latour, B., & Woolgar, S. (1979). *Laboratory life: The social construction of scientific facts.* Beverly Hills, CA: Sage.

Leary, D. E. (1987). Telling likely stories: The rhetoric of the new psychology, 1880–1920. *Journal of the History of the Behavioral Sciences, 23*, 315–31.

McCloskey, D. N. (1985). *The rhetoric of economics.* Madison: University of Wisconsin Press.

Mair, M. (1977). Metaphors for living. In A. W. Landfield (Ed.), *Nebraska Symposium on Motivation* (pp. 243–290). Lincoln: University of Nebraska Press.

Mills, J. C., & Crowley, R. J. (1986). *Therapeutic metaphors for children and the child within.* New York: Brunner-Mazel.

Mooney, M. (1985). *Vico in the tradition of rhetoric.* Princeton, NJ: Princeton University Press.

Morawski, J. G. (1988). Impossible experiments and practical constructions: The social bases of psychologists' work. In J. G. Morawski (Ed.), *The rise of experimentation in American psychology* (pp. 72–93). New Haven, CT: Yale University Press.

Nelson, J. S., & Megill, A. (1986). Rhetoric of inquiry: Projects and prospects. *Quarterly Journal of Speech, 72*, 20–37.

Nelson, J. S., Megill, A., & McCloskey, D. N. (Eds.) (1987). *The rhetoric of the human sciences: Language and argument in scholarship and public affairs.* Madison: University of Wisconsin Press.

O'Donnell, J. M. (1985). *The origins of behaviorism: American psychology, 1870–1920.* New York: New York University Press.

Overington, M. A. (1977). The scientific community as audience: Toward a rhetorical analysis of science. *Philosophy and Rhetoric, 10*, 143–64.

Payne, H. C. (1981). Malinowski's style. *Proceedings of the American Philosophical Society, 125*, 416–40.

Pepper, S. C. (1942). *World hypotheses: A study in evidence.* Berkeley and Los Angeles: University of California Press.

Perelman, C., & Olbrechts-Tyteca, L. (1969). *The new rhetoric: A treatise on argumentation* (J. Wilkinson & P. Weaver, Trans.). Notre Dame, IN: University of Notre Dame Press. (Original work published 1959.)

Polkinghorne, D. E. (1988). *Narrative knowing and the human sciences.* Albany: State University of New York Press.

Quine, W. V. O. (1979). A postscript on metaphor. In S. Sacks (Ed.), *On metaphor* (pp. 159–60). Chicago: University of Chicago Press.

Rorty, R. (1982). *Consequences of pragmatism.* Minneapolis: University of Minnesota Press.

Rosenberg, C. E. (1976). *No other gods: On science and American social thought.* Baltimore, MD: Johns Hopkins University Press.

Sapir, J. D., & Crocker, J. C. (Eds.). (1977). *The social use of metaphor: Essays on the anthropology of rhetoric.* Philadelphia: University of Pennsylvania Press.

Sarbin, T. R. (Ed.). (1986). *Narrative psychology: The storied nature of human conduct.* New York: Praeger.

Scarr, S. (1985). Constructing psychology: Making facts and fables for our times. *American Psychologist, 40,* 499–512.

Schank, R. C., & Abelson, R. P. (1977). *Scripts, plans, goals and understanding.* Hillsdale, NJ: Erlbaum.

Schön, D. A. (1979). Generative metaphor: A perspective on problem setting in social policy. In A. Ortony (Ed.), *Metaphor and thought* (pp. 254–83). Cambridge University Press.

Schuster, J. A., & Yeo, R. R. (Eds.). (1986). *The politics and rhetoric of scientific method: Historical studies.* Dordrecht: Reidel.

Simons, H. W. (1981). The management of metaphor. In C. Wilder-Mott & J. H. Weakland (Eds.), *Rigor & imagination: Essays from the legacy of Gregory Bateson* (pp. 127–48). New York: Praeger.

(Ed.) (1989). *Rhetoric in the human sciences.* Beverly Hills, CA: Sage.

Sontag, S. (1978). *Illness as metaphor.* New York: Farrar, Straus & Giroux.

(1988). *AIDS and its metaphors.* New York: Farrar, Straus & Giroux.

Spence, D. P. (1982). *Narrative truth and historical truth: Meaning and interpretation in psychoanalysis.* New York: Norton.

Star, S. L. (1983). Simplification in scientific work: An example from neuroscience research. *Social Studies of Science, 13,* 206–28.

Toulmin, S. (1958). *The uses of argument.* Cambridge University Press.

(1988). The recovery of practical philosophy. *American Scholar, 57,* 337–52.

Turner, V. (1974). *Dramas, fields, and metaphors: Symbolic action in human society.* Ithaca, NY: Cornell University Press.

Vico, G. (1948). *The new science of Giambattista Vico* (rev. ed.; T. G. Bergin & M. H. Fisch, Eds. and Trans.). Ithaca, NY: Cornell University Press. (Original work published 1744.)

Vidich, A. J., & Lyman, S. M. (1985). *American sociology.* New Haven, CT: Yale University Press.

Weimer, W. B. (1977). Science as a rhetorical transaction: Toward a nonjustificational conception of rhetoric. *Philosophy and Rhetoric, 10,* 1–29.

(1979). *Notes on the methodology of scientific research.* Hillsdale, NJ: Erlbaum.

White, G. M. (1987). Proverbs and cultural models: An American psychology of problem solving. In D. Holland & N. Quinn (Eds.), *Cultural models in language and thought* (pp. 151–72). Cambridge University Press.

Yearley, S. (1981). Textual persuasion: The role of social accounting in the construction of scientific arguments. *Philosophy of Social Science, 11,* 409–35.

Name index

Abbott, A., 51 n52
Abelson, R. P., 86, 285, 363 n5
Abrams, M. H., 27 n9
Adams, G., 51 n53
Adams, J., 274
Adams, J. A., 194–7, 215
Adkins, A. W. H., 31 n17, 145, 307
Adler, M., 7
Aeschylus, 142
Agassi, J., 335, 352 n2
Agnew, J. C., 36 n24
Albrecht, D. G., 91
Alexander, H. G., 32 n18
Alford, J. A., 36 n24
Allen, D. C., 30 n16
Allen, V. L., 124
Allport, F., 282
Alston, W. P., 115
Altman, I., 278
Amundson, R., 259
Anderson, J. R., 38 n27, 86, 205, 206, 209, 211
Appleman, P., 35 n21
Aquinas, T., 143
Arbib, M. A., 1, 28 n11, 31 n16, 41 n35, 54 n54
Aristotle, 1, 3–5, 8, 23 nn1,2, 24 n4, 30 n14, 46 n45, 136, 143, 145, 149, 154, 163 n5, 164 n14 n15, 165 n18, 231, 232, 239, 273, 277, 278, 339, 340, 341, 345, 352 nn1,2, 353 nn3,5
Arkes, H. R., 158
Arnheim, R., 35 n22

Arter, J. A., 23 n2
Asch, S. E., 14, 39 n33, 55 n54, 178, 275
Ashby, R. W., 293
Ashby, W. R., 82, 87, 88
Atkinson, J. W., 32 n18
Attneave, F., 184, 196, 198
Augustine, St., 110–11, 143, 164 n15
Averbach, E., 186
Averill, J. R., 105, 118, 120, 123, 126, 127, 129 n8, 357
Avila, Teresa of (Teresa of Jesus), 301–2

Baars, B. J., 39 n35
Bacon, F., 30 n16, 39 n33, 138, 152–3
Badalamenti, A. F., 44 n40
Baernstein, H. D., 250
Bahrick, H. P., 210, 211
Baillarger, J. G. F., 305
Bailyn, B., 319
Bain, A., 3, 26 n6, 332, 339, 351, 352 n2
Baker, H., 15
Bales, R. F., 32 n18
Bambrough, R., 8, 36 n24
Barbour, I. G., 1, 5
Barbu, Z., 140, 142
Barfield, O., 28 n11, 30 n14
Barker, P., 361 n2
Barlow, H. B., 87, 89
Barlow, J. M., 178
Barnes, B., 35 n23
Baron, R., 90
Barrett, P. H., 10, 34 n20
Barrough, P., 303

369

Subject index

381